People and Plants
in Ancient Western North America

Alison Parry

People and Plants
in Ancient Western
North America

EDITED BY PAUL E. MINNIS

Smithsonian Books
Washington

Dedicated to the memory of Volney H. Jones,
scholar, mentor, and colleague

©2004 by the Smithsonian Institution
All rights reserved

Copy Editor: Linda Forman
Production Editor: Joanne Reams
Designer: Janice Wheeler

Library of Congress Cataloging-in-Publication Data
   People and plants in ancient western North America / edited by
Paul Minnis.
      p.   cm.
   Includes bibliographical references and indexes.
   ISBN 1-58834-173-9 (cloth. : alk. paper) – ISBN 1-58834-174-7
(paper. : alk. paper)
      1. Paleo-Indians—Ethnobotany—West (US). 2. Paleo-Indians—
Ethnobotany—Southwest, New. 3. Paleoethnobotany—West (US).
4. Paleoethnobotany—Southwest, New. 5. Plant remains (Archaeology) —
West (US). 6. Plant remains (Archaeology)—Southwest, New. 7. Plants,
Useful—West (US). 8. Plants, Useful—Southwest, New.
I. Minnis, Paul E.

E78.W5P46   2004
581.6′3′08997078—dc22   2003061115

British Library Cataloging-in-Publication Data is available

Manufactured in the United States of America
10 09 08 07 06 05 04   1 2 3 4 5
⊚ The paper used in this publication meets the minimum requirements
of the American National Standard for Information Sciences—
Permanence of Paper for Printed Library Materials ANSI Z39.48-1992.

Contents

List of Figures

List of Tables

Foreword

This second of two volumes dedicated to the study of the prehistoric ethnobotany of North America is the culmination of 70 years of paleo-ethnobotanical research throughout the western North American continent north of Mexico. Although future articles may present additional details about archaeological plants from particular sites, the chapters in this volume provide the regional baselines concerning identified plants and their cultural interpretations. Paul E. Minnis has provided an indispensable ecological and historical introduction that serves as a guide for reading this multi-authored volume with its wide geographical sweep. It is doubtful that such encyclopedic coverage of western North American paleoethnobotany based on charred or desiccated plant remains will ever again be presented in a single volume.

In the United States ethnobotany began in 1895 with the identification of plant remains from dry shelters in southwest Colorado and southeast Utah that had been exhibited at the Chicago World's Fair. Dr. John Harshberger, a University of Pennsylvania faculty botanist, identified the remains and designated the new science of "ethno-botany." Thus began the methodological trend to account for archaeological plant remains. Megaremains, which are plant parts visible with the naked eye in archaeological contexts, began to be physically removed from rockshelters and from soil deposits and sent to botanists for identification. The remains were mostly domesticated plant parts—corn, cucurbit and gourd rinds, and beans—although wood was sometimes collected.

At the start of the 20th century dried plant remains from shelters in the North American Southwest contributed the most to a slowly expanding inventory of prehistoric plant information. Three decades later, macroremains in the form of waterlogged plants from anaerobic environments on the West Coast and from human feces would be considered important data for the nascent archaeological plant specialists. Regional patterns of prehistoric plant use, however, could not yet be discerned.

By 1930 anthropologically trained plant specialists were identifying archaeobotanical specimens. Archaeological field recovery methods now included the use of sieves of various sizes, and, consequently, the volume of recovered remains increased while the individual specimen sizes decreased. Archaeologists recovered mostly charred plant parts that were only visible after the soil matrix had been mechanically removed. These specimens are considered macroremains but require some form of magnification to aid in their identification. Beyond providing genus or species identifications, plant specialists used ethnographic analogy to interpret the botanical remains. Because of the availability of numerous ethnographic studies of Native western groups, this basis for plant interpretation seemed logical. Several institutions became associated with archaeological plant analyses. First the Ethnobotanical Laboratory at the University of Michigan provided identifications gratis as a professional service. Later, the Harvard Botanical Museum and the Missouri Botanical Garden did the same as part of their research programs.

When archaeological plant remains were recognized as holding answers to important questions related to sequences of crop evolution, botanical specialists began to concentrate on producing crop histories of individual domesticated species, from their indigenous hearth areas in Latin America to their diffusion into the North American Southwest (Fish, this volume) and Great Basin (Cummings, this volume). Individual botanists became associated with particular domesticated plants: Paul Mangelsdorf and Walton Galinat with maize, Thomas Whitaker with cucurbits, Hugh Cutler with corn and cucurbits, and Lawrence Kaplan with beans. The impact of their work was enormous, and archaeologists organized field expeditions specifically to seek remains representing the beginnings of plant domestication. Richard S. MacNeish did this in Tamaulipas and Tehuacan, Mexico, and Herbert Dick did the same when he returned for several seasons to Bat Cave, New Mexico.

Interest in plant domestication has not ceased, as we read in the chapter by Suzanne K. Fish. It is noteworthy that prior to concentrating on tropical domesticates, pioneer archaeological plant specialists were discovering macroremains from dry shelters in eastern North America that suggested the domestication or, at least, the intensive cultivation of indigenous plants. Melvin R. Gilmore suggested such schema for the Ozark Bluff Shelters, and Volney H. Jones did the same for Red River valley shelters in Kentucky. Western North America has not produced evidence of similar patterns of prehistoric plant domestication.

An innovation in plant recovery popularly called flotation, or water separation, had a tremendous impact on the growth of paleoethnobotany. This approach allows plant parts to be retained in fine screens while the water-saturated soil washes away. The use of flotation resulted in a quantitative increase in the volume of plant remains, mostly charred, for paleoethnobotanists to analyze.

Although the beginnings of flotation can be traced to the recovery of plant parts from mold-formed, adobe bricks from missions in California and the North American Southwest, those two areas were not the first to benefit from collection of greater varieties of genera and statistically significant quantities of plant remains. Midwestern archaeological sites secured that distinction. In fact, the amount of plant remains recovered from midwestern sites quickly overwhelmed existing laboratories, and archaeologists had to establish local laboratories to handle the volume of plant remains their excavations produced. Archaeologically trained paleoethnobotanists were accepted as specialists within anthropological archaeology, first in eastern North America and subsequently in the West. The increasing importance of paleoethnobotanical research within western North American archaeology is demonstrated by all of the contributors to this volume, who wrote dissertations based on the impact flotation had on their respective study regions.

Following quickly on the benefits flotation offered for recovering plant parts that otherwise would be lost, federally funded contract archaeology expanded under new legislation. Flotation became part of cultural resource management, and contractors could not secure approval of research designs without including flotation as a recovery method. By the 1970s, flotation was well established in parts of the United States. The information contained in all of the chapters in this volume to some degree reflects the recovery of water-separated plant remains. The chapter on wild plant use in the North American Southwest (Huckell and Toll, this volume) would not have much detail or authority without flotation. It is equally clear that some geographical areas have benefited to a greater degree than other areas from the extensive application of flotation. Although later than their colleagues in the eastern United States, researchers in the North American Southwest led the way, followed by those in the Great Basin (Cummings, this volume), in deriving new plant subsistence and ecological knowledge from the employment of this rather simple recovery method. Archaeologists in California (Hammett and Lawlor, this volume) and the Northwest (Lepofsky, this volume) have more recently applied it to their excavations despite earlier harangues by paleoethnobotanists to do so. Flotation has revolutionized paleoethnobotanical interpretations and transformed paleoethnobotany in those areas. A review of the regional histories provided by this volume's authors and a perusal of the bibliographies they provide reveal the importance flotation had in the construction of the chapters. In the end, all of the chapters are dependent on flotation.

Microremains, whose recovery requires the use of chemical methods, include microscopic plant parts like pollen, spores, phytoliths, starch grains, and stone cells. Their identification necessitates the use of high-powered microscopes. Although microremains have been recovered from sites in all areas, they do not constitute the major data bases used to draw the conclusions presented in the regional overviews in this volume. In the West, however, paleofeces have yielded microremains important for reconstructing diets, and pollen from paleofeces is an important component of the paleoethnobotanical record in the North American Southwest and Great Basin.

Paleoethnobotanical evidence has been primary in addressing a variety of research problems about prehistoric human cultural adaptations. The most common questions concern subsistence patterns over time, the evolution and importance of domesticated crops, and the human impact on the plant environment. The last-mentioned topic has only recently become a focus of research, but its investigation is guided by many ethnobotanical (and ethnologically based) models of human manipulations of plant species, populations, and ecological communities (Adams, this volume). Once these models are substantiated, paleoethnobotany will find a complementary and indispensable relationship with the sciences of ecosystem reconstruction and conservation biology.

This volume concludes a century of very profitable analyses of identified plants. As the chapters demonstrate, this tradition has successfully defined subsistence patterns, measured the impact of agriculture in human economies, and addressed the transformation of the biotic landscape. The methodologies of all of the authors have proven useful in revealing variation in crop plants that reflects the plants' histories, local adaptations, and farming methods. To briefly recapitulate, paleoethnobotanical data have expanded during the twentieth century to include smaller plant parts and microscopic remains and biochemical evidence of diets and plant evolution.

The next major summary of western North American paleoethnobotany, still a few decades away, will concentrate on the biochemistry and ancient DNA of plants manipulated by humans. Biochemical analysis will focus on residues in vessels, chemicals on implements, and soil associated with food preparation and consumption areas. Subsistence patterns will be described in terms of culturally processed nutrients. In addition, genetic analyses will provide a more accurate evolutionary history of domesticated plants and indicate which native plant species were modified as a result of cultural practices of harvest and management. It is expected that some of the crop histories postulated from morphometric examination now underway will prove accurate but that others will be modified and that patterns of parallel evolution will be revealed. Paleoethnobotany has great potential to contribute to mapping environmental dynamics, especially anthropogenic ones. Until the results of such future work are available, this indispensable volume will stand as the authoritative word on western North American paleoethnobotany.

—RICHARD I. FORD

Chapter 1

People and Plants in Prehistoric Western North America: An Introduction

PAUL E. MINNIS

The environmental diversity of Western North America—from the wind-scoured tundra of the high mountains to the seemingly desolate lowland deserts—is matched by the cultural and historical diversity of the continent's inhabitants. Humans have lived in North America for over 12 millennia, comprising thousands of very different indigenous groups. For the vast majority of that long time span, people extracted their livelihood—food, shelter, fuel, and other facets of material culture—solely from their surroundings. The record of plant use by indigenous North Americans is astounding. Moerman's 1998 compendium (which is still a work in progress) enumerates 2,582 plant species used as medicines, 1,649 for food, 442 for fiber, 217 as dyes, and 1,074 used in other ways, including 704 used "ceremonially." More North American data, both ethnographic and archaeological, remain to be recorded.

Indigenous ecology extended beyond the use of plants for food, medicine, and material needs. For example, worldviews and ideologies often were bound to local environments and recognized human interdependence with the natural world (e.g.,

1

Anderson 1996; Berkes 1999; Rappaport 1979). Other cultural factors of importance for understanding how peoples interacted with their environments include population size, composition, and distribution and technology, among others.

Ethnobotany is about more than plant uses and their cultural context. All human activity occurs within an ecological setting. Acknowledging an ideology of interdependence with nature does not mean accepting that human actions were ecologically passive or neutral; prehistoric North Americans were active manipulators of their biotic settings. Sometimes the manipulations, for example, large-scale burning (e.g., Krech 1999; Mills 1986; Peacock and Turner 2000), were quite obvious, whereas others, like altering individual trees or shrubs (e.g., Bohrer 1983; Fowler 2000; Nichols and Smith 1965), were subtle.

Native North Americans, then, like all peoples throughout the world, developed complex interrelationships with their natural environments. If we are to understand the dynamic ecological experiences of humans in North America, we must look to the archaeological record, if for no other reason than most human history occurred before European contact. Written records of North America did not begin until about AD 1500, only 500 years ago, yet, as noted, people had lived in North America by that time for no less that 12,000 years and probably for thousands of years beyond that. Therefore, the historical record accounts, most optimistically, for less than 5 percent of human occupation of this diverse continent. The other 95 percent is the domain of prehistorians and oral historians. The story of the rich, intricate, and many-faceted relationships between the prehistoric peoples of North America and their biotic environments is important and holds practical and ethical lessons for today—although the lessons are not always what we might expect.

This volume is the second of two that summarize the ethnobotany of the prehistoric peoples of North America. This volume covers western North America, that is, the area of the continent that lies to the west of the Great Plains. It focuses on the North American Southwest, because that region has been the most intensively studied. The Great Basin, California, and the Northwest also receive critical attention. The first volume, *People and Plants in Ancient Eastern North America* (Minnis 2003), covers the rest of North America: the Eastern Woodlands, Northeast, Plains, and Caribbean. The definitions of these regions generally follow the "culture areas" used for decades in anthropology and cultural geography.

Plant remains from archaeological sites comprise basic data types for the study of prehistoric ethnobotany. As might be expected, early archaeologists did not expect to find many plant remains, because plants are, after all, perishable. From their beginning as rare archaeological and botanical curiosities, however, prehistoric plant remains have now become important information sources, their recovery and study a standard part of archaeological research. During the 1960s, archaeobotanical research accelerated greatly, resulting in a fuller knowledge of how prehistoric Native Americans lived, earned a living, and interacted with their environments and each other. This volume and its companion attempt to capture our current understanding of ancient North American ethnobotany and provide the first continent-wide paleoethnobotanical overview.

Nature of People-Plant Relationships in Prehistory

Paleoethnobotanical relationships are both diverse and complex (see Ford 1979 for a fuller explication of the intellectual foundations of paleoethnobotanical research). The best-known type of ethnobotanical research focuses on the economic use of plants, especially for foods, medicines, and material needs. What types of plants did people use, how did they use them, and when? This "economic botany" tradition is ethnobotany's historical core, but the relationships between plants and people have many aspects. Ethnobotanical interactions are systemic and reciprocal—that is, coadaptational—and they take place within complex cultural, ideological, and ecological frameworks, each intertwined with its own contingent history (Crumley 1994). Even the apparently simple act of harvesting naturally available resources such as piñon nuts can have profound biological implications for the distribution, adaptation, and evolution of the plants collected, and resource gathering itself is largely determined by behavioral, social, and cultural considerations.

For example, many years ago, while living in the mountains of central Arizona, I awoke one Saturday morning to find a Western Apache family gathering acorns from a grove of trees around the house in which I was staying. The family had had to drive several hundred kilometers to collect the acorns from these specific oaks, and they had driven past thousands of square kilometers of oak forests with edible acorns located much closer to their home. Nevertheless, they were collecting the acorns around my house because they recognized the acorns from this grove as especially good for an important ritual meal. Of course, the availability of efficient transportation in the form of a pickup truck made long-distance travel much easier than in the past. Nonetheless, the ritual significance of acorn meal is important, as are the biochemistry and nutritional composition of the nuts, for understanding how these Western Apaches related to the oak.

This volume concerns itself with a whole range of ethnobotanical relationships, including, but not restricted to, plant use. We specifically focus on three topics: the use of native plants, the history of crops, and anthropogenic ecology. Although not the only issues of interest to paleoethnobotanists, these topics are the foundations of current research and have been the most fully studied. Furthermore, these topics are of interest to allied disciplines in the natural sciences, social sciences, and humanities.

Thousands of native plants were essential resources for many Native American needs, from fuelwood to foods. As impressive as Moerman's (1986, 1998) inventories of ethnohistorically documented native North American plant uses are, prehistoric plant-use lists would surely be much longer, reflecting knowledge lost in historic times. Native plants were major foods for peoples who never farmed and even for groups who did farm. The size, nutritional status, and distribution of human populations across the landscape, as well as human (pre)history, were influenced by the biogeography and ecology of native plants.

Many ancient Native North Americans were farmers for millennia (e.g., Ford 1981; Hurt 1987). It is commonly assumed that native North Americans simply adopted Mesoamerican crops, particularly maize, various beans, squash, and a few others. Although these crops were the major ones used by some indigenous peoples of North America, this image of plant adoption is far too simplistic. In western North America, particularly in the North American Southwest, Mesoamerican-derived crops were incorporated into indigenous economies early on. Mesoamerican domesticates, however, were not the only plants cultivated by Native Americans. In the Eastern Woodlands, where the topic of indigenous cultigens has been studied most intensively, a whole suite of native plants was domesticated well before the introduction of Mesoamerican cultigens, and it was not until late in prehistory that maize became a staple in the region. Not only did the plants change with farming, but human society and health changed as well, and the lives and successes of many indigenous communities became closely tied to farming.

One of the most interesting issues involving the study of human ecology and paleoethnobotany revolves around the third topic of concern in this volume, anthropogenic ecology, that is, how people, including indigenous groups, affect their natural environments. This issue is ideologically and politically charged, and stereotypical images shape how we think not only about the past but also about the present and the future. There tend to be two conflicting views about anthropogenic ecology. Arguably, the most common perception is that Native Americans were loving caretakers of their environments and had little or no ecological impact on their natural surroundings, in stark contrast to images of environments increasingly despoiled by modern industrial and postindustrial economies. Those who take this "Edenic" view often present three reasons for their perspective. First, they point out that Native American population densities were low; simply put, fewer people meant fewer environmental impacts. Second, Native Americans made their living from their immediate surroundings, so they had powerful incentives not to foul their local environments. The third reason cited in support of the Edenic view is that all Native Americans share an ethos of environmental conservation. Whereas some who take this position are incurable romantics, the view has its academic defenders. Hughes, for example, writes, "When Indians alone cared for the American earth, this continent was clothed in green robes of forests, unbroken grasslands, and useful desert plants, filled with an abundance of wildlife. Changes have occurred since people with different attitudes have taken over" (1983:1–2). A more recent example is Grinde and Johansen's *Ecocide of Native America* (1995). These authors' main goal is to show how current environmental degradation affects modern Native American communities more adversely than others in North America, a position that is quite supportable. Although not logically necessary to their primary point, they argue, like Hughes, that Native Americans had little adverse impact on the natural environments of North America before European conquest and colonization:

> While some scholars may argue that the idea of the Indian as ecologist is simply stereotyping and wishful thinking among present-day environmental advocates, the written and oral histories of many Native American peoples indicate that their cultures evolved over thousands of years largely in symbiosis with the earth that sustained them. Often these customs were incorporated into religious rituals that held the earth to be the sustainer of all things and linked the welfare of the earth to the survival of people who lived upon it. [Grinde and Johansen 1995:52]

Grinde and Johansen voice the common assumption that what people believe directly translates into what they do; when a culture is dependent on a local environment, then ideologies and behaviors will develop that foster respect for the environment and encourage environmental homeostasis. There are a number of reasons why this assumption may not be correct. For example, people cannot foresee the consequences of their actions, especially actions having a cumulative effect beyond a person's lifetime. In addition, there was probably a significant amount of migration in the past, and so the ties between a specific group and a specific locale may have been weaker than many now recognize. In addition, environments are dynamic, often maddeningly so (Botkin 1990). It is not likely that indigenous ecologies—like scientific ecology—had adequate knowledge of how "natural" changes articulate with human actions.

The literature documenting indigenous North American environmental impacts has some antiquity and is abundant (e.g., Denevan 1992; Doolittle 2000; Krech 1999; Redman 1999; Thomas 1956). Some view documented adverse effects as supporting the opposite position from the Edenic view, that is, the "Lapsarian" position holding that people usually despoil their environments. The best-known current example in this genre is Krech's *The Ecological Indian, Myth and History* (1999), a volume that has received much popular attention. An ethnohistorian, Krech draws most heavily on data from the European-contact and postcontact eras. Only two of his examples, megafauna extinctions and Hohokam agriculture, are archaeological, and neither is especially persuasive. Another recent book, Redman's *Human Impact on Ancient Environments* (1999), focuses specifically on the impacts of prehistoric peoples on their natural environments. Redman argues that ancient humans did adversely affect their environments, often to the point that the sustainability of their lifeways was severely compromised. Although he emphasizes regions and times with dense populations, complex polities, and market economies, Redman provides other case studies, two from the prehistoric North American Southwest: Kohler's (1992) work on the Colorado Plateau and the human ecology of the Hohokam of the Sonoran Desert. Redman consciously chooses to focus on the most serious environmental problems: "The perspective I believe to be most useful is that the *environmental crisis* is not strictly a recent problem uniquely tied to contemporary politics, economies, or technology, but rather centers more on the nature of human decision-making and the forces that shape those decisions" (2000:xiii). Redman's emphasis on crisis can obscure other valuable lessons to be learned from the study of prehistoric human ecology. We do not know that ecological manipulations by indigenous people always, or usually, adversely affect environments. The study of the anthropogenic ecology of past eras may provide useful ecological and economic lessons about environmental conservation.

Each of these opposing perspectives has its own interpretive pitfalls. The

Edenic view can lead to the misconception that all indigenous peoples at all times lived in harmony with their environments. The Lapsarian perspective can lead to a view that all environmental manipulations by native peoples are always deleterious. Native people do actively manipulate their environments, at differing scales of intensity and over varying lengths of time, and yet such manipulations are, a priori, neither harmonious management, on the one hand, nor environmental rape, on the other.

The study of anthropogenic ecology is, unfortunately, also embedded in wider political issues so that it too is often emotionally and political charged. This need not be so. Rather, the task is to learn how indigenous peoples, including those in prehistoric western North America, have affected their environments and what this means for ecological dynamics and environmental conservation. Admitting that Native Americans manipulated their environments in no way argues against the conclusions, ceteris paribus, (1) that large populations with industrial economies affect environments more than small-scale societies, (2) that modern indigenous peoples throughout the world are disproportionately affected by environmental damage, and (3) that modern environmental damage is therefore justified, a concern Fritz (2000) raises. The criteria for determining whether the ecological effects of humans, whether members of indigenous communities or not, are "good" or "bad" are not easily drawn, nor are they especially amenable to scientific definition. What is possible is for paleoethnobotanists to document the effects of human management and suggest what implications these effects have for environments and for the people themselves.

Although we may never understand fully the decisions made by prehistoric peoples or the "indigenous science" behind their choices, study of the effects of people's actions on the biotic environment allows us to glimpse pivotal ecological changes that affected both people and the biotic environment. Consideration of prehistoric anthropogenic ecology, therefore, is important for understanding prehistoric ethnobotany. The three interrelated topics of native plant usage, agroecology, and anthropogenic ecology, then, form the foundation for understanding the relationships between people and plants in the past.

Archaeobotanical Data

The primary data of paleoethnobotany, plant remains from archaeological sites, can be divided into two broad categories, "microbotanical" ("microplant" or "microfossil") and "macrobotanical" ("macroplant" or "macrofossil").

The distinction between microbotanical and macrobotanical remains follows Ford (1979) as well as others. Microbotanical remains are those that are too small to be seen by the naked eye and require sophisticated techniques to recover and identify. Pollen, pollenlike structures (e.g., spores), phytoliths, and leaf cuticle/epidermal fragments are the most common microbotanical remains. Macrobotanical remains are those that are large enough to be seen by the naked eye, and the most commonly studied are propagules (seeds, fruits, and nuts) and wood, especially in the form of charcoal. They can be recovered directly in the excavation process or by simple techniques such as flotation.

Some define prehistoric ethnobotany as the study of the plant remains themselves. I join many of my colleagues in preferring a definition that emphasizes the study of relationships—economic, ecological, and cultural—between people and plants. This places paleoethnobotany in line with the definition of ethnobotany, its parent discipline (Ford 1979; Jones 1941). Central to ethnobotanical research as they may be, plant remains themselves comprise only one type of data that can be used to infer ethnobotanical relationships. Others include paleoenvironmental, biogeographical, botanical, and archaeological data. The distribution of ancient fields, for example, can tell us as much about prehistoric agroecology as the recovery of a few fragments of prehistoric crops.

Obviously, some types of data are more direct indications of prehistoric behavior than others. For example, remains in ancient feces are direct indicators of what was eaten, more direct than burned seeds from trash deposits, because it can be difficult to determine exactly what actions resulted in the deposition of remains in trash. Similarly, the wood remains from hearths probably reflect the local prehistoric woody environment more closely than do beams used in house construction. Fuelwood was a constant need among indigenous peoples, especially those living in one location for many years. It is likely that people tended to use the closest woods rather than preferred woods farther from a settlement. In contrast, construction beams would have been collected less frequently, would have been curated for multiple uses, and are more likely to have been obtained from farther away than fuelwood. If so, then fuelwood is more likely to have sampled the local woody environment than wood used for beams.

Still, the study of any archaeological data is fraught with analytic traps and interpretive uncertainty. Consequently, the use of multiple, independent analyses is important for any successful archaeological research. Ultimately, inferences drawn from these different analyses can be compared to build more confident interpretations of prehistoric ethnobotany. Fortunately, there are many prehistoric ethnobotanical data sets, plant remains as well as other data, that can be compared to draw stronger inferences about the past. Thus, this overview of a few archaeological data sets is best understood in conjunction with other archaeological data, such as architecture, chipped stone, ceramics, animal bones, and so on. We can hope that archaeologists who do not study plant remains can use this volume to guide them in contrasting their work with ours.

History of Prehistoric Ethnobotany

Research on the prehistoric ethnobotany of North America is a little over a hundred years old. J. W. Harshberger (1896) coined the term "ethnobotany" during a study of macrobotanical remains recovered from an archaeological site in the Four Corners area of the North American Southwest. Yet, the study of plant remains continued to be a peculiarity for most archaeologists for many decades after Harshberger. An occasional dry cave or waterlogged site might have yielded an abundance of plants remains, and archaeologists often recovered a few burnt plant remains from the excavation of open sites; otherwise, plant remains were considered rare, odd, and slightly exotic discoveries. Fortunately, a small group of pioneering scholars, especially Melvin Gilmore, Volney Jones, Vorsila Bohrer, Hugh Cutler, and Richard Yarnell, extended the range and quality of paleoethnobotanical research during this time and deepened our understanding of prehistory. In addition, a number of botanists analyzed plant remains of specific archaeologically significant taxa: Lawrence Kaplan focused on beans, Thomas Whitaker on squashes and gourd, and Paul Mangelsdorf and Walton Galinat on maize. At the same time, scholars demonstrated the archaeological value of microbotanical remains, especially pollen, thus adding to the scope of paleoethnobotanical research.

Beginning around 1960, archaeobotanical research increased exponentially. Largely fueled by theoretical interest in human ecology, archaeologists began to look in earnest for plant remains rather than waiting for their serendipitous discovery. Archaeobotanists discovered that macrobotanical remains were easily concentrated through use of the flotation technique, that is, placing archaeological deposits in water, causing the plant remains to float to the surface (Pearsall 2000; Struever 1968). The dried flotation remains could then be sent to increasing numbers of experts trained specifically in botanical identification and interpretation. An archaeological excavation without plant remains now has become the exception, not the rule. Today, many students in a dozen labs are learning to study plant remains from archaeological sites in ways little different from their colleagues who analyze pottery, chipped stone, or other artifact categories more traditionally associated with archaeology. More paleoethnobotanical studies are being published (e.g., Gremillion 1997; Hastorf and Popper 1988; Pearsall 2000; Smith 1992). The study of plant remains, in short, has matured from a curiosity to an integral part of archaeological research. Yet, these prehistoric ethnobotanical data and their interpretation have rarely been drawn together in one source, a deficiency we hope this volume in part remedies.

The Need for Prehistoric Ethnobotany

There are more archaeological data to be analyzed than people, time, and money to do the work, so a basic question remains: Why study prehistoric ethnobotany? Bluntly, prehistoric ethnobotanists need to explain clearly why what we do is important. Fortunately, prehistoric ethnobotany has a number of "relevancies," both academic and practical (Minnis 1999, 2001). On the academic side, such research is relevant to understanding and appreciating the efforts and accomplishments of past peoples, cultures traditionally understudied in North America and elsewhere. Second, such research is of potential benefit to other disciplines. Archaeobotanical data, for example, can help biogeographers map changing distributions of plant species, data not readily available elsewhere. An overview like the one presented in this volume provides a single point-in-time perspective that can be used as a baseline for integrating future work within a wide region. On a more immediate level, the present overview draws broad conclusions about a rapidly expanding topic of interest, thus countering the tendency of ethnobotanical analyses to be focused on individual data sets or on small areas within North America. This work is not an encyclopedia that discusses every detail of prehistoric ethnobotany and covers all of the data. Instead, it attempts to reveal and review major trends and address problems of concern to archaeologists and others interested in the prehistory of North America.

The study of ancient peoples and their human ecology is not just an academic topic. Rather, prehistoric ethnobotanical knowledge is relevant to a variety of environmental and economic issues. For example, much effort is expended to preserve and conserve the "natural environments" of North America. Unfortunately, many think that environments before European colonization were largely unchanging and unaffected by indigenous peoples and that precontact environments should constitute the ecological baseline for ecosystem preservation. They argue that what was here before Europeans was *the* natural environment. People, however, are a part of "nature," and indigenous peoples who inhabited all parts of North America often influenced the distribution and abundance of plants and were active ecological managers. Cronin's (1983) consideration of the Northeast is the most widely read case study of anthropogenic ecology in North America, but examples are known from all over the continent (e.g., Blackburn and Anderson 1993; Delcourt 1987; Denevan 1992; Doolittle 2000; Krech 1999; Minnis and Elisens 2000; Redman 1999; Stahl 1996). Investigations of low-density hunting and gathering groups in western North America—groups one might think would have had minimal effects on their biotic environments—demonstrate the significant anthropogenic effects of such groups' activities. As examples, see Fowler's (2000) study of the Great Basin and Peacock and Turner's (2000) discussion of the Interior Plateau. These ethnographically documented cases are compelling, and similar situations surely occurred prehistorically. Therefore, it is necessary to understand prehistoric anthropogenic ecology to better model environmental change and to design successful conservation programs. As Hunter observes, "Conservationists often refer to restoring an ecosystem to its condition before it was colonized by technologically advanced people. Choosing this particular time marker makes no sense in the face of climate change; we are always dealing with a moving target" (1996: 696). Part of the target's movement is also due to the ecological effects of prehistoric humans.

Knowledge of the prehistoric ethnobotany of North America may be useful in expanding the range of resources available to modern people. Although there may well be practical modern applications to be derived from information about how ancient peoples used plants for medicines, weaving, and other purposes, such applied interests most commonly focus on food. Many are concerned with the narrowing of the human food base; fewer crops and crop varieties are becoming more and more important as sources of human food (e.g., Fowler and Mooney 1990; Orlove and Brush 1996). Fewer than 20 crops supply the majority of human food today, even though thousands of plants have been domesticated, among which are tens of thousands of crop varieties. Furthermore, the expansion of industrial agriculture in many locations has replaced traditional crop varieties, resulting in the loss of genetic diversity (Nabhan 1989). Archaeological data can expand our inventory of crop foods. One of the most important contributions of the study of prehistoric ethnobotany of North America has been the documentation of a whole suite of ancient crops, most of which are now extinct as domesticated plants but whose wild ancestors still exist. Such crops have been most intensively studied in eastern North America, but examples are also known from western North America. These ancient crops could, at some point, be revived, expanding the inventory of crops available for modern use. It may well be possible to redomesticate these plants, if need be, or at least to add selected DNA to the gene pool of cultivated plants.

This Volume

All prehistoric time periods are considered in this overview. Some are better studied than others. For example, little is known about the ethnobotany of the Paleoindians, the earliest well-documented peoples in North America, and ethnographic analogies must be used to draw inferences about Paleoindian ethnobotany. Generally, the closer to the present, the better the ethnobotanical documentation in the archaeological record. The exception is the often murky protohistoric period, a time of often dramatic change in indigenous lifeways because of European contact and colonization. We do not know, for example, how the very icon of southwestern cuisine, the chile (*Capsicum annuum*), was introduced in the North American Southwest by the Spanish.

Some geographic areas have been investigated more fully then others. The North American Southwest is the most intensively studied region in western North America. Consequently, four chapters are devoted to that region. The first introduces the area's natural environments, history, and cultural diversity (Minnis). Following chapters focus on the use of native plants (Huckell and Toll), agroecology (Fish), and, anthropogenic environmental change (Adams). Other regions—less intensively studied, although no less important—receive coverage in individual chapters. Specific chapters focus on California (Hammett and Lawlor), the Great Basin (Cummings), and the Northwest (Lepofsky). So little is known about the paleoethnobotany of the Subarctic and Arctic that these areas are not covered.

One of the major strengths of prehistoric ethnobotany is that ideas, perspectives, and methodologies are interdisciplinary, derived from a number of traditionally separated disciplines. This has resulted in an intellectual "heterosis" and an exciting interchange among scholars. The cross-disciplinary nature of ethnobotany, however, has resulted in two problems that are relevant to this volume. The first is that individual researchers have their own biases, interests, and training limitations. Most of the contributors to this volume were trained primarily in anthropology and archaeology. Although all of us have worked intimately with botanists, geographers, and others in interdisciplinary teams, our training and interests reflect our own disciplinary background.

The second problem with multidisciplinary research is that one must juggle two or more sets of professional jargon. Botanical nomenclature, in particular, is well developed and is not readily decipherable by those not trained in its use. "Pome," "achene," "legume," "multiple fruit," "berry," "aggregate fruit," "cariopsis," "capsule," "follicle," "cone," "hesperidium," "samora," "drupe," "nut," "schizocarp," "pepo," and "pyxis" are all botanical names for structures that, in modern American folk nomenclature, are "fruits," "seeds," or "nuts." Although the precision of botanical nomenclature is necessary for understanding taxonomic and phylogenetic relationships, it only confuses those with minimal botanical training. To simplify matters, botanical nomenclature in this volume is more "folk" than "scientific." I also hope that we have kept archaeological and anthropological jargon to a minimum. For example, a variety of terms have been used for the study of prehistoric plant-people interactions: "paleoethnobotany," "archaeobotany," "prehistoric ethnobotany," "archaeoethnobotany," and simply, "ethnobotany." All of these terms are used synonymously in this volume.

This volume comes, we believe, at an auspicious time, when we now have established a reasonable foundation of research from North America, although some regions are far more fully studied than others. Summarizing decades of intensive research, this volume surveys how ancient peoples of western North America survived, prospered, and sometimes failed, and it points to the lessons that prehistoric ethnobotany has for the modern world. This work does not constitute a definitive statement; research is progressing too rapidly for that. Rather, we hope that this volume provides a baseline, summarizing what we know, what we do not know, and what we should know, and that it points toward better ways of finding out what we need to know.

Acknowledgments

Until recently the study of prehistoric ethnobotany in North America was in the hands of a very few dedicated scholars, most of whom were Volney Jones's students, students of his students, his colleagues, or his close friends. The volume, then, is a tribute, as inadequate as any tribute can be, to his legacy.

Richard Ford, Volney Jones's most active student, has trained and mentored nearly every author in this volume. As editor, I would like to acknowledge all of the contributors for their patience—they have waited a long time for this volume to go to press; I cannot thank them enough. Susan de Quevado, Ryan Rowles, and Heather Szarka deserve special thanks for editorial preparation.

References Cited

Anderson, Eugene N.
  1996   *Ecologies of the Heart: Emotion, Belief, and the Environment.* Oxford University Press, Oxford.
Berkes, Fikret
  1990   *Sacred Ecology, Traditional Ecological Knowledge and Resource Management.* Taylor and Francis, Philadelphia.
Blackburn, Thomas C., and Kat Anderson
  1993   *Before the Wilderness: Environmental Management by Native Californians.* Ballena Press, Menlo Park, California.
Bohrer, Vorsila L.
  1983   New Life from Ashes: The Tale of the Burnt Bush (*Rhus trilobata*). *Desert Plants* 5:122–124.
Botkin, Daniel D.
  1990   *Discordant Harmonies: A New Ecology for the Twenty-First Century.* Oxford University Press, Oxford.
Cronon, William
  1983   *Changes in the Land: Indians, Colonists, and the Ecology of New England.* Hill and Wang, New York.
Crumley, Carole L.
  1994   *Historical Ecology: Cultural Knowledge and Changing Landscapes.* School of American Research Press, Santa Fe.
Delcourt, Hazel R.
  1987   The Impact of Prehistoric Agriculture and Land Occupation on Natural Environments. *Trends in Ecology and Evolution* 2:39–44.
Denevan, William M.
  1992   The Pristine Myth: The Landscape of the Americas in 1492. *Annals of the Association of American Geographers* 82:369–385.
Doolittle, William E.
  2000   *Cultivated Landscapes of Native North America.* Oxford University Press, Oxford.
Ford, Richard I.
  1979   Paleoethnobotany in American Archaeology. *Advances in Archaeological Method and Theory* 2:285–336. Academic Press, New York.
  1981   Gardening and Farming before A.D. 1000: Patterns of Prehistoric Cultivation North of Mexico. *Journal of Ethnobiology* 1:6–27.
Fowler, Cary, and Pat Mooney
  1990   *Shattering: Food, Politics, and the Loss of Genetic Diversity.* University of Arizona Press, Tucson.
Fowler, Catherine S.
  2000   "We Live by Them": Native Knowledge of Biodiversity in the Great Basin of Western North America. In *Biodiversity and Native America*, edited by Paul Minnis and Wayne Elisens, pp. 99–132. University of Oklahoma Press, Norman.

Gremillion, Kristen J.

    1997   *People, Plants, and Landscapes: Studies in Paleoethnobotany.* University of Alabama Press, Tuscaloosa.

Grinde, Donald A., and Bruce E. Johansen

    1995   *Ecocide in Native America: Environmental Destruction of Indian Lands and Peoples.* Clear Light, Santa Fe.

Harshberger, John W.

    1896   The Purposes of Ethnobotany. *Botanical Gazette* 21:146–154.

Hastorf, Christine A., and Virginia S. Popper (editors)

    1988   *Current Paleoethnobotany: Analytic Methods and Cultural Interpretations of Archaeological Plant Remains.* University of Chicago Press, Chicago.

Hughes, J. Donald

    1983   *American Indian Ecology.* Texas Western Press, El Paso.

Hunter, M.

    1996   Benchmarks for Managing Ecosystems: Are Human Activities Natural? *Conservation Biology* 10:695–697.

Hurt, R. Douglas

    1987   *Indian Agriculture in America: Prehistory to the Present.* University Press of Kansas, Lawrence.

Jones, Volney H.

    1941   The Nature and Status of Ethnobotany. *Chronica Botanica* 6(10):219–221.

Kohler, Timothy A.

    1992   Prehistoric Human Impact on the Environment in Upland North American Southwest. *Population and Environment* 13:235–268.

Krech, Shepard, III

    1999   *The Ecological Indian, Myth and History.* W. W. Norton, New York.

Mills, Barbara

    1986   Prescribed Burning and Hunter-Gatherer Subsistence Systems. *Haliksa'i: UNM Contributions to Anthropology* 5:1–26.

Minnis, Paul E.

    1991   Famine Foods of the North American Desert Borderlands in Historical Context. *Journal of Ethnobiology* 11:231–258.

    1999   Sustainability: A Long View from Archaeology. *New Mexico Journal of Science* 39:23–41.

    2001   One Possible Future of Paleoethnobotany. In *Ethnobiology at the Millennium*, edited by Richard Ford, pp. 35–48. Anthropological Papers 91. Museum of Anthropology, University of Michigan, Ann Arbor.

    2003   (editor) *People and Plants in Ancient Eastern North America.* Smithsonian Books, Washington, DC.

Minnis, Paul E., and Wayne J. Elisens (editors)

    2000   *Biodiversity and Native America.* University of Oklahoma Press, Norman.

Moerman, Daniel E.

    1986   *Medicinal Plants of Native America.* Technical Reports 19. Museum of Anthropology, University of Michigan, Ann Arbor.

    1998   *Native American Ethnobotany.* Timber Press, Portland, Oregon.

Nabhan, Gary P.

    1989   *Enduring Seeds: Native American Agriculture and Wild Plant Conservation.* North Point Press, Berkeley.

Nichols, Robert F., and David G. Smith

    1965   Evidence of Prehistoric Cultivation of Douglas-Fir Trees at Mesa Verde. *Memoirs* 31:57–64. Society for American Archaeology, Washington, DC.

Orlove, Benjamin S., and Stephen B. Brush

    1996   Anthropology and the Conservation of Biodiversity. *Annual Review of Anthropology* 25:329–352.

Peacock, Sandra L., and Nancy Turner

    2000   "Just Like a Garden": Traditional Resource Management and Biodiversity Conservation in the Interior Plateau of British Columbia. In *Biodiversity and Native America*, edited by Paul Minnis and Wayne Elisens, pp. 133–179. University of Oklahoma Press, Norman.

Pearsall, Deborah M.

    2000   *Paleoethnobotany: A Handbook of Procedures.* 2nd ed. Academic Press, San Diego.

Redman, Charles L.

    1999   *Human Impacts on Ancient Environments.* University of Arizona Press, Tucson.

Rappaport, Roy A.

    1979   *Ecology, Meaning, and Religion.* North Atlantic Books, Berkeley.

Smith, Bruce D.

    1992   *Rivers of Change: Essays on Early Agriculture in Eastern North America.* Smithsonian Institution Press, Washington, DC.

Stahl, Peter W.

    1996   Holocene Biodiversity: Archaeological Perspectives from the Americas. *Annual Review of Anthropology* 25:105–126.

Struever, Stuart

    1968   Flotation Techniques for the Recovery of Small-Scale Archaeological Remains. *American Antiquity* 33:353–362.

Thomas, William L., Jr.

    1956   *Man's Role in Changing the Face of the Earth.* University of Chicago Press, Chicago.

Chapter 2

Southwest Overview: History, Archaeology, and Environment

Paul E. Minnis

*H*umans have lived in the United States Southwest and northwestern Mexico (together also known as the Greater Southwest or Southwest/Northwest, and herein called the North American Southwest) for at least the past 12,000 years. People in the North American Southwest now obtain the resources needed for survival by importing them from outside the area, over the years using increasingly efficient modes of transportation—first mule, then wagon, railroad, truck, and now plane. By contrast, nearly all of the resources used by prehistoric human occupants came from the local area. Given the area's supposedly limited floral and faunal resources, it has been a source of amazement to many that ancient peoples of the North American Southwest could sustain themselves. This popular image masks the great historical, cultural, and environmental diversity and dynamic history of the North American Southwest. True, there were times when traditional ways of living were unsustainable; nonetheless, study of the area's ancient ethnobotanical record offers important lessons about the often successful interactions between people and their environments, a historical glimpse of ingenious lifeways and adaptations.

Paleoethnobotany in the North American Southwest is as old

as southwestern archaeology itself. Two decades before Nelson's stratigraphic work at San Cristobal in the Galisteo Basin and Kidder's excavations at Pecos—the two projects in New Mexico that defined the beginnings of archaeology in the North American Southwest—J. W. Harshberger (1896) reported on plant remains from Mancos Canyon that had been collected by the Wetherill brothers. This assemblage, the Hazard Collection, was exhibited at the Columbian Exposition in 1893. Harshberger, a botanist at the University of Pennsylvania, secured this collection and reported on his analysis of it. In describing this work, he introduced the term "ethnobotany," which has won widespread and enduring use in the New World and beyond. Harshberger envisioned ethnobotany to include ethnography and archaeology. Although he was not the first in the world to study archaeological plant remains, his contribution established the North American Southwest as an early center of prehistoric ethnobotanical research. With one of the earliest regional syntheses (Carter 1945), a rich ethnographic record, a large corpus of paleoethnobotanical research, and the data to consider significant questions in archaeology and botany, the North American Southwest continued to be an intensively studied region.

Generally speaking, only the largest and most durable plant remains were recovered during the earliest archaeological investigations in the North American Southwest. Maize cobs, fiber artifacts (sandals and basketry fragments), a small amount of squash, maybe a piñon pine nut or two, and an occasional cache of small seeds such as goosefoot constituted the typical assemblage of plant remains from sites. The predominance of the remains of cultivated plants reinforced the assumption that prehistoric peoples in the North American Southwest had an agricultural economy not unlike the modern day Puebloans or some O'odham (Pimans). This view was expressed by Hough: "It is not difficult to ascertain the materials entering into the subsistence of ancient Pueblo, as conditions in the region have changed little during the human occupancy. Pueblo economy has been perpetuated by the less modified groups of the Hopi and Zuni, so that knowledge of their domestic life is easily accessible" (1930:67).

Hough's complacency about reconstructing prehistoric subsistence practice became less secure as more archaeological work was undertaken. Archaeologists began to work more frequently with sites representing more mobile, less agricultural groups. The analogies with modern Puebloan groups did not fit these Archaic and pithouse-dwelling groups well and perhaps did not fit as well as one might have assumed the ancient Puebloan groups themselves. Yet, archaeologists' concern for plant remains was slow in developing.

Since the late 1960s a noticeable increase has occurred in the number of analyses of North American Southwest plant remains. This increase can be traced to several factors. First, the explosive growth in contractual archaeology has meant more archaeologists doing more research with larger budgets. And paleoethnobotany has become a standard part of the archaeological research protocol. Unfortunately, this has not been uniform throughout the region. Whereas our understanding of the prehistory of the Sonoran Desert, in particular, has grown greatly, northern Mexico has not benefited from contract archaeology. Second, many archaeologists in the North American Southwest embraced human ecology as an important theoretical underpinning for their work and thus viewed the study of human-environmental interactions as essential. Human diet and settlement patterning over the landscape have become common research topics. Third, the introduction of flotation techniques increased the number of plant remains recovered from types of sites once thought to be lacking macrobotanical material and expanded the diversity of remains collected.

If one work were to be singled out as emblematic of these changes, it would be Bohrer's (1970) innovative analysis of material from the site of Snaketown, a major Hohokam site south of Phoenix. In this work, Bohrer integrated three data sets, pollen, wood charcoal, and seeds, to devise a quantitative methodology for dealing with macrobotanical remains and to derive archaeologically meaningful conclusions about the adaptive success of Hohokam farming practices. This innovative work set a new analytic and interpretive standard for paleoethnobotanists.

Within the past several decades, research on North American Southwest paleoethnobotany has broadened in focus. Concern with anthropogenic environmental change, use of plants in material culture, the symbolic/ideological/iconic nature of ethnobotanical relationships, gender differences in plant knowledge and use, and diversity within and between ancient populations have been added to the traditional archaeological focus on prehistoric dietary and settlement patterns. Another recent trend is archaeologists' efforts to secure greater direct involvement of Native Americans in research.

Archaeology

Too often, the prehistoric Puebloan remains of the Four Corners define our image of the prehistoric North American Southwest (see Figures 2.1 and 2.2 for geographic and temporal overviews of the area). Yet, the prehistoric cultural diversity of the North American Southwest matches its environmental

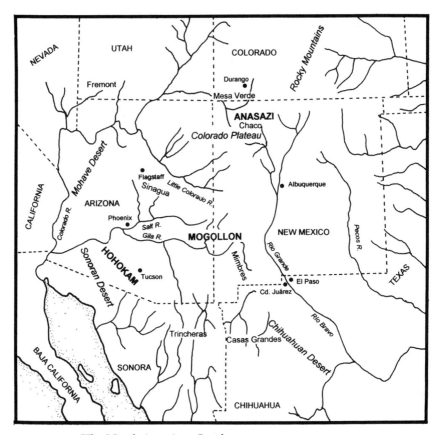

FIGURE 2.1   The North American Southwest

diversity. For detailed academic and popular summaries of this diversity, see
Cordell (1994, 1997), Plog (1997), and Reid and Whittlesey (1997). Even
within prehistoric traditions ("cultures"), such as the well-known "big three"—
Anasazi, Hohokam, and Mogollon—there was substantial variation. Adding
lesser-known archaeological traditions such as the Sinagua, Fremont, Salado,
Chihuahuan, and Trincheras allows a glimpse of regional, cultural, and historic
diversity. These designations of archaeological traditions are troublesome and
hard-to-define terms whose meanings have changed through time. "Mogollon," for example, once referred only to pithouse dwellers occupying a restricted area before AD 1000, but the term has now come to refer to nearly
all archaeological remains east of the Hohokam area, south of the Anasazi
area, and west of the Southern Plains. And some area specialists even argue
that the remains now called "Anasazi," the grandfather of southwestern archaeological terms, should be renamed "Ancestral Pueblo." Given all of these

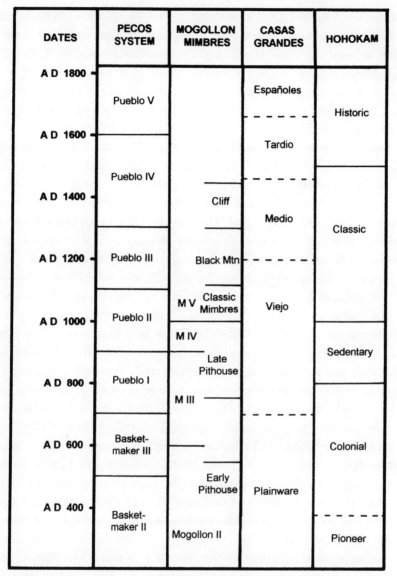

DATES	PECOS SYSTEM	MOGOLLON MIMBRES	CASAS GRANDES	HOHOKAM
A D 1800	Pueblo V		Españoles	Historic
A D 1600			Tardio	
	Pueblo IV			
A D 1400		Cliff	Medio	Classic
A D 1200	Pueblo III	Black Mtn		
		M V Classic Mimbres	Viejo	
A D 1000	Pueblo II	M IV		
		Late Pithouse		Sedentary
A D 800	Pueblo I	M III		
A D 600	Basket-maker III			Colonial
		Early Pithouse	Plainware	
A D 400	Basket-maker II	Mogollon II		Pioneer

FIGURE 2.2   Generalized chronology of the North American Southwest

issues and to avoid getting bogged down in archaeological systematics, culture area terms used here are defined loosely and often refer more to geographical areas than to cultural domains. Remains of the Anasazi tradition
center on the Colorado Plateau and adjacent regions of the northern North
American Southwest, the Hohokam tradition is found in the Sonoran Desert
and surrounding mountains, and the core areas of the Mogollon are the high-

lands of south-central Arizona and west-central New Mexico and the nearby deserts of the southern North American Southwest. Even the North American Southwest as a whole is not a tightly bounded cultural unit. Rather, the archaeological remains along its peripheries often blend with those of adjacent regions. Some researchers suggest, for example, that farming groups in the Southern Plains, such as those of the Antelope Creek focus, had "Puebloan" architecture.

Some time periods are better studied than others. Little is known about the ethnobotany of the Paleoindian period, and ethnographic analogies must be used to draw inferences about the ethnobotany of that early time span. Generally, the closer to the present, the better the ethnobotanical documentation in the archaeological record. The exception is the protohistoric period, a time of radical changes that are often hard to detect in the archaeological record and for which written records are sparse and often ambiguous.

Despite the image of the North American Southwest as a region of spectacular archaeological remains being studied by hundreds of archaeologists, great disparity characterizes the intensity of archaeological investigations in different areas. The Four Corners has had a long history of intensive research. Some areas of the Sonoran Desert, once an archaeological tabula rasa, have witnessed an astonishing increase in research. In contrast, the more remote deserts of western Arizona, nearly all of northwestern Mexico, and large swaths of the eastern edges of the North American Southwest have not seen proportional increases in archaeological research. As an example, Casas Grandes in northwestern Chihuahua—one of the largest sites in that area, if not the largest, and certainly an exceptionally influential prehistoric pueblo community—was not investigated again for a quarter century after Charles Di Peso (1974) concluded his excavation there in 1961. During the same quarter century thousands of sites north of the border in the US Southwest were recorded and studied.

One other issue regarding the interpretation of prehistoric ethnobotany of the North American Southwest requires mention. It is true that many indigenous peoples in the North American Southwest live on their ancestral homelands, have maintained cultural continuity, and have been the subjects of rich ethnographic documentation. It also true that ethnographic analogy is a central interpretive tool for archaeologists. Our understanding of the ancient past has been enriched greatly and deepened by references to and collaboration with modern indigenous communities. All people change, however, the indigenous peoples of the North American Southwest no less than others. Southwestern peoples have faced severe challenges from within their own groups, from outsiders, and from their natural environments. A pernicious tendency exists among too many scholars and others to uncritically read the ethnographic present into the North American Southwest past. This problem has been widely recognized by archaeologists working in the area, but it also affects paleoethnobotanical research. How researchers have perceived indigenous use of low-preference foods during food shortages is an ethnobotanical example of this problem (Minnis 1992b). Many foods known ethnographically in the northern North American Southwest as "famine foods" are common in archaeological sites. Such ubiquity may be evidence for sustained and widespread food provisioning problems in the past. Although there is little doubt that shortages occurred, it is more reasonable to conclude that this pattern actually reflects a subtle shift in food preference patterns from the ancient past to the ethnographic present, largely because of the effects of Euro-Mexican-American occupation. Therefore, it is important that prehistoric ethnobotanists not use the abundant ethnographic and ethnohistoric data available as an intellectual smorgasbord from which to simply pick information without sufficient consideration of its applicability to the past.

The initial and defining archaeological work in the North American Southwest focused on the prehistoric and protohistoric peoples of the northern North American Southwest, the remains of communities generally recognized to have been ancestral to modern Puebloan peoples. The Pecos Conference in 1927 established an archaeological sequence that became reified as *the* archaeological sequence for the North American Southwest (Kidder 1927). Until just a few decades ago, archaeologists routinely tried to fit other prehistoric traditions into this framework. Furthermore, the sweeping generalizations about cultural developments during specific time periods demarcated within the Pecos Classification are now being questioned as more diverse data have accumulated within the Anasazi regions.

Painted broadly, prehistoric groups throughout the North American Southwest followed similar paths, even though each group had its own unique history and identity. This should not be surprising for two reasons. First, no ancient groups were isolated. People traded, fought, married, and arranged other social and cultural relationships with distant groups as well as with their neighbors. Second, communities throughout the world often respond to similar conditions in generally similar ways. To frame the discussions of North American Southwest prehistory that appear in the following chapters,

I consider three issue-related topics rather than geographic or "cultural" units: Archaic lifeways and the origins of farming, the formation of village life and agricultural economies, and the development of regional polities.

The Archaic and the Origins of Farming

From the first human occupation of the North American Southwest until about AD 200 people generally lived as small, mobile groups of hunters and foragers scattered thinly over the entire region. The late glacial and immediately postglacial natural environments were much different from today. Unfortunately, those millennia have been of little concern to paleoethnobotanists of the North American Southwest, largely because of the meager data available for early time periods outside of pollen records and a few cave sites. One exception to such general disinterest is the study of the origins of agriculture in the region. Dick's (1965) research at Bat Cave and Mangelsdorf's (1954) subsequent analysis of the maize remains from this site spurred further research on the topic and were central for evaluating early models of maize evolution. More recent reconsiderations of the development of maize and of Bat Cave itself (Wills 1988) have recast the historical significance of this site and its plant assemblage. A resurgent interest in the origin of farming and/or early domesticated plants in the North American Southwest began several decades ago (e.g., Berry 1982; Ford 1981; Matson 1991; Minnis 1985b, 1992a; Wills 1988, 1992) and continues today, with recent discoveries that have changed our understanding of agricultural origins.

As discussed in detail in Suzanne K. Fish's chapter, work in the Tucson area as well as northern Chihuahua is altering our understanding of these issues. The first millennium BC may, in places, have witnessed far greater population aggregation and crop dependence than previously thought. Scholars are now sorting through the data and arguments to evaluate such claims and to determine how widespread these processes were in the North American Southwest.

Formation of Village Life and Farming Economies

Whereas in some areas ancient peoples continued mobile hunting and gathering lives, many areas in the North American Southwest saw the formation of village farming societies in the first millennium AD. Such changes occurred in the Sonoran Desert among the Hohokam, in the Mogollon region, especially in the Mimbres region of southwestern New Mexico, and throughout the Anasazi Colorado Plateau. Architecture, pottery styles, and a whole range of other material and organizational characteristics varied regionally. Yet, a broad pattern of small, largely autonomous villages based on farming and scattered over the landscape took root in the North American Southwest at that time. One of the most important early paleoethnobotanical reports focusing on initial farming was Jones and Fonner's (1954) study of plant remains from Basketmaker sites near Durango, Colorado. Disagreement has been voiced about the relative dietary contribution of crops and the degree to which farming determined economic strategies during the initial period of village farming. Even those who tend to minimize the role of farming and argue for greater degrees of residential mobility recognize that agriculture was still a significant activity at the time (e.g., Gilman 1987).

The study of the prehistoric ethnobotany of early farming groups is important. Early farmers fine-tuned crops and agricultural techniques to a variety of specific environmental settings that allowed for subsequent historical developments. These people developed, for example, ways of growing crops in the high elevations near Chimney Rock Pueblo in southwest Colorado, with its mesic, short growing season, as well as in the low deserts of central Arizona, characterized by long, but dry growing seasons. Their archaeological legacy is valuable for understanding human behavior and movement in relation to changing environmental conditions. The North American Southwest offers especially good opportunities to study how environmental variation, such as in precipitation, affected the economic, demographic, and social conditions of prehistoric people (e.g., Dean et al. 1985; Euler et al. 1979; Gumerman 1988; Minnis 1985a; Peterson 1988; Van West 1994).

Development of Regional Polities

Although not developed to the degree as in contemporary Eastern Woodlands prehistory, clear examples exist in the North American Southwest of prehistoric intermediate-scale (or "chiefdom") societies, those characterized by some elite coordination, integration of communities within regional polities, large population aggregates, and, to a limited degree, economic specialization. The latter attribute is especially interesting to paleoethnobotanists because such specialization can lead to strategic changes and standardization for surplus production, as well as changes in dietary patterns (e.g., Hastorf 1992). Some intermediate-scale societies are difficult to recognize archaeologically, because the first indicators of their existence can be subtle and fall

along a continuum of social characteristics with no obvious breaks. Consequently, arguments have arisen as to whether archaeological remains from
many areas in the North American Southwest represent such systems. Most
would agree, I suspect, that there were at least three clear examples of intermediate-scale organizations in the North American Southwest. The first, the
longest studied, and the most enigmatic was the Chaco phenomenon centered in the San Juan Basin of the Four Corners (e.g., Crown and Judge 1991;
Neitzel 1999). The explosion of research on the Hohokam of the Sonoran
Desert, especially near what is now Phoenix, Arizona, has demonstrated that
Pre-Classic and Classic Hohokam populations exhibited characteristics of
intermediate-scale development (e.g., Crown and Judge 1991; Gumerman
1991; Neitzel 1996). The third and least studied example was a polity centered at Casas Grandes in northwestern Chihuahua, Mexico, in an area called
the International Four Corners (e.g., Di Peso 1974; Schaafsma and Riley 1999;
Whalen and Minnis 2001). Southwestern paleoethnobotanists have only begun
to address the ethnobotanical aspects of prehistoric complex traditions.

Indigenous ethnobotany in the North American Southwest has not been
static but continually changing. Changes, so evident in prehistory, continued
during the protohistoric and early historic times and continue today. The
very icon of what is now considered "southwestern" cuisine, the chile (*Capsicum annuum*), was not used prehistorically in the North American Southwest; rather, the best evidence suggests that it was brought into the region by
the Spanish. In fact, the chile is one of a very few Mesoamerican crop plants
that could have been easily grown prehistorically in the North American
Southwest but was not (Minnis 1992a). And, of course, the postcontact introduction of Euro-Asian domesticates such as wheat changed the diet and
economies of native peoples of the North American Southwest. As interesting as these changes are, they remain largely outside the scope of this volume.

Environments

The environments of the North American Southwest form a complex mosaic, ranging from majestic mountain ranges and photogenic "badlands" to
topography that drew this complaint from Bartlett: "One becomes sickened
and disgusted with the ever-recurring sameness of plain and mountain, plant
and living things" (1854:8). Often abrupt changes in soil composition, hydrology, and elevation are chiefly responsible for this environmental complexity. Although many academic and popular references about the natural

environments of the North American Southwest are available, the best detailed summaries are by Brown (1982, 1994).

The topography of the North American Southwest is composed of plains and mountains, the latter as isolated desert peaks and as enormous continental ranges. Although some plains are lower in elevation, the majority lie above 900 m, and they can extend for thousands of square kilometers. In other cases, moderately small mountain ranges are interspersed among the level floors. Many of the southwestern mountain ranges are among the most spectacular in North America. Peaks up to 4,200 m high form the apex of this topography, but most mountains do not rise above 3,400 m. The abrupt changes in slope and orientation create conditions of remarkable biotic diversity.

Most drainages are dry channels much of the year. But major rivers often were loci of prehistoric human occupation. Notable among these are the Salt, Gila, Colorado, Little Colorado, Rio Grande/Río Bravo del Norte, Pecos, and Casas Grandes, and their tributaries.

Some parts of the North American Southwest are truly arid, but most areas are semiarid. Deserts may receive less that 20 cm of precipitation per year, whereas the higher mountainous areas may be blessed with more than 100 cm. Precipitation increases with elevation, and with abrupt changes in altitude precipitation can change radically over short distances. For example, Española, in the Rio Grande drainage just north of Santa Fe, receives 25.4 cm of precipitation annually, but only 24 km away, the Jemez Mountains average up to 100 cm. Generally, for every 3,000-m increase in elevation, there is a corresponding increase in precipitation of 10 to 13 cm (Lowe 1964).

Precipitation in the North American Southwest is neither random nor evenly distributed throughout the year. There are two seasons of precipitation when "drought conditions are less severe than usual" (Sellers and Hill 1974:8). These seasons differ in terms of the origin of the moisture and the localized nature of the precipitation. The summer monsoons extend from July through September. This summer rainy season is preceded by the two driest months, May and June (Sellers and Hill 1974; Tuan et al. 1973). The second precipitation spike occurs during winter cyclonic storms, which affect large areas. A west to east gradient in the bimodality of precipitation characterizes the North American Southwest. The further west, the greater the contribution of winter precipitation (Lowe 1964; Tuan et al. 1973).

Other climatic factors such as length of the growing season, as well as variables related to hydrology and soils, are critical to plant growth, especially to growth of cultivated plants. The upper limit for farming, as an example, tends to be determined by a short growing season, although prehistoric farm-ers could increase the growing season by planting on south-facing slopes, as may have happened at Chimney Rock Mesa, Colorado (Minnis and Ford 1977), and by the use of other strategies.

As a result of changes in climate, soils, hydrology, and topography, the vegetation of the North American Southwest is complex. This diversity is con-sidered below in the context of four vegetation zones: desertscrub/grasslands, woodlands, forests, and tundra. Human occupation of each zone was affected by the unique conditions found there, including the presence of hundreds of edible and useful plants, as discussed in Lisa Huckell and Mollie Toll's chapter.

Desertscrub/Grasslands

Desertscrub/grasslands occupy most of the level plains and are the most arid of the four vegetation categories, receiving less than 30 cm of rain annually. The most familiar image of deserts in the North American Southwest, the columnar cacti such as saguaro (*Carnegiea gigantea*), occur only in a small area. More common are shrub-dominated plains or grasslands. It is not clear how extensive grasslands and shrub/grasslands were in the past. Desert shrubs, particularly mesquite (*Prosopis*), have invaded what were formerly grasslands in the southern deserts, and in the "cold" desert greasewood (*Sarcobatus ver-miculatus*) and saltbush (*Atriplex*) are now more common (e.g., Bahre 1991; Hastings and Turner 1965; Humphrey 1987).

Three deserts within the study area have been described: Mojave, Sono-ran, and Chihuahuan. The Mojave (or Great Basin) Desert of the northwest-ern North American Southwest is "cold," with severe winter weather and much of the precipitation occurring as snow. A number of shrubs dominate this desert formation. Saltbush, blackbrush (*Coleogyne ramosissima*), grease-wood, shadscale (*Atriplex confertifolia*), mormon tea (*Ephedra*), and sagebrush (*Artemesia*) are the most common. Interspersed among these shrubs are a wide variety of forbs and grasses. Cacti and leguminous plants are compara-tively rare in this desert.

The vegetation of the Sonoran Desert of the southwestern part of the region is composed of two major assemblages. The paloverde (*Cercidium*)-saguaro community is characterized by small legume trees, shrubs, and a di-versity of cacti. This community is most common on gentle slopes. The second vegetation type in the Sonoran Desert, the creosotebush (*Larrea tridentata*)-bursage (*Franseria*) community, occurs on the flatter desert plains. The Chihuahuan Desert is dominated by creosotebush and tarbush (*Flourensia cernua*). Mesquite often forms dense stands in the Sonoran and Chihuahuan Deserts. Unlike the Sonoran Desert, the Chihuahuan Desert does not have an abundance or diversity of columnar cacti and leguminous trees, although cholla (*Opuntia*), prickly pears (*Opuntia*), and mesquite are common.

Ribbons of riparian vegetation are present in desertscrub and grasslands. Dense stands of greasewood and saltbush are particularly common along water channels in the cool deserts. Other streamside-specific shrubs are also common, especially desert hackberry (*Celtis reticulata*) and desert willow (*Chilopsis linearis*). Where water is dependable, cottonwoods (*Populus*), willows (*Salix*), and other trees can line watercourses.

Prehistoric human occupations of many desertscrub/grassland areas were quite substantial. Hohokam and desert Mogollon sites are usually found along the major river valleys and tributaries in these zones. In other desert locations, prehistoric occupation was limited to scattered, ephemerally used campsites.

Woodlands

Woodlands are often sparsely populated stands of trees. These formations grade into the desertscrub and grassland communities and occur on the lower slopes of mountain ranges, generally above 1,520 m. Precipitation is higher than in grasslands, generally averaging 30–50 cm a year. An imprecise but important distinction can be drawn between the woodlands of the southern part of the study area and those of the north. The familiar piñon (*Pinus edulis*)-juniper (*Juniperus*) woodlands—what most people think of as North American Southwest woodlands—are most common in the northern portion of this region. In the southern part of the North American Southwest, with its higher temperatures, piñon is less common and oaks (*Quercus*) are featured more prominently in the vegetation. Agavacious plants (including sotol [*Dasylirion*], beargrass [*Nolina*], agave [*Agave*], and yucca [*Yucca*]) are particularly common in southern woodlands. Shrubs, grasses, and forbs vary in density, depending on a number of factors such as canopy coverage.

Like the deserts, a robust riparian assemblage often occurs along streams. Cottonwoods, willows, walnuts (*Juglans*), alder (*Alnus*), sycamores (*Platanus wrightii*), and ashes (*Fraxinus*) are characteristic of this riparian vegetation. Along perennial watercourses, this assemblage forms a distinctive green ribbon snaking its way among the scarcer hillside vegetation. It is in the woodlands that many of the Anasazi and Mogollon occupations were densest.

Forests

Forest vegetation is found higher up in the mountains than are woodlands, generally between 1,525 m and 3,400 m. Annual precipitation averages 40–75 cm. There is a marked altitudinal continuum of conifers from pine (*Pinus*) at the low end to fir (*Picea*) and then spruce (*Abies*) with increasing elevation. Low temperatures are the primary factors defining the lower limit of this zone.

The lower-elevation forest vegetation in the northern part of the North American Southwest is dominated by ponderosa pine (*Pinus ponderosa*), which can form nearly pure stands with an open understory. In the forests of the southern part of the North American Southwest, ponderosa is commonly joined by a large number of woody plants, including other conifers, mesophytic oaks, and madron (*Arbutus arizonica*). Other trees and shrubs are abundant. In the more northerly parts of the study area, a less diverse assemblage of plants is found with ponderosa. Gambel's oak (*Quercus gambelii*), aspen (*Populus tremuloides*), and Rocky Mountain juniper (*Juniperus scopulorum*) are prominent among these plants. Grasses and forbs thrive in the open canopy often formed by ponderosa pine forests.

At higher elevations ponderosa pine gives way to Douglas-fir (*Pseudotsuga menziesii*) forests. Other conifers such as white fir (*Abies concolor*) are common along with the Douglas-fir. Above the Douglas-fir-dominated forests are stands of spruce, fir, and other cold-tolerant plants. Fewer mountain ranges are tall enough to extend into the spruce forests in the southern part of the study area. A significant number of prehistoric settlements were located in the lower elevations of the forest zone, but few habitation sites are found above the ponderosa pine belt. Seasonal occupations of the higher forest elevations occurred, and specialized-use sites are present.

Tundra

Tundra vegetation occupies a very small part of the study area. Generally lying above 3,500 m, this zone receives upwards of 100 cm of precipitation annually. The severe climate limits growth to low-growing plants. Snow remains on the ground for much of the year, reducing the length of the growing season. There is little documented prehistoric use of tundra zones in the North American Southwest.

Environmental Changes through Time

Natural environments are not static. What may appear as a stable climax plant community is often a fragile assemblage of plants that is easily altered. Substantial evidence exists of both natural and anthropogenic vegetation changes in the North American Southwest. The thousands of square kilometers of desertscrub-dominated plains are a comparatively recent phenomenon. Understanding vegetational changes is a critical goal of North American Southwest paleoethnobotany, not only to reconstruct the environments where prehistoric peoples lived but also to better model ecological change. Karen R. Adams's chapter deals with the important issue of anthropogenic change.

Environmental changes during the early postglacial period in the North American Southwest were significant and included a retreat of mesic plants to the higher elevations where they are now found. This early postglacial period is not the focus of this volume, but substantial detailed scholarship analyzing major postglacial environmental changes in the North American Southwest is available (e.g., Betancourt et al. 1990; Hall 1985; Martin 1963; Van Devender and Spaulding 1979).

Compared with the pre-1000 BC period, the environmental history of the post-BC era is better known, and the scale of environmental reconstruction is more precise. Yearly and even seasonal changes can be studied in some locations. Dendroclimatology has become a primary source of information for understanding climatic changes after about 300 BC. Environmental fluctuations measurable with tree-ring studies help researchers understand the role of precipitation variation in the prehistory of the North American Southwest. Some studies have measured fine-scale changes. For example, Rose et al. (1981) reconstructed the prehistoric annual and spring precipitation changes in the Santa Fe region as a part of the Arroyo Hondo Archaeological Project. Various studies have analyzed how prehistoric human demography and behavior were affected by climatic and environmental variation (e.g., Dean et al. 1985; Euler et al. 1979; Gumerman 1988; Minnis 1985a; Peterson 1988; Van West 1994).

The vegetation of the North American Southwest has undergone substantial change within the last hundred years. A decline in grasslands and an invasion of shrubs have been documented widely. Interestingly, York and Dick-Peddie (1965) suggested that the original historic stands of mesquite were locations where this plant was established as a result of its prehistoric use. The apparent correlation between the locations of mesquite stands and archaeological sites can also be explained as due to sites having been established near already existing mesquite groves.

Historic changes in woodland vegetation are less well documented than changes in desert grasslands. Studies have documented two major changes in vegetation patterning within piñon-juniper woodlands, a reduction in grass cover and an increase in shrubs and trees. Two causes have been posited for these recent changes, fire suppression and the effects of grazing pressure from livestock.

Other plant distributions have changed in the North American Southwest within the last 100 years. Some plants such as cholla, snakeweed (*Gutierrezia sarothra*), and a number of ruderals have increased substantially because of human-induced soil disturbance (Harris 1965). This disturbance is most common around settlements and in extremely overgrazed ranges. In addition to the reduction of grasses due to overgrazing, a number of other plants have been adversely affected. Bohrer (1978) cataloged seven plants that have become locally extinct in areas of the Colorado Plateau: stickleaf (*Mentzelia albicaulis*), purslane (*Portulaca*), winged pigweed (*Cycloloma atriplicifolium*), contrayerba (*Kallstroemia*), buffalo gourd (*Cucurbita foetidissima*), wild onion (*Allium*), and spiderwort (*Tradescantia occidentalis*). The presence of these plants in archaeological sites in regions where they no longer seem to occur attests to the changes in plant distributions. Undoubtedly, many times this number of plants have been affected by historic land use; for many we have no archaeological or botanical evidence of prehistoric distribution or abundance.

In addition to changes in native flora, numerous exotics have been introduced within the past century. Saltcedar or tamarack (*Tamarix*) and Russian olive (*Elaeagnus angustifolia*) have become established along watercourses throughout much of the North American Southwest and are crowding out native riparian plants. And livestock often destroy young native riparian plants such as cottonwoods and willows.

Water is an especially important resource in arid to semiarid environments. A number of modern factors have led to the depletion of surface and underground water resources throughout the North American Southwest. The effects differ depending on the hydrology of each locality. With this reduction, there should be a reduction in vegetation that depends on surface soil moisture. Throughout the North American Southwest, hydrophytic plants, such as the common reed (*Phragmites australis*), have been recovered from archaeological sites in areas where the plants now do not occur, indicating a profoundly altered hydrology from the past to the present.

Conclusion

The North American Southwest has made many contributions to prehistoric ethnobotany, and the area continues to hold much research potential for archaeologists and paleoethnobotanists. The preservation of plant remains from southwestern archaeological sites is often good, an enviable ethnographic and historic record exists for the area, the quantity and quality of archaeological work is high, paleoenvironmental reconstructions of the area's substantial environmental diversity are often superb, and a diversity of prehistoric human lifeways is available for study. Thus, paleoethnobotanists of the North American Southwest can investigate a wealth of anthropologically and biologically important topics. The following chapters—Lisa W. Huckell and Mollie S. Toll's discussion of the use of native plants, Suzanne K. Fish's examination of ancient crops, and Karen R. Adams's summary of anthropogenic ecology—clearly illustrate the value of studying the prehistoric human ecology of the North American Southwest. The value of such study can be measured on the basis of its utility for understanding the past and also its significance for dealing with practical problems in the present and future. Although it would be presumptuous to predict where North American Southwest paleoethnobotany will go in the future, it is clear that early scholars such as Jones and Bohrer, as well as current practitioners, have laid an excellent foundation.

References Cited

Bahre, Conrad J.
   2000   *A Legacy of Change: Historic Human Impact on Vegetation of the Arizona Borderlands.* University of Arizona Press, Tucson.
Bartlett, John R.
   1854   *Personal Narrative of Explorations and Incidences in Texas, New Mexico, California, Sonora, and Chihuahua,* vol. 1. D. Appleton Press, New York.
Berry, Michael S.
   1982   *Time, Space, and Transition in Anasazi Prehistory.* University of Utah Press, Salt Lake City.
Betancourt, Julio H., Thomas R. Van Devender, and Paul S. Martin
   1990   *Pack Rat Middens: The Last 40,000 Years of Biotic Change.* University of Arizona Press, Tucson.
Bohrer, Vorsila L.
   1970   Ethnobotanical Aspects of Snaketown, a Hohokam Village in Southern Arizona. *American Antiquity* 35:413–430.

1978 Plants That Have Become Locally Extinct in the Southwest. *New Mexico Journal of Science* 18:10–19.

Brown, David E. (editor)

1982 Biotic Communities of the American Southwest—United States and Mexico. Special issue, *Desert Plants* 4(1–4).

1994 *Biotic Communities, Southwest United States and Northwest Mexico.* University of Utah Press, Salt Lake City.

Carter, George F.

1945 *Plant Geography and Culture History in the American Southwest.* Publications in Anthropology 5. Viking Fund, New York.

Cordell, Linda S.

1994 *Ancient Pueblo Peoples.* Smithsonian Institution Press, Washington, DC, and St. Remy Press, Montreal.

1997 *Archaeology of the Southwest.* 2nd ed. Academic Press, San Diego.

Crown, Patricia L., and W. James Judge (editors)

1991 *Chaco and Hohokam: Prehistoric Regional Systems of the American Southwest.* School of American Research Press, Santa Fe.

Dean, Jeffrey S., Robert C. Euler, George J. Gumerman, Fred Plog, Richard H. Hevley, and Thor N. V. Karlstrom

1985 Human Behavior, Demography, and Paleoenvironment on the Colorado Plateaus. *American Antiquity* 50:537–554.

Dick, Herbert W.

1965 *Bat Cave.* Monograph 27. School of American Research, Santa Fe.

Di Peso, Charles C.

1974 *Casas Grandes: A Fallen Trading Center of the Gran Chichimeca.* Northland Press, Flagstaff.

Euler, Robert C., George J. Gumerman, Thor N. V. Karlstrom, Jeffery S. Dean, and Richard H. Hevley

1979 The Colorado Plateaus: Cultural Dynamics and Paleoenvironment. *Science* 205:1089–1101.

Ford, Richard I.

1981 Gardening and Farming before A.D. 1000: Patterns of Prehistoric Cultivation North of Mexico. *Journal of Ethnobiology* 1:6–27.

Gilman, Patricia A.

1987 Architecture as Artifact: Pitstructures and Pueblos in the American Southwest. *American Antiquity* 52:538–564.

Gumerman, George J. (editor)

1988 *The Anasazi in a Changing Environment.* Cambridge University Press, Cambridge.

1991 *Exploring the Hohokam: Prehistoric Desert Dwellers of the American Southwest.* University of New Mexico Press, Albuquerque.

Hall, Stephen A.

1985 Quaternary Pollen Analysis and Vegetational History of the Southwest. In *Pollen Records of Late-Quaternary North American Sediments*, edited by Vaughn M. Bryant Jr. and Richard G. Holloway, pp. 95–123. American Association for Stratigraphic Palynologists Foundation, Dallas.

Harris, David R.

1960 Recent Plant Invasions in the Arid and Semiarid Southwest of the United States. *Annals of the Association of American Geographers* 56:408–422.

Harshberger, John W.

1896 The Purposes of Ethnobotany. *Botanical Gazette* 21:146–154.

Hastings, James Rodney, and Raymond M. Turner

1965 *The Changing Mile: An Ecological Study of Vegetation Change with Time in the Lower Mile of an Arid and Semi-Arid Region*. University of Arizona Press, Tucson.

Hastorf, Christine A.

1992 *Agriculture and the Onset of Political Inequality before the Inka*. Cambridge University Press, Cambridge.

Hough, Walter

1930 Ancient Pueblo Subsistence. *Proceedings of the International Congress of Americanists* 23: 39–48.

Humphrey, Robert R.

1987 *90 Years and 535 Miles: Vegetation Change along the Mexican Border*. University of New Mexico Press, Albuquerque.

Jones, Volney H., and Robert L. Fonner

1954 Plant Remains from Sites in the Durango and La Plata Areas, Colorado. In *Basket Maker II Sites near Durango, Colorado*, by Earl H. Morris and Robert F. Baugh, pp. 93–115. Publication 604. Carnegie Institution of Washington, Washington, DC.

Kidder, Alfred V.

1927 Southwestern Archaeological Conference. *Science* 68:489–491.

Lowe, Charles

1964 *Arizona's Natural Environment*. University of Arizona Press, Tucson.

Mangelsdorf, Paul C.

1954 New Evidence on the Origin and Ancestry of Maize. *American Antiquity* 19:409–410.

Martin, Paul S.

1963 *The Last 10,000 Years*. University of Arizona Press, Tucson.

Matson, R. G.

1991 *The Origins of Southwestern Agriculture*. University of Arizona Press, Tucson.

Minnis, Paul E.

1985a *Social Adaptation to Food Stress: A Prehistoric Southwestern Example*. University of Chicago Press, Chicago.

1985b Domesticating People and Plants in the Greater Southwest. In *Prehistoric Food Production in North America*, edited by Richard I. Ford, pp. 309–341. Anthropological Papers 75. Museum of Anthropology, University of Michigan, Ann Arbor.

1992a Earliest Plant Cultivation in the Desert Borderlands of North America. In *The Origins of Agriculture: An International Perspective*, edited by C. Wesley Cowan and Patty Jo Watson, pp. 121–141. Smithsonian Institution Press, Washington, DC.

1992b Famine Foods of the North American Desert Borderlands in Historical Context. *Journal of Ethnobiology* 11:231–258.

Minnis, Paul E., and Richard I. Ford

1977 Analysis of Plant Remains from Chimney Rock Mesa. In *Archaeological Investigations at Chimney Rock Mesa: 1970–72*, edited by Frank W. Eddy, pp. 81–91. Memoir 1. Colorado Archaeological Society, Boulder.

Neitzel, Jill E. (editor)

1999 *Great Towns and Regional Polities in the Prehistoric Southwest and Southeast*. University of New Mexico Press, Albuquerque.

Petersen, Kenneth Lee

1988 *Climate and the Dolores River Anasazi*. University of Utah Press, Salt Lake City.

Plog, Stephen

1997 *Ancient Peoples of the American Southwest*. Thames and Hudson, London.

Reid, Jefferson, and Stephanie Whittlesey
    1997   *The Archaeology of Ancient Arizona*. University of Arizona Press, Tucson.
Rose, Martin R., Jeffrey S. Dean, and William J. Robinson
    1981   *The Past Climate of Arroyo Hondo, New Mexico, Reconstructed from Tree Rings*. School of
            American Research Press, Santa Fe.
Schaafsma, Curtis F., and Carroll L. Riley (editors)
    1999   *The Casas Grandes World*. University of Utah Press, Salt Lake City.
Sellers, William D., and Richard H. Hill
    1974   *Arizona Climate*. University of Arizona Press, Tucson.
Tuan, Yi-Fu, Ciril E. Everard, Jerold G. Widdison, and Iven Bennett
    1973   *The Climate of New Mexico*. New Mexico State Planning Office, Santa Fe.
Van Devender, Thomas R., and W. Geoffrey Spaulding
    1979   Development of Vegetation and Climate in the Southwestern United States. *Science*
            204:701–710.
Van West, Carla R.
    1994   *Modeling Prehistoric Agricultural Productivity in Southwestern Colorado: A GIS Approach*.
            Reports of Investigations 67. Department of Anthropology, Washington State University,
            Pullman.
Whalen, Michael E., and Paul E. Minnis
    2001   *Casas Grandes and Its Hinterland: Prehistoric Regional Organization in Northwest Mexico*.
            University of Arizona Press, Tucson.
Wills, Wirt H.
    1988   *Early Prehistoric Agriculture in the American Southwest*. School of American Research Press,
            Santa Fe.
    1992   Plant Cultivation and the Evolution of Risk-Prone Economies in the Prehistoric Ameri-
            can Southwest. In *Transitions to Agriculture in Prehistory*, edited by Anne Birgitte Gebauer
            and T. Douglas Price, pp. 153–176. Prehistory Press, Madison.
York, John C., and William A. Dick-Peddie
    1965   Vegetation Changes in Southern New Mexico during the Past One Hundred Years. In
            Arid Lands in Perspective, edited by William G. McGinnies and Bram J. Goldman,
            pp. 157–166. University of Arizona Press, Tucson.

Chapter 3

Wild Plant Use in the North American Southwest

LISA W. HUCKELL AND MOLLIE S. TOLL

*T*he past 30 years of archaeobotanical research have witnessed quantum leaps in recovery techniques, sampling, the application of new procedures to obtain new lines of evidence, and attempts to interpret and synthesize the accumulating data base. In the North American Southwest, as elsewhere in the continent, we owe the remarkable amount of new data largely to cultural resources management (CRM). We benefit, ironically, from the legislated requirement that archaeological sites facing destruction from certain kinds of economic development must first be recorded and investigated. In a few short decades, paleoethnobotanical studies have made the transition from species lists and reviews of the artifactual high points at a few particularly well preserved sites to routine inclusion of pollen and flotation analyses at myriad projects throughout the region. A hidden boon of CRM is that it necessitates dealing with small and perhaps individually unexciting sites throughout the region. The emerging data base is not only extensive and detailed but also far more representative of the full range of site types and economic activities undertaken than indicated by previous research. This information has made significant contributions to our understanding of settlement subsistence systems and the nature and extent of the flexible adaptive strategies people employed through time and across space.

The Southwest is characterized by considerable geographic and cultural variation. Prior to the emergence of distinct regional cultures, the Southwest was occupied by nomadic hunter-gatherers. The first unequivocal occupants were the Paleoindian hunters of now-extinct Pleistocene megafauna such as mammoth. These hunters first appeared around 11,500 years ago and disappeared 3,000 years later. No plant remains from that period have been reported. The 6,000-year-long Archaic period followed, during which small, mobile bands of people living in ephemeral brush structures practiced a very successful generalized hunting and gathering adaptation. A small record for the early and middle portions of the period comes from both rockshelters and open sites. Maize cultivation appeared during the Late Archaic around 1500–1000 BC, along with new adaptive strategies that involved the integration of farming, foraging, and hunting. These strategies are reflected in major changes in subsistence-settlement systems, with pithouse villages making their first appearance. The introduction of ceramic vessels initiated the ceramic period during the early centuries AD, a time when agriculture-based communities living in pithouse villages or masonry buildings developed into three major regionally distinct cultures. The Anasazi occupied the extensively dissected Colorado Plateau, the Mogollon domain was centered on the rugged mountains of southeastern Arizona and southwestern New Mexico, and the Hohokam occupied the low desert valleys of southern Arizona. This relatively short, latest period in the prehistory of the Southwest is by far the best documented archaeobotanically. For incompletely understood reasons, the ceramic period came to an end with the abandonment of much of the Southwest by the middle of the fifteenth century.

The diverse environments and site types found in this vast region create highly variable conditions for the accumulation and preservation of cultural botanical debris. Much of the southwestern archaeobotanical record comes from open sites that are characterized by poorly preserved remains that devolve primarily from chance and accident. Rare even in the arid Southwest, exceptional preservation situations such as dry shelters can provide valuable insights into the subsistence repertoire and environmental background of any period. In addition to yielding reeds (*Phragmites australis*), cactus pads (*Opuntia*), grass (Poaceae) bundles, corn (*Zea mays*) husks and tassels, squash rind, and a host of other floral materials missing from most archaeobotanical assemblages, optimal preservation conditions result in exceptional recovery of pollen, macrofossils, and coprolites, or paleofeces, which contribute unique direct evidence of prehistoric diet. Variation in the quality and amount of paleobotanical information available from southwestern sites is remarkable. Assemblages range from the two metric tons of vegetal debris recovered from sheltered Antelope House in Canyon de Chelly (Ambrose 1986) to the single charred grass seed recovered from 48 flotation samples taken from small, open Archaic and Anasazi sites in the Navajo Indian Irrigation Project (NIIP) (Donaldson and Toll 1981). This variability exerts a profound influence on the accuracy and reliability of subsistence reconstructions and synthetic efforts at every level.

In this chapter we present a summary of the archaeobotanical record of wild plant use for the North American Southwest, placing emphasis on those areas offering the most extensive archaeobotanical documentation. The focus is on macrofossil evidence, particularly as it relates to foods, although where possible, we also consider coprolite, pollen, and bone chemistry studies. We begin our overviews with the preceramic Archaic period, followed by the three major culture areas: Anasazi, Mogollon/Western Pueblo, and Hohokam. We conclude by reviewing two smaller subregional areas with growing archaeobotanical records and briefly comment on several other areas that offer a wide range of macrofossil data. Table 3.1 provides the common and scientific names of the plants mentioned in the text and tables along with the plant parts of each that are usually recovered. Because of the large number of sites and projects discussed, it is impossible to represent the location of each on a single map; instead, we present generalized zones to which multiple sites can be assigned (Figure 3.1). To provide a more complete picture of the range of plants exploited in the areas discussed, archaeobotanical assemblages of a selected number of representative sites are detailed in tabular form for the Archaic and Basketmaker II/Early Agricultural periods (Table 3.2); Anasazi and Sinagua (Table 3.3); Mogollon/Western Pueblo and Mimbres (Table 3.4); and Hohokam and Tonto Basin Salado (Table 3.5).

Archaic Period

The Archaic period in the Southwest began at roughly 6000 BC and extended to AD 1–500. The boundary between the Early and Middle Archaic periods falls around 3500 BC (Huckell 1996a). The majority of Archaic period sites are small surface manifestations generally lacking formally constructed features

Table 3.1

Plants Mentioned in the Text and Tables, with Parts Recovered

Common Name	Scientific Name	Part Recovered
Acacia	*Acacia* spp.	seed, wood
Acorn	*Quercus* spp.	shell
Agave	*Agave* spp.	leaf, terminal spine, marginal tooth, fiber, quid, epidermis, wood, caudex (heart)
Amaranth	*Amaranthus* sp.; cultigen?	seed
Amaranth, dye	*Amaranthus cruentus*	seed
Amaranth, grain	*Amaranthus hypochondriacus*	seed, inflorescence
Barberry	*Berberis* spp.	seed
Barnyard grass	*Echinochloa crusgalli*	seed
Barrel cactus	*Ferocactus* sp.	seed
Bean, common	*Phaseolus vulgaris*	seed, fruit
Bean family	Fabaceae (Leguminosae)	seed, fruit
Bean, jack	*Canavalia ensiformis*	seed
Bean, lima	*Phaseolus lunatus*	seed, fruit
Bean, tepary	*Phaseolus acutifolius* var. *latifolius*	seed
Beargrass	*Nolina* sp.	wood, leaf
Bedstraw	*Galium* sp.	fruit
Beeweed	*Cleome* spp.	seed
Bentgrass/muhly	*Agrostis/Muhlenbergia*	seed
Bladderpod	*Lesquerella* spp.	seed
Bluestem	*Andropogon* sp.	culm
Borage family	Boraginaceae	seed
Bristlegrass	*Setaria* sp.	inflorescence, seed
Brome/wheatgrass	*Bromus/Agropyron*	seed
Buckwheat, wild	*Eriogonum* spp.	seed
Bugseed	*Corispermum* spp.	seed
Bulrush	*Scirpus* spp.	seed
Bursage	*Ambrosia* spp.	fruit
Cactus family	Cactaceae	seed
Cañaigre	*Rumex hymenosepalus*	root
Canarygrass	*Phalaris* sp.	panicle, seed
Caper family	Capparidaceae	seed
Carpetweed	*Mollugo verticillata*	seed
Carrot family	Apiaceae (Umbelliferae)	seed
Catchfly/campion	*Silene/Lychnis*	seed
Catclaw	*Acacia greggii*	seed
Cattail	*Typha* sp.	leaf
Cheno-am	*Chenopodium/Amaranthus*	seed
Chia	*Salvia* spp.	seed
Chokecherry	*Prunus serotina*	seed
Cholla	*Opuntia* spp.	seed, bud, joint
Clammyweed	*Polanisia trachysperma*	seed

Table 3.1 *continued*

Common Name	Scientific Name	Part Recovered
Cocklebur	*Xanthium* spp.	fruit
Cosmos	*Cosmos* sp.	seed
Cotton	*Gossypium hirsutum* var. *punctatum*	seed, boll, fiber, carpel, stem
Cottonwood	*Populus* spp.	wood
Creosotebush	*Larrea tridentata*	seed, leaf, wood
Cucumber, wild	*Marah gilensis*	seed
Desert willow	*Chilopsis linearis*	wood
Devil's claw	*Proboscidea* spp.	seed, capsule
Dicoria	*Dicoria* spp.	seed
Dock/knotweed	*Rumex/Polygonum*	seed
Doveweed	*Croton* sp.	seed
Dropseed	*Sporobolus* spp.	seed
Elderberry	*Sambucus* spp.	seed, wood
Elymoid grass	*Elymus* and other genera	seed
Evening primrose	*Oenothera* sp.	fruit, seed
False purslane	*Trianthema portulacastrum*	seed
Feathergrass	*Stipa neomexicana*	chaff
Fiddleneck	*Amsinckia* sp.	seed
Fishhook cactus	*Coryphantha* spp.	seed
Four o'clock	*Mirabilis multiflora*	root
Globemallow	*Sphaeralcea* spp.	seed
Goosefoot	*Chenopodium* spp.	seed
Gourd, bottle	*Lagenaria siceraria*	rind, peduncle, seed
Gourd, buffalo	*Cucurbita* spp.	seed, rind
Grama grass	*Bouteloua* spp.	seed
Grass family	Poaceae (Gramineae)	seed, floret
Greasewood	*Sarcobatus vermicularis*	fruit, seed
Gromwell	*Lithospermum* spp.	seed
Groundcherry	*Physalis* sp.	seed
Gourd, wild	*Cucurbita digitata*; *C. foetidissima*	seed, rind
Grape, wild	*Vitis* spp.	seed, fruit
Hackberry	*Celtis* spp.	seed, wood
Hedgehog cactus	*Echinocereus* spp.	seed, stem
Horsetail	*Equisetum* sp.	stem
Iodine bush	*Allenrolfea*	seed
Jimsonweed	*Datura* spp.	seed
Jojoba	*Simmondsia chinensis*	seed, wood
Juniper	*Juniperus* spp.	seed, fruit, wood
Kallstroemia	*Kallstroemia* sp.	seed
Knotweed	*Polygonum* spp.	seed
Little barleygrass	*Hordeum pusillum*	seed, spikelet
Littleleaf paloverde	*Cercidium microphyllum*	fruit, seed
Locoweed	*Astragalus* spp.	seed
Lovegrass	*Eragrostis* spp.	seed

Continued on next page

Wild Plant Use in the North American Southwest

Table 3.1 *continued*

Common Name	Scientific Name	Part Recovered
Maize	*Zea mays*	seed, embryo, ear, cob, cupule, tassel, shank, stalk
Mallow family	Malvaceae	seed, carpel
Manzanita	*Arctostaphylos* spp.	seed, wood
Maygrass	*Phalaris*	seed
Mesquite	*Prosopis* sp.	seed, fruit, wood, endocarp
Mexican crucillo	*Condalia warnockii*	seed
Milkvetch	*Astragalus nuttaliana*	seed
Morning glory	*Ipomoea* sp.	seed
Morning glory family	Convolvulaceae	seed
Mustard family	Brassicaceae (Cruciferae)	seed
Navajo tea	*Thelesperma* spp.	stem, leaf
Nightshade	*Solanum* spp.	seed
Nightshade family	Solanaceae	seed, fruit
Oak	*Quercus* spp.	nutshell, wood
Oat, wild	*Hordeum jubatum*	seed
Onion	*Allium* sp.	tissue
Oshá	*Ligusticum porteri*	root
Panic grass	*Panicum* spp.	seed
Paspalum	*Paspalum* spp.	seed
Peppergrass	*Lepidium* spp.	seed
Phacelia	*Phacelia* spp.	seed
Pigweed	*Amaranthus* spp.	seed
Pincushion cactus	*Mammillaria* spp.	seed
Pink family	Caryophyllaceae	seed
Piñon	*Pinus* spp.	nutshell, cone scale, wood
Plantain	*Plantago* spp.	seed
Plum	*Prunus* sp.	seed
Ponderosa pine	*Pinus ponderosa*	wood
Potato, wild	*Solanum* sp.	seed, tuber
Prickly pear	*Opuntia* spp.	seed, pad, bud, fruit
Prickly poppy	*Argemone* sp.	seed
Primrose	*Oenothera* spp.	fruit, seed
Pumpkin	*Cucurbita pepo*	fruit, rind, seed, peduncle
Purslane	*Portulaca* spp.	seed
Ragweed	*Ambrosia* sp.	fruit
Red sage	*Kochia americana*	seed
Reed	*Phragmites australis*	stem
Ricegrass	*Oryzopsis hymenoides*	seed
Rose	*Rosa* sp.	seed
Rush	*Juncus* sp.	seed
Sage	*Salvia* spp.	seed
Sagebrush	*Artemisia* spp.	seed, wood, leaf, twig, flower
Saguaro	*Carnegiea gigantea*	seed, wood, spine

Table 3.1 *continued*

Common Name	Scientific Name	Part Recovered
Saltbush	*Atriplex* spp.	seed, fruit, wood
Screwbean mesquite	*Prosopis pubescens*	seed, fruit, wood
Sedge family	Cyperaceae	seed
Seepweed	*Suaeda* sp.	seed
Silktassel	*Garrya wrightii*	leaf, twig
Snakeweed	*Gutierrezia sarothrae*	seed
Soapberry	*Sapindus saponaria*	seed
Sotol	*Dasylirion wheeleri*	wood, leaf
Spiderling	*Boerhaavia* spp.	fruit
Sprangletop	*Leptochloa* sp.	seed
Spruce	*Picea* spp.	seed
Spurge	*Euphorbia* spp.	seed
Squash	*Cucurbita* spp.	seed, rind, peduncle,
Squash, crookneck	*Cucurbita argyrosperma* (= *C. moschata*)	fruit, rind, seed, peduncle
Squash, cushaw	*Cucurbita mixta*	fruit, rind, seed, peduncle
Squash/gourd	*Cucurbita* sp.	rind, seed
Squaw-apple	*Peraphyllum ramossisimum*	seed
Stickleaf	*Mentzelia* spp.	seed
Stickseed	*Lappula* sp.	seed
Sumac	*Rhus trilobata*	seed, wood
Sumpweed	*Iva* spp.	seed
Sunflower	*Helianthus* spp.	seed
Sunflower family	Asteraceae (Compositae)	seed
Sycamore	*Platanus wrightii*	wood
Tansy mustard	*Descurainia* sp.	seed
Thistle	*Cirsium* spp.	seed, capitulum
Tick clover	*Desmodium* sp.	seed
Tobacco	*Nicotiana* spp.	seed, leaf, stem
Turk's head cactus	*Echinocactus horizonthalonius*	spine cluster
Verbena	*Verbena* spp.	seed
Vetch	*Astragalus* sp.	seed
Walnut	*Juglans major*	nutshell, wood
Wild ryegrass	Elymoid group (Poaceae)	seed
Willow	*Salix* spp.	wood
Winged pigweed	*Cycloloma atriplicifolium*	seed
Wolfberry	*Lycium* spp.	seed, fruit
Yerba mansa	*Anemopsis californica*	seed
Yucca	*Yucca* spp.	seed, fruit, leaf, fiber, terminal spine
Yucca, banana	*Yucca baccata*	seed, leaf, fruit, fiber, terminal spine

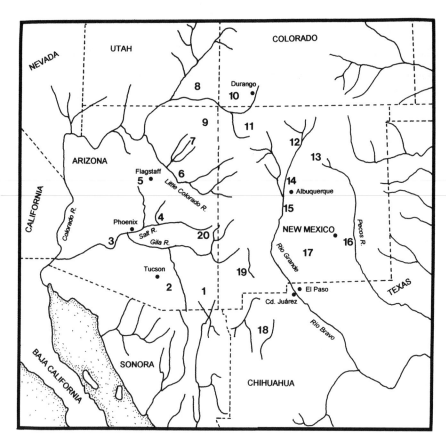

FIGURE 3.1   The North American Southwest: 1. Sulphur Springs and
San Simon Valleys; 2. Tucson Basin and Cienega Creek; 3. Salt River and
Gila River Basin; 4. Tonto Basin; 5. Flagstaff region and Upper Verde River
Valley; 6. Middle Little Colorado River; 7. Hopi Mesas and Black Mesa;
8. southeastern Utah and Kayenta; 9. Chuska Mountains, Red Rock Valley,
Canyon de Chelly; 10. Mesa Verde, Dolores Project; 11. San Juan Basin, Chaco;
12. Northern Rio Grande Valley, Chama Valley; 13. Upper Pecos River Valley,
Galisteo Basin; 14. Central Rio Grande Valley; 15. Rio Abajo; 16. Hondo
Valley, Lower Pecos River Valley; 17. Jornada Mogollon, Tularosa Basin;
18. northwestern Chihuahua, Casas Grandes; 19. Mimbres region;
20. Upper Gila River Valley, Mogollon highlands

apart from hearths, although a few larger, more established residential sites with pit structures have been found (Huckell 1995, 1996a). Current views of Archaic subsistence are based primarily on site distributions, ground stone and flaked stone tool kits, and ethnographic analogy. Prolonged exposure, deflation, and erosion of sites have left very little direct evidence of subsistence. Although this description fits many Late Archaic sites as well, it is becoming clear that some time around 1500 BC, a significant change took place throughout much of the Southwest that corresponded with the appearance of maize agriculture. Traditionally referred to as the Basketmaker II period in the northern region and, more recently, as the Early Agricultural period (Huckell 1996a), the archaeological record of this time span is marked by the appearance of large-scale storage features and more substantial habitations, all of which indicate shifts in mobility and subsistence patterns.

Early–Middle Archaic: Northern Southwest

On the Colorado Plateau, flotation samples from small, open Archaic sites (Toll 1983) tend to contain seeds of cheno-ams, other disturbed-ground annuals, and two principal grasses, ricegrass (*Oryzopsis hymenoides*) and dropseed (*Sporobolus*) (Reed 1999). Where assemblages consist of a very small number of charred seeds (Donaldson 1982; Gasser 1981b), we have no way of determining whether the narrow taxonomic array and the emphasis on taxa that naturally produce large numbers of seeds are the products of cultural selection or of sample size bias. In the few open sites with preserved macrofossils, assemblages appear to represent variability in a hunting and gathering adaptation by small, mobile bands. In the Navajo Mines area in northwest New Mexico, flotation remains document plant gathering during a single segment of the growing season, with ricegrass (obtained in spring) occurring at some sites and goosefoot and dropseed (collected in late summer) at others (Toll 1983). Evidence for short-term occupation includes fuelwood obtained from the immediate site area and the absence of substantial hearths, storage facilities, and structures. Other Archaic floral assemblages represent the whole growing season, as exemplified by the spring ricegrass, mustard, and late-summer cheno-ams recovered from a large site on the Navajo Indian Irrigation Project (NIIP) in the San Juan Basin of northwestern New Mexico (Streuver and Knight 1983) and by the spring ricegrass found with late-summer cheno-ams, prickly pear cactus (*Opuntia*), and beeweed (*Cleome serrulata*) at a deeply buried site on Black Mesa in northeastern Arizona

(Trigg 1985). Sites with broader plant-use spectra may indicate a longer occupation period or successive episodes of reuse.

Most of the limited archaeobotanical evidence related to Early and Middle Archaic subsistence in the northern Colorado Plateau area comes from a small number of caves located in northern Arizona and southeastern Utah, from which well-preserved macrofossils, pollen, and coprolites have been studied. Chief among the sites are Cowboy Cave (Hogan 1980; Schroedl and Coulam 1994), Sudden Shelter (Coulam and Barnett 1980), Dust Devil Cave (Van Ness 1986) (Table 3.2), and Old Man Cave (Hansen 1994; Van Ness and Hansen 1996) (Table 3.2), all in southeastern Utah. Although, as expected, some variability occurs in assemblage composition, a suite of consistently utilized plants has been identified that includes cheno-ams, sunflower (*Helianthus*), grasses—among which dropseed and wildrye (Elymoid group spp.) are prominent—and prickly pear cactus (Hansen 1994:Table 10). Seasonality data suggest a winter occupation of the shelters, and a number of the taxa are known from the ethnographic record for their use during times when preferred foods are not available. A similar pattern is found in northern New Mexico, where coprolites from Atlatl Cave at Chaco Canyon (Table 3.2) indicate consumption of sunflower, dropseed, mustard, and piñon (*Pinus*) nuts (Toll 1981). The overall subsistence adaptation reconstructed for the San Juan Basin is one of broad-spectrum foraging with preferential status given weedy annuals that produce abundant small seeds.

A very different aspect of Middle Archaic plant use has been identified at rockshelters in parts of Arizona, California, Nevada, and Utah. These protected locations have served as ritual repositories for twig segments and split-twig zoomorphic figurines, some of which are pierced with twig spears. Ingeniously constructed of single, long shoots of willow (*Salix*), cottonwood (*Populus*), or sumac (*Rhus*) (Bohrer 1992; Euler 1984), the artifacts probably functioned in sympathetic hunting magic directed at procurement of large game such as deer, bighorn sheep, and mountain goat (Emslie et al. 1987).

Early–Middle Archaic: Central Southwest

Wild plant remains unequivocally attributable to the Early and Middle Archaic periods have yet to be recovered from the Mogollon highlands region. Most sites are surface lithic scatters that offer no opportunities for organic preservation. The earliest record comes from the Late Archaic/Early Agricultural period, which is widely known because of the extraordinarily well preserved and abundant plant remains recovered from three famous sites located in and near the Mogollon highlands: Tularosa, Cordova, and Bat Caves in west-central New Mexico (Dick 1965; Martin et al. 1952). Despite the sheer volume of material obtained from these caves (more than 30,000 maize cobs were recovered from Tularosa Cave alone) and despite the researchers' primary focus on cultigens as part of the investigation of the evolution of corn and the spread of agriculture, only brief, preliminary reports have been issued (Cutler 1952; Dick 1965; Kaplan 1963) (Table 3.2). Significant portions of the wild plant components of the assemblages are unevenly and incompletely reported. Furthermore, the problem of isolating unmodified Archaic-age materials was complicated by excavation by arbitrary levels, multicomponent occupations, and ongoing bioturbation of deposits over time. The reports that exist do not provide the contextual data needed for reliable evaluation of the temporal affiliation of the wild plants recovered. Regrettably, much of the material remains unanalyzed. Plant taxa yielding edible and medicinal parts that may be related to the Archaic occupations include juniper (*Juniperus*), piñon, several grasses, two species of yucca (*Yucca*), walnut (*Juglans*), acorns (*Quercus*), chenopods, winged pigweed (*Cycloloma*), pigweed (*Amaranthus*), tansy mustard (*Descurainia*), stickleaf (*Mentzelia*), various cacti, buffalo gourd (*Cucurbita foetidissima*), sunflower, thistle (*Cirsium*), wild tobacco (*Nicotiana*), oshá (*Ligusticum*), and primrose (*Oenothera*) (Cutler 1952). Bat Cave was re-excavated in 1981 and 1983 (Wills 1988), but the wild plant component of the recovered botanical remains has yet to be reported.

Early–Middle Archaic: Southern Southwest

In the southern Southwest, the Early and Middle Archaic periods are poorly known, primarily because of the near-complete absence of caves in the region and poor preservation at open sites. Further complications arise from re-cently identified major erosional events in several river valleys in the Salt, Gila, Tucson, and Tonto Basins that may have eliminated the geological units and surfaces on which sites of these time periods were established. The two most influential places in terms of defining the material and chronological character of the area's Early Archaic are Ventana Cave (Haury 1950), located on the Tohono O'odham reservation in southwestern Arizona, and a series of buried sites in Whitewater Draw in the Sulphur Spring Valley of southeast-ern Arizona (Sayles and Antevs 1941). Stratified deposits were found in Ven-tana Cave, but organic materials in the lower units had been destroyed by chronic exposure to moisture. Charcoal suitable for radiocarbon dating was obtained from some early sites, but no other plant remains were recovered

Table 3.2

Macrofossil and Coprolite Records from Selected Archaic, Early Agricultural, and Basketmaker II Period Sites

Location/Site	Map Location	Date	Plants (References)
Tsosie Shelter	7	Early Archaic	w: purslane, goosefoot, saltbush, pigweed, prickly pear, ricegrass, juniper (Trigg 1985)
Dust Devil Cave[a]	8	Early Archaic	w: cf. onion, hackberry, goosefoot, cheno-am, sunflower, sunflower family, cf. stickseed, mallow family, prickly pear, ricegrass, piñon, grass family, knotweed, purslane, nightshade family, dropseed (Van Ness 1986; Van Ness and Hansen 1996)
Old Man Cave[a]	8	Early Archaic	w: prickly pear, dropseed, sumpweed, sunflower, goosefoot, beeweed, purslane, juniper, cf. knotweed, sumac, grass family (Hansen 1994; Van Ness and Hansen 1996)
Picacho Peak Arroyo site	3	Middle Archaic	w: cheno-am, saguaro, hedgehog cactus, purslane, tansy mustard, grass family (Raymer and Minnis 1986)
Los Pozos	2	Middle Archaic	w: cheno-am, bentgrass/muhly, tansy mustard, lovegrass, dropseed, mesquite, mustard family (Diehl 1999)
Keystone Dam	17	Middle Archaic	w: saltbush, cheno-am, Turk's head cactus, grass family, prickly pear, poppy family, purslane, smartweed, screwbean mesquite, dock, bulrush, mesquite/acacia (O'Laughlin 1980)
UII/Navajo Mine	11	Archaic	w: goosefoot, pigweed, bugseed, tansy mustard, globemallow, ricegrass, dropseed, saltbush (Knight 1980; Toll 1983)
Atlatl Cave[a]	11	Archaic	w: piñon, dropseed, sunflower, tansy mustard (Toll 1981a)
Transwestern Pipeline	11	Archaic/BMII	c: maize; w: goosefoot, pigweed, purslane, bugseed, peppergrass, plantain, ricegrass, hedgehog cactus, prickly pear, juniper, piñon, wolfberry (Hammett and McBride 1993b)
Lukachukai	9	Late Archaic/BMII	c: maize; w: cheno-am, goosefoot, bugseed, winged pigweed, mustard family, purslane (Gilpin 1994)
Black Mesa sites	7	BMII	c: maize; w: juniper, piñon, saltbush, goosefoot, purslane, red sage, pigweed, ricegrass, grass family, sunflower, globemallow, buckwheat, milkvetch, prickly pear, cactus family (Ford 1984)
San Jose de Cabezon LA 110946	14	Early Agricultural	c: maize; w: pigweed, cf. sagebrush, saltbush, cheno-am, goosefoot spp., sunflower family, bugseed, cholla, tansy mustard, spurge, grass family, cf. rush, juniper, bean family, ricegrass, groundcherry/nightshade, piñon, prickly pear, knotweed, purslane, dock/knotweed, cf. sage, cf. greasewood, bulrush, globemallow, dropseed, banana yucca (Huckell and McBride 1999)

Site	No.	Period	Plants
NM 90: 2 sites	19	Late Archaic/ Early Agricultural	c: maize; w: pigweed, goosefoot, cheno-am, winged pigweed, mustard family, bugseed, tansy mustard, grass family, sunflower family, walnut, juniper, stickleaf, tobacco, prickly pear/cholla, groundcherry/nightshade, cf. pine, purslane, acorn, dock/knotweed, dropseed, yucca (Huckell 2000b)
Tularosa Cave	20	Early Agricultural	c: maize, beans, squash, bottle gourd, wild gourd; w: yucca, hedgehog cactus, primrose, thistle, agave, yucca, grass family spp. (Cutler 1952)
Cordova Cave	20	Early Agricultural	c: maize; w: wild gourd, bottle gourd, walnut, yucca, agave (Kaplan 1963)
Fresnal Shelter	17	Early Agricultural	c: maize, common bean; w: saltbush, wild gourd, juniper, four o'clock, grass family, screwbean mesquite, dropseed, feathergrass, Turk's head cactus, pigweed, prickly pear (Bohrer 1981a; Tagg 1996)
Santa Cruz Bend	2	Early Agricultural	c: maize; w: cf. agave, pigweed, saltbush, saguaro, cheno-am, goosefoot, tansy mustard, hedgehog cactus, grass family, bean family, stickleaf, prickly pear/cholla, purslane, mesquite, sage, globemallow, dropseed, seepweed, false purslane (Huckell 1998a)
Stone Pipe	2	Early Agricultural	c: maize; w: tobacco, cf. agave, pigweed, saguaro, cheno-am, goosefoot, sunflower family, tansy mustard, spurge, grass family, rush, bean family, stickleaf, mesquite, sage, dropseed, seepweed, false purslane (Huckell 1998a)
Matty Canyon: Cienega Creek	2	Early Agricultural	c: maize; w: sedge family, dropseed, cf. brome/wheatgrass, rush, acorn, purslane, false purslane, juniper, cheno-am, mesquite, rush, squash/gourd, cf. golden eye, sage, morning glory, bean family, agave, kallstroemia, ragweed, walnut, cf. dock/knotweed, mallow family, saguaro, spurge, carpetweed, prickly pear, sumac, yucca spp., saltbush, cf. groundcherry/nightshade (Huckell 1995a)
Cerro Juanaqueña	18	Early Agricultural	c: maize, amaranth; w: wild gourd, chia, plains lovegrass, grass family spp., milkvetch, bulrush, globemallow, false purslane, barrel cactus, groundcherry, cf. spurge (Hard and Roney 1998, 1999)

Note: BM = Basketmaker; c = cultivated, w = wild.

For map locations, refer to Figure 3.1.

[a]coprolites

49

from any of these sites. Although the debut and continued presence of milling stones points to the processing of plant products, no direct evidence currently exists as to what those plant foods may have been.

The Middle Archaic period is almost as poorly known as the preceding period. Materials of this period tend to appear as components within stratified sites or as shallow surface manifestations that occasionally achieve considerable artifact density and areal extent (Agenbroad 1970) but offer virtually no preserved plant remains. Three exceptions include the Arroyo site located halfway between Phoenix and Tucson (Table 3.2), the Boatyard site in the Tonto Basin northeast of Phoenix, and Los Pozos in the Tucson Basin (Table 3.2). The Arroyo site assemblage consists of small quantities of cheno-ams, grasses, saguaro (*Carnegiea gigantea*), hedgehog cactus (*Echinocereus*), purslane (*Portulaca*), and tansy mustard (Raymer and Minnis 1986). The Middle Archaic component at the Boatyard site produced grass, hedgehog cactus, and possible mustard family seeds (Huckell 2000a). Los Pozos contained cheno-ams, three grass species, tansy mustard, and mesquite (*Prosopis*) (Diehl 1999) (Table 3.2). These modest records suggest the exploitation of widely available annual and perennial taxa that appear consistently in assemblages of later time periods, reflecting their universally recognized value as dietary components.

Basketmaker II/Late Archaic/Early Agricultural Period

The conceptual structure of the period between 1500 BC and AD 500 in the North American Southwest has undergone a remarkable transformation over the last 15 years, with infusions of new data coming from northern and southern Arizona and northern Mexico (Carpenter et al. 1997; Gilpin 1994; Hard and Roney 1998; Huckell 1990, 1995; Huckell et al. 1995; Mabry et al. 1997; Matson 1991; Smiley and Parry 1990). This time period is now seen as one of profound change in most of the region, with the widespread adoption of maize the signature event. Once called the Late Archaic, it is now widely referred to as the Early Agricultural or Basketmaker II period, with "Late Archaic" reserved for sites of the period that lack evidence of agriculture (Huckell 1995).

Northern Southwest

In the northern Southwest, maize was firmly integrated into the subsistence regime during the Basketmaker II period, as initially revealed by exceptionally well preserved materials from a series of caves in the Kayenta and Durango areas (Guernsey and Kidder 1921; Jones and Fonner 1954; Kidder and Guernsey 1919; Matson 1991). The wild plant record from these sites is minimal because of recovery bias, making assessments of the dietary role of wild plants impossible. Stable carbon isotope studies carried out on skeletal remains of Basketmaker II (BMII) individuals from several sites indicate that C4/CAM plants were central dietary elements, with maize the primary contributor (Chisholm and Matson 1994; Martin 1999; Martin et al. 1991).[1] Coprolite data for the same period from southeastern Utah also demonstrate the staple status of maize, but consumption of a variety of wild plants was also documented, with cheno-ams, ricegrass, purslane, prickly pear, beeweed, saltbush (*Atriplex*), and bursage (*Ambrosia*) present. The dietary profile created by the macrofossil and pollen records matches those of later Puebloans (Aasen 1984), an indication of continuity in the farming/foraging economy established during the Basketmaker II period.

The macrobotanical record for this period is growing steadily, offering an expanding inventory of economic wild taxa that is dominated by weedy annuals and grasses. Recurring annual taxa include cheno-ams, bugseed (*Corispermum*), tansy mustard, and purslane, with dropseed and ricegrass the most frequent grasses. Whether actively encouraged or simply naturally abundant on the landscape, these plants served as subregional staples (Brandt 1994, 1995; Cummings et al. 1996; Dean 1991; Huckell and McBride 1999; Reed 1999). The importance of wild plants to residents of areas characterized by great variability in growing conditions is discussed by Ford (1984), who proposed that in the Black Mesa area, an environment lacking in resource diversity and density, concentrated weedy resources such as goosefoot, pigweed, and purslane growing in anthropogenic environments such as fallow or abandoned fields significantly increased edible biomass and yield predictability (Table 3.2).

Central and Southern Southwest

The early work at the classic cave sites in the Mogollon highlands area formed the basis for an early model of the arrival of agriculture as a localized montane event, with cultigens first largely restricted to the Mogollon area and then slowly diffusing to lower elevations with more arid environments (Haury 1962; Minnis 1985b, 1992). More recent work has provided the basis for an alternative model proposing the rapid spread of maize via lowland river valleys. Recently investigated sites in southern Arizona along the floodplains of the Santa Cruz River and its tributaries (Mabry 1998) as well as in the San Pedro River valley immediately to the east (Huckell 1990) have produced evidence of dramatic and rapid changes in settlement pattern, architecture, storage technology, material items, projectile point styles, and subsistence systems in the basin floors. Most significant is the appearance of extensive pithouse villages that include hundreds of intramural and extramural storage pits that are consistently associated with maize. Maize has appeared in almost all of the recently investigated sites of this time period, usually in extremely high ubiquities (Huckell 1995b, 1998a). Extensively terraced hillside *trincheras* sites in northern Chihuahua also appear to be large habitation sites situated adjacent to fertile river floodplains where maize agriculture was undertaken (Hard and Roney 1998a, 1999). The preferential location of these villages along floodplains is significant, as this allowed for optimal access to arable land and reliable water supplies. A recent investigation into middle to late Holocene stream behavior in the major drainages in southeastern Arizona suggests that the arrival of maize agriculture was correlated with a change in stream flow regime from one of degradation to one of aggradation, creating the floodplains requisite for successful farming (Huckell 1996b). Aggradation also promoted unusually good site preservation through the rapid burial of settlements established along the floodplain margins.

Because of the excellent preservation at Early Agricultural riverine sites, a much more complete picture of the wild plant component of the economy can be constructed. An examination of the macroplant inventory from six sites in the Tucson Basin and an additional four sites from the Cienega Creek and San Pedro River valleys to the south and east, respectively, reveals the presence and inferred use of more than 40 wild taxa (Huckell 1995a, 1998a: Tables 3.21, 3.22) (Table 3.2). Over half are annuals, with the remainder divided among perennial shrubs, cacti, and trees. Common taxa found at several sites in the Tucson Basin floor include cheno-ams, grasses, tansy mustard, false purslane (*Trianthema*), mesquite, and saguaro. The Cienega Creek (Table 3.2) and San Pedro River sites are located at higher elevations and in different biotic communities, but they too yielded cheno-ams, grasses, and mesquite. They also produced a number of taxa not readily available in the Tucson Basin floodplain settlements, such as acorns, yucca, manzanita (*Arctostaphylos*), walnut, and sumac (*Rhus*). Lowland sites also provide evidence of logistical mobility for the procurement of upland resources such as probable agave, probable acorn, juniper, and manzanita (Huckell 1998a:Table 3.21). Several of the same taxa have been recovered from the Chihuahuan Cerro Juanaqueña *trinchera* site (Table 3.2), where the record consists of barrel cactus (*Ferocactus*), wild gourd, bulrush (*Scirpus*), grasses, sage (*Salvia*), and vetch

(*Astragalus*), along with cheno-ams, false purslane, groundcherry (*Physalis*), and globemallow (*Sphaeralcea*), all of which are annuals (Hard and Roney 1998, 1999) (Table 3.2).

The high visibility of cheno-ams, grasses, and weedy annuals in Early Agricultural period records may have been promoted by expanding anthropogenic habitats such as fields, gardens, burned areas, and middens, in which economically significant taxa were tolerated and probably encouraged. One of the tolerated plants may have been tobacco (*Nicotiana*), which made its earliest known regional appearance to date at the Stone Pipe site, where it was found in an exceptionally large late Early Agricultural period pithouse in association with a finely carved stone pipe (Huckell 1998a). Whether the tobacco was a true cultigen or an encouraged wild species remains to be determined. Minimal evidence is present thus far for the exploitation of riparian and aquatic plants, although preservation bias may play a significant role in their archaeological visibility (Table 3.2); taxa such as cattail are better represented in the pollen record.

The growing record for this period indicates that, as early as 1500–1000 BC, maize agriculture was successfully integrated with plant gathering to create a highly successful, diversified farming/foraging economy in which a wide range of wild plant resources continued to be exploited, initiating perhaps the most successful and durable risk-minimization strategy adopted in the arid Southwest.

The Ceramic Period

Anasazi

Anasazi territory is centered on the Colorado Plateau in the Four Corners area, the meeting place of Arizona, New Mexico, Colorado, and Utah. The rugged topography of the Colorado Plateau consists of incised tablelands punctuated by mountain ranges, creating interspersed basins and small plateaus. Distinctive subregional Anasazi branches include the Kayenta (Figure 3.1, Nos. 7, 8, 9), Mesa Verde (Figure 3.1, No. 10), Virgin, Middle Rio Grande (Figure 3.1, No. 14), and the Chaco/San Juan Basin (Figure 3.1, No. 11) (Cordell 1997:188). Puebloan occupation of the region was characterized by the emergence of regionally complex sociopolitical systems and increasing population size, aggregation, and resettlement. The area was largely abandoned by the early 15th century AD. Frequent migrations were primarily driven by extreme climatic shifts or events that made farming a marginal and often unsuccessful endeavor in a region of short growing seasons, intermittent water flow, and limited agricultural lands. Economically significant wild resources were generally limited in quantity and dispersed within vegetation characterized by high resource redundancy (Cordell 1997:283; Dean et al. 1994).

The emergence of a Puebloan identity commenced during the Basketmaker III (BMIII) period at approximately AD 400–600 (Cordell 1997:249). Ceramic containers appeared, with divergent characteristic local design styles evolving over the ensuing centuries. Settlements initially consisted of pithouses that, by AD 1000, were largely but not completely replaced by surface masonry rooms that formed pueblos.

The shift from pit structures occupied by seasonally mobile populations to surface masonry rooms constructed by more sedentary inhabitants resulted in a marked change in patterning of archaeobotanical data. As a result of the greater duration and intensity of occupation, accumulation of plant debris greatly increased. The plant remains at long-term habitation sites and residential field houses provide the bulk of the evidence for subsistence activities during the ceramic period. Low macrofossil productivity characterizes smaller, less intensively occupied site types such as isolated storage structures, day-use field houses, and short-term habitations associated with gathering or processing specific food and raw material resources.

Plant utilization of the late Basketmaker II–early Pueblo occupation is richly but incompletely documented in cave sites of the Four Corners area, where remarkable BMII perishable materials were found in the Kayenta subarea (Guernsey and Kidder 1921; Kidder and Guernsey 1919). Investigation of caves in the Prayer Rock area provided examples of basketry, clothing, and utilitarian and wooden artifacts (Hays-Gilpin et al. 1998; Morris 1980). Only large or familiar plant remnants that were visible to excavators were collected; these remains included corn, squash (_Cucurbita_), bottle gourd (_Lagenaria_), beans (_Phaseolus_), and piñon nuts. Myriad small utilized wild plant remains went unrecorded. Data from open sites of this period have been far less informative than those from caves, but recent analyses of early Chaco area sites provide useful insights into subsistence and economics (Toll 1993b) (Table 3.3). These sites offer substantial evidence of farming but contain a meager representation of the range of economic annuals consistently recovered from later Pueblo II (PII) and Pueblo III (PIII) sites in the Chaco Basin. Economic annuals include goosefoot, winged pigweed, pigweed, purslane, cocklebur (_Xanthium_), tobacco, and possibly groundcherry, stickleaf, and beeweed, all of which have been recovered only as unburned seeds. The array is very similar to the taxa found with far greater frequency at later sites. Grasses and perennials consistently appear in low frequencies in the larger and later Chacoan flotation assemblage; their low profile to date in the earlier material may be due to sampling error. To the west, sites with ties to Chaco Canyon show that this early Anasazi period of successful farming was accompanied by a robust foraging effort, with both maize and wild economic plants at their highest ubiquity, density, and diversity (Winter 1993b).

Although some parts of the San Juan Basin show signs of an economic slump having occurred as early as the PII period, the long-term picture is one of increasing intensity and diversity of subsistence effort with time. The number of taxa utilized and array of habitats exploited were greater in PII occupations at both large and small sites in the Chaco Basin and Four Corners area compared with earlier periods (Donaldson 1982; McBride 1993; Toll 1983, 1985) (Table 3.3). So much of the observed variation in density and diversity of plant remains may be affected by differential preservation conditions at different site types that it is useful to look at time shifts within a single, well-sampled site, Pueblo Alto, occupied from AD 1020 to 1150. Here the earliest PII occupation is marked by particularly high occurrences of some important wild perennials (piñon, prickly pear, hedgehog cactus) and some weedy annuals, such as sunflower, together with the lowest percentage of samples with corn (Toll 1987a:Table 11.35). At Salmon Ruin, a large PIII pueblo roughly 50 km north of Pueblo Alto on the banks of the San Juan River, wild plants also show an inverse quantitative relationship with corn (Doebley 1981), but in many parts of the Colorado Plateau analysts find no conclusive evidence that corn was produced intensively at the expense of wild plants (Hammett 1993b:459). Detailed studies of corn morphometrics have suggested that people in many areas within the San Juan Basin may have been experiencing difficulties producing corn in the PIII period. Evidence points to a second focus on corn agriculture as the main subsistence element during this period, this time based on desperation rather than success. In their effort to sustain their increasing population, the inhabitants of the San Juan Basin seem to have invested even more effort in farming, with fewer wild plants incorporated into the diet. This effort ultimately failed, and much of Chaco and the central San Juan Basin were abandoned in the mid-11th century.

Perhaps the most salient aspect of wild plant use in the San Juan Basin was its consistency from one era to the next. We see an array of weedy annuals

Table 3.3
Macrofossil Records from Selected Anasazi and Sinagua Sites

Location/Site	Map Location	Date	Plants (References)
Chaco Canyon	11	BMIII–PIII	c: maize, common bean, squash, bottle gourd; w: goosefoot, pigweed, purslane, beeweed, bugseed, winged pigweed, tansy mustard, sunflower, stickleaf, tobacco, groundcherry, globemallow, wild potato, ricegrass, dropseed, hedgehog cactus, prickly pear, yucca, walnut, juniper, piñon, sumac, saltbush, wild grape, horsetail, rush, reed, sedge family, cattail (Toll 1985, 1993b)
UII/Navajo Mines	11	BMIII–PIII	c: maize; w: goosefoot, pigweed, purslane, beeweed, bugseed, winged pigweed, tansy mustard, stickleaf, plantain, globemallow, ricegrass, dropseed, juniper, saltbush (Knight 1980; Toll 1983)
Transwestern Pipeline	11	BMIII–PIII	c: maize, squash, bottle gourd; w: goosefoot, pigweed, purslane, beeweed, bugseed, winged pigweed, tansy mustard, sunflower, tobacco, groundcherry, globemallow, wild potato, ricegrass, dropseed, hedgehog cactus, prickly pear, yucca, walnut, juniper, piñon, saltbush, reed (McBride 1993a)
Salmon Ruin	11	PII–PIII	c: maize; w: cf. pigweed, cf. yerba mansa, cf. sedge, cheno-am, goosefoot, beeweed, sunflower family, gourd/squash, cf. winged pigweed, cf. tansy mustard, cf. tick clover, spurge, grass family, juniper, mallow family, bean family, cf. groundcherry, cf. stickleaf, cf. ricegrass, piñon, clammyweed, cf. knotweed, purslane, cf. screwbean mesquite, plum/chokecherry, cf. sumac, cf. sage, cf. bulrush, nightshade family, cf. dropseed, cf. false purslane, banana yucca (Doebley 1981)
Rowe Pueblo	13	PIII–PIV	c: maize, squash, tobacco; w: piñon, juniper, dropseed, grass family, cactus family, pigweed, goosefoot, cheno-am, mustard family, tansy mustard, nightshade family, purslane, sunflower, bulrush, hedgehog cactus, bugseed, prickly pear, groundcherry, globemallow, ricegrass, dropseed, chokecherry, sedge (Toll 1998a)
Arroyo Hondo	13	PIV	c: maize, common bean, squash; w: purslane, cheno-am, winged pigweed, beeweed, sunflower, groundcherry, ricegrass, hedgehog cactus, pincushion cactus, banana yucca, chokecherry, piñon (Wetterstrom 1986)
Antelope House	9	PII–PIII	c: maize, common bean, squash, bottle gourd, cotton; w: goosefoot, pigweed, purslane, beeweed, bladderpod, peppergrass, globemallow, wild potato, groundcherry, dropseed, knotweed, four o'clock, Navajo tea, devil's claw, onion, yucca, walnut, juniper, piñon, saltbush, reed, sedge (Hall and Dennis 1986)
Dolores Project	10	BMIII–PIII	c: maize, common bean, squash, bottle gourd; w: goosefoot, pigweed, purslane, beeweed, tansy mustard, sunflower, stickleaf, tobacco, knotweed, plantain, verbena, groundcherry, globemallow,

Site			
Duckfoot	10	PI	wild potato, ricegrass, prickly pear, yucca, juniper, piñon, sumac, saltbush, horsetail, rush, reed, sedge, cattail (Matthews 1986)
Homol'ovi II	6	PIV	c: maize, cf. common bean; w: juniper, cf. sagebrush, cf. saltbush, cf. caper family, cheno-am, sunflower family, cf. tansy mustard, cf. hedgehog cactus, cf. bedstraw, grass family, bean family, mallow family, cf. stickleaf, cf. prickly pear, cf. squaw-apple, reed, cf. groundcherry, purslane, sumac, cf. bulrush, cf. ricegrass, cf. banana yucca (Adams 1993)
Lizard Man[a]	5	PII–PIII	c: maize, common bean, tepary bean, lima bean, squash, cotton; w: ricegrass, dropseed, tansy mustard, pigweed, goosefoot, greasewood, locoweed, buckwheat, purslane, beeweed, globemallow, cholla, yucca, knotweed, sumac, juniper, piñon, barberry, hedgehog cactus, fishhook cactus, grama grass (Miksicek 1991)
Walnut Canyon[a]	5	PII–PIII	c: maize, common bean, tepary bean, squash, bottle gourd, cotton; w: bugseed, purslane, pigweed, goosefoot, sunflower, snakeweed, knotweed, juniper spp., grass family spp., saltbush, peppergrass, manzanita, elderberry, dropseed, sagebrush, wild oat, barnyard grass, fishhook cactus, cf. wolfberry, cf. rose, prickly pear, walnut, acorn, piñon, groundcherry/nightshade, cactus family, beargrass, agave, unknown tuber (Hunter et al. 1999)
Elden Pueblo[a]	5	PIII	c: maize, squash, common bean spp., tepary bean, cotton; w: piñon, walnut, banana yucca, reed, juniper, agave, beargrass, juniper spp., ricegrass, dropseed, grass family, acorn, saltbush, goosefoot, bugseed, winged pigweed, pigweed, purslane, barberry, rose, sumac, grape, cholla, prickly pear, manzanita, stickseed, gromwell, elderberry, sunflower family, cf. cosmos, dicoria, wild gourd (Huckell 1999b; Rixey and Voll 1962); c: maize, common bean spp., squash, bottle gourd, cotton; w: goosefoot, grama grass, sunflower, pigweed, juniper, purslane, agave, piñon, acorn, walnut, bugseed, catchfly, elderberry, spruce, cf. stickleaf, grass family spp., goosefoot family, sunflower family, nightshade family, cactus family, unknown tuber (Hunter and Wright 1998)
Winona and Ridge Ruins[a]	5	PII	c: maize, squash, common bean, tepary bean, cotton; w: banana yucca, goosefoot, beargrass, reed, walnut, acorn (Jones 1941)
Montezuma Castle area[a]	5	PIII	c: maize, squash, squash spp., bottle gourd, lima bean, common bean, cotton; w: wild gourd, yucca, acorn, walnut, mesquite, acacia, jimsonweed, reed (Cutler and Kaplan 1956; Pierson 1956)

Note: BM = Basketmaker, P = Pueblo; c = cultivated, w = wild.

For map locations, refer to Figure 3.1.

[a]Sinagua

utilized from early on, including taxa with both edible greens and tiny seeds, whose growth habits encouraged proliferation in disturbed areas such as habitation perimeters and fields. Goosefoot was the most common such taxon, appearing with purslane in as many as 62 percent of samples in the southern reaches of the Colorado Plateau (Minnis 1982; Toll and Donaldson 1982). Pigweed, winged pigweed, beeweed, and tansy mustard were also of wide-spread importance; bugseed, sunflower, groundcherry, and stickleaf appear less often among recovered remains. The record of tobacco use now extends securely back into the Basketmaker/Pueblo I period as well (Adams and Toll 2000). Several perennials such as cacti, reeds, and sedges (Cyperaceae) appear occasionally. The recovery of piñon nutshells is more consistent in the south, where this important resource was locally available. Farming was a vital part of Basketmaker/early Pueblo economic life in the basin, as shown by some of the largest and most uniform corn recovered from small sites, and by bean and squash seed morphometrics that are consistent with specimens from later periods. Both construction and fuelwood inventories show early utilization of conifer species in the central basin. The PII record in Chaco shows considerable pressure on local resources, as seen in the use of local conifers for fuel (Toll 1993b). Compelling evidence indicates that, from this period on, as building progressed rapidly and population levels also presumably rose, Chaco beams came increasingly from mountain forests outside the San Juan Basin, where ponderosa pine (*Pinus ponderosa*) logs were cropped from stands characterized by rapid, uniform growth (Windes and Ford 1996; Windes and McKenna 2001). The shrub component of charcoal in heating features and trash decreases in quantity and diversity over time, whereas piñon and juniper increase, suggesting that firewood may also have been imported late in the Chaco sequence.

In the northern Rio Grande Valley, early ceramic period sites tend to be small, shallow, and open, the brief occupations providing few opportunities for good preservation. Plant remains typically include those of both canyon bottom habitats—annuals, sedge, sumac, chokecherry (*Prunus*)—and taxa of drier, rockier uplands, such as piñon and juniper (Toll 1984). Both agricultural and wild plant food products point to summer occupation and early fall harvests; spring taxa such as ricegrass, tansy mustard, and stickleaf are rarely encountered. Use of locally available weedy taxa such as goosefoot, amaranth, purslane, sunflower, and sumpweed (*Iva*), along with dropseed and piñon, has been documented at Rowe Pueblo (Toll 1998) (Table 3.3). In the succeeding PII and PIII periods, mixed farming and foraging economies continued to be the rule. In the Pueblo IV (PIV) period, population increased significantly toward the end of the Coalition period (AD 1200–1325), reaching its height during the Classic period (AD 1325–1600), when large aggregated communities were formed (Cordell 1997:198–199).

Poor recovery of perishables in the northern Rio Grande area (Figure 3.1, No. 12) presents interesting interpretive problems. Miserable preservation may not be the only culprit behind the area's scanty archaeobotanical record. Of particular significance is the near-absence of fragmentary corncob debris in small sites, this uniquely durable category of plant waste barely evident. But cob fragments are ubiquitous at large sites such as Agua Fria School House and Pindi Pueblo, Arroyo Hondo in the Galisteo Basin south of Santa Fe (Figure 3.1, No. 13; Table 3.3), and Rowe (Figure 3.1, No. 13; Table 3.3) and Pecos Pueblos further east in the Upper Pecos Valley. Additional crop plant remnants at these large pueblos include beans and cucurbit peduncles, rind, seeds, and flesh at Arroyo Hondo (Wetterstrom 1986); cucurbit pollen at Agua Fria (Cummings 1989); a cucurbit seed at Rowe Pueblo (Toll 1998); and cucurbit peduncles and an entire pot of beans at Pindi Pueblo (Jones 1953). This disjunctive pattern is reasonable confirmation that at least some categories of plant resources were processed and utilized in entirely different patterns at small sites than at the few much larger pueblos of the Coalition and early Classic periods. Dean (1993a, 1993b) notes that the consistently disappointing recovery of plant remains from ephemeral sites in the Santa Fe area may be a reflection of site function. Small sites were an important component in the regional use of the prehistoric landscape. Such sites could represent localities used briefly by people in transit from one location to another or while collecting wild plants or other resources that were then carried back "home" to be processed.

A rich array of wild taxa complements the inventory of farm crops at the large pueblos, including piñon; juniper; chokecherry; cholla, prickly pear, pincushion, and hedgehog cacti; yucca; ricegrass; dropseed grass; and the weedy annuals pigweed, goosefoot, beeweed, bugseed, purslane, and sunflower (Toll 1998:Tables 20, 22; Wetterstrom 1986:175–183) (Table 3.3). Over the 125-year history of Arroyo Hondo, two major occupations took place, both of which corresponded with higher-moisture periods (Table 3.3). Although a large population is suggested at the site, the area was marginal for maize production, resulting in a meager and precarious cultivated food base that was susceptible to recurring droughts. Evidence of continuous nutritional stress in the skeletal population and indications of faunal procurement at ever-increasing distances from the site suggest a chronic state of fluctuating dietary adequacy. Poor preservation limits diachronic interpretation of the plant record, although the range of perennial and annual taxa suggests foraging efforts in all local biotic communities (Table 3.3). No unequivocal famine foods could be identified in the assemblage, but the high visibility of weedy annuals could reflect production intensification efforts. Supporting evidence for the importance of goosefoot and pigweed comes from the Arroyo Hondo pollen record (Bohrer 1986), which also suggests the harvesting, if not the local management, of cholla cactus for buds and joints.

The development during the Classic period of new subsistence strategies to accommodate increasing food demands can be seen in the Rio Chama/El Rito area (Figure 3.1, No. 12) northwest of Santa Fe, where large numbers of rock border and rock/cobble mulch features have been recorded on terraces away from the river floodplains. Characteristically associated with very large villages, the features exhibit varied construction and represent a significant labor investment (Maxwell and Anschuetz 1992). They were part of a larger array of soil- and water-control systems developed as risk-buffering strategies to diversify or intensify plant food production in areas away from the flood-prone floodplains, where crop losses were frequent events. Pollen records from some of these features indicate that maize and cotton (*Gossypium*) were grown (Dean 1995; Smith 1998), but large quantities of cheno-ams, beeweed, and other plants suggest that the plots also may have acted as sources for wild plant harvests. High ubiquities for prickly pear, cholla, and purslane pollen suggest the possibility of deliberate concentration and management of these taxa, as well (Smith 1998).

Centered in the southwestern corner of Colorado, the Mesa Verde branch (Figure 3.1, No. 10) is best known for the suite of spectacular cliff dwellings that form the core of Mesa Verde National Park. Despite intensive investigation of the cliff dwellings and several of the many open sites found in the park area, little detailed information has been published on the wild food plants exploited by the inhabitants (Cattanach 1980; Colyer and Osborne 1965; Cutler and Meyer 1965; Kaplan 1965). Superb preservation in the large cliff dwellings, however, resulted in the recovery of abundant evidence of cultigen and utilitarian plant use (Cutler and Meyer 1965; Kaplan 1965; Nordenskiöld 1990; Osborne 1980).

Detailed temporal and spatial data are available from the Dolores Archaeological Project area west of Durango and north of Mesa Verde. Large-scale systematic flotation and pollen analyses were carried out in a large study area with sites that span the period AD 600–1250 (Matthews 1986). Maize and beans were found to be of continuing importance, with use of squash decreasing dramatically because of increasingly frequent colder, shorter growing seasons. An important subsistence role for early colonizing weedy taxa was documented (Matthews 1986:Table 4.6). Of the 24 taxa classified as agrestals, amaranth, goosefoot, cheno-am, mustard family, tansy mustard, groundcherry, and purslane were preferred, consistently utilized resources through time. Additional wild taxa with significant temporal ubiquities include sedge family, *Opuntia*/Cactaceae, yucca, sagebrush (*Artemisia*), juniper, and piñon (Table 3.3). Projectwide ubiquity increases in disturbance taxa were viewed as indicators of the status of these taxa as valuable coproducts of agricultural intensification from AD 840 to 920 (Matthews 1986:Tables 4.14–4.17), reflecting deliberate encouragement as a "least-cost" strategy during a time of increasing population growth and persistent climatic stress. Despite a paucity of macrobotanical evidence, the economic importance of beeweed as a green was evident from the exceptionally high pollen ubiquities that persisted through the occupation period (Peterson 1986:Table 4.26). Exploitation of other wild taxa also increased and appears to have continued after AD 920, when local population levels rapidly declined in response to frequent droughts and abbreviated growing seasons (Schlanger 1988). Evidence in some sites suggests changes in wood use for fuel and construction that may have resulted from overexploitation and from continuous land clearing in limited arable land belts (Kohler and Matthews 1988); a reduction in piñon nut use and corresponding population increases are viewed as evidence for piñon tree loss as a casualty of intensified maize production.

Coprolite-derived macrofossil and pollen data from other Mesa Verde area sites (Scott 1979; Stiger 1979) support the observed trends, documenting high ubiquities for maize and the presence, particularly, of chenopods, groundcherry, piñon, prickly pear, beeweed, and purslane. Macrofossil data also show a reduction in the presence of piñon and squash by the PIII period (Stiger 1979). Dietary composition estimates for maize and wild plants were placed at 50 percent each on the basis of the macrofossil study, but the pollen record and stable carbon isotope data for BMIII through PIII individuals (Decker and Tieszen 1989) suggest a much higher maize component, placed at 70 to 80 percent.

Similar basic patterns can be seen to the west and southwest at Black Mesa (Figure 3.1, No. 7) (Gleichman 1982; Trigg 1985; Wagner et al. 1984), in the Kayenta area (Figure 3.1, No. 8) at Jeddito (McBride 1998), and at Antelope

Lisa W. Huckell and Mollie S. Toll

House (Fry and Hall 1975; Hall and Dennis 1986; Sutton and Reinhard 1995; Williams-Dean and Bryant 1975) in Canyon de Chelly (Figure 3.1, No. 9), northeastern Arizona, where the record suggests continuing reliance on maize agriculture. Field weeds such as cheno-ams, beeweed, purslane, and ground-cherry continue to occupy a prominent place in the record, again as probable coproducts of agricultural intensification. Several gathered perennial plant products that cannot be linked to the proliferation of farm fields show increased use with time. For instance, ricegrass, considered to have been especially important during the Archaic period, increases regionally in frequency at BMIII sites and is present at a large number of later Pueblo period sites. These data make it clear that, far from farming to the near-exclusion of other subsistence pursuits, these agriculturalists depended on wild plants just as their predecessors did, with growing populations a compelling impetus to maximize resource exploitation. For the period following AD 1150, when areal expansion ceased, large-scale abandonment took place, and populations concentrated in fewer core areas, increased investment in maize production was a clear trend, as seen in the widespread appearance of water- and soil-control features and a concurrent reduction in the numbers of small, specialized, nonagricultural resource-procurement sites dating to the PIII period.

An exceptional record is available for evaluating Anasazi subsistence through time and across space. Although sample sizes are thoroughly weighted toward later periods, general diachronic trends have been suggested. The growing record of macrofossil, pollen, coprolite, and stable carbon isotope data (Brand 1994; Chisholm and Matson 1994; Decker and Tieszen 1989; Kirkpatrick and Ford 1977; Martin 1999; Matson and Chisholm 1991; Minnis 1989; Sutton and Reinhard 1995) for the northern Southwest indicates continuity in the mixed farming/foraging adaptation first seen in the Early Agricultural/Basketmaker II period. Maize was important from its first appearance, exhibiting consistently high ubiquities in pollen, coprolite, and macrofossil data. Bone chemistry studies also indicate a strong maize dependence, which, by some estimates, exceeded 80 percent (Decker and Tieszen 1989; Martin et al. 1991). The importance of beans and squash is more difficult to determine because of poor preservation; the roles of these cultigens may have fluctuated considerably. Disturbance taxa form a core group of consistently recovered economic annuals, co-occurring with locally available perennials such as ricegrass, prickly pear, and piñon that assume varying levels of importance. Some researchers, assuming adverse climatic impacts on wild plant availability, have posited a trend of diminished gathering, reductions in nonagricultural, limited-activity sites during PIII times, and an increased focus on agricultural production (Gumerman and Dean 1989). Macrofossil data in some areas, however, suggest that greater diversity in wild plant taxa tended to occur prior to abandonment, reflecting efforts to diversify the available resource base. Studies suggesting diversification and intensification of wild plant use over time include those based on work in the Coronado Project area in northeastern Arizona (Gasser 1982), at Salmon Ruin (Doebley 1976, 1981) (Table 3.3), and at Chaco Canyon (Toll 1985) (Table 3.3), and on the coprolite evidence from Antelope House in Canyon de Chelly (Fry and Hall 1975; Sutton and Reinhard 1995) and from Mesa Verde (Stiger 1977, 1979). Both views are probably correct in that they reflect variable local responses rather than a monolithic regional trend. Wild plant remains continue to appear in larger archaeobotanical assemblages, suggesting that sampling and preservation biases may be obscuring the visibility of such remains in some cases. Based on the extensive regional coprolite record, Minnis (1989) has proposed a "generally stable dietary regime" over time in which a flexible mixed farming and foraging economy proved to be a successful adaptation in a chronically unstable environment.

Mogollon/Western Pueblo

The Mogollon region covers a vast territory from north-central Arizona and central New Mexico south to eastern Sonora and western Chihuahua (Figure 3.1, Nos. 1, 17, 18, 19, 20). The area is dominated by rugged basin and range topography, with steep mountains and narrow valleys in the north and broad, arid intermontane basins in the southern portion. The considerable physiographic and biotic diversity within the region is the basis for the definition of a number of distinctive subtraditions or branches (Cordell 1997: 202–203), but for this discussion, we consider two general subdivisions: upland and desert. The Mogollon tradition began sometime around AD 200–550 with the appearance of brownware and redware pottery; these ceramics mark the Early Pithouse period. In the upland region, early, small pithouse settlements were located on bluffs, knolls, and other easily defended positions, but beginning with the Late Pithouse period, locations on first terraces adjacent to drainages with arable floodplains appear to have been preferred (Minnis 1985a).

Upland Mogollon

This area includes east-central Arizona and west-central New Mexico (Figure 3.1, No. 20). Botanical information for six upland sites from the Early Pithouse period (Diehl and Minnis in press) documents the presence of three cultigens—corn, beans, and squash—and a wild plant inventory consisting of chenopod and pigweed species, piñon, juniper, walnut, sunflower, dropseed, purslane, prickly pear, and grasses. Although most of the records are minimal, as is typical of open sites, the Gallo Mountain site in the Quemado-Reserve in west-central New Mexico offers rare insight into the importance of wild foods (Toll and McBride 1998) (Table 3.4). There a catastrophically burned pithouse yielded 21 ceramic, basket, and gourd storage containers and their contents. A sample of nine containers revealed that, in addition to large amounts of squash, beans, and maize, significant quantities of goosefoot, pigweed, winged pigweed, and sunflower had been amassed. Walnuts and piñon nuts were also present, as were groundcherry and purslane. The weedy taxa list indicates a strong exploitative focus on summer annual plants that likely would have been encountered in anthropogenic environments such as fields, field margins, and trash mounds, where they may have been encouraged to grow in readily harvestable concentrations. The recovery of 7 m³ of maize kernels from a storage pit near the burned house suggests that fields were locally maintained on nearby prime floodplain soils. Recent investigations at an Early Pithouse period site located along NM 90 northeast of Lordsburg, New Mexico, yielded nine taxa, three of which—spurge (*Euphorbia*), stickleaf, and acorn—are new additions to the Early Pithouse plant inventory (Huckell 2000b) (Table 3.4).

Although a large number of upland sites from the Late Pithouse period (AD 550–1000) have been investigated, most of the available botanical record comes from a small portion of the region centered on the Mimbres Valley in southwestern New Mexico (Minnis 1978:Fig. 2) (Figure 3.1, No. 19). Many more sites are known to date to the Late Pithouse than to the Early Pithouse period. People used valley floor floodplains more intensively and expanded into additional areas offering arable land of lesser quality (terraces, side drainages, and mountain parks), a shift attributed to increasing population pressure (Diehl 1996; Minnis 1985a). High ubiquities for maize in the macrofossil record suggest a central subsistence role for the crop, but the record is inadequate to reveal reliable production trends through time. Morphological changes in ground stone artifacts during the Pithouse period and subsequent Pueblo period (Hard et al. 1996) also suggest a trend toward greater dependence on maize, perhaps accompanied by a reduction in reliance on wild plants. The existing macrobotanical record, however, is insufficient to support or refute this position (Diehl 1996; Hard 1990), and no other available evidence indicates a change in the nature of wild plant exploitation or a shift in dietary importance. The wild plant inventories at contemporaneous sites in the Mimbres Valley and along the NM 90 highway to the west indicate that, at a minimum, 28 taxa were probably utilized (Table 3.4), suggesting an eclectic foraging strategy that encompassed a variety of locally available annual and perennial resources (Huckell 2000b; Minnis 1985a).

Sometime between AD 950 and 1150, pithouses were replaced by surface cobble masonry pueblos, and brownware and redware pottery traditions came to be dominant or were replaced by a white-slipped brownware bearing black designs. It was during that time that the most famous and most intensively studied Mogollon component, the Classic Mimbres, emerged. Today known worldwide for their pictorial black-on-white bowls, the Mimbres people occupied a limited area in southwestern New Mexico that encompassed upland biotic resources in the north and desert biotic resources in the south. Intensive work over the last 20 years has produced an archaeobotanical record that suggests specific diachronic trends in plant use. A large wild plant inventory was found at sites in the Mimbres Valley, with goosefoot, purslane, juniper, grasses, amaranth, sunflower, and various cacti the most frequently recovered taxa (Minnis 1985a) (Table 3.4). These and other resources used were largely local in origin. Weedy species predominated, a predictable consequence of the replacement of native vegetation by anthropogenic communities such as cultivated fields. No absolute changes in wild plant use could be detected for the 125-year Mimbres occupation. Nevertheless, a comparison of the estimated regional population size with the percentage of the seed assemblage consisting of weed (goosefoot, amaranth, and purslane) seeds for the entire 1,200-year occupation of the area shows a strong correlation, with population and weed seeds both peaking during the Classic Mimbres period (Minnis 1978:Fig. 7). Cheno-am pollen frequencies for the same 1,200-year period show a similar trend. Such patterns were attributed to the growing population's demand for land and to the need for larger landholdings to compensate for inadequate harvests resulting from increasingly unreliable rainfall and water availability. This contention is supported by the appearance of irrigation canals and of agricultural rock features that accompanied Mimbres expansion into previously unused lands.

Wood charcoal species composition also reflects human impact on the landscape. A dramatic reduction in riparian taxa at Classic Mimbres phase sites, for instance, is felt by Minnis (1978, 1985a) to indicate land clearing and the exhaustion of local floodplain wood resources, necessitating a shift to reliance on higher-elevation conifers, particularly for construction wood

Table 3.4

Macrofossil Records from Selected Mogollon and Western Pueblo Sites

Location/Site	Map Location	Date	Plants (References)
Mimbres Valley	19	Early Pithouse	c: maize; w: goosefoot, purslane, juniper (Minnis 1985a)
Mimbres Valley	19	Late Pithouse	c: maize, bean; w: goosefoot, pigweed, purslane, peppergrass, bugseed, sunflower, knotweed, juniper, piñon, chokecherry, saltbush, grape, prickly pear, lovegrass, nightshade, paspalum, cactus family, mallow family, bean family, sunflower family (Minnis 1985a)
Mimbres Valley	19	Classic Mimbres	c: maize; w: goosefoot, pigweed, purslane, peppergrass, bugseed, sunflower, tansy mustard, knotweed, walnut, juniper, saltbush, mesquite, stickleaf, hedgehog cactus, prickly pear, banana yucca, grama grass, ricegrass, cactus family, morning glory family, sunflower family (Minnis 1985a)
Mimbres Valley	19	Animas	c: maize, bean, cotton; w: goosefoot, pigweed, purslane, knotweed, walnut, juniper, saltbush, mesquite, hedgehog cactus, prickly pear, banana yucca, grama grass, ricegrass, dropseed, bulrush, cactus family, sunflower family (Minnis 1985a)
Mimbres Valley	19	Salado	c: maize, bean, squash, cotton; w: goosefoot, pigweed, purslane, peppergrass, sunflower, tansy mustard, beeweed, walnut, juniper, acacia, hedgehog, grama grass, dropseed, cactus family, bean family, morning glory family, sunflower family (Minnis 1985a)
Western Pueblo Point of Pines	20	AD 1250–1325	c: maize, bean, squash, cotton; w: juniper, walnut, reed, beargrass, cf. yucca, acorn, buckwheat, cheno-am, winged pigweed, pigweed, mesquite, doveweed, stickleaf, cholla, prickly pear, cf. bottle gourd, sunflower family (Bohrer 1973)
Grasshopper Pueblo	20	AD 1300–1400	c: maize, bean, cotton; w: manzanita, cheno-am, goosefoot, beeweed, sunflower family, winged pigweed, grass family, sunflower, walnut, juniper, cholla/prickly pear, piñon pine, purslane, acorn, sumac, sage, grape (Bohrer 1982; Welch 1996)
SCARP: 2 sites	20	AD 1050–1150	c: maize, squash; w: pigweed, manzanita, cheno-am, goosefoot, beeweed, sunflower family, bugseed, winged pigweed, tansy mustard, hedgehog cactus, grass family, walnut, juniper, stickleaf, prickly pear, groundcherry/nightshade, piñon, purslane, sage, dropseed (Huckell 1999a)

SCARP: 2 sites	20	AD 1200–1330	c: maize, common bean, squash, cotton; w: pigweed, elymoid grasses, manzanita, cheno-am, goosefoot, beeweed, sunflower family, bugseed, winged pigweed, tansy mustard, grass family, walnut, juniper, stickleaf, prickly pear, groundcherry/nightshade, plantain, purslane, acorn, sage (Huckell 1999a)
Mogollon			
Gallo Mtn, LA 5407	20	Early Pithouse	c: maize, common bean, squash; w: goosefoot, sunflower, purslane, winged pigweed, reed, walnut, piñon, yucca, groundcherry, grass family (Toll and McBride 1998)
NM 90: LA 121210	19	Early Pithouse	c: maize; w: goosefoot, cheno-am, winged pigweed, spurge, walnut, juniper, stickleaf, acorn (Huckell 2000b)
NM 90: 2 sites	19	Late Pithouse	c: maize; squash/gourd; w: goosefoot, cheno-am, winged pigweed, tansy mustard, spurge, grass family, sunflower family, juniper, stickleaf, prickly pear/cholla, purslane, acorn, dock/knotweed, dropseed (Huckell 2000b)
Jornada Mogollon			
Turquoise Ridge	17	Formative	c: maize, common bean; w: mesquite/acacia, screwbean mesquite, prickly pear, hedgehog cactus, banana yucca, cf. sumac, cheno-am, purslane, sunflower, purslane, dropseed, bugseed, grass family, mustard family, bean family, pink family (Whalen 1994)
Three Lakes Pueblo	17	El Paso	c: maize, cushaw squash, common bean, tepary bean; w: agave, pigweed, goosefoot, cf. summer cypress, mesquite, Mexican buckeye (Ford 1977)
La Cabraña Pueblo	17	El Paso	c: maize, common bean, tepary bean, lima bean, squash; w: mesquite, screwbean mesquite, false purslane, prickly pear, cheno-am, buffalo gourd, reed, hoary pea (Foster et al. 1981)
Northern Mexico			
Casas Grandes/Paquimé	18	all periods	c: maize, cotton, squash, bottle gourd; w: panic grass, hackberry, false purslane, saltbush, mesquite, grass family, walnut, agave, piñon, goosefoot, cf. cañaigre (Di Peso et al. 1974 vol. 8)

Note: c = cultivated, w = wild.

For map locations, refer to figure 3.1.

(Minnis 1986:Fig. 11.7). Considerably smaller populations living in the area in the centuries following the Classic Mimbres collapse by AD 1150 seem to have exerted a minimal effect on the environment in comparison with their predecessors (Minnis 1986), and riparian wood taxa appear in sufficient quantities at later sites to suggest the recovery of riverine vegetation.

During the ensuing centuries, material and social changes of sufficient magnitude took place as a result of Puebloan influence that the name "Western Pueblo" is often used in place of "Mogollon" in referring to the region (Cordell 1997). Driven in large measure by the Great Drought of AD 1276–1299, Puebloan people emigrated into the Mogollon region from the Colorado Plateau on a massive scale, resulting in the wholesale abandonment of some areas of the plateau along with a drastic reduction in the number of dispersed small sites. The primary consequence of such population movement in the Mogollon area was the development of large, aggregated settlements composed of large, multistoried pueblos that may have served in a defensive capacity. Smaller pueblos were abandoned, often after being burned, with people subsequently congregated in a few very large sites (Cordell 1997). Sites exemplifying this transition for which archaeobotanical data are available are located in the uplands of east-central Arizona and date to the end of the 13th century. For reasons not yet fully understood, the system began to collapse toward the end of the 14th century, with abandonment of the area completed by AD 1400.

Located on and just above the Mogollon escarpment, these site locations offered exceptional access to resources in several biotic communities, ranging from lower-elevation Sonoran desertscrub, through chaparral and grassland, to forests of piñon/juniper and ponderosa pine. Use of these communities is confirmed by the archaeobotanical record, particularly by the occurrence of perennial taxa such as manzanita, juniper, acorns, prickly pear and cholla cactus, walnuts, mesquite, grapes (*Vitis*), and sumac. Familiar annuals and weedy species are also conspicuous, with cheno-ams, beeweed, sunflower, winged pigweed, wild buckwheat (*Eriogonum*), grasses, purslane, and sage identified (Bohrer 1973, 1982; Huckell 1999a; Welch 1996) (Table 3.4).

Efforts have been made, using the macrobotanical and pollen records, to discern temporal changes in wild plant exploitation between the establishment/expansion stages (PIII) and the dispersion/abandonment stages (PIV) that might be expressions of the aggregation process, but such efforts have met with limited success because of the small size and biased nature of the data base (Welch 1996). Although intensification of maize production and consumption is suggested, the degree of reliance on maize cannot be deduced from macrofossil or pollen records. What can be seen is continuity in the suite of wild resources exploited (Welch 1996). The surprisingly consistent trend in the regional record of low recovery rates for high-caloric-value foodstuffs such as acorns, piñon nuts, and walnuts may be a product of preservation, storage, or processing biases. It may also reflect the choice to adopt a strategy of intensified maize production rather than relying on the erratic, unpredictable vagaries of annual nut mast production.

Exceptional evidence of wild plant use comes from the investigation of dietary practices at Grasshopper Pueblo, a 500-room settlement occupied for 125 years in east-central Arizona. Macrobotanical and pollen records are modest for a site of this size, offering limited information (Bohrer 1982; Welch 1996) (Table 3.4). Bone chemistry studies reveal dramatic temporal, spatial, and gender differences in the consumption of wild and cultivated plants (Ezzo 1993, 1994). Inhabitants of early room blocks maintained a higher level of maize consumption than those of subsequently constructed room blocks, among whom wild plants played a greater dietary role, suggesting differential access to farmland and resources between founder populations and later arrivals. Gender differences were most acutely visible in the early population, where male diets included considerably more maize and meat than the wild plant-focused female diets; this discrepancy diminished over time as game became less abundant. Late female diets show decreased consumption of wild plant products, suggesting either a reduced range of available foods or the greater availability of maize through intensified production to meet the demands of an escalating population.

Desert Mogollon

The southern desert Mogollon subregion includes the San Simon (Figure 3.1, No. 1) and Jornada (Figure 3.1, No. 17) branches, which encompass portions of the arid Sonoran and Chihuahuan Deserts. Little formal archaeological work has been done in the western San Simon branch area in southeastern Arizona, with plant remains obtained from a single project in the Timber Draw area (Hurst et al. 1997). The modest assemblage spans the period AD 650–1150. All of the sampled loci produced maize and a combined wild plant inventory that includes familiar weedy annuals, such as false purslane, cheno-ams, globemallow, and purslane, along with the perennial mesquite. All of these resources would have been locally available to the mobile forager/farmers who occupied the sites seasonally during the summer and fall. Readily available acacia/mesquite was the dominant wood type selected for both construction and fuel uses.

Adjacent to the San Simon branch to the east lies the Jornada Mogollon branch, which occupies much of southern New Mexico, westernmost Texas, and part of northern Chihuahua. Most of the region today is inhospitably arid, characterized by erratic and highly variable seasonal summer rainfall that fills ephemeral small playas, or shallow basins, in the valley floors. Paleo-environmental records (Van Devender and Riskind 1979) indicate that the late Holocene environment probably consisted of grasslands with some perennial shrubs present on the surrounding mountain slopes, a dramatic contrast to the degraded, scrub-dominated community encountered today (Whalen 1994). A small but growing number of archaeological investigations have documented the use of the area by residentially mobile, Formative period pithouse dwellers as early as AD 500. Their small settlements are consistently found on the basin floors and margins, with the former interpreted as summer seasonal camps and the latter as winter base camps. Around AD 1100, a Puebloan occupation appeared featuring fewer but larger settlements optimally located in the best-watered land around the basin margins. The settlements suggest some degree of permanence through prolonged or repeated use, although the exact nature of the adaptation is still open to debate (Whalen 1994). Here, too, the Puebloans ultimately abandoned the area, their exodus completed by AD 1400.

The archaeobotanical record (Table 3.4) suggests that the Formative occupants engaged in maize agriculture while also exploiting locally available basin floor annuals along with succulent plant products found some distance away in neighboring mountains. Annual taxa include sunflower, purslane, dropseed and other grasses, cheno-ams, and bugseed. Perennials include lower-elevation mesquite and screwbean mesquite and the higher-elevation sumac, prickly pear, hedgehog cactus, agave (*Agave*), and banana yucca (*Yucca baccata*) (Table 3.4). Based on higher ubiquities of cultigens, the Puebloans appear to have capitalized more fully than their predecessors on the agricultural potential of the basin margins to obtain maize, several kinds of beans, and squash, but they, too, continued to rely on many of the same wild taxa (Ford 1977; O'Laughlin 1977; Whalen 1994:Table 44). Cheno-ams and purslane are particularly ubiquitous in Puebloan sites and may have been summer staple foods (Browning et al. 1993:Table 21; Cummings 1993; Ford 1977:201; Phelps 1968). Fuelwood remains from El Paso phase hearths and roasting pits indicate an overwhelming preference for mesquite wood (Cummings 1993; Ford 1977).

Mogollon in Mexico

Although cultural/ethnic affiliations and chronological sequences for northern Chihuahua are still in the early stages of definition and refinement, the area's archaeological record has clear linkages with the Mogollon. Until recently, a small handful of Chihuahuan sites provided a modest record of wild plant use. The best-known and largest site is Paquimé, or Casas Grandes, a highly influential regional center dating from AD 1200 to the late 1400s that is situated in a broad, arid valley (Dean and Ravesloot 1993) (Figure 3.1, No. 18). The extant plant assemblage comes from a very small portion of the site. It consists primarily of cultigens—maize, cucurbits, and cotton—and a small suite of wild plant remains (Cutler and Blake 1974; Di Peso et al. 1974) (Table 3.4), a result attributable to work carried out prior to the use of flotation. The list of wild plant remains includes walnuts, piñon nuts, mesquite pods, agave, and possible cañaigre (*Rumex*) root fragments along with seeds of grasses, an annual saltbush (*Atriplex*), and false purslane (Table 3.4). This limited inventory suggests the exploitation of both local resources and more distant upland species as well as the use of perennial resources with good storage qualities. The agave remains are of particular interest, as it appears that several huge roasting pits and an associated room block at the edge of the site represent a specialized agave-cooking area (Minnis 1988). The resulting food and fiber products may have been locally consumed or used as trade commodities. Local cultivation of the plants may have occurred, a phenomenon that was widespread in other parts of the southern North American Southwest during the Classic period.

A handful of additional projects that have yielded archaeobotanical information have been done in northern Chihuahua. Upland cave sites on the eastern slope of the Sierra Madre Occidental to the west of Paquimé have provided limited records of human exploitation of wild resources (Lister 1958; Montúfar López 1985, 1992; Montúfar López and Reyes Landa 1995). Although preservation of plant materials at these sites is excellent, contextual problems deriving from a paucity of direct radiocarbon dates, bioturbation, and disturbance from continued human use of the caves during the historic period act to compromise the research value of the wild plants recovered. Ongoing research in west-central Chihuahua (Kelley et al. 1999) is providing new data on the southern frontier of the Casas Grandes/Chihuahuan culture territory. Preliminary archaeobotanical analysis has produced a small inventory of wild plant resources that includes piñon, cheno-ams, grasses, walnut, groundcherry, purslane, and acorns (Adams 1992).

Hohokam

The Hohokam occupied the arid desert valleys lying between the Mogollon Rim scarp to the north and northern Sonora, Mexico, to the south. Superb agriculturalists, the Hohokam amassed the most extensive inventory of cultivated and managed wild plants of the three major southwestern cultures. Recent investigations in the Tucson Basin have provided new insights into the poorly known beginnings of Hohokam culture. A small but growing number of sites have been identified as belonging to the Early Ceramic or Formative period, which falls roughly from AD 1 to 650 and is marked by the advent of plainware and redware ceramics. Few single-component sites attributable to this period have been found; diagnostic materials usually appear as components of larger sites whose superimposed successive occupations have disturbed and masked the character of these early occupations. The archaeobotanical record is a small one drawn from a handful of sites with unusually good preservation. In the Hohokam core area of the Salt and Gila River valleys (Figure 3.1, No. 3), a pit structure of this period, assigned to the earliest—Red Mountain—phase, was found during work at Pueblo Patricio in Phoenix; floor-contact flotation samples yielded maize, sunflower family, and legume remains (Gasser 1985). A small Red Mountain phase component at La Cuenca del Sedimento (Miksicek 1989) in the Tempe area produced maize, pigweed, seepweed (*Suaeda*), tansy mustard, grass, dropseed, iodine bush (*Allenrolfea*), sage, and fishhook cactus (*Mammillaria*).

In the Tucson Basin (Figure 3.1, No. 2) eight investigated sites either date to or have substantial components of the Early Ceramic period (Fish, Fish, Madsen, et al. 1992; Huckell 1998a:Table 3.23, 1998b; Miksicek and Bernard-Shaw 1989, 1990). The collective wild plant inventory is lengthy, with 35 taxa or types identified (Table 3.5). Taxa that are found at all or most of the sites include saguaro, cheno-ams, tansy mustard, hedgehog cactus, grasses, mesquite, globemallow, dropseed, and false purslane, a pattern that suggests the widespread importance of these plants and the systematic collection of wild resources from early spring through fall. The Houghton Road site, located on the Catalina Mountain piedmont in the eastern part of the basin, also yielded manzanita, juniper, agave, and probable acorn obtained from nearby upland locales (Huckell 1998b). Agave is also found in the northern basin at several sites where the recovery of vegetative parts suggests that local cultivation may already have begun (Fish, Fish, Madsen, et al. 1992; Miksicek and Bernard-Shaw 1989, 1990). During the Early Ceramic period, wild plants continued to contribute significantly to subsistence even as more cultigens— cotton and two species of beans—were added to the inventory.

The importance of wild plants is apparent in the paleoethnobotanical record dating to the earliest identifiable appearance of the Hohokam and their distinctive red-on-buff ceramics. Evidence suggests that a large inventory of wild species was used (Table 3.5). Subregional staples varied, but consistently important foods included mesquite pods, saguaro fruits and seeds, cholla buds, and the seeds of pigweed and goosefoot. Evidence also exists to suggest that, from the beginning, manipulation and cultivation of wild plant species took place, especially of cool-season annuals, as exemplified by the recovery of little barleygrass (*Hordeum*) from several sites and contexts dating from the early Preclassic through the Classic periods (Gasser and Kwiatkowski 1991a). Management, if not domestication, of amaranth, tobacco, and possible groundcherry has also been proposed (Bohrer 1991). Additional taxa suspected of having been manipulated include goosefoot, tansy mustard, vetch (*Astragalus*), maygrass (*Phalaris*), and panic grass (*Panicum*) (Bohrer 1991; Nabhan 1985; Nabhan and de Wet 1984). The significantly higher productivity of annuals over perennials noted by Bohrer (1991) suggests that Hohokam experimentation with controlling annuals was an efficient strategy for increasing and diversifying production as well as for enhancing the probability of food availability during late winter and spring, when stores were low or exhausted.

Perennials, possibly including Mexican crucillo (*Condalia*), agave, and cholla, may also have been manipulated (Bohrer 1991). Pollen evidence from a large number of sites in the Salt and Gila River valleys (Fish 1984; Gish 1991) suggests that cholla and, possibly, prickly pear were transplanted to habitation sites, probably to ensure a reliable supply of edible cholla buds and prickly pear fruit and pads. A similar phenomenon has been described for the Jemez area of northwestern New Mexico, where disjunct populations of cholla found outside their natural elevational range correlate with prehistoric habitation sites (Housley 1974). Although agave remains identified in Early Colonial contexts at La Ciudad in Phoenix (Bohrer 1987) appear to belong to wild species, possible evidence of cultivation found at one of the

Table 3.5
Representative Macrofossil Records from Selected Hohokam and Tonto Basin Salado Sites

Location/Site	Map Location	Date	Plants (References)
Snaketown	3	Preclassic period	c: maize, bean, bottle gourd, cotton; w: cholla/prickly pear, saguaro, hedgehog cactus, cocklebur, wild gourd, goosefoot, little barley, panic grass, mesquite, screwbean, sedge, false purslane, walnut, tansy mustard, pigweed (Bohrer 1970)
Les Hornos	3	Preclassic period	c: maize, agave, little barley; w: milkvetch, spiderling, tansy mustard, peppergrass, cactus family, cheno-am, winged pigweed, hedgehog cactus, wild buckwheat, spurge, groundcherry, brome grass/elymoid grasses, sprangletop, canarygrass, dropseed, purslane, mesquite, globemallow, seepweed, false purslane (Kwiatkowski and Smith 1993)
Las Colinas	3	Preclassic period	c: maize, cotton, common bean, little barley, tepary bean, squash, agave, amaranth; w: mesquite, false purslane, globemallow, goosefoot, dropseed, saltbush, plantain, saguaro, brome grass, groundcherry, hedgehog cactus, prickly pear, spurge, kallstroemia, cholla, wild tobacco, sunflower, clammyweed, tansy mustard, purslane, legume family, iodine bush, sunflower family, spiderling, wild gourd, nightshade family, grass family, dock, peppergrass, locoweed, catchfly, filaree (Miksicek and Gasser 1989)
Las Colinas	3	Classic period	c: maize, agave, cotton, common bean, little barley, tobacco, amaranth; w: mesquite, false purslane, globemallow, goosefoot, saguaro, dropseed, saltbush, Indian wheat, brome grass, groundcherry, hedgehog cactus, prickly pear, sunflower, clammyweed, tansy mustard, purslane, bean family, iodine bush, sunflower family, locoweed, wild buckwheat (Miksicek and Gasser 1989)
Grand Canal	3	Classic period	c: maize, bean, cotton, agave; w: cheno-am, mesquite, hedgehog cactus, grass family, saguaro, seepweed, false purslane, purslane, saltbush, cactus family, plantain, mustard family, spurge, globemallow, spiderling, prickly pear, vetch, bursage, knotweed, nightshade family (Kwiatkowski 1989)

Pueblo Grande	3	Classic period	c: maize, agave, little barley, cotton, tepary bean, common bean, jack bean; w: mesquite, cheno-am, mustard family, tansy mustard, peppergrass, cf. bentgrass, cf. lovegrass, canarygrass, cf. sprangletop, saguaro, hedgehog cactus, pincushion cactus, cactus family, purslane, plantain, false purslane, globemallow, chia, spurge, saltbush, seepweed, winged pigweed, wild tobacco, spiderling, nightshade (Miller 1994)
Tonto Basin	4	Early Ceramic period	c: maize, bean, cotton, grain amaranth, agave, little barley; w: pigweed, clammyweed/beeweed, cheno-am, goosefoot, buckwheat, globemallow, bentgrass/muhly, bromegrass, panic grass, dropseed, cholla, hedgehog cactus, prickly pear, mesquite, yucca, grass family (Huckell 2000a; Miksicek 1995)
Tonto Basin	4	Preclassic period	c: maize, bean, lima bean, jack bean, squash, bottle gourd, cotton, agave, little barley; w: amaranth, prickly poppy, vetch, spiderling, borage family, clammyweed/beeweed, catchfly/campion, cheno-am, goosefoot, sunflower family, mustard family, sedge family, tansy mustard, spurge, stickleaf, phacelia, plantain, knotweed, purslane, chia, groundcherry/nightshade, globemallow, false purslane, bentgrass/muhly, grama grass, elymoid grass, grass family, cf. ricegrass, panic grass, maygrass, dropseed, cactus family, cholla, hedgehog cactus, pincushion cactus, prickly pear, catclaw, manzanita, walnut, juniper, mesquite, jojoba, grape (Adams 1994; Huckell 2000a; Kwiatkowski 1992; Miksicek 1995)
Tonto Basin: Salado	4	Classic period	c: maize, bean, tepary bean, jack bean, squash, bottle gourd, cotton, dye amaranth, grain amaranth, agave, little barley; w: pigweed, fiddleneck, prickly poppy, vetch, saltbush, borage family, clammyweed/beeweed, catchfly/campion, cheno-am, goosefoot, sunflower family, mustard family, tansy mustard, buckwheat, spurge, mallow family, tobacco, phacelia, plantain, purslane, devil's claw, chia, groundcherry/nightshade, globemallow, false purslane, carrot family, bentgrass/muhly, bromegrass, elymoid grass, lovegrass, grasses, sprangletop, maygrass, dropseed, cactus family, saguaro, cholla, hedgehog cactus, prickly pear, catclaw, manzanita, saltbush, hackberry, walnut, juniper, mesquite, acorn, jojoba, seepweed, arrow-weed, yucca (Adams 1994; Dering 1998; Huckell 2000a; Kwiatkowski 1992; Miksicek 1995)

Continued on next page

Table 3.5 *continued*

Location/Site	Map Location	Date	Plants (References)
Tonto Natl Mon: Salado	4	Classic period	c: maize, common bean, tepary bean, lima bean, jack bean, cotton, pumpkin, cushaw squash, crookneck squash, bottle gourd, grain amaranth, little barley; w: juniper, piñon, reed, saguaro, willow, screwbean mesquite, agave, sotol, yucca, bluestem, hackberry, silktassel, sagebrush, devil's claw, acorn, prickly pear, catclaw, bristlegrass, cocklebur, jojoba, mesquite, littleleaf paloverde, thistle, walnut, grape, canarygrass, soapberry, wild cucumber (Bohrer 1962; Sauer 1967; Sauer and Kaplan 1969)
Tucson Basin: 8 sites	2	Early Ceramic period	c: maize, common bean, tepary bean, squash, cotton; w: tobacco, agave, pigweed, manzanita, saltbush, spiderling, borage family, saguaro, hackberry, cheno-am, goosefoot, sunflower family, mustard family, tansy mustard, hedgehog cactus, spurge, grass family, rush, juniper, bean family, mallow family, pincushion cactus, carpetweed, plantain, prickly pear, clammyweed, purslane, mesquite, cf. acorn, sage, globemallow, seepweed, dropseed, false purslane (Fish, Fish, Madsen, et al. 1992; Huckell 1998a, 1998b; Miksicek and Bernard-Shaw 1989, 1990)
Hodges Ruin	2	Preclassic period	c: maize, tepary bean, jack bean, cotton; w: agave, cf. mesquite, saguaro, barrel cactus, hedgehog cactus, purslane, false purslane, spiderling, cheno-am, goosefoot family, tansy mustard, grass family, sunflower family (Huckell 1986a)
Tanque Verde Wash	2	Preclassic period	c: maize, tepary bean, common bean spp., jack bean, squash spp.; bottle gourd, cotton, amaranth, goosefoot; w: dropseed, prickly pear, tansy mustard, globemallow, spiderling, purslane, grama grass (Miksicek 1986a)
West Branch	2	Preclassic period	c: maize, common bean, jack bean, squash, cotton, tobacco, agave; w: pigweed, tansy mustard, dropseed, goosefoot, false purslane, purslane, globemallow, spiderling, wild tobacco, mesquite, saguaro, prickly pear, cholla, fishhook cactus (Miksicek 1986b)
Gibbon Springs	2	Classic period	c: maize, bean; w: tansy mustard, saguaro, saltbush, grass family, prickly pear, reed (Puseman 1996)
San Xavier Bridge	2	Classic period	c: maize, bean, cotton, agave; w: pigweed, cheno-am, goosefoot, saltbush, mustard family, globemallow, false purslane, grass family, mesquite, saguaro, cholla, hedgehog cactus, prickly pear, acacia, vetch, wild buckwheat, spurge, bean family, cf. bulrush (Gasser 1987)

Note. c = cultivated, w = wild.

For map locations, refer to figure 3.1.

Salt-Gila Aqueduct Project sites dates to as early as the Late Colonial–Early Sedentary period (Gasser and Kwiatkowski 1991a; Miksicek 1984a). Agave was an attractive resource because it produced both durable, long leaf fibers and a sweet food made by roasting the heart. Particular species were chosen for manipulation, all of which produce either bulbils or offsets that are easily transported and planted. The locations of modern northern disjunct populations near archaeological habitation sites reflect this close link to humans (Hodgson and Slauson 1995; Minnis and Plog 1976). Over time, agave cultivation assumed considerable economic importance, the maximum extent occurring in the Classic period, when the use of this xerophyte to convert marginal into productive land proved a highly successful economic strategy (Fish et al. 1985).

Regional and Diachronic Trends

Although the Hohokam regional system encompassed considerable territory in addition to the core Salt/Gila Valleys and the Tucson Basin, these two areas offer the largest data bases from which subregional comparisons can be made. Gasser and Kwiatkowsi (1991a) observed differences in the distribution of sites containing domesticated beans and those containing little barley. Beans were relatively common in the Tucson Basin but rare to the north, a condition Gasser and Kwiatkowski propose was attributable to Tucson's milder climate, which would have been more favorable for bean production. Little barley shows the opposite trend, being rare in the Tucson Basin and much more common to the north, suggesting that demand or need for this crop was greater in the latter region. The Tucson Basin assemblage also lacks obvious morphological evidence for use of the other plants identified by Bohrer as probably manipulated, again suggesting that the introduction of nonlocal plants into habitation or farming areas was unnecessary because of better local availability of wild resources. The frequency with which tansy mustard occurs, however, and the often large quantities that are recovered (Huckell 1986) have prompted Gasser and Kwiatkowski (1991b) to consider it a signature plant for the Tucson Basin.

The physiographic character of the Salt and Gila Valleys may offer a clue to the observed differences, as both valley floors are extremely broad and flat and are bounded by low mountains lacking the elevationally controlled vegetation diversity found in higher ranges. The valley floors are dominated by broad expanses of saltbush and creosotebush (*Larrea*) flats, communities that are not very productive for human needs unless cleared, planted, and watered.

Through the use of irrigation technology, the Hohokam were able to transcend the limited quantity of arable floodplain land and convert large tracts of marginal lands into productive fields. Resources found on the bajada slopes, such as saguaro, hedgehog cactus, cholla/prickly pear, and arborescent legumes, would have been limited in quantity and probably increasingly difficult to obtain in the face of burgeoning demand, the establishment of local political boundaries, and careful control over access to valuable wild commodities (Mitchell 1989). To ensure a dependable supply of supplemental wild foods, the Hohokam created suitable habitats in which many such plants could be grown. Pollen and macrobotanical evidence suggest that this was accomplished through the use of burning for large-scale land clearing or field maintenance (Bohrer 1992), the transplanting of economically desirable plants such as cholla to habitation areas (Fish 1984), and controlled water diversion and allocation beyond natural channels through extensive canal systems (Fish 1995). These tactics would have provided the means to establish and maintain wild populations, often well outside their normal ranges, as has been demonstrated for cholla and agave. Specialized production of some of these plants may have evolved as a means of generating trade goods; temporal trends in the specialization of plant products such as cotton and agave have been postulated for some sites (Gasser and Miksicek 1984).

Access to wild resources in places other than the core Hohokam area may have been more easily accomplished, especially in areas like the Tucson Basin, where a narrow, long valley is flanked by mountain ranges that are close to riverine settlements. The more compact vertical zonation of such settings would have offered ready access to several different biotic communities. Continued efforts by the Hohokam to intensify production by exploiting marginal lands are demonstrated by late Preclassic evidence for the incipient cultivation of agave on landforms largely unsuitable for maize agriculture. The success of this strategy is seen in the Classic period after AD 1150, when immense tracts of land were placed under agave cultivation in and around the Tucson Basin as well as in many other parts of the Hohokam region (Fish et al. 1985).

Gasser and Kwiatkowski (1991a, 1991b) found little significant regional diachronic change in wild plant use. They do note that little barley use appeared to decline during the Classic period and that agave utilization increased in importance in the nonriverine area north of the Tucson Basin. They attribute variability in plant use to (1) variation in local resource availability; (2) different ethnic food preferences; (3) culturally dictated variability to create mechanisms for exchange; and (4) the effects of formation processes on site records.

Local variation can be proposed for some areas where site-level trends in resource use may also indicate intersite variability in decision-making (Gasser and Kwiatkowski 1991a, 1991b; Miksicek 1984a). Pollen records for several sites in the northern Hohokam territory indicate general similarities in plant assemblages, but local variations in resource emphasis can be seen (Gish 1991: Fig. 2) that may indicate ethnic food preferences or behavioral choices to fully exploit specific local resources. Resource fluctuation through time was proposed by Bohrer (1970), who devised a seed/charcoal index to show that use of certain species fluctuated through time at Snaketown, a large Preclassic pithouse village located along the Gila River that was occupied from about AD 600 to 1100. Bohrer linked such fluctuations to Hohokam responses to periodic crop failures. A subsequent macrofossil presence value analysis of the same data (Gasser 1981a) supported Bohrer's results. At Las Canopas near Phoenix, use of maize apparently increased over time, whereas at Los Hornos, a few kilometers away, evidence suggests a steady decrease in corn consumption. At Frogtown on Queen Creek, Miksicek (1984b) noted that decreased use of maize corresponded with a more broadly based diet in the later periods of occupation. At other sites in the Gila River area, there are indications of increased use of tended wild species during the later periods (Fish 1984; Miksicek 1984a). Increasing dependence on nonagricultural foods during the Classic period has been proposed for the Hohokam in general; recent studies, however, indicate that, if true, such a trend was definitely not a regional one (Gasser and Kwiatkowski 1991a; Mitchell 1989). In evaluating the validity of these trends, one must take into account the following factors: highly variable period sample sizes, kinds of sampled contexts, preservation biases, and the size and quality of the area record into which the results will be integrated.

Data for interpreting wood use largely relate to fuel and construction categories. In broad terms, mesquite was preferred for both construction and fuel needs, although other riparian species such as cottonwood/willow and desert willow (*Chilopsis linearis*) were also used for main structural elements (Miksicek 1983, 1984b). Long, straight saguaro ribs were used as roofing material. Hearths and roasting pits show consistent use of mesquite, although creosotebush and saltbush are also frequently recovered from hearths. Roasting pit contents also indicate a preference for mesquite wood, although mixtures have been noted of several wood species, reflecting the expedient collecting of taxa obtained either locally or perhaps as driftwood in flood deposits.

Through the use of a diverse array of farming techniques that included sophisticated irrigation technology, the Hohokam were able to significantly alter their environment on a large scale, thereby greatly expanding the range of habitats available to them. Consummate agriculturalists, they continued to acquire domesticated crops from the south, with the final list of cultigens including several maize varieties, three species of squash (pumpkin, cushaw, and crookneck), bottle gourd, four species of beans (common, tepary, lima, and jack), cotton, grain amaranth, possible dye amaranth, and a possible cultivated chenopod (Gasser and Kwiatkowski 1991a). At the same time, they were also adept at capitalizing on the wealth of wild plant products available in the Sonoran Desert, both by deliberately manipulating wild species and by opportunistic wild harvesting, creating a successful blend that sustained their culture for nearly a millennium (Cordell 1997; Dean et al. 1994).

Other Areas

Two small parts of the North American Southwest in Arizona have benefited from new investigations over the last decade and merit discussion because of the increasingly detailed botanical records that have been developed there. They are the Tonto Basin, located northeast of Phoenix, which was the heartland of what has been called the Salado culture, and the area around Flagstaff south to the Upper Verde River valley, the territory of the Sinagua.

Tonto Basin—Salado

The Tonto Basin (Figure 3.1, No. 4) is of considerable archaeological interest because of the ongoing debate over the nature of the Salado phenomenon, which appeared with the advent of the Classic period at AD 1250 and is principally defined by the presence of distinctive red, white, and black polychrome pottery (Cordell 1997; Crown 1994). Extensive contract archaeology work in what is considered the Salado heartland has generated an exceptional botanical record that documents 3,000 years of prehistory from the Middle Archaic period through the Classic period (Adams 1994; Bohrer 1962, 1997; Dering 1998, 2000; Fish 2000; Halbirt and Gasser 1987; Huckell 2000a; Kwiatkowski 1992; Miksicek 1995). The record reveals the appearance of maize agriculture during the Early Agricultural period, followed by the establishment of a fundamentally Hohokam subsistence system that integrated a large suite of cultigens, a group of managed or cultivated plants, and a broad array of wild taxa (Table 3.5). The advent of the Classic period ushered in the same profound changes in material culture, architecture, and sociopolitical organization seen elsewhere, driven by the arrival of Puebloan immigrants (Stark et al. 1995). Corresponding dramatic increases in maize, agave, and cotton, along with construction of large-scale storage granaries, suggest a rapidly growing population. Intensification of key food and fiber crops points toward greater demand for basic foods and raw materials for consumption and exchange. Evidence of craft specialization is also suggested, perhaps reflecting economic activities of newcomers with less access to limited agricultural lands. Surviving examples of Salado textiles reveal extraordinary skill and artistry (Kent 1983) and suggest that woven items were important trade commodities. Cultivated wild or incipiently domesticated plants also played an important economic role, and management strategies are indicated for agave, several cactus species, and little barley. The macrofossil and pollen records indicate that wild plant use varied through time in different parts of the basin, plant selection being mediated by cultural, economic, and climatic variables. As an example, little barley use declined dramatically in the northern basin, but it persisted in the southern basin, especially during the Classic period (Huckell 2000a:Table 11.8).

Wood needs for fuel and construction were primarily met by juniper; mesquite was utilized in much smaller quantities and is more evident at sites in the southern basin. Notable exceptions to this pattern that may reflect ethnic or religious preferences were found in limited mortuary contexts and some of the platform mounds that formed the nuclei for settlements along the drainages. Cribbing elements for certain inhumations and some structural beams were found to be high-elevation conifers such as spruce and pine, procurement of which required arduous expeditions into surrounding mountains (Elson et al. 1995). Similar commitments to obtaining high-elevation beams have been observed in a contemporary platform mound in the northern Tucson Basin (Stark et al. 1995) and at Chaco Canyon (Windes and McKenna 2001); the trees' symbolic association with rain clouds may have provided the incentive for such a laborious task (Huckell 2000a). The Tonto Basin was abandoned at the end of the Classic period for unknown reasons, although climatic fluctuations and escalating social conflict may have been contributing factors.

Sinagua

The area surrounding Flagstaff and the Upper Verde Valley was occupied by the Sinagua (Cordell 1997) (Figure 3.1, No. 5). As in so many other places, much of the initial archaeological work in the area was done prior to use of flotation (Cutler and Kaplan 1956; Jones 1941; Kent 1954; Pierson 1956; Rixey and Voll 1962), resulting in a biased record that is only now being amended. Sinagua territory posed major challenges to subsistence farmers, as it has thin soils, limited biotic resources, and little surface water; in fact, the name "Sinagua" means "without water." The eruption of Sunset Crater in AD 1064 was a pivotal event, as it deposited a layer of ash several centimeters thick over a 2,100-km² area that acted as a mulch, retaining precious soil moisture (Berlin et al. 1977; Berlin et al. 1990). An abundance of small farmstead sites appeared following the eruption, which suggests that the population dispersed seasonally from large home settlements to these small field sites. The farmsteads offer little evidence of sustained habitation, however, probably reflecting rapidly exhausted soil fertility (Sullivan and Downum 1991).

The botanical record indicates that the Sinagua grew a variety of cultigens (Table 3.3). Cotton is a major presence, a surprising trend given the high elevation and short growing season that characterizes much of the territory. Microclimatic advantages in some lower areas appear to have provided an adequate growing season to permit the arid-adapted plants to mature (Wright 2000). Wild plant resources are dominated by small-seeded annuals, with members of the goosefoot family the most prominent (Huckell 1999b; Hunter et al. 1999; Hunter and Wright 1998). In particular, bugseed has been recovered consistently and in quantities that suggest deliberate cultivation (Hunter et al. 1999). Pollen studies of several kinds of agricultural features found in the ash zones identified some maize and abundant cheno-ams (Berlin et al. 1977; Hasbargen 1997), suggesting that, although maize could have been grown there, weedy species that provided both seed and greens crops in a short time span were very likely the focus of cultivation. Wood use was eclectic, with locally available pines, oak, and juniper preferred for fuel and construction. Shrub species also appear as common inclusions in thermal features (Hunter et al. 1999; Hunter and Wright 1998).

Lesser Known Areas

Other parts of the North American Southwest have not received the kind of intensive investigation efforts devoted to the preceding areas and offer highly variable records of plant use.

Northern Mexico remains largely unknown archaeobotanically. Chihuahua has benefited in recent years from renewed investigations in the Paquimé area, in the northern Sierra Madre Occidental caves, and in the southern part of the state, all of which have produced paleoethnobotanical records. Almost no plant studies are available for Sonora, the neighboring state to the west. Excavation projects have been limited until recently. Work conducted in the northeastern part of the state by Richard Pailes during the 1970s resulted in the definition of the Río Sonora culture; although flotation samples were taken from a number of sites, analysis results have yet to be published (Pailes 1984). Preliminary excavations at La Playa, an immense Late Archaic/Early Agricultural site located in the Boquillas Valley roughly 100 km southwest of the international border from Nogales, Arizona, yielded a disappointing, small floral record, suggesting that poor preservation may be a problem in reconstructing plant subsistence activities at the site (Carpenter et al. 1997). Continuing work at La Playa and at some of the *trincheras* sites found nearby may eventually produce useful archaeobotanical records.

The Patayan area is poorly known culturally and geographically; even its cultural boundaries are subject to considerable disagreement. In very general terms, this area includes the parts of southeastern California and western Arizona that flank the Colorado River (Cordell 1997), but the eastern limit in Arizona remains to be determined. Little direct information is available on prehistoric wild plant use (Hammett 1993a; Kaemlein 1963).

The Virgin Anasazi area lies west of the Kayenta region; it encompasses the portion of Arizona from the Colorado River north into southern Utah around the Virgin River drainage. The plant record from this poorly known peripheral area is too limited to assess patterns and trends in wild plant use (Allison 1990; Martin 1999; Nusbaum 1922; Van Ness 1987). Recent isotope studies suggest a consistently high degree of reliance on maize and the minor exploitation of wild plants from Basketmaker II through late Pueblo II, when the area was abandoned; options for dietary diversification based on wild plants may have been limited in this chronically marginal environment (Martin 1999).

The Middle Little Colorado includes the area flanking the Little Colorado River from the Puerco River confluence to Oraibi Wash (Figure 3.1, No. 6). It includes a small number of investigated sites; the most prominent are two large, late, ancestral Hopi pueblo sites, Homol'ovi II and Homol'ovi III (Adams 1996; Miksicek 1991) (Table 3.3). Both have yielded extensive plant records because of unusually good preservation. A large crop inventory, in which cotton is unusually prominent, suggests that the settlements were heavily invested in agricultural production and may have been major producers of the fiber, perhaps as a trade commodity. Wild plants include agrestals and a significant riparian component, a benefit of close proximity to the perennial Little Colorado. Generally smaller and ranging in age from Late Archaic/Basketmaker II through Pueblo IV, the remaining sites are summarized by Adams (1996). Their smaller sample sizes and poorer preservation make proposed diachronic trends for the area based on the exceptional late record from Homol'ovi II and III tentative at best.

Bounded on the west by the Sangre de Cristo Mountains, the northeastern portion of New Mexico supports grasslands in which the cultural transition from Pueblo to Plains takes place. The area is poorly known archaeobotanically; reports are available from the Cimarron area (Kirkpatrick and Ford 1977) and the Vermejo River (Judges-Edwards 1997).

A surprisingly modest number of archaeobotanical reports are available for the Central Rio Grande area around Albuquerque north to the vicinity of Bernalillo (Figure 3.1, No. 14). The record spans the Archaic through the late Pueblo periods (Brandt 1991; Galinat et al. 1970; Garber 1980; Knight 1994; Toll 1982, 1987b, 1994), but the records from sampled sites are insufficient to address wild plant use trends in time and space. Most of the frequently encountered disturbance taxa noted elsewhere appear here consistently, with goosefoot, pigweed, winged pigweed, and bugseed the most visible. Perennials include ricegrass, dropseed, and cholla, hedgehog, and other small cereoid cacti. Differences in assemblage composition have been noted from site to site, but their significance cannot be assessed apart from an apparent emphasis on local resource procurement.

The Rio Abajo section of the Rio Grande Valley encompasses the area to the north and south of Socorro, New Mexico (Figure 3.1, No. 15). Little excavation has been carried out, and few reported macrobotanical studies are available (Toll 1987b, 1995, 1997).

In southeastern New Mexico, the area around Roswell and the Rio Hondo Valley to the west also represents an environmental and cultural transition area in which the Jornada Mogollon interfaces with the Plains (Figure 3.1, No. 16). A number of projects have been carried out, most of which are not yet fully reported (Powell 2001; Toll 1993a, 1996).

Although many researchers feel that west Texas falls outside the boundaries of the North American Southwest, we include the Big Bend/Trans-Pecos region here because of the extensive record of wild plant use that has been compiled for the area. Hunter-gatherer adaptations have been explored through pollen, macrobotanical remains, and coprolites from a series of well-stocked dry caves (Bryant 1969; Edwards 1990; Holloway 1985; Sobolik 1991; Sobolik and Gerick 1992; Stock 1983). The exploitation of wild succulents such as agave, yucca, and cacti has been documented, with distinctive rock middens and hearths providing macrobotanical confirmation of their widespread use (Dering 1999).

Ritual Use Determined from Imagery

This chapter has focused on the subsistence use of wild plants. The treatment of medicinal plants or ritual plants has been minimal because of the paucity of unequivocal information on their uses (Harrison 2002; Toll and McBride 1997). The assumption that most plants identified from macrofossil and pollen remains were used for food almost certainly is not justified, but evidence for alternative functions can be elusive, with pollen and coprolite data offering the most potential in this regard (Reinhard et al. 1991). Insights into important nonfood uses of wild plants can also be obtained from sources other than the archaeobotanical record, one of which is representational art. Two examples of plants depicted in art are sunflower and jimsonweed (*Datura*).

Sunflower

The sporadic presence, small quantities, and generally low ubiquities of sunflower remains in the prehistoric Southwest suggest that this plant served as little more than a supplemental food. Among the Hohokam and Mimbres, anthropomorphic and zoomorphic elements were often employed in Preclassic period ceramic decoration, but plant representations are extremely rare. Just two cases of Hohokam use of floral motifs are currently known: on three or four sherds from Snaketown (Haury 1976:Fig. 12.85) and on a shallow, imported buffware bowl from the Hardy site in the Tucson Basin (Gregonis and Reinhard 1979:40) (Figure 3.2). Both images are executed in the same style, are contemporaneous in age (AD 500–700), and appear to portray sunflowers. Although among the Mimbres, flowers were seldom rendered, several ceramic designs appear to depict the sunflower (Anyon and LeBlanc 1984: Plates 21a, 27d, 65f, 74c, 92c, 99f; Davis 1995; Fewkes 1923:Figs. 50, 51, 112, 121) (Figure 3.2). Sunflowers have also been identified on a Western Pueblo White Mountain redware bowl (Carlson 1970:Figs. 40h, 59a) (Figure 3.2) and in more abstract form on Salado polychromes (Crown 1994:158). Sunflowers were painted on stone slabs in rooms containing ritual artifacts at Kinishba Pueblo in east-central Arizona (Crown 1994:201; Cummings 1940).

At least one rock art site in northern Arizona includes a sunflower petroglyph (Kelley Hays-Gilpin, personal communication 2001). The sunflower theme can also be seen in prehistoric caches of ritual items from Sunflower Cave in the Kayenta Anasazi area in northeastern Arizona (Kidder and Guernsey 1919: 145–147, Plates 60, 61) and from a cave near Bonita Creek in east-central Arizona (Wasley 1962). Both caches contained elaborately constructed, multipetaled, composite wooden sunflowers, painted yellow or white in the Sunflower Cave cache and either blue, green, or unpainted in the Bonita Creek cache. Both caches date to the end of the 13th century.

Crown (1994:214–225) proposes that floral images were elements of belief systems that were in place prior to the Great Drought of AD 1275. The widespread population relocations that took place throughout the North American Southwest in the wake of the drought were the impetus behind a reformulation of what had been a kin-based ancestor cult as the Southwest Regional Cult, in which symbols such as flowers assumed new importance. This new system promoted social harmony and integration manifested as concern with the well-being of the earth, as shown by the increased use of icons representing the universe, fertility, and weather: the sun, Venus, stars, flowers, the sky, clouds, lightning, rain, and the wind. Floral representations also may have evoked the Flower World, a concept of a spiritual paradise afterworld that is found today among Uto-Aztecan speakers in Mexico and in southwestern pueblos (Hays-Gilpin and Hill 1999; Hill 1992). Sunflowers have also figured prominently in prehistoric and historic kiva murals (Smith 1952:230; Stephen 1936:1225) and as components of historic altar furnishings and kachina dancer costumes (Hays-Gilpin and Hill 1999; Smith 1952:230). The sunflower was the most important and consistently used floral icon in this complex; with the exception of maize, no other plant approaches it in artistic visibility.

Jimsonweed

Like sunflower, jimsonweed has a minimal macrobotanical presence in the Southwest, known from rare recoveries of seeds and pollen. Small, spiny ceramic vessels whose forms resemble jimsonweed capsules have been recovered from more than 40 sites (Huckell and VanPool 2002). They are best represented in Anasazi sites dating to the PI–PIII periods in the Mesa Verde area and in Colonial or Classic period Hohokam sites in southern Arizona (Fish, Fish, Brennan, et al. 1992; Gladwin et al. 1965:Plate CXXXVII; Litzinger 1979; Yarnell 1959). At the Classic period Hohokam Marana platform mound in the northern Tucson Basin, fragments of six different small vessels

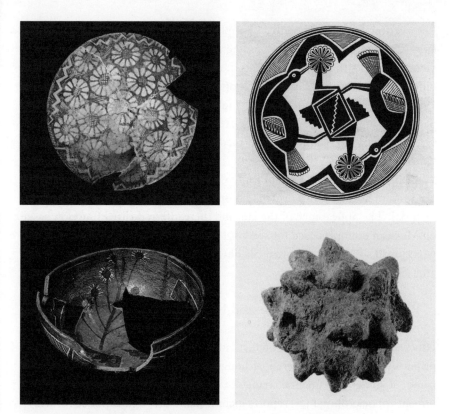

FIGURE 3.2 Graphic representations of sunflowers and jimsonweed:
(*upper left*) Hohokam Colonial period Red-on-Buff bowl with sunflower design
(Arizona State Museum, University of Arizona, Helga Teiwes, photographer);
(*upper right*) Mimbres Black-on-White bowl with birds and sunflowers
(illustration by Harriet S. Cosgrove, courtesy of C. Burton Cosgrove);
(*lower left*) Western Pueblo Point of Pines Polychrome bowl with paired sunflower plants (Arizona State Museum, University of Arizona, Geoffrey Ashley,
photographer); (*lower right*) Hohokam jimsonweed capsule effigy bead (Arizona
State Museum, University of Arizona, Ken Matesich, photographer)

bearing appliqued conical tubercles or spines were recovered from the top of
the mound in a sample of fewer than 700 sherds. In contrast, just two spiny
ceramic items were found among thousands of pieces obtained from the surrounding trash mounds and residential areas (Suzanne K. Fish, personal communication 2001; Fish, Fish, Brennan, et al. 1992). The most unusual specimen is a complete, small, capsule effigy bead with a longitudinal suspension
hole (Figure 3.2). A similar bead or spindle whorl was found on the Ak Chin

Reservation south of Phoenix; 12 appliqued sherds were recovered from a large Colonial period site in the same area (Fryman 1990:Fig. 16.11). This record suggests the ritual exploitation of the powerful hallucinogenic capability of jimsonweed, a practice rooted in antiquity in Mexico (Schultes 1976). Early ethnographers noted the use of the dangerous, alkaloid-rich plants by a number of traditional societies in the North American Southwest, Great Basin, and California for medicinal and hallucinogenic purposes (Curtin 1984:85–87; Rea 1991:220–222; Russell 1975:300; Safford 1922; Whiting 1966:89). Ethnographically documented preparation methods do not require heat and thus provide no opportunities for preservation of plant material. The appearance of the jars and their inferred ritual function based on Mexican examples used for seed or leaf storage may indicate a potentially widespread southwestern ritual use of the plants that is not evident from the archaeobotanical record alone.

Research Issues: Present and Future

Issues addressed by archaeobotanists in the North American Southwest are primarily subsistence centered, although questions regarding the paleoenvironment and environmental change may be discussed as well. Routine components of macrobotanical reports include plant-based subsistence records at the site and project levels and consideration of seasonality of occupation, feature function, and identification of wood used for fuel and construction. Examination of environmental change centers mainly on diachronic changes in wood use that may indicate preferred resource use or overexploitation. Efforts to address longitudinal vegetation change have been made, but they can be risky endeavors because of the cultural filter through which the samples have passed. Pollen and phytolith analyses are better tools for such analyses. More detailed investigations relating to questions such as patterning of activities within domestic space are seldom carried out. Exceptional cases can be cited in which intensive sampling has resulted in highly detailed, informative reconstructions of localized activities and of the impacts of natural processes on floor assemblages (Adams 1980; Benz and Matthews 1983; Scott 1980; Toll and McBride 1998). Regrettably, time and monetary constraints make these kinds of studies rare.

Topical issues in which paleoethnobotany plays a significant role include the timing of the arrival of maize and other cultigens, the transition from hunting and gathering to a mixed foraging/food production economy, and storage technology (Minnis 1992; Smiley 1993; Wills and Huckell 1994); management of wild plants and evidence for the in situ domestication process involving wild plants (Bohrer 1991, 1992; Hodgson and Slauson 1995; Matthews 1986; Nabhan and de Wet 1984); identification of plants associated with manifestations of local and subregional subsistence strategies that indicate diversification and intensification (Berlin et al. 1977; Clary 1987; Dean 1995; Hasbargen 1997); degree of dependence on maize and wild plants through time (Chisholm and Matson 1994; Decker and Tieszen 1989; Martin 1999; Stiger 1979); mobility and sedentism (Huckell 1990, 1996a; Huckell 1995a, 1998a); diet and nutrition (Cummings 1994; Ezzo 1994); human impacts on the landscape (Anschuetz 1995; Fish 1995; Fish et al. 1985; Lang 1995; Minnis and Plog 1976; Woodbury 1961); production and exchange (Fish and Donaldson 1991); and medicinal plant use (Reinhard et al. 1991).

The basis for current understanding of the economic role of wild plants comes from macrofossils, pollen, coprolites, and bone chemistry analyses. Ideally, all of these complementary lines of evidence should be brought to bear on subsistence questions, but, in fact, this is currently feasible only in the Anasazi area. Coprolites have yet to be found in southern Arizona, where environments conducive to preservation are rare. Almost no published data are available for the Mogollon region, despite its many caves (Reinhard et al. 1991). Of the handful of bone chemistry studies that have been done (Chisholm and Matson 1994; Decker 1989; Ezzo, 1993, 1994; Martin et al. 1991; Martin 1999; Matson and Chisholm 1991), almost none pertain to sites in the southern Southwest (Katzenberg and Kelley 1991; MacNeish and Marino 1993). Such studies may prove increasingly difficult to conduct because of Native American objections to destructive analyses of human remains. The potential of other lines of evidence such as phytoliths, crystals, starch grains, and residues should also be investigated to determine their relevance and applicability to southwestern research issues.

Experimental studies are an underutilized tool for developing new insights into formation processes, for improving identification accuracy, and for challenging and modifying entrenched but untested assumptions (Adams et al. 1999; Greenhouse et al. 1981; Osborne 1965; Rylander 1994; Smith and Geib 2000). Issues such as isolating botanical evidence for various steps in the processing of plant products, documenting the morphological effects of carbonization, and evaluating storage methods and their effectiveness can be directly addressed through carefully constructed experiments. Publication of the results is imperative.

Lisa W. Huckell and Mollie S. Toll

Archives and museums constitute a relatively untapped source of new archaeobotanical knowledge; curated materials are literally buried treasure. Materials obtained from dry caves and rockshelters may reflect recovery biases, but they are still important parts of the subsistence record. Opportunities to apply current analytical techniques, capitalize on AMS radiocarbon dating to obtain precise chronological data, and evaluate plant assemblages from new theoretical perspectives should be pursued and reported. Museum collections may prove to be important sources of coprolites as well.

Summary

General trends can be identified in the archaeobotanical record in the North American Southwest. It is clear that maize agriculture was effectively integrated into a hunting and gathering adaptation that had been in place for 8,000 years. Isotope and coprolite data from the northern Southwest and macrofossil data that represent the rest of the region indicate that over the ensuing 3,000 years maize assumed an integral place in subsistence systems from the Early Agricultural period through the Pueblo IV/Classic periods. Evidence is also accruing that intensification of maize production was widely employed as a strategy for coping with increasing or aggregating populations and recurrent environmental stress during the late ceramic period.

Despite the increased or continued strong reliance on maize as a central component, wild plants continued to be important dietary constituents. Subregional and regional wild staples can be identified. Anasazi plants with high archaeological ubiquity included ricegrass, cheno-ams, piñon, various mustards, sunflower, prickly pear, groundcherry, beeweed, and grasses (Brand 1994). Among the upland Mogollon/Western Pueblo, preferred or conspicuous resources included cheno-ams, grasses, juniper, sunflower, and cacti (Huckell 1999a:Table 24; Minnis 1985a). Purslane and goosefoot were the most frequent Jornada Mogollon wild plant foods (Cummings 1993; Whalen 1994). Hohokam gatherers consistently relied on cheno-ams, purslane, tansy mustard, cholla, prickly pear, saguaro, and mesquite (Gasser and Kwiatkowski 1991a), with intensified production of managed wild species such as agave and little barley taking place during the Sedentary and Classic periods, if not earlier. Certain plants now appear to have been important throughout the Southwest, among them, tansy mustard, dropseed, purslane, cheno-ams, groundcherry, cholla, and prickly pear. These wild plant foods contributed diversity and, perhaps more importantly, vital nutritional elements to maize-centered diets. For example, the critical amino acid lysine is lacking in maize but is abundant in pigweed/amaranth, and the large amount of calcium packed into cholla buds exceeds the value of milk (Meals for Millions/Freedom from Hunger Foundation 1985; National Research Council 1984; Ross 1941). Some perennial crops (piñon nuts in woodland areas, agave in upland regions, saguaro fruits and seeds in the Sonoran Desert) were concentrated resources that served as important seasonal staples often obtained through long-distance foraging expeditions.

Preservation biases are particularly important in shaping the use record of wild plants, as off-site processing, the ephemeral quality of greens and other foodstuffs, high susceptibility to decay, and other factors act to reduce the visibility of some taxa and make accurate evaluations of diet breadth extremely difficult. Assessments of maize use suffer from the opposite bias, with a high potential for overrepresentation devolving from the extraordinarily durable and large cob that was deliberately carbonized when used for fuel. The extreme differences in the two records complicate drawing conclusions about the roles played by both cultigens and wild species in local economies.

One of the most intriguing regionwide patterns to emerge is the growing record of the management or encouragement of wild taxa. Although no unequivocal evidence yet exists for true in situ domestication of any species by prehistoric people in the Southwest, as is seen in the eastern United States, the Anasazi and Hohokam records provide evidence for active manipulation as part of diversification and intensification strategies. The record is less clear for the Mogollon/Western Pueblo area, but the increased presence of chenoams, which correlates with increasing population, suggests the possibility of manipulation there as well (Minnis 1978). This strategy appears to have extended beyond food production to include raw materials as well (Bohrer 1992; Nichols and Smith 1965). The ethnographic record contains abundant references to such practices, and it is not surprising to see antecedents of this behavior in prehistory as well (Bye 1979, 1981; Lawton et al. 1976; Rea 1978; Winter and Hogan 1986).

Wild plants were integral components of prehistoric subsistence economies. Although the importance or significance of individual taxa may have ebbed and flowed, wild plants were indispensable to the well-being and survival of prehistoric peoples. Together with maize, they offered a suite of options from which solutions could be fashioned for the day-to-day and long-term problems of making a living in a region characterized by environmental fluctuations and uncertainty. An increasing dependence on maize did not result in

Lisa W. Huckell and Mollie S. Toll

independence from wild plants; no one can survive on a diet composed solely of maize. Rather, wild plant foods served agriculturalists as backup crops, dietary supplements, starvation foods, and staples, and could be used in different ways as need dictated. The value of wild plants to meet utilitarian needs—providing everything from simple string to construction timbers and fuel—has barely been addressed here, but raw material availability was also a critical consideration in socioeconomic decision-making processes.

The archaeobotanical record in some more intensively studied areas is just now beginning to provide us with the tools to develop basic models of wild plant use, but more work remains to be done before the data are in place that will permit more accurate, nuanced, large-scale cultural, local, and regional syntheses. At the least, larger samples of macrofossil and pollen data are required to assess current concepts, and the collaborative efforts of analysts and archaeologists will be required to generate the high-quality data that are needed for this purpose. As their potential is explored, contributions from other lines of evidence such as phytoliths and starch grains will also provide valuable insights. Together, these sources of plant data will provide the means for ongoing evaluation, expansion, and refinement of the records and ideas summarized here.

Acknowledgments

We would like to thank Karen Adams, Suzanne Fish, Kelley Hays-Gilpin, Art MacWilliams, and Pamela McBride for graciously sharing unpublished papers, reports, and information. Vaughn Bryant, Phil Dering, Scott Kwiatkowski, Janet McVickar, and Mark Slaughter provided reports, references, and data. Helpful comments on the manuscript were made by Vaughn Bryant, Bruce Huckell, and an anonymous reviewer. Paul Fish generously provided the Marana Mound jimsonweed capsule effigy photograph that was taken by Ken Matesich of the Arizona State Museum, University of Arizona. Kathy Hubenschmidt, photoarchivist at the Arizona State Museum, provided two vessel photographs: the Hohokam sunflower bowl (ASM Neg. No. 49809), Helga Teiwes, photographer, and the White Mountain polychrome sunflower bowl (ASM Neg. No. C-58428), Geoffrey Ashley, photographer. Carolyn O'Bagy Davis and C. Burton Cosgrove graciously made available the Mimbres birds and sunflowers vessel illustration by Harriet S. Cosgrove. Finally, thanks to Bob Gasser for contributing to the first version of this chapter.

Note

C3, C4 and CAM are the three photosynthetic pathways used by plants to convert water and atmospheric CO_2 to oxygen and complex sugars that provide energy for the plant. Each pathway is an adaptation to environmental conditions: C3 plants are temperate, cool-season plants that appear in the spring (e.g., mustard, barley); C4 plants are tropical, warm-season plants that appear in the summer (e.g., maize); and CAM plants are adapted to extreme heat and aridity (e.g, agave, cacti, yucca). See Chisholm and Matson (1994) and Ezzo (1993) for more information.

References Cited

Aasen, Diane Katien
1984   *Pollen, Macrofossil, and Charcoal Analyses of Basketmaker Coprolites from Turkey Pen Ruin, Cedar Mesa, Utah.* Unpublished master's thesis, Department of Anthropology, Washington State University, Pullman.

Adams, Karen R.
1980   *Pollen, Parched Seeds and Prehistory: A Pilot Invesigation of Prehistoric Plant Remains from Salmon Ruin, a Chacoan Pueblo in Northwestern New Mexico.* Contributions in Anthropology 9. Eastern New Mexico University, Portales.

1992   Archaeobotanical and Modern Ecological Perspectives on Ancient Sites in West-Central Chihuahua, Mexico: Preliminary Report of 1990 and 1991 Field Seasons. Manuscript on file, Department of Anthropology, University of Calgary, Calgary.

1993   Carbonized Plant Remains. In *The Duckfoot Site: 1. Descriptive Archaeology*, edited by Ricky R. Lightfoot and Mary C. Etzkorn, pp. 195–220. Occasional Paper 3. Crow Canyon Archaeological Center, Cortez, Colorado.

1994   Macrobotanical Analyses. In *Changing Land Use in the Tonto Basin*, vol. 3, edited by Richard S. Ciolek-Torello and John R. Welch, pp. 167–187. Technical Series 28. Statistical Research, Tucson.

1996   Archaeobotany of the Middle Little Colorado River. In *River of Change: Prehistory of the Middle Little Colorado River Valley, Arizona*, edited by E. Charles Adams, pp. 163–186. Archaeological Series 185. Arizona State Museum, Tucson.

Adams, Karen R., Deborah A. Muenchrath, and Dylan M. Schwindt
1999   Moisture Effects on the Morphology of Ears, Cobs and Kernels of a Southwestern U.S. Maize (*Zea mays* L.) Cultivar, and Implications for the Interpretation of Archaeological Maize. *Journal of Archaeological Science* 26:483–496.

Adams, Karen R., and Mollie S. Toll
2000   Tobacco Use, Ecology, and Manipulation in the Prehistoric and Historic Southwestern United States. In *Tobacco Use by Native North Americans: Sacred Smoke and Silent Killer*, edited by Joseph C. Winter, pp. 143–170. University of Oklahoma Press, Norman.

Agenbroad, Larry D.
1970   *Cultural Implications from the Statistical Analysis of a Prehistoric Lithic Site in Arizona.* Unpublished master's thesis, Department of Anthropology, University of Arizona, Tucson.

Allison, James R.
  1990   *Anasazi Subsistence in the St. George Basin, Southwestern Utah.* Unpublished master's thesis,
          Department of Anthropology, Brigham Young University, Provo.

Ambrose, James E., Jr.
  1986   The Past Environment of Canyon de Chelly. In *Archeological Investigations at Antelope
          House*, edited by Don P. Morris, pp. 84–109. National Park Service, US Department of
          the Interior, Washington, DC.

Anschuetz, Kurt F.
  1995   Saving a Rainy Day: The Integration of Diverse Agricultural Technologies to Harvest
          and Conserve Water in the Lower Rio Chama Valley, New Mexico. In *Soil, Water,
          Biology, and Belief in Prehistoric and Traditional Southwestern Agriculture*, edited by
          H. Wolcott Toll, pp. 25–39. Special Publication 2. New Mexico Archaeological Council,
          Albuquerque.

Anyon, Roger, and Stephen A. LeBlanc
  1984   *The Galaz Ruin.* Maxwell Museum of Anthropology and University of New Mexico Press,
          Albuquerque.

Benz, Bruce, and Meredith H. Matthews
  1983   Bulk Soil Samples from a Basketmaker III Pithouse Floor at Windy Wheat. Paper pre-
          sented at the 48th Annual Meeting of the Society for American Archaeology, Pittsburgh.

Berlin, G. Lennis, J. Richard Ambler, Richard H. Hevly, and Gerald G. Schaber
  1977   Identification of a Sinagua Agricultural Field by Aerial Thermography, Soil Chemistry,
          Pollen/Plant Analysis, and Archaeology. *American Antiquity* 42:588–600.

Berlin, G. Lennis, David E. Salas, and Phil R. Geib
  1990   A Prehistoric Sinagua Agricultural Site in the Ashfall Zone of Sunset Crater, Arizona.
          Journal of Field Archaeology 17:1–16.

Bohrer, Vorsila L.
  1962   Nature and Interpretation of Ethnobotanical Materials from Tonto National Monument.
          In *Archaeological Studies at Tonto National Monument, Arizona*, edited by Charlie R. Steen,
          L. M. Pierson, Vorsila L. Bohrer, and Kate P. Kent, pp. 79–114. Technical Series 2.
          Southwestern Monuments Association, Globe, Arizona.

  1970   Ethnobotanical Aspects of Snaketown, a Hohokam Village in Southern Arizona. *Ameri-
          can Antiquity* 35:413–430.

  1973   Ethnobotany of Point of Pines Ruin, Arizona W:10:50. *Economic Botany* 27:423–437.

  1981   Former Dietary Patterns of People as Determined from Archaic-Age Plant Remains from
          Fresnal Shelter, South-Central New Mexico. *Artifact* 19:41–50.

  1982   Plant Remains from Rooms at Grasshopper Pueblo. In *Multidisciplinary Research at Grass-
          hopper Pueblo, Arizona*, edited by William A. Longacre, Sally J. Holbrook, and Michael W.
          Graves, pp. 97–105. Anthropological Papers 40. University of Arizona, Tucson.

  1986   The Ethnobotanical Pollen Record at Arroyo Hondo Pueblo. In *Food, Diet, and Population
          at Prehistoric Arroyo Hondo Pueblo, New Mexico*, edited by Wilma Wetterstrom, pp. 187–220.
          Arroyo Hondo Archaeological Series 6. School of American Research Press, Santa Fe.

  1987   The Plant Remains from La Ciudad, a Hohokam Site in Phoenix. In *La Ciudad*, edited by
          Jo Ann E. Kisselburg, Glen E. Rice, and Brenda L. Shears, pp. 67–178. Anthropological
          Field Studies 20(3). Arizona State University, Tempe.

  1991   Recently Recognized Cultivated and Encouraged Plants among the Hohokam. *Kiva*
          56:227–235.

  1992   New Life from Ashes II: A Tale of Burnt Brush. *Desert Plants* 10:122–125.

  1997   Flotation Analysis: Prehistoric Plant Use and Subsistence Strategies in the Upper Tonto

Basin. In *The Mazatzal Rest Area Archaeological Data Recovery Project: Archaic and Salado Settlement and Subsistence Patterns along Hardt Creek, Upper Tonto Basin, Gila County, Arizona*, edited by Matthew H. Bilsbarrow and Gregory R. Woodall, pp. 277–298. Project Report 95:14C. Archaeological Research Services, Phoenix.

Brand, Michael James
    1994   *Prehistoric Anasazi Diet: A Synthesis of Archaeological Evidence.* Unpublished master's thesis, Department of Anthropology and Sociology, University of British Columbia, Vancouver.

Brandt, Carol B.
    1991   The River's Edge Archaeobotany Analysis: Phase II Data Recovery. In *At the River's Edge: Early Puebloan Settlement in the Middle Rio Grande Valley Phase II Report: Results of the 1989 Field Season*, edited by Matthew F. Schmader, pp. 274–319. Zuni Archaeology Program Ethnobiological Technical Series 91-14. Amrep Southwest, Rio Grande, and Rio Grande Consultants, Albuquerque.
    1994   Analysis of Plant Macroremains. In *Excavations along the Arkansas Loop Pipeline Corridor, Northwestern New Mexico*, edited by Linda Honeycutt and Jerry Fetterman, pp. 26-1–26-13. Woods Canyon Archaeological Consultants, Yellowjacket, Colorado.
    1995   Analysis of Plant Macro-Remains from Site LA 12954. In *Excavations at Site LA 12954: An Early Lithic Heat-Treatment Facility Overlooking the San Juan River, on Navajo Route 36(6b) South of Farmington, San Juan County, New Mexico*, prepared by Patricia A. Ruppé, Elizabeth Skinner, and Karol Stoker, pp. 69–83. Report 419. Zuni Cultural Resource Enterprise, Zuni, New Mexico.

Browning, Cody, Mark Sale, David T. Kirkpatrick, and Karl W. Laumbach
    1993   MOTR Site: Excavation at Site LA 72859, an El Paso Phase Structure on Fort Bliss, Otero County, New Mexico. *Artifact* 31(3):1-74.

Bryant, Vaughn M., Jr.
    1969   *Late Full-Glacial, and Post-Glacial Pollen Analysis of Texas Sediments.* Unpublished PhD dissertation, Department of Botany, University of Texas, Austin.

Bye, Robert A., Jr.
    1981   Quelites-Ethnoecology of Edible Greens-Past Present and Future. *Journal of Ethnobiology* 1:109–123.
    1979   Incipient Domestication of Mustards in Northwest Mexico. *Kiva* 44:237–256.

Carlson, Roy L.
    1970   *White Mountain Redware: A Pottery Tradition of East-Central Arizona and Western New Mexico.* Anthropological Papers 19. University of Arizona Press, Tucson.

Carpenter, John P., Guadalupe Sanchez de Carpenter, and Elisa Villalpando Canchola
    1997   Rescate Arqueológico La Playa (SON F:10:3), Municipio de Trincheras, Sonora, México. Manuscript on file, Director General of INAH, Mexico City, and Centro INAH Sonora, Hermosillo.

Cattanach, George S., Jr.
    1980   Refuse. In *Long House, Mesa Verde National Park, Colorado*, edited by George S. Cattanach Jr., pp. 369–398. Publications in Archeology 7H, Wetherill Mesa Studies. National Park Service, US Department of the Interior, Washington, DC.

Chisholm, Brian, and R. G. Matson
    1994   Carbon and Nitrogen Isotopic Evidence on Basketmaker II Diet at Cedar Mesa, Utah. *Kiva* 60:239–255.

Clary, Karen
    1987   Pollen Evidence for the Agricultural Utilization of Early Classic Period (A.D. 1350–1500) Anasazi Gravel Mulch Terrace Gardens, the Rio Chama, in the Vicinity of Medanales,

Lisa W. Huckell and Mollie S. Toll

New Mexico. Manuscript on file, Laboratory of Anthropology, Museum of New Mexico, Sante Fe.

Colyer, Marilyn, and Douglas Osborne
1965   Screening Soil and Fecal Samples for Recovery of Small Specimens. *American Antiquity* 31:186–192.

Cordell, Linda
1997   *Archaeology of the Southwest*. 2nd ed. Academic Press, New York.

Coulam, Nancy J., and Peggy R. Barnett
1980   Paleoethnobotanical Analysis. In *Sudden Shelter*, edited by Jesse D. Jennings, Alan R. Schroedl, and Richard N. Holmer, pp. 171–194. Anthropological Papers 103. University of Utah, Salt Lake City.

Crown, Patricia L.
1994   *Ceramics and Ideology: Salado Polychrome Pottery*. University of New Mexico Press, Albuquerque.

Cummings, Byron
1940   *Kinishba*. Hohokam Museums Association and the University of Arizona, Tucson.

Cummings, Linda Scott
1989   Pollen and Macrofloral Analysis at LA 2, Agua Fria Schoolhouse, Northern New Mexico. In *Limited Excavations at LA 2, the Agua Fria Schoolhouse Site, Agua Fria Village, Santa Fe County, New Mexico*, edited by R. W. Lang and Cherie L. Scheick, pp. 149–160. Southwest Report 216. Southwest Archaeological Consultants, Santa Fe.
1993   Pollen and Macrofloral Analysis. *Artifact* 31(3):83–99.
1994   Anasazi Diet: Variety in the Hoy House and Lion House Coprolite Record and Nutritional Analysis. In *Paleonutrition: The Diet and Health of Prehistoric Americans*, edited by Kristin D. Sobolik, pp. 134–150. Occasional Paper 22. Center for Archaeological Investigations, Southern Illinois University, Carbondale.

Cummings, Linda Scott, Kathryn Puseman, and Thomas E. Moutoux
1996   Pollen and Macrofloral Analysis at Bluff Bench, Site 42SA17725, Southeast Utah. Manuscript on file, Abajo Archaeology, Bluff, Utah.

Curtin, Leonora S. M.
1984   *By the Prophet of the Earth, Ethnobotany of the Pima*. Reprinted. University of Arizona Press, Tucson. Originally published 1949, San Vicente Foundation, Santa Fe.

Cutler, Hugh C.
1952   A Preliminary Survey of Plant Remains of Tularosa Cave. In *Mogollon Cultural Continuity and Change, the Stratigraphic Analysis of Tularosa and Cordova Caves*, edited by Paul S. Martin, John B. Rinaldo, Elaine Bluhm, Hugh C. Cutler, and Roger Grange Jr., pp. 461–479. Fieldiana: Anthropology 40. Chicago Natural History Museum, Chicago.

Cutler, Hugh C., and Leonard W. Blake
1974   Corn from Casas Grandes. In *Casa Grandes: A Fallen Trading Center of the Gran Chichimeca*, vol. 8, edited by Charles C. Di Peso, John B. Rinaldo, and Gloria J. Fenner, pp. 308–322. Amerind Foundation, Dragoon, Arizona, and Northland Press, Flagstaff.

Cutler, Hugh C., and Lawrence Kaplan
1956   Some Plant Remains from Montezuma Castle and Nearby Caves (NA 4007 B and C on Dry Beaver Creek). *Plateau* 28(4):98–100.

Cutler, Hugh C., and Winton Meyer
1965   Corn and Cucurbits from Wetherill Mesa. *American Antiquity* 31:136–152.

Davis, Carolyn O'Bagy
1995   *Treasured Earth: Hattie Cosgrove's Mimbres Archaeology in the American Southwest*. Sanpete Publications and the Old Pueblo Archaeology Center, Tucson.

Dean, Glenna

1991   Analysis of Pollen and Flotation Samples from Archaic Archeological Sites LA 16197, LA 16198, and LA 16663, Bolack Exchange Lands, San Juan County, New Mexico. Manuscript on file, Office of Contract Archaeology, University of New Mexico, Albuquerque.

1993a   Pollen and Flotation Analyses of Archaeological Samples from Estates I, Estates II, and the West Golf Course at Las Campanas de Santa Fe, Santa Fe County, New Mexico. Manuscript on file, Southwest Archaeological Consultants, Santa Fe.

1993b   Flotation Analyses of Two Archeological Samples from LA 101101 and I.O. 59, Frijoles Survey, Santa Fe County, New Mexico. Archeobotanical Services Technical Series 934. Manuscript on file, Department of Anthropology, University of New Mexico, Albuquerque.

1995   In Search of the Rare: Pollen Evidence of Prehistoric Agriculture. In *Soil, Water, Biology, and Belief in Prehistoric and Traditional Southwestern Agriculture*, edited by H. Wolcott Toll, pp. 353–359. Special Publication 2. New Mexico Archaeological Council, Albuquerque.

Dean, Jeffrey S., William H. Doelle, and Janet D. Orcutt

1994   Adaptive Stress, Environment, and Demography. In *Themes in Southwest Prehistory*, edited by George J. Gumerman, pp. 53–86. School of American Research Press, Santa Fe.

Dean, Jeffrey S., and John C. Ravesloot

1993   The Chronolgy of Cultural Interaction in the Gran Chichimeca. In *Culture and Contact: Charles C. Di Peso's Gran Chichimeca*, edited by Ann I. Woosley and John C. Ravesloot, pp. 83–103. University of New Mexico Press, Albuquerque.

Decker, Kenneth W., and Larry L. Tieszen

1989   Isotopic Reconstruction of Mesa Verde Diet from Basketmaker III to Pueblo III. *Kiva* 55:33–46.

Dering, J. Phil

1998   Macrobotanical Remains from Classic Period Farming Villages in the Tonto Basin. In *Environment and Subsistence in the Classic Period Tonto Basin, Roosevelt Platform Mound Study*, edited by Katherine A. Spielmann, pp. 87–132. Roosevelt Monograph Series 9. Anthropological Field Studies 39. Office of Cultural Resource Management, Arizona State University, Tempe.

1999   Earth-Oven Plant Processing in Archaic Period Economies: An Example from a Semi-Arid Savanna in South-Central North America. *American Antiquity* 64:659–674.

2000   Botanical Remains. In *Archeological Investigation of Rooms 15 and 16 at the Upper Cliff Dwelling (AZ U:8:48[ASM])*, Tonto National Monument, by Gregory L. Fox, pp. 197–232. Western Archeological and Conservation Center Publications in Anthropology 73. National Park Service, US Department of the Interior, Tucson.

Dick, Herbert W.

1965   *Bat Cave*. Monograph 27. School of American Research, Santa Fe.

Diehl, Michael W.

1996   The Intensity of Maize Processing and Production in Upland Mogollon Pithouse Villages, A.D. 200–1000. *American Antiquity* 61:102–115.

1999   Paleobotanical Remains. In *Excavations in the Santa Cruz Floodplain: The Middle Archaic Component at Los Pozos*, edited by David A. Gregory, pp. 49–59. Anthropological Papers 20. Center for Desert Archaeology, Tucson.

Diehl, Michael W., and Paul E. Minnis

In press   Paleobotanical Remains. In *Early Pithouse Villages of the Mimbres Valley and Beyond, the McAnally and Thompson Sites in Their Cultural and Ecological Contexts*, edited by Michael W. Diehl and Stephen A. LeBlanc. Maxwell Museum of Anthropology, Albuquerque.

Di Peso, Charles C., John B. Rinaldo, and Gloria J. Fenner
  1974   *Casas Grandes, a Fallen Trading Center of the Gran Chichimeca*, vol. 8. The Amerind Foundation, Dragoon, Arizona, and Northland Press, Flagstaff.

Doebley, John F.
  1976   *A Preliminary Study of Wild Plant Remains Recovered by Flotation at Salmon Ruin, New Mexico.* Unpublished master's thesis, Department of Biology, University of New Mexico, Albuquerque.
  1981   Plant Remains Recovered by Flotation from Trash at Salmon Ruin, New Mexico. *Kiva* 46:169–188.

Donaldson, Marcia L.
  1982   Flotation Analysis Samples from Six Archaeological Sites in the Gallo Wash Mine Lease. In *Prehistoric Adaptive Strategies in the Chaco Canyon Region, Northwestern New Mexico: 1. Introduction, Environmental Studies, and Analytical Approaches*, edited by Alan H. Simmons, pp. 143–172. Navajo Nation Papers in Anthropopogy 9. Navajo Nation Cultural Resource Management Program, Window Rock, Arizona.

Donaldson, Marcia L., and Mollie S. Toll
  1981   A Flotation Study with Implications for the Planning of Archaeological Testing Programs: Navajo Indian Irrigation Project Blocks VIII and IX. Manuscript on file, Navajo Nation Cultural Resource Management Program, Window Rock, Arizona.

Edwards, Sherrian K.
  1990   *Investigations of Late Archaic Coprolites: Pollen and Macrofossil Remains from Hinds Cave (41VV456), Val Verde County, Texas.* Unpublished master's thesis, Department of Anthropology, Texas A&M University, College Station.

Elson, Mark D., Suzanne K. Fish, Steven R. James, and Charles H. Miksicek
  1995   Prehistoric Subsistence in the Roosevelt Community Development Study Area. In *The Roosevelt Community Development Study: 3. Paleobotanical and Osteological Analyses*, edited by Mark D. Elson and Jeffery J. Clark, pp. 217–260. Anthropological Papers 14. Center for Desert Archaeology, Tucson.

Emslie, Steven D., Robert C. Euler, and Jim I. Mead
  1987   A Desert Culture Shrine in Grand Canyon, Arizona, and the Role of Split-Twig Figurines. *National Geographic Research* 3:511–516.

Euler, Robert C.
  1984   The Archaeology and Geology of Stanton's Cave. In *The Archaeology, Geology, and Paleobiology of Stanton's Cave*, edited by Robert C. Euler, pp. 7–32. Grand Canyon Natural History Association, Flagstaff.

Ezzo, Joseph A.
  1993   *Human Adaptation at Grasshopper Pueblo, Arizona, Social and Ecological Perspectives.* Archaeological Series 4. International Monographs in Prehistory, University of Michigan, Ann Arbor.
  1994   Paleonutrition at Grasshopper Pueblo, Arizona. In *Paleonutrition: The Diet and Health of Prehistoric Americans*, edited by Kristin D. Sobolik, pp. 265–279. Occasional Paper 22. Center for Archaeological Investigations, Southern Illinois University, Carbondale.

Fewkes, Jesse W.
  1923   Designs on Mimbres Pottery from the Mimbres Valley, New Mexico. *Miscellaneous Collections* 74(6):1–47. Smithsonian Institution, Washington, DC.

Fish, Paul R., Suzanne K. Fish, Curtiss Brennan, Douglas Gann, and James Bayman
  1992   Marana: Configuration of an Early Classic Period Hohokam Platform Mound Site. In *Proceedings of the Second Salado Conference, Globe, AZ 1992*, edited by Richard C. Lange and Stephen Germick, pp. 62–68. Arizona Archaeological Society, Phoenix.

Fish, Paul R., Suzanne K. Fish, John H. Madsen, Charles H. Miksicek, and Christine R. Szuter
  1992   The Dairy Site: Occupational Continuity on an Alluvial Fan. In *The Marana Community in the Hohokam World*, edited by Suzanne K. Fish, Paul R. Fish, and John H. Madsen, pp. 64–72. Anthropological Papers 56. University of Arizona Press, Tucson.

Fish, Suzanne K.
  1984   Agriculture and Subsistence Implications of the Salt-Gila Aqueduct Project Pollen Analysis. In *Hohokam Archaeology along the Salt-Gila Aqueduct, Central Arizona Project: 7. Environment and Subsistence*, edited by Lynne S. Teague and Patricia L. Crown, pp. 111–138. Archaeological Series 150. Arizona State Museum, Tucson.
  1995   Mixed Agricultural Technologies in Southern Arizona and Their Implications. In *Soil, Water, Biology, and Belief in Prehistoric and Traditional Southwestern Agriculture*, edited by H. Wolcott Toll, pp. 101–116. Special Publication 2. New Mexico Archaeological Council, Albuquerque.
  2000   Pollen Analysis. In *Tonto Creek Archaeological Project: 2. Stone Tool and Subsistence Studies*, edited by Jeffery J. Clark, pp. 629–639. Anthropological Papers 23. Center for Desert Archaeology, Tucson.

Fish, Suzanne K., and Marcia Donaldson
  1991   Production and Consumption in the Archaeological Record: A Hohokam Example. *Kiva* 56:255–275.

Fish, Suzanne K., Paul R. Fish, Charles Miksicek, and John Madsen
  1985   Prehistoric Agave Cultivation in Southern Arizona. *Desert Plants* 7:100, 107–112.

Ford, Richard I.
  1977   Archaeobotany of the Fort Bliss Maneuver Area II, Texas. In *Settlement Patterns of the Eastern Hueco Bolson*, edited by Michael E. A.Whalen, pp. 199–205. Anthropological Paper 4. El Paso Centennial Museum, University of Texas, El Paso.
  1984   Ecological Consequences of Early Agriculture in the Southwest. In *Papers on the Archaeology of Black Mesa, Arizona*, vol. 2, edited by Stephen Plog and Shirley Powell, pp. 127–138. Southern Illinois University Press, Carbondale.

Foster, Michael S., Ronna J. Bradley, and Charlotte Williams
  1981   Prehistoric Diet and Subsistence Patterns of La Cabraña Pueblo. *Artifact* 19(3–4):151–168.

Fry, Gary, and H. J. Hall
  1975   Human Coprolites from Antelope House: Preliminary Analyses. *Kiva* 41:87–96.

Fryman, Leslie R.
  1990   Worked Sherd and Miscellaneous Ceramic Artifacts. In *Archaeology of the Ak-Chin Indian Community West Side Farms Project: Material Culture and Human Remains*, edited by Robert E. Gasser, C. K. Robinson, and C. D. Breternitz, pp. 16.1–16.23. Publications in Archaeology 9(4). Soil Systems, Phoenix.

Galinat, Walton C., Theodore R. Reinhart, and Theodore R. Frisbie
  1970   Early Eight-Rowed Maize from the Middle Rio Grande Valley, New Mexico. *Botanical Museum Leaflets* 22(9):313–331. Harvard University, Cambridge.

Garber, Emily
  1980   Analysis of Plant Remains. In *Tijeras Canyon, Analyses of the Past*, edited by Linda S. Cordell, pp. 71–87. Maxwell Museum of Anthropology and University of New Mexico Press, Albuquerque.

Gasser, Robert E.
  1981a   Hohokam Plant Use at La Ciudad and other Riverine Sites: The Flotation Evidence. In *Archaeological Investigations, Arizona Department of Transportation, Phoenix, Testing at La Ciudad (Group III), West Papago-Inner Loop (I-10), Maricopa County, Arizona*, by Ronald K. Yablon, pp. 341–380. Museum of Northern Arizona, Flagstaff.

Lisa W. Huckell and Mollie S. Toll

1981b Flotation Analysis. In *Prehistory of the St. John's Area, East-Central Arizona: The TEP St. John's Project*, by Deborah A. Westfall, pp. 309–319. Archaeological Series 153. Arizona State Museum, Tucson.

1982 Anasazi Diet. In *The Coronado Project Archaeological Investigations, the Specialists' Volume: Biocultural Analyses*, edited by Robert E. Gasser, pp. 8–95. Research Paper 23. Coronado Series 3. Museum of Northern Arizona, Flagstaff.

1985 Macrobotanical Analysis. In *City of Phoenix Archaeology of the Original Townsite Block 24-East*, edited by John S. Cable, K. S. Hoffman, David E. Doyel, and F. Ritz, pp. 391–392. Publications in Archaeology 8. Soil Systems, Phoenix.

1987 Macrofloral Analysis. In *The Archaeology of the San Xavier Bridge Site (AZ BB:13:14), Tucson Basin, Southern Arizona*, edited by John C. Ravesloot, pp. 303–318. Archaeological Series 171. Arizona State Museum, Tucson.

Gasser, Robert E., and Scott M. Kwiatkowski

1991a Food for Thought: Recognizing Patterns in Hohokam Subsistence. In *Exploring the Hohokam*, edited by George J. Gumerman, pp. 417–459. Amerind Foundation and University of New Mexico Press, Dragoon, Arizona, and Albuquerque.

1991b Regional Signatures of Hohokam Plant Use. *Kiva* 56:207–226.

Gasser, Robert E., and Charles H. Miksicek

1984 The Specialists: A Reappraisal of Hohokam Exchange and the Archaeobotanical Record. In *Proceedings of the 1983 Hohokam Symposium*, Part II, edited by Donald Dove and Alfred E. Dittert Jr., pp. 483–498. Occasional Paper 2. Arizona Archaeological Society, Phoenix.

Gilpin, Dennis

1994 Lukachukai and Salina Springs: Late Archaic/Early Basketmaker Habitation Sites in the Chinle Valley, Northeastern Arizona. *Kiva* 60:203–218.

Gish, Jannifer W.

1991 Current Perceptions, Recent Discoveries, and Future Directions in Hohokam Palynology. *Kiva* 56:237–254.

Gladwin, Harold S., Emil W. Haury, Edwin B. Sayles, and Nora Gladwin

1965 *Excavations at Snaketown: Material Culture*. Reprinted. University of Arizona Press, Tucson. Originally published 1938, Gila Pueblo Medallion Papers 25. Globe, Arizona.

Gleichman, Peter J.

1982 Botanical Remains. In *Anasazi Archaeology on Central Black Mesa, Northeastern Arizona: The Piñon Project*, edited by Laurance D. Lindford, pp. 387–401. Navajo Nation Papers in Anthropology 10. Navajo Nation Cultural Resource Management Program, Window Rock, Arizona.

Greenhouse, Ruth, Robert E. Gasser, and Jannifer W. Gish

1981 Cholla Bud Roasting Pits: An Ethnoarchaeobiological Example. *Kiva* 46:227–242.

Gregonis, Linda M., and Karl J. Reinhard

1979 *Hohokam Indians of the Tucson Basin*. University of Arizona Press, Tucson.

Guernsey, Samuel J., and Alfred V. Kidder

1921 Basket-Maker Caves of Northeastern Arizona. *Papers of the Peabody Museum of American Archaeology and Ethnology* 7(2):1–121. Harvard University, Cambridge.

Gumerman, George J., and Jeffrey S. Dean

1989 Prehistoric Cooperation and Competition in the Western Anasazi Area. In *Dynamics of Southwest Prehistory*, edited by Linda S. Cordell and George J. Gumerman, pp. 99–148. Smithsonian Institution Press, Washington, DC.

Halbirt, C. D., and Robert E. Gasser

1987 Archaeobotanical Analyses. In *Archaeology of the Mazatzal Piedmont, Central Arizona*, vol. 1, edited by Richard Ciolek-Torello, pp. 282–327. Museum of Northern Arizona Research Paper 33. Museum of Northern Arizona Press, Flagstaff.

Hall, Robert L., and Arthur E. Dennis
   1986   Cultivated and Gathered Plant Foods. In *Archeological Investigations at Antelope House*, by Don P. Morris, pp. 110–141. National Park Service, US Department of the Interior, Washington, DC.

Hammett, Julia E.
   1993a   Patayan Paleoethnobotany along the Transwestern Pipeline. In *Across the Colorado Plateau: Anthropological Studies for the Transwestern Pipeline Expansion Project: 15. Subsistence and Environment*, edited by Joseph C. Winter, pp. 471–480. Office of Contract Archeology and Maxwell Museum of Anthropology, University of New Mexico, Albuquerque.
   1993b   Sinaguan Paleoethnobotany along the Transwestern Pipeline. In *Across the Colorado Plateau: Anthropological Studies for the Transwestern Pipeline Expansion Project: 15. Subsistence and Environment*, edited by Joseph C. Winter, pp. 459–469. Office of Contract Archeology and Maxwell Museum of Anthropology, University of New Mexico, Albuquerque.

Hammett, Julia E., and Pamela J. McBride
   1993   Paleoethnobotanical Evidence from Aceramic Sites. In *Across the Colorado Plateau: Anthropological Studies for the Transwestern Pipeline Expansion Project: 15. Subsistence and Environment*, edited by Joseph C. Winter, pp. 429–442. Office of Contract Archeology and Maxwell Museum of Anthropology, University of New Mexico, Albuquerque.

Hansen, Eric
   1994   *Early Archaic Diet at Old Man Cave: A Perspective on Archaic Subsistence in Southeastern Utah*. Unpublished master's thesis, Department of Anthropology, Northern Arizona University, Flagstaff.

Hard, Robert J.
   1990   Agricultural Dependence among the Mountain Mogollon. In *Perspectives on Southwestern Prehistory*, edited by Paul Minnis and Charles Redman, pp. 135–149. Westview Press, Boulder.

Hard, Robert J., Raymond P. Mauldin, and Gerry R. Raymond
   1996   Mano Size, Stable Carbon Isotope Ratios, and Macrobotanical Remains as Multiple Lines of Evidence of Maize Dependence in the American Southwest. *Journal of Archaeological Method and Theory* 3:253–318.

Hard, Robert J., and John R. Roney
   1998   A Massive Terraced Village Complex in Chihuahua, Mexico, 3000 Years Before Present. *Science* 279:1661–1664.
   1999   *An Archaeological Investigation of Late Archaic Cerros de Trincheras Sites in Chihuahua, Mexico*. Special Report 25. San Antonio Center for Archaeological Research, University of Texas, San Antonio.

Harrison, Merry L.
   2002   The Patterson Bundle, an Herbalist's Discoveries in a 500-Year-Old Native American Bundle. *HerbalGram* 55:34–39.

Hasbargen, Jim
   1997   *Identification of Prehistoric Fields through Palynological Evidence*. Unpublished master's thesis, Department of Anthropology, Northern Arizona University, Flagstaff.

Haury, Emil W.
   1950   *The Stratigraphy and Archaeology of Ventana Cave*. University of Arizona Press, Tucson, and University of New Mexico Press, Albuquerque.

1962   The Greater American Southwest. In *Courses toward Urban Life: Some Archaeological Considerations of Cultural Alternates*, edited by Robert J. Braidwood and Gordon R. Willey, pp. 106–131. Publications in Anthropology 32. Viking Fund, New York.

1976   *The Hohokam, Desert Farmers and Craftsmen*. University of Arizona Press, Tucson.

Hays-Gilpin, Kelley Ann, Ann Cordy Deegan, and Elizabeth A. Morris

1996   *Prehistoric Sandals from Northeastern Arizona, the Earl H. Morris and Ann Axtell Morris Research*. Anthropological Papers 62. University of Arizona Press, Tucson.

Hays-Gilpin, Kelley, and Jane H. Hill

1999   The Flower World in Material Culture: An Iconographic Complex in the Southwest and Mesoamerica. *Journal of Anthropological Research* 55:1–37.

Hill, Jane H.

1992   The Flower World of Old Uto-Aztecan. *Journal of Anthropological Research* 48:117–144.

Hodgson, Wendy C., and Liz Slauson

1995   *Agave delamateri* (Agavaceae) and Its Role in the Subsistence Patterns of Pre-Columbian Cultures in Arizona. *Haseltonia* 3:130–140.

Hogan, Patrick F.

1980   The Analysis of Human Coprolites from Cowboy Cave. In *Cowboy Cave*, edited by Jesse D. Jennings, pp. 201–211. Anthropological Papers 104. University of Utah Press, Salt Lake City.

Holloway, Richard G.

1985   Diet and Medicinal Plant Useage of a Late Archaic Population from Culberson County, Texas. *Bulletin of the Texas Archaeological Society* 54:319–329.

Housley, Lucile Kempers

1974   Opuntia imbricata *Distribution on Old Jemez Indian Habitation Sites*. Unpublished master's thesis, Department of Biology, University of New Mexico, Albuquerque.

Huckell, Bruce B.

1990   *Late Preceramic Farmer-Foragers in Southeastern Arizona: A Cultural and Ecological Consideration of the Spread of Agriculture into the Arid Southwestern United States*. Unpublished PhD dissertation, Department of Arid Lands Resource Sciences, University of Arizona, Tucson.

1995   *Of Marshes and Maize, Preceramic Agricultural Settlements in the Cienega Valley, Southeastern Arizona*. Anthropological Papers 59. University of Arizona Press, Tucson.

1996a   The Archaic Prehistory of the North American Southwest. *Journal of World Prehistory* 10:305–373.

1996b   Middle to Late Holocene Stream Behavior and the Transition to Agriculture in Southeastern Arizona. In *Early Formative Adaptations in the Southern Southwest*, edited by Barbara J. Roth, pp. 27–36. Monographs in World Archaeology 25. Prehistory Press, Madison.

Huckell, Bruce B., Lisa W. Huckell, and Suzanne K. Fish

1995   *Investigations at Milagro, a Late Preceramic Site in the Eastern Tucson Basin*. Technical Report 94-5. Center for Desert Archaeology, Tucson.

Huckell, Lisa W.

1986   Botanical Remains. In *The 1985 Excavations at the Hodges Site, Pima County, Arizona*, edited by Robert W. Layhe, pp. 241–269. Archaeological Series 170. Arizona State Museum, Tucson.

1995a   Farming and Foraging in the Cienega Valley: Early Agricultural Period Paleoethnobotany. In *Of Marshes and Maize, Preceramic Agricultural Settlements in the Cienega Valley, Southeastern Arizona*, edited by Bruce B. Huckell, pp. 74–97. Anthropological Papers 59. University of Arizona, Tucson.

1995b   Paleoethnobotanical Analysis. In *Investigations at Milagro, a Late Preceramic Site in the Eatern Tucson Basin*, edited by Bruce B. Huckell, Lisa W. Huckell, and Suzanne K. Fish, pp. 33–40. Technical Report 94-5. Center for Desert Archaeology, Tucson.

1998a Macrobotanical Remains. In *Archaeological Investigations of Early Village Sites in the Middle Santa Cruz Valley: Analysis and Synthesis, Part I*, edited by Jonathan B. Mabry, pp. 57–148. Anthropological Papers 19. Center for Desert Archaeology, Tucson.

1998b Paleoethnobotany. In *Early Farmers of the Sonoran Desert, Archaeological Investigations at the Houghton Road Site, Tucson, Arizona*, edited by Richard Ciolek-Torrello, pp. 327–344. Technical Series 72. Statistical Research, Tucson.

1999a Paleoethnobotany. In *Living on the Edge of the Rim: Excavations and Analysis of the Silver Creek Archaeological Research Project 1993–1998*, vol. 2, edited by Barbara J. Mills, Sarah A. Herr, and Scott Van Keuren, pp. 459–504. Archaeological Series 192. Arizona State Museum, Tucson.

1999b Plant Remains. In *Archaeological Sandal Recovery and Test Excavations at NA 324, Walnut Canyon National Monument*, edited by Christian E. Downum, pp. 4.1–4.26. Archaeological Report 1186. Northern Arizona University, Flagstaff.

2000a Archaeobotanical Analysis. In *Tonto Creek Archaeological Project: 2. Stone Tool and Subsistence Studies*, edited by Jeffery J. Clark, pp. 571–627. Anthropological Papers 23. Center for Desert Archaeology, Tucson.

2000b Paleoethnobotany. In *A Highway through Time: Archaeological Investigations along NM 90*, compiled by Christopher A. Turnbow, pp. 509–564. Technical Series 2000-3. TRC, Albuquerque.

Huckell, Lisa W., and Pamela J. McBride
1999 Paleoethnobotany. In *Data Recovery along the 1995 MAPCO Four Corners Pipeline: Sites in the San Juan Basin/Colorado Plateau, Sandoval, San Juan, and McKinley Counties, New Mexico*, vol. 2, compiled by Kenneth L. Brown, pp. 155–196. Office of Contract Archeology, University of New Mexico, Albuquerque.

Huckell, Lisa W., and Christine S. VanPool
2002 Toloatzin and Shamanic Journeys: Exploring the Ritual Role of Sacred Datura in the Prehistoric Southwest. Paper presented at the 67th Annual Meeting of the Society for American Archaeology, Denver.

Hunter, Andrea, Kathryn Kamp, and John Whitaker
1999 Plant Use. In *Surviving Adversity, the Sinagua of Lizard Man Village*, by Kathryn A. Kamp and John C. Whitaker, pp. 139–151. Anthropological Papers 120. University of Utah Press, Salt Lake City.

Hunter, Andrea A., and Karen A. Wright
1998 Paleoethnobotanical Analysis of Sinagua Subsistence Strategies at Elden Pueblo. Manuscript on file, Laboratory of Paleoethnobotany, Department of Anthropology, Northern Arizona University, Flagstaff.

Hurst, Samantha, Karen R. Adams, and Patricia A. Gilman
1997 Macrobotanical Remains. In *Wandering Villagers: Pit Structures, Mobility and Agriculture in Southeastern Arizona*, by Patricia A. Gilman, pp. 139–148. Anthropological Research Papers 49. Arizona State University, Tempe.

Jones, Volney H.
1941 The Plant Materials from Winona and Ridge Ruin. In *Winona and Ridge Ruin, Part 1, Architecture and Material Culture*, edited by John C. McGregor, pp. 295–300. Bulletin 18. Museum of Northern Arizona, Flagstaff.

1953 Desiccated or Charred Material from Pindi. In *The Excavation of Pindi Pueblo, New Mexico*, by Stanley A. Stubbs and W. S. Stallings, pp. 140–142. Monographs 18. School of American Research and Laboratory of Anthropology, Santa Fe.

Jones, Volney H., and Robert L. Fonner
1954 Plant Materials from Sites in the Durango and La Plata Areas, Colorado. In *Basket-Maker*

II Sites near Durango, Colorado, by Earl H. Morris and Robert F. Burgh, pp. 93–115. Publication 604. Carnegie Institution of Washington, Washington, DC.

Judges-Edwards, G.

1997   Flotation Analysis of Archaeobotanical Samples from Twenty-Two Sites in the Ancho Canyon Complex, Raton, New Mexico. In *Cultural Definition on the Southern Park Plateau of Northeast New Mexico: The Ancho Canyon Archaeological Project*, vol. 2, edited by Jan V. Biella and Wetherbee B. Dorshow, pp. 701–748. Southwest Archaeological Consultants, Santa Fe.

Kaemlein, Wilma

1963   A Prehistoric Twined-Woven Bag from the Trigo Mountains, Arizona. *Kiva* 28:1–13.

Kaplan, Lawrence

1963   Archeoethnobotany of Cordova Cave. *Economic Botany* 17:350–359.

1965   Beans of Wetherill Mesa. *American Antiquity* 31:153–155.

Katzenberg, M. Anne, and Jane H. Kelley

1991   Stable Isotope Analysis of Prehistoric Bone from the Sierra Blanca Region of New Mexico. In *Mogollon V*, edited by Patrick H. Beckett, pp. 207–219. COAS Publishing, Las Cruces.

Kelley, Jane H., Joe D. Stewart, A. C. MacWilliams, and L. C. Neff

1999   West-Central Chihuahuan Perspective on Chihuahuan Culture. In *The Casas Grandes World*, edited by Curtis F. Schaafsma and Carroll L. Riley, pp. 63–77. University of Utah Press, Salt Lake City.

Kent, Kate Peck

1954   *Montezuma Castle Archeology, Part 2: Textiles*. Technical Series 3(2). Southwestern Monuments Association, Globe, Arizona.

1983   *Prehistoric Textiles of the Southwest*. School of American Research, Santa Fe, and University of New Mexico, Albuquerque.

Kidder, Alfred V., and Samuel J. Guernsey

1919   *Archaeological Explorations in Northeastern Arizona*. Bulletin 65. Bureau of American Ethnology, Smithsonian Institution, Washington, DC

Kirkpatrick, David T., and Richard I. Ford

1977   Basketmaker Food Plants from the Cimarron District, Northeastern New Mexico. *Kiva* 42:257–269.

Knight, Paul J.

1980   Flotation and Macrobotanical Analysis. In *Human Adaptations in a Marginal Environment: the UII Mitigation Project*, edited by James L. Moore and Joseph C. Winter, pp. 310–336. Office of Contract Archaeology, University of New Mexico, Albuquerque.

1994   Ethnobotanical Analysis. In *Archaeological Excavations at Three Sites within the Proposed Rio Bravo Blvd. and Paseo del Volcan Corridors, Bernalillo County, New Mexico*, by Michael P. Marshall and Christina L. Marshall, pp. 111–129. Cibola Research Report 97. Cibola Research Consultants, Albuquerque.

Kohler, Timothy A., and Meredith H. Matthews

1988   Long-Term Anasazi Land Use and Forest Reduction: A Case Study from Southwest Colorado. *American Antiquity* 53:537–564.

Kwiatkowski, Scott M.

1989   The Paleoethnobotany of the Grand Canal Ruins: Results from Flotation, Macrobotanical and Wood Charcoal Analyses. In *Archaeological Investigations at the Grand Canal Ruins: A Classic Period Site in Phoenix, Arizona*, edited by Douglas R. Mitchell, pp. 497–558. Publications in Archaeology 12. Soil Systems, Phoenix.

1992   The Rye Creek Flotation and Macrobotanical Analyses. In *The Rye Creek Project: Archaeology in the Upper Tonto Basin*, by Mark D. Elson and Douglas B. Craig, pp. 325–407. Anthropological Papers 11. Center for Desert Archaeology, Tucson.

Kwiatkowski, Scott M., and Susan N. Smith

1993   Flotation Results from La Ciudad de los Hornos. In *In the Shadow of South Mountain: The Pre-Classic Hohokam of La Ciudad de los Hornos, Part 1*, edited by Mark L. Chenault, Richard V. N. Ahlstrom, and Thomas N. Motsinger, pp. 389–434. Archaeological Report 93-30. SWCA Environmental Consultants, Tucson.

Lang, Richard W.

1995   The Fields of San Marcos: Agriculture at a Great Town of the Galisteo Basin, Northern New Mexico. In *Soil, Water, Biology, and Belief in Prehistoric and Traditional Southwestern Agriculture*, edited by H. Wolcott Toll, pp. 41–76. Special Publication 2. New Mexico Archaeological Council, Albuquerque.

Lawton, Harry W., Philip W. Wilke, Mary Decker, and W. M. Mason

1976   Agriculture among the Paiute of Owens Valley. *Journal of California Archaeology* 3(1): 13–50.

Lister, Robert H.

1958   *Archaeological Excavations in the Northern Sierra Madre Occidental, Chihuahua and Sonora, Mexico*. University of Colorado Studies, Series in Anthropology 7. University of Colorado Press, Boulder.

Litzinger, William Joseph

1979   Ceramic Evidence for the Prehistoric Use of Datura in Mexico and the Southwestern United States. *Kiva* 44:145–158.

Mabry, Jonathan B.

1998   *Archaeological Investigations of Early Village Sites in the Middle Santa Cruz Valley*. Anthropological Papers 19. Center for Desert Archaeology, Tucson.

Mabry, Jonathan B., Deborah L. Swartz, Helga Wöcherl, Jeffery J. Clark, Gavin H. Archer, and Michael W. Lindeman

1997   *Archaeological Investigations of Early Village Sites in the Middle Santa Cruz Valley: Descriptions of the Santa Cruz Bend, Square Hearth, Stone Pipe, and Canal Sites*. Anthropological Papers 18. Center for Desert Archaeology, Tucson.

MacNeish, Richard S., and Bruno Marino

1993   Carbon 13/12 and Nitrogen 15/14 Isotope Ratios on Skeletons from the Jornada Area. In *Preliminary Investigations of the Archaic in the Region of Las Cruces, New Mexico*, edited by Richard S. MacNeish, pp. 117–122. Historic and Natural Resources Report 9. United States Army Air Defense Artillery Center, Fort Bliss, Texas.

Martin, Debra L., Alan H. Goodman, George J. Armelagos, and Ann L. Magennis

1991   *Black Mesa Anasazi Health: Reconstructing Life from Patterns of Death and Disease*. Occasional Paper 14. Center for Archaeological Investigations, Southern Illinois University, Carbondale.

Martin, Paul S., John B. Rinaldo, Elaine Bluhm, Hugh C. Cutler, and Roger Grange Jr.

1952   *Mogollon Cultural Continuity and Change, the Stratigraphic Analysis of Tularosa and Cordova Caves*. Fieldiana: Anthropology 40. Chicago Natural History Museum, Chicago.

Martin, Steve L.

1999   Virgin Anasazi Diet as Demonstrated through the Analysis of Stable Carbon and Nitrogen Isotopes. *Kiva* 64:495–514.

Matson, R. G.

1991   *The Origins of Southwestern Agriculture*. University of Arizona Press, Tucson.

Lisa W. Huckell and Mollie S. Toll

Matson, R. G., and Brian Chisholm
  1991   Basketmaker II Subsistence: Carbon Isotopes and Other Dietary Indicators from Cedar
          Mesa, Utah. *American Antiquity* 56:444–459.
Matthews, Meredith H.
  1986   The Dolores Archaeological Program Macrobotanical Data Base: Resource Mix and
          Availability. In *Dolores Archaeological Program: Final Synthetic Report*, compiled and edited
          by David A. Breternitz, C. K. Robinson, and T. G. Gross, pp. 184–199. Bureau of Recla-
          mation, US Department of the Interior, Denver.
Maxwell, Timothy D., and Kurt F. Anschuetz
  1992   The Southwestern Ethnographic Record and Prehistoric Agricultural Diversity. In *Gar-
          dens of Prehistory, the Archaeology of Settlement Agriculture in Greater Mesoamerica*, edited by
          Thomas W. Killion, pp. 35–68. University of Alabama Press, Tuscaloosa.
McBride, Pamela J.
  1993   Description of Anaszi Archeobotanical Remains. In *Across the Colorado Plateau: Anthropo-
          logical Studies for the Transwestern Pipeline Expansion Project: 15. Subsistence and Environment*,
          edited by Joseph C. Winter, pp. 443–457. Office of Contract Archeology and Maxwell
          Museum of Anthropology, University of New Mexico, Albuquerque.
  1998   Archaeobotanical Remains. In *Ethnohistoric Interpretation and Archaeological Data Recovery
          along Navajo Route 9101, Jeddito Road, Navajo County, Arizona*, by David C. Eck, pp. 393–
          427. Report 562. Zuni Cultural Resource Enterprise, Zuni, New Mexico.
Meals for Millions/Freedom from Hunger Foundation
  1985   *O'odham I:waki, Wild Greens of the Desert People*. Meals for Millions/Freedom from
          Hunger Foundation, Tucson.
Miksicek, Charles H.
  1983   Plant Remains from Smiley's Well (AZ U:14:73, Locus A). In *Hohokam Archaeology along
          the Salt-Gila Aqueduct, Central Arizona Project: 5. Small Habitation Sites on Queen Creek*, ed-
          ited by Lynne S. Teague and Patricia L. Crown, pp. 87–97. Archaeological Series 150(5).
          Arizona State Museum, Tucson.
  1984a   Historic Desertification, Prehistoric Vegetation Change, and Hohokam Subsistence in
          the Salt-Gila Basin. In *Hohokam Archaeology along the Salt-Gila Aqueduct Central Arizona
          Project: 7. Environment and Subsistence*, edited by Lynne S. Teague and Patricia L. Crown,
          pp. 563–590. Archaeological Series 150. Arizona State Museum, Tucson.
  1984b   Archaeobotanical Remains from Frogtown. In *Hohokam Archaeology along the Salt-Gila
          Aqueduct, Central Arizona Project: 4. Prehistoric Occupation of the Queen Creek Delta*, edited
          by Lynne S. Teague and Patricia L. Crown, pp. 563–590. Archaeological Series 150. Ari-
          zona State Museum, Tucson.
  1986a   Plant Remains from the Tanque Verde Wash Site. In *Archaeological Investigations at the
          Tanque Verde Wash Site, a Middle Rincon Settlement in the Eastern Tucson Basin*, by Mark D.
          Elson, pp. 371–394. Anthropological Papers 7. Institute for American Research, Tucson.
  1986b   Plant Remains. In *Archaeological Investigations at the West Branch Site Early and Middle Rin-
          con Occupation in the Southern Tucson Basin*, by Frederick W. Huntington, pp. 289–313.
          Anthropological Papers 5. Institute for American Research, Tucson.
  1989   Snails, Seeds and Charcoal: Biological Remains from La Cuenca del Sedimento. In *Pre-
          historic Agricultural Activities on the Lehi-Mesa Terrace: Excavations at La Cuenca del Sedi-
          mento*, edited by T. Kathleen Henderson, pp. 222–242. Northland Research, Flagstaff.
  1991   Paleoethnobotany. In *Homol'ovi II: Archaeology of an Ancestral Hopi Village, Arizona*, edited
          by E. Charles Adams and Kelley A. Hayes, pp. 88–102. Anthropological Paper 55. Uni-
          versity of Arizona, Tucson.

1995 Temporal Trends in the Eastern Tonto Basin: An Archaeobotanical Perspective. In *The Roosevelt Community Development Study: 3. Paleobotanical and Osteological Analyses*, edited by Mark D. Elson and Jeffery J. Clark, pp. 43–83. Anthropological Papers 14. Center for Desert Archaeology, Tucson.

Miksicek, Charles H., and Mary Bernard-Shaw
1989 Plant Remains. In *Archaeological Investigations at the Redtail Site, AA:12:149 (ASM), in the Northern Tucson Basin*, edited by Mary Bernard-Shaw, pp. 159–164. Technical Report 89-8. Center for Desert Archaeology, Tucson.

1990 Plant Remains. In *Archaeological Investigations at the Lonetree Site, AA:12:120 (ASM), in the Northern Tucson Basin*, edited by Mary Bernard-Shaw, pp. 149–156. Technical Report 90-1. Center for Desert Archaeology, Tucson.

Miksicek, Charles H., and Robert E. Gasser
1989 Hohokam Plant Use at Las Colinas: The Flotation Evidence. In *The 1982–1984 Excavations at Las Colinas: Environment and Subsistence*, by Donald A. B. Graybill, David A. Gregory, Fred L. Nials, Suzanne K. Fish, Charles H. Miksicek, Robert E. Gasser, and Christine R. Szuter, pp. 95–115. Archaeological Series 162(5). Arizona State Museum, Tucson.

Miller, JoAnne
1994 Pueblo Grande Flotation, Macrobotanical, and Wood Charcoal Analysis. In *The Pueblo Grande Project: 5. Environment and Subsistence*, edited by Scott Kwiatkowski, pp. 127–204. Publications in Archaeology 20. Soil Systems, Phoenix.

Minnis, Paul E.
1978 Paleoethnobotanical Indicators of Prehistoric Environmental Disturbance: A Case Study. In *The Nature and Status of Ethnobotany*, edited by Richard I. Ford, pp. 347–366. Anthropological Papers 67. Museum of Anthropology, University of Michigan, Ann Arbor.

1982 The Ethnobotanical Remains. In *The Tsaya Project: Archeological Excavations near Lake Valley, San Juan County, New Mexico*, by Regge N. Wiseman, pp. 64–82. Note 308. Laboratory of Anthropology, Santa Fe.

1985a *Social Adaptation to Food Stress: A Prehistoric Example*. University of Chicago Press, Chicago.

1985b Domesticating People and Plants in the Greater Southwest. In *Prehistoric Food Production in North America*, edited by Richard I. Ford, pp. 309–339. Anthropological Papers 75. Museum of Anthropology, University of Michigan, Ann Arbor.

1986 Macroplant Remains. In *Short-Term Sedentism in the American Southwest: The Mimbres Salado*, by Ben A. Nelson and Stephen A. LeBlanc, pp. 205–218. Maxwell Museum of Anthropology and University of New Mexico, Albuquerque.

1988 Four Examples of Specialized Production at Casas Grandes, Northwestern Chihuahua. *Kiva* 53:181–193.

1989 Prehistoric Diet in the Northern Southwest: Macroplant Remains from Four Corners Feces. *American Antiquity* 54:543–563.

1992 Earliest Plant Cultivation in the Desert Borderlands of North America. In *The Origins of Agriculture, an International Perspective*, edited by C. Wesley Cowan and Patty Jo Watson, pp. 121–141. Smithsonian Institution Press, Washington, DC.

Minnis, Paul E., and Stephen E. Plog
1976 A Study of the Site Specific Distribution of *Agave parryi* in East Central Arizona. *Kiva* 41:299–308.

Mitchell, Douglas R.
1989 La Lomita Pequeña: Relationships between Plant Resource Variability and Settlement Patterns in the Phoenix Basin. *Kiva* 54:127–146.

Montúfar López, Aurora

1985   Estudio de los Restos Vegetales en la Cueva de las Ventanas, Chihuahua. In *Estudios Pale-oecológicos y Paleoetnobotánicos*, pp. 113–133. Científica 147. Instituto Nacional de Antropología e Historia, Mexico City.

1992   Arqueobotánica de la Sierra de Chihuahua. In *Historia General de Chihuahua: 1. Geología, Geografía y Arqueología*, edited by Arturo Márquez-Alameda, pp. 215–227. Universidad Autónoma de Ciudad Juárez, Ciudad Juarez.

Montúfar López, Aurora, and María Luisa Reyes Landa

1995   Estudios de los Restos Botánicos de la Cueva de la Olla, Chihuahua. In *Investigaciones Re-cientes en Paleobotánica y Palinología*, edited by Aurora Montúfar López, pp. 29–36. Serie Arqueología. Instituto Nacional de Antropología e Historia, Mexico City.

Morris, Earl A.

1980   *Basketmaker Caves in the Prayer Rock District, Northeastern Arizona*. Anthropological Papers 35. University of Arizona, Tucson.

Nabhan, Gary P.

1985   Native Crop Diversity in Aridoamerica: Conservation of Regional Gene Pools. *Economic Botany* 39:387–399.

Nabhan, Gary P., and Jan M. J. de Wet

1984   *Panicum sonorum* in Sonoran Desert Agriculture. *Economic Botany* 38:65–68.

National Research Council

1984   *Amaranth: Modern Prospects for an Ancient Crop*. National Academy Press, Washington, DC.

Nichols, Robert F., and David G. Smith

1965   Evidence of Prehistoric Cultivation of Douglas-Fir Trees at Mesa Verde. *American Antiquity* 31:57–64.

Nordenskiöld, Gustof E. A.

1990   *The Cliff Dwellers of the Mesa Verde, Southwestern Colorado, Their Pottery and Implements*. Reprinted. Mesa Verde Museum Association, Mesa Verde, Colorado. Originally published 1893, P. A. Norstedt & Söner, Stockholm.

Nusbaum, Jesse L.

1922   *A Basket-Maker Cave in Kane County, Utah*. Indian Notes and Monographs. Museum of the American Indian, Heye Foundation, New York.

O'Laughlin, Thomas C.

1977   Excavation of Two Caves in the Mountain Zone of Fort Bliss Maneuver Area II. In *Settlement Patterns of the Eastern Hueco Bolson*, by Michael E. Whalen, pp. 169–189. Anthropological Paper 4. El Paso Centennial Museum, University of Texas, El Paso.

1980   *The Keystone Dam Site and Other Archaic and Formative Sites in Northwest El Paso, Texas*. Publications in Anthropology 8. El Paso Centennial Museum, University of Texas, El Paso.

Osborne, Carolyn M.

1965   The Preparation of Yucca Fiber: An Experimental Study. *American Antiquity* 31:45–50.

1980   Objects of Perishable Materials. In *Long House, Mesa Verde National Park, Colorado*, by George S. Cattanach Jr., pp. 317–367. Publications in Archeology 7H. Wetherill Mesa Studies. National Park Service, US Department of the Interior, Washington, DC.

Pailes, Richard A.

1984   Agricultural Development and Trade in the Río Sonora Valley. In *Prehistoric Agricultural Strategies in the Southwest*, edited by Suzanne K. Fish and Paul R. Fish, pp. 309–325. Anthropological Research Papers 33. Arizona State University, Tempe.

Peterson, Kenneth L.

1986   Temporal Patterns in Resource Use. In *Dolores Archaeological Program: Final Synthetic*

Report, compiled and edited by David A. Breternitz, C. K. Robinson, and T. G. Gross, pp. 184–199. Bureau of Reclamation, US Department of the Interior, Denver.

Phelps, Alan L.

1968   A Recovery of Purslane Seeds in an Archaeological Context. *Artifact* 6(4):1–9.

Pierson, Lloyd M.

1956   The Archaeology of Richards Caves, Arizona. *Plateau* 28(4):91–97.

Powell, Gina S.

2001   *Hunting and Farming between the Plains and the Southwest: Analysis of Archaeobotanical Remains from the Henderson Site, Roswell, New Mexico.* Unpublished PhD dissertation, Department of Anthropology, Washington University, St. Louis.

Puseman, Kathryn

1996   Macrofloral Analysis. In *Excavation of the Gibbon Springs Site, a Classic Period Village in the Northeastern Tucson Basin*, edited by Mark C. Slaughter and Heidi Roberts, pp. 449–471. Archaeological Report 94–97. SWCA, Tucson.

Raymer, Leslie, and Paul E. Minnis

1986   Macroplant and Ethnobotanical Studies. In *Prehistoric Hunter-Gatherers of South Central Arizona: The Picacho Reservoir Archaic Project*, edited by Frank E. Bayham, Donald H. Morris, and M. Steven Shackley, pp. 299–314. Anthropological Field Studies 13. Office of Cultural Resource Management, Department of Anthropology, Arizona State University, Tempe.

Rea, Amadeo

1978   The Ecology of Pima Fields. *Environment Southwest* 484:8–13.

1991   Gila River Pima Dietary Reconstruction. *Arid Lands Newsletter* 31:3–10.

Reed, Alan C.

1999   Archaeobotanical Analysis. In *Pipeline Archaeology 1990–1993: The El Paso Natural Gas North System Expansion Project, New Mexico and Arizona*, vol. 7, edited by Timothy M. Kearns and Janet L. McVickar, pp. 12-1–12-141. Western Cultural Resource Management, Farmington, New Mexico.

Reinhard, Karl J., Donny L. Hamilton, and Richard H. Hevly

1991   Use of Pollen Concentration in Paleopharmacology: Coprolite Evidence of Medicinal Plants. *Journal of Ethnobiology* 11:111–132.

Rixey, Raymond, and Charles B. Voll

1962   Archaeological Materials from Walnut Canyon Cliff Dwellings. *Plateau* 34(3):85–96.

Ross, Winifred

1941   *The Present Day Dietary Habits of the Papago Indians.* Unpublished master's thesis, Department of Home Economics, University of Arizona, Tucson.

Russell, Frank

1975   *The Pima Indians.* Reprinted. University of Arizona Press, Tucson. Originally published 1908, 26th Annual Report of the Bureau of American Ethnology for the Years 1904–1905, Smithsonian Institution, Washington, DC.

Rylander, Kate A.

1994   Corn Preparation among the Basketmaker Anasazi: A Scanning Electron Microscope Study of *Zea mays* Remains from Coprolites. In *Paleonutrition: The Diet and Health of Prehistoric Americans*, edited by Kristin D. Sobolik, pp. 115–133. Occasional Paper 22. Center for Archaeological Investigations, Southern Illinois University, Carbondale.

Safford, William E.

1922   Daturas of the Old World and New. *Smithsonian Report for 1920*, pp. 537–567. Smithsonian Institution, Washington, DC.

110

Sauer, Jonathan D.
　1967　The Grain Amaranths and Their Relatives: A Revised Taxonomic and Geographic Survey. *Annals of the Missouri Botanical Garden* 54:103–137.

Sauer, Jonathan D., and Lawrence Kaplan
　1969　Canavalia Beans in American Prehistory. *American Antiquity* 34:417–424.

Sayles, Edwin B., and Ernst Antevs
　1941　*The Cochise Culture*. Medallion Papers 29. Gila Pueblo, Globe, Arizona.

Schlanger, Sarah H.
　1988　Patterns of Population Movement and Long-Term Population Growth in Southwestern Colorado. *American Antiquity* 53:773–793.

Schroedl, Alan R., and Nancy J. Coulam
　1994　Cowboy Cave Revisited. *Utah Archaeology* 7(1):1–34.

Schultes, Richard E.
　1976　*Hallucinogenic Plants*. Golden Press, New York.

Scott, Linda
　1997　Dietary Inferences from Hoy House Coprolites: A Palynological Interpretation. *Kiva* 44:257–281.
　1980　A Basketmaker III Pithouse Floor at Windy Wheat. Paper presented at the 3rd Annual Conference of the Society of Ethnobiology, Tucson.

Smiley, Francis E.
　1993　Early Farmers in the Northern Southwest: A View from Marsh Pass. In *Anasazi Basketmaker: Papers from the 1990 Wetherill-Grand Gulch Symposium*, edited by Victoria M. Atkins, pp. 243–254. Cultural Resource Series 24. Bureau of Land Management, Salt Lake City.

Smiley, Francis E., and William J. Parry
　1990　Early, Rapid, Intensive: Rethinking the Agricultural Transition in the Northern Southwest. Paper presented at the 54th Annual Meeting of the Society for American Archaeology, Las Vegas.

Smith, Susan J.
　1998　AR-03-0-02-0460 (LA111461) Pollen Analysis. In *Pre-Columbian Pueblo Agricultural Plots (AR-03-0-02-0460 [LA111461]) within the Proposed Las Clinicas del Norte Special-Use Permit Parcel, El Rito Ranger District, Carson National Forest, Rio Arriba County, New Mexico*, edited by Kurt F. Anschuetz, pp. 73–84, 168–171. Community and Cultural Landscape Contribution 2. Rio Grande Foundation for Communities and Cultural Landscapes, Santa Fe.

Smith, Susan J., and Phil R. Geib
　2000　Pollen Washes from Seeds and Metates: An Experimental Study. Paper presented at the 9th Southwest Paleoethnobotany Workshop, Santa Fe.

Smith, Watson
　1952　*Kiva Mural Decorations at Awatovi and Kawaika-a*. Papers of the Peabody Museum of American Archaeology and Ethnology 37. Harvard University, Cambridge.

Sobolik, Kristin D.
　1991　A Nutritional Analysis of Diet as Revealed in Prehistoric Human Coprolites. *Texas Journal of Science* 42(1):23–36.

Sobolik, Kristin D., and Deborah J. Gerick
　1992　Prehistoric Medicinal Plant Usage: A Case Study from Coprolites. *Journal of Ethnobiology* 12:182–194.

Stark, Miriam T., Jeffery J. Clark, and Mark D. Elson
　1995　Causes and Consequences of Migration in the 13th Century Tonto Basin. *Journal of Anthropological Archaeology* 14:212–246.

Stephen, Alexander M.

1936   *Hopi Journal of Alexander M. Stephen.* Contributions to Anthropology 23. Columbia University, New York.

Stiger, Mark A.

1977   *Anasazi Diet: The Coprolite Evidence.* Unpublished master's thesis, Department of Anthropology, University of Colorado, Boulder.

1979   Mesa Verde Subsistence Patterns from Basketmaker to Pueblo III. *Kiva* 44:133–144.

Stock, Janet Ann

1983   *The Prehistoric Diet of Hinds Cave (41VV456), Val Verde County, Texas: The Coprolite Evidence.* Unpublished master's thesis, Department of Anthropology, Texas A&M University, College Station.

Struever, Mollie, and Paul J. Knight

1983   Analysis of Flotation Samples and Macrobotanical Materials Recovered from Block III. In *Human Adaptation and Cultural Change: The Archaeology of Block III, N.I.I.P.,* vol.1, edited by Laurance E. Vogler, pp. 1653–1749. Navajo Nation Papers in Anthropology 15. Navajo Nation Cultural Resources Management Program, Farmington, New Mexico.

Sullivan, Alan P., III and Christian E. Downum

1991   Aridity, Activity, and Volcanic Ash Agriculture: A Study of Short-Term Prehistoric Cultural-Ecological Dynamics. *World Archaeology* 22:271–287.

Sutton, Mark Q., and Karl J. Reinhard

1995   Cluster Analysis of the Coprolites from Antelope House: Implications for Anasazi Diet and Cuisine. *Journal of Archaeological Science* 22:741–750.

Tagg, Martyn D.

1996   Early Cultigens from Fresnal Shelter, Southeastern New Mexico. *American Antiquity* 61:311–324.

Toll, Mollie S.

1981   *Macro-Botanical Remains Recovered from Chaco Canyon Coprolites.* Technical Series 38. Castetter Laboratory for Ethnobotanical Studies, Department of Biology, University of New Mexico, Albuquerque.

1982   Flotation Analysis of Outlying Structures at Nuestra Señora de Dolores Pueblo (LA 677). In *Excavations at Nuestra Señora de Dolores Pueblo (LA 677), a Preshistoric Settlement in the Tiguex Province,* by Michael P. Marshall, pp. 149–159. Office of Contract Archaeology, University of New Mexico, Albuquerque.

1983   Changing Patterns of Plant Utilization for Food and Fuel: Evidence from Flotation and Macrobotanical Remains. In *Economy and Interaction along the Lower Chaco River: The Navajo Mine Archeological Program, Mining Area III, San Juan County, New Mexico,* edited by Patrick Hogan and Joseph C. Winter, pp. 331–350. Office of Contract Archeology and Maxwell Museum of Anthropology, University of New Mexico, Albuquerque.

1984   Archaic and Historical Botanical Materials from Cerrososo Canyon Sites. Manuscript on file, Carson National Forest, New Mexico, Albuquerque.

1985   An Overview of Chaco Canyon Macrobotanical Materials and Analyses to Date. In *Environment and Subsistence at Chaco Canyon,* edited by Frances Joan Mathien, pp. 247–277. Chaco Canyon Studies Publications in Archeology 18E. National Park Service, US Department of the Interior, Santa Fe.

1987a   Plant Utilization at Pueblo Alto: Flotation and Macrobotanical Analysis. In *Investigations at the Pueblo Alto Complex, Chaco Canyon,* vol. 3, part 2, edited by Frances Joan Mathien and Thomas C. Windes, pp. 691–784. Chaco Canyon Studies Publications in Archeology 18F. National Park Service, US Department of the Interior, Santa Fe.

Lisa W. Huckell and Mollie S. Toll

1987b Floral Evidence for Subsistence Practices at the Piro Pueblo of Qualacu (LA 757). In *Qualacu: Archaeological Investigations of a Piro Pueblo*, by Michael P. Marshall, pp. 111–118. US Fish and Wildlife Service, Albuquerque.

1993a Plant Utilization at a 13th c. Pithouse Village (The Fox Place, LA 68188) on the Edge of New Mexico's Eastern Plains. Manuscript on file, Office of Archaeological Studies, Museum of New Mexico, Santa Fe.

1993b Botanical Indicators of Early Life in Chaco Canyon: Flotation Samples and Other Plant Materials from Basketmaker and Early Pueblo Occupations. Manuscript on file, National Park Service, US Department of the Interior, Santa Fe.

1994 Flotation, Macrobotanical Remains, and Charcoal. In *Archaeological Excavations at LA 15260: The Coors Road Site, Bernalillo County, New Mexico*, by Richard B. Sullivan and Nancy J. Akins, pp. 121–128. Archaeology Notes 147. Office of Archaeological Studies, Museum of New Mexico, Santa Fe.

1995 Botanical Study. In *The Belen Bridge Site and the Late Elmendorf Phase of Central New Mexico*, by Regge N. Wiseman, pp. 139–167. Archaeology Notes 137. Office of Archaeological Studies, Museum of New Mexico, Santa Fe.

1996 Picacho: A Record of Diverse Plant Use in a Diverse Ecological Setting. In *The Land in Between: Archaic and Formative Occupations along the Upper Rio Hondo of Southeastern New Mexico*, by Regge N. Wiseman, pp. 125–156. Archaeology Notes 125. Office of Archaeological Studies, Museum of New Mexico, Santa Fe.

1997 Analysis of Botanical Remains. In *Excavation of a Jornada Mogollon Pithouse along US 380, Socorro County, New Mexico*, by Daisy L. Levine, James L. Moore, Susan M. Moga, Linda Mick-O'Hara, and Mollie S. Toll, pp. 95–107. Archaeology Notes 138. Office of Archaeological Studies, Museum of New Mexico, Santa Fe.

1998 Plant Use and Subsistence at Rowe Pueblo. In *Before Pecos, Settlement Aggregation at Rowe, New Mexico*, by Linda S. Cordell, pp. 153–160. Maxwell Museum of New Mexico, Albuquerque.

Toll, Mollie S., and Marcia L. Donaldson

1982 Flotation and Macrobotanical Analyses of Archeological Sites on the McKinley Mine Lease: A Regional Study of Plant Manipulation and Natural Seed Dispersal over Time. In *Anasazi and Navajo Land Use in the McKinley Mine Area near Gallup, New Mexico: 1. Archeology*, edited by Christina G. Allen and Ben A. Nelson, pp. 712–786. Office of Contract Archeology, University of New Mexico, Albuquerque.

Toll, Mollie S., and Pamela J. McBride

1997 Healer vs. Shaman: Evidence for the Practice of Medicine in 17th Century New Mexico. Paper presented at the 20th Annual Ethnobiology Conference, University of Georgia, Athens.

1998 Flotation and Macrobotanical Materials. In *Excavations at the Gallo Mountain Sites, NM 32, Catron County, New Mexico*, by Nancy J. Akins, pp. 263–281, 452–480. Archaeology Notes 65. Office of Archaeological Studies, Museum of New Mexico, Santa Fe.

Trigg, Heather B.

1985 Ethnobotanical Analysis of D:7:2085. In *Excavations on Black Mesa, 1983, a Descriptive Report*, edited by Andrew L. Christenson and William J. Parry, pp. 489–511. Research Paper 46. Center for Archaeological Investigations, Southern Illinois University, Carbondale.

Van Devender, Thomas R., and David H. Riskind

1979 Late Pleistocene and Early Holocene Plant Remains from Hueco Tanks State Historical Park: The Development of a Refugium. *Southwestern Naturalist* 24:127–140.

Van Ness, Margaret A.

    1986   *Desha Complex Macrobotanical Fecal Remains: An Archaic Diet in the American Southwest.* Unpublished master's thesis, Department of Anthropology, Northern Arizona University, Flagstaff.

    1987   Flotation Analysis of the Pinenut Site. In *The Pinenut Site: Virgin Anasazi Archaeology on the Kanab Plateau of Northwestern Arizona*, edited by Deborah A. Westfall, pp. 173–180. Cultural Resources Series 4. Arizona State Office, Bureau of Land Management, US Department of the Interior, Phoenix.

Van Ness, Margaret A., and E. Hansen

    1996   Archaic Subsistence in the Glen Canyon Region. In *Glen Canyon Revisited*, by Phil R. Geib, pp. 117–125. Anthropological Papers 119. University of Utah Press, Salt Lake City.

Wagner, Gail, Tristine Smart, Richard I. Ford, and Heather Trigg

    1984   Ethnobotanical Recovery, 1982: Summary of Analysis and Frequency Tables. In *Excavations on Black Mesa, 1982, Descriptive Report*, edited by Deborah L. Nichols and Francis E. Smiley, pp. 613–632. Research Paper 39. Center for Archaeological Investigations Southern Illinois University, Carbondale.

Wasley, William W.

    1962   A Ceremonial Cave on Bonita Creek, Arizona. *American Antiquity* 27:380–394.

Welch, John Robert

    1996   *The Archaeological Measures and Social Implications of Agricultural Commitment.* Unpublished PhD dissertation, Department of Anthropology, University of Arizona, Tucson.

Wetterstrom, Wilma

    1986   *Food, Diet, and Population at Prehistoric Arroyo Hondo Pueblo, New Mexico.* Arroyo Hondo Archaeological Series 6. School of American Research Press, Santa Fe.

Whalen, Michael E.

    1994   *Turquoise Ridge and Late Prehistoric Residential Mobility in the Desert Mogollon Region.* Anthropological Papers 118. University of Utah Press, Salt Lake City.

Whiting, Alfred F.

    1966   *Ethnobotany of the Hopi.* Northland Press, Flagstaff.

Williams-Dean, Glenna, and Vaughn M. Bryant

    1975   Pollen Analysis of Human Coprolites from Antelope House. *Kiva* 41:97–111.

Wills, Wirt H., III

    1988   *Early Prehistoric Agriculture.* School of American Research Press, Santa Fe.

Wills, Wirt H., III and Bruce B. Huckell

    1994   Economic Implications of Changing Land Use Patterns in the Late Archaic. In *Themes in Southwest Prehistory*, edited by George J. Gumerman, pp. 33–52. School of American Research Press, Santa Fe.

Windes, Thomas C., and Dabney Ford

    1996   The Chaco Wood Project: Chronometric Reappraisal of Pueblo Bonito. *American Antiquity* 61:295–310.

Windes, Thomas C., and Peter J. McKenna

    2001   Going against the Grain: Wood Production in Chacoan Society. *American Antiquity* 66:119–140.

Winter, Joseph C.

    1993   Environment and Subsistence across the Colorado Plateau. In *Across the Colorado Plateau: Anthropological Studies for the Transwestern Pipeline Expansion Project, Parts 4 and 5: 5. Subsistence and Environment*, edited by Joseph C. Winter, pp. 601–648. Office of Contract Archaeology and Maxwell Museum of Anthropology, University of New Mexico, Albuquerque.

Lisa W. Huckell and Mollie S. Toll

Winter, Joseph C., and Patrick F. Hogan
  1986   Plant Husbandry in the Great Basin and Adjacent Northern Colorado Plateau. In *Anthropology of the Desert West, Essays in Honor of Jesse D. Jennings*, edited by Carol J. Condie and Don D. Fowler, pp. 115–144. Anthropological Papers 110. University of Utah Press, Salt Lake City.
Woodbury, Richard B.
  1961   Prehistoric Agriculture at Point of Pines, Arizona. *American Antiquity* 26:1–48.
Wright, Karen A.
  2000   *Archaeobotanical Evidence of Cotton*, Gossypium hirsutum *var.* punctatum, *on the Southern Colorado Plateau*. Unpublished master's thesis, Department of Anthropology, Northern Arizona University, Flagstaff.
Yarnell, Richard A.
  1959   Evidence for Prehistoric Use of Datura. *El Palacio* 66:176–178.

Chapter 4

Corn, Crops, and Cultivation in the North American Southwest

Suzanne K. Fish

*G*rowing crops of tropical origin in hot desert basins, wind-swept plateaus, and rugged uplands had far-reaching implications for the lifestyles of prehistoric cultivators in the southwestern United States and adjacent northwest Mexico (Figure 4.1). Their commitment to agriculture is a fundamental attribute distinguishing southwestern farmers from neighboring peoples to the north, east, and west. The same key contrast underlies the traditional delineation of the "Greater Southwest" as a coherent cultural entity (Fish and Fish 1994:83; Kirchhoff 1954). As the farthest extensions of a continuum of agriculturists stretching north from central Mexico, the farming societies of the North American Southwest formed a peninsula with temporally shifting boundaries among surrounding North American groups, who were primarily foragers rather than food producers. Widespread adherence to the Mesoamerican-derived domesticates of corn, beans, and squash set southwestern groups apart from populations on their peripheries, among whom such crops were typically rare or absent. The primacy of these domesticates in prehistoric southwestern

Suzanne K. Fish

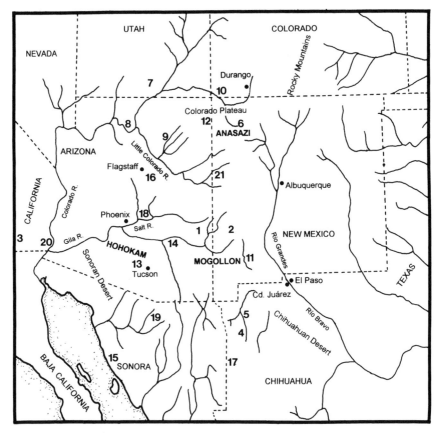

FIGURE 4.1   The North American Southwest: 1. Apache; 2. Bat Cave;
3. Cahuila; 4. Casas Grandes; 5. Cerro Juanaqueña; 6. Chaco; 7. Fremont;
8. Grand Canyon; 9. Hopi; 10. Mesa Verde; 11. Mimbres; 12. Navajo; 13. Pima;
14. Salado; 15. Seri; 16. Sinagua; 17. Tarahumara; 18. Tonto; 19. Trincheras;
20. Yuma; 21. Zuni

economies was linked, in turn, with contrastive levels of population, sedentism, and organizational complexity.

A pervasive theme in characterizations of the indigenous agriculture of the
North American Southwest is the marginality and precariousness of farming
in the face of aridity and other environmental challenges. This perception
arose with the beginnings of regional archaeology north of the international
border. In the decades surrounding the turn of the 20th century, when pioneering ethnographers and archaeologists embarked on detailed studies, an
era of capital investment and technological virtuosity had just begun to make

western basins and plateaus bloom for cultivators and crops from temperate climes. Like most of their countrymen who had resided in the North American Southwest for fewer than 50 years, these early scholars harbored expectations based in the agricultural experience of the eastern United States and ultimately rooted in European traditions. By comparison, the hard-won harvests of Indian peoples served mainly to illustrate the vicissitudes that these cultivators had had to overcome.

Notwithstanding these perceptions of marginality, the North American Southwest is rich in the remains of ancient farmers, whose postcontact descendants occupied only limited segments of the vast territory once inhabited by their forebears. Although dispossessed of many prime arable locations first by Hispanic and then by Anglo encroachment, Native American enclaves of historic times continued to follow a legacy of agricultural lifeways stretching back more than three millennia. Even the earliest Spanish observers arrived too late, however, to witness the most populous and complex late prehistoric societies and the means by which they had been supported. Such intensive precontact agricultural practices ranged from the capture of surface runoff in extensive complexes of cobble features to the construction of the most massive irrigation networks in the New World north of Peru (Doolittle 1990). Evidence for these impressive indigenous efforts to counter the agricultural constraints of regional environment is confined to the archaeological record.

The practices of indigenous agricultural societies of historic times offer invaluable analogs for assessing the role played by crops in past societies. Nevertheless, postcontact forces impacted the economic orientations of even the most isolated and conservative groups. Factors precipitating far-reaching change included the rapid incorporation of Old World crops and livestock, population loss in the wake of disease and disruption, accelerated raiding due to the acquisition of guns and horses, territorial encroachment by Europeans and displaced native peoples, and the proliferation of economic alternatives.

Southwestern Environment and Agriculture

Even though it is customary to view the prehistoric inhabitants of the North American Southwest as distinctive from other such inclusive cultural groupings, these populations exhibited marked internal differentiation over time and space as measured by material remains. As is the case today among the region's culturally and linguistically diverse Native Americans, many practices and preferences regarding crops and farming undoubtedly were expressed along ethnic lines. Interdigitating with cultural boundaries, environments of the North American Southwest also offered highly varied opportunities and limitations for agriculturalists.

The latitudinal extent of the prehistoric societies discussed in this chapter stretches from central Utah and Colorado to southern sectors of Sonora and Chihuahua and encompasses significant differences from north to south in day length, temperature, and other seasonal parameters affecting agriculture. Variables in Table 4.1 provide an overview of environment in conjunction with the geographic position and topographic setting of four of the major cultural subdivisions in southwestern archaeology. Ancestral Puebloan peoples classified as Western Anasazi were centered on the Colorado Plateau in northeastern Arizona and adjacent northwestern New Mexico. Eastern Anasazi occupations extended from the southeastern Colorado highlands through central and eastern portions of New Mexico. Hohokam and closely related groups covered much of central and southern Arizona, mainly in low desert basins. Inhabitants of the Casas Grandes sphere, usually considered as possessing a variant of Mogollon culture, occupied the higher desert basins in northwest Chihuahua and immediately adjoining southeastern Arizona and southwestern New Mexico. The Mountain Mogollon, another variant, lived in the mountainous country along the Mogollon Rim in east-central Arizona.

Elevation differs dramatically from the low basin floor of 225 m (700 ft) at Gila Bend, Arizona, occupied by the Hohokam, to the high mesas of 2,155 m (6,600 ft) at Mesa Verde, Colorado, occupied by the Eastern Anasazi (Table 4.1). The influence of elevation on temperature and precipitation is reflected in the contrast between two exemplary locations; Gila Bend averages 146 mm (6 in) of annual precipitation and a 275-day growing season, whereas Mesa Verde averages 450 mm (18 in) of rainfall annually and a 131-day growing season. Environmental diversity is greatest at the scale of the macroregion, but it is also substantial within individual cultural subdivisions. Although no single subdivision spans the elevational extremes for agricultural settlement in the North American Southwest, internal differences between uppermost and lowermost elevations present varying challenges for cultivators (Table 4.1).

Precipitation throughout the North American Southwest is low compared with temperate regions, but amounts vary substantially from the 146-mm (6-in) low for the Hohokam at Gila Bend to more than 400 mm (16 in) at upper elevations in Eastern Anasazi, Western Anasazi, and Casas Grandes territories (Table 4.1). Only in the most favored upland districts could farmers have attempted to grow crops without some form of supplemental water. Reinforcing the harshness of areas with lower annual precipitation is the correspondingly greater variability in amount of rainfall from year to year in those locations. Heightened evaporation due to high temperatures is also encountered at low elevations and in more southerly latitudes.

The seasonality of rainfall in the North American Southwest is more critical to the success of crops than are yearly totals. Seasonal proportions of rainfall generally trend along an east-west gradient, with summer-dominant precipitation to the east and winter-dominant precipitation to the west. Rainfall during the summer agricultural season may be relatively low despite high annual totals, as is the case for the Eastern Anasazi, especially when compared with the more favorable seasonal distribution around Casas Grandes in Chihuahua, Mexico. Individual locations within the Western Anasazi and Hohokam domains receive the lowest amounts of summer rainfall, but internal variation is appreciable within these subareas (Table 4.1).

Given the frequently cited requirement of 120 days for corn to mature (e.g., Carter 1945:88–89; Cordell 1997:133; Hack 1942:23; Schoenwetter and Eddy 1964), the length of the growing season as determined by the frost-free interval in itself seldom constitutes a limiting factor even at the highest elevations or northernmost extent of the region. In these situations the timing of summer rains may be a critical factor in crop maturation, however, because the onset is predominantly from late June onward. Snowmelt and its contribution to runoff and streamflow, on the other hand, often counterbalance late spring and early summer moisture deficiencies by providing sources of agricultural water earlier in the year.

The topographically controlled drainage of cold air into low elevations creates localized but compelling conditions that often override more general measures of climate. For example, the frost-free growing season in mountainous Flagstaff, Arizona, is 70 days shorter at one weather station where cold air subsides than at a second station only 36 m (120 ft) higher (Adams 1979:290). Even in low desert basins to the south, cold air drainage may inhibit early spring or late summer plantings in prime farming zones along major watercourses that correspond to topographic low points. During five years of record in Tucson, Arizona, the average frost-free interval was 121 days shorter along the river than on an adjacent hill only 105 m (330 ft) above the floodplain (Hastings and Turner 1965:17). Whereas cold air drainage in Flagstaff would have prohibited Western Anasazi cultivation in the affected locale, the same phenomenon would have impeded two floodplain crops per

Table 4.1

Environmental Variables Associated with Four Major Southwestern Cultural Traditions

Cultural Tradition	Weather Station	Elevation (m)	Average Annual Precip. (mm)	Average Summer Precip. (mm)	Average Growing Season (days)	25% Prob. Late Freezing Temps.	25% Prob. Early Freezing Temps.
Eastern Anasazi	Mesa Verde, CO	2,155	450	171	131	6-Jun	23-Sep
	Yellow Jacket, CO	1,554	472	200	134	27-May	25-Sep
	Cortez, CO	1,883	293	102	128	14-Jun	15-Sep
	Aztec, NM	1,719	242	105	148	27-May	21-Sep
	Taos, NM	2,124	321	171	141	30-May	27-Sep
	Santa Fe, NM	2,147	362	223	157	15-May	28-Sep
	Mountainaire, NM	1,987	328	223	154	19-May	30-Sep
Western Anasazi	Kayenta, AZ	1,725	194	94	165	11-May	8-Oct
	Jeddito, AZ	2,042	274	123	152	21-May	29-Sep
	Moenkopi, AZ	1,504	157	73	171	4-May	13-Oct
	Winslow, AZ	1,492	202	112	185	2-May	19-Oct
	Zuni, NM	1,966	289	147	136	1-Jun	22-Sep

Group	Location						
Hohokam	Tonto, AZ	672	394	134	322	19-Feb	1-Dec
	Gila Bend, AZ	225	146	57	275	14-Mar	19-Nov
	Phoenix, AZ	339	171	68	265	16-Mar	13-Nov
	Sacaton, AZ	392	219	96	243	29-Mar	7-Nov
	Florence, AZ	459	248	98	250	26-Mar	9-Nov
	Tucson, AZ	787	278	140	256	27-Mar	13-Nov
	Sells, AZ	733	302	181	267	16-Feb	14-Nov
	Tumacacori, AZ	996	367	228	206	28-Apr	2-Nov
Mogollon: Casas Grandes and Mountain Mogollon	Casa Grandes, Chih	1,487	381	264	NA	NA	NA
	La Junta, Chih	2,062	427	362	NA	NA	NA
	Animas, NM	1,343	263	162	189	12-May	9-Nov
	Douglas, AZ	1,310	341	228	217	14-Apr	4-Nov
	Cibecue, AZ	1,506	447	195	147	10-May	7-Oct
	Sierra Ancha, AZ	1,554	652	239	208	28-Apr	28-Oct

Note: NA = not available.

year in the warmer Tucson climate and might have impacted even a single Hohokam harvest if summer rains were long delayed.

Because crops of Mexican origin need warmth and substantial moisture, but adequate amounts of rainfall are largely restricted to cool upper elevations, opportunities for routine double cropping were not the norm among prehistoric societies of the North American Southwest, particularly those inhabiting uplands and northern regional sectors. Staggered corn crops were possible in some southern areas with a fortunate coincidence of frost-free climate and abundant water in the spring, for example, on lands irrigated from the lower reaches of the Gila River. Even in higher and cooler environments, however, minor plantings to supplement later main-season harvests might have been accomplished through careful attention to microclimatic effects. Such practices enabled the Hopi, a Western Pueblo group of recent centuries, to produce limited amounts of early-season corn. In rock-walled canyons where corn could be planted well before the spring frosts had ended elsewhere, the Hopi constructed terraces at considerable effort because they valued fresh produce for seasonal feasts and ceremonies (Hack 1942:30). Options for double cropping expanded significantly in postcontact times with the introduction of frost-resistant wheat.

Hydrology was another powerful determinant in regional patterns of prehistoric farming. Watersheds draining the snowy plateaus of the northern Southwest carried spring flows that the Eastern and Western Anasazi could divert for planting prior to the summer rains. Hopi practices exemplify additional use of stored winter precipitation. They watered fields with springs that tapped upland aquifers, and they farmed sand dune plots overlying shallow water tables that were fed by runoff from surrounding mesas (Hack 1942). Huge watersheds in mountainous zones produced spring floods and year-round flow in the Salt and Gila Rivers as they traversed the low deserts of central and southern Arizona. The Hohokam and other groups who filled canals from these rivers thus overcame daunting agricultural disadvantages of low rainfall and extreme heat (Fish and Nabhan 1991). In contrast, the still vaster drainage of the Colorado River produced downstream volumes of flow beyond the capacity of prehistoric technologies for diversion. The fields of cultivators along its lower reaches on the western edges of the region were confined to the limits of natural inundation and recession of seasonal floods.

Hohokam who lived south of the Salt and Gila, residents of the Casas Grandes sphere, and the other southerly societies responded to different seasonal hydrological regimes than did residents in the northern sector. With lesser contributions from upland snowmelt and runoff, major drainages in southern Arizona and adjoining Mexico to the south and west tend to carry maximal flows following summer rains. On the east, in a Chihuahuan Desert area of summer-dominant rainfall paralleling the international border and extending south, drainages of moderate size frequently do not join through-flowing rivers but, instead, terminate in seasonal lakes, or playas.

Distributions of archaeological cultures during agricultural times mirror broad environmental configurations to some extent and, notably, the division in the US Southwest between the higher plateaus north of the Mogollon Rim and the lower, warmer basin and range country to the south of the rim. Ceramic and architectural styles and other markers of cultural differentiation proliferated following the initial centuries of reliance on Mexican cultigens. It is not surprising that diversity in regional environment would be reflected in the material culture of increasingly sedentary farmers. Likewise, the environmental diversity of the North American Southwest was reflected in the variety of their crops.

Southwestern Crops and Crop Complexes

In two influential syntheses of information on prehistoric crops in North America, Richard Ford (1981, 1985) defined three agricultural complexes within the southwestern United States that reflected distinctive origins and archaeological patterns. Ford's Upper Sonoran Complex, believed to have diffused to the southwestern United States from western Mexico, consisted of corn, common beans (*Phaseolus vulgaris*), a cucurbit with both squash and pumpkin varieties (*Cucurbita pepo*), and bottle gourd (*Lagenaria siceraria*). The first three became the foremost food crops throughout the region in subsequent periods. Ford named the complex after the Upper Sonoran Life Zone, in the belief that these first crops were transmitted along an upland route through northern Mexico to the Mogollon highlands of New Mexico, a biotic zone that could accommodate their presumed need for relatively cool and moist conditions. Cave sites yielding some of the earliest dated cultigens known up to 1985 are also clustered in these New Mexico highlands.

Ford's Lower Sonoran Agricultural Complex consisted of cultigens that could withstand the high temperatures of the low-elevation southern deserts when irrigated. Cultigens in this complex entered the hotter basins of the Sonoran Desert in southern Arizona along lowland routes from Mexico at a later date than those of the Upper Sonoran Complex. This most diverse Lower

Sonoran Complex included cotton (*Gossypium hirsutum*) and tepary beans (*Phaseolus acutifolius*), and such later arrivals as jackbeans (*Canavalia ensiformis*), lima beans (*Phaseolus lunatus*), possibly scarlet runner beans (*Phaseolus coccineus*), green-striped or cushaw squash (in older literature *Cucurbita mixta* and now *Cucurbita argyrosperma*), warty or butternut squash (*Cucurbita moschata*), and grain amaranth (*Amaranthus hypochondriacus*).

The Southwest Complex consisted of confirmed and suspected indigenous domesticates of late prehistoric and historic times. The most probable candidates for cultigen status in this complex included prehistoric Sonoran panic grass (*Panicum sonorum*) and little barley (*Hordeum pusillum*) and post-contact devil's claw (*Proboscidea parviflora*). Devil's claw was domesticated to enhance desired characteristics and availability as a basketry raw material. Based on archaeological patterns and ethnographic practice, Ford also included beeweed (*Cleome serrulata*), native tobaccos (*Nicotiana trigonophylla* and *N. attenuata*), and an agave, or century plant (*Agave parryi*), among the plants that likely were cultivated.

The current need to revise these agricultural complexes reflects information on southwestern agricultural history obtained since the time of Ford's definitions. Chronologically equivalent and earlier instances of corn in many other environmental zones throughout the North American Southwest and adjoining Mexico and at lower elevations than the Mogollon highlands challenge the validity of the geographically and climatically delimited Upper Sonoran Complex. The earliest corn is noteworthy for its wide ecological tolerance rather than its narrow compatibility with cool, moist uplands or with any single environmental zone.

Common beans, *Phaseolus vulgaris*, and the relatively hard-shelled squash or pumpkin, *Cucurbita pepo*, still represent the initial species in these two cultigen categories to be grown in the Southwest. The earliest radiocarbon date on common beans reveals their presence about 2,500 years ago in the uplands of New Mexico (Wills 1988). A recent ^{14}C determination nearly five centuries older from the lower, hotter deserts of southern Arizona (Mabry in press) demonstrates that very early beans also were not restricted to the highlands. *Cucurbita pepo* is directly dated in northern New Mexico to about 2,800 years ago (Simmons 1986). The earliest cucurbits in southern Arizona are of undetermined species (e.g., Huckell 1998). Bottle gourd as old as the other three crops of the Upper Sonoran Complex is as yet unconfirmed by direct dating.

Amaranth has now been added to the earliest crops as a result of new identifications. An unknown species with a thin seed coat indicative of domestication was present in northern Chihuahua by 1000 BC (Fritz et al. 1999). Cultivated *Amaranthus cruentus* has been noted in New Mexico and dates to about 500 years later (Bohrer 1983; Tagg 1996). Spotty later records of grain amaranth, *Amaranthus hypochondriacus*, exist in the southern Southwest (e.g., Bohrer 1962; Huckell 1993), still in keeping with Ford's placement of this crop in the group of second-wave arrivals from Mexico. Probable domesticate morphologies have also been described in several cases for amaranths used by the Hohokam and nearby groups in southern Arizona during the ceramic era (e.g., Bohrer 1962; Gasser and Kwiatkowski 1991). Because pale seed color, a definitive trait of domestication, cannot be determined from charred remains, distributional knowledge about cultivated amaranths is incomplete and biased toward rare instances of their nonburned preservation.

With the exception of amaranths, evidence for crops of the Lower Sonoran Complex is still later than for corn, common beans, and the first cucurbit. As analyzed samples from the earliest agricultural occupations increase, the ages of other domesticates in this complex may also be pushed back in time. Currently, the earliest directly dated cotton comes from the Tonto Basin of east-central Arizona and is as old as the third to fourth centuries AD (Elson et al. 1995:228), but indirectly dated remains of equivalent and greater age have been recovered in southern Arizona (e.g., P. Fish et al. 1992; Fish 1998a, 1998b). Cotton likely arrived relatively soon after the first Mexican cultigens and was prized for its edible, oily seeds as well as for its fiber. Cotton (primarily in the form of burned seeds) is commonly encountered throughout the Hohokam sequence and elsewhere in the southern deserts, but a few instances also occur in the north, dated as early as AD 500–700 (Wright 2000). Cotton remains suggestive of cultivation are more widespread in occupations postdating AD 900 across northern Arizona, northern New Mexico, and southern Utah (Huckell 1993; Kent 1983; Wright 2000). It was apparently grown at elevations over 1,800 m (6,000 ft) (e.g., Hunter 1997; Teague 1998:6). In the following centuries abundant cotton characterized several northern sectors, including the Flagstaff vicinity and ancestral Hopi sites in northeastern Arizona. Spanish explorers observed its importance among Puebloan peoples of the Colorado Plateau and the Rio Grande Valley of eastern New Mexico.

Regional patterns of viability and preference for the less common types of beans in the Lower Sonoran Complex are not known in detail because beans often are not preserved in open-air sites. Tepary beans may have been domesticated from wild progenitors in the North American Southwest as well as from wild species farther south in Mexico (Ford 1981:18; Nabhan and Felger 1978). They are most frequently encountered in Hohokam sites (e.g., Gasser and Kwiatkowski 1991) but eventually were grown as far east as El Paso, Texas, and as far north as southern Colorado (Ford 1985:355). The small lima, or sieva, bean seems to have had a limited regional presence, being primarily identified at sites in southern Arizona and the Hopi area dating to late ceramic times (Ford 1985:355). Jack beans, which require appreciable water, appear at a number of Hohokam sites and may be associated with irrigation (Ford 1981:18–19). Recovery is most notable in the Tucson Basin (Gasser and Kwiatkowski 1991:431). Identifications of scarlet runner beans are few and tentative. It is unclear whether these beans were cultivated in the North American Southwest in precontact times.

Green-striped, or cushaw, squash, one of the two cucurbits in the Lower Sonoran Complex, became the more widespread member after its appearance in Hohokam territory, perhaps because it yields abundantly with irrigation (Ford 1981:19). In the north varieties with thick rinds may have provided containers in colder climates where bottle gourds grow poorly (Cutler and Meyer 1965). The warty, or butternut, squash has a more restricted temporal and spatial distribution and has not been recovered in earlier ceramic sites or those on the northern and eastern regional peripheries (Ford 1985:19).

The Southwest Agricultural Complex has expanded in the years since Ford defined it and now encompasses a wider variety of potential and confirmed crops derived from wild ancestors in the region. Extensive research in the Hohokam area has contributed disproportionately to this expansion. Agave of probable indigenous origin is now recognized as an important prehistoric crop in southern and central Arizona. The cooked base of this versatile succulent provides a sugary food that also may be fermented for alcoholic beverages. Its leaves supply fibers for cordage and textile crafts. There also is convincing evidence for cultivation of little barley (*Hordeum pusillum*) for its seeds and of cholla cactus (*Opuntia* sp.) for its edible buds (Bohrer 1991; Fish and Nabhan 1991).

Ethnographic practice, modern and archaeological distributions, and morphology departing from that of extant wild populations have been cited to suggest the intensive manipulation or cultivation of additional native species in both the northern and southern Southwest. These plants include shrubs furnishing fruits, such as wolfberry (*Lycium pallidum*) and Mexican crucillo (*Condalia warnockii*), and a variety of herbaceous, often weedy native species furnishing seeds, greens, and edible roots, including chenopods (*Chenopodium*), amaranths, (*Amaranthus*), groundcherry (*Physalis*), spiderling (*Boerhaa-*

via), tansy mustard (*Descurainia*), and hog potato (*Hoffmanseggia*) (e.g., Bohrer 1991; Fish and Nabhan 1991; Winter and Hogan 1986; Yarnell 1977). Incipient cultivation of weedy species probably was closely linked with the cultivation of domesticates, with both categories of plants benefiting from supplemental water.

Recent recognition of agave's former prominence as a crop in addition to its postcontact status as a widely gathered wild resource underscore the potential both for significant differences between prehistoric and historic agriculture and for deriving major new insights from archaeological studies. The remains of specialized fields with cobble features intended to enhance agave growth and of roasting pits for cooking the harvest provide conclusive evidence for large-scale agave cultivation by the Hohokam (Fish et al. 1985; S. Fish et al. 1992). Plantings of these desert succulents on otherwise marginal land had begun by AD 700, and production was expanded substantially after the 11th century (e.g., Elson et al. 1995; S. Fish et al. 1992). Also in keeping with its status as a crop, agave has been recovered in abundance from Phoenix area settlements that lacked ready access to wild populations (e.g., Gasser and Kwiatkowski 1991). *Agave murpheyi* is the foremost candidate for the common Hohokam cultivar, based on its archaeological associations, botanical attributes, ethnographic transplantation, and modern disjunct distributions (Crosswhite 1981; Gentry 1982; Nabhan 1995). Several additional cultivated species appear to be indicated by variability in charred spines and epidermal tissues from archaeological sites (Bohrer 1987; Fish et al. 1985) and by modern relict agave populations from Phoenix to the Grand Canyon in Arizona (Hodgson et al. 1989; Hodgson and Slauson 1995). It is quite possible that Mexican as well as native species were cultivated prehistorically.

Ford's complex of crops introduced to the North American Southwest by the Spanish has changed little in recent years. It is composed of cultigens from the Old World and distant parts of the New World. Old World wheat (*Triticum*), barley, peaches, apricots, plums, peas, chickpeas, broad beans, grapes, watermelons, and melons were adopted by indigenous groups as a result of Spanish contact in the 16th century. Documents and remains from both indigenous and mixed historic occupations reveal rapid incorporation (Ford 1985:359). To some degree, early plantings of wheat and barley stem from the preference of the Spanish for foods derived from these crops and from Spanish insistence on their cultivation at missions and in other colonial settlements. Indian farmers undoubtedly also found many of these crops attractive and were quick to appreciate the greater tolerance for cold temperatures of wheat and barley than corn, their tropically derived staple. Thus, these new cultigens provided more viable winter or early spring crops than previously had been available. Wheat became as important as corn or more so among Indian and Hispanic populations of the North American Southwest in an area centered on northern Sonora, and wheat was widely grown throughout the region.

Crops introduced from other parts of the Americas, mostly in the postcontact era, also came to be prominent in Native American communities. Chiles, now a standard ingredient in Indian cuisine throughout the southwestern United States, have not been securely documented north of the border in prehistoric contexts, in spite of the fact that wild populations of berrylike "chiltepines," *Capsicum annuum* var. *aviculare*, extend north from Mexico into southwestern Arizona and were widely used historically (Nabhan 1985). Remains of domesticated chiles were recovered from 17th-century mission pueblos (Ford 1985:359), suggesting that their earlier archaeological absence is not simply a result of sampling error, even though these plants are not readily preserved. The Spanish or their Indian allies from central Mexico who accompanied them on the first expeditions to the north may have transported the seeds.

Infusions of Mexican dent corn influenced the morphology of postcontact Puebloan varieties (Adams 1994a; Ford 1985:359–360). Sunflower seeds from southwestern archaeological sites are relatively infrequent and no larger than those of wild species; large-seeded domesticated sunflowers planted by the Hopi, Havasupai, and others in more recent times suggest postcontact introduction from Mexico or the eastern United States (Heiser 1985; Nabhan 1979, 1983).

Ford (1981, 1985) considered domesticated tobacco, *Nicotiana rustica*, to be a Spanish introduction from Mexico. Prehistoric tobacco seeds in the size range of this domesticate have since been noted in Arizona and New Mexico (e.g., Hammett 1993; Miksicek and Gasser 1989), with a tentative occurrence dating to the first centuries of farming in southern Arizona (Huckell 1998:73–79). Further confirmation is needed of the presence of prehistoric domesticated tobacco in the region and of the effects of intense manipulation of native species (Adams and Toll 2001).

Traditions of Southwestern Crop Use

Traditional modes of crop production and consumption among historic southwestern societies are the culmination of influences, preferences, and practices stretching back many centuries. This continuous chain of experience provides insights into the richness and diversity that crops contributed to prehistoric lifestyles. As a facet of regional identity both before and after European contact, the manner in which southwesterners used tropical cultigens reflected a more direct connection with central Mexico than was the case in adjoining regions to the north.

The most extensive and complex culinary activities developed around corn. Southwestern cultivators universally ate fresh corn both when it was mature and when it was still somewhat unripe, boiled and roasted on the cob, and with or without husks. Major parts of harvests were roasted in large pits or open fires to enhance preservation as a prelude to subsequent storage and cooking. Parched and ground corn was consumed in gruels, both as a thicker mush and diluted to a thinner consistency for drinking. Among southern groups such as the Tarahumara and Tepehuan of Chihuahua and the Pimans of Arizona, such gruels furnished a substantial part of the diet (Castetter and Bell 1942:188; Pennington 1963:76, 1969:99). Travelers elsewhere often resorted to a gruel beverage because finely ground, lightweight meal could be conveniently carried and mixed with water on demand (e.g., Cushing 1974: 266, 342–343). Native Americans consumed popcorn directly off the cob. In addition, the Zuni finely ground popcorn for use in a beverage (Stevenson 1915:76), and the Hopi soaked kernels in saltwater before parching them in hot sand (Whiting 1939:15).

Throughout the North American Southwest, boiling or soaking corn in ashes or weak lime solutions was a first step in making hominy and many kinds of gruels and dough. This step improved the nutritional value of corn, particularly adding calcium and enhancing the availability of essential amino acids, which are typically low in high-corn diets (Katz et al. 1974; Kuhnlein 1986:21–23). This process could be quite specific, as, for example, among the Hopi, who made hominy by soaking white corn with juniper ashes (Whiting 1939:15). In a less commonly recorded modification, Zuni cooks masticated corn to initiate fermentation for the production of natural leavening agents and sweet dough (Cushing 1974:294, 300, 304). Members of Yuman, Piman, Puebloan, and other traditions wrapped corn dough and even kernels in both green and dry husks in the manner of tamales, to be cooked by boiling or baking in ashes (Castetter and Bell 1942:187; Cushing 1974: 301, 304; Spier 1970:63). The Hopi and Zuni favored boiled dumplings (Cushing 1974:298–301; Stevenson 1915: 75–76; Whiting 1939:15), which were also made by the Pima (Russell 1975:68). Corn in many of these forms was everywhere a major or minor ingredient in soups and stews (e.g., Hernandez 1985).

Breadlike foods were also common. Some were relatively thick, resembling cakes, and were baked in ashes or on stone and pottery griddles (Cushing 1974:301–304; Russell 1975:73; Spier 1970:63). Thinner, tortilla-like wafers were baked on a pottery plate griddle, or *comal*, by the Pimans, Yumans, and more southerly groups and on flat stones by Puebloans (e.g., Castetter and Underhill 1935:46; Lange 1960:114–115; Spier 1970:63). At Hopi, Zuni, Cochiti, and other pueblos, skilled cooks made waferlike breads as thin as paper.

After harvest and drying for storage, beans were usually boiled, alone or with other foods in stews and mixed dishes. Boiled beans were sometimes added to corn dough recipes (Stevenson 1915:69–70). The Hopi dried string beans in the pod (Whiting 1939:81). The Zuni, Tepehuan, and Tarahumara also sometimes boiled and consumed unshelled beans (Cushing 1974:561; Pennington 1963:83, 1969:104), as did the Pima, who cooked immature pods in times of scarcity (Castetter and Bell 1942:194). In addition to boiling, Yumans and Tarahumara parched and then ground beans into flour to be cooked in water or added to other dough products; in fact, this method predominated over boiling whole beans among the Tarahumara (Castetter and Bell 1951:107–108; Pennington 1963:82). Yumans stored parched and ground white tepary beans as dried lumps of flour, and the Hopi parched white tepary beans before boiling (Whiting 1939:80).

Fresh pumpkin and squash were roasted in ashes, boiled, or added to soups and stews. Most southwestern groups cut the flesh in strips and sun dried it for storage and eventual rehydration by soaking and boiling. After parching, the seeds were eaten whole, ground for use in mush or in toasted cakes, and added to stews and other dishes (Castetter and Bell 1942:113; Cushing 1974: 561; Pennington 1963:82; Russell 1975:71; Whiting 1939:93). Hopi cooks used the oily squash seeds to prepare the flat stones for baking *piki*, a paper-thin bread. The Navajo, Yumans, Hopi, Tepehuan, Pimans, and others prized squash or pumpkin flowers, sometimes storing them in jars and consuming them in soups, stews, fried, and as flavorings in corn-dough recipes (Castetter and Bell 1942:190, 1951:112; Pennington 1969:104; Vestal 1952:46; Whiting 1939:93). Hard-shelled cucurbits were sometimes used as containers, like true gourds (*Lagenaria siceraria*), which were also widely cultivated.

Cotton was prehistorically cultivated for its fiber where growing seasons were of sufficient length. In postcontact times, cotton was raised by farmers at Hopi and several Rio Grande pueblos and by most indigenous peoples to the south (Huckell 1993:175). Cotton producers wove cotton textiles, as did groups, such as the Zuni, who acquired the raw materials by trade (e.g., Cushing 1974:357, 449). The Hopi were particularly noted for fine weavings prized by their neighbors. Oily cottonseeds were widely toasted for eating (Beaglehole 1937; Castetter and Underhill 1935:37; Gentry 1963:87; Russell 1975:77). Pimans pounded the seeds in a mortar, adding them to other dough products or making cakes cooked in ashes (Castetter and Bell 1942:198).

Agave cultivation has not been observed historically in the North American Southwest beyond recent instances of minor transplantings near homes among southern cultures (e.g., Nabhan 1995; Pennington 1969:268, 1980: 177). Information is plentiful, however, on the use of wild agave species (e.g., Castetter et al. 1938; Cushing 1974:235–237; Russell 1975:68, 93). Carbohydrates stored over the plant's lifetime in stem tissues were converted to a sugary, nutritious food by lengthy baking in pits. The cooked tissue was both consumed directly and dried for storage and later rehydration. Sweet drinks were made by soaking dried and sometimes ground agave in water. Pimans roasted dried agave cakes, and they also made a syrup by boiling the extracted juice (Russell 1975:68, 93). The Tarahumara, Tepehuan, and the Lower Pima of Sonora extracted juice from baked agave before or after fermentation to make *tesguiño*, an alcoholic beverage essential for ritual and hospitality (Pennington 1963:153–154, 1969:109, 1980:186–187). Apaches, Pimans, and other groups as far north as the Grand Canyon and as far east as Zuni made fermented agave beverages during historic times (Castetter et al. 1938). Prehistoric fermented equivalents probably were made in these areas but are poorly documented archaeologically. A second important agave product was fiber, extracted from leaves and crafted into twine, bags, baskets, nets, and textiles.

Crop Source and Transmission

The precise relationship of the earliest corn and other tropical cultigens in the North American Southwest to the cultigens of source areas in Mexico is open to question. As corn is the undisputed staple crop and the only one of the major Mesoamerican crop triad commonly recovered from archaeological sites, its Mexican heritage is central to this inquiry. Southwestern archaeological corn is classified on the basis of morphological (and not necessarily genetic) resemblance to named categories of modern maize, leaving much room for debate about the implied relationships and the significance of the classification. The time gap between the appearance of domesticated corn in Mexico and the earliest corn in the North American Southwest has important implications both for genetic relationships and for the manner in which archaeologists conceptualize processes of transmission and adoption in the north. Accepted facts of chronology in both Mexico and the North American Southwest have changed dramatically in recent years. An age for corn of 5,000 years, based on estimates from Bat Cave in New Mexico, was discounted (Berry 1982; Wills 1988). Subsequently, the time span has been shortened to approximately 4,000 years.

The earliest corn from caves in the Tehuacan Valley in central Mexico was initially assigned an age of 8,000 to 10,000 years ago, based on stratigraphic association with dated wood charcoal. The antiquity of Tehuacan corn was reevaluated in 1989 by direct determinations on corn remains from appropriate proveniences; none of the material could be placed earlier than 4,700 years ago (Long et al. 1989). Recent direct dates on beans in highland Mexico are no greater than 2,500 years old (Kaplan and Lynch 1999)—now exceeded by dates in the US Southwest! Recently, unequivocally domesticated cucurbits from a cave in the state of Oaxaca have been directly dated to between 8,000 and 10,000 years ago, an age similar to the original estimate for Tehuacan corn (Smith 1997). Cucurbits may indeed have been domesticated millennia prior to corn and beans, but the disparity between the current earliest dates for these three important crops in their Mexican homeland suggests that further chronological revision may well be forthcoming.

Because the mode and rate of transmission of domesticated crops to the north from central Mexico cannot be traced with existing archaeological data, the issue of timing is a crucial one in modeling the process by which it occurred. The oldest date on corn in the North American Southwest is now about 4,000 years ago (Gregory 1999), less than 1,000 years after the revised initial date for Tehuacan corn. If farming villages in the North American Southwest began producing corn only 1,000 years after its domestication in central Mexico and were producing demonstrably abundant corn only about 500 years later, the crop's spread and integration into local economies should be viewed differently than if that diffusion spanned 4,000 to 6,000 years. Other poorly known factors critical to understanding the adoption of agriculture are the range of subsistence orientations among Late Archaic populations in the North American Southwest and adjoining areas to the south, and the manner of crop transmission, whether by exchange from group to group, through migrations of farmers, or by a spatially and temporally complex combination of both processes.

Very few well-studied sites of relevant age from central through northern Mexico are available to delineate the "route" by which corn and other crops were transmitted into the US Southwest. Nevertheless, essentially linear pathways of transmission have long been envisioned, reflecting the implicit assumption of a corridor of cultivators or the actual movement of farmers through surrounding populations of mobile hunters and gatherers. The now-discounted 5,000-year age for cultigens at Bat Cave and their preceramic presence in other caves in the Mogollon highlands of New Mexico gave primacy to an upland route to the US Southwest along the north-south-trending Sierra Madre. Emil Haury (1962), among others, posited that corn adapted to relatively cool and moist environments in Mexico was transported to environmentally similar New Mexico locales. Only after a period of ecological adjustment was this initial corn thought to have spread into lower elevations (Ford 1985).

A second route, to the west of the Sierra Madre, has been discussed, with agriculturalists seen as moving along lower, warmer river valleys into southern Arizona (Haury 1962, 1976; Huckell 1995; Matson 1991). Whether or not continuing research supports an initial entry of crops into the North American Southwest along exclusive pathways, the massive spine of the Sierra Madre, the extremely arid Mexican coastal strip on the far west, and increasing continental aridity to the east undoubtedly served to channel successive northward infusions of southern cultigens (e.g., Sanchez-Gonzalez 1994), and perhaps cultivators, throughout the agricultural era.

Presently emerging distributional patterns for the earliest southwestern corn challenge previous notions about linear "routes" for the first entry of crops. Instances of directly dated corn are increasingly widespread across the North American Southwest for the interval between 3,000 and 2,500 years ago. Remains of this age occur above the Mogollon Rim in the north and in eastern and western sectors of the southern deserts on both sides of the international border. Significantly, outlier dates 500 or more years older likewise come from sites dispersed across the North American Southwest (e.g., Gilpin 1994; Gregory 1999; Hard and Roney 1998; Smiley 1994; Smiley and Parry 1990; Upham et al. 1987; Wills 1988).

If a single category of early corn (almost uniformly described as resembling the modern Chapalote type) was equally viable in such diverse environmental sectors, there is little reason to assume that points of entry were restricted by narrow ecological tolerances. Rather, the broad distribution of this early and indistinguishable corn implies that it could have been exchanged readily among a multiplicity of groups in contact all across the southern edges of the region. The role of agricultural populations in central and northern Mexico as transmitters of southern domesticates is unknown, although early cultigens have long been reported from several highland caves in Tamaulipas in the east and in northern Chihuahua and Sonora in the west (e.g., Lister 1958; MacNeish 1958; Mangelsdorf and Lister 1956).

Archaeologists working in northern Chihuahua (Hard and Roney 1998) and northern Sonora (Carpenter et al. 1998) recently identified populous settlements of preceramic farmers in prime basin locations dating to approximately 2,000–3,300 years ago. One of these sites in Chihuahua, Cerro Juanaqueña, is surprising for the amount of effort expended by cultivators near the beginning of this interval in constructing an impressive complex of more than 450 stone terraces on a large hill, and there are other such hill sites in the area (Hard and Roney 1998, 1999). As yet, these northern Mexican occupations have produced no dates as old as the earliest dates from agricultural sites much farther north; it is doubtful that they represent the very first farming settlements in the southern part of the North American Southwest.

The Transition to Agriculture

Relatively little is known about the settlement and subsistence systems of Late Archaic residents of the North American Southwest before the advent of Mexican cultigens. These populations are much less visible archaeologically than their immediate successors, the first farmers, whose occupations are now undergoing investigation throughout the region. Subsistence information is sufficiently spotty that it is difficult to characterize preagricultural Late Archaic economies for any locale in detail. The traditional model for many years in southwestern archaeology posited a band of mobile foragers, moving periodically to take advantage of sequentially available seasonal resources. The exploitation of resource diversity by means of an annual seasonal round across environmental zones was a corollary.

Predominantly nonagricultural groups within and around the North American Southwest provide a continuum of likely ethnographic analogs for Late Archaic foragers, ranging from the highly mobile Seri of the extremely arid Sonoran coast (Felger and Moser 1985) to the village-dwelling Cahuilla at the region's western boundary, who maintained stable settlements by storing the prolific yields of riparian mesquite groves (Bean and Saubel 1972). Intensive manipulations of native species included burning, pruning, and transplanting. Some practices approached conventional cultivation, such as Yuman broadcasting of panic grass seed along the Colorado River margins in western Arizona and Paiute ditch irrigation of sedges in the Owens Valley in eastern California. As in other parts of the world (Freeman 1968), immediate ethnographic analogs are lacking for preagricultural groups in those locations that later proved most favorable for agriculture; such locations in the North American Southwest were persistently occupied by cultivators after the inception of farming. Variable ethnographic patterns among foragers serve as a reminder that the timing and degree to which Archaic societies incorporated Mexican cultigens undoubtedly varied in conjunction with prior subsistence orientations and environmental settings.

Some formulations posit a transition to agriculture in which cultigens were added in minor increments to mobile lifestyles without effecting immediate, fundamental change (e.g., Minnis 1985, 1992; Wills 1988). Alternative reconstructions focus on a more wholesale incorporation of cultigens by groups preconditioned to farming by virtue of minimal mobility and dependence on plentiful, predictable, and perhaps intensively manipulated key resources (e.g., Fish and Fish 1991; Fish et al. 1990) or on the transmission of agriculture to new areas through the migration of farmers (e.g., Huckell 1995; Matson 1991). The timing of the transition to agriculture has been linked in the south with aggrading floodplains that created conditions conducive to farming (e.g., Huckell 1995; Mabry 1998) and, in the north, with the emergence of genetically adapted corn varieties in the southern Southwest that could then tolerate the cooler climate and shorter days of the Colorado Plateau when transmitted further north (Matson 1991). Dates on corn in the northern Southwest (e.g., Gilpin 1994) that approach the very early dates in the south bring into question the time lag for genetic adjustment posited in this last scenario. The various models of the transition to agriculture need not be mutually exclusive. Choosing among them conclusively for any specific time and place demands archaeological sequences bridging the transition, a requirement seldom met with present data.

Where investigations are sufficient to reveal a comprehensive settlement context, the first corn in regional sequences within the North American Southwest is usually associated with pithouses, storage facilities, and in some cases extensive domestic middens, cemeteries, and irrigation canals (e.g., Gilpin 1994; Mabry 1998; Wills and Huckell 1994). At present, the most comprehensive settlement data for early cultivators are available in southern Arizona and include all of these elements (e.g., Mabry 1998, in press). Hundreds of pithouses spanning the interval before and soon after the routine use of pottery have been uncovered in excavations along the Santa Cruz River in Tucson. Analyses of botanical remains from these sites reveal plentiful corn. Still older corn, dated to about 4,000 years ago, has now been discovered in limited exposures stratigraphically below these occupations. Compatible with a model of rapid wholesale incorporation of corn by relatively settled foragers in resource-rich environments, this earliest evidence of cultigens is accompanied by remains of gathered plants that would have been available over an extended period encompassing the summer agricultural season (Gregory 1999:118).

Cultural Significance of Corn

As elsewhere in the Americas, corn played a central role in the ideology of farmers in the North American Southwest. Similarities between beliefs and observances surrounding corn in southwestern and Mesoamerican traditions, such as the association of corn colors with the cardinal directions (Bohrer 1994), suggest southwestern adoption of ideological elements along with Mexican crops. Although corn only occasionally appears in prehistoric southwestern art and iconography, primarily in the more representational images on Mimbres painted bowls from southern New Mexico and in Puebloan kiva murals, it figures prominently in the oral history and ideologies of all indigenous agricultural societies. For example, corn pollen and cornmeal are widely used as ritual substances, and origin stories typically recount how a group supernaturally received the gift of corn (Ford 1994; Ortiz 1994).

Ethnographic perceptions and practices offer insights into the realm of culturally meaningful variation in prehistoric corn. As recorded by Frank Cushing (1974) in the late 1800s, the Zuni of northwest New Mexico exhibited an intimate and intricate concern for corn that must have had roots in the more distant past. The Zuni of that time distinguished six colors of corn: yellow, blue, red, white, speckled, and black. Seeds of each of these colors were ceremonially planted in a patterned manner near the center of a field at the beginning of the growing season; four of the colors were associated with each of the cardinal directions, and two were placed in adjacent "upper" and "lower" positions. The success of these first special plantings predicted the success of the crop of each respective color of corn. Cobs were sorted by color at harvest and stored separately to facilitate selective use as seed stock and in cooking. Thin, flat bread baked on smooth stone slabs was made in six colors corresponding to the color of the type of corn used as the major ingredient. Cooks deemed corn of each color to possess variants of flavor, texture, and other properties appropriate in Zuni cuisine; for example, red corn was appropriate for a sweet, paper-thin bread, and blue cornmeal was the definitive ingredient for a particular kind of dumpling.

Color was still a principal means of distinguishing corn when E. F. Castetter and W. H. Bell (1942) recorded agricultural practices during the early decades of the 20th century. However, the Pima of south-central Arizona maintained fewer color categories than had the Zuni a few decades earlier. White, yellow, and blue varieties of corn were common among the Pima. Occasional red ears appeared among plantings, but the status of red corn as a separate variety was acknowledged only for ancient times. Previously, corn of different colors had been planted in different plots and separated carefully at harvest. The Pima still made an effort to sort harvested corn in this manner despite many ears of mixed color. Farmers selected seed corn on the basis of pure color and set apart cobs for future planting. Informants designated blue corn as used mostly for parching, white as best for pinole (a liquid gruel), and yellow as most suitable for tortillas (Castetter and Bell 1942:187–188).

A diversity of maize persists among traditional subsistence farmers of northwest Mexico in an area surrounding the Sierra Madre Occidental (Hernandez 1985). Inhabitants of this area include isolated populations of indigenous and mixed heritage who maintain older, noncommercial varieties of corn because these types have different ecological tolerances and superior qualities in cuisine. Hernandez (1985:423) relates crop diversity to the constant consumption of corn as a staple and to the related need for variety in an otherwise monotonous diet. Color, distinguished as two shades of white, yellow, pink, red, dark blue, and black, is used in combination with kernel texture to identify types best suited for consumption in a host of corn-based foods. Among these foods are green corn, tortillas, pinole (a thin gruel beverage), popcorn, corn cookies, pozole (a stew), and alcoholic drinks made from fermented corn.

Categories of corn that are linguistically designated according to color also encode corresponding sets of genetically differentiated traits in addition to color. Genetic diversity in these other traits is maintained as a consequence of maintaining distinct corn colors, thus ensuring a range of responses to environmental conditions and options with respect to planting strategies (Ford 1980). For example, traditional farmers of northwest Mexico use categories based primarily on color and secondarily on texture to select the proper corn for planting rituals, for dry areas and poorer soils, and for early, intermediate, or late planting seasons with particular moisture and temperature conditions. As among traditional southwesterners in general, careful northwest

Mexican farmers still sort harvested corn by these categories for storage, and they select seed from ears of homogeneous color and morphology. Recognized as ancient and increasingly scarce, varieties of corn with special colors and textures are planted in separate rows and along the upper limits of fields on slopes to prevent interbreeding with the dominant commercial crops (Hernandez 1985:425). The Hopi exemplify northern versions of these practices, similarly selecting cobs with homogeneous kernels for seed, planting the same corn types in segregated fields year after year, and recognizing differences among varieties in quality, seasonality, and other characteristics (Whiting 1939:11–12).

Prehistoric Southwestern Corn

Archaeobotanists do not customarily describe and categorize prehistoric southwestern corn according to variables such as color or culinary suitability that are prominent in ethnographic classification. Rather, attributes amenable to measurement and qualitative criteria such as overall shape are favored because of preservation constraints. The great majority of maize remains are both fragmentary and burned. Based on more complete specimens and on the distinctive characters of commonly recovered cob fragments and kernels, archaeobotanists usually classify archaeological corn by its resemblance to morphologically defined categories still grown in the North American Southwest, Mexico, and elsewhere in the Americas. These categories have names such as "Chapalote," "Onaveño," and "Reventador."

Karen Adams (1994a) cites eight types of prehistoric southwestern corn in addition to Chapalote that have been distinguished by archaeobotanical analysts on morphological grounds. These southwestern types are variously attributed to the diffusion of Mexican types from the south, genetic evolution within the North American Southwest, and later admixtures of established regional varieties with subsequent arrivals. Nomenclature is not standardized or applied in the same manner by all analysts. Soft-cob pod or pop, flint, flour, and dent corns have been identified, with row numbers varying from eight to 16 (Adams 1994a:277). With the possible exception of a very early eight-rowed type in southern New Mexico (Upham et al. 1987), corn with lower row numbers is most often reported as postdating the era of initial farming but still relatively early in archaeological sequences (e.g., Cutler 1952; Cutler and Blake 1986; Galinat et al. 1970), although not necessarily at the same time throughout the region. Analysts have observed what could be a shift toward lower row numbers related to the arrival of such corn in upland portions of the North American Southwest (e.g., Cutler 1952; Cutler and Meyer 1965). Corn of the Hohokam tradition of southern Arizona, on the other hand, exhibits little variation in types through time.

Since its early appearance, Chapalote-like corn has remained important through the present. It has been identified throughout the region in sites of many periods and locations (Adams 1994a). Another widely reported category of corn is the Pima/Papago series that includes flint and flour types. It has been recognized in every state in the southwestern United States and among all major cultural divisions. A floury member of the series, Maíz Blando, had appeared by AD 500–700 in northern Arizona (Cutler and Blake 1986). Harinoso de Ocho, Reventador, and Chapalote, representing floury, flint, and flint or pop types, respectively, often co-occur with Pima/Papago corn (Adams 1994a). Variable combinations of this set of types were common throughout Arizona, New Mexico, Colorado, and Utah for much of prehistoric time.

Two distinctive and localized types of southwestern corn are found in Utah and Colorado. Fremont Dent, named after the Fremont variant of Western Pueblo culture, occurred in Utah by approximately AD 400 (Winter 1973). Apparently not related to a Mexican dent corn introduced by the Spanish, Fremont Dent has been variously attributed to an untraced northward diffusion of dent corn from Mexico (Anderson 1948; Cutler 1966) and to an in situ development in the North American Southwest (Galinat and Gunnerson 1963; Winter 1973). Similarly, corn resembling Mexican Pyramidal types is reported from sites in western Utah, although a passage north from Mexico, again, cannot be documented. Morphological variability in preceding San Juan Basketmaker corn and other early corn in this general area is an alternative means of accounting for these two comparatively localized types (Adams 1994a:292; Winter 1973).

Pueblo corn, a late type with typically large cobs and large shanks, is recovered over much of the North American Southwest, usually at sites postdating the 12th century AD. Early examples date between AD 1000 and 1150 in New Mexico (Cutler 1961). Especially large varieties of Pueblo corn became common among Puebloan groups after the Pueblo Revolt of 1690, when Spanish settlers introduced Mexican dent and other new corn types into the North American Southwest (Ford 1985:359–360).

It is difficult to specify the corn varieties and the diversity of types that were used by a prehistoric southwestern household or by the inhabitants of a single settlement. Only limited insights into variability, whether simply morphological or genetic, can be derived from the charred and blackened kernels and cupules (durable cup-shaped structures of the cob that hold the kernels) that make up the vast majority of archaeologically recovered corn remains. Situations of unusual preservation, such as dry caves and cliff dwellings or catastrophically burned structures, provide more diverse and intact remains and thus more attributes for assessing diversity. Situations of enhanced preservation are relatively rare, however, and, particularly in the case of caves, may not be fully representative of preferences and diversity in more ordinary situations.

Crop Storage

Farmers of the North American Southwest satisfied the universal need of agriculturalists for substantial, secure storage by a wide variety of means. A hallmark of sites yielding early cultigens is the presence of many large pits in residential areas and often in the more specialized occupations of caves (Huckell 1990, 1995; Mabry 1998; Matson 1991; Simmons 1986; Wills 1988). On the Colorado Plateau of the upland north, a slab-lined version of such pits is often termed a "cist." Bruce Huckell (1995:120) estimates that a typical storage pit with a .5-m^3 capacity at a southern Arizona early farming site could hold as many as 9,200 unshelled ears, enough to meet one adult's total caloric requirements for about a year. A capability for bulk storage was demonstrably a concern of early agriculturalists in this region. Less permanently settled cultivators of historic times, such as the Navajo and Tohono O'odham, also used large storage pits, and, by analogy, some archaeologists have suggested that Late Archaic pits are indicative of concealed storage for groups who left farming locations during a mobile seasonal round (Gilman 1983; Young 1996). Even the most sedentary early farmers, however, were more likely to have used pits than their successors, who had additional storage options in the form of ceramic vessels and specialized structures.

Equally critical to farmers as the storage of food supplies was the secure maintenance of seed, on which harvests in succeeding years depended. Ethnographically, seed selected for planting was often separated from other crop products and stored in a special manner with heightened care and ritual. Among the earliest ceramic vessels in the North American Southwest are shapes termed "seed jars" that may have served to store seed. These are neckless jars with tops rounding inward to an orifice smaller than the maximum vessel diameter. Large storage jars produced by later potters routinely held household resources, as revealed by contents burned in catastrophic fires. Wild resources as well as cultigens were preserved by sealing in jars. Assemblages of large jars mark storage among the Hohokam; the numbers of such vessels occasionally found in individual structures virtually would have filled available interior space, indicating a specialized storage function (e.g., Elson 1986; Fish and Fish 2000).

Rooms dedicated primarily to subsistence storage were common among postcontact Puebloans who lived in buildings with contiguous rooms of adobe or stone (e.g., Adams 1983; Cushing 1974; Mindeleff 1891). Separate storage structures among several houses in a household cluster are also widely recorded among peoples of the southern Southwest such as the Piman-speaking groups of southern Arizona and their Yuman neighbors to the west. Archaeologists often identify specialized storage space by the absence of facilities for general domestic activities, most frequently a hearth for cooking and heating. Some catastrophically burned structures provide evidence confirming such spatially segregated storage, for example in a room filled with burned food supplies at Arroyo Hondo near Santa Fe, New Mexico (Wetterstrom 1986). Among Puebloan populations, architectural specialization has a long history. Household units consisting of rooms devoted to general habitation functions or to storage have long been recognized, beginning with the transition from earlier pithouse to later pueblo architecture (e.g., Lipe 1989; Prudden 1903).

Storage bins made of coarse basketry or brush and earth were common during the postcontact era below the Mogollon Rim. Cylindrical to rounded facilities of this sort were constructed outdoors by the O'odham, Tarahumara, Yumans, and others, either free-standing or placed on the roofs of houses (Castetter and Bell 1942:183). They were capped or had roofs of brush and thatch and often were coated on the outside with a layer of hardened mud. Well-known prehistoric examples are preserved as a result of their protected situation in the Cave of the Olla in Chihuahua (Di Peso 1974:2:609; Lumholtz 1902:62–66). The Pima used another kind of large, coiled basket indoors in specialized storage structures. Both indoor and outdoor storage in bins or granaries is archaeologically identified for late prehistoric Salado occupations of the Tonto Basin in central Arizona. Platforms composed of flat stones mark the bases of former granaries, and portions of basketry superstructures have been preserved in collapsed rooms (Lindauer 1992). Because the bases of historic bins were often made of perishable materials rather than stone (e.g.,

Castetter and Bell 1942:183–186), such storage practices may have been more widespread prehistorically than has been archaeologically detected.

Food Technology and Cuisine

The Mexican cultigens are central elements in southwestern technologies for food processing and preparation. It would be very difficult, however, to archaeologically reconstruct the kind of complexity and sophistication that has been ethnographically recorded for southwestern cooking. Much food preparation must have occurred outdoors to keep fuel, smoke, and debris out of dwellings. Extramural hearths, roasting pits, and shelters for outdoor processing and preparation are often encountered.

In the dry climate of the North American Southwest, air drying is usually a sufficient means to preserve cultigens for future use, although parching and pit roasting also are employed to enhance the storability of corn. Rehydrating can be accomplished by soaking, steaming, or boiling at the time of consumption. Corn requires the additional step of grinding when consumed in most forms other than whole kernels. Unexpected fires in the past have preserved corn stored both as kernels and as whole ears; in the latter case removal of kernels from the cob would have taken place at the time of preparation. Kernels could have been removed from dried ears for storage, but in some cases the appearance of well-preserved examples suggests a process of scraping or cutting while the kernels were still moist (e.g., Anderson 1950: 162; Cutler 1961:92, 1969:373; Hall 1975:55).

Grinding as a routine method of food preparation in the North American Southwest predates the appearance of corn by millennia. Metates with flat to basin-shaped grinding surfaces, accompanied by handstones, or manos, are plentiful in Archaic contexts. Change in these tools was not instantaneous or dramatic with the advent of corn. Indeed, early styles of manos and metates, consisting largely of stones with appropriate natural shapes that were further shaped through use, never disappeared even as the variety of ensuing ground stone implements increased. More formally manufactured shapes, more selective use of raw materials, and implements with larger working surfaces (e.g., Hard et al. 1996; Lancaster 1983; Morris 1990) likely denote a greater investment of time in preparing corn by grinding. Grinding per se and increasingly finer grinding offer the advantages of decreasing the amount of fuel needed for cooking while increasing nutritional benefits by aiding more complete digestion of smaller particles (Stahl 1989).

Formally shaped trough metates with rims enclosing the grinding surface became common in the North American Southwest sometime after AD 300 (e.g., Doyel 1991; Wills 1996). Occasional trough shapes occur in still earlier southwestern sites (Adams 1998), and these types are of greater antiquity in Mexico. Larger manos were often used in conjunction with the enlarged grinding surfaces in later metates. Women in some parts of the Puebloan Southwest still used slab metates with flat surfaces after AD 900. In many instances, these were permanently positioned within fixed grinding bins that had stone or adobe rims, thus containing kernels and meal in the same manner as the upright walls of trough metates. Groups of bins in special mealing rooms and other site locations mark shared facilities enabling Puebloan women to work in company with others while performing the repetitive and time-consuming task of grinding. Sets of two to four metates, grading from coarser to finer stone, may have been used sequentially to produce progressively finer meal or flour (Lancaster 1983).

Ethnographically documented food preparation provides only partial insight into the ways cultigens were prepared prior to the advent of ceramic cooking vessels, an interval lasting centuries in some cases. As in later times, farmers may have consumed green corn directly from the cob or may have roasted and parched kernels in basketry trays with hot coals to prepare it for storage and consumption. Pit baking and bulk roasting in surface fires also have been employed for both purposes by various groups (Castetter and Bell 1942:181–182; Cushing 1974:204–208; Russell 1975:72; Vestal 1952:18). It is unclear how boiling or simmering might have been accomplished without pottery; boiling with heated stones in perishable containers such as watertight baskets and hide bags is one method that possibly was used. The appearance of beans several centuries before pots suitable for extended boiling is of particular interest, given that boiling later became the most common method of cooking beans. Initially, beans may have been roasted and ground, as among postcontact Tarahumara and Yumans. Although bowls and neckless seed jars, presumably designed for storage of agricultural seeds, predominate among the earliest ceramic vessels throughout the southwestern United States, a few moderate-sized jars with shapes potentially suitable for boiling also appear in early assemblages (e.g., Blinman 1993; Burton 1991; Heidke et al. 1998; Whittlesey 1998). By AD 500, regional potters were producing vessels capable of processing, storing, cooking, and serving a wide range of cultigen products.

Undoubtedly, after pottery became the foremost medium for cooking containers, diversification in vessel raw materials, shape, size, thickness, orifice diameter, and surface treatments such as corrugation or smudging was at least partially related to a prehistoric elaboration of cuisine and cookware akin to that of the postcontact record. For example, in addition to generalized cooking vessels of globular shape, Pima at the turn of the 20th century made distinctive bean pots with flange handles, shallow vessels with handles for parching, and shapes resembling plates for cooking thin wafers resembling tortillas (Russell 1975:128, Plates XVII, XIX). For parching and other culinary purposes, they also selected large broken pieces of unsmoothed cooking pots that would not become slippery when wet (Russell 1975:128). The complex Zuni cuisine required a variety of vessels such as little, narrow-necked pots that were placed near the hearth to ferment masticated corn dough to make leavened dishes, small pots that were set in ashes to cook a sweet mush resembling bread pudding, and shallow pans to hold hot sand for parching corn (Cushing 1974:294, 304–305). Zuni manufacture and seasoning of the polished flat stones for baking paper-thin bread represented the height of labor-intensive, specialized, and socially mandatory equipment for cultigen-based cookery (Cushing 1974:326–333).

Roasting pits and fire-cracked rock, the heat-fractured fragments of stones placed in pits to retain heat, are common features of southwestern archaeological sites, particularly in the south. Pit roasting makes efficient use of the scarce fuels of arid landscapes and transforms plant resources into more consumable and fully nutritious products (Wandsnider 1997). Roasting pits occur in the settlements of the earliest agriculturalists in the southern Southwest (e.g., Mabry 1998; Sanchez de Carpenter 1998) and at sites dating throughout most regional sequences. Roasting pits in residential sites undoubtedly were reused again and again for cooking multiple resources, including domesticates, wild plants, and game. Other roasting pits had more specialized functions such as the large-scale baking of cultivated agave hearts in field areas (e.g., S. Fish et al. 1992).

Roasting, steaming, parching, and boiling appear to have been the major alternatives for cooking corn prior to the relatively late prehistoric development of methods for baking thin, flat forms akin to tortillas and Puebloan paper bread. Soaking in limewater or ash solutions is a pretreatment for such products. Snow (1990) identifies the combination of smooth, rectangular stone slabs, rectangular hearths, and "fire dogs," or andirons, to support the slabs over hearths, as specialized equipment for cooking tortilla-like products in the Rio Grande area from the 13th century into postcontact times. In relative synchroneity with these Eastern Pueblo patterns, flat *piki* stones for preparing the Western Pueblo version of wafer bread appeared in northeastern Arizona in conjunction with specialized *piki* rooms with facilities for making *piki* (Adams 1983). Flat ceramic plates resembling the Mexican comal used to cook tortillas also appeared among the Hohokam of southern Arizona at about the same time (Haury 1945). Comals never constituted common shapes in Hohokam ceramic assemblages, however, nor did tortilla-like products remain widespread among the Eastern Pueblos during the historic period (Snow 1990:193).

Some of the variability in southwestern culinary equipment undoubtedly corresponds to the characteristics of the predominant type of corn with which the equipment was used. As previously noted, grinding implements did not change significantly for many centuries after corn entered the picture, nor did farmers immediately begin to make pots. Early corn appears to have included flint or dent types (Adams 1994a). The later entry, dispersal, and genetic influence of floury types are known only in rough outline. It is likely that increasingly formal shapes of grinding tools and more efficient designs with large grinding surfaces were related to extensive use of floury corn, as well as dent varieties also containing substantial soft endosperm, because these types are most amenable to the production of finely ground meal and flour. Likewise, late prehistoric equipment for making thin wafer bread and tortilla-like products likely is correlated with preferential use of floury types. Other considerations probably account for the continuing retention of hard-kernel varieties along with floury types in spite of the greater difficulty of grinding. Hard-kernel corn is much less vulnerable to insect damage during extended storage, an asset in maintaining annual stores and longer-term supplies against unpredictable shortfalls (e.g., Whiting 1939:11).

Archaeological evidence for technology related to cotton and agave is oriented toward use of fiber more than food. Spindle whorls for spinning cotton thread tend to be smaller and lighter than those used for the generally coarser agave fiber, but absolute discrimination on these bases is questionable. Flat disk whorls of such perishable materials as wood and gourd or cucurbit rinds are known ethnographically and from dry caves. Perforated disks made from sherds were the common ceramic forms after AD 500, and stone disks were used regularly but less commonly in subsequent times. After AD 1000, modeled three-dimensional whorls of Mesoamerican style appeared among the Hohokam, Trincheras of Sonora, and cultures further to the south (Teague 1998:51–56). Stone "knives" with ground and serrated edges, like those used ethnographically to sever tough, spiny leaves at harvest are scattered on the surfaces of Hohokam agave fields (S. Fish et al. 1992). A similar type of knife with a smooth edge and a handle or haft was used for depulping leaves to extract fiber. These artifacts tend to be found in residential sites. Additional archaeological evidence for cotton and agave textiles includes bone weaving tools and posthole patterns indicating loom supports.

Diet and Dependence

The relative importance of cultigens in the diet and the degree to which past farming societies relied on agriculture are recurring questions. The answers are not necessarily matters of consensus for the region as a whole or for individual time periods, developmental stages, cultural traditions, or even sites (Fish and Fish 1994). Archaeologists working in the North American Southwest often address these issues indirectly by considering related variables such as the nature of storage facilities, residential duration and architecture, and annual mobility. Another recent approach relies on the measurement of grinding tools, primarily manos, or handstones, and is based on the premise that the average size of the grinding surface increases with the proportion of corn in the diet (e.g., Hard et al. 1996; Morris 1990).

A direct indication of the cumulative contribution of corn to the diet of prehistoric populations potentially can be obtained by analyzing human skeletal remains (Schoeninger and Moore 1992). Corn takes in atmospheric carbon dioxide and fixes carbon according to a distinctive photosynthetic pathway termed the C4 pathway. A plant's photosynthetic pathway determines the ratio of stable carbon isotopes fixed in its tissues, and this ratio is also reflected in the bone biochemistry of humans who consume the plant. Unfortunately, agave, cacti, and other wild plants in the southwestern diet fix stable carbon isotopes in a manner overlapping that of corn, thus hindering efforts to infer corn input from bone (e.g., Schoeninger and Schurr 1994; Van de Merwe 1982). Although occasional southwestern bone analyses have been reported and debated over the years (e.g., Chisholm and Matson 1994; Hard et al. 1996; Martin 1999; Matson and Chisholm 1991), results have failed to conclusively resolve regionwide issues of dietary importance.

Plant residues preserved in archaeological sites offer indirect but significant insights into the dietary importance of crops and the degree of dependence on them. Table 4.2 presents data based on macrobotanical remains because they are the most commonly recovered plant materials. Macrobotanical remains are plant residues, usually preserved by burning, that retain sufficient integrity to allow identification based on the morphology of the plant's primary structures. Table entries were derived mainly from flotation analyses, in which buoyant carbonized remains were separated from soil samples by floating in water. However, the values for cultigens are by no means unqualified proxies for the relative quantities or proportions in which resources were produced or consumed. Many intervening factors affect the relationship between amounts of resources present during site occupations and amounts recovered or tabulated from archaeological samples. Such factors include the inherent likelihood of a resource's preservation by burning, site-specific conditions affecting deposition and preservation of charcoal, kinds of site contexts sampled, such as house floors, pits, or middens, and the volume of soil floated per sample. Nonstandardized methods of identification and tabulation also pose many difficulties in comparing different analysts' results. Nevertheless, broad patterns are apparent.

The groupings of sites in Table 4.2 reflect a cross section of times and places in the North American Southwest. Cultural, geographical, and chronological coverage is tempered by the accessibility of reports, analysis of sufficient samples, and the presentation of data in an appropriately quantified format. Sites were included only if the occurrence of a particular crop could be determined among all analyzed samples, a simple criterion but one that often is not met. Although the entries do not in any way comprise a rigorously or exhaustively drawn sample, neither do they reflect any systematic bias; many investigators selected the contexts to be sampled, and a variety of archaeobotanists generated the results.

Each series in Table 4.2 represents a set of analyses spanning early to late periods within one regional subdivision. Categories correspond to the major geographic and cultural subdivisions listed in Table 4.1, with the exception of a more geographically circumscribed series for the Tonto Basin. Extensive recent research in this portion of east-central Arizona has produced an abundant, relatively localized record of plant remains in an area designated as being of both Hohokam and Salado affiliation.

Corn is the foremost botanical indicator for tracing the history of agriculture in the North American Southwest and the role of cultigens in the subsistence systems of prehistoric southwestern societies. It is the only one of the three major food crops that is encountered with sufficient consistency in the archaeological record to permit comprehensive quantitative and distributional evaluation. Beans and squash are inherently less durable, were pre-

Table 4.2
Ubiquity and Presence Values for Macrobotanical Remains of Cultigens in Five Southwestern Sequences

Cultural Tradition	Time Period	Site Type	No. of Samples	Corn (Ubiquity)	Agave (Ubiquity)	Beans	Cucurbits	Cotton	Reference
Eastern Anasazi	AD 200–400	cave	28	90.0			X		Matson and Chisholm 1991
	AD 500–700	rockshelter	20c	60.0		X	X	X	Minnis 1989; Stiger 1979
	AD 900–1100	rockshelter	27c	90.0		X	X	X	Minnis 1989; Stiger 1979
	AD 1100–1300	rockshelter	139c	90.0		X	X	X	Minnis 1989; Stiger 1979
	AD 1000–1200	large and small pueblos	70	60.0					Toll 1984, 1985
	AD 1200–1250	pithouse	58	96.0		X	X	X	Toll 1988
	AD 1300–1425	large pueblo	174	86.0		X	X		Wetterstrom 1986
	AD 1350–1650	large pueblo	30	100.0		X	X		Toll 1987
Western Anasazi	200 BC–AD 200	pithouse	308	35.0					Ford et al. 1985; Wagner et al. 1984
	AD 200–400	pithouse	8	62.5					Donaldson 1991; Huckell 1987a
	AD 500–900	pithouse	13	100.0		X			Adams 1996
	AD 700–1100	pithouse	13	38.5					Adams 1994b, 1996
	AD 1070–1220	pithouse/pueblo	12	94.0		X	X	X	Hunter 1997
	AD 1300–1450	large pueblo	21	100.0		X	X	X	Miksicek 1991
	AD 1300–1450	large pueblo	92	85.0		X	X	X	Adams 1996
	AD 1300–1450	large pueblo	20	90.0		X	X	X	Donaldson and Miksicek 1990

	Date	Site type	n					Reference
Hohokam/Salado: Tonto Basin	AD 400–600	pithouse	12	75.0	16.7		X	Miksicek 1995
	AD 600–700	pithouse	16	31.5	12.5		X	Miksicek 1995
	AD 900–1100	pithouse	20	75.0	30.0		X	Miksicek 1995
	AD 1100–1250	compound/pueblo	98	69.4	60.2	X	X	Miksicek 1995
Hohokam	900–700 BC	pithouse	24	100.0	4.2			Huckell 1990
	700–300 BC	pithouse	109	81.5	1.2			Huckell 1998
	AD 1–300	pithouse	33	63.5			X	Huckell 1998
	AD 1–300	pithouse	41	73.2			X	Huckell 1987b
	AD 300–600	pithouse	32	53.1				Huckell 1998
	AD 300–600	pithouse	29	72.0	10.0	X		P. Fish et al. 1992
	AD 600–1100	pithouse	444	39.9	8.6		X	Bohrer 1987
	AD 600–1100	pithouse	128	60.9	21.1	X	X	Miksicek 1992
	AD 800–1400	pithouse/compound	582	73.9	27.1	X	X	Miksicek and Gasser 1989
Mogollon/ Casas Grandes	1300–800 BC	terraced hill	50	84		X	X	Hard and Roney 1999
	AD 250–900	pithouse	38	55.8			X	Minnis 1981
	AD 900–1100	pithouse/pueblo	35	57.1				Minnis 1981
	AD 1100–1300	pueblo	25	84.0			X	Minnis 1981
	AD 1300–1500	pueblo	52	76.9			X	Minnis 1981
	AD 1300–1500	pueblo	27	81.0	18.0	X	X	Whalen and Minnis 1997

Note: X = present, c = coprolite.

pared in ways less likely to produce carbonized remains, and are preserved quite sporadically in the majority of archaeological sites. Excavators recover seeds, rind, and stem fragments of squash and pumpkin most frequently in dry caves or other situations of unusual preservation. Such contexts and catastrophic fires are responsible for many of the instances of plentifully preserved beans. In contrast, charred corn kernels and cupules are regularly present in even the shallowly buried deposits of open-air sites. Carbonized cupules were generated by empty cobs used as fuel as well as by the accidental burning of cobs in the course of food preparation.

Values for corn and agave are presented in Table 4.2 as measures of ubiquity or presence. Ubiquity is calculated as the percentage of samples containing corn among all samples yielding charred remains. Ubiquity provides a useful means of comparison because very high quantities of a resource in only one or a few samples do not unduly influence the resulting distributional profile of a site or other sampling universe. Moreover, the ubiquity value for a cultigen is independently derived; it is not affected by the abundance or distribution of any other resource. Beans, squash, and cotton, on the other hand, are designated in Table 4.2 only as present or absent, in view of their inconsistent recovery and their low likelihood of preservation under many archaeological circumstances. These cultigens are generally better registered in analyses in which many rather than few samples were examined. Based on ethnographic analogy across the North American Southwest, it is unlikely that most prehistoric agriculturalists did not regularly consume squash and beans, yet there are many sites in which one or both of these crops were not identified. This sort of sporadic recovery contrasts strongly with that of corn. Conversely, a failure to recover corn would constitute compelling evidence that corn was not used.

The distribution of cotton among the analyses in Table 4.2 is more complicated. Like beans and squash, cotton fibers are less amenable to routine preservation than corn cupules and kernels, but the edible seeds are subject to accidental charring when roasted. Seeds are fairly common both in southern settlements such as those of the Hohokam and Salado and in areas farther north, such as later prehistoric Western Pueblo sites along the Little Colorado River in northern Arizona (e.g., Adams 1996; Gasser and Kwiatkowski 1991; Miksicek 1991). A further factor to consider in the overall distribution of cotton in the North American Southwest is its vulnerability to cold temperatures in locations with short growing seasons. For example, it would be much riskier, if not impossible in most years, to grow cotton in the uplands of southern Colorado at Mesa Verde than at low-lying Phoenix, Arizona. Nevertheless, cottonseeds and vegetative parts such as bolls have been recovered in locations of high elevation and cool climate, suggesting cultivation in the past at the extremes of environmental viability.

Two circumstances account for the restricted appearance of agave in Table 4.2. Ethnographic and, presumably, prehistoric use coincides fully with the natural geographic range of this succulent. Preliminary or well-established evidence for cultivation, however, a prerequisite for inclusion in Table 4.2, is at present limited to Arizona and surrounding areas in the south. For the cultural sequences in which cultivation is indicated, values for agave predating evidence of cultivation are also listed. The second factor affecting the representation of agave is the fact that identifications are usually missing from older flotation reports. Remains retrieved by this technique are sorted with a primary focus on seeds and wood charcoal. Agave seeds are seldom present because both wild and cultivated plants are typically harvested before a massive flower stalk emerges as the final event in the plant's life cycle, thereby depleting stored carbohydrates available for human consumption. Only in the mid-1980s did archaeobotanist Charles Miksicek pioneer the systematic search for burned tissue fragments and fibers, the most common agave residues. Flotation analysts have not yet standardized the recognition, identification, and quantification of these kinds of agave remains.

The most striking pattern in Table 4.2 is that of corn. Although some of the oldest assemblages containing corn in each cultural sequence are included in the table, no overall temporal trend is apparent in this crop's prominence from earlier to later times. Only in the Western Pueblo tradition is there a suggestion that households in the initial listing had significantly less access to corn than those in most succeeding entries. In both the Hohokam and Mimbres/Casas Grandes sequences, very early sites produce ubiquity values as high as those of any ensuing period. Early ubiquity values of this sort imply that regional inhabitants had even earlier experience with this cultigen than is currently documented. Although models of gradual incorporation of corn into foraging economies may simply be pushed farther back in time or be found to apply in other instances, the most comprehensive and fully reported analyses at present do not conform to expectations for these models.

After the initial time when charred plant assemblages with abundant corn are reported for an area, few exceptions to this emphasis occur in assemblages of the following sequence. Even though sample size varies greatly among entries in Table 4.2, ubiquity values exhibit a strong tendency toward the presence of corn in a majority of samples. Where ubiquity falls below this threshold, it is not in a context of sustained downward trends.

Beans, cucurbits, and cotton tend to be more fully represented in later segments of regional sequences. This tendency may be partially due to the larger number of analyzed samples from later sites and to the better preservation afforded by the more substantial architecture of later times. In Table 4.2 the Eastern Anasazi sequence provides a cautionary note. By considering only flotation results, the inference could be drawn that common and widespread use of these cultigens was delayed well into the first millennium AD. Results from another class of remains contradicts that timetable. The designation "c" following the number of samples in three instances indicates the results not of flotation but of analyses that identify the plant remains in prehistoric human feces, or coprolites. These "packages" encapsulating the constituents of short-term diet are usually recovered only under circumstances of unusually good preservation. Although coprolite sample numbers are much lower for the first two of the three Eastern Anasazi chronological divisions, beans, cucurbits, and cotton were identified in each set of coprolites, beginning with the earliest from AD 500–700. In general, beans are identified somewhat more frequently than cucurbits and cotton. However, even the highest sample numbers do not ensure the recovery of beans, cucurbits, and cotton from individual sites within regional sequences in which these cultigens are encountered over long time spans.

The analyses producing generally substantial ubiquity values for corn in Table 4.2 are drawn from sequences within the geographic core of the North American Southwest rather than from occupations along its peripheries. The results of these analyses concur with those reported by Robert Gasser (1982), who evaluated the contents of 417 flotation samples and 155 coprolites from areas throughout the northern Southwest. Corn was the most commonly recovered remain, occurring in 60 percent of flotation samples and 85 percent of the coprolites. It is certainly possible to find reports of low corn recovery from sites in the North American Southwest heartland, but in keeping with the agricultural contrasts that are fundamental to regional identity, such reports are more likely to come from sites near the area's borders. For example, a study assessing agricultural dependencies in southwestern sequences considered the combined variables of corn ubiquity, mano size, and human bone chemistry. In only one of four regional sequences with sufficient data for analysis did the authors detect a long period of minor corn use preceding increased dependence rather than substantial dependence from the start (Hard et al. 1996). That sequence is the Southern Jornada Mogollon, located near El Paso, Texas, on the eastern boundary of archaeological manifestations traditionally included within the sphere of southwestern cultures.

Crops, Agriculture, and Southwestern Societies

Involvement in agriculture and dependence on crops were central facts of life for ancient southwesterners, shaping their activities and relationships day after day. The joint pursuit of supplemental water for successful harvests linked individuals, households, and settlements in an arid region where opportunities for independent, rain-fed cultivation were exceptions rather than the rule. Massive irrigation networks on perennial rivers that connected multiple settlements are the well-known cases necessitating maximal interdependency among farmers, but simpler floodwater and runoff techniques also entailed close cooperation to fulfill needs for timely supplies of water. Exchange of agricultural labor also bridged households, kin groups, and even larger social units, entailing reciprocation of prepared foods, produce, or labor obligations.

Continuities in land tenure from postcontact times suggest that a parallel structure existed in the more distant past (Fish 2001). Puebloan farmers had claims to fields through clan membership defined by kinship through either the mother's or father's line. Farmers in southern groups gained use rights through more flexible bilateral kin relations, participation in agricultural improvements such as the construction of canals, and the consensus of village leaders and residents. Prehistoric societies undoubtedly followed similarly prescribed rules regulating access to agricultural land and production. The efforts of farmers to strengthen claims to productive land in the northern Southwest and sometimes elsewhere are apparent in stone markers and strategically placed rock art resembling the territorial markers of their postcontact descendants. The remains of seasonally occupied field houses dotting arable land in many regional sectors attest to the constant concern of farming households with labor-intensive yet vulnerable crops and fields.

During recent centuries, men have played the more visible role in southwestern agricultural labor. Social and demographic disruption following Spanish contact and the constant threat of mounted raiders may have deepened a previous regional tendency for men to have primary responsibility for fields. Heavy domestic demands on women—Hopi women, for instance, ground corn three to five hours per day (Bartlett 1933)—are another pertinent aspect of this pattern. Women's workloads associated with food processing and preparation appear to have increased during late prehistoric times (Crown 2001). Women also planted garden plots near their homes in which they grew crops requiring extra attention or filling special needs (Maxwell and Anscheutz 1992). At the household level, men are usually described as controlling agricultural land and crops in the field, whereas women are more often noted as controlling harvested and stored supplies and guiding the distribution of prepared food (Fish 2001).

Levels of nonessential production and accumulation permitted by agricultural economies are integral elements of hierarchical structures and power relations in the North American Southwest. Ethnographically, leaders were coordinators of communal hospitality and group welfare. In Eastern and Western Pueblo societies, rights to land, harvests, and communal labor were awarded to civic and ceremonial officeholders in support of these obligations. An association between public architecture and amassed subsistence supplies is indicated by such evidence as concentrations of crop remains (Fish 1989, 1998b) and substantial proportions of storage space in Hohokam platform mound compounds (Doyel 1974), burned granaries in Salado mound rooms (Lindaur 1992), and large numbers of nonresidential storage rooms at Chaco Canyon great houses (Lekson 1986; Windes 1987). Public areas contained cooking facilities of communal scale, as exemplified by large roasting pits at Casas Grandes in Chihuahua and Pueblo Grande in southern Arizona and by oversized hearths at Pueblo Bonito in Chaco Canyon, New Mexico. Archaeologists are currently investigating feasting in many parts of the region as an activity of aspiring elites to reinforce social prominence, create reciprocal obligations, and maintain power relations (e.g., Blinman 1989; Crown 1994; Graves and Eckert 1998; Mills 1999).

Cultigens in general, but particularly corn, are at the heart of rich, agriculturally oriented southwestern ideologies. A Mesoamerican flavor in symbolism and ritual regarding crops is a hallmark of regional belief systems. Accounts of the supernatural bestowal of corn and other cultivated plants on a favored human group are universal, as are planting, harvest, and storage rituals. Cotton is widely associated with urgently awaited clouds and water. Calendrics revolve around tracking and celebrating agricultural events and seasons. Southwestern ideologies underscore the central place of crops in indigenous societies and express unifying themes that reflect centuries of lifetimes spent in farming.

References Cited

Adams, E. Charles
    1979   Cold Air Drainage and Length of Growing Season in the Hopi Mesa Area. *Kiva* 44: 285–266.
    1983   The Architectural Analogue to Hopi Social Organization and Room Use, and Implications for Prehistoric Southwestern Culture. *American Antiquity* 48:44–61.

Adams, Jenny L.
    1998   Ground Stone Artifacts. In *Archaeological Investigations of Early Village Sites in the Middle Santa Cruz Valley*, edited by Jonathan Mabry, pp. 357–413. Anthropological Papers 19. Center for Desert Archaeology, Tucson.

Adams, Karen R.
    1994a   A Regional Synthesis of *Zea mays* in the Prehistoric American Southwest. In *Corn and Culture in the Prehistoric New World*, edited by Sissel Johannessen and Christine A. Hastorf, pp. 273–302. Westview Press, Boulder.
    1994b   Macrofloral Plant Remains from the Archer Site (AZ P:4:22 ASM), Holbrook, Arizona. In *River, Rain, or Ruin: Intermittent Prehistoric Land Use along the Middle Little Colorado River*, edited by Carla Van West, pp. 187–204. Technical Series 53. Statistical Research, Tucson.
    1996   Archaeobotany of the Middle Little Colorado River. In *River of Change: Prehistory of the Middle Little Colorado River Valley, Arizona*, edited by E. Charles Adams, pp. 163–186. Archaeological Series 185. Arizona State Museum, University of Arizona, Tucson.

Adams, Karen, and Mollie Toll
    2001   Tobacco (*Nicotiana*) Use and Manipulation in the Prehistoric and Historic Southwest. In *Tobacco Use by Native North Americans: Sacred Smoke and Silent Killer*, edited by Joseph C. Winter, pp. 145–170. University of Oklahoma Press, Norman.

Anderson, Edgar
    1948   Racial Identity of the Corn from Castle Park. In *The Archaeology of Castle Park, Dinosaur National Monument*, edited by Robert F. Burgh and Charles R. Scoggin, pp. 91–92. Series in Anthropology 2. University of Colorado, Boulder.
    1950   Food, Cultivated. In *The Stratigraphy and Archaeology of Ventana Cave, Arizona*, edited by Emil W. Haury, pp. 161–163. University of New Mexico Press, Albuquerque.

Bartlett, Katharine
    1933   *Pueblo Milling Stones of the Flagstaff Region and Their Relation to Others in the Southwest.* Museum of Northern Arizona, Flagstaff.

Beaglehole, Ernest
    1937   *Notes on Hopi Economic Life.* Publications in Anthropology 15. Yale University, New Haven.

Bean, Lowell J., and Katherine S. Saubel
    1972   *Temalpakh, Cahuilla Indian Knowledge and Usage of Plants.* Morongo Indian Reservation and Malki Museum Press, Banning, California.

Berry, Michael S.
    1982   *Time, Space, and Transition in Anasazi Prehistory.* University of Utah Press, Salt Lake City.

Blinman, Eric
    1989   Potluck in the Protokiva: Ceramics and Ceremonialism in Pueblo I Villages. In *The Architecture of Social Integration in Prehistoric Pueblos*, edited by William Lipe and Michelle Hegmon, pp. 113–124. Occasional Papers 1. Crow Canyon Archaeological Center, Cortez, Colorado.
    1993   Anasazi Pottery: Evolution of a Technology. *Expedition* 35:14–22.

Bohrer, Vorsila L.

1962   Nature and Interpretation of Ethnobotanical Materials from Tonto National Monument. In *Archaeological Studies at Tonto National Monument, Arizona*, vol. 2, edited by Charlie R. Steen, Lloyd M. Pierson, Vorsila L. Bohrer, and Kate Peck Kent, pp. 75–114. Technical Series. Southwestern Monuments Association, Globe, Arizona.

1983   And Before Crops Came: The Fresnal Shelter. *El Palacio* 89:13–14.

1987   The Plant Remains from La Ciudad, a Hohokam Site in Phoenix. In *La Ciudad: Specialized Studies in the Economy, Environment, and Culture of La Ciudad, Part III*, edited by Jo Ann E. Kisselburg, Glen E. Rice, and Brenda Shears, pp. 67–202. Anthropological Field Studies 20. Arizona State University, Tempe.

1991   Recently Recognized Cultivated and Encouraged Plants among the Hohokam. *Kiva* 56: 227–235.

1994   Maize in Middle American and Southwestern United States Agricultural Traditions. In *Corn and Culture in the Prehistoric New World*, edited by Sissel Johannessen and Christine Hastorf, pp. 469–512. Westview Press, Boulder.

Burton, Jeffery F.

1991   *The Archaeology of Sivu'ovi: The Archaic to Basketmaker Transition at Petrified Forest National Park*. Publications in Anthropology 55. Western Archaeological and Conservation Center, National Park Service, Tucson.

Carpenter, John P., Guadalupe Sánchez de Carpenter, and Elisa Villalpando

1998   Rescate Arqueológico La Playa (SON F: 10:3) Municipio de Trincheras, Sonora, México. Manuscript on file, Arizona State Museum Library, University of Arizona, Tucson.

Carter, George F.

1945   *Plant Geography and Cultural History in the American Southwest*. Publications in Archaeology 5. Viking Fund, New York.

Castetter, Edward F., and Willis M. Bell

1942   *Pima and Papago Indian Agriculture*. University of New Mexico Press, Albuquerque.

1951   *Yuman Indian Agriculture: Primitive Subsistence on the Lower Colorado and Gila Rivers*. University of New Mexico Press, Albuquerque.

Castetter, Edward F., Willis M. Bell, and Alvin R. Grove

1938   *Ethnobiological Studies in the American Southwest VI: The Early Utilization and the Distribution of Agave in the American Southwest*. Bulletin, Biological Series 5. University of New Mexico, Albuquerque.

Castetter, Edward F., and Ruth M. Underhill

1935   *Ethnobiological Studies in the American Southwest II: The Ethnobiology of the Papago Indians*. Bulletin, Biological Series 4. University of New Mexico, Albuquerque.

Chisholm, Brian, and R. G. Matson

1994   Carbon and Nitrogen Isotopic Evidence on Basketmaker II Diet at Cedar Mesa, Utah. *Kiva* 60:239–255.

Cordell, Linda

1997   *Archaeology of the Southwest*. 2nd ed. Academic Press, San Diego.

Crosswhite, Frank S.

1981   Desert Plants, Habitat, and Agriculture in Relation to the Major Pattern of Cultural Differentiation in the O'odham People of the Sonoran Desert. *Desert Plants* 3:47–76.

Crown, Patricia

1994   *Ceramics and Ideology*. University of New Mexico Press, Albuquerque.

2001   Women's Role in Changing Cuisine. In *Women and Men in the Prehispanic Southwest*, edited by Patricia Crown, pp. 221–266. School of American Research Press, Santa Fe.

Cushing, Frank H.

1974   *Zuni Breadstuff*. Museum of the American Indian, New York.

Cutler, Hugh C.

1952   A Preliminary Survey of Plant Remains of Tularosa Cave. In *Mogollon Cultural Continuity and Change*, edited by Paul Martin, John Rinaldo, Elaine Bluhm, Hugh Cutler, and Roger Grange, pp. 461–479. Fieldiana: Anthropology 40. Chicago Natural History Museum, Chicago.

1961   Vegetal Remains: Corn and Cucurbits. In *A Survey and Excavation of Caves in Hidalgo County, New Mexico*, edited by Marjorie Lambert and J. Richard Ambler, pp. 90–94. Monograph 25. School of American Research, Santa Fe.

1966   *Corn, Cucurbits, and Cotton from Glen Canyon*. Anthropological Papers 80. University of Utah Press, Salt Lake City.

1969   Plant Remains from Sites near Navajo Mountain. In *Survey and Excavation North and East of Navajo Mountain, Utah, 1959–1962*, edited by Alexander J. Lindsay Jr., J. Richard Ambler, Mary Ann Stein, and Phillip M. Hobler, pp. 371–378. Bulletin 45. Museum of Northern Arizona, Flagstaff.

Cutler, Hugh C., and Leonard Blake

1986   Botanical Analyses, Corn Analysis. In *The Kayenta Anasazi Archaeological Investigations along the Black Mesa Railroad Corridor*, edited by Sara Stebbins, Bruce Harrill, William Wade, Marsha Gallagher, Hugh Cutler, and Leonard Blake, pp. 88–103. Research Paper 30. Museum of Northern Arizona, Flagstaff.

Cutler, Hugh C., and Winton Meyer

1965   Corn and Cucurbits from Wetherill Mesa. In *Contributions of the Wetherill Mesa Project*, compiled by H. Douglas Osborne, pp. 136–152. Memoir 19. Society for American Archaeology, Menasha, Wisconsin.

Di Peso, Charles C.

1974   *Casas Grandes, a Fallen Trading Center of the Gran Chichimeca: 2. Medio Period*. Northland Press, Flagstaff.

Donaldson, Marcia L.

1991   Floral Remains. In *The Archaeology of Sivu'uovi: The Archaic to Basketmaker Transition at Petrified Forest National Park*, edited by Jeffrey F. Burton, pp. 85–90. Publications in Anthropology 55. Western Archaeological and Conservation Center, National Park Service, Tucson.

Donaldson, Marcia L., and Charles H. Miksicek

1990   Floral Remains. In *Archaeological Investigations at Puerco Ruin, Petrified Forest National Park, Arizona*, edited by Jeffrey F. Burton, pp. 231–254. Publications in Anthropology 54. Western Archaeological and Conservation Center, National Park Service, Tucson.

Doolittle, William W.

1990   *Canal Irrigation in Prehispanic Mexico: The Sequence of Technological Change*. University of Texas Press, Austin.

Doyel, David E.

1974   *Excavations in the Escalante Ruin Group, Southern Arizona*. Archaeological Series 37. Arizona State Museum, University of Arizona, Tucson.

1991   Hohokam Cultural Evolution in the Phoenix Basin. In *Exploring the Hohokam: Prehistoric Desert Peoples of the American Southwest*, edited by George J. Gumerman, pp. 231–278. University of New Mexico Press, Albuquerque.

Elson, Mark D.

1986   *Archaeological Investigations at the Tanque Verde Wash Site: A Middle Rincon Settlement in the Eastern Tucson Basin*. Anthropological Papers 7. Institute for American Research, Tucson.

Suzanne K. Fish

Elson, Mark D., Suzanne Fish, Steven James, and Charles Miksicek
   1995   Prehistoric Subsistence in the Roosevelt Community Development Study Area. In *The Roosevelt Community Development Study: 3. Paleobotanical and Osteological Analyses*, edited by Mark Elson and Jeffery Clark, pp. 217–260. Anthropological Papers 14. Center for Desert Archaeology, Tucson.

Felger, Richard S., and Mary Beck Moser
   1985   *People of the Desert and Sea: Ethnobotany of the Seri Indians*. University of Arizona Press, Tucson.

Fish, Paul R., and Suzanne K. Fish
   2000   The Marana Mound Site: Patterns of Social Differentiation in the Early Classic Period. In *The Hohokam Village Revisited*, edited by David Doyel, Suzanne Fish, and Paul Fish. American Association for the Advancement of Science, Glenwood Springs, Colorado.

Fish, Paul R., Suzanne K. Fish, John Madsen, Charles Miksicek, and Christine Szuter
   1992   The Dairy Site: Occupational Continuity on an Alluvial Fan. In *The Marana Community in the Hohokam World*, edited by Suzanne Fish and Paul Fish, pp. 64–72. Anthropological Papers 56. University of Arizona Press, Tucson.

Fish, Suzanne
   1989   Hohokam Plant Use at Las Colinas: The Pollen Evidence. In *The 1982–1984 Excavations at Las Colinas: Environment and Subsistence*, edited by D. A. Graybill, David A. Gregory, F. Nials, Suzanne Fish, Charles Miksicek, Robert Gasser, and Christine Szuter, pp. 79–93. Archaeological Series 162. Cultural Resource Management Division, Arizona State Museum, University of Arizona, Tucson.

   1998a   Cultural Pollen. In *Archaeological Investigations of Early Village Sites in the Middle Santa Cruz Valley*, edited by Jonathan Mabry, pp. 149–164. Anthropological Papers 19. Center for Desert Archaeology, Tucson.

   1998b   A Pollen Perspective on Variability and Stability in Tonto Basin Subsistence. In *Environment and Subsistence in the Classic Period Tonto Basin*, edited by Katherine A. Spielmann, pp. 49–86. Anthropological Field Studies 39. Office of Cultural Resource Management, Department of Anthropology, Arizona State University, Tempe.

Fish, Suzanne K., and Paul R. Fish
   1991   Comparative Aspects of Paradigms for the Neolithic Transition in the Levant and the American Southwest. In *Perspectives on the Past: Theoretical Biases in Hunter-Gatherer Research*, edited by Geoffrey A. Clark, pp. 396–410. University of Pennsylvania Press, Philadelphia.

   1994   Prehistoric Desert Farmers of the Southwest. *Annual Review of Anthropology* 23:83–109.

   2001   Farming, Foraging, and Gender. In *Women and Men in the Prehispanic Southwest*, edited by Patricia Crown, pp. 169–196. School of American Research Press, Santa Fe.

Fish, Suzanne K., Paul R. Fish, and John Madsen
   1990   Sedentism and Settlement Mobility in the Tucson Basin Prior to AD 1000. In *Perspectives on Southwestern Prehistory*, edited by Paul Minnis and Charles Redman, pp. 76–91. Westview Press, Boulder.

   1992   Evidence for Large-Scale Agave Cultivation in the Marana Community. In *The Marana Community in the Hohokam World*, edited by Suzanne Fish, Paul Fish, and John Madsen, pp. 73–87. Anthropological Papers 56. University of Arizona Press, Tucson.

Fish, Suzanne K., Paul Fish, Charles Miksicek, and John Madsen
   1985   Prehistoric Agave Cultivation in Southern Arizona. *Desert Plants* 7:107–113.

Fish, Suzanne K., and Gary P. Nabhan
   1991   Desert as Context: The Hohokam Environment. In *Exploring the Hohokam: Prehistoric*

Desert People of the American Southwest, edited by George Gumerman, pp. 29–60. University of New Mexico Press, Albuquerque.

Ford, Richard I.
  1980   The Color of Survival. *Discovery* 1980:17–30.
  1981   Gardening and Farming before AD 1000: Patterns of Prehistoric Cultivation North of Mexico. *Journal of Ethnobiology* 1:6–27.
  1985   Patterns of Prehistoric Food Production in North America. In *Prehistoric Food Production in North America*, edited by Richard I. Ford, pp. 341–364. Anthropological Papers 75. University of Michigan, Museum of Anthropology, Ann Arbor.
  1994   Corn Is Our Mother. In *Corn and Culture in the Prehistoric New World*, edited by Sissel Johannessen and Christine Hastorf, pp. 513–526. Westview Press, Boulder.

Freeman, L. G., Jr.
  1968   A Theoretical Framework for Interpreting Archaeological Materials. In *Man the Hunter*, edited by Richard Lee and Irven DeVore, pp. 262–267. Aldine, Chicago.

Fritz, Gayle, Karen R. Adams, Robert Hard, and John Roney
  1999   Evidence for Cultivation of *Amaranthus* sp. (Amaranthaceae) 3,000 Years ago at Cerro Juanaqueña, Chihuahua. Paper presented at the 22nd Annual Conference, Society of Ethnobiology, Oaxaca, Mexico.

Galinat, Walton C., and James H. Gunnerson
  1963   Spread of Eight-Rowed Maize from the Prehistoric Southwest. *Harvard University Botanical Museum Leaflets* 20:117–160.

Galinat, Walton C., Theodore Reinhart, and Theodore Frisbie
  1970   Early Eight Rowed Maize from the Middle Rio Grande Valley, New Mexico. *Harvard University Botanical Museum Leaflets* 22:313–331.

Gasser, Robert E.
  1982   Anasazi Diet. In *The Coronado Project Archaeological Investigations, the Specialists' Volume: Biocultural Analyses*, edited by Robert E. Gasser, pp. 8–95. Research Paper 23. Museum of Northern Arizona, Flagstaff.

Gasser, Robert E., and Scott M. Kwiatkowski
  1991   Food for Thought: Recognizing Patterns in Hohokam Subsistence. In *Exploring the Hohokam: Prehistoric Desert Peoples of the American Southwest*, edited by George Gumerman, pp. 417–460. University of New Mexico Press, Albuquerque.

Gentry, Howard Scott
  1963   *The Warihio Indians of Sonora-Chihuahua: An Ethnographic Survey*. Bulletin 186. Bureau of American Ethnology, Smithsonian Institution, Washington, DC.
  1982   *Agaves of Continental North America*. University of Arizona Press, Tucson.

Gilman, Patricia A.
  1983   *Changing Architectural Forms in the Prehistoric Southwest*. Unpublished PhD dissertation, Department of Anthropology, University of New Mexico, Albuquerque.

Gilpin, Dennis
  1994   Lukachukai and Salinas Springs: Late Archaic/Early Basketmaker Habitation Sites in the Chinle Valley, Northeastern Arizona. *Kiva* 60:203–218.

Graves, William, and Suzanne Eckert
  1998   Decorated Ceramic Distributions and Ideological Developments in the Northern Rio Grande Valley, New Mexico. In *Migration and Reorganization: The Pueblo IV Period in the American Southwest*, by Katherine Spielmann, pp. 264–284. Anthropological Research Paper 51. Arizona State University, Tempe.

Suzanne K. Fish

Gregory, David
  1999   *Excavations in the Santa Cruz River Floodplain: The Middle Archaic Component at Los Pozos.*
          Anthropological Papers 20. Center for Desert Archaeology, Tucson.
Hack, John T.
  1942   *The Changing Physical Environment of the Hopi Indians of Arizona.* Papers of the Peabody
          Museum of American Archaeology and Ethnology 35. Harvard University, Cambridge.
Hall, Robert L.
  1975   Cultivars from Antelope House. *Kiva* 41:49–56.
Hammett, Julia
  1993   Paleoethnobotanical Evidence of Tobacco Use along the Transwestern Pipeline. In *Across
          the Colorado Plateau: Anthropological Studies for the Transwestern Pipeline Expansion Project:
          25. Subsistence and Environment*, edited by Jannifer Gish, Julia Hammett, M. Brown,
          Pamela McBride, Joseph Winter, K. Brown, J. Ponczynski, and J. DeLanois, pp. 509–518.
          Office of Contract Archaeology, University of New Mexico, Albuquerque.
Hard, Robert J., Raymond Mauldin, and Gerry Raymond
  1996   Mano Size, Stable Carbon Isotope Ratios, and Macrobotanical Remains as Multiple
          Lines of Evidence of Maize Dependence in the American Southwest. *Journal of Archaeo-
          logical Method and Theory* 3:253–318.
Hard, Robert J., and John R. Roney
  1998   A Massive Terraced Village Complex in Chihuahua, Mexico, 3000 Years Before Present.
          Science 279:1661–1664.
  1999   *An Archaeological Investigation of Late Archaic Cerros de Trincheras Sites in Chihuahua,
          Mexico.* Special Report 25. Center for Archaeological Research, University of Texas, San
          Antonio.
Hastings, James Rodney, and Raymond M. Turner
  1965   *The Changing Mile: An Ecological Study of Vegetation Change with Time in the Lower Mile of
          an Arid and Semi-Arid Region.* University of Arizona Press, Tucson.
Haury, Emil W.
  1945   *The Excavations of Los Muertos and Neighboring Ruins in the Salt River Valley, Southern Ari-
          zona.* Papers of the Peabody Museum of American Archaeology and Ethnology 24. Har-
          vard University, Cambridge.
  1962   The Greater American Southwest. In *Courses Toward Urban Life: Some Archaeological Con-
          siderations of Cultural Alternatives*, edited by Robert J. Braidwood and Gordon R. Willey,
          pp. 106–131. Publications in Anthropology 32. Viking Fund, New York.
  1976   *The Hohokam: Desert Farmers and Craftsmen.* University of Arizona Press, Tucson.
Heidke, James M., Elizabeth Miksa, and Michael Wiley
  1998   Ceramic Artifacts. In *Archaeological Investigations of Early Village Sites in the Middle Santa
          Cruz Valley*, edited by Jonathan Mabry, pp. 471–544. Anthropological Papers 19. Center
          for Desert Archaeology, Tucson.
Heiser, Charles B., Jr.
  1985   Some Botanical Considerations of the Early Domesticated Plants North of Mexico. In
          Prehistoric Food Production in North America, edited by Richard I. Ford, pp. 57–72. An-
          thropological Papers 75. Museum of Anthropology, University of Michigan, Ann Arbor.
Hernandez, Efraim
  1985   Maize and Man in the North American Southwest. *Economic Botany* 39:416–430.
Hodgson, Wendy, Gary P. Nabhan, and Liz Ecker
  1989   Prehistoric Fields in Central Arizona: Conserving Rediscovered Agave Cultivars. *Agave*
          3(3):9–11.

Hodgson, Wendy, and Liz A. Slauson

1995   *Agave delamateri* (Agavaceae) and Its Role in the Subsistence Patterns of Pre-Columbian Cultures in Arizona. *Haseltonia* 3:130–140.

Huckell, Bruce B.

1990   *Late Preceramic Farmer-Foragers in Southeastern Arizona: A Cultural and Ecological Consideration of the Spread of Agriculture into the Arid Southwestern United States.* PhD dissertation, Arid Lands Resource Sciences, University of Arizona, Tucson.

1995   *Of Marshes and Maize: Preceramic Agricultural Settlements in the Cienega Valley, Southeastern Arizona.* Anthropological Papers 59. University of Arizona Press, Tucson.

Huckell, Lisa W.

1987a   Plant Remains from an Archaic Site (AZ K:13:60 ASM) in Petrified Forest National Park. In *Contributions to the Archaeology of Petrified Forest National Park, 1985–1986*, edited by A. Trinkle Jones. Publications in Anthropology 45. Western Archaeological and Conservation Center, National Park Service, Tucson.

1987b   Archaeobotanical Remains. In *The Corona de Tucson Project: Prehistoric Use of a Bajada Environment*, edited by Bruce B. Huckell, Martyn D. Tagg, and Lisa W. Huckell, pp. 221–259. Archaeological Series 174. Arizona State Museum, University of Arizona, Tucson.

1993   Plant Remains from the Pinaleño Cotton Cache. *Kiva* 59:147–204.

1998   Macrobotanical Remains. In *Archaeological Investigations of Early Village Sites in the Middle Santa Cruz Valley*, edited by Jonathan Mabry, pp. 57–148. Anthropological Papers 19. Center for Desert Archaeology, Tucson.

Hunter, Andrea

1997   Seeds, Cucurbits, and Corn from Lizard Man Village. *Kiva* 62:221–244.

Kaplan, Lawrence, and Thomas Lynch

1999   *Phaseolus* (Fabaceae) in Archaeology: AMS Radiocarbon Dates and Their Significance for Pre-Columbian Agriculture. *Economic Botany* 53:261–272.

Katz, S. H., M. L. Hediger, and L. A. Valleroy

1974   Traditional Maize Processing Techniques in the New World. *Science* 184:765–773.

Kent, Kate Peck

1983   *Prehistoric Textiles of the Southwest.* School of American Research, Santa Fe.

Kirchhoff, Paul

1954   Gatherers and Farmers of the Greater Southwest. *American Anthropologist* 56:529–550.

Kuhnlein, Harriet V.

1986   Food Sample Collection for Nutrient Analyses in Ethnobiological Studies. *Journal of Ethnobiology* 6:19–25.

Lancaster, James W.

1983   *An Analysis of Manos and Metates from the Mimbres Valley, New Mexico.* Unpublished master's thesis, Department of Anthropology, University of New Mexico, Albuquerque.

Lange, Charles

1960   *Cochiti: A New Mexico Pueblo, Past and Present.* University of Texas Press, Austin.

Lekson, Stephen H.

1986   *Great Pueblo Architecture of Chaco Canyon, New Mexico.* University of New Mexico Press, Albuquerque.

Lindauer, Owen

1992   Centralized Storage: Evidence from a Salado Platform Mound. In *Developing Perspectives on Tonto Basin Prehistory*, edited by Charles L. Redman, Glen E. Rice, and K. Pedrick, pp. 33–44. Anthropological Field Studies 26. Department of Anthropology, Arizona State University, Tempe.

Lipe, William D.
  1989   Social Scale of Mesa Verde Anasazi Kivas. In *The Architecture of Social Integration in Pre-*
          historic Pueblos, edited by William D. Lipe and Michelle Hegmon, pp. 53–71. Occasional
          Papers 1. Crow Canyon Archaeological Center, Cortez, Colorado.
Lister, Robert H.
  1958   *Archaeological Excavations in the Northern Sierra Madre Occidental, Chihuahua and Sonora,*
          Mexico. Series in Anthropology 7. University of Colorado, Boulder.
Long, Austin, Bruce F. Benz, D. J. Donahue, A. J. T. Jull, and L. J. Toolin
  1989   First Direct AMS Dates on Early Maize from Tehuacan, Mexico. *Radiocarbon* 31:1035–1040.
Lumholtz, Carl
  1902   *Unknown Mexico.* Charles Schribner's Sons, New York.
Mabry, Jonathan B.
  1998   *Archaeological Investigations of Early Village Sites in the Middle Santa Cruz Valley.* Anthropo-
          logical Papers 19. Center for Desert Archaeology, Tucson.
  In press Excavations at Las Capas, AA:12:111 (ASM). Anthropological Papers 28. Center for
          Desert Archaeology, Tucson.
MacNeish, Richard S.
  1958   *Preliminary Archaeological Investigations in the Sierra de Tamaulipas, Mexico.* Transactions of
          the American Philosophical Society 44. Philadelphia.
Mangelsdorf, Paul C., and Robert H. Lister
  1956   Archaeological Evidence on the Diffusion and Evolution of Maize in Northern Mexico.
          Harvard University Botanical Museum Leaflets 17:151–178.
Martin, Steve L.
  1999   Virgin Anasazi Diet as Demonstrated through the Analysis of Stable Carbon and Nitro-
          gen Isotopes. *Kiva* 64:495–514.
Matson, R. G.
  1991   *The Origins of Southwestern Agriculture.* University of Arizona Press, Tucson.
Matson, R. G., and Brian Chisholm
  1991   Basketmaker II Subsistence: Carbon Isotopes and Other Indicators from Cedar Mesa.
          American Antiquity 56:444–459.
Maxwell, Timothy D., and Kurt F. Anschuetz
  1992   The Southwestern Ethnographic Record and Prehistoric Agricultural Diversity. In *Gar-*
          dens in Prehistory, edited by Thomas Killion, pp. 35–69. University of Alabama Press,
          Tuscaloosa.
Miksicek, Charles H.
  1991   Paleoethnobotany. In *Homol'ovi II: The Archaeology of an Ancestral Hopi Village*, edited by
          E. Charles Adams and Kelley Ann Hays, pp. 88–102. Anthropological Papers 55. Univer-
          sity of Arizona Press, Tucson.
  1992   The Verde Bridge Project: A View from Float Tank. In *Prehistoric and Historic Occupation*
          of the Lower Verde River Valley: The State Route 87 Verde Bridge Project, edited by Mark R.
          Hackbarth, pp. 313–338. Northland Research, Flagstaff.
  1995   Temporal Trends in the Eastern Tonto Basin: An Archaeological Perspective. In *The*
          Roosevelt Community Development Study: 3. Paleobotanical and Osteological Analyses, edited by
          Mark D. Elson and Jeffrey J. Clark, pp. 43–84. Anthropological Papers 14. Center for
          Desert Archaeology, Tucson.
Miksicek, Charles H., and Robert E. Gasser
  1989   Hohokam Plant Use at Las Colinas: The Flotation Evidence. In *The 1982–1984 Exca-*
          vations at Las Colinas: Environment and Subsistence, edited by D. A. Graybill, D. A. Gre-

gory, F. L. Nials, Suzanne Fish, Robert Gasser, Charles Miksicek, and Christine Szuter, pp. 115–145. Archaeological Series 162. Arizona State Museum, Tucson.

Mills, Barbara J.
    1999   Ceramics and the Social Contexts of Food Consumption in the Northern Southwest. In *Pottery and People: Dynamic Interactions*, edited by James Skibo and Gary Feinman, pp. 99–114. University of Utah Press, Salt Lake City.

Mindeleff, Victor
    1891   A Study of Pueblo Architecture in Tusayan and Cibola. *Eighth Annual Report of the Bureau of American Ethnology for the Years 1886–1887*, pp. 3–228. Smithsonian Institution, Washington, DC.

Minnis, Paul E.
    1981   *Economic and Organizational Responses to Food Stress by Non-Stratified Societies: A Prehistoric Example*. Unpublished PhD dissertation, Department of Anthropology, University of Michigan, Ann Arbor.
    1985   *Social Adaptation to Food Stress: A Prehistoric Southwestern Example*. University of Chicago Press, Chicago.
    1989   Prehistoric Diet in the Northern Southwest: Macroplant Remains from Four Corners Feces. *American Antiquity* 54:543–563.
    1992   Early Plant Cultivation in the Desert Borderlands of the American West. In *The Origins of Agriculture: An International Perspective*, edited by C. Wesley Cowan and Patty Jo Watson, pp. 121–141. Smithsonian Institution Press, Washington, DC.

Morris, Donald H.
    1990   Changes in Groundstone Following the Introduction of Maize into the American Southwest. *Journal of Anthropological Research* 46:177–194.

Nabhan, Gary Paul
    1979   Southwestern Indian Sunflowers. *Desert Plants* 1:23–26.
    1983   Hopi Protection of *Helianthus anomalus*, a Rare Sunflower. *Southwestern Naturalist* 28:231–235.
    1985   *Gathering the Desert*. University of Arizona Press, Tucson.
    1995   Finding the Hidden Garden. *Journal of the Southwest* 37:401–413.

Nabhan, Gary Paul, and Richard Felger
    1978   Teparies in Southwestern North America: A Biogeographical and Ethnohistorical Study of *Phaseolus acutifolius*. *Economic Botany* 32:2–19.

Ortiz, Alfonso
    1994   Some Cultural Meanings of Corn in Aboriginal North America. In *Corn and Culture in the Prehistoric New World*, edited by Sissel Johannessen and Christine Hastorf, pp. 527–544. Westview Press, Boulder.

Pennington, Cambell W.
    1963   *The Tarahumar of Mexico: Their Environment and Material Culture*. University of Utah Press, Salt Lake City.
    1969   *The Tepehuan of Chihuahua: Their Material Culture*. University of Utah Press, Salt Lake City.
    1980   *The Pima Bajo of Central Sonora, Mexico*. University of Utah Press, Salt Lake City.

Prudden, T. Mitchell
    1903   The Prehistoric Ruins of the San Juan Watershed of Utah, Arizona, Colorado, and New Mexico. *American Anthropologist* 5:224–228.

Russell, Frank
    1975   *The Pima Indians*. Reprinted. University of Arizona Press, Tucson. Originally published,

1908, 26th Annual Report of the Bureau of American Ethnology for the Years 1904–
1905. Smithsonian Institution, Washington, DC.

Sánchez de Carpenter, Guadalupe
1998   *Of Roasting Pits and Plants: A Preliminary Analysis of Archaeobotanical Remains from La Playa,
Sonora, Mexico.* Unpublished master's thesis, Department of Anthropology, University of
Arizona, Tucson.

Sánchez-Gonzalez, Jose L.
1994   Modern Variability and Patterns of Maize Movement in Mesoamerica. In *Corn and Culture in the Prehistoric New World,* edited by Sissel Johannessen and Christine A. Hastorf,
pp. 135–156. Westview Press, Boulder.

Schoeninger, Margaret J., and Katherine Moore
1992   Bone Stable Isotope Studies in Archaeology. *Journal of World Prehistory* 6:247–296.

Schoeninger, Margaret J., and Mark R. Schurr
1994   Interpreting Carbon Stable Isotope Ratios. In *Corn and Culture in the Prehistoric New World,*
edited by Sissel Johannessen and Christine A. Hastorf, pp. 57–66. Westview Press, Boulder.

Schoenwetter, James, and Frank W. Eddy
1964   *Alluvial and Palynological Reconstruction of Environments, Navajo Reservoir District.* Papers in
Anthropology 13. Laboratory of Anthropology, Museum of New Mexico, Santa Fe.

Simmons, Alan
1986   New Evidence for the Early Use of Cultigens in the American Southwest. *American Antiquity* 51:73–88.

Smiley, Francis E.
1994   The Agricultural Transition in the Northern Southwest: Patterns on the Current
Chronometric Data. *Kiva* 60:165–189.

Smiley, Francis E., and William J. Parry
1990   Early, Intensive, and Rapid: Rethinking the Agricultural Transition in the Northern
Southwest. Paper presented at the 55th Annual Meeting of the Society for American Archaeology, Las Vegas.

Smith, Bruce D.
1997   The Initial Domestication of *Cucurbita pepo* in the Americas 10,000 Years Ago. *Science*
276:932–934.

Snow, David H.
1990   Tener Comal y Metate: Prothistoric Rio Grande Maize Use and Diet. In *Perspectives on
Southwestern Prehistory,* edited by Paul E. Minnis and Charles L. Redman, pp. 289–300.
Westview Press, Boulder.

Spier, Leslie
1970   *Yuman Tribes of the Gila River.* Cooper Square, New York.

Stahl, Ann B.
1989   Plant-Food Processing: Implications for Dietary Quality. In *Foraging and Farming:
The Evolution of Plant Exploitation,* edited by David R. Harris and Gordon C. Hillman,
pp. 171–186. Unwin Hyman, London.

Stevenson, Matilda Coxe
1915   *Ethnobotany of the Zuni Indians.* 30th Annual Report of the Bureau of American Ethnology, 1901–1902, pp. 1–634. Smithsonian Institution, Washington, DC.

Stiger, Mark A.
1979   Mesa Verde Subsistence Patterns from Basketmaker to Pueblo III. *Kiva* 44:133–144.

Tagg, Martyn D.
1996   Early Cultigens from Fresnal Shelter, Southeastern New Mexico. *American Antiquity*
61:311–325.

Teague, Lynne

1998   *Prehistoric Southwestern Textiles*. University of New Mexico Press, Albuquerque.

Toll, Mollie

1984   Taxonomic Diversity in Flotation and Macrobotanical Assemblages from Chaco Canyon. In *Recent Research on Chaco Prehistory*, edited by W. James Judge and John D. Schelberg, pp. 241–250. Reports of the Chaco Center 8. National Park Service, US Department of the Interior, Albuquerque.

1985   An Overview of Chaco Canyon Macrobotanical Materials and Analyses to Date. In *Environment and Subsistence of Chaco Canyon, New Mexico*, edited by F. J. Mathein, pp. 247–277. National Park Service, US Department of the Interior, Albuquerque.

1987   Floral Evidence for Subsistence Practices at the Piro Pueblo of Qualacu. In *Qualacu: Archaeological Investigation of a Piro Pueblo*, edited by Michael P. Marshall, pp. 111–119. Office of Contract Archaeology, University of New Mexico, Albuquerque.

1988   *Botanical Studies at an Extensive 13th Century Pithouse Village in the Southern Rio Grande Valley, New Mexico: LA 53662, Belen Bridge*. Technical Series 235. Castetter Laboratory for Ethnobotanical Studies, University of New Mexico, Albuquerque.

Upham, Steadman, Richard S. MacNeish, Walton Galinat, and Christopher M. Stevenson

1987   Evidence Concerning the Origin of Maiz de Ocho. *American Anthropologist* 89:410–419.

Van der Merwe, N. J.

1982   Carbon Isotopes, Photosynthesis, and Archaeology. *American Scientist* 70:596–606.

Vestal, Paul A.

1952   *Ethnobotany of the Ramah Navajo*. Papers of the Peabody Museum of American Archaeology and Ethnology 40. Harvard University, Cambridge.

Wandsnider, LuAnn

1997   The Roasted and the Boiled: Food Composition and Heat Treatment with Special Emphasis on Pit-Hearth Cooking. *Journal of Anthropological Archaeology* 16:1–48.

Wetterstrom, Wilma

1986   *Food, Diet, and Population at Prehistoric Arroyo Hondo Pueblo, New Mexico*. Arroyo Hondo Archaeological Series 6. School of American Research Press, Santa Fe.

Whalen, Michael E., and Paul E. Minnis

1997   Investigaciones Especializadas Sobre El Sistema Regional de Paquimé, Chihuahua, México. Informe Técnico al Consejo de Arqueología, Instituto Nacional de Antropología e Historia, Mexico. Manuscript on file at the University of Oklahoma, University of Tulsa, and INAH Chihuahua.

Whiting, Alfred

1939   *Ethnobotany of the Hopi*. Bulletin 15. Museum of Northern Arizona, Flagstaff.

Whittlesey, Stephanie M.

1995   Early Formative Stage Ceramics and Cultural Affiliation. In *Early Farmers of the Sonoran Desert: Archaeological Investigations of the Houghton Road Site, Tucson, Arizona*, edited by Richard Ciolek-Torrello, pp. 209–228. Technical Series 72. Statistical Research, Tucson.

Wills, Wirt H.

1988   *Early Prehistoric Agriculture in the American Southwest*. School of American Research Press, Santa Fe.

1996   The Transition from the Preceramic to Ceramic Period in the Mogollon Highlands of Western New Mexico. *Journal of Field Archaeology* 23:335–359.

Wills, Wirt H., and Bruce B. Huckell

1994   Economic Implications of Changing Land-Use Patterns in the Late Archaic. In *Themes in Southwest Prehistory*, edited by George Gumerman, pp. 33–52. School of American Research Press, Santa Fe.

Windes, Thomas C.
  1987   *Investigations at the Pueblo Alto Complex, Chaco Canyon, New Mexico, 1975–1979.* Publications in Archaeology 18F, Chaco Studies. National Park Service, US Department of the Interior, Santa Fe.
Winter, Joseph C.
  1973   The Distribution and Development of Fremont Maize Agriculture: Some Preliminary Interpretations. *American Antiquity* 38:439–452.
Winter, Joseph C., and Patrick F. Hogan
  1986   Plant Husbandry in the Great Basin and Adjacent Northern Colorado Plateau. In *Anthropology of the Desert West: Essays in Honor of Jesse D. Jennings*, edited by Carol J. Condie and Don D. Fowler, pp. 117–144. Anthropological Papers 110. University of Utah Press, Salt Lake City.
Wright, Karen
  2000   *Archaeobotanical Evidence of Cotton,* Gossypium hirsutum *var.* punctatum, *on the Southern Colorado Plateau.* Unpublished master's thesis, Department of Anthropology, Northern Arizona University, Flagstaff.
Yarnell, Richard A.
  1977   Native Plant Husbandry North of Mexico. In *Origins of Agriculture*, edited by Charles A. Reed, pp. 861–875. Mouton, The Hague.
Young, Lisa C.
  1996   Pits, Rooms, Baskets, Pots: Storage among Southwestern Farmers. In *Interpreting Southwestern Diversity: Underlying Principles and Overarching Patterns*, edited by Paul Fish and J. Jefferson Reid, pp. 201–210. Anthropological Research Papers 48. Department of Anthropology, Arizona State University, Tempe.

Anthropogenic Ecology of the North American Southwest

KAREN R. ADAMS

nthropogenic ecology documents the nature and scale of human modifications to the land, and the many interrelationships that exist between humans and landscapes. Assessing anthropogenic effects on ancient environments, however, can be quite complicated. For example, how prehistoric humans intentionally and unintentionally affected lands around them is frequently interpreted via the archaeobotanical record of plants preserved in dwellings and communities, a record heavily biased toward cultural perceptions and uses of plants and only indirectly reflecting human actions on the land. Complicating the task, landscapes are continually changing for natural reasons, such as climate shifts, short-term events, and evolution (Betancourt et al. 1993). The passage of centuries both mutes and blends the evidence of human and natural actions. Finally, modern environmental assessments are unable to provide direct analogs for interpreting prehistoric land alteration because of factors such as historic fire suppression, extensive domestic animal grazing, use of the steel plow and fertilizers, and the presence of a weedy, alien flora, all unknown before Columbus.

Because of the difficulties in recognizing human effects on long past environments, I assess anthropogenic ecology in the prehistoric North American Southwest from two interwoven points of view. An ethnographic perspective that provides a rich reservoir of historical Native American interactions with the land offers a starting framework for understanding the range and diversity of prehistoric land modifications. I then combine this framework with archaeological case studies, whenever possible, to suggest the breadth of past human impacts on southwestern environments. For reference, Table 5.1 contains all common plant names and their scientific counterparts reported here, and Figure 5.1 locates all major geographic landmarks, prehistoric culture areas, and modern groups.

Biological Organization

Rather than a traditional prehistoric culture area or chronological perspective, I employ a biological organization here to consider human impacts on entire *ecosystems*, then on specific plant *populations*, and finally on individual *organisms*. Landscape impacts are assumed to be most significant when an entire ecosystem is affected, for example, by intentional burning, by extensive cultivation, or through repeated collecting of major resources such as wood. Activities that foster, suppress, or otherwise alter a particular plant population would have a less immediate, but perhaps cumulative impact on an environment over time. Direct manipulations of individual plants would be least likely to lead to any long-lasting environmental changes but were nevertheless undoubtedly practiced widely in prehistoric times. Another format for considering anthropogenic effects on past environments, exemplified by Hammett (1992), is that of landscape ecology (Forman and Gordon 1986).

Ecosystems

An ecosystem comprises nonliving (sun, substrate, water, heat) and living (producers, consumers, decomposers, transformers) components, in which the exchange of most components follows circular paths (Odum 1966). Ecosystems are considered to be self-perpetuating. Humans can be viewed as one species cycling energy and matter between plants, animals, and inorganic matter within ecosystems (Lewis 1973:13).

As an ecosystem moves toward a state of stability, the biotic communities work through a series of changes termed "succession." When this process occurs in an area previously inhabited by biotic organisms, the recovery is con-

Table 5.1

Common and Scientific Names of Plants

Common Name	Scientific Name
Agave	*Agave; A. parryi*
Aspen	*Populus tremuloides*
Barberry	*Berberis*
Bean	*Phaseolus*
Beeweed	*Cleome serrulata*
Bitterbrush	*Purshia*
Box elder	*Acer negundo*
Buckbrush	*Ceanothus*
Cattail	*Typha*
Cholla	*Opuntia*
Contrayerba	*Kallstroemia*
Corn	*Zea mays*
Cottonwood	*Populus*
Creosotebush	*Larrea*
Cucurbita	*Cucurbita; C. foetidissima*
Devil's claw	*Martynia*
Dropseed grass	*Sporobolus*
Evening primrose	*Oenothera*
Globemallow	*Sphaeralcea*
Goosefoot	*Chenopodium*
Grass	Gramineae
Groundcherry	*Physalis*
Juniper	*Juniperus*
Lemonadeberry	*Rhus aromatica; R. trilobata*
Mint	*Salvia; S. dorrii*
Mountain mahogany	*Cercocarpus*
Mustard	*Schoencrambe*
Mutton grass	*Poa fendleriana*
New Mexico locust	*Robinia neomexicana*
Onion	*Allium*
Panic grass	*Panicum sonorum*
Piñon	*Pinus edulis*
Ponderosa pine	*Pinus ponderosa*
Princess plume	*Stanleya pinnata; S. elate*
Purslane	*Portulaca*
Ragweed	*Ambrosia*
Redbud	*Cercis occidentalis*
Spiderling	*Boerhaavia*
Spiderwort	*Tradescantia occidentalis*
Stickseed	*Mentzelia albicaulis*
Tobacco	*Nicotiana attenuata; Nicotiana*
Willow	*Salix*
Winged pigweed	*Cycloloma atriplicifolium*
Woolly wheat	*Plantago*

Karen R. Adams

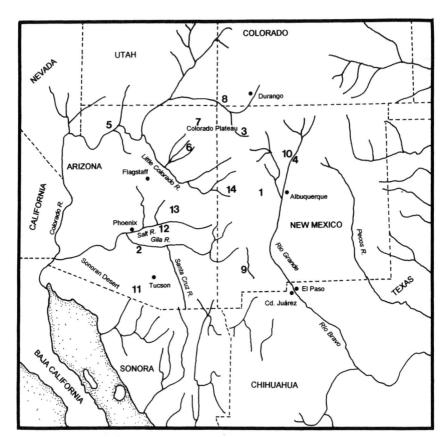

FIGURE 5.1   The North American Southwest: 1. Acoma; 2. Akimel O'odham (Pima), Casa Grande; 3. Chaco Canyon; 4. Cochiti; 5. Havasupai; 6. Hopi; 7. Kayenta, Navajo, and Tsegi Canyon; 8. Mesa Verde and Sand Canyon Pueblo; 9. Mimbres; 10. Sia; 11. Tohono O'odham (Papago) and Quitobaquito; 12. Tonto National Monument; 13. White Mountain Apache; 14. Zuni

sidered secondary succession. Humans living in any ecosystem comprising early, intermediate, and mature stages of plant succession would essentially reap the benefits offered by a mosaic habitat. Mature or climax communities offer high diversity, high stability, and an enhanced capacity to buffer environmental changes (Odum 1966). Young communities, on the other hand, provide high productivity (net organic matter produced per unit area) facilitated by high energy input. Human disturbance provides open habitats that suit certain plants with early successional adaptations. Boundaries between communities can have additional beneficial edge effects for humans, often in the form of increased biotic diversity.

Human Impacts on Ecosystems

Humans impact ecosystems in many ways. Three major anthropogenic effects discussed here are (1) manipulation of vegetation by fire, (2) clearing for agriculture, including water and soil control, and (3) harvesting wood resources for fuel and construction timbers. Although I discuss each activity separately, humans maintain mosaic habitats around them by multiple landscape modifications. By keeping plant communities in stages of secondary succession, humans increase the heterogeneity of plants and animals (Anderson and Nabhan 1991). Two good, modern examples of human-fostered mosaic habitats include the Sonoran Desert oases of Quitovac, Sonora, and Quitobaquito, Arizona. In recent times, Tohono O'Odham (Papago) families living in southwestern Arizona and northern Mexico employed fire, flood irrigation, transplanting, and seed sowing to promote a variety of vegetation patches, which together nurtured a diversity of plant and animal species that was greater than in the surrounding natural desert (Nabhan et al. 1982).

Examples exist of the diverse nature of effects of prehistoric human impact on the environment. Here I mention two. In the first example, the prehistoric Hohokam in Arizona lived in a culturally modified, mosaic landscape. Their environment, as indicated by pollen analysis, was richer and more varied than the modern one. It contained plant resources in proximity, diversity, and abundance that could have been fostered only by human activities (Fish 1984a). Larger plant materials from Hohokam sites support this conclusion (Miksicek 1984), as do faunal remains, which indicate a reliance on small animals attracted to human disturbance (Szuter 1984a, 1984b). In the second example, farming by the Dolores River Valley Ancestral Puebloans (Anasazi) of southwestern Colorado is shown to have influenced the distribution of native flora and fauna in multiple ways, likely surpassing the effects of climate change (Petersen and Matthews 1987). In a nearby area, the human impacts reflected in the prehistoric plant record of a locale occupied over the 13th century do not appear to have been severe enough to explain complete abandonment of the region (Adams and Bowyer 1999).

Fire

Fire was a major ecological force in the formation of some landscapes prior to human arrival on the continent. Sparked primarily by lightning, fires were also started by vulcanism and spontaneous combustion. Southwestern states, particularly Arizona and New Mexico, have a high incidence of lightning-caused fires, reflected by the widespread occurrence of fire-adapted ponderosa pine (*Pinus ponderosa*) trees (Komarek 1969:18).

Fires generally promote grasslands at the expense of shrublands and forests and reduce woody vegetation in well-established communities. A mosaic environment that consists of a variety of young-to-mature plant communities is better protected against the incursions of fires, disease, and bug infestation than are more uniform stands of aging brush and trees (Lewis 1980:83). The ecological consequences of fire are influenced by its periodicity, intensity, seasonality, and the nature of the vegetation burned. Humans can directly affect fire periodicity and seasonality and can indirectly affect its intensity.

A modern study of the early successional trajectory after fire in piñon-juniper woodland and sagebrush-bitterbrush (*Artemisia-Purshia*) shrubland on Mesa Verde in southwestern Colorado reveals some ecological effects of fire that have important implications for humans (Adams 1991, 1993). For example, a postfire mosaic habitat of contiguous burned and unburned areas offers a much wider range of resources, in varying densities and with differing qualities, than unburned mature vegetation alone. Some species of interest to humans, such as tobacco (*Nicotiana attenuata*), goosefoot (*Chenopodium*), mustard (*Schoencrambe*), and mutton grass (*Poa fendleriana*), display significant vigor and vitality early in fire recovery. Flexible stems for technological uses become available via vigorous postfire stump-sprouting of shrubs, and abundant amounts of sound deadwood are available for a short while.

NATIVE AMERICAN USE OF FIRE

The role of human burning in the formation of the landscape of the North American Southwest has been debated (Wickstrom 1987). Some researchers believe that, at least in some areas, the majority of the ignitions for the past several thousand years have been set by Native Americans (Christensen et al. 1987; Dobyns 1981; Stewart 1956) and that plant communities have adapted to this anthropogenic force. A contrasting view suggests aboriginal human-caused fires have had minimal impact on the evolution or perpetuation of western plant communities (Wickstrom 1987:3).

Much of the information on Native American burning comes from modern accounts that cite a wide variety of reasons humans set fires to their landscape (Bahre 1985; Barrett 1979; Blackburn and Anderson 1993; Dobyns 1981; Lewis 1973, 1985; Pyne 1982; Reynolds 1959; Wickstrom 1987). These include increasing seed yield, driving game, stimulating growth of certain plants, opening up land for agriculture, improving game forage, facilitating travel and visibility, and a variety of other reasons (Stewart 1956).

The ethnographic record in the North American Southwest offers numerous examples of purposeful burning. At Acoma in late July or early August of every fifth year, the Fire Katsina Ceremony of the Corn Clans was intended to exert a beneficial influence on crops and health, as well as supply new fire to the households of the village (Curtis 1926a:90–191; White 1932: 94–96). As part of this ceremony, four groups traveled in different directions up to 19 km (12 mi) away from the village, and as they returned they lit fires all along the way by means of smoldering masses of shredded juniper bark. In the origin legend of this ceremony, a fire katsina told a member of the Corn Clan, "This is my work. I do this every 5 or 10 years. I am not doing this to burn (i.e., to destroy) the world, but to heat Mother Earth to make her more fertile" (White 1943:314). In ecological terms, the katsinas were creating a large mosaic of burned and unburned vegetation patches, including open habitats, and were increasing edge areas between burned and unburned land. An ecosystem burned every five to 10 years existed in a state of perpetual secondary succession.

Southwestern groups also burned during animal drives. In New Mexico, at Cochiti, north of Albuquerque, a deer hunter offered meal to Fire Old Woman, saying "Fire the oldest, today let us have deer, all animals" (Parsons 1939:1:312). Numerous Sonoran Desert groups hunted rabbits, deer, and antelope with fire drives (Dobyns 1981:42). The Zuni in west-central New Mexico set fires in a circle, and then hunters closed toward the center of the circle, capturing rabbits as they went (Curtis 1926b:149). Sometimes the katsinas set fires to grass and vegetation as they traveled to a focal point, where hunters formed a circle to kill the rabbits, and katsinas used firebrands to drive the rabbits from their hiding places (Parsons 1939:2:759–760; Stevenson 1904:91–92). Ecologically, this Zuni use of fire in animal drives created irregular patches and corridors of burned vegetation leading toward focal areas.

Evaluating whether prehistoric fires can be attributed to human actions is difficult, because human ignition must be separated from lightning in fire regime analysis (Swetnam et al. 1987). The following examples, however, suggest ways to assess human actions and prehistoric fires.

TREE-RING FIRE-SCAR RECORDS: FREQUENCY

Fire frequency intervals are naturally influenced by climate, flood events that alter the ability of fires to spread, and biological phenomena (e.g., pathogens, insect infestations). If these relationships can be recognized in long-term tree-ring records, signatures attributable to human burning might stand out. A study of fire history, flood history, and climatic data encoded in tree rings in Rhyolite Canyon in the Chiricahua Mountains of southeastern Arizona demonstrated how long-term tree-ring records can be used to assess the possible roles of nature and humans in past fire regimes (Swetnam et al. 1991). An anomalous century (AD 1800–1900) for which little correlation can be seen between fire history and climatic conditions in the lower canyon and a notably high fire frequency during the AD 1850s and 1860s led researchers to postulate a role for human ignitions during that particular short period. Because stands of old trees continue to vanish in the North American Southwest, portions of the history of human-caused fires may never be known.

TREE-RING FIRE-SCAR RECORDS: SEASONALITY

Humans may use fire as a management tool in seasons that do not normally receive lightning strikes (Lewis 1980). Researchers can sometimes assess the season of a burn in fire-scarred trees by the position of a scar in relation to early wood and late wood formation or inferred dormancy (Swetnam et al. 1987:18). Archaeological fire-scar records of increased incidence of fires in nonlightning seasons could have an anthropogenic explanation.

POLLEN CORES: JUXTAPOSITION OF CHARCOAL INFLUX

Pollen cores monitor fire history through time via amounts and frequencies of charcoal deposited along with pollen. Cultural explanations might be invoked for increased frequency of charcoal influx or occurrences coinciding with specific archaeological manifestations. A pollen profile dating to the AD 600s in the Dolores River valley of southwestern Colorado documents a burn just prior to the appearance of corn (*Zea mays*) pollen, suggesting that the Ancestral Puebloans cleared the area with fire prior to planting their maize crop (Petersen 1985:238).

MULTIPLE LINES OF EVIDENCE FOR PREHISTORIC BURNING

The consequences of burning vegetation can be reflected in archaeobotanical and archaeofaunal records (Crites 1987:725). An excellent example of purposeful burning in the prehistoric North American Southwest rests on multiple paleobiological data bases meshed with modern fire ecology insights. Specialists in archaeological pollen (Fish 1983, 1984b), seeds and charcoal (Miksicek 1983, 1984), and faunal remains (Szuter 1984a) provided key evidence and insights that Bohrer (1992) then combined with modern fire ecology data to suggest that the Hohokam in south-central Arizona used fire to manipulate pristine Sonoran Desert vegetation near Queen Creek, east of Florence, and near Phoenix. She suggests that, as an agricultural tool, fire may have been "as much respected as a digging stick" (Bohrer 1992:123). By burning, the Hohokam cleared irrigation ditches of potentially clogging vegetative matter, provided short-term increases in the fertility of agricultural soils, and promoted an increase in diversity of available flora and fauna. The evidence for Hohokam use of fire derives from agricultural features, where elevated pollen and seed frequencies of plants able to increase after fire, such as globemallow (*Sphaeralcea*), spiderling (*Boerhaavia*), contrayerba (*Kallstroemia*), woolly wheat (*Plantago*), and evening primrose (*Oenothera*), accompany lowered frequencies of plants known to be reduced by fire, such as ragweed (*Ambrosia*), creosotebush (*Larrea*), and cholla cacti (*Opuntia*), and by an abundance of burned grass (Poaceae) stems (Bohrer 1992). When considering Hohokam impacts to the Sonoran Desert environment, Fish (1997, 2000) suggests that targeted, as opposed to broad-scale, applications of fire would have provided optimal access to plant and animal resources, including fuelwood. Elsewhere in the northeastern Hohokam region, prehistoric groups burned chaparral to draw animals to new growth of shrubs such as mountain mahogany (*Cercocarpus*) (Adams 1998; Bohrer 1997).

Agricultural Field Systems

Agriculture creates anthropogenic landscapes. Early agriculture in the North American Southwest created concentrated areas of edible biomass that included not only the domesticated crops of interest but also weedy opportunistic species and various animals attracted to these anthropogenic habitats (Ford 1984). A wide variety of farming strategies were practiced in prehistoric times, and many of them are still in use today (summarized in Maxwell and Anschuetz 1992). Each is distinctive in terms of its potential impact on a landscape.

Removing unwanted vegetation to increase field area will have varied effects, depending on how it is accomplished (e.g., by fire or tools) and on whether all native plants are removed. The resulting disturbed area encourages the growth of weedy taxa, many of whose leaves, seeds, and other parts might be of as much interest to humans as the domesticated crops themselves. Selective weeding during the growing season will cause the assemblage of plants in the field to further diverge from the composition of any natural community.

Abandoned fields are often colonized by annuals and perennials in greater densities than occur naturally, and both active and abandoned fields attract cottontails, jackrabbits, and other small mammals of interest to humans (Szuter 1984b, 1986). If fire is used to clear fields or enhance fertility, the successional trajectory would be different than if no burning had occurred at all. It is also easy to envision lasting impacts resulting from prehistoric manipulations to enhance moisture delivery (e.g., rock diversions, cobble contour terraces, check dams, spreaders) or to retard moisture loss (e.g., gravel mulches, rock piles).

One difficulty in assessing how prehistoric agricultural activities affected humans is that the weedy status of plants has not necessarily been constant through time (Bohrer 1991a:37). In the North American Southwest, introduced domestic grazing animals have established a camp-follower flora that is unknown archaeologically. Weedy taxa of the past may be unable to compete in a regime of reduced fires, different types or amounts of grazing pressure, and the introduction of aggressive foreign annuals (Bohrer 1991a:37–38). Pollen frequencies from Lower Sonoran Desert archaeological agricultural loci and habitation sites, that is, disturbed habitats expected to promote weedy floras, are unmatched by present natural weedy plant associations in the same region (Fish 1984a:45).

The first settled agricultural communities in the North American Southwest are older than previously thought. Along the Middle Santa Cruz River in southern Arizona near Tucson, early village sites with residential architecture, storage facilities, and abundant corn remains date to the Late Archaic period, 800 BC–AD 150 (Mabry 1998; Mabry et al. 1997). Human effects on the environment due to agriculture likely accompanied these efforts. The presence of abundant seeds of weedy plants in later Hohokam archaeological contexts reflects continued disturbance because of farming, as well as the importance of weedy resources as food (Kwiatkowski 1994:344).

IRRIGATION AGRICULTURE

Some of the anthropogenic effects of irrigation are suggested by modern reports on Arizona groups who have harvested crops, wild plants, and animals in irrigated fields, ditches, hedgerows, and abandoned fields (Fish and Nabhan 1991). Akimel O'odham (Pima) groups living along the Gila River in central Arizona increased biological productivity and diversity via management of field, ditch, and fencerow (Rea 1979, 1997). Their activities expanded the area and diversity of mesic vegetation types and provided new oases for wildlife. Annual plants produced abundant quantities of seeds for birds, animals, and people. Other plants provided basketry material and greens or offered moist vegetation for lining roasting pits. Intentionally planted living fencerows contained species with edible fruit that attracted high densities and diversities of breeding birds and other game (Rea 1979). Although the diversity and varied canopy levels of these fields mimicked native mesic habitats, the presence of domesticated crops and selective weeding by humans made them unique. Elsewhere in the Sonoran Desert, Tohono O'odham created a series of both large-scale and small-scale vegetation associations around two perennial water sources (Nabhan et al. 1982). The richness of biota in these managed oases offered a diversity of foods, medicines, and ceremonial paraphernalia not matched in unaltered native habitats.

Natural habitats on the edges of irrigated fields can come under occasional human influence. Extra water from irrigated Akimel O'odham (Pima) fields along the Gila River in Arizona was often allowed to sheet across the nearby desert floor to produce a "second garden" of wild and semiwild salt-tolerant annual and perennial plants (Crosswhite 1981:64). Greens were eaten as available, though some young plants were left to mature edible seed and others were encouraged to seed along irrigation ditches and in waste places.

One potential long-term environmental effect of irrigation agriculture could be persistent and increasing salt levels. Some researchers have suggested that salt buildup ruined many prehistoric Hohokam fields (Woodbury and Ressler 1962). Yet modern Akimel O'odham know how to flood their fields to leach out salts (Russell 1975:87). Even if prehistoric groups shared this insight, clear archaeological evidence of salt leaching might be difficult to find.

Clearly, there are multiple anthropogenic effects of irrigation agriculture. Canals and other water diversion structures allow corridors of riparian vegetation to cross arid lands to reach patches of irrigated fields. Increases in mesic habitat area, plant and animal productivity, and plant and animal diversity may all result from this type of farming. Edible biomass goes up, open habitats and edge areas between vegetation types are increased, and patches of previously farmed land may be left in various states of secondary succession. A mosaic of vegetation types prevails. Soils that experience increased salt levels may become permanently altered. Also, the stage is set for repeated associations between humans and plants that may eventually lead to mutualistic relationships such as domestication.

Archaeologically, canal irrigation is best known among Lower Sonoran Desert Hohokam groups in the Phoenix and Tucson Basins of southern Arizona. Along the Salt and Gila Rivers, the Hohokam constructed elaborate canal systems that transported water laterally as well as downstream for miles beyond the source (Fish and Nabhan 1991:48–49). Other canal systems were constructed along intermittent streams, such as in the Tucson Basin, where water carried in a ditch from the Santa Cruz River crossed many miles of desert floor to reach the Marana community (Fish et al. 1992). Some of the earliest known Sonoran Desert canals include those at Las Capas, dating to the period 1200–1100 BC (Mabry 1999), and one along the Middle Gila River in Arizona dated to AD 185 (Waters and Ravesloot 2000). Less complex water-control systems are described for Ancestral Puebloan groups in the Kayenta, Mesa Verde, Chaco Canyon, and Upper Little Colorado-Zuni areas (Vivian 1974).

Some aspects of agricultural technology do not preserve archaeologically, but perspectives on anthropogenic effects of these systems can be offered by ethnographic descriptions. The ethnographic record, however, is not likely to record the total repertoire or the potential variability in prehistoric agricultural strategies practiced. For example, agricultural features comparable to gravel-mulched fields found archaeologically in the Chama area of New Mexico northwest of Santa Fe are absent from modern agricultural descriptions, and it is clear that sophisticated prehistoric field systems included micro-topographic water control (Anschuetz 1995; Maxwell and Anschuetz 1992). The archaeological record also suggests a high degree of localized variability in aproaches to Ancestral Puebloan agricultural production (Maxwell and Anschuetz 1992).

OTHER TYPES OF WATER ENHANCEMENT

Other farming strategies exist to enhance water availability, and each creates a different type of anthropogenic environment. The diversity of ethnographically documented fields includes seepage, water-table, slope-wash, ak-chin, floodplain, arroyo-bottom, terrace, dry-farming, and sand-dune (Hack 1942; Maxwell and Anschuetz 1992). Ak-chin fields, for example, are developed on broad alluvial fans at the mouths of small canyons or arroyos that have shallow slopes. Although these fields may not receive enough water to mature a domesticated crop every season, they can still produce important and diverse "second garden" harvests of useful weeds if the crops fail. In southern Arizona, water-enhancement strategies include shallow ditches, rock/brush diversion weirs, rock/brush water spreaders, living cottonwood or willow fencerow silt traps, multicourse cobble terraces, and single-course alignments, some of which would leave little trace in the archaeological record (Fish and Nabhan 1991:47–48).

Prehistoric groups were probably also quite adept at sizing up a landscape in terms of optimal temperatures for growth. It is likely that some of their water-enhancement materials were also intended to optimize temperature conditions for their crops. For example, dark rocks that absorb heat might be selected for or against, depending on circumstance. Placement of agricultural features also must have been considered carefully in relation to cold-air drainage patterns.

Extensive archaeological systems that augmented soil moisture by diversion or surface preparation are still visible on the southwestern landscape, as represented by the following examples. Near Hovenweep in southeastern Utah, researchers have identified over 68 water-control fields via a variety of structural features, floral cover, and pollen associations (Winter 1978). Domesticated maize and beans were apparently supplemented with native harvests of beeweed, milkweed, rushes, sedges, cattail, dock, wolfberry, and groundcherry. Modern Puebloans still encourage or manipulate many of these same plants (summarized in Winter 1978:87–88).

In the northern Rio Grande area of New Mexico, investigators have identified widespread cobble-bordered grids in association with Ancestral Puebloan villages. For example, groups inhabiting the lower Rio Chama from the 13th to 15th centuries AD extensively modified the natural landscape (Anschuetz 1995). Extant features relating to their agricultural technologies include cobble-bordered contour terraces, floodwater-irrigated fields at the mouths of washes, circular borrow pits and reservoirs, check dams, ditch irrigation systems, spreaders to slow and diffuse surface runoff across planting areas, and simple snow- and rainfall-fed fields. It seems that many of these features were integrated into coherent systems of land use, evidenced by hydrological links between separate field facilities within spatially restricted microwatersheds. The use of basalt or quartzite gravel mulches in prehistoric times, a practice not recorded in modern documents, may have offered significant soil moisture and temperature conservation properties that ameliorated both drought and frost.

In the Sonoran Desert of southern Arizona, other researchers have documented rock piles, small check dams, stone alignments, terraces, and other features on mountain and *bajada* slopes in the Marana community (Fish et al.

1992). In middle *bajada* areas, simple mulches of piled cobbles increased and conserved soil moisture for vast fields of drought-adapted agave (*Agave*). On lower *bajadas*, it is speculated that brush, earth, and stone diversion structures, along with ditches and canals of moderate length, distributed water for crop production.

In southern Arizona and northern Mexico after AD 1100, agriculturalists constructed a number of extensive terrace, or *trinchera*, systems on the slopes of flat-topped, volcanic hills (Johnson 1963). Other terrace features in Chihuahua, Mexico, still serve to retain more moisture than nearby alluvial settings where the only source of water is direct rainfall (Herold 1992). In southern New Mexico, soil moisture measurements taken before and after a runoff event suggested increased available water in terraced soils when compared with nearby unterraced control locations (Sandor et al. 1990:74).

Evidence from pollen cores gives some insight into the extent of prehistoric land disturbance by humans, primarily via agriculture. For example, pollen data from Mummy Lake at Mesa Verde demonstrated postabandonment secondary forest succession of plants onto land previously cleared, cultivated, and apparently water enhanced by the Ancestral Puebloan population (Breternitz 1999; Martin and Byers 1965; Wycoff 1977). Additional examples of prehistoric water reservoirs in the Mesa Verde region of Colorado (Wilshusen et al. 1997) suggest long-term commitments to certain locales by specific communities, likely resulting in increasingly disturbed landscapes in their vicinities.

Some of the ecological consequences of prehistoric water-enhanced agriculture are still operating on southwestern landscapes. The widespread presence of small patches of rock piles, cobble terraces of various sizes, check dams, alignments, and depressions continues to affect local moisture availability, temperature conditions, infiltration, and fertility. Researchers have only recently begun to document the variety of differences that can exist between prehistoric farmland and adjacent unfarmed control plots (see Soil Fertility discussion below).

DIRECT RAINFALL FIELDS

A small number of prehistoric fields were probably able to produce crops with direct rainfall only, without modifications to concentrate water. Such fields would be difficult to recognize archaeologically, so the extent of prehistoric direct rainfall agriculture is unknown. If such fields were not planted annually, for example, if groups opted to plant only when winter moisture levels were adequate (Russell 1983), the potential anthropogenic effects to the land would have been low.

DOORYARD GARDENS

Although dooryard gardens were introduced by the Spanish in historic times, the concept of locating some plants near dwellings to receive more tending likely existed in prehistory. Such loci may be enhanced with organic debris by virtue of their proximity to communities and increased human presence. Soil changes in and near prehistoric habitations may in part explain why some archaeological sites today have floras unlike those of surrounding areas (Yarnell 1965). Gardens located near dwellings are also likely to receive extra water from people able to monitor their condition on a daily basis.

Soil Fertility

Native American agricultural regimes have varying effects on soil fertility. On the one hand, centuries of continuous cultivation of lowland Akimel O'odham fields attest to successful strategies that keep fertility levels up (Castetter and Bell 1942:172). For the Tohono O'Odham of southwestern Arizona, plant nutrients carried primarily in floodwater debris (stems, leaves, partially decomposed organic litter, feces, and silt) and, to a lesser extent, in the floodwater itself, replenish nutrient stocks depleted by crops and also enhance soil moisture-holding capacities (Nabhan 1979:249, 1983). Rather than facing fertility problems, these irrigators instead contend with having too much debris or sediment deposited on fields, or with flood loss of irrigation systems and fields.

On the other hand, upland, dryland agricultural activities undertaken by people who are constrained in their movements are more likely to result in long-term deficits of nitrogen, phosphorus, and soil organic matter and in increased accumulations of elements such as manganese (Berlin et al. 1977; Sandor et al. 1990). Soil compaction and accelerated erosion lasting for eight centuries have been recorded at Mimbres fields in New Mexico (Sandor et al. 1990). Elsewhere, local plant succession on archaeological fields north of Sunset Crater near Flagstaff, Arizona, has not fully established the probable preagricultural shrub community, apparently because of differences existing between field and nonfield soils (Berlin et al. 1977).

In upland locales, nutrient management may be especially necessary as fields experience slowly decreasing productivity with use. Nutrient depletion

Anthropogenic Ecology of the North American Southwest

of upland soils can be offset by nutrient additions or by planting strategies that conserve nutrients.

NUTRIENT ADDITIONS

People can add various components to their fields, such as residential garbage, ashes, and urine. Use of household garbage as fertilizer is known in the Americas, though southwestern pollen profiles do not document pollen intentionally introduced through such an activity (Fish et al. 1984:67). Gardens located close to dwellings would be the likeliest recipients of such household debris. On occasion plants might be specifically taken to the fields to decay. For example, presently among the New Mexico pueblos, Douglas-fir trees used in social or ceremonial dances are sometimes taken to gardens or farms and left to decompose and serve as fertilizer while returning to Mother Earth (Sando 1992:33). The Tohono O'Odham in Arizona rejuvenate soil by adding green manure and by plowing under crop stubble (Nabhan 1983:165).

The southwestern literature reveals use of ashes in fields, either by transporting them in or by starting fires in the fields themselves. Ashes contain an excess of basic ions ($K+$, $Ca++$, $Mg++$) and contribute phosphorous to plant growth (Wells et al. 1979). As wood ashes leach, they also liberate various potassium salts. Stevenson recorded how the Zuni took 10 days worth of ashes and sweepings to the fields, with the admonition "I now deposit you as sweepings, but in one year you will return to me as corn. I now deposit you as ashes, but in one year you will return to me as meal" (1904:108–132). Zia (or Sia) have been known to pack wood ashes overtopped with soil rich in clay around the bases of young corn plants (Euler 1954:29). The Tohono O'Odham recognize the plowing under of ashes as a soil rejuvenating technique (Nabhan 1983:165).

Field burning can have a notable impact on agricultural efforts. Field burns affect microorganisms, mineral content, organic matter, pH, erosion, and subsequent field temperatures (Wells et al. 1979). In the seasons immediately following a fire, agricultural crops benefit both from reduced competition with native plants and from increased available nutrients (Bohrer 1992), though these effects may be relatively short-lived. In the North American Southwest, southern Arizona groups burned fields to increase soil fertility (Castetter and Bell 1942). A White Mountain Apache in central Arizona spoke of burning grama grass on a field because the ashes were good for corn (Buskirk 1986:25). In the past, the Hohokam in the Queen Creek area of central Arizona manipulated pristine Sonoran Desert vegetation by fire prior to planting their crops (Bohrer 1992), though the interval at which they may have burned a particular field is unknown.

One nutrient rapidly leached from ashes is nitrogen, which is also reduced in amount when volatilized during burning (Wells et al. 1979:11). Nitrogen is perhaps the most important limiting element in desert ecosystems (Felker and Clark 1980; Romney et al. 1978). A good-yielding corn crop may carry away in its harvested grains as much as 128 kg/ha of nitrogen (Delwiche 1971). Therefore, nitrogen must be replaced in many agricultural fields. One natural replacement route is slow accumulation via atmospheric deposition at the rate of 1–12 kg/ha/year (Wells et al. 1979:13). Another includes various biological processes of nitrogen fixation (discussed below).

Cultural enhancement of nitrogen can be achieved through judicious addition of urine to soil. The urea in urine offers nitrogen in a readily available form, though it must not be put directly on the plants or developing seedlings in too concentrated an amount. It can be diluted or perhaps added to ditch water. In the mid-1500s, Castenada observed that pueblo villages collected urine in clay vessels, which they emptied some distance from the village (Hodge 1946:354). Bandelier reported the same practice three centuries later, adding the critical comment that the urine was carried "out into the fields" (Lange and Riley 1966:104).

NUTRIENT CONSERVATION STRATEGIES

Planting strategies to conserve nutrients in the fields include spacing and rotation of crops, resting periods, and planting in areas where biological nitrogen fixation is high. Wide spacing of corn "hills" and their movement within the field from year to year lets all areas of each field "rest" periodically, even while the fields are in constant use. The Hopi planted in widely spaced hills with a cluster of several stalks per hill (Stephen 1936:955). Each season the new crop was planted between the rows of stubble from the preceding harvest (Beaglehole 1937:40; Forde 1931:390). Leaving organic matter (roots, stalks, leaves) in the fields promotes recycling of nutrients directly back into the field, as well as soil and moisture retention. Fields were on occasion left fallow (Forde 1948:230). Some Western Apache claim that they have always fallowed (or "rested") a field for a year, once every two or three years (Buskirk 1986:23). Some Tohono O'odham also follow fallow/rotation sequences (Nabhan 1983:165).

Companion planting of corn and beans (*Phaseolus*) benefits the maize because of the nitrogen-fixing abilities of the beans. Bean plants, however, may require some of the nitrogen they fix, funneling it into the beans (seeds), which are then removed from the field by humans. Nitrogen taken into weeds and maize leaves will be rereleased into the field as the standing plants slowly decay. Various shrubs such as mountain mahogany, bitterbrush (*Purshia*), and buckbrush (*Ceanothus*), in the rose and buckthorn families, and numerous plants in the legume family (Fabaceae) may contribute significant net inputs of soil nitrogen over time, especially in areas where these nitrogen-fixing plants are an important component of the surrounding plant communities (Berry 1992; Wells et al. 1979). The importance of these contributions may be significant for the long-term fertility of a given area.

Regardless of how humans culturally enhance soil fertility, the ecological consequences include increased productivity, especially of the edible portion of the biomass. Depletion of certain elements to repeated cropping might alter the composition of future plant communities.

Fuelwood and Construction Timbers

Ecosystems can be affected by prolonged or intensive plant collecting. This is especially true when both fuelwood and construction timbers are harvested. Depletion of dominant tree and shrub members lowers standing biomass. Collection of fuelwood can significantly reduce ground litter cover and promote erosion. Whether trees are regularly cut down for timbers or selectively pruned for their usable beams and for deadwood useful as fuel, the character of plant community composition will shift as the understory opens and provides an altered habitat.

FUELWOOD

Modern records reveal the role of cultural choice in fuelwood gathering. Wood types are not necessarily selected in proportion to their relative availability on a landscape but, rather, to satisfy human needs in relation to known qualities. One seasoned fire builder observed, "The knack of finding what we want in a firewood lies a good deal in knowing what we *don't* want" (Kephart 1988:236). Among the Kiowa Apache, for example, good firewood for cooking meats was one that burned readily, produced a hot blaze, and formed a bed of long-lasting coals with abundant heat (Jordon 1965). Navajo preferred piñon (*Pinus edulis*) wood for open fires, and juniper (*Juniperus*) for enclosed heating (Russell and Dean n.d.). Timbisha Shoshone of Death Valley never camped where they could not get the right type of wood for a planned activity (C. Fowler, personal communication March 28, 1994). Such examples of fuelwood preference guide what woods are collected and what woods are left around a dwelling. The ecosystem may be affected, however subtly, by such selective deadwood removal.

Deadwood seems to be preferred among modern groups, as green wood will "scarcely burn" (Kephart 1988:236). Elders of the Timbisha Shoshone claim that no one kills a living tree for wood if he or she can possibly avoid it (C. Fowler, personal communication March 28, 1994). Rather, one extensively prunes the lower branches and clears all underbrush from campsites, thus opening the understory and promoting tree health and new tree seedling establishment.

Types of available fuelwood can change through time, especially as people live in a place for a long period and alter their choices. Some landscapes become so altered that the available fuelwood is primarily the result of human activities, with people eventually producing much of their fuel (Johannessen and Hastorf 1990:71). Amounts of fuel burned can also differ notably among groups. For example, in his general history of the New World, Padre Cobo (1891–93[1639]) commented in 1639 that Spanish household fuel use was many times greater than that of indigenous peoples. Such differences can clearly impact the rate at which a landscape is denuded of deadwood around a human community.

Keeping warm and daily cooking probably placed great demands on prehistoric fuelwood supplies. For Ancestral Puebloans in the Dolores River valley of southwestern Colorado, several lines of evidence suggest significant human impact on the environment during a 300-year occupation between AD 600 and 900 (Kohler 1992; Kohler and Matthews 1988). Fuelwood use changed in a patterned way, as charcoal from slow-growing piñon and juniper shows decreases in ubiquity at later sites, whereas charcoal of various woody shrubs and cottonwood shows increases (Kohler and Matthews 1988). Hunting appears to have taken place in progressively more open and disturbed habitats (Neusius and Gould 1988), and seeds of pioneer plants increased in ubiquity in flotation samples dating later in that period (Matthews 1988). By the end of the occupation, availability of fat- and protein-rich piñon seeds had decreased relative to other wild plant resources and to maize (Floyd and Kohler 1990). In concert, these changes were thought to reflect increasingly disturbed local environments and agricultural intensification. The human impact eventually led to abandonment of the area (Kohler 1992).

In Chaco Canyon, northwestern New Mexico, packrat midden evidence suggests that middle and late Holocene vegetation consisted of a form of piñon-juniper woodland until the Ancestral Puebloans occupied the area (Betancourt and Van Devender 1981). Marginal stands of piñon and juniper were unable to support the relentless needs to meet fuelwood demands over a two-century span. An effort to model the long-term effects of fuelwood harvests on piñon-juniper woodlands in Chaco Canyon (Samuels and Betancourt 1982) supports the hypothesis that woodcutting by the resident population overtaxed and reduced the local conifer trees. The diminished woodland underwent a shift in species dominance as it was replaced by Great Basin desertscrub following Ancestral Puebloan occupation. Researchers now wonder if the modern "invasion" of piñon-juniper woodland into southwestern grasslands is not so much an invasion as a recovery of woodlands from heavy use by large prehistoric settlements (Betancourt et al. 1993; Samuels and Betancourt 1982).

Elsewhere in New Mexico, in the Mimbres area, environmental disturbance is suggested by charcoal and seed evidence and by other studies. Changes through time in ratios of floodplain to upland fuelwood types suggest that increasing population pressure reduced available floodplain fuelwood as people removed woody vegetation to open new agricultural fields (Minnis 1978, 1985). Relative percentages of carbonized weed seeds followed the same basic pattern as the fuelwood types, suggesting that greater agricultural clearing increased growth opportunities for plants preferring disturbed habitats. For this case study the analysis of faunal remains, pollen, and lithics, as well as catchment analysis, reached similar conclusions (Minnis 1978:364, 1985).

Less regularly, perhaps, fuel was needed to process specific plant resources or to fire pottery. The numerous archaeological roasting pits still scattered on the Sonoran Desert landscape must have used up large amounts of fuelwood during the roasting of various products (Dobyns 1981:91–96), including corn, agave, and cholla flower buds. In the same area, during the Classic period, large amounts of fuel must have been required for cremation ceremonies. The appearance of prehistoric agave roasting pits throughout the natural range of agave in the North American Southwest suggests high fuel needs beyond the Sonoran Desert (Castetter et al. 1938; Greer 1965). Ancestral Puebloan pit kilns probably required large amounts of wood to fire the massive quantities of ceramics known from the Pueblo III time period. Modern experiments to replicate Ancestral Puebloan black-on-white pottery required 128–168 kg of juniper wood to successfully fire 30–34 small to medium-sized vessels (Edminster 1993).

Modern southwestern groups utilize wood for construction of permanent dwellings and for temporary structures such as ramadas, turkey pens, windbreaks, and brush shades for field houses. Prehistoric needs may have been similar, although wood use behavior may have changed through time as new tools and techniques for handling wood were acquired, as new uses for wood were developed, and as local habitats changed (Russell and Dean n.d.).

In general, modern Puebloan patterns of wood use are conservative. Construction techniques minimize the quantity of wood required, and structural timbers are recycled many times, eventually becoming fuel. For example, at the Hopi pueblo of Walpi, researchers believe there has been a significant amount (up to 40 percent) of beam reuse (Ahlstrom et al. 1991).

The archaeological record can be examined for wood-use patterns such as stockpiling, reuse, processing of live timber or deadwood, seasonal timing of acquisition, and species preference (Russell and Dean n.d.). Dean (1969) and Cattanach (1980) document beam reuse in Tsegi Canyon and Long House (Mesa Verde), respectively. Although beam reuse may have been a consequence of construction timber scarcity within a culturally modified landscape, it could also simply reflect expedient acquisition of already prepared and still useful beams, regardless of current roof timber availability.

In terms of anthropogenic ecology, the archaeological record of construction timber use reflects woodland impacts. For example, fewer than 150 inhabitants of Kiet Siel in Tsegi Canyon, northern Arizona, nearly denuded the area of trees within a 20-year period in the late AD 1200s (Dean 1969:147–148). The aspens (*Populus tremuloides*) and box elders (*Acer negundo*) in the canyon bottoms were the first to go, as people cleared agricultural land and acquired roof timbers.

Efforts to model construction timber supply versus demand for the late Pueblo III site of Sand Canyon Pueblo in southwestern Colorado revealed that certain larger beam sizes occurred in limited numbers in the surrounding woodland (Hovezak 1992). Beam needs of earlier Puebloan occupants in the area also may well have reduced numbers of the more common smaller-sized roof timbers. Archaeological evidence in the area suggests beam recycling occurred by late Pueblo III times (Bradley 1992:93; Varien 1999), so some amount of forest impact is suspected.

In the past, construction beams were also acquired at some distance from a dwelling or community. Such transport is documented at sites in Chaco Canyon (Bannister 1973; Betancourt et al. 1986; Durand et al. 1999), at Mesa Verde (Hayes 1964), Salmon Ruin (Adams 1980), Tonto National Monument (Bohrer 1962:81), Casa Grande Ruin (Wilcox and Shenk 1981), and elsewhere. Such a strategy would have reduced human impact on local ecosystems, transferring it instead to more distant areas.

Plant Populations

Anthropogenic effects can be felt at levels smaller than that of the ecosystem, for instance, at the population level. A population includes a group of individuals of one kind of organism. Humans can promote range loss or reduction for a plant population through relentless pressure. Range extension occurs when a plant species or variety is transported into an area where it does not grow naturally. Transplanting can set up the potential for various types of hybridization when two related plant populations come into contact with each other after long isolation. Sometimes interactions between human and plant populations coevolve into an association termed "mutualism" that is necessary for the survival of both (Crites 1987). Clear cases of prehistoric southwestern human-plant mutualism include plant domestication, discussed elsewhere in this volume (see Fish, this volume).

Disturbed Landscapes

Disturbed landscapes such as agricultural fields, slowly accumulating trash mounds, or edges of frequently traveled paths can foster weedy species that catch human interest. In Hopi cornfields, beeweed (*Cleome serrulata*) plants "are allowed to mature and seed . . . insuring a supply for the following spring" of edible greens and the material from which organic pottery paint is made (Whiting 1966:77–78). Devil's claw (*Martynia*) plants are also purposefully left in Hopi agricultural fields so that their fruit can be gathered for basket making (Whiting 1966:17). Zuni women encouraged a species of groundcherry (*Physalis*) to grow in their gardens so that they could add the ripe fruit to a salsa dish (Stevenson 1915). A wild barley grass (*Hordeum pusillum*), suspected of having undergone some degree of prehistoric domestication in central Arizona (Adams 1987; Bohrer 1987, 1991b), is a species endemic to "swales, roadsides, and other disturbed soils" (Gould 1951:107). Humanly disturbed landscapes would have drawn the barley plant into open niches closer to human attention.

Some plant parts may thrive when regularly thinned by harvesting (Butzer 1982:187). For example, digging underground plant parts loosens and aerates the soil and reduces competition among the parts left behind. Repeated cutting of reed grass (*Phragmites*) induces strengthened stem walls through increased lignification (Stant 1953). Prehistoric groups may have recognized this when gathering materials for manufacture of "reed grass cigarettes" (Adams 1990).

Pruning

In the North American Southwest, groups have cut or burned back lemonadeberry plants (*Rhus aromatica*, or *Rhus trilobata*) in the fall to induce the growth of long, straight, flexible shoots to be harvested the following spring for basketry and other purposes (Bohrer 1983). Elsewhere, in the Sierra Nevada of California, elders still prune redbud plants (*Cercis occidentalis*) to stimulate the production of long and supple blood-red sprouts to use in basketry designs (Anderson 1991). Timbisha Shoshone of Death Valley prune princess plume (*Stanleya pinnata*, *S. elate*) and willow (*Salix*) (C. Fowler, personal communication, March 28, 1994). Tubatulabals living in California pruned and weeded tobacco plants to encourage growth (Voegelin 1938:36–38).

Fire to Encourage Individual Species

In addition to the ecosystemwide effects of fire already discussed, southwestern groups set fires to encourage growth of specific plants. For example, the Tohono O'Odham burned patches of dropseed grass (*Sporobolus*) and then swept up the parched seeds from the ground (Castetter and Underhill 1935:24). Havasupai in Arizona cut down mesquite trees, burned them, and then threw tobacco seeds in the ashes for a future harvest (Spier 1928:105). These groups had undoubtedly witnessed the flourishing of native tobacco plants following natural fires in certain vegetation types (Adams 1991, 1993).

Broadcasting

Broadcasting of wild seeds may once have been a very common Native American practice (Shipek 1989:162). Nequatewa (1936:99) noted that in the North American Southwest the Hopi broadcast the seeds of a variety of plants. For example, someone occasionally scattered tobacco seeds on a convenient and favorable spot, thus ensuring a goodly supply for ceremonial purposes (Whiting 1966:16). Groups living along the Lower Colorado River broadcast seeds of a native panic grass (probably *Panicum sonorum*) as the river receded in the spring (Nabhan and De Wet 1984; Palmer 1871). Later in the year the planters returned and harvested the ripe heads.

Range Extensions, Reductions

Humans are capable of promoting species range extensions or reductions. For example, the Hopi brought cottonwood (*Populus*), willows, and cattails (*Typha*) into washes nearer their dwellings (Whiting 1966:64, 72). Transplanting plants closer to dwellings may encourage hybridization if related species grow nearby. If progeny of such hybridization can find their way into the open niches that usually surround human settlements, these genetically altered plants may adaptively radiate and promote permanent and irreversible changes in plant communities (Bohrer 1991a).

Evidence of range extension is often based on anomalous distributions of plants on archaeological sites. For example, in the New River Mountains and Tonto Basin of central Arizona, two species of agave grow today on prehistoric agricultural terraces and in rock piles, where they are associated with mescal knives, turtleback scrapers, and multiroom foundations (Bohrer 1991b; Hodgson et al. 1989). These plants are definitely growing at lower elevations than other naturally occurring agave species and may well represent relict populations testifying to prehistoric efforts to cultivate agaves. The presence of abundant carbonized agave remains in Classic period sites and in roasting pit features located outside the range of modern agave populations strengthens this story (Bohrer 1991b; Fish et al. 1985; Gasser and Miksicek 1985; Miksicek 1984). Farther to the northeast in Arizona, the association of *Agave parryi* with archaeological sites above the Mogollon Rim, beyond what appears to be the northern natural limits of the species, led researchers to speculate that humans had extended its range in prehistoric times (Minnis and Plog 1976).

Impressively high cholla pollen frequencies near archaeological Hohokam hamlets in central Arizona suggest that cholla cactus plants were transplanted close to dwellings so that their young flower buds could be easily gathered as a spring vegetable (Fish 1984b:120, 134–135). The ubiquity of cholla pollen in house and trash pit samples at the Hohokam community of La Ciudad in the Phoenix area (Bohrer 1987:169; Gish 1987:43–48) may also represent intentional transplanting (Bohrer 1991b). Elsewhere, at the prehistoric pueblo of Arroyo Hondo near Santa Fe, New Mexico, Bohrer (1986:212, 250) interpreted variation in cholla pollen size to represent the former presence of two cholla species or their hybrids. In the nearby Jemez Mountains, cholla plants growing outside their normal elevational range on abandoned pueblo ruins are thought to be the descendants of cacti transplanted in prehistoric times (Housley 1974).

Prehistoric range extensions are also suggested by the presence of distinctive modern flora growing on Puebloan ruins in New Mexico. For example, a species of mint (*Salvia*), strikingly associated with Puebloan ruins in Bandelier National Monument outside of Santa Fe, occurs more than 300 m above its known range and is suspected of having been introduced into the area by prehistoric peoples (Yarnell 1965:669). Another mint (*Salvia dorrii*) may owe its current distribution in central Arizona to prehistoric human influences (Huisinga 1999). The role of prehistoric groups as dispersal agents is also suggested by unusual patterning of secondary chemical compounds in piñon. Trees from southeastern Arizona and southwestern New Mexico have compounds very similar to those in trees growing hundreds of miles north in the front range of the Rocky Mountains (Betancourt et al. 1993:49). Compounds in piñon populations between these two locations differ considerably. People may have carried or traded piñon nuts a long distance from the south, with some of these nuts establishing a new population far from their home base. Molecular assessments might shed additional light on such questions of range extensions.

The archaeological record also suggests human-induced reductions in species range. The case for Chaco Canyon peoples' impact on a form of piñon-juniper woodland has already been presented (Betancourt and Van Devender 1981; Samuels and Betancourt 1982). Elsewhere in southwestern Colorado, prehistoric packrat samples contained evidence of barberry (*Berberis fendleri*) and New Mexican locust (cf. *Robinia neomexicana*), two species that are rare in the area today. Van Devender (1985:204) suggested that the reduced occurrence of these species may be due to heavy human impact during prehistoric times.

Ironically, the archaeological record can also shed light on reductions in plant range due to modern land-use strategies. The southwestern archaeobotanical record on the Colorado Plateau, in concert with modern distributional data, suggests prehistoric groups had access to larger populations than currently exist of stickseed (*Mentzelia albicaulis*), winged pigweed (*Cycloloma atriplicifolium*), purslane (*Portulaca*), contrayerba, wild cucurbita (*Cucurbita foetidissima*), onion (*Allium*), and spiderwort (*Tradescantia occidentalis*) (Bohrer 1978). This situation may be due to differences in disturbance forces that encouraged these plants in prehistory and discourage them today. Similarly, in southern Arizona there are no modern plant associations that produce frequencies of pollen types comparable to archaeological agricultural loci and habitation sites (Fish 1984a:45). These differences may result from different prehistoric and modern land-use strategies, including prehistoric efforts to encourage certain plants.

Individual Organisms

Individual organisms begin life, age, reproduce sexually or asexually, and die within a matter of weeks to decades. They have both a habitat, or living space, and a niche, or role, to play in the larger ecosystem. Humans can certainly impact the habitat of an organism and perhaps, over time, its niche as well.

Manipulation of individual plants may not result in significant anthropogenic effects to a landscape, unless such actions are repeated over time and involve enough plants to affect a population. Chances of recognizing cases of individual plant manipulation in the archaeological record are understandably small. Yet examples of prehistoric interactions with individual plants do exist in the record of conifer use in the North American Southwest.

Prehistoric manipulation of Douglas-fir (*Pseudotsuga menziesii*) trees at Mesa Verde National Park in southwestern Colorado to facilitate acquisition of roof timbers has been documented (Nichols and Smith 1965). One tree in particular was bent when young (either naturally or by human hands), and, using stone axes, humans subsequently removed two separate lateral (now leader) branches at 15-year intervals. Such manipulations could have fostered a supply of roof beams of the length, straightness, and strength required of construction timbers. Perhaps the preceding centuries of Ancestral Puebloan occupation had reduced the natural supply of available construction timbers.

The consumption of cambial tissue from large slabs of conifer bark, either as an emergency or starvation food or as a delicacy or sweet, has been documented for Native American groups over the past two centuries (Martorano 1989; Swetnam 1984). There is no reason to assume that this was not a prehistoric practice as well. Evidence occurs in the form of large, somewhat oval or rectangular scars on living trees. The timing and season of bark-peeling episodes can often be revealed by dendrochronological analysis. Most peeled trees healed these wounds and continued to grow. Overuse of bark in famine times, however, resulting in death of multiple trees, presumably would have altered local landscapes.

Summary

Prehistoric groups in the North American Southwest knew that their inhabited natural landscapes could be made even *more* productive through their own actions. Specific effects depended on the nature, intensity, seasonality, and duration of the many different activities humans engaged in. Modern and archaeological evidence documents human impacts to ecosystems, plant populations, and even to individual plants.

Use of fire, agriculture, and repeated harvesting of natural dominant plant resources such as trees altered ecosystems. Such activities promoted high diversity and productivity by maintaining a mosaic of open habitats, undisturbed surrounding territory, and land in varying stages of secondary succession. Trails provided disturbed corridors connecting the different patches of land. Changes in species dominance and plant population characteristics were consequences of ecosystem manipulation. Heavily modified landscapes offered opportunities for the development of mutualistic relationships between humans and plants, including those involving management and domestication of plant species.

Some prehistoric ecosystems were permanently altered as the result of human activity. Partly degraded agricultural fields in Arizona and New Mexico today have lowered levels of nutrients and organic matter and are subject to increased erosion and soil compaction. Prehistoric water-control and enhancement features in many areas of the North American Southwest still affect local landscapes. Irrigated fields may have experienced long-lasting effects from increased salinization. The effects of deforestation of a Chacoan woodland still endure centuries after the area's initial clearance.

Plant populations were affected by human activity as well. The ethnographic record documents such activities as pruning, use of fire, broadcasting, and general disturbance. People found some native plant taxa of enough interest to have extended the ranges of those taxa in prehistoric times. These included species of agave, cholla cactus, mints, and others. Yet other taxa experienced a reduction in range. Wild resources recovered repeatedly in the North American Southwest archaeological record, for example, groundcherry and ricegrass (*Oryzopsis hymenoides*), should be closely scrutinized for any morphological evidence of increased human selection pressure.

Attention received by individual plants constituted the lowest level of anthropogenic impact to prehistoric landscapes. Very subtle changes occurred when human manipulation affected the vigor and vitality of individual plants.

Of course, when any activity was applied to many individual plants, a population was affected.

Additional prehistoric landscape changes will undoubtedly be recognized beyond the ones cited in this review. Archaeological case studies of changing resource availability, coupled with modern environmental studies, will contribute to this effort. The remains of prehistoric crops may be found to retain chemical signatures relevant to declines in nutrient levels. Chemical and physical analyses of sediment might help pinpoint farmed areas and assess any long-lasting changes in soil properties. Molecular studies could be brought to bear on questions regarding plant population manipulation and the geographic movements of plants by humans. Archaeologists may not at present fully recognize the nature and scale of anthropogenic effects on prehistoric southwestern landscapes.

Acknowledgments

I appreciate reviews and comments on this review provided by Catherine Fowler, Suzanne Fish, Carla Van West, and Vorsila Bohrer.

References Cited

Adams, Karen R.
  1980 Pines and Other Conifers from Salmon Ruin, Northwestern New Mexico: Their Identification and Former Role in the Lives of the Ancient People. In *Investigations at the Salmon Site: The Structure of Chacoan Society in the Northern Southwest III*, edited by Cynthia Irwin-Williams and Phillip H. Shelley, pp. 355–562. Eastern New Mexico University, Portales.
  1987 Little Barley (*Hordeum pusillum* Nutt.) as a Possible New World Domesticate. In *Specialized Studies in the Economy, Environment and Culture of La Ciudad, Part III*, edited by JoAnn E. Kisselburg, Glen E. Rice, and Brenda L. Shears, pp. 203–237. Anthropological Field Studies 20. Arizona State University, Tempe.
  1990 Prehistoric Reedgrass (*Phragmites*) "Cigarettes" with Tobacco (*Nicotiana*) Contents: A Case Study from Red Bow Cliff Dwelling, Arizona. *Journal of Ethnobiology* 10:123–139.
  1991 Mesa Verde Fire Effects: An Ecological and Ethnobotanical Study of Vegetation Recovery after the Long Mesa Fire of July 1989. Annual Report, Study Period July–October 1990. Manuscript on file, Mesa Verde National Park, Colorado.
  1993 Mesa Verde Fire Effects: An Ecological and Ethnobotanical Study of Vegetation Recovery after the Long Mesa Fire of July 1989. Second Annual Report, Study Period July 1990–October 1992. Manuscript on file, Mesa Verde National Park, Colorado.
  1998 Plant Remains from State Route 87 Sites. Manuscript on file, Statistical Research, Tucson.
Adams, Karen R., and Vandy E. Bowyer
  1999 Subsistence and Human Impact on the Environment: The 13th Century and Abandon-

ment as Viewed from the Archaeobotanical Record. Paper presented at the 64th Annual Meeting of the Society for American Archaeology, Chicago.

Ahlstrom, Richard V. N., Jeffrey S. Dean, and William J. Robinson
1991 Evaluating Tree-Ring Interpretations at Walpi Pueblo, Arizona. *American Antiquity* 56:628–644.

Anderson, M. Kat
2001 California Indian Horticulture: Management and Use of Redbud by the Southern Sierra Miwok. *Journal of Ethnobiology* 11:145–157.

Anderson, M. Kat, and Gary P. Nabhan
1991 Gardeners in Eden. *Wilderness Magazine* fall:27–30.

Anschuetz, Kurt F.
1995 Saving a Rainy Day: The Integration of Diverse Agricultural Technologies to Harvest and Conserve Water in the Lower Rio Chama Valley New Mexico. In *Soil, Water, Biology, and Belief in Prehistoric and Traditional Southwestern Agriculture*, edited by H. Wolcott Toll, pp. 25–39. Special Publication 2. New Mexico Archaeological Council, Albuquerque.

Bahre, Conrad J.
1985 Wildfire in Southeastern Arizona between 1959–1890. *Desert Plants* 7:190–194.

Bannister, Bryant
1973 *Tree-Ring Dating of the Archaeological Sites in the Chaco Canyon Region, New Mexico.* Technical Series 6, Pt. 2. Southwest Parks and Monuments Association, Tucson.

Barrett, Stephen W.
1979 *Ethnohistory of Indian Fire Practices in Western Montana. First Annual Report: Relationship of Indian-Caused Fires to the Ecology of Western Montana Forests.* Intermountain Forest and Range Experiment Station, USDA Forest Service Missoula.

Beaglehole, Ernest
1937 *Notes on Hopi Economic Life.* Yale University Publications in Anthropology 15. Yale University Press, New Haven.

Berlin, G. Lennis, J. Richard Ambler, Richard H. Hevly, and G. G. Schaber
1977 Identification of a Sinagua Agricultural Field by Aerial Thermography, Soil Chemistry, Pollen/Plant Analysis, and Archaeology. *American Antiquity* 42:588–600.

Berry, Alison M.
1992 Biological Nitrogen Fixation and Soil Fertility in Southwestern Lands: Implications for Anasazi Agriculture. Paper presented at the New Mexico Archaeological Council Agricultural Symposium, Santa Fe.

Betancourt, Julio L., Jeffrey S. Dean, and Herbert M. Hull
1986 Prehistoric Long-Distance Transport of Construction Beams, Chaco Canyon, New Mexico. *American Antiquity* 51:370–375.

Betancourt, Julio L., E. A. Pierson, Kate A. Rylander, James A. Fairchild-Parks, and Jeffrey S. Dean
1993 Influence of History and Climate on New Mexican Pinon-Juniper Woodlands. In *Managing Piñon-Juniper Ecosystems for Sustainability and Social Needs*, Earl F. Aldon and Douglas W. Shaw, technical coordinators, pp. 42–62. General Technical Report RM-236. USDA Forest Service, Albuquerque.

Betancourt, Julio L., and Thomas R. Van Devender
1981 Holocene Vegetation in Chaco Canyon, New Mexico. *Science* 214:656–658.

Blackburn, Thomas C., and M. Kat Anderson
1993 *Before the Wilderness: Environmental Management by Native Californians.* Anthropological Papers 40. Ballena Press, Menlo Park, California.

Karen R. Adams

Bohrer, Vorsila L.

1962 Nature and Interpretation of Ethnobotanical Materials from Tonto National Monument. In *Archaeological Studies at Tonto National Monument, Arizona*, edited by Louis R. Caywood, pp. 80–114. Technical Series 2. Southwestern Monuments Association, Tucson.

1978 Plants That Have Become Locally Extinct in the Southwest. *New Mexico Journal of Science* 18(2):10–19.

1983 New Life from Ashes: The Tale of the Burnt Bush (*Rhus trilobata*). *Desert Plants* 5:122–124.

1986 The Ethnobotanical Pollen Record at Arroyo Hondo Pueblo. In *Food, Diet and Population at Arroyo Hondo Pueblo, New Mexico*, edited by Wilma Wetterstrom, pp. 187–220. Arroyo Hondo Archaeological Series 6. School of American Research Press, Santa Fe.

1987 The Plant Remains from La Ciudad, a Hohokam Site in Phoenix. In *Specialized Studies in the Economy, Environment and Culture of La Ciudad*, edited by JoAnn E. Kisselburg, Glen E. Rice, and Brenda L. Shears, pp. 67–237. Anthropological Field Studies 20. Arizona State University, Tempe.

1991a Commentary on "The Ecological Genetics of Domestication and the Origins of Agriculture," by M. Blumler and R. Byrne. *Current Anthropology* 32:37–38.

1991b Recently Recognized Cultivated and Encouraged Plants among the Hohokam. *Kiva* 56:227–235.

1992 New Life from Ashes II: A Tale of Burnt Brush. *Desert Plants* 10:122–125.

1997 Pieces of the Landscape: Flotation Analysis of Plant Remains from Sites in the Vicinity of Kitty Jo Canyon. In *Rocks, Roasters, and Ridgetops: Data Recovery across the Pioneer Road Landscape, State Route 87 Segment F, Maricopa and Gila Counties, Arizona*, edited by G. R. Woodall, D. D. Barz, and M. P. Neeley, pp. 295–314. Project Report 94:77B. Archaeological Research Services, Tempe.

Bradley, Bruce A.

1992 Excavations at Sand Canyon Pueblo. In *The Sand Canyon Archaeological Project, a Progress Report*, edited by William D. Lipe, pp. 79–97. Occasional Paper 2. Crow Canyon Archaeological Center, Cortez, Colorado.

Breternitz, David A.

1999 *The 1969 Mummy Lake Excavations, Site 5MV833*. Wright Paleohydrological Institute, Boulder.

Buskirk, Winifred

1986 *The Western Apache: Living with the Land before 1950*. University of Oklahoma Press, Norman.

Butzer, Karl W.

1982 *Archaeology as Human Ecology: Method and Theory for a Contextual Approach*. Cambridge University Press, Cambridge.

Castetter, Edward F., and Willis H. Bell

1942 *Pima and Papago Indian Agriculture*. University of New Mexico Press, Albuquerque.

Castetter, Edward F., Willis H. Bell, and A. R. Grove

1938 *The Early Utilization and Distribution of Agave in the American Southwest*. Bulletin 335. University of New Mexico, Albuquerque.

Castetter, Edward F., and Ruth M. Underhill

1935 *Ethnobiological Studies in the American Southwest II: The Ethnobiology of the Papago Indians*. Bulletin 275, Biological Series 4(3). University of New Mexico Press, Albuquerque.

Cattanach, George S., Jr.

1980 *Long House, Mesa Verde National Park*. Publications in Archeology 7H, Wetherill Mesa Studies. National Park Service, US Department of the Interior, Washington, DC.

Christensen, N. L., L. Cotton, T. Harvey, R. Martin, J. McBride, P. Rundel, and R. Wakimoto
1987 Final Report: Review of Fire Management Programs for Sequoia-Mixed Conifer Forests of Yosemite, Sequoia, and Kings Canyon National Parks. Unpublished report on file, US Department of the Interior, National Park Service, Western Regional Office, San Francisco.

Cobo, Bernabé de
1891–93 [1639] *Historia del Nuevo Mundo*. Seville, E. Rasco, 1890–95. Sociedad de Bibliófiles Andaluces.

Crites, Gary D.
1987 Human-Plant Mutualism and Niche Expression in the Paleoethnobotanical Record: A Middle Woodland Example. *American Antiquity* 52:725–740.

Crosswhite, Frank S.
1981 Desert Plants, Habitat and Agriculture in Relation to the Major Pattern of Cultural Differentiation in the O'odham People of the Sonoran Desert. *Desert Plants* 3: 47–76.

Curtis, Edward S.
1926a *The North American Indian: 16. The Tiwa, the Keres*. Plimpton Press, Norwood, Massachusetts.
1926b *The North American Indian: 17. The Tewa, the Zuni, Mythology*. Plimpton Press, Norwood, Massachusetts.

Dean, Jeffrey S.
1969 *Chronological Analysis of Tsegi Phase Sites in Northeastern Arizona*. Papers of the Laboratory of Tree-Ring Research 3. University of Arizona Press, Tucson.

Delwiche, C. C.
1971 Man and Mineral Cycles. *Yale Science* 46(2):12–20.

Dobyns, Henry F.
1981 *From Fire to Flood: Historic Human Destruction of Sonoran Desert Riverine Oases*. Anthropological Papers 20. Ballena Press, Socorro, New Mexico.

Durand, Stephen R., Phillip H. Shelley, Ronald C. Antweiler, and Howard E. Taylor
1999 Trees, Chemistry and Prehistory in the American Southwest. *Journal of Archaeological Science* 26:185–203.

Edminster, S. C.
1993 Third Annual Kiln Conference Crow Canyon Archaeological Center, May 1993. Manuscript on file, Crow Canyon Archaeological Center, Cortez, Colorado.

Euler, Robert C.
1954 Environmental Adaptation at Sia Pueblo. *Human Organization* 12(4):27–30.

Felker, P., and P. R. Clark
1980 Nitrogen Fixation (Acetylene Reduction) and Cross Inoculation in 12 *Prosopis* (Mesquite) Species. *Plant and Soil* 57:177–186.

Fish, Suzanne K.
1983 Pollen from Agricultural Features. In *Hohokam Archaeology along the Salt-Gila Aqueduct Central Arizona Project: 3. Specialized Activity Sites*, edited by Lynn S. Teague and Patricia L. Crown, pp. 575–603. Archaeological Series 150. Cultural Resource Management Section, Arizona State Museum, Tucson.
1984a The Modified Environment of the Salt-Gila Aqueduct Project Sites: A Palynological Perspective. In *Hohokam Archaeology along the Salt-Gila Aqueduct Central Arizona Project: 7. Environment and Subsistence*, edited by Lynn S. Teague and Patricia L. Crown, pp. 39–51. Archaeological Series 150. Cultural Resource Management Section, Arizona State Museum, Tucson.

Karen R. Adams

1984b   Agriculture and Subsistence Implications of the Salt-Gila Aqueduct Project Pollen Analysis. In *Hohokam Archaeology along the Salt-Gila Aqueduct Central Arizona Project: 7. Environment and Subsistence*, edited by Lynn S. Teague and Patricia L. Crown, pp. 111–138. Archaeological Series 150. Cultural Resource Management Section, Arizona State Museum, Tucson.

1997   Modeling Human Impacts to the Borderlands Environment from a Fire Ecology Perspective. In *Effects of Fire on Madrean Province Ecosystems*, edited by H. Hambre, pp. 125–134. General Technical Report RM-GTR-289. Rocky Mountain Forest and Range Experiment Station, US Department of Agriculture, Albuquerque.

2000   Hohokam Impacts on Sonoran Desert Environment. In *Imperfect Balance: Landscape Transformations in the PreColumbian Americas*, edited by David Lentz, pp. 251–280. Columbia University Press, New York.

Fish, Suzanne K., Paul R. Fish, and Christian Downum

1984   Hohokam Terraces and Agricultural Production in the Tucson Basin. In *Prehistoric Agricultural Strategies in the Southwest*, edited by Suzanne K. Fish and Paul R. Fish, pp. 55–71. Anthropology Research Papers 33. Arizona State University, Tempe.

Fish, Suzanne K., Paul R. Fish, and John H. Madsen

1992   Parameters of Agricultural Production in the Northern Tucson Basin. In *The Marana Community in the Hohokam World*, edited by Suzanne K. Fish, Paul R. Fish, and John H. Madsen, pp. 41–52. Anthropological Papers 56. University of Arizona, Tucson.

Fish, Suzanne K., Paul R. Fish, Charles Miksicek, and John H. Madsen

1985   Prehistoric Agave Cultivation in Southern Arizona. *Desert Plants* 7:107–112.

Fish, Suzanne K., and Gary P. Nabhan

1991   Desert as Context: The Hohokam Environment. In *Exploring the Hohokam, Prehistoric Desert Peoples of the American Southwest*, edited by George J. Gumerman, pp. 29–60. Amerind Foundation Publication. University of New Mexico Press, Albuquerque.

Floyd, M. Lisa, and Timothy A. Kohler

1990   Current Productivity and Prehistoric Use of Piñon (*Pinus edulis*, Pinaceae) in the Dolores Archaeological Project Area, Southwestern Colorado. *Economic Botany* 44:141–156.

Ford, Richard I.

1984   Ecological Consequences of Early Agriculture in the Southwest. In *Papers on the Archaeology of Black Mesa, Arizona*, vol. 2, edited by Stephen Plog and Shirley Powell, pp. 127–138. Southern Illinois University Press, Carbondale.

Forde, Cyril Daryll

1931   Hopi Agriculture and Land Ownership. *Journal of the Royal Anthropological Institute* 61:357–405.

1948   The Hopi and Yuma: Flood Farmers in the North American Desert. In *Habitat, Economy, and Society: A Geographical Introduction to Ethnology*, 6th ed., edited by Cyril Daryll Forde, pp. 220–259. Methuen, London.

Forman, Richard T. T., and Michael Godron

1986   *Landscape Ecology*. John Wiley and Sons, New York.

Gasser, Robert, and Charles Miksicek

1985   The Specialists: A Reappraisal of Hohokam Exchange and the Archaeobotanical Record. In *Proceedings on the 1983 Hohokam Symposium*, edited by Alfred E. Dittert and Donald E. Dove, pp. 483–498. Occasional Paper 2. Arizona Archaeological Society, Phoenix.

Gish, Jannifer W.

1987   Structured Diversity in the Resource Base of a Hohokam Village: The Pollen Evidence from La Ciudad. In *Specialized Studies in the Economy, Environment and Culture of La Ciudad*, edited by Jo Ann F. Kisselburg, Glen E. Rice, and Brenda L. Shears, pp. 1–66. Anthropological Field Studies 20. Arizona State University, Tempe.

Gould, Frank W.
1951　*Grasses of Southwestern United States.* University of Arizona Press, Tucson.

Greer, John W.
1965　A Typology of Midden Circles and Mescal Pits. *Southwestern Lore* 31(3):41–55.

Hack, John T.
1942　*The Changing Physical Environment of the Hopi Indians of Arizona.* Papers of the Peabody Museum of American Archeology and Ethnology 59(2). Harvard University, Cambridge.

Hammett, Julia E.
1992　The Shapes of Adaptation: Historical Ecology of Anthropogenic Landscapes in the Southeastern United States. *Landscape Ecology* 7:121–135.

Hayes, Alden C.
1964　*The Archaeological Survey of Wetherill Mesa, Mesa Verde National Park, Colorado.* Archaeological Research Series 7-A. National Park Service, US Department of the Interior, Washington, DC.

Herold, Laurance C.
1992　Soil Moisture Conditions in Agricultural Terraces Associated with a Highland Variant of the Casas Grandes Culture, Chihuahua, Mexico. Paper presented at the New Mexico Archaeological Council Agricultural Symposium, Santa Fe.

Hodge, Frederick W.
1946　*Spanish Explorers in the Southern United States, 1528–1543.* Barnes and Noble, New York.

Hodgson, Wendy, Gary P. Nabhan, and Liz Ecker
1989　Prehistoric Fields in Central Arizona: Conserving Rediscovered Agave Cultivars. *Agave* 3(3):9–11.

Housley, Lucile Kempers
1974　Opuntia imbricata *Distribution on Old Jemez Indian Habitation Sites.* Unpublished master's thesis, Department of Botany, Pomona College, Claremont, California.

Hovezak, Mark J.
1992　*Construction Timber Economics at Sand Canyon Pueblo.* Unpublished master's thesis, Department of Anthropology, Northern Arizona University, Flagstaff.

Huisinga, Kristin D.
1999　*Cultural and Biological Factors that Contribute to the Distribution of* Salvia dorrii *Subspecies* mearnsii. Unpublished master's thesis, Department of Biology, Northern Arizona University, Flagstaff.

Johannessen, Sissel, and Christine A. Hastorf
1990　A History of Fuel Management (AD 500 to the present) in the Mantaro Valley, Peru. *Journal of Ethnobiology* 10:61–90.

Johnson, Alfred E.
1963　The Trinchera Culture of Northern Sonora. *American Antiquity* 29:174–186.

Jordon, Julia Ann
1965　*Ethnobotany of the Kiowa Apache.* Unpublished master's thesis, Department of Anthropology, University of Oklahoma, Norman.

Kephart, Horace
1988　*Camping and Woodcraft.* Reprinted. University of Tennessee Press, Knoxville. Originally published 1917, Macmillan, New York.

Kohler, Timothy A.
1992　Prehistoric Human Impact on the Environment in the Upland North American Southwest. *Population and Environment: A Journal of Interdisciplinary Studies* 13:255–268.

Kohler, Timothy A., and Meredith H. Matthews

1988   Long-Term Anasazi Land Use and Forest Reduction: A Case Study from Southwestern Colorado. *American Antiquity* 53:537–564.

Komarek, E. V., Sr.

1969   Fire and Man in the Southwest. *Proceedings of the Symposium on Fire Ecology and the Control and Use of Fire in Wild Land Management*, edited by R. F. Wagle, pp. 3–22. Arizona Academy of Science, University of Arizona, Tuscon.

Kwiatkowski, Scott

1994   Some Thoughts about the Prehistoric Environment and Subsistence Practices at Pueblo Grande. In *The Pueblo Grande Project: 5. Environment and Subsistence*, edited by Scott Kwiatkowski, pp. 335–348. Publications in Archaeology 20. Soil Systems, Phoenix.

Lange, Charles H., and Carroll L. Riley

1966   *The Southwestern Journals of Adolph F. Bandelier, 1880–1882.* University of New Mexico Press, Albuquerque.

Lewis, Henry T.

1973   *Patterns of Indian Burning in California: Ecology and Ethnohistory.* Anthropological Papers 1. Ballena Press, Ramona, California.

1980   Indian Fires of Spring. *Natural History* 89:76–83.

1985   Why Indians Burned: Specific Versus General Reasons. *Proceedings, Symposium and Workshop on Wilderness Fire, Missoula, Montana, November 1983*, pp. 75–80. General Technical Report INT-182. USDA Forest Service, Albuquerque.

Mabry, Jonathan B.

1998   *Archaeological Investigations of Early Village Sites in the Middle Santa Cruz Valley: Analyses and Synthesis.* Anthropological Papers 19(1-2). Center for Desert Archaeology, Tucson.

1999   Las Capas and Early Irrigation Farming. *Archaeology Southwest* 13(1):14.

Mabry, Jonathan B., D. L. Swartz, H. Wocherl, J. J. Clark, G. H. Archer, and M. W. Lindeman

1997   *Archaeological Investigations of Early Village Sites in the Middle Santa Cruz Valley. Descriptions of the Santa Cruz Bend, Square Hearth, Stone Pipe, and Canal Sites.* Anthropological Papers 18. Center for Desert Archaeology, Tucson.

Martin, Paul S., and William Byers

1965   Pollen and Archaeology at Wetherill Mesa. *American Antiquity* 31:122–135.

Martorano, Marilyn A.

1989   So Hungry They Ate the Bark Off a Tree. *Canyon Legacy* 1(1):9–12.

Matthews, Meredith H.

1988   The Macrobotanical Data Base: Applications in Testing Two Models of Socioeconomic Change. In *Dolores Archaeological Program: Anasazi Communities at Dolores: Grass Mesa Village*, edited by William D. Lipe, James N. Morris, and Timothy A. Kohler, pp. 1137–1158. Bureau of Reclamation, US Department of the Interior, Denver.

Maxwell, Timothy D., and Kurt F. Anschuetz

1992   The Southwestern Ethnographic Record and Prehistoric Agricultural Diversity. In *Gardens of Prehistory*, edited by Thomas W. Killion, pp. 35–68. University of Alabama Press, Tuscaloosa.

Miksicek, Charles H.

1983   Plant Remains from Agricultural Features. In *Hohokam Archaeology along the Salt-Gila Aqueduct Central Arizona Project: 3. Specialized Activity Sites*, edited by Lynn S. Teague and Patricia L. Crown, pp. 604–620. Archaeological Series 150. Arizona State Museum, Tucson.

1984   Historic Desertification, Prehistoric Vegetation Change, and Hohokam Subsistence in the Salt-Gila Basin. In *Hohokam Archaeology along the Salt-Gila Aqueduct Central Arizona*

    Project: 7. Environment and Subsistence, edited by Lynn S. Teague and Patricia L. Crown, pp. 53–80. Archaeological Series 150. Arizona State Museum, Tucson.

Minnis, Paul E.
    1978   Paleoethnobotanical Indicators of Prehistoric Environmental Disturbance: A Case Study. In *The Nature and Status of Ethnobotany*, edited by Richard I. Ford, pp. 347–366. Anthropological Papers 67. Museum of Anthropology, University of Michigan, Ann Arbor.

    1985   *Social Adaptation to Food Stress: A Prehistoric Example*. University of Chicago Press, Chicago.

Minnis, Paul E., and Stephen E. Plog
    1976   A Study of the Site Specific Distribution of *Agave Parryi* in East Central Arizona. *Kiva* 41:299–308.

Nabhan, Gary P.
    1979   The Ecology of Floodwater Farming in Arid Southwestern North America. *Agro-Ecosystems* 5:245–255.

    1983   *Papago Fields: Arid Lands Ethnobotany and Agricultural Ecology*. Unpublished PhD dissertation, Arid Lands Resource Sciences Committee, University of Arizona, Tucson.

Nabhan, Gary P., and J. M. J. de Wet
    1984   *Panicum sonorum* in Sonoran Desert Agriculture. *Economic Botany* 38:65–82.

Nabhan, Gary P., A. M. Rea, K. L. Reichhardt, E. Mellink, and C. F. Hutchinson
    1982   Papago Influences on Habitat and Biotic Diversity: Quitovac Oasis Ethnoecology. *Journal of Ethnobiology* 2:124–143.

Nequatewa, Edmund
    1936   *Truth of a Hopi and Other Clan Stories of Shung-opovi*. Bulletin 8. Museum of Northern Arizona, Flagstaff.

Neusius, Sarah W., and M. Gould
    1988   Faunal Remains: Implications for Dolores Anasazi Adaptations. In *Dolores Archaeological Program: Anasazi Communities at Dolores: Grass Mesa Village*, edited by William D. Lipe, James N. Morris, and Timothy A. Kohler, pp. 1049–1136. Bureau of Reclamation, US Department of the Interior, Denver.

Nichols, Robert F., and David G. Smith
    1965   Evidence of Prehistoric Cultivation of Douglas-Fir Trees at Mesa Verde. *Memoir* 31(2, Part 2):57–64. Society for American Archaeology, Washington, DC.

Odum, Eugene P.
    1966   *Ecology*. Holt, Rinehart and Winston, New York.

Palmer, E.
    1871   Food Products of the North American Indians. *Report of the Commissioner of Agriculture for 1870*, pp. 404–428. Government Printing Office, Washington, DC.

Parsons, Elsie C.
    1939   *Pueblo Indian Religion*, vol. 1 and 2. University of Chicago Press, Chicago.

Petersen, Kenneth L.
    1985   The History of the Marsh in Sagehen Flats: The Pollen Record. In *Dolores Archaeological Program: Studies in Environmental Archaeology*, edited by Kenneth Lee Petersen, Vickie L. Clay, Meredith H. Matthews, and Sarah W. Neusius, pp. 229–238. Bureau of Reclamation, US Department of the Interior, Denver.

Petersen, Kenneth L., and Meredith H. Matthews
    1987   Man's Impact on the Landscape: A Prehistoric Example from the Dolores River Anasazi, Southwestern Colorado. *Journal of the West* 26(3):4–16.

Pyne, Stephen J.
    1982   *Fire in America: A Cultural History of Wildland and Rural Fire*. Princeton University Press, Princeton.

Rea, Amadeo M.

    1979   *The Ecology of Pima Fields*. Environment Southwest 484. San Diego Natural History Society, San Diego.

    1997   *At the Desert's Green Edge: An Ethnobotany of the Gila River Pima*. University of Arizona Press, Tucson.

Reynolds, Richard Dwan

    1959   *Effect of Natural Fires and Aboriginal Burning upon the Forests of the Central Sierra Nevada*. Unpublished master's thesis, Department of Geography, University of California, Berkeley.

Romney, E. M., A. Wallace, and R. B. Hunter

    1978   Plant Response to Nitrogen Fertilization in the Northern Mohave Desert and Its Relation to Water Manipulation. In *Nitrogen in Desert Ecosystems*, edited by N. E. West and J. Skujins, pp. 232–242. Dowden, Hutchinson and Ross, Stroudsburg, Pennsylvania.

Russell, Frank

    1975   *The Pima Indians*. University of Arizona Press, Tucson.

Russell, Scott C.

    1983   *Factors Affecting Agricultural Production in a Western Navajo Community*. Unpublished PhD dissertation, Department of Anthropology, Arizona State University, Tempe.

Russell, Scott C., and Jeffrey S. Dean

    n.d.   Navajo Wood Use Behavior: Archaeological and Dendrochronological Data. Manuscript on file, Laboratory of Tree-Ring Research, Tucson.

Samuels, M. L., and Julio L. Betancourt

    1982   Modeling the Long-Term Effects of Fuelwood Harvests on Pinyon Juniper Woodlands. *Environmental Management* 6:505–515.

Sando, Joe S.

    1992   *Pueblo Nations. Eight Centuries of Pueblo Indian History*. Clear Light, Santa Fe.

Sandor, Jonathan A., Paul L. Gersper, and John W. Hawley

    1990   Prehistoric Agricultural Terraces and Soils in the Mimbres Area, New Mexico. *World Archaeology* 22:70–86.

Shipek, Florence C.

    1989   An Example of Intensive Plant Husbandry: The Kumeyaay of Southern California. In *Foraging and Farming, The Evolution of Plant Exploitation*, edited by David R. Harris and Gordon C. Hillman, pp. 159–170. Unwin Hyman, London.

Spier, Leslie

    1928   *Havasupai Ethnography*. Anthropological Papers 29, Pt. 3. American Museum of Natural History, New York.

Stant, M. Y.

    1953   Variations in Reed Structure in Relation to Thatching. *Kew Bulletin* 2:231–238.

Stephen, Alexander M.

    1936   *Hopi Journal of Alexander M. Stephen*, edited by Elsie C. Parsons. Contributions in Anthropology 23, Pts. 1 and 2. Columbia University Press, New York.

Stevenson, Matilda C.

    1904   *The Zuni Indians*. 23rd Annual Report for the Years 1901–1902. Bureau of American Ethnology, Smithsonian Institution, Washington, DC.

    1915   *Ethnobotany of the Zuni Indians*. Annual Report (1908–1909) 30:35–102. Bureau of American Ethnology, Smithsonian Institution, Washington, DC.

Stewart, Omer C.

    1956   Fire as the First Great Force Employed by Man. In *Man's Role in Changing the Face of the Earth*, edited by William L. Thomas, pp. 115–133. University of Chicago Press, Chicago.

Swetnam, Thomas W.
  1984   Peeled Ponderosa Pine Trees: A Record of Inner Bark Utilization by Native Americans. *Journal of Ethnobiology* 4:177–190.
Swetnam, Thomas W., C. H. Baisan, P. M. Brown, and A. C. Caprio
  1987   *Fire History of Rhyolite Canyon, Chiricahua National Monument.* Technical Report 32. Co-operative National Park Resources Studies Unit, Tucson.
Swetnam, Thomas, C. H. Baisan, A. C. Caprio, A. McCord, and P. Brown
  1991   Fire and Flood in a Canyon Woodland: The Effects of Floods and Debris Flows on the Past Fire Regime of Rhyolite Canyon, Chiricahua National Monument. Manuscript on file, Laboratory of Tree-Ring Research, Tucson.
Szuter, Christine R.
  1984a Paleoenvironment and Species Richness along the Salt-Gila Aqueduct. In *Hohokam Archaeology along the Salt-Gila Aqueduct Central Arizona Project: 7. Environment and Subsistence*, edited by Lynn S. Teague and Patricia L. Crown, pp. 81–93. Archaeological Series 150. Arizona State Museum, Tucson.
  1984b Faunal Exploitation and the Reliance on Small Animals. In *Hohokam Archaeology along the Salt-Gila Aqueduct Central Arizona Project: 7. Environment and Subsistence*, edited by Lynn S. Teague and Patricia L. Crown, pp. 139–170. Archaeological Series 150. Arizona State Museum, Tucson.
  1986   Lagomorph and Artiodactyl Exploitation among the Inhabitants of the West Branch Site. In *Archaeological Investigations at the West Branch Site: Early and Middle Rincon Occupation in the Southern Tucson Basin*, edited by Frederick W. Huntington, pp. 273–288. Anthropological Paper 3. Institute for American Research, Tucson.
Van Devender, Thomas R.
  1985   Late Holocene Plant Records from the Dolores River Area, Montezuma County, Colorado. In *Dolores Archaeological Program: Studies in Environmental Archaeology*, edited by Kenneth Lee Petersen, Vickie L. Clay, Meredith H. Matthews, and Sarah W. Neusius, pp. 203–206. Bureau of Reclamation, US Department of the Interior, Denver.
Varien, Mark D.
  1999   *The Sand Canyon Archaeological Project: Site Testing.* Version 1.0. Available online at http://www.crowcanyon.org/ResearchReports/SiteTesting/start.htm. Crow Canyon Archaeological Center, Cortez, Colorado.
Vivian, R. G.
  1974   Conservation and Diversion Water-Control Systems in the Anasazi Southwest. In *Irrigation's Impact on Society*, edited by Theodore E. Downing and McGuire Gibson, pp. 95–112. Anthropological Papers 25. University of Arizona, Tucson.
Voegelin, Erminie W.
  1938   *Tubatulabal Ethnography.* Anthropological Records 2(1). University of California Press, Berkeley.
Waters, M. R., and John C. Ravesloot
  2000   Late Quaternary Geology of the Middle Gila River, Gila River Indian Reservation, Arizona. *Quaternary Research* 54:49–57.
Wells, C. G., R. E. Campbell, L. F. De Bano, C. E. Lewis, R. L. Fredriksen, E. C. Franklin, R. C. Froelich, and P. H. Dunn
  1979   *Effects of Fire on Soil. A State-of-Knowledge Review.* General Technical Report WO-7. USDA Forest Service, Albuquerque.
White, Leslie A.
  1932   *The Acoma Indians.* 47th Annual Report (1929–1930), pp. 18–192. Bureau of American Ethnology, Smithsonian Institution, Washington, DC.

Karen R. Adams

1943   *New Material from Acoma.* Bulletin 136. Anthropological Papers 32. Bureau of American Ethnology, Smithsonian Institution, Washington, DC.

Whiting, Alfred F.

1966   *Ethnobotany of the Hopi.* Reprinted. Northland Press, Flagstaff. Originally published 1939, Bulletin 15, Museum of Northern Arizona, Flagstaff.

Wickstrom, C. K. Roper

1987   *Issues Concerning Native American Use of Fire: A Literature Review.* Publications in Anthropology 6. Yosemite Research Center, Yosemite National Park, California.

Wilcox, David R., and Lynette O. Shenk

1981   *The Architecture of Casa Grande and Its Interpretation.* Archaeological Series 115. Arizona State Museum, Tucson.

Wilshusen, Richard H., Melissa J. Churchill, and James M. Potter

1997   Prehistoric Reservoirs and Water Basins in the Mesa Verde Region: Intensification of Water Collection Strategies during the Great Pueblo Period. *American Antiquity* 62:664–681.

Winter, Joseph C.

1978   *Anasazi Agriculture at Hovenweep, Field Systems.* Contributions to Anthropological Studies 1. Center for Anthropological Studies, Albuquerque.

Woodbury, Richard B., and J. Q. Ressler

1962   Effects of Environmental and Cultural Limitations upon Hohokam Agriculture, Southern Arizona. In *Civilizations in Desert Lands*, edited by Richard B. Woodbury, pp. 41–55. Anthropological Papers 62. University of Utah, Salt Lake City.

Wycoff, Don G.

1977   Secondary Forest Succession Following Abandonment of Mesa Verde. *Kiva* 42:215–231.

Yarnell, Richard A.

1965   Implications of Distinctive Flora on Pueblo Ruins. *American Anthropologist* 67:662–674.

Great Basin Paleoethnobotany

LINDA SCOTT CUMMINGS

*T*he boundaries of the Great Basin traditionally have been identified as the Sierra Nevada Mountains on the west and the Rocky Mountains on the east (Figure 6.1). Over 1 million square kilometers (400,000 square miles) of land are included in the area, which encompasses all of the states of Nevada and Utah, most of western Colorado to the western border of the Rocky Mountains, western Wyoming, portions of southern Idaho and southeastern Oregon, and smaller parts of eastern California and northern Arizona and New Mexico (d'Azevedo 1986:1). In this volume, the Owens Valley, Death Valley, and other areas of California normally included in the Great Basin are treated in the California chapter by Julia Hammett and Elizabeth Lawlor.

Physiographically, this large interior basin is part of a more extensive basin and range province, in which mountain ranges alternate with long, narrow valleys and basins (Jennings 1986: 113). Humans occupying the prehistoric Great Basin adapted to widely varying microenvironments. Large portions of the Great Basin were occupied by people practicing an Archaic lifestyle, dependent on hunting and gathering and "generally

Linda Scott Cummings

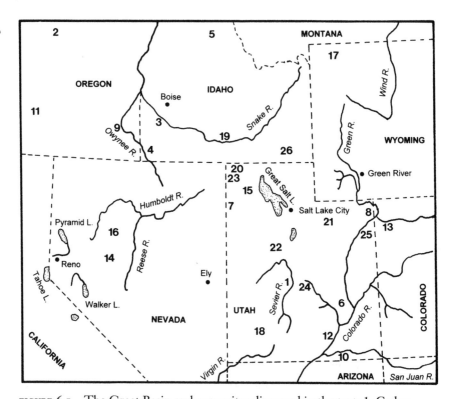

FIGURE 6.1　The Great Basin and some sites discussed in the text: 1. Cedar
Siding Shelter, Fremont, Innocents Ridge, and Trough Cave; 2. central and
northern Oregon sites; 3. Cave 1; 4. Columbet Rockshelter and Kitty's Hot
Hole site; 5. Corn Cave; 6. Cowboy Cave; 7. Danger Cave; 8. Deluge Shelter
and Dinosaur National Monument; 9. Dirty Shame Rockshelter; 10. Dust
Devil Cave and Sanddune Cave; 11. Fort Rock Basin; 12. Glen Canyon;
13. Hell's Midden; 14. Hidden Cave; 15. Hogup Cave; 16. Lovelock Cave;
17. Mummy Cave; 18. Parowan Fremont; 19. Pence-Duerig Cave; 20. Rampart
Cave; 21. San Raphael Fremont; 22. Sevier/Fremont; 23. Swallow Shelter;
24. Sudden Shelter; 25. Thorne Cave; 26. Wahmuza and Aviator's Cave

lacking domesticated animals, horticulture, or permanent villages" (Jennings 1986:113). Cultural diversity over this large geographic area is exemplified by the contrast between the agricultural economy of Fremont groups
and the hunting and gathering economy of Archaic groups.

The Fremont occupied large portions of Utah, "as well as adjacent portions of eastern Nevada, western Colorado, and southern Idaho" (Marwitt
1986:161) and probably portions of southwest Wyoming. The sedentary life-

style of the Fremont was aberrant within the Great Basin. The Fremont occupied portions of the Colorado Plateau, where environmental diversity fostered regional specialization. Although the unifying trait among Fremont peoples was a pattern of village farming, which developed from an Archaic base, "horticulture and sedentary villages were never developed by the Fremont people to the extent that they were by their neighbors in the prehistoric Southwest. Hunting and gathering remained important economic activities for all groups during the entire span of the Fremont culture" (Marwitt 1986: 161). The Fremont in the southern and eastern portions of their range were more heavily dependent on horticulture than were the people living in the northern and western areas, where reliance on native game and plants was more important.

The Archaic hunters and gatherers of the Great Basin exploited such widely varying habitats as dry valleys, spring-fed marshes, deserts, and forested mountains. The specialized and often rich environments provided variety in the plant and animal populations available for exploitation. The degree of annual mobility of different groups, the makeup of their tool assemblages, and major food and other resources they exploited varied greatly across the Great Basin. Local adaptations by occupants of the Great Basin have led researchers to construct separate prehistoric chronologies for six discretely defined areas in the region (Figure 6.1). For the northern area, which includes portions of southeastern Oregon, northeastern California, and northwestern Nevada, two chronologies have been put forth. For the western area, which encompasses most of the state of Nevada, as well as the easternmost portion of California, numerous temporal subdivisions have been proposed for the Archaic occupations (Elston 1986:135). The chronology for the southwestern area, which includes the southern tip of Nevada and southern portion of eastern California, is divided into the following sequence: Clovis during the Pre-Archaic period, Lake Mojave and Pinto during the Early Archaic, Gypsum during the Middle Archaic, and Fremont-Anasazi and ethnographic peoples during the Late Archaic. The southeastern area, which includes the eastern portion of the southern tip of Nevada, northwestern Arizona, and southwestern Utah is divided into Pre-Archaic, Early Archaic, Middle Archaic, and Late Archaic segments, the latter being the period of Fremont-Anasazi and ethnographic peoples. The sequence in the eastern area, which includes the eastern portion of Nevada, most of the state of Utah, and portions of Colorado and southwestern Wyoming, begins with possible Clovis during the Pre-Archaic period, followed by Bonneville and Windover phases during the Early Archaic, Black Rock phase during the Middle Archaic, a Fremont-

Anasazi occupation, and, finally, ethnographic peoples practicing a Late Archaic lifestyle. The Upper Snake and Salmon River area encompasses southern Idaho, as well as the central and northern portions of western Wyoming. The culture chronological divisions for this area include Clovis, Folsom, and Plano during the Pre-Archaic period, a short Early Archaic period, a Middle Archaic period, a Fremont-Anasazi period, and, finally, the ethnographic period, during which people practiced a Late Archaic lifestyle. The Pre-Archaic lifestyle appears to have continued longer in the Upper Snake and Salmon River area than in any of the other geographic areas.

Natural Environment

The alternation of mountains and valleys in the Great Basin produces a complex pattern of environmental variability. In general, precipitation rises and temperature decreases with increasing elevation (Daubenmire 1979). The southwest quarter of the Great Basin experiences the lowest precipitation and the most severe evaporative stress. Plant cover is extremely scant. Temperatures decrease and available moisture increases on a gradient from south to north across the region. Cacti and succulents comprise a greater proportion of the vegetation in the southwest, decreasing to a minor component in the plateau area. The mountains are the least arid, standing as "humid islands above parched lowlands" (Harper 1986:51).

Total annual precipitation is most variable in the drier areas of the Great Basin, resulting in plant resources that are both small in size and unpredictable in availability. The highly variable precipitation is responsible for a generalist adaptive strategy on the part of the area's Native inhabitants, who utilized available resources rather than developing specialization leading to subsequent reliance on relatively few resources.

The Colorado River drainage supports a mosaic of sagebrush (*Artemisia*) and grasses (mainly *Agropyron*, *Festuca*, and *Poa*), which vary in relative frequency (see Table 6.1 for a listing of plant names appearing in the text). Internal basins are common within the Great Basin as a result of the lack of external drainage. This drainage pattern is largely responsible for the concentric fluctuations in soil texture and salinity that also influence local vegetation.

The Mojave Desert areas in southern Nevada and adjacent California are often dominated by creosote (*Larrea tridentata*). The colder deserts of the Great Basin, Colorado Plateau, and Snake River plain are dominated by sagebrush (*Artemisia*). Fluctuations in the quantities of sagebrush and grass are

Table 6.1

Common and Scientific Names Used in the Text

Common Name	Scientific Name
Agave	*Agave*
Alder	*Alnus*
Alder, thin-leaf	*Alnus tenuifolia*
Amaranth	*Amaranthus*
Arrowweed	*Sagittaria*
Aspen, quaking	*Populus tremuloides*
Bean, common	*Phaseolus vulgaris*
Bean, cultivated	cf. *Phaseolus*
Bean family	Fabaceae
Bedstraw, cleavers	*Galium*
Beeweed	*Cleome*
Bitterbush	*Purshia*
Birch	*Betula*
Birch, water	*Betula occidentalis*
Blueberry	*Vaccinium*
Bluegrass	*Poa*
Brodiaea	cf. *Brodiaea* (*Dichelostemma*)
Bulrush	*Scirpus*
Bulrush, alkali	*Scirpus maritimus* var. *paludosus* (*Scirpus paludosus*)
Bulrush, panicled	*Scirpus microcarpus*
Bulrush, three-square	*Scirpus americanus*
Bunchgrass	*Festuca*
Bunchgrass, blue; wheatgrass	*Agropyron spicatum*
Bur reed	*Sparganium*
Buttercup family	Ranunculaceae
Cactus family	Cactaceae
Camas	*Camassia quamash*
Cane	*Phragmites communis*
Cattail, common	*Typha latifolia*
Cattail, narrowleaf	*Typha angustifolia*
Cheno-ams	amaranth and pigweed family
Cherry, wild	*Prunus*
Chokecherry	*Prunus virginiana*
Cliffrose	*Cowania*
Collomia	*Collomia*
Corispermum; bugseed	*Corispermum hyssipfolium*
Cottonwood; poplar; aspen	*Populus*
Cow-parsnip	*Heracleum lanatum*
Creosote	*Larrea tridentata*
Cryptanth	*Cryptantha*
Desert almond	*Prunus fasciculatus*
Dicoria	*Dicoria*
Ditchgrass	*Ruppia*

Continued on next page

Table 6.1 *continued*

Common Name	Scientific Name
Dock	*Rumex*
Dogbane; Indian hemp	*Apocynum*
Dogbane, low	*Apocynum androsaemifolium*
Dogwood	*Cornus*
Dogwood, red-osier	*Cornus stolinifera*
Douglas-fir	*Pseudotsuga*
Dropseed	*Sporobolus*
Dropseed, sand	*Sporobolus cryptandrus*
Elder; elderberry	*Sambucus*
Evening primrose	*Oenothera*
Fir	*Abies*
Fishhook cactus	*Sclerocactus*
Flax	*Linum*
Galleta grass	*Hilaria*
Glasswort	*Salicornia rubra*
Goldenweed	*Haplopappus*
Gooseberry	*Ribes*
Goosefoot	*Chenopodium*
Grass family	Poaceae
Greasewood	*Sarcobatus, Sarcobatus vermiculatus*
Green ephedra	*Ephedra* cf. *viridis*
Hackberry	*Celtis*
Hedgehog cactus	*Pediocactus simsoni*
Heath family	Ericaceae
Hedgehog or strawberry cactus	*Echinocereus*
Hopsage	*Grayia*
Horsebrush	*Tetradymia*
Horsetail	*Equisetum*
June grass	*Koeleria*
Juniper	*Juniperus*
Knotweed	*Polygonum*
Knotweed/smartweed family	Polygonaceae
Leather biscuitroot	*Lomatium*
Lily family	Liliaceae
Maize; corn	*Zea mays*
Manzanita; kinnickinnick	*Arctostaphylos*
Maple	*Acer*
Maple, big-tooth	*Acer glabrum*
Maple, rocky	*Acer grandidentatum*
Marsh marigold	*Caltha leptosepala*
Mesquite	*Prosopis*
Milkvetch	*Astragalus*
Milkweed	*Asclepias*
Mock-orange	*Philadelphus, Philadelphus lewisii*

Table 6.1 *continued*

Common Name	Scientific Name
Mormon tea	*Ephedra, Ephedra torreyena*-type
Mormon tea, Nevada	*Ephedra nevadensis*-type
Mountain lilac	*Ceanothus*
Mountain mahogany	*Cercocarpus*
Mountain mahogany, alder leaf	*Cercocarpus montanus*
Mountain mahogany, curl leaf	*Cercocarpus ledifolius*
Muhly	*Muhlenbergia*
Mule ears	*Wyethia amplexicaulis*
Mustard family	Brassicaceae
Needle grass	*Stipa*
Ninebark	*Physocarpus malvaceous*
Oak	*Quercus*
Oak, gambel's; scrub oak	*Quercus gambelli*
Onion, wild	*Allium*
Onion, wild/beargrass	cf. *Allium/Nolina*
Orache	*Atriplex* cf. *patula*
Peppergrass; pepperweed	*Lepidium*
Phacelia	*Phacelia*
Phlox	*Phlox*
Pickleweed	*Allenrolfea*
Pincushion cactus	*Mammillaria*
Pine	*Pinus*
Pine, lodgepole	*Pinus contorta*
Pine, piñon	*Pinus edulis*
Pine, ponderosa	*Pinus ponderosa*
Pine, single leaf piñon	*Pinus monophylla*
Pinkweed	*Polygonum pennsylvanicum*-type
Plane tree; sycamore	*Platanus*
Plum, wild	*Prunus americana*
Pondweed	*Potamogeton*
Potato, wild	*Solanum jamesii*
Poverty weed	*Monolepis*
Prickly pear cactus	*Opuntia*
Rabbitbrush	*Chrysothamnus*
Raspberry	*Rubus*
Redmaids	*Calandrinia*
Reed	*Phragmites, Phragmites australis*
Reed, hardstem tule	*Scirpus acutus*
Reed, knotted; braided reed	*Scirpus olneyii*
Ricegrass	*Oryzopsis*
Rose family	Rosaceae
Rose, wild	*Rosa*
Rush	*Juncus*
Sage, bud	*Artemisia spinescens*

Continued on next page

Table 6.1 *continued*

Common Name	Scientific Name
Sagebrush	*Artemisia*
Sagebrush, big	*Artemisia* cf. *tridentata*
Saltbush	*Atriplex*
Saxifrage family	Saxifragaceae
Seepweed; sea-blite; suaeda	*Suaeda*
Sedge	*Carex*
Sedge family	Cyperaceae
Sego lily	*Calochortus*
Serviceberry	*Amelanchier alnifolia*
Shadscale; saltbush	*Atriplex canescens*
Shadscale; sheep fat; spiny saltbush	*Atriplex confertifolia*
Shooting star	*Dodecatheon*
Silverberry	*Elaeagnus argentia*
Snapweed	*Balsamorhiza sagittata*
Snowberry	*Symphoricarpus*
Spruce	*Picea*
Spruce, Engelmann	*Picea engelmannii*
Squash; pumpkin; gourd	*Cucurbita*
Squawberry	*Rhus trilobata*
Strawberry	*Fragaria*
Sunflower	*Helianthus*
Sunflower family	Asteraceae
Tansy mustard	*Descurainia*
Umbel or parsley family	Apiaceae
Valerian	*Valeriana edulis*
Water lily, native	*Nuphar polysepalum*
Western wintergreen	*Gaultheria humifusa*
Wheat	*Triticum aestivum*
Whipworm (parasite)	*Trichuris*
White sage	*Eurotia*
Wildrye	*Elymus*
Willow	*Salix*
Willow, sandbar	*Salix exigua*
Wolfberry	*Lycium pallidum*
Wood rush	*Luzula*
Yampah	*Perideridia*
Yucca	*Yucca*
Yucca, narrowleaf	*Yucca angustissima*

the basis for descriptive subdivisions within this area, including sagebrush, sagebrush-grass, and grassland. Sagebrush-grass steppe is the most common vegetation. A wider variety of herbaceous plants is expected to have existed during the prehistoric period than in modern years, given a decrease in broad-leafed herbs after contact (Barrett 1980; Cottam 1961; Harper 1986:52–53; Leopold 1950; Sauer 1950; Stewart 1955).

Mountains in the southeastern and eastern portion of the Great Basin support vegetation that varies by altitude and that consists primarily of sagebrush-grasslands on the lower slopes. "Successively higher elevations support forests of juniper (*Juniperus osteosperma*) and pinyon (*Pinus edulis*), followed by zones of scrub oak (*Quercus gambelii*), ponderosa pine (*Pinus ponderosa*) forest, aspen (*Populus tremuloides*) forest, spruce (*Picea engelmannii*) and fir (*Abies lasiocarpa*) forest, and finally open herblands above timberline" (Harper 1986:53).

The mountains of central Nevada exhibit a less complex altitudinal sequence of vegetation. Vegetation on the lower slopes is again dominated by sagebrush. With increasing elevation, this zone is replaced by juniper (*Juniperus*) and single-leaf piñon (*Pinus monophylla*) woodland, then by another sagebrush zone that includes more perennial herbs and grasses than the lower sagebrush zone. Scattered open forests of conifers are noted at higher elevations.

The mountains in the northern portion of the Great Basin along the plains of the Snake River and in western Wyoming exhibit a brushy grassland community on their lower slopes. With increasing elevation, brushland increases and may include such shrubby plants as mountain mahogany (*Cercocarpus montanus*), Rocky Mountain juniper (*Juniperus osteosperma*), serviceberry (*Amelanchier alnifolia*), maple (*Acer grandidentatum* or *A. glabrum*), snowberry (*Symphoricarpus*), ninebark (*Physocarpus malvaceous*), or chokecherry (*Prunus virginiana*) (Harper 1986:55). Closed forests occur at some higher elevations and may include Douglas-fir (*Pseudotsuga menziesii*), ponderosa or lodgepole pine (*Pinus contorta*), aspen, or spruce and fir. Alpine herblands are found above these forests at the highest elevations.

Small marshes, freshwater seeps, and springs are noted in the hydrologic basin province and in Death Valley basins of former Pleistocene lakes. Biological diversity is usually great in these areas, and plant species may include rushes (*Scirpus*), grasses (*Distichlis spicata*, *Phragmites australis*, and *Puccinellia nuttaliana*), and various succulent halophytes (*Allenrolfea occidentalis* and *Salicornia virginica*, among others). These wet areas are likely to have been of great importance to the prehistoric occupants of the Great Basin. Salinity, as well as depth of flooding, affects local vegetation in wet areas.

Saline-tolerant plants such as alkali bulrush (*Scirpus paludosus*), glasswort (*Salicornia rubra*), and saltgrass (*Distichlis spicata*) are affected by varying quantities of water. Fresh water supports cattails (*Typha latifolia*), hardstem bulrush (*Scirpus acutus*), and three-square bulrush (*Scirpus americanus*). These plants are sensitive to water depth and are variably sensitive to salinity.

In northwestern Utah and northeastern Nevada, "only 11% of the [archaeological] sites occurred on the deserts below 5000 feet, while 7% appeared above 7000 feet. The intervening elevations supported the remaining 82% of the sites" (Harper 1986:58). Vegetation zones dominated by sagebrush, juniper-piñon, and mountain brush vegetation were utilized the most by the prehistoric occupants of this portion of the Great Basin. Of the Nevada native plants with medicinal properties, the majority occur in the more moderate vegetation zones. Alpine and marsh environments support the fewest medicinal plants. Forests and deserts support moderate numbers of medicinal plants, and mountain brush, juniper-piñon, and sagebrush-grass communities support larger numbers of such plants. "The majority of known food and fiber plants also occur within the mid-elevational zones previously described as centers of human activity on the basis of dwelling-place and medicinal plant criteria" (Harper 1986:58). The most common of these plants are listed in Table 6.2.

Stream-bank and marsh communities also would have been important to prehistoric peoples. Not only are the marsh plants themselves economically useful, but they also attract native fauna, making marshes good places for hunting. Fleshy rhizomes, greens, and seeds all could have been collected from these riparian habitats. Valuable fibers for mats and cordage also would have been available from plants gathered in marshes, such as tule reeds (*Scirpus acutus*), dogbane (*Apocynum*), and milkweed (*Asclepias*).

Higher-elevation forests and meadows provided such fruits as gooseberries (*Ribes*), serviceberries (*Amelanchier*), strawberries (*Fragaria*), raspberries (*Rubus*), western wintergreen (*Gaultheria humifusa*), and blueberries (*Vaccinium*). High-elevation plant resources probably included native water lily (*Nuphar polysepalum*) rhizomes and seeds, greens from the marsh marigold (*Caltha leptosepala*), and perhaps the edible and medicinally valuable valerian root stalks (*Valeriana edulis*). Cow-parsnip (*Heracleum lanatum*) roots also were valuable as food or for medicinal use.

Horticulture was practiced in the southeastern portion of the Great Basin on the lower Colorado Plateau and included cultivation of such crops as corn (*Zea mays*), cucurbits (*Cucurbita mixta*, *C. pepo*), beans (*Phaseolus vulgaris*), and

Table 6.2

Common Food and Fiber Plants of the Great Basin

Common Name	Scientific Name	Use	Location
Amaranth	*Amaranthus* spp.	seeds	disturbed
Beeweed	*Cleome serrulata, C. lutea*	seeds	disturbed
Bitterroot	*Lewisia rediviva*	roots	north
Blue elderberry	*Sambucus caerulea*	fruits	foothills/riparian
Bluegrass	*Poa* spp.	seeds	
Bracken fern	*Pteridium aquilinum*	greens	north
Camas	*Camassia quamash*	roots	north
Chenopods	*Chenopodium* spp.	seeds	disturbed
Chokecherry	*Prunus virginiana*	fruits	foothills/riparian
Cliffrose	*Cowania mexicana*	fiber	
Cottonwood	*Populus fremontii*	fiber	
Currants	*Ribes* spp.	fruits	foothills/riparian
Dogbane	*Apocynum* spp.	fiber	
Groundcherry	*Physalis* spp.	fruits	foothills/riparian
Indian potato	*Orogenia linearifolia*	roots	north
Indian ricegrass	*Oryzopsis hymenoides*	seeds	
Juniper	*Juniperus*	fiber	
Milkweed	*Asclepias speciosa*	fiber	
Miner's lettuce	*Claytonia perfoliata*	greens	north
Oak	*Quercus* spp.	nuts	foothills/riparian
Oregon-grape	*Berberis repens*	fruits	foothills/riparian
Piñon pine	*Pinus edulis, P. monophylla*	nuts	foothills
Sagebrush	*Artemisia* spp.	fiber	
Sand dropseed grass	*Sporobolus cryptandrus*	seeds	
Sego lily	*Calochortus* spp.	roots	north
Serviceberry	*Amelanchier*	fruits	foothills/riparian
Silver buffaloberry	*Shepherdia argentea*	fruits	foothills/riparian
Sunflower	*Helianthus annuus*	seeds (achenes)	especially profuse on burned areas
Sweet cicely	*Osmorhiza* spp.	greens	north
Violets	*Viola* spp.	greens	north
Wild caraway	*Perideridia gairdneri*	roots	north
Wild flax	*Linum perenne*	fiber	
Wild grape	*Vitis arizonica*	fruits	foothills/riparian
Wild onion	*Allium* spp.	roots	north
Wild rose	*Rosa* spp.	fruits	foothills/riparian
Wild ryegrass	*Elymus* spp.	seeds	
Yellow bells	*Fritillaria pudica*	roots	north

Source: Fowler 1986.

cotton (*Gossypium*). Weeds common to disturbed ground, such as amaranths (*Amaranthus*), goosefoot (*Chenopodium*), groundcherry (*Physalis*), and beeweed (*Cleome*), were probably common at villages, in middens, and perhaps in or at the edges of agricultural fields. Greens, seeds, or fruits from these plants would have been harvested. It is possible that these plants were manipulated or encouraged to grow in certain areas near sites to concentrate these weedy resources for harvest. "Jennings (1966) suggests that certain fleshy-fruited prickly pears (*Opuntia* spp.) and sunflowers (*Helianthus*) were wild plants that were deliberately cultivated" (Harper 1986:60). Wolfberry (*Lycium pallidum*) is frequently noted to grow around prehistoric dwellings, suggesting that it, too, may have been cultivated (Harper 1986:60; Yarnell 1965). Irrigation appears to have been rare in the prehistoric, as well as in the early historic, occupation of the southeastern portion of the Great Basin (Harper 1986:60; Woodbury 1954).

Brief Review of Dietary Patterns

Three sequential climatic episodes—the relatively cool, moist Anathermal, the hot, dry Altithermal, and the cooler, more mesic Medithermal—proposed by Antevs (1948) provide a background for understanding paleoenvironmental change that influenced prehistoric cultures in the Great Basin. "Most instability of the last 10,000 years is mirrored in the ecological variation encountered by Great Basin inhabitants within a single year" (Mehringer 1986:50). The first studies of plant remains and pollen in the Great Basin were undertaken to identify paleoenvironmental conditions. These studies identified plant remains from ancient woodrat middens (Wells and Jorgensen 1964) and laid a foundation for palynological studies to address archaeological questions in the southern Great Basin and the North American Southwest (Martin 1963).

Early coprolite studies provided a wealth of information concerning diet and subsistence in the Great Basin, as well as guidelines for further coprolite studies throughout the American West for several decades. Pollen, macrofloral, and, usually, parasite studies of coprolites were conducted. Studies of coprolites from Hogup and Danger Caves focused on the "varieties and importance of foods (Kelso 1970; Wilke 1978), their preparation (Napton and Kelso 1969:26), and the season and region of their collection (Fry 1976; Heizer and Napton 1969; Wilke 1978)" (Mehringer 1986:43). Studies of seeds and pollen recovered from coprolites also addressed both time of harvest and potential for storage of foods (Mehringer 1986:43; Wigand and Mehringer 1985).

The first analysis of coprolites from Danger Cave was conducted "by Charles C. Sperry at the Wildlife Research Laboratory, U.S. Fish and Wildlife Service, Denver, Colorado" (Fry 1978:111). These results are presented in Appendix B in Jennings's (1957) monograph on the site. Four specimens tentatively identified as bear coprolites were then submitted to Robert L. Fonner at the Ethnobotanical Laboratory at the University of Michigan for analysis. The results of Fonner's study are presented in Appendix B in Jennings's (1957) monograph. Fonner implied a human origin for the four "bear" coprolites. Neither Fonner nor Sperry discussed methods used for analysis, although Fry (1978:111) assumes that they were dry analyses. Analysis of coprolites from Lovelock Cave, Nevada, "has been undertaken by Heizer (1960, 1966, 1967), Ambro and Cowan (1966), Ambro (1967), Cowan (1967), Follet (1967), Roust (1967), Tubbs and Berger (1967), and Lewis K. Napton (personal communication) at the University of California at Berkeley" (Fry 1978:112).

Gary Fry (1968, 1977, 1978) is responsible for several studies of coprolites from Danger Cave (Archaic and Desert Archaic tradition), Hogup Cave (Archaic, Fremont, and Shoshone occupations), and Glen Canyon (both Fremont and Anasazi occupations). Twenty-seven coprolite samples from Hogup Cave were examined for quantitative chemical assays of calcium, sodium, nitrogen, phosphate, and potassium. Fry examined seeds and parasites from coprolites from Glen Canyon, and pollen analysis was performed by Martin and Sharrock (1964). Ten of the Glen Canyon coprolites were examined for macrofossils by Callen (Callen and Martin 1969). Macrofloral and pollen analyses of coprolites from Hogup Cave are presented by Fry (1970:247–250) and Kelso (1970:251–262), respectively. Harper and Alder (1972) also report on remains from Danger Cave coprolites.

Rising waters in the lakes in the Great Basin after 3100 BC (Elston 1982; Mehringer 1986:36) attracted humans to the expanding marsh and lake resources. Evidence of marsh plants in the human diet was recovered from Lovelock Cave (Heizer and Napton 1969; Loud and Harrington 1929; Mehringer 1986:36; Wigand and Mehringer 1985).

Dunes are found on the leeward side of the remnants of most of the Great Basin pluvial lakes and rivers. Food plants are particularly abundant on these dunes, which support mesquite (*Prosopis juliflora, P. pubescens*) and Indian ricegrass (*Oryzopsis hymenoides*). When dunes dam spring-fed drainages, they produce marshes, with the attendant vegetation and fauna. Waterfowl and mammals also are attracted (Mehringer 1986:41).

A general review of plants documented to have been used by historic groups in the Great Basin is provided in Fowler (1986:64–97). Complexes identified as important to historic cultures include the piñon complex, the acorn complex, the mesquite complex, and the agave complex. Agave and mesquite are restricted to the southern hot deserts of the Great Basin. A variety of seeds, roots, berries, and leaves also are noted to have contributed to the historic diet. These complexes represent relatively modern vegetation zones, typical in the Great Basin since approximately the middle Holocene.

Pine nuts from piñons were an important resource in the Great Basin. "The lack of flotation so far in Great Basin archaeology has seriously skewed the archaeological record in favor of animals and against plant foods in general, but the truth is that pine nuts have been found at plenty of Great Basin sites. Unfortunately, the behavioral importance of pinyon procurement is simply not reflected in the archaeological record at either the artifact or feature level" (Thomas 1983:64). The single-leaf piñon, common in the western portions of the Great Basin, produces a larger cone and larger seed than does the two-needle piñon common in the southeastern portion of the area. The larger nuts of the single-leaf piñon appear to have played a much more important role in the diet than did the smaller nuts common on the Colorado Plateau. The single-leaf piñon appeared in the Great Basin after approximately 4000 BC (Harper 1986:59; Lanner 1983; Thompson and Hattori 1983; Wells 1983). Both piñons produce nut crops irregularly, making this resource undependable on a yearly basis. The cones require 26 months to mature, and individual stands of trees are not capable of producing bumper crops every year because of depletion of energy reserves in individual trees. Climatic variability during the two consecutive years required for cone maturation is a major cause of variability in nut production. Mobility of prehistoric peoples in the Great Basin would have compensated for local poor production of this resource, ensuring an opportunity to harvest at least some nuts every year from the foothill communities. Predictability of harvest during the 26-month maturation cycle contributed to successful planning of seasonal rounds by the Archaic and ethnographic inhabitants of the Great Basin.

Climbing is important in harvesting piñon nuts, which are collected before they drop to the ground. Because the nuts mature over a period of three growing seasons (26 months) abundance at harvest may be predicted in advance. Potential harvest size is predictable approximately 18 months in advance, when the red conelets (female flowers) are visible. Still, between this point and harvest a number of factors may affect a potentially good yield, including "weather, jays, insects, and rodents" (Thomas 1983:62). A poor harvest, however, may be recognized 18 months in advance. Piñon nut harvesting is often limited to approximately 10 days to two weeks in any one area because of competition from local jays and rodents. Thomas (1983) provides good descriptions of expected recovery for pine nuts and Indian ricegrass in the Monitor Valley.

Ricegrass (*Oryzopsis*) was a common food in the central and southern portions of the Great Basin. Ricegrass harvesting also is limited in time, because once ricegrass seeds fall to the ground, they can no longer be retrieved. Direct competition with birds, rodents, and rabbits also reduces the available crop.

Utilitarian resources such as *Salix* (willow) for basketry and *Apocynum* (Indian hemp or dogbane) for cordage and twine also would have required scheduling for harvesting. Willows could only be found in the proper condition for use in basketry between the fall, when the leaves dropped, and the spring, when the buds began to swell. Once harvested, "slender willow wands were scraped and carefully wrapped into bundles, together with coils of willow sap wood" (Thomas 1983:68). Only wands one year old were selected for harvest (Coville 1892). *Apocynum* puts up new, green stalks each year, which turn brown and brittle with age. *Apocynum* fibers may be collected only when the stalks are green and covered with reddish brown fibers (Heizer 1970; Thomas 1983:68; Wheat 1967:55). Large quantities of both *Salix* and *Apocynum* were collected and stored by historic period groups.

An attempt at identifying changing resource use through time in the Great Basin is based on the recovery of small seeds from such plants as goosefoot, cactus, and grass from features or deposits dated prior to AD 1000. Examination of specific prehistoric diets will rely on pollen, macrofloral, phytolith, and starch studies in conjunction with archaeological investigations. Phytolith and starch analyses are relatively new studies in the Great Basin. Pollen and macrofloral analyses, on the other hand, have contributed for several decades to understanding the subsistence patterns of the area's prehistoric occupants. The Great Basin is a large and diverse geographic area. Therefore, I provide the following review of the paleoethnobotanical evidence related to diet as well as to changes in subsistence through time on a regional basis.

Northern Area

Fort Rock Basin

Situated in the south-central portion of Oregon, Fort Rock Basin occupies the northwestern portion of the northern Great Basin. This large, flat basin includes three subbasins—the Fort Rock Valley, Christmas Valley, and Silver

Lake Valley. Models based on ethnographic data have been developed to test the hypothesis that intensive root crop harvests supported prehistoric villages (Prouty 1994). A study of root crop exploitation at upland habitation sites has focused on subsistence/settlement and mobility (Prouty 1994). Ethnographic records of historically exploited root grounds in the Fort Rock Basin provide evidence of the exploitation of a large variety of plant roots, tubers, nuts, seeds, and berries in many diverse environments around marshes, lakes, and playas, and in desert lowlands and upland forests. Seasonal mobility facilitated plant collection as resources became available. Examination of the paleoethnobotanical record from long-term settlements or villages at upland sites in the Fort Rock Basin has yielded excellent data. This study includes air photo interpretation, a survey and census of plant resources, site catchment analysis, experimental archaeology, and flotation or macrobotanical analysis (Prouty 1994:588).

In the Fort Rock Basin, Early and Middle Archaic villages were commonly located along marsh peripheries. The only modern marsh system in the Fort Rock Basin is located in the Silver Lake Valley. "Reduction in the reliability of these resources and increases in human populations apparently led to a gradual increase in the exploitation of upland root crops and a shift in residence to upland 'root ground' villages" (Jenkins 1994:599). This shift appears to have begun as early as 1000 to 2000 BC, with a cluster of villages dating between 1359 to 1450 BC, although the pattern became far more common after AD 450. The Western Pluvial Lakes tradition (9000–6000 BC) is identified from cave sites around early Holocene lakes and marshes, and the assumption is that subsistence focused on resources available in and around these wetlands. These lakes and marshes dried up during the Altithermal (ca. 5550–2500 BC), and people moved away from the caves to occupy areas around the most favorable springs and marshes. With the Medithermal (ca. 2500 BC to present), for which moister climatic conditions are postulated, people reoccupied the caves. Utilization of small, hard seeds was postulated to have accompanied the increase in ground stone artifacts between 3000 and 1000 BC. Differential utilization of upland and lowland resources is the focus of current research in the Fort Rock Basin (Jenkins 1994:600).

Macrobotanical analysis in the Fort Rock Basin was conducted of samples from five village sites ranging in age from 2900 BC to AD 450 (Stenholm 1994). Stenholm attempted to identify tissue fragments from roots such as biscuitroot (*Lomatium*) and yampah (*Perideridia*). Recovery of a complete charred root (biscuitroot or yampah) at Boulder Village was fortuitous. The outer root covering was missing, supporting an interpretation that roots were cleaned before being cooked. Accidental loss undoubtedly resulted in charring of this single specimen. Charred *Atriplex* cf. *patula* seeds recovered at Boulder Village from two structures, including a historic wickiup, suggest utilization of *Atriplex* as a food or seasoning. Charred goosefoot (*Chenopodium*) seeds from Carlon Village and Boulder Village indicate that these seeds also were collected and processed. *Suaeda* seeds also were recovered at Boulder Village and Scotts Village. Suaeda is a common food plant of the Great Basin, growing in marshy areas and on more or less saline or alkaline soil. A single, charred, probable legume embryo suggests the possibility that a member of the pea family was harvested during the early summer. Charred specimens indicate that occupants of these villages utilized such grass seeds as wheatgrass (*Agropyron*), bunchgrass (*Festuca*), and, probably, bluegrass (*Poa*). A single, charred *Polygonum* seed was noted and may be present as a result either of economic activity or accidental introduction. Woods that were burned as fuel in these villages include *Artemisia*, *Juniperus*, *Philadelphus*, *Cercocarpus*, and *Purshia*. Charred Cyperaceae seeds that may represent either *Carex* or *Luzula* were recovered and are suggestive of inclusion in the diet. Charred wood has been divided into probable fuel (*Artemisia*, *Juniperus*, and *Pinus*) and probable construction material (*Juniperus* and *Cercocarpus*). Stenholm postulates a pattern of early season root gathering and late season small seed procurement for these villages. Table 6.3 provides a summary of archaeobotanical information from some of the Fort Rock Basin sites.

Paleoenvironmental pollen studies have been conducted in the Fort Rock Basin to provide a basis for understanding subsistence and settlement records. These studies (Mehringer 1985; Wigand 1987) provide the foundation on which current and ongoing paleoethnobotanical studies of the pollen, starch, and macrofloral records may be interpreted. Although the authors of these studies discuss settlement strategies as the direct result of resource exploitation, their interpretations are based on historical ethnographic and ethnobotanical studies. Examination of pollen, phytolith, starch, and macrofloral records in the Fort Rock Basin has very recent beginnings. Fortunately it is well guided by research designs, specific research questions, and theoretical modeling. Exploratory pollen and starch analysis at the Big M Site (2950–2550 BC) in Fort Rock Basin found evidence of grass seed starch in all samples, as well as Cyperaceae pollen and *Typha* raphids, indicating utilization of wetland resources. Recovery of *Typha* raphids in the pollen record indicates that extraction for phytoliths would likely be quite productive (Cummings 1993a). A pollen record from the uplands (Paquat Gulch—35WS125) exhibits definite evidence of the exploitation of root crops in the Apiaceae family

Table 6.3
Pollen and Macrofloral Remains from the Fort Rock Basin

Scientific Name	Common Name	Big M Site	Boulder Village	Carlon Village	Christmas Lake Valley	Indian Grave Spring Site	Paquat Gulch	Scotts Village	Zane Church
Agropyron	wheatgrass		seeds					seeds	
Apiaceae	parsley family						pollen		
Artemisia	sagebrush		charcoal					charcoal	
Artemisia cf. *spinescens*	bud-sage				charcoal				
Artemisia cf. *tridentata*	sagebrush				charcoal				charcoal
Atriplex	shadscale				charcoal				charcoal
Atriplex canescens	saltbush								charcoal
Atriplex confertifolia	shadscale								
Atriplex cf. *patula*	shadscale		seeds						
Camassia quamash	camas					bulbs			
Cercocarpus	mountain mahogany		constr. material					constr. material	
Chenopodium	goosefoot		seeds	seeds					

Cyperaceae	sedge family			seeds
Carex	sedge	pollen		seeds
Luzula	wood rush	seeds		seeds
Festuca	bunchgrass	seeds		seeds
Grayia	hopsage		charcoal	
Juniperus	juniper	charcoal, constr. material		charcoal, constr. material
Lomatium	biscuitroot	root		
Perideridia	yampah	root		
Philadelphus	mock-orange	charcoal		charcoal
Pinus	pine	seeds		seeds
Poa	bluegrass	seed		seed
Polygonum	smartweed, knotweed			
Purshia	antelope brush	charcoal		charcoal
Sarcobatus	greasewood		charcoal	
Suaeda	seepweed	seeds		seeds
Typha	cattail	raphids		
Starch	grass seed			

(Cummings 1993b). An abundance of Apiaceae pollen suggests the practice of processing or drying root crops that were brought into structures with their leaves and flowers intact. Macrofloral analysis in the Fort Rock Basin (the Big M Site, Carlin Village, and Squaw Butte) provides evidence that the diet included a mixture of small seeds and roots. Small seeds that appear to have been exploited as food include saltsage (*Atriplex*), goosefoot (*Chenopodium*), suaeda (*Suaeda*), grasses (*Agropyron* and/or *Festuca*), and juniper (*Juniperus*). Roots for which evidence of exploitation exists include biscuitroot (*Lomatium*) and yampah (*Perideridia*). Woods that may have been used as fuel or possibly fabrication material include juniper (*Juniperus*), pine (*Pinus*), sagebrush (*Artemisia*), bitterbush (*Purshia*), mountain mahogany (*Cercocarpus*), and mock-orange (*Philadelphus*). Wood fragments representing artifacts include *Juniperus* and *Cercocarpus* (Stenholm 1992).

BERGEN SITE (35LK3175) AND CLAIM A1 (35LK3176)

Houses from lowland sites (35LK3175 [Bergen] and 35LK3176 [Claim A1]) and from a site in the Boulder Village Uplands yielded macrofloral evidence of plant use. Charred *Scirpus* seeds recovered from the Bergen site indicate exploitation of riparian resources. Occupants of Claim A1 appear to have used *Atriplex* seeds. Charcoal documented at these sites includes *Juniperus*, *Chrysothamnus*, *Artemisia*, *Atriplex*, *Sarcobatus*, Salicaceae, and an unidentified hardwood. The upland site yielded evidence of processing *Atriplex* and Poaceae seeds. *Juniperus* dominated the charcoal record, and *Cercocarpus*, *Artemisia*, and Asteraceae charcoal also were recovered (Puseman and Ruggiero 1999a). A recent study of a middle Holocene house floor at the Bergen site using samples provenienced to grid squares yielded evidence of patterning of bulrush (*Scirpus*) and cheno-am seeds across the floor, clustering around the hearth in the center of the room and near the entryway (Helzer 2000).

CHRISTMAS LAKE VALLEY

Macrofloral analysis in Christmas Lake Valley has been undertaken of samples from undated hunter-gatherer sites. Charcoal recovered indicates that among the fuels used were *Artemisia* cf. *tridentata* and *Artemisia spinescens*. Shadscale (*Atriplex*) was also noted, as was either *Grayia* or *Sarcobatus* (Stenholm n.d.).

ZANE CHURCH

Macrofloral analysis at Zane Church yielded charcoal from shadscale (*Atriplex confertifolia*) or saltbush (*A. canescens*) and a small quantity of sagebrush

(*Artemisia* cf. *tridentata*). Charred seeds from bunchgrass (*Festuca*), notchgrass (*Polygonum*), and juniper (*Juniperus occidentalis*) complete the charred assemblage from a single hearth. The quantity of charred grass seeds recovered was relatively large, indicating intentional collection and processing (Stenholm 1989a).

RATZ NEST HOUSE RING (35LK2468)

The botanical assemblage recovered at the Ratz Nest House Ring (35LK2468) was large. Charred juniper nutlets were common, and the charcoal assemblage included juniper, Douglas-fir, sagebrush, and mountain mahogany. Wild cherry pit fragments also were recovered. Charred grass seeds assigned to the *Agropyron/Festuca* group complete the paleobotanical assemblage (Stenholm 1989b). In addition to reporting the customary charred seeds and charcoal fragments, Stenholm also recorded charred plant tissue and coined the term "processed edible tissue" (PET) to refer to softer tissue types, such as starchy parenchymoid or fruity epitheloid tissues. PET starchy tissues are usually starchy roots or tubers, and PET fruity tissues resemble sugar-laden fruit or berry tissue without the seeds, as well as tissue from succulent plant parts such as cactus pads.

DUNN SITE

Archaeobotanic investigations at the Dunn site (35HA1261) in the Ft. Rock Basin relate to occupation of a semisubterranean house pit dated to about 3060 ± 65 BC. Preservation of charcoal was poor, but charred seeds were noted. Charred juniper seeds and juniper fruit tissue appear to represent economic activity in the house. A hearth yielded charred *Chenopodium* and juniper seeds, as well as a single charred mustard (Brassicaceae) seed. All of these seeds represent edible resources. Wood recovered in the charcoal record includes Pinaceae and *Artemisia* (Stenholm 1990). Macrobotanical analysis at nearby 35HA1263 recovered evidence of plants useful as fuel (*Artemisia tridentata*), construction material (*Salix, Populus,* and *Philadelphus lewisii*), flooring and structural material (bluebunch wheatgrass [*Agropyron spicatum*]), and other grasses as cordage (low dogbane [*Apocynum androsaemifolium*]) and seeds and fruits from such edible resources as goosefoot (*Chenopodium*), western juniper (*Juniperus occidentalis*), wheatgrass (*Agropyron*), and knotweed (*Polygonum*). It also is possible that the knotweed and dogbane seeds, recovered as single specimens, may represent accidental intrusions from nearby plants. The macrofloral record exhibits evidence for late summer and fall harvesting. The fuel of choice appears to have been sagebrush, which was locally abundant. Small quantities of poplar or aspen and a Douglas-fir needle tip indicate that these trees also were used, at least occasionally (Stenholm 1990).

LINES SITE

The Lines site (35HH2692) in southeastern Oregon was a temporary campsite occupied at approximately AD 750. Pollen and macrofloral analyses indicate use of Poaceae, cheno-am, and *Descurainia* seeds, as well as probable Camas root, all available in the uplands. In addition, PET fragments were recovered that might represent starchy tubers. Charcoal included *Artemisia*, Chenopodiaceae, *Chrysothamnus, Juniperus, Pinus*, Rosaceae, *Amelanchier*, and *Purshia* (Cummings et al. 1998a).

DRAWS VALLEY

Pollen analysis at five sites in the Draws Valley, south-central Oregon, in the northwestern portion of the Great Basin, provides evidence of the use of Camas and other members of the Liliaceae, including *Calochortus* and perhaps *Brodiaea*, all upland resources. In addition, members of the Apiaceae family were available and apparently used. Recovery of starch granules indicates that grass seeds also were processed at this root-processing site (Cummings 1995).

INDIAN GRAVE SPRING SITE

In a study of macrobotanical remains from the Indian Grave Spring site in Harley County, southeastern Oregon, charred camas (*Camassia quamash*) bulbs were recovered, indicating their roasting. No other charred remains are reported, although uncharred remains document modern plants in the area that also may have been available for exploitation prehistorically (Prouty n.d.:Appendix A).

DIRTY SHAME ROCKSHELTER

Located on the Owyhee Plateau, Dirty Shame Rockshelter sits in the extreme southeastern corner of Oregon not far from the headwaters of the Owyhee River. Excavations yielded coprolites, macrofloral remains, basketry, and sandals representing a 9,000-year record with a hiatus between approximately 3950 and 750 BC (Aikens et al. 1977). One of the structures inside Dirty Shame Rockshelter consisted of large bundles of grass laid horizontally around the outside of a framework of vertical willow branches. Bent willow "pins" attached these bundles to the frame. Artifacts recovered beneath structures included ground stone and fragments of textiles and wooden specimens. Grass-lined pits held a few seeds and tubers or rhizome fragments, as well as ground stone, bone, and mussel and crayfish shells. These pits represent the earliest cultural features in Cultural Zone II. A grass-lined basin contained stone tools and a mat fragment.

A small patch of grass was associated with sandal and net fragments in Cultural Zone III. This zone also contained evidence of an extensive scatter of sandals, wooden shafts, and textile fragments and a large grass-lined pit that contained a textile fragment and stone tools. Cultural Zone IV also included grass-lined pits that contained stone tools, and clusters of sandals and netting fragments were recovered from this zone. Zone VI included basketry, sandal, and netting fragments.

Structures identified in Dirty Shame Rockshelter resemble winter houses built by the northern Paiute, suggesting an occupation that might have included the colder months. This interpretation is consistent with evidence of food storage in the rockshelter. Occupation of the rockshelter is interpreted to have occurred during the late summer and fall, probably lasting through the winter. The south-facing overhang would have provided one of the most hospitable locations to spend the cold months in this portion of the northern Great Basin. Preservation of large quantities of perishable materials such as "grass, leaves, bark, twigs, inflorescences, husks, seeds, and organic residue from plant decay represent food, fuel, bedding, and manufacturing materials brought into the shelter, where they were used, discarded, and fragmented underfoot through countless seasons of use" (Aikens et al. 1977:16).

Foods represented in human feces all could have been obtained locally from the moist canyon-bottom habitat. The vegetable portion of the diet, as recovered from coprolites, includes wild onion bulbs (*Allium*) and sego lily bulbs (*Calochortus*), wild cherry (*Prunus*) fruits represented by seeds, wild rose (*Rosa*), and sedge seeds (Cyperaceae). Goosefoot (*Chenopodium*), sunflower (*Helianthus*), and prickly pear cactus (*Opuntia*) may have been harvested either in the upland or along Antelope Creek. The seeds, including the cherry seeds, had been cracked and broken, indicating that they had been milled. Fragments of charred prickly pear epidermis indicate that cactus pads had been baked in a fire, presumably to remove the spines. Additional plant macrofloral remains and pollen analysis from the rockshelter deposits further expanded the number of plants interpreted to have been utilized by the occupants. Indian hemp (*Apocynum*) and milkweed (*Asclepias*) yielded fiber for cordage. Soft woods such as willow (*Salix*), cottonwood or aspen (*Populus*), birch (*Betula*), alder (*Alnus*), and juniper (*Juniperus*) were noted. Other food plants for which evidence was recovered include ryegrass (*Elymus*), buckwheat (*Eriogonum*), reed (*Phragmites*), rush (*Scirpus* and *Juncus*), arrowweed (*Sagittaria*), cattail (*Typha*), sedge (Cyperaceae), lily (Liliaceae), evening primrose (*Oenothera*), and horsetail (*Equisetum*). It also is possible that *Equisetum* was used as a medicinal or utility item. Recovery of perishable nonfood botanical remains included twined basketry and coiled ware, representing containers probably used for gathering and preparing vegetal foods. Cordage made from twisted plant fibers was common, as were sandals. Metates and manos indicate seed processing and perhaps also were used for grinding bulbs. The presence of "cut or twisted but otherwise unmodified plant fibers may represent raw materials for the making of cordage, or the weaving of baskets or sandals" (Aikens et al. 1977:19). These items indicate manufacture at the site from local resources. Recovery of small quantities of sagebrush bark from human coprolites "may represent the practice of stripping, between the teeth, this favored raw material for sandal-making" (Aikens et al. 1977:19).

Coprolite analysis indicates that the population "at Dirty Shame was infected by the common pinworm (*Enterobius vermicularis*) and may have occasionally hosted the giant thorny-headed worm [*Acanthocephala*]" (Hall 1977: cover). Although pinworm infection is irritating, its effects are not as severe as those of infection involving thorny-headed worm. Giant thorny-headed worm parasitizes various small rodents and uses the camel cricket, and perhaps other insects, as its intermediate host. Recovery of giant thorny-headed worms from coprolites at Dirty Shame always coincided with the recovery of small mammal bones, indicating the probability that it was these small animals, rather than the site's human occupants, that hosted these parasites. Because insects formed part of the diet at Dirty Shame, it also is possible that people occasionally became infected by consuming the intermediate host (Hall 1977:10). Recovery of *Muhlenbergia* grass fiber from coprolites and identification of *Muhlenbergia* in quids from Dirty Shame indicates that fibers from the quids were occasionally swallowed. *Opuntia* fibers, epidermis, and singed spines all were recovered from the coprolites and attest to the practice of burning spines off prior to consumption. The fragments of wild cherry pit may represent the ethnographically documented technique of pulverizing wild cherries, including both the fruit and pit, then sun drying the resulting pulp for storage in grass-lined pits for winter consumption (Hall 1977:5). Moderately large quantities of wild rosehip skins and seeds (*Rosa fendleri*) were recovered from the coprolites, indicating that rosehips were consumed by occupants of all three zones represented.

Nine sites along the PGT-PG&E Pipeline, which represent Early Archaic, Middle Archaic, Late Archaic, and Historic periods of use, were sampled for macrofloral remains (Puseman 1994). Four of the sites, and possibly a fifth, were interpreted to represent winter residential sites. The macrofloral record was consistent with this interpretation, yielding evidence of use of a variety of seeds, berries, and roots, all of which could be stored.

The Early Archaic period is represented at three sites (35DS263, 35DS557, and 35JE231). *Pinus* charcoal was recovered at sites 35DS263 and 35DS557. Site 35JE231 was located on a canyon floor and yielded evidence of pre-Mazama (pre-5000 BC) vegetation including monocots, conifers, wild cherries (*Prunus*), Salicaceae, and Apiaceae.

The Middle Archaic period is represented at sites 35GM25, 35SH140, 35WS231, 35JE51B, and 35DS33. Several house pits at 35GM25, located on a low terrace near the confluence of Thirtymile Creek and the John Day River in northern Oregon, appeared to represent winter residences. Recovery of charred cheno-am embryos, *Chenopodium* seeds, Poaceae seeds, *Arctostaphylos* seeds, *Juniperus* seeds, PET fruity tissue (representing berries), and charred PET starchy tissue (representing roots) indicates that these resources were processed. Grass also might have been used for making mats or as thatching material. Charcoal recovered at this site included *Alnus*, *Artemisia*, *Chrysothamnus*, *Juniperus*, *Pinus*, and Salicaceae. The Middle Archaic occupation at 35SH140 yielded a charred, unidentified seed embryo, as well as *Artemisia*, *Juniperus*, and *Pinus* charcoal, representing local resources.

Both Middle and Late Archaic features were excavated at 35WS231, another winter residential site or perhaps a long-term habitation site. The Middle Archaic features (Nos. 6, 7, 9, and 14) contained charred Asteraceae, Fabaceae, Poaceae, Cyperaceae, *Galium*, *Phacelia*, probable *Collomia*, cheno-am, and unidentified seeds. Bone fragments and lithic flakes also were present in pit fill. Charcoal included *Artemisia*, *Purshia tridentata*, and Salicaceae, indicating use of sagebrush, bitterbrush, and willow/cottonwood for fuel. Recovery of uncharred remains in pits filled with waterlogged sediments also might represent resources used at the site. These include uncharred probable *Juncus*, Poaceae stem fragments, *Alnus* wood, Salicaceae twigs, and *Prunus* twigs. Feature 5 represents a Late Archaic occupation and yielded charred Fabaceae, Poaceae, and unidentified seeds, as well as a weathered, uncharred *Descurainia* seed and probable *Juncus* stem fragments. Charcoal included conifer and Salicaceae, as well as partially charred *Prunus* twigs. In addition, uncharred *Prunus* twigs were recovered. The presence of partially charred twigs points to the probability that weathered remains from this feature were present at the time of abandonment. Undated pit features yielded charred Cyperaceae, Poaceae, and unidentified seeds, as well as uncharred, weathered *Calandrinia* and *Sambucus* seeds, a charred PET starchy tissue fragment, Salicaceae charcoal, and uncharred probable *Juncus* and Poaceae stem fragments.

Site 35JE51B also contained features and house pits dating to both the Middle and Late Archaic periods. This site, located at the base of cliffs that rise above a broad floodplain drained by Trout Creek, probably also represents a winter residence. Charred remains recovered from Middle Archaic features include a cheno-am embryo, *Juniperus* seeds, and a *Quercus* acorn cap. The charcoal record was dominated by *Juniperus* and *Alnus* charcoal, and Salicaceae and *Pinus* charcoal were present in smaller quantities. The Late Archaic occupation yielded charred cheno-am embryos, *Chenopodium* seeds, Cyperaceae seeds, a Fabaceae seed, a *Galium* seed, a *Calandrinia* seed, Poaceae seeds, PET fruity tissue, PET starchy tissue, and probable Poaceae stems. The charcoal record was dominated by Salicaceae charcoal, although *Alnus* charcoal also was abundant. Other types of charcoal that were recovered include *Artemisia*, *Juniperus*, and *Purshia tridentata*. Undated features from this site yielded charred *Chenopodium*, *Calandrinia*, and Poaceae seeds, as well as *Alnus*, *Artemisia*, *Juniperus*, *Purshia tridentata*, and Salicaceae charcoal.

A Middle Archaic hearth at 35DS33, situated on the High Lava Plains in central Oregon, yielded a charred, unidentified seed embryo, as well as charred Poaceae, *Arctostaphylos*, and *Pinus* remains. A collapsed lava tube contained charred *Arctostaphylos*, *Ceanothus*, *Pinus*, and *Purshia tridentata* remains, indicating that these plants were part of the local vegetation.

Late Archaic occupation also was noted at 35WS225 and 35JE50. Site 35WS225, located on a terrace on the south side of Cow Canyon in north-central Oregon, contained prehistoric residential structures and other cultural features indicating it probably was occupied throughout the winter. Charred Brassicaceae, *Descurainia*, *Galium*, *Juniperus*, Poaceae, *Polygonum*, probable *Prunus virginiana* seeds, and a probable *Suaeda* embryo, as well as charred PET starchy and fruity tissue fragments, were recovered. Charcoal from the two structures examined includes *Alnus*, *Artemisia*, *Atriplex*, *Juniperus*, *Pinus*, and Salicaceae. Charred monocot stems were recovered in both structures and might represent either mats or thatching material that burned. Site 35JE50, situated on a small ridge in north-central Oregon, yielded *Juniperus* and *Artemisia* charcoal and might have been a field camp used for processing animal remains and perhaps for tool maintenance, because a feature included a concentration of charcoal, animal bone, and lithic debitage.

One historic feature from 35SH140 yielded a charred *Triticum aestivum* seed, indicating that wheat might have been grown or purchased as whole seed by the occupants of the historic ranch complex located near the head of the canyon.

Western Area

Hidden Cave, Nevada

The paleoethnobotanical record at Hidden Cave, Nevada, includes both pollen and seeds (Wigand and Mehringer 1985:108–124). Stratigraphic pollen analysis provided a record of vegetation in the vicinity of Hidden Cave during much of the Holocene as well as evidence of human activity, identifying cattails as an important resource for the cave's occupants (Madsen 1979; Wigand and Mehringer 1985:124). Pollen and seed content of coprolites place occupation of Hidden Shelter during midsummer to fall and identifies marsh plants as important foods. Cattail (*Typha*) pollen was a major component of coprolites, indicating that the pollen was consumed. Cheno-am pollen occurring in large quantity indicated that a member of this group also was important in the diet. Local chenopods that may have been consumed include *Allenrolfea* and *Chenopodium*. Charred but unmilled *Scirpus* seeds were recovered, and a large quantity of *Typha* pollen and abundant *Scirpus* seeds were present in the coprolites. Because cattails pollinate at least six weeks before mature fruits of *Scirpus maritimus* are available, either the *Scirpus* seeds had been stored since the previous fall or the *Typha* pollen had been saved for several weeks or months. Recovery of large quantities of two foods not available at the same time indicates storage of one or the other food rather than differential transit times through the digestive system. Other possible elements of the diet of people living in caves in the Western Area are listed in Table 6.4.

Stillwater Marsh

Robert L. Kelly (2001) presents evidence for environment, mobility, and subsistence in Stillwater Marsh in the Carson Desert and Stillwater Mountains. Pollen (Wigand 2001:252–254), phytolith (Cummings 2001a:251–

Table 6.4
Pollen and Macrofloral Remains from Shelters in the Northern and Western Great Basin

Scientific Name	Common Name	Hidden Cave Pollen	Hidden Cave Macro	Gatecliff Shelter Macro	Lovelock Cave Pollen	Lovelock Cave Macro	Danger Cave Pollen	Danger Cave Macro	Alta Toquima Village Macro
Asteraceae (Compositae)	sunflower family								
Artemisia									charcoal
Cheno-ams		copro			copro				
Amaranthus				X					
Chenopodiaceae									
Allenrolfea									
Atriplex									
Chenopodium				X					X
Suaeda									
Cyperaceae	sedge family	copro			copro				
Scirpus			copro			copro			
Scirpus maritimus									X
Ephedra viridis	green ephedra								X
Juniperus	juniper			X					X
Pediocactus simpsoni	hedgehog cactus								X
Pitularia americana	pellwort	copro							
Pinaceae	pine family			X					
Pinus monophylla	piñon pine							seeds	X
	limber pine								
Poaceae (Gramineae)	grass family		copro	X	copro	copro[a]	copro		charcoal
Elymus				X	fiber				
Festuca				X					
Rosaceae	rose family								
Holodiscus	oceanspray	copro							
Ramex	dock	copro							
Typha	cattail	copro			copro				

Note: copro = recovered from coprolite; X = present in pollen or macrofloral record.

[a] Seeds and stems

252), and macrofloral analyses (Rhode 2001:254–262) indicate a fluctuating marsh and intermittent flooding, the presence of *Phragmites* grass as well as other grasses in the festucoid and chloridoid groups, and use of marsh plant resources including cattail, bulrush, common reed (*Phragmites*), bur-reed (*Sparganium*), pondweed (*Potamogeton*), and ditchgrass (*Ruppia*). Plants typically found growing in the margins of marshes and alkali flats also were represented, including *Atriplex, Allenrolfea, Suaeda, Chenopodium, Rumex*, and *Heliotropium*. No remains of plants growing in drier habitats or uplands were recovered from the macrofloral record.

Ward Charcoal Ovens State Park

Macrofloral analysis of samples from the Ward Charcoal Ovens State Park indicates food processing involving cheno-am seeds, *Descurainia* seeds, and grass seeds. Charcoal included *Juniperus, Pinus*, and *Artemisia* (Puseman 1995).

Southwestern Area

Lovelock Cave

Napton and Kelso (1969) note *Typha* as a dominant element of the pollen record in coprolites from Lovelock Cave (Table 6.4). One coprolite contained *Typha* pollen that appeared to have been charred and may reflect the cooking of such pollen, perhaps in cattail leaves roasted in ashes or on hot coals. This preparation is supposed to yield a candylike food (Loud and Harrington 1929:156–158). Grass pollen and seeds and *Elymus* fibers also were occasionally recovered from Lovelock coprolites (Napton and Kelso 1969). Recovery of Cyperaceae pollen and abundant *Scirpus* seeds (Napton and Kelso 1969) from Lovelock Cave coprolites indicates the importance of sedges in the diet. Grass stems and leaves were recovered in a few of the Lovelock coprolites (Napton and Kelso 1969). An abundance of cheno-am pollen and the recovery of cheno-am seeds from the Lovelock coprolites indicate that seeds of this group, including *Suaeda* and, possibly, *Atriplex* and *Amaranthus*, were consumed. At Lovelock Cave (Napton and Kelso 1969) grass was noted to have been an important element of the diet, as indicated by two coprolites, one dated to ca. AD 750 and the other to ca. AD 1800. Analyses of coprolites from Lovelock Cave by a variety of researchers produced evidence of *Chenopodium, Scirpus*, and *Atriplex* seeds and *Opuntia* tissues (Fry 1978:112).

Flaherty Rockshelter

Pollen and macrofloral analyses for Flaherty Rockshelter (26CK415) in southern Nevada provide a record of Archaic through Late Prehistoric (3240 BC to AD 1820) activity. Charred remains of various cacti, including *Echinocereus*, a rush or rushlike plant, Solanaceae, *Plantago*, *Yucca*, and a fleshy fruit or berry indicate that a variety of native plants were used. Uncharred *Cucurbita* seed fragments suggest cultivation or perhaps trade. Recovery of *Nicotiana*-type pollen might reflect use of tobacco by native peoples in this rockshelter. A variety of charcoal was recovered, including *Alnus*, Asteraceae, *Pluchea*-type, *Ephedra*, *Juniperus*, Fabaceae, *Prosopis*, *Larrea tridentata*, Rosaceae, *Coleogyne ramosissima*, *Cowania*-type, *Prunus*, and *Salix* (Puseman and Cummings 1999).

Southern Area

Black Dog Cave

Pollen and macrofloral analyses of material from Black Dog Cave (26CK5686) in southeastern Nevada provide information concerning Virgin Anasazi Basketmaker II/Basketmaker III occupation. This cave was extremely rich in remains. These remains indicate that white bursage, the dominant plant today, was not as abundant during the Anasazi occupation. Instead, members of the cheno-am group were more abundant in archaeological deposits, suggesting that these weedy plants might have been better competitors in the disturbed vegetation community. *Typha* pollen was abundant, indicating availability of cattails from the local riparian community. Other native plants used by occupants of this cave included grasses, *Opuntia*, *Amaranthus*, *Atriplex*, *Chenopodium*, *Monolepis*, *Suaeda*, Cyperaceae, *Descurainia*, Fabaceae, *Helianthus*, *Juniperus*, *Opuntia* (cholla), *Phacelia*, *Pinus edulis*, Poaceae, *Portulaca*, *Prosopis*, *Rumex*, *Solanum*, and *Ranunculus*. These plants undoubtedly contributed a variety of seeds, greens, and berries to the subsistence base. Woods used as fuel included Asteraceae, *Atriplex*, *Larrea tridentata*, *Prosopis*, Salicaceae, *Salix*, and possibly others (Puseman and Cummings 2001).

Eastern Area

Evidence for the recovery of botanic specimens from the eastern Great Basin is sprinkled through archaeological reports and review volumes such as Jennings (1978). Large amounts of data may be extracted from these reports, although none include formal summaries of the botanic remains. Jennings (1978), however, provides an excellent review of the Desert Archaic cultures as represented by material recovered from Danger and Hogup Caves, Sanddune and Dust Devil Caves, Thorne Cave, and Hell's Midden site, among others. The majority of archaeological work in the caves of western Utah, which exposed much of the Desert Archaic evidence, was conducted between the early 1900s and the 1950s (Jennings 1978:29). Sites in western Utah tend to be located in caves around the periphery of Pleistocene Lake Bonneville. The most famous of these, Danger and Hogup Caves, are south-facing caverns.

Danger Cave

Radiocarbon ages at Danger Cave indicate occupation between 8300 BC and AD 20 (Jennings 1978:35, 41). "Probably the most numerous artifacts found at Danger Cave were those made from wood or vegetal materials—fibers, twigs, branches, bark, and stems. These artifacts include all basketry, cloth, propulsive weapon shafts, spear throwers, knife and scraper handles, cordage, quids, digging tools, snares or traps, fire drills and hearths, and other items" (Jennings 1978:41). Jennings presents photographs of many of these items, although he provides no information to tie the individual artifacts or classes of artifacts to stratigraphic layers that have been radiocarbon dated.

A summary of plant remains recovered from Danger Cave is presented in tabular form (Jennings 1978:86–87). The table divides the remains into several categories, such as food collected for immediate use, food that was stored, cordage, basketry/textiles, artifacts, medicine, narcotics, and fuel. Again, no mention is made of association with stratigraphic levels. The list of plant types recovered is impressive. A minimum of 78 different species is represented. Changes in popularity of resources were noted through time on the basis of abundance of recovered remains. Hemp (*Apocynum*), cedar/juniper (*Juniperus*), and flax (*Linum*) were commonly used for cordage in Layer III times (5200–4670 BC) but were not recovered in Layer IV (3150–900 BC), where all cordage found was manufactured from sagebrush (*Artemisia*) bark. In Layer V (3050 BC–AD 20) milkweed (*Asclepias*) and bulrush (*Scirpus*) were commonly recovered cordage materials. The most common cordage materials through all time periods represented were *Asclepias* and *Apocynum*. *Artemisia*, *Juniperus*, and *Cowania* were noted less frequently (Jennings 1978:84). Sandbar willow (*Salix exigua*) was most commonly used for basketry. White sage (*Eurotia*) also was noted in Layer V but was not as common as willow. Willow also was the preferred basketry manufacturing material at Hogup Cave.

Jennings (1978:247) notes that the diet at Danger Cave was consistent from 8000 BC until about the time of Christ and that the vegetal portion of the diet included pickleweed (*Allenrolfea*) seed, cactus, and a few other species. A similar diet was noted at Hogup Cave, where a decline in pickleweed seed and an increase in grass and sagebrush seed utilization was noted as occurring around 6400 BC.

Hogup Cave

Occupation at Hogup Cave spanned 8400 BC to AD 1470 (Jennings 1978: 49). Photographs of archaeological botanic remains from the site are presented in Jennings (1978) and are invaluable. Twining and netting are pictured, as are dart foreshafts made of serviceberry. Hogup Cave exhibits evidence of Fremont occupation. The textile collection from Hogup is larger than from Danger Cave, although remains from both shelters are similar.

In the archaeological report on Hogup Cave, Aikens (1970) describes numerous artifacts, including those made from plants. Worked plant fibers that are documented include sagebrush bark and grass pads, a finely shredded sagebrush bark bundle, knotted sagebrush bark bundles, wrapped shredded sagebrush bark bundles, wrapped fiber rings of sagebrush bark, wrapped fiber bundles, knotted reed (*Scirpus olneyii* or *Scirpus* spp.), braided reed (*Scirpus olneyii*) objects, wrapped reeds (*Scirpus olneyii*), anthropomorphic figurines made of wrapped plant fiber identified as either sagebrush bark or reed, cordage from an unidentified plant fiber, and a complete net as well as netting fragments made of *Apocynum* fiber. The most abundant cordage fibers included *Asclepias*, followed by *Apocynum, Artemisia, Juniperus*, and *Cowania* (Aikens 1970:127). Textiles and twined and coiled basketry were examined by Adovasio (1970:133–153). *Salix* was the most commonly used material for basketry. *Asclepias* was noted occasionally in basketry and in twined bags and mats either alone or in combination with *Apocynum* and *Artemisia. Apocynum*, as well as *Yucca* and *Juniperus*, was reportedly used for bundles in one-rod and bundlewear. *Scirpus* was present as matting but was not very common.

Wooden artifacts from Hogup Cave, which were examined by Dalley (1970:153–186), represent a wide variety of apparently local woods. Wooden artifacts were made from the following woody plants, in descending order of occurrence: *Sarcobatus vermiculatus, Salix, Phragmites, Cercocarpus ledifolius, Artemisia, Populus, Sambucus, Betula occidentalis, Cornus stolonifera, Juniperus osteosperma, Juniperus, Tetradymia, Ephedra, Atriplex, Acer grandidentatum, Allenrolfea, Alnus tenuifolia, Amelanchier alnifolia,* and *Prunus fasciculatus* (Dalley 1970:153).

At Hogup Cave, pickleweed and cactus appear to have been important foods, although pickleweed became less popular after approximately AD 0. An increase in dietary complexity was also noted through time at Hogup Cave (Fry 1968). Coprolites from contexts in which chenopods, grasses, and *Celtis* were present in the seed records and *Opuntia* plant fibers and epidermis were common indicate greater reliance on plant materials in the diet.

Both Fremont and Shoshone coprolites recovered from Hogup Cave are too few to provide accurate statements of dietary significance. Observed trends, however, include a decrease in utilization of *Opuntia* and an increase in utilization of grass seeds. Tables of seed and plant tissue recovery are presented as appendices in Fry (1977). Minor components of the coprolite record include *Celtis, Poa, Lepidium, Phlox,* and *Scirpus* seeds, as well as seeds and leaves of both *Artemisia* and *Atriplex*. Although the Fremont peoples practiced horticulture and grew *Zea, Cucurbita,* and *Phaseolus,* only *Zea* was present in the macrofloral record at Hogup Cave. Corn from Hogup Cave is reviewed by Cutler (1970:271), who separated corn kernels into numerous classes for tabulation.

Danger and Hogup Caves Compared

Kelso (1970) conducted pollen analysis on coprolites from both Hogup and Danger Caves, as well as from cave fill from Hogup Cave, for which he presents pollen diagrams. Fry (1968, 1977, 1978) examined macrofloral remains from coprolites recovered in both Danger and Hogup Caves. *Allenrolfea* seeds were abundant in the macrofloral record, *Allenrolfea* chaff was abundant in cave fill, and cheno-am pollen was dominant in most of the coprolites examined from both caves. These records combine to indicate that the local riparian resources adapted to the alkaline conditions in this portion of the Great Basin constituted an extremely important component of the diet for the occupants of both Danger and Hogup Caves. In addition to charred pickleweed (*Allenrolfea*) seeds, cactus pad epidermis, charred cactus spines, rabbitbrush seeds, saltbush seeds and leaves, bulrush seeds, charcoal, and grit were recovered.

The preliminary analysis of the Danger Cave coprolites demonstrates no major changes in dietary patterns for a period of 9,000 years. A continual but gradually decreasing use of chenopod seed is apparent and appears to coincide with a gradual increase in dietary complexity. The use of the same plant and animal resources (e.g., chenopod, cactus, antelope, and probably rabbit) throughout this great span of time and a slow increase in dietary complexity indicate the human ecological adaption was gradually cumulative. [Fry 1978:116]

Fry presents his macrofloral data in tables using number of occurrences per level, weight, and percentage weights. *Pinus* seed appeared to have been a staple resource at Danger Cave (Fry 1977:13). Minor components of the coprolites include *Chrysothamnus* and possibly other members of the Asteraceae, *Cornus*, *Phlox*, and *Scirpus*. *Pinus* was not a major component of the coprolites. The presence of large quantities of *Cornus stolonifera* bark in a Late Archaic coprolite has been interpreted to represent ingestion of a narcotic, as smoking this bark is noted to produce an effect similar to that of opium (Fry 1977:13). Madsen and Rhode (1990) report evidence that occupants of Danger Cave exploited piñon nut (*Pinus monophylla*) for at least 7,500 years. Their study documents the movement of *Pinus monophylla* from the southern portion of the Great Basin into the area around Danger Cave by about 5900 BC. Coprolite evidence suggests that the diet of occupants of Danger Cave became more varied in later occupations. The Archaic coprolites from Danger and Hogup Caves exhibited a decrease in the utilization of pickleweed after Middle Archaic times.

Pollen and macrofloral data recovered between strata 1 and 9 have been interpreted to suggest that Hogup Cave (occupied between 6450 BC and AD 1470) was occupied only during the fall. During that time it appears to have functioned as an *Allenrolfea* seed collection station (Kelso 1970:261). Elevations are noted in *Artemisia* pollen frequencies that recall the presence of sagebrush leaves and seeds in some of the coprolites. It is the presence of the macrofloral remains that makes interpretation of the *Artemisia* pollen as representative of intentionally ingested items possible. The presence of Cyperaceae pollen was interpreted as an indicator that sedges were part of the local plant community. Such pollen may have been ingested with the drinking water or possibly with seeds, which were recovered from several of the coprolites. Cyperaceae species pollinate in the spring or early summer, suggesting the possibility of an extension of the seasonality of occupation. *Artemisia* and Poaceae pollen are most abundant in coprolites from the upper strata, suggesting an increase in utilization of these plants later in time. A concomitant increase in grass pollen was noted in fill samples from Hogup Cave, which correlates with a sharply increased quantity of bison in the faunal record. These data are suggestive of changes in local vegetation resulting, in turn, in changes in resources available for exploitation.

Grass appears to have been a more important element of the diet at Hogup Cave than at Danger Cave, since this pollen was more abundant throughout most of the record. *Polygonum pensylvanicum*-type pollen was noted at both Danger and Hogup Caves, although no edible modern analog is noted in Gosiute plant usage (Chamberlin 1911). *Ephedra* pollen recovered from a single coprolite at Danger Cave suggests the possible medicinal use of this plant. Elevated *Sarcobatus* pollen amounts were noted in a few coprolites from both Danger and Hogup Caves. *Sarcobatus* is noted to have been an important raw material for fuel, construction, or other uses. Evidence for utilization of *Sarcobatus* as a food or medicine is scant, although the bark may have been used medicinally (Kelso 1970:259). Because *Sarcobatus* is noted as an important raw material, elevated *Sarcobatus* pollen frequencies might represent collection of the wood or branches for utilitarian use while the plants were in flower (pollinating) and, thus, that the ingestion of *Sarcobatus* pollen was accidental.

Lander County, Nevada

In the first study of its kind, pollen, starch, and blood residue analyses were conducted on ground stone from several sites in Lander County, Nevada, including site 26LA2387 (Cummings and Puseman 1993a, 1993b). The research design, developed by Intermountain Research in Nevada, included specific examination of artifacts for starch granules and possible blood or protein residues in addition to pollen analysis. Pollen and starch granule analyses were performed on manos and metates, and blood residue analysis was performed on mortars and pestles. Recovered starch granules augmented interpretation of the subsistence record. Combined pollen and starch records from the manos and metates indicated that grass seeds were probably the most important vegetal resources that were ground. "Recovery of large solid starch granules consistent with those produced by seeds of *Elymus, Agropyron,* and *Hordeum* suggests that one or all of these grasses figured in the diets of these occupants of the village at 26LA2387" (Cummings and Puseman 1993b: 11). Other plants for which evidence of processing was recovered include cheno-ams, perhaps *Artemisia*, perhaps a member of the High-spine Aster-aceae group, *Eriogonum*, a member of the Fabaceae, a member of the Lili-aceae, perhaps *Gilia*, perhaps *Polemonium*, perhaps *Amelanchier*, a member or members of the Apiaceae, and *Yucca*.

Glen Canyon

Fremont coprolites from Glen Canyon contained such foods as yucca pod, *Artemisia* fiber, *Juniperus* fiber, *Phaseolus*, *Equisetum* stems, conifer bark, *Amelanchier* seeds, *Cucurbita*, *Zea*, *Opuntia*, Poaceae, an unidentified seed, *Amaranthus*, several types of *Chenopodium*, Asteraceae, *Lepidium*, and *Scirpus* (Fry 1977:15). Fry (1977) published photos of several types of plant materials from coprolites examined from Danger and Hogup Caves, as well as from Glen Canyon.

Martin and Sharrock (1964) present a review of pollen analysis of 54 pre-historic human feces or perhaps quids from the Glen Canyon area. Primary pollen types representing foods consumed by these people include *Cleome*, *Zea mays*, and *Cucurbita*. Other pollen that probably reflects foods eaten by these people includes cheno-ams, Gramineae (Poaceae), *Opuntia*, and Cruciferae (Brassicaceae). The pollen record reflects a diet that included at least the cultigens maize and squash/pumpkin, as well as the native plants bee-weed, goosefoot, and probably amaranth (probably both seeds and greens), grass seeds, prickly pear cactus, and a member or members of the mustard family.

Swallow Shelter

Swallow Shelter is located in the extreme northwestern corner of Utah on an unnamed tributary of Grouse Creek approximately 97 km northwest of Hogup Cave. The archaeological report on Swallow Shelter describes plant remains recovered during excavation, such as juniper bark concentrations (Dalley 1976:21). The Fremont and Archaic occupations at Swallow Shelter are not separated in the description of paleoethnobotanic remains. Worked wood and plant materials also are described in the report and occasionally depicted in photographs. *Phragmites* was utilized for arrow and atlatl shafts. Arrow foreshafts were made, in descending order of frequency, of *Cercocarpus*, *Atriplex*, *Prunus fasciculatus*, *Rosa*, and *Sarcobatus vermiculatus*. Miscellaneous shafts were constructed, also in descending frequency, of *Cercocarpus*, *Prunus*, *Rosa*,

Ribes, Sarcobatus vermiculatus, Chrysothamnus, Cornus stolonifera, and *Juniperus*. Peeled and split wood was identified as *Salix* and *Cercocarpus*. Promontory pegs were constructed of *Atriplex, Cercocarpus*, or *Salix*. A section of cactus (*Opuntia*) pad was skewered by a peg, suggesting a method of burning off spines or perhaps another use. Four juniper berries are noted to have been skewered on a tiny *Salix* twig, which probably represents a portion of a larger artifact. Compound fire-drilled foreshafts were made of *Artemisia, Salix*, or other unidentified woods. Simple fire drills were made of *Cercocarpus*. A possible basal firestick, termed a "firehearth" in the report, was made of *Prunus*. It exhibited two charred, round depressions at one end. Digging sticks were made of *Cercocarpus, Atriplex*, or *Salix*. A single spatula made of *Juniperus* was recovered. A slotted stick was identified as *Rosa*, and circumferentially grooved sticks were identified as *Ribes, Juniperus*, or *Rosa*. A single composite artifact consisting of a long tube of *Phragmites* with a pointed splinter of *Juniperus* inserted in one end was also recorded. A possible awl was made of *Prunus virginiana*. A small bundle of grass was secured with twisted juniper bark. Bent branch forms were identified as *Salix*. Lashed sticks included *Cercocarpus* and *Prunus*, as well as *Salix*. Worked reed (*Phragmites*) fragments were noted, as were reed (*Phragmites*) elements with designs. Worked wood fragments included *Cercocarpus, Juniperus, Prunus, Salix, Quercus, Rosa*, and unidentified taxa. String and net fragments were recovered, as was twisted and knotted bark (Dalley 1976:58–65).

Botanical specimens collected from screens included seeds, fibers, and cactus pads, among others. *Opuntia* remains were abundant, and *Juniperus* remains included bark, berries, seeds, and twigs. Grasses included *Elymus, Koeleria, Oryzopsis*, and *Poa*. Other plants represented were *Asclepias, Astragalus, Atriplex confertifolia, Balsamorhiza sagittata, Phragmites communis, Polygonum, Rhus trilobata, Scirpus microcarpus, Typha latifolia*, and *Wyethia amplexicaulis* (Dalley 1976:69). Woody plant materials represented at Swallow Shelter included *Acer, Arctostaphylos, Artemisia, Atriplex, Cercocarpus, Chrysothamnus, Cornus, Juniperus, Prunus, Pseudotsuga, Purshia, Quercus, Rhus, Ribes, Rosa, Salix, Sambucus*, and *Sarcobatus* (Dalley 1976:70). The large number of *Opuntia* pads recovered indicates the importance of these pads, probably in the diet. Botanical remains are consistent with use of this site during late summer or early fall (Dalley 1976:72).

The heavy dependence on local seeds, particularly pickleweed (*Allenrolfea*), noted at Hogup Cave is not apparent at Swallow Shelter, where the most important activity appears to have been hunting. Strata 9 and 10 at

Swallow Shelter represent Fremont occupations. The greater variety of botanic remains recovered from the Fremont strata may reflect the fact that these strata were dry rather than wet, as were the Archaic levels. Based on quantities of artifacts recovered, particularly when adjusted to reflect 1,000-year intervals, Fremont occupation at Swallow Shelter appears more intense, which implies an increase in intensity of resource utilization.

A stratigraphic pollen record exists for Swallow Shelter, and although impacted by cultural activities, it is not interpreted to reflect economic activity (Dalley 1976:171–174).

Rampart Cave

Rampart Cave, located in the Grouse Creek Mountains of northwestern Utah, yielded radiocarbon ages spanning 2900 BC to AD 1545. Rampart Cave appears to have been occupied between approximately 3000 and 500 BC by Archaic hunter-gatherers. After a hiatus, the cave was reoccupied by Fremont groups beginning at approximately AD 1000. Wooden artifacts were recovered and identified, including composite arrow fragments in which *Phragmites* was used for the main shaft and *Cercocarpus* for the foreshaft. Dart shaft fragments reveal that *Salix* was used for the mainshafts and *Cercocarpus* for the foreshafts. Three end-cut sticks of *Ribes* and *Pinus* were recorded. A cylinder fragment of *Rosa* had been split longitudinally and bore grooves around the circumference at each end. Possible juniper bark was painted, and a single promontory peg made of *Atriplex* was recovered. Miscellaneous wood fragments were identified as *Haplopappus*, *Cercocarpus*, *Salix*, *Artemisia*, *Juniperus*, *Cornus stolonifera*, and *Atriplex*. Because they were unmodified and usually partially burned, these fragments were interpreted as pieces of firewood. Basketry made of unidentified material and a twilled mat probably made of yucca fiber or juniper bark were recovered (Berry 1976: 115–127).

The pollen record from Rampart Cave has been examined with the aim of paleoenvironmental reconstruction. Cultural "contamination" was noted in the higher frequencies of Poaceae pollen exhibited by some coprolite samples from Rampart Cave, which indicate consumption of grass seeds (Hull 1976: 175–179). Interpretation of the coprolite results is minimal, but some coprolites exhibit elevated *Artemisia* pollen frequencies, a single elevated chenoam frequency occurs, and single instances of elevated Rosaceae and Liliaceae pollen frequencies occur. Most other pollen frequencies are consistent with abundance of pollen from cave fill samples. It is possible that the peaks in these types of pollen represent consumption of foods or medicines by occupants of Rampart Cave.

Fremont

David Madsen and Steven Simms (1998:255–336) provide a recent overview of the Fremont complex of farmers and foragers who occupied the Great Basin and Colorado Plateau. They place occupation between approximately 150 BC and AD 1800. Nearly every subsistence variation from full-time farming to full-time foraging is attributed to the Fremont people. Episodic shifts in subsistence strategies are noted to have occurred through time, making any single description of the Fremont people inappropriate.

The Sevier/Fremont groups shared traits with the preceding Archaic peoples. The Sevier culture often is referred to as a Great Basin culture, whereas the Fremont is often assigned to the Colorado Plateau (Madsen 1982:217).

> The Sevier/Fremont settlement pattern is characterized by villages located on alluvial fans in intermontane valleys adjacent to marsh or riverine ecosystems and by temporary encampments spread throughout other environmental zones surrounding these centrally located villages. The subsistence economy is based on the collecting of wild flora and fauna, primarily from marsh environments, and is supplemented by corn agriculture. [Madsen 1982:217]

Variations within this culture are noted along a north–south gradient and may reflect both environmental constraints and differences in cultural-historical factors. Marshes are few and small in the southern Fremont area, where reliance on domesticates was relatively high. Groups in that area also appear to have had a significant amount of interaction with Virgin Anasazi groups farther south. In contrast, marshy areas are far more numerous and larger in the northern part of the Fremont area, and groups there made limited use of domesticates and interacted with Plains groups. Madsen (1982: 217) places emergence of the Sevier/Fremont culture in the AD 350–650 time span, acknowledging that corn may have been introduced in some areas prior to changes in settlement patterns identified as Sevier/Fremont.

Jennings's (1978) review of the Fremont indicates that this culture was identifiable between AD 500 and AD 1250. The Fremont appears to have developed from Desert Archaic cultures, probably in response to influence from southwestern cultures. Horticulture appears to have been laid on top of the wild-plant-gathering subsistence base. General traits of the Fremont culture include the pithouse as the most common dwelling type, pottery, and granaries or storage rooms, which often were numerous. These facilities were built primarily of stone and may be seen scattered on ledges throughout canyons. Fremont dent is the race of maize attributed to the Fremont. It is highly resistant to drought and adapted both to extremes in climate and to a short growing season (Jennings 1978:156). Villages are often small, usually including two or three pithouses, as well as a series of surface storage rooms or possible dwelling structures made of jacal, coarse adobe, or even stone masonry. Sites are usually located near arable land. Jennings (1978:162) subdivided the Fremont into regional groups, which include the Great Salt Lake Fremont, Uintah Fremont, San Raphael Fremont, Sevier Fremont, and Parowan Fremont.

Jennings (1978:246) notes that the Fremont cultivated corn, beans, and squash. He cites five primary reasons that vegetal foods always made up the major portion of the diet for gathering populations: "(1) Plants are fixed in position, (2) they normally fruit every year (pinyon is an exception) although abundance may vary, (3) they fruit at the same time each year (4) collecting fruits does *not* endanger the species and the permanent availability is thus assured and (5) much vegetal food can be saved or stored" (Jennings 1978:246).

Hunting is not as predictable as plant gathering and although estimates of animal population size and location may be made on the basis of past experience, animal populations are not rooted like plants. Both cultural and climatic changes are likely to have contributed to dietary variation.

Sevier/Fremont occupations in the vicinity of the Great Salt Lake and Utah Lake are associated with the Bear River or are located in marsh areas on saline soils, precluding agriculture (Jennings 1978:162; Madsen 1982:218). Sites represent special-use, temporary camps as well as permanent villages. Plants noted to have been utilized include bulrush (*Scirpus*), which has been found cached, and goosefoot (*Chenopodium*), recovered from coprolites. Only one site in this area, at Willard, Utah (Judd 1926), exhibits adobe story structures and charred corn cobs (Madsen 1982:218). This permanent horticultural village appears to be the exception in this region, as most other sites exhibit no evidence of agriculture, even as a minor component of the subsistence economy.

42SL98

Macrofloral analysis at a Fremont site (42SL98) in Salt Lake City, Utah, yielded evidence for the use of the cultigens *Zea mays* and *Phaseolus*, as well as native plants including cheno-ams, *Atriplex, Chenopodium*, Poaceae, *Oryzopsis*, probable *Prunus, Scirpus*, and *Typha*. A wide variety of charcoals were identified, including *Acer, Alnus*, Asteraceae, *Artemisia, Atriplex, Betula*, conifer, *Pinus, Quercus*, Rosaceae, *Amelanchier, Prunus, Rosa*, Salicaceae, *Populus*, and *Ulmus* (Puseman and Ruggiero 1999b).

42SL285

Recent excavation of a Fremont village (42SL285) in Salt Lake City, Utah, has yielded abundant evidence of both maize agriculture and exploitation of cattails. *Typha* pollen is present in nearly every sample examined from pithouses, ramadas, pits, and big depressions, indicating the importance of cattails in the diet. Other edible riparian plants also are represented by Cyperaceae and *Sagittaria* pollen. Other plants apparently important in the local diet included cheno-ams, *Cleome*, and Apiaceae. Poaceae was abundant in the pollen and macrofloral records and probably contributed to the diet, as well as being used for various utilitarian purposes such as lining storage pits and constructing basketry and matting. Plants that appear to have played a lesser role in the local Fremont diet include Liguliflorae (chicory tribe Asteraceae), Brassicaceae, *Calochortus*, arrowweed, Solanaceae, and *Urtica*. In addition to cultivated maize, beans (*Phaseolus*) are part of the subsistence record, represented in both the pollen and macrofloral records. A single large pit contained evidence for the probable use of *Chenopodium, Helianthus*, Poaceae, *Scirpus*, and possible *Atriplex* (Cummings and Puseman 2001a). In addition, examination of a single pit at 42SL285yielded evidence that both *Zea mays* and *Phaseolus* probably were stored. Grasses might have been used to line the pit. In addition, recovery of Apiaceae, Low-spine Asteraceae, Liguliflorae, Cyperaceae, *Geranium*, and *Typha* pollen indicates availability of plants in the nearby riparian habitat. If grasses used to line the pit were collected in the riparian area, they might account for the presence of these pollen types as well as for the *Spirogyra* algal spore recovered in the sample. Recovery of a variety of charred macrofloral remains, including both *Zea mays* and *Phaseolus*, points to the possibility that trash was placed in this pit. Other charred remains included *Chenopodium, Helianthus*, Poaceae, *Scirpus*, and *Atriplex* seeds, as well as numerous types of charcoal, including Asteraceae, *Artemisia, Chrysotham-nus, Atriplex, Betula, Juniperus, Platanus*-type, *Quercus*, Rosaceae, *Cercocarpus*, and Salicaceae (Puseman et al. 1999).

American Fork Cave

Pollen and macrofloral analyses at several sites in the Utah Valley examined Archaic records. Archaic occupants of the American Fork Cave (42UT135) probably collected and processed *Atriplex, Chenopodium*, other cheno-ams, Cyperaceae, Brassicaceae, Poaceae, *Polygonum, Rosa, Vicia*, and *Cleome* seeds. The recovered charcoal indicates that *Acer, Cercocarpus, Juniperus, Pseudo-tsuga, Quercus*, and Salicaceae were burned as fuel. Macrofloral remains from several sites along the shore of Utah Lake yielded evidence that *Atriplex, Chenopodium*, and *Rumex* were important resources. In addition, *Juniperus*, Poaceae, *Scirpus, Typha*, monocots, fleshy fruits such as rosehips or juniper berries, and, possibly, *Sarcobatus* were used. Woods used as fuel included *Artemisia, Chrysothamnus*, Asteraceae, *Atriplex, Sarcobatus, Juniperus, Salix*, and Salicaceae (Puseman and Cummings 2000a).

Baker Village

Pollen analysis at Baker Village (26WP63), a Fremont site located in eastern Nevada, yielded evidence of use of *Zea mays* during both the early and late occupations, as well as *Cucurbita* during the late occupation. Native plants that were used included cheno-ams, *Cleome*, Lamiaceae, Poaceae, and *Typha* during the early occupation and Apiaceae, *Cylindropuntia, Mammillaria*-type, *Opuntia*, cheno-ams, Poaceae, and *Typha* during the late occupation (Cummings and Moutoux 1997). All samples examined represent the floors of several pithouses, as well as those of storage structures.

42CB507

Combined pollen and macrofloral analyses at 42CB507, the easternmost known Fremont village, produced evidence of *Zea mays* in the pollen, macrofloral, and starch records, as well as native plants, including cheno-am and goosefoot seeds, ricegrass, and possibly other grass seeds, and perhaps *Opuntia*. *Agave* pollen was recovered, suggesting that this resource might have been traded into the area, given that Carbon County, where the site is located, is currently outside the range for *Agave* (Cummings et al. 1998b).

42CB1302

Pollen and macrofloral analyses at 42CB1302, located north of Price, Utah, included examination of a two-handed mano. A hearth or roasting pit appears to have been used to process cheno-ams, *Oryzopsis*, and, possibly, other grasses, *Sclerocactus* fruits, and perhaps *Opuntia*. *Juniperus* and *Pinus* (piñon pine) were burned as fuel (Cummings et al. 1999).

42CB1407

Pollen and macrofloral analysis at 42CB1407, a prehistoric camp in the uplands of Castle Valley, central Utah, indicates that the site's occupants might have parched *Chenopodium* seeds. Alternatively, *Chenopodium* greens and *Atriplex* might have been part of a buffering plant layer in a pit used to roast foods such as wild potato (*Solanum jamesii*), represented in the pollen record. Cheno-am seeds appear to have been ground on a metate that was examined for pollen. *Juniperus* and *Pinus* were used as fuel (Cummings and Nepstad-Thornberry 2000).

10-42-1

Macrofloral analysis of a single Fremont hearth at site 10-42-1 in Emery County, Utah, yielded evidence of the processing of *Zea mays* as well as of native plants, including *Sclerocactus*, cheno-ams, *Chenopodium*, and *Helianthus*. *Juniperus*, *Pinus*, and *Salix* charcoal was recovered (Puseman 1999).

42EM2568, 42EM2569, 42EM2570, and 42EM2571

Pollen and macrofloral analyses at four sites in central Utah (42EM2568, 42EM2569, 42EM2570, and 42EM2571) indicate that Fremont people processed *Chenopodium* seeds, cheno-ams, *Opuntia*, *Atriplex*, *Juniperus*, and *Zea mays*. Saltbush and juniper berries might have been used as flavorings, and prickly pear cactus pads might have been roasted. Woods burned as fuel included *Juniperus*, *Pinus*, *Populus*, and *Salix* (Puseman and Cummings 2000b).

Crazy Bird Shelter

Pollen analysis at Crazy Bird Shelter (42SV896) in central Utah yielded evidence of *Zea mays* only from Formative period sediments. In addition, wild potato starch was recovered from Late Archaic and Formative occupations. A single *Trichuris* parasite egg was recovered in the Formative sediments, suggesting whipworm infection (Cummings and Moutoux 1999a).

Backhoe Village

Farther south in central Utah, Sevier/Fremont sites contain evidence of reliance on cattail, as well as use of maize, cheno-ams, and other plants. Madsen (Madsen and Lindsey 1977) appears to have been the first palynologist to examine a structure floor by grid squares to determine the spatial distribution of pollen that might point to economic activities by occupants of the structure. He plotted the distribution of cattail pollen across the floor of Structure 3 at Backhoe Village and found conclusive evidence of concentration of this pollen toward the center of the structure. This floor was a basin-shaped depression. Examining structure floors by grid squares has been valuable in other archaeobotanical studies in the North American Southwest (Scott 1983) and in the extreme northwest portion of the Great Basin in Fort Rock Valley (Helzer 2000).

At Backhoe Village Madsen and Lindsey (1977) also recorded probable *Celtis, Opuntia, Helianthus*-type, Liliaceae, and *Agave* pollen that might represent foods processed. In addition, maize cobs and kernels, Chenopodiaceae seeds, and a variety of woods were documented. Madsen and Lindsay (1977: 88) argue for a Fremont economy that relied primarily on wild foods, with secondary use of cultigens such as maize, citing additional information from the midden at Evans Mound (Dalley 1972) and a storage pit at Pharo Village. They postulate that wild resources are renewed with sufficient frequency in the Sevier area that they would have provided a stable resource base to support sedentary villages (Madsen and Lindsay 1977:88), and they note that marsh ecosystems are highly productive. At 5,500 kg/ha (5,500 lbs/ac), productivity of cattail roots, which rival maize in nutritive value, is much higher than maize productivity (Classen 1919; Madsen and Lindsay 1977:88). About 8 ha (20 ac) of postulated marsh in the vicinity of Backhoe Village at the time of occupation would have produced more than 45,400 kg (100,000 lbs) of cattail flour, which could have supported a much larger population than the one that lived in the village. This harvest would have freed occupants of Backhoe Village and similar villages to pursue seasonal resources, using the village as the primary camp and still growing small quantities of agricultural crops.

Backhoe Village was reexamined recently, and additional archaeobotanical samples were examined in 2000 and 2002. New evidence indicates that Fremont inhabitants relied on a mixture of nature plants and cultivated maize and beans (Cummings and Puseman 2003a). Native resources noted to have been used include *Typha* (cattail), cheno-ams (including amaranth, goosefoot, and greasewood), *Helianthus* (sunflower) seeds, *Yucca* seeds, Brassicaceae (a member of the mustard family) seeds, *Oryzopsis* (ricegrass) seeds, other grass seeds, *Phacelia* seeds, *Prunus* fruits, *Physalis* fruits, Cyperaceae (sedge) seeds, *Epilobium* (fireweed) seeds, and *Nicotiana* (wild tobacco). Winter-dominant precipitation was noted for this area, interpreted through the presence of ratios of *Ephedra nevadensis*-type and *E. torreyana*-type pollen. Charcoal types most common in this record are juniper, greasewood, pine, saltbush, piñon pine, mountain mahogany, rabbitbrush, antelopebrush, and other woody members of the rose family, and members of the willow family, probably including both willow and cottonwood.

Although *Typha* pollen was recovered on the floor of a structure examined recently, large quantities of *Typha* pollen were not present in any of the samples, which led to a correlation of field observations and another possible explanation of the symmetrical and concentric patterning of increasing quantities of *Typha* in the earlier study. Water collecting in basin-shaped areas, such as an abandoned pithouse from which the superstructure had been removed, provides an excellent pollen trap. Pollen collecting on puddles during the spring and early summer often makes a yellow scum. If a structure had been open and filled with water when cattails were pollinating, cattail pollen would have accumulated on the water, then become more concentrated toward the lowest (central) portion of the floor as the water dried. Although it is not possible to identify which scenario is correct, it is appropriate to examine all avenues of explanation for patterns of pollen distribution. Although the original study by Madsen and Lindsay (1977) might have evaluated a natural phenomenon mixed with a cultural record, it introduced the concept of sampling floors on a much more intensive basis, using grids, and served to inspire further, more complete understanding of human activity within structures.

42SV2304 and 42SV2229

Sites 42SV2304 and 42SV2229, located at the north end of Fish Lake in Sevier County, yielded pollen and macrofloral remains indicating that the sites' Fremont occupants used both cultivated and native resources, including *Zea mays*, cheno-ams, Asteraceae, *Opuntia*, *Rhus*, *Sambucus*, Cyperaceae, and starchy roots. Woods that were burned included *Populus*, *Abies*, Salicaceae, *Artemisia*, *Pseudotsuga*, and conifer (Puseman et al. 1996).

Uintah Fremont

The Uintah Fremont also includes such sites as Boundary Village, the Goodridge Site, Shelter Hill, Flattop Butte, Whole Place Village, Fremont Playhouse, Deluge Shelter, and the Dam site (Jennings 1978:179). Although Jennings illustrates ground stone artifacts and pottery vessels from Uintah Fremont sites, he does not discuss botanical remains.

San Raphael Fremont

San Raphael Fremont sites include the Nine-Mile Canyon sites, Snakerock, Old Woman, Poplar Knob, Windy Ridge, Crescent Ridge, and Powerpole Knoll (Jennings 1978:184, 187). Gates Roost, a San Raphael site in Glen Canyon, yielded bushels of cornhusks and corncobs, along with dozens of figurine fragments (Jennings 1978:206). Coprolites examined from Clyde's Cavern in the San Rafael Swell yielded a variety of foods. Seeds noted to have been consumed by the site's occupants include Indian ricegrass, ryegrass, bulrush, and composites (Jennings 1978:247–248). In the western portion of the Great Basin in Nevada and eastern Oregon, riparian plants and seeds are well documented in the diet after 2500 BC (Jennings 1978:248).

Parowan Fremont

Parowan Fremont sites are located in southwestern Utah and include Garrison, Kanosh, Paragonah, Parowan, and Median Village (formerly Summit Village), as well as the Evans site (Jennings 1978:206). Surface coil-adobe granaries are common in this area. Plant remains at the Evans site included "pickleweed seed, amaranth, serviceberry, sagebrush, saltbush, bromegrass, sedge, lambsquarter, beeweed, *Cryptantha*, sunflower, Indian ricegrass, piñon nuts, globe mallow, and bulrush seeds" (Jennings 1978:213).

42GA3817

Pollen and macrofloral analysis has been undertaken on material from 42GA3817, Bear Creek Canyon, Utah, a Fremont lithic activity area in the Parowan Valley. A radiocarbon age of AD 960 ± 40 anchors this data base.

The site is located in the uplands above Evans Mound. The pollen record indicates the possibility that woodland resources were being overused during the Fremont occupation, resulting in a reduction of woody resources, destruction of habitats, and, possibly, reduction of wildlife populations that might have been important game resources. It is likely that expanding open areas that supported sagebrush would have allowed increases in other animal populations. Plants available for exploitation included cheno-ams, *Cleome*, *Opuntia*, *Salix*, *Pinus*, *Juniperus*, *Quercus*, *Artemisia*, *Ephedra*, Poaceae, Rosaceae, *Cercocarpus*, and *Sphaeralcea*. The macrofloral record documents use of *Chenopodium* and cheno-am seeds (Cummings and Puseman 2000).

Sudden Shelter

Pollen (Lindsay 1980a) and macrofloral (Coulam and Barnett 1980) analyses were conducted at Sudden Shelter in east-central Utah. Evidence for plant utilization at Sudden Shelter includes pollen from such plants as cheno-ams, grasses, Asteraceae, *Ephedra*, Liliaceae, and Rosaceae. It also is possible that *Artemisia*, Cactaceae (including *Opuntia*), and members of the Liliaceae (probably *Allium* and *Yucca*), as well as members of the Rosaceae (including *Rosa*, *Amelanchier*, *Cercocarpus*, and *Prunus*) and Saxifragaceae (probably *Ribes*) were utilized. Although not interpreted as such by Lindsay, the fluctuations in Apiaceae pollen might represent economic activity. Coulam and Barnett (1980) present the macrofloral data as ubiquity values (presence/absence of a taxon in individual samples). They recovered a considerable variety of seeds and tissue fragments, as well as other plant parts. They examined seasonal availability of food and reviewed biotic communities in the vicinity of the site. An ethnobotanical inventory is included in their report, which reviews the habitats of individual plants, details the plant parts used and for what purposes, notes seasonal availability, and occasionally comments on attributes such as ease of collection and nutritional value. At Sudden Shelter, "four plant families constitute more than half (55 percent) of all the floral remains recovered: Chenopodiaceae, Amaranthaceae, Gramineae, and Cactaceae. This seems to support Flannery's [1968] contention that people adapt not to microenvironments within a zone, but rather to a select series of plants whose ranges cross-cut several environments, as do these four plant families" (Coulam and Barnett 1980:194). Occupations appear to have been brief, probably occurring during the summer months, with a possible range of occupation from April to September.

Cowboy Cave

At Cowboy Cave in central eastern Utah, paleoethnobotanical research included analysis of fiber artifacts (Hewitt 1980:49–74), examination of wood and reed artifacts (Janetski 1980:75–96), macrofloral analysis (Barnett and Coulam 1980:127–133), examination of piñon pine (Hewitt 1980:135) and of corn (Winter 1980:191–192), analysis of human coprolites (Hogan 1980: 201–211), and pollen analysis of cultural deposits (Lindsay 1980b:213–224). The lowest levels of Cowboy Cave contain dung from Pleistocene megafauna, including mammoth, bison, horse, camel, and sloth. The oldest sediments date to between 11,000 and 9000 BC. The shelter has produced the following radiocarbon dates: 6740 BC, 6325 BC, 5265 BC, 4725 BC, 1685 BC, 1610 BC, AD 60, and AD 370. Jennings (1980) documents the presence of plant remains in his general archaeological description of the site, describing cedar bark bundles that comprised the chinking in a cist, a thick layer of loose grass extending outward from this cist, and two skin bags of shelled corn inside a pit, which were overlain with layers of cedar bark and grass and covered with a mat of *Sporobolus* grass. Wood and reed artifacts are not only thoroughly described and identified to genus of wood used, but many are also represented by photographs (Janetski 1980). Plant macrofossils recovered from Cowboy Cave were abundant and diverse and included, in diminishing order of frequency, Poaceae, *Juniperus*, *Chenopodium*, *Corispermum hyssipfolium*, and Cactaceae. Remains from other plants were recovered less frequently. All are detailed, by ubiquity, in tables. In addition, season of availability is listed for each of the remains recovered (Barnett and Coulam 1980).

Basketry recovered from Cowboy Cave is described in detail by Hewitt (1980), who details each type of basketry, the technique of manufacture, the type of stitch, and the working direction, and provides additional comments and comparisons with other basketry described in the literature. In addition to basketry, sandals also were recovered and described. Other fiber artifacts include two hairbrushes, a string apron, and a bark-wrapped ring, all of which Hewitt illustrates with photographs. Cordage materials are both described and pictured, as are some worked plant fibers. Hewitt makes no identification of materials used in most of the basketry. Both the rods and stitching elements of five pieces were identified as *Rhus trilobata*. Sandals were commonly made of yucca. Cordage was made from such diverse plants as *Apocynum/Asclepias*, grass, yucca, *Artemisia*, *Linum*, *Juniperus*, and *Cowania* (Hewitt 1980:68). Of the identifiable grasses, *Sporobolus* was most abundant, and

Stipa and *Hilaria* also were present. Cordage types are listed in descending order of abundance. Worked plant fibers included grass and sagebrush bark pads, a shredded sagebrush bark bundle, a heterogeneous group of fiber bundles, torches made of juniper bark, coiled fibers, wrapped rings, elongated split rings, buttons, bent twigs and splits, and problematical objects made of split *Rhus trilobata* that appear to be fringed, yucca strips and knots, and yucca leaf bundles. The hairbrushes were composed of rigid grass stems. Hewitt (1980) also details the occurrence by stratum of pine pitch, pitched basketry, sticks and gypsum points with pitch adhering, botanical remains of piñon, and pitched spindle whorls.

Janetski (1980) describes the wood artifacts from Cowboy Cave and identifies them by genus. An atlatl made of *Cercocarpus* was recovered, as were atlatl dart shafts made of *Cornus*, *Populus*, and *Cercocarpus*. Arrow shafts were made of *Phragmites*. Snares included scissor snares made of *Chenopodium* sticks and noose snares made of *Phragmites* reed and cord. An awl appears to be made of *Chenopodium*. Wooden gaming pieces were made of juniper. A wooden cup made of porous *Populus* root was also recovered. Wooden fire-hearths were recovered, but the types of wood represented remain unidentified. A digging stick packed with a large number of cheno-am seeds has been interpreted as having been used to beat seed-bearing plants. Six sticks were recovered with pitch gobbets adhering to them; one of these sticks was identified as *Phragmites* reed. Sticks identified as waste from woodworking activities also were recovered, one of which was identified as *Quercus*. A hoop made of a twig of *Rhus trilobata* and decorated sections of *Phragmites* reed also were described. *Phragmites* wrapped with fibrous bark or thin strips of split wood were recovered, and sections of worked *Phragmites* were noted. Split-twig figurines were made of *Salix* or *Rhus trilobata*. Numerous photos of the split-twig figurines and other floral artifacts accompanied Janetski's discussion.

Animal skin bags from Cowboy Cave were noted to contain items made from plants or plant fibers. A wad of grass (*Sporobolus*) was recovered from such a bag and yielded a radiocarbon age of 1380 BC. The bag was fashioned of the unsplit skin from a fawn's head (Hull 1980:137–139). Patches had been sewn over the natural openings with fine yucca twine (*Yucca angustissima*). Contents of the bag also included a dropseed (*Sporobolus cryptandrus*) grass net, two other grass nets, and a seed necklace. Large beads on the necklace were wild plum (*Prunus americana*), and the small, striped beads with ground ends were identified as silverberry (*Elaeagnus argentia*). The smallest beads were *Juniperus* cf. *osteosperma*. Corn recovered from one of two skin bags

254

Linda Scott Cummings

sewn with yucca fiber yielded a radiocarbon age of about AD 350. Both bags were fashioned from the skins of marmots.

The pollen record from metates and coprolites from Cowboy Cave indicated that grass seeds were important in the diet. *Zea mays* was recovered from coprolites from a depositional unit dating to AD 60, as well as from soil samples from that unit. Maize pollen was absent, however, from metate samples. The cheno-am frequency for the metate samples and for two of the coprolites from a unit dating to AD 100 was consistently higher than in the soil samples, indicating cheno-am consumption. Recovery of cf. *Cleome* pollen from a coprolite associated with a level yielding a radiocarbon age of 1685 BC indicates that this plant was probably part of the subsistence base at a relatively early date. Elevated *Artemisia* and *Helianthus*-type Asteraceae pollen in another coprolite from the same sample level suggests that this coprolite represents deposition during the summer or early fall, when sagebrush and various members of the sunflower family pollinate, and possible consumption of sunflower seeds. Economic diversity is apparently associated with the appearance of *Zea mays* in the pollen record (Lindsay 1980b:213–224).

Hogan (1980:201–211) examined the macrofloral component of human coprolites from Cowboy Cave. *Helianthus* and *Sporobolus* were suggested as dietary staples, with cheno-ams becoming more important in Levels IVc (1685 BC) and Vb (AD 60). Plants that appear to have had secondary importance include *Dicoria*, *Corispermum*, and *Carex*, as well as cactus pads. Seeds recovered from coprolites support the interpretation of Cowboy Cave as a seasonal camp that functioned primarily as a seed-processing station. Seed fragments and cactus pad fragments compose the bulk of the botanical material in the coprolites. On the basis of the seed record, occupation was interpreted to have taken place from late summer and early fall (Hogan 1980: 208). *Helianthus* appears to have been eaten "unroasted and frequently whole with the hulls present but split away [suggesting] that the seeds were consumed hull and all" (Hogan 1980:209). *Sporobolus* seeds are interpreted to have been consumed both as meal and as whole seeds. The presence of *Carex* seeds was used to posit the exploitation of a nearby wetland by the occupants of Cowboy Cave. Between 4750 and 1650 BC, cheno-ams gradually emerged as an important dietary component, becoming codominant with sunflower and dropseed by 1600 BC and the dominant resource by AD 50. Cheno-am seeds always appeared to have been ground prior to consumption. Hogan (1980) noted that both *Chenopodium* and *Amaranthus* tend to ripen later than sunflower or dropseed in the study area. He further suggested "that the increasing emphasis on Cheno-Ams arose as a result of a scheduling conflict between the gathering of sunflower and dropseed and the harvesting of maize" (Hogan 1980:210). The presence of corn pollen and macrofossils by AD 60 indicated the possibility of such a scheduling conflict.

Trough Hollow

Numerous sites in central to eastern Utah have produced evidence only of Fremont occupation. Trough Hollow, located in central Utah, was occupied during the Fremont to Shoshone/Ute time periods. The seed record from sites in this area contained burned seeds only of *Chenopodium* and cheno-ams. The pollen record, however, indicated utilization of a wider variety of plants, including *Cleome*, Fabaceae, *Opuntia*, cheno-ams, Poaceae, and *Typha* (Scott 1983:200–213). It may be that the Fremont limited-activity/hearth sites in the Trough Hollow study area represent the exploitation of a narrow range of local plant resources by small groups from larger base camps in the area.

Cedar Siding Shelter

Pollen analysis at Cedar Siding Shelter (42EM1533), an Archaic and Fremont site located approximately 60 miles northeast of Trough Hollow, yielded evidence of the probable Fremont utilization of *Pinus*, *Echinocereus*, cheno-ams, *Artemisia*, and a member of the Rosaceae family (Scott 1983).

Fremont Use of Cultigens

Zea mays is noted palynologically as the only cultigen in Fremont occupations at Clyde's Cavern (Lindsay n.d.) and Innocents Ridge (Lindsay 1975). *Cucurbita* (squash) rinds also were recovered in Fremont levels at Clyde's Cavern (Winter and Wylie 1974). At Clyde's Cavern, Poaceae and *Zea mays* (maize) were the dominant plants represented in the macrofloral record (Winter and Wylie 1974).

Innocents Ridge

At Innocents Ridge in central Utah, a broad variety of vegetal foods supplemented the use of *Zea mays* in the diet. These included cheno-ams, Poaceae, *Juniperus*, *Artemisia*, and *Typha* (Lindsay 1975). The subsistence pattern reflected in the pollen record, which did not indicate heavy reliance on grasses and agriculture, suggests that "at least a portion of the population was engaged in subsistence activities elsewhere during a part of the year" (Lindsay 1975:64).

Pint-Size Shelter

Pint-Size Shelter is a Fremont site in central eastern Utah. It is located in Castle Valley to the north of the San Raphael Swell at the confluence of Ivy and Muddy Creeks, a few miles northeast of Trough Hollow. The site produced no pollen evidence of *Zea mays* (maize), although cheno-ams and Poaceae appear to have been utilized heavily. In addition, greasewood and a member of the lily family also appear to have been consumed. A very large quantity of *Sarcobatus* pollen was recovered from a coprolite at this site (Lindsay 1976:68–70). The absence of *Zea mays* pollen at Pint-Size Shelter led Lindsay (1976) to conclude that the site was not directly associated with cultivation of that crop.

Dinosaur National Monument, 42UN1103

Macrofloral analysis at Mantle's Cave (42UN1103), a small rockshelter in Dinosaur National Monument, reflects a late Fremont and a Shoshonean occupation. Juniper bark is noted as a lining material for storage structures at Mantle's Cave (Burgh and Scoggin 1948). The macrofloral assemblage may represent either or both occupations.

Wild plant remains at 42UN1103, including juniper (*Juniperus utahensis*), *Pinus edulis, Opuntia, Echinocereus, Oryzopsis, Coryspermum, Cleome, Amaranthus,* and *Chenopodium*, might have been introduced through human or animal activity. The only unequivocally cultural remains recovered were corncobs and corn kernels. Toll (1985:62–80) reviews the morphology of the kernels and cobs recovered. She compares her results with those of Winter (1973), who presents a case for in situ evolution of Fremont dent rather than diffusion of germ plasm from Mexico via a western Arizona corridor. A primitive popcorn recovered from late Desert Archaic levels at Clyde's Cavern and early occurrence of dent corn throughout Utah and western Colorado provide the basis for Winter's hypothesis.

A single pollen sample was examined from a juniper bark level at 42UN1103. No *Zea mays* pollen was recovered from this sample. Cully (1984:

82–90) combines this evidence with the absence of non-ear plant parts to suggest that corn was never prepared for storage or consumption at 42UN1103 (Toll 1985:73–75).

Dinosaur National Monument, Deluge Shelter

Deluge Shelter (Leach 1970) yielded Archaic through Fremont remains on a tributary of the Green River in Dinosaur National Monument (Jennings 1978:81).

Dinosaur National Monument, 42UN1724

Granaries in northeastern Utah and northwestern Colorado frequently contain evidence of *Zea mays* or *Cucurbita*, or both. Site 42UN1724 contained both, as well as portions of a woven juniper basket and basket strap, and flax thread and cordage (Cummings 1993c:47–61; Truesdale 1993:12, 22–29). In addition, pollen and macrofloral analyses yielded additional evidence of *Zea mays*, *Cucurbita pepo* seed and rind, charred cactus spines and embryos, cheno-am seeds, grass seeds, juniper seeds, and wood. Single specimens of Fremont dent *Zea mays* and *Cucurbita* were identified at a later date from this same site (Cummings 1990). A radiocarbon age of AD 850 is reported for the Fremont occupation, which contained a single, shallow, bowl-shaped feature containing a charred grub and grasshopper fragments. Fremont dent-type maize kernels, however, were recovered from a layer dating to 380 BC. Native plants that appear to have been utilized include *Juniperus*, *Pinus*, cheno-ams, Asteraceae, Brassicaceae, *Eriogonum*, Poaceae, Malvaceae, *Sambucus*, and Cactaceae, including *Opuntia*.

Mummy Cave

Cordage and other artifacts recovered from Mummy Cave in northwestern Wyoming near Yellowstone Park (Wedel et al. 1968, cited in Jennings 1978: 81) indicate relationship to the Great Basin cultures.

42UN2012

A cradleboard recovered at 42UN2012 was made of split willow twigs with vertical cottonwood (*Populus*) support sticks. Horizontal cradleboard sticks were *Prunus*. The support for the head was made of juniper bark and deer hide, and the cordage was made from native flax (*Linum*) (Cummings and Puseman 1992; Truesdale 1992:18–25).

42UN1999

A prehistoric fishhook, recovered from a wattle and daub storage facility at 42UN1999 (AD 754), was made from *Atriplex*. Cordage attached to the fishhook was made from *Linum* (Cummings 1992).

Willow Creek, East Tavaputs Plateau

Cordage made from *Linum* is reported from a site on the western side of Willow Creek in the East Tavaputs Plateau (Cummings 2001b).

Rimrock Hamlet and Sky Aerie

Pollen, phytolith, and macrofloral analyses were conducted of material from Rimrock Hamlet (4RB2792) and Sky Aerie (5RB104), Fremont sites located in western Colorado. Macrofossil analysis yielded evidence of charred wild potatoes. Identification was confirmed using starch analysis. *Zea mays* was represented in both the pollen and macrofloral records. Cheno-ams, including both *Chenopodium* and *Amaranthus*, and ricegrass (*Oryzopsis*) were processed at one or both of these sites (Cummings et al. 1998).

Dutch John

Pollen analysis of four features at the Dutch John site on the Ashley National Forest near Vernal, Utah, indicates use of cheno-ams, *Opuntia*, and Poaceae. Recovery of starch granules points to the use of *Elymus* and *Agropyron* grasses, as well as a member of the Apiaceae family, such as biscuitroot (Cummings 1999a).

Examination of curated basketry from the Ashley National Forest yielded evidence for use of *Rhus* as construction material. Wood was used for rods and bundle material. In addition, *Salix* wood was noted in some of the basketry. *Asclepias* and *Apocynum* also were used in making fiber and cordage. Examination of the ends of two snares led to identification of four woods: *Salix*, *Artemisia*, *Sarcobatus*, and Rosaceae. The cordage used for one of the snares was identified as *Apocynum* and for the other as *Asclepias*. Identifications were made using a combination of macro- and microtechniques. Wood was examined in cross section, and fibers were examined using a light microscope and cross-polar illumination (Cummings and Puseman 2001b).

Douglas Creek

The Douglas Creek drainage in northwestern Colorado, particularly the Canyon Pintado area, contains an abundance of archaeological sites, many of which have been studied for archaeobotanical remains. Fremont sites, complete with evidence of *Zea mays*, are present throughout this area. For instance, *Zea mays* pollen has been recovered at the Brady site (5RB726) and Dripping Brow Cave site (5RB699) (Scott 1979) and at the Texas Creek Overlook site (5RB2435) (Scott and Rood 1986). Cheno-am seeds also were processed at the Texas Creek Overlook site.

Starch analysis of a mano from the Hanging Hearth site (5RB454) indicated grinding of grass seeds, whereas high cheno-am pollen frequencies point to use of a member of this group for its seeds, greens, or both (Cummings 1999b).

Hauck et al. (1993) examined five sites in Douglas Creek. Two of the sites (5RB3298 and 5RB3499) appear to have been short-term cheno-am processing sites. Hadden (1994; also Hauck et al. 1997) examined the occurrence of cheno-am seeds at Fremont sites in the Douglas Creek drainage at Hanging Hearth (5RB454), Hardings Hearths (5RB3498 and 3499), White Rock Shelters (5RB2829), and Alimony Alcove (5RB3657). Cheno-am seeds outnumbered all other types of seeds recovered in 53 of the 54 samples examined, sometimes by an order of magnitude. At Alimony Alcove, 1-liter float samples taken from the floor in a systematic grid revealed the presence of large numbers of cheno-am seeds. The number of seeds increased with increasing proximity to the hearth, with a single 1-liter sample of the hearth contents yielding over 59,000 seeds (Hadden 1994). This study provides another example in which archaeobotanical data were examined by systematic grid sampling from a floor. Hadden (1998, 1999) conducted experimental *Chenopodium* seed collection and processing, resulting in a yield of 4,500 calories per hour of work expended. Collection alone can produce between 3,600 and 7,100 calories of food per hour, depending on patch density and the experience of the forager. *Chenopodium* seeds are a highly nutritious food. These seeds are higher in protein and lower in carbohydrates than cultivated grains such as maize, making them a superior food for human consumption.

Kuck Rock Shelter (5RB3157)

The Fremont occupation at this rockshelter left behind hearths, ash pits, and a room of beam construction dated to AD 870–1025 (calibrated to AD 860). A grass mat, used in the construction of the shelter, yielded a radiocarbon age of AD 820. An earlier occupation also is represented outside the structure area, with radiocarbon ages of 1580 BC, 1440 BC, and 1280 BC. Pollen and macrofloral analysis yielded evidence of maize cobs and use of a variety of native plants, including cheno-am seeds (*Chenopodium*), *Helianthus* seeds, *Lepidium*-type Brassicaceae seeds, Poaceae seeds, and possibly *Juniperus* seeds. Phytoliths were extracted from maize cobs of different sizes to examine the cellular record for environmental conditions when the maize was grown and also to define a proxy for the genetic signature of the maize. Shape parameters held relatively constant between these cobs of different sizes, whereas cell size varied considerably. This pattern was interpreted to indicate that a single variety of maize, probably Fremont dent, was grown in two different habitats with differing water availability, one yielding relatively large ears and the other smaller ears (Cummings and Puseman 2003b).

Southwest Wyoming

Thompson and Pastor (1995) summarize archaeological work in southwestern Wyoming that has resulted in a record representing approximately the past 10,000 years. They synthesize reported remains by time period and discuss floral resources reported by archaeobotanists. Their Appendix B provides a valuable reference to the age and seasonality of occupations, fauna and flora reported, and archaeological literature related to work in the Moxa Arch study area. Archaeobotanical studies are usually included as appendices or chapters within the archaeological works cited by Thompson and Pastor, although they are not referenced individually. The contract archaeobotanical literature is voluminous (well over 100 reports) because pollen and macrofloral analyses have been conducted on a regular basis in this area since 1980. Thompson and Pastor (1995:96–98) discuss the possibility that a wide variety of plants was used, including (but not limited to) Apiaceae, Brassicaceae, *Calochortus*, *Carex*, *Chenopodium*, *Cleome*, Asteraceae, *Eriogonum*, Fabaceae, *Fragaria*, *Helianthus*, *Juniperus*, *Monolepis*, *Opuntia*, *Polygonum*, *Potentilla*, *Prunus*, *Rosa*, *Rumex*, and *Typha*, and they note the months during which these resources are available.

Highlights of work in southwestern Wyoming include the examination of pollen from house pits, pits, and ground stone at site 48FR1602 (Scott 1986). This study points to the importance of spatial analysis of archaeobotanical data. Concentrations of cheno-am, Poaceae, and other pollen types at the site indicate the locations of work areas and probable storage areas.

Other sites such as Buffalo Hump (48SW5057) provide evidence of use of *Cleome*, Poaceae, *Opuntia*, Solanaceae, and possibly *Polygonum sawatchense* (Scott 1986b).

Close-interval stratigraphic pollen sampling at 48LN1468 provided an unprecedented look at paleoenvironmental conditions during approximately the past 3,000 years and a less detailed look at conditions between approximately 3300 BC and 1000 BC. Prior to AD 450 conditions appear to have been cooler and/or moister than today, supporting a larger population of sagebrush. Between approximately AD 450 and 1000 conditions appear to have been similar to today, although that time span was punctuated by a severe warm and/or dry episode at one point. Cheno-ams, including saltbush, were the dominant vegetation types. After AD 1000 vegetation varied considerably, representing fluctuating conditions (Scott 1988).

The practice of examining both stratigraphic column samples and feature and floor samples for pollen has enhanced interpretations of the plant use record for this area. Evidence for processing plants has been subtle in the pollen records of features, floors, and ground stone. Only through comparison with the stratigraphic pollen record has it been possible to identify this subtle evidence of plant use.

Given the paucity of obvious information concerning plant use in some sites in southwestern Wyoming and northwestern Colorado, one project set out to examine mostly ground stone to obtain information concerning plant processing (Cummings and Moutoux 1999b). Pollen frequencies were instructive concerning the kinds of plants probably ground, and starch granules, recovered more often from ground stone washes than from accompanying sediments, also represented a suite of plants probably processed. Not surprisingly, grass seeds were commonly exploited in this area. The pollen record pointed to exploitation of cheno-ams, *Cleome*, Liliaceae, *Opuntia*, Poaceae, *Rhamnus*, Rosaceae, *Shepherdia*, and *Typha*. The starch record also pointed to the use of *Dodecatheon* roots, Poaceae seeds, and *Solanum jamesii*-type (wild potato) roots (Cummings and Moutoux 1999b).

Upper Snake and Salmon River Area

Kitty's Hot Hole Site

Limited recovery of macrofloral remains at Kitty's Hot Hole Site (10-OE-64) in Owyhee County, southern Idaho, included charred *Scirpus* and cheno-am seeds in association with charred wood and fire-cracked rock. No ash was recovered from this deposit. A single charred *Juniperus* wood fragment was reported (Heath 1992). Feature 1, which was sampled for macrofloral remains, was associated with diagnostic artifacts that indicated a possible age range for use of this feature of 300 BC to AD 650 (Holmer 1985, cited in Meatte et al. 1992).

Columbet Creek Rockshelter

Perishable remains recovered at the Columbet Creek Rockshelter in Owyhee County, southern Idaho, included a wooden shaft, fragments of a worked wood promontory peg, a notched shaft fragment, several twigs, and sagebrush or juniper bark twine. Matting was recorded in several different areas but was not identified. Tightly twisted vegetable cord was also noted but remains unidentified (Lynch and Olsen 1964).

Cave 1

Perishable macrofloral remains also are reported from Cave 1 in southwestern Idaho (Shellbach 1967:63–72), where excavation was conducted in 1929. Numerous forked sticks recovered along the rear wall appear to have been cultural. Heavy grass and organic layers were noted in portions of the cave, but no further identification was made. A string mat that had been woven over wooden rods was folded and placed beneath a grass covering in the cave. This object was identified as a backrest similar to those used by the Plains Indians. Material used in its construction was not identified. A layer of straw contained a small fragment of basketry weaving and an antler point fishhook. The straw layer was interpreted as representing a bed. A wooden fishhook or foreshaft with original cord lashings and barb was recovered near the bed. Three stone sinkers wrapped in rush and bound with string also were recovered in the vicinity of the bed. More woven matting was encountered in other contexts. Ash layers inside the cave may represent volcanic eruptions of Mount Mazama or Newberry Crater. This cave was interpreted as a fishing station where tools and personal effects such as a harpoon line, a backrest, and fishing hooks were left for seasonal use.

Wahmuza

Excavations at Wahmuza (10BK26) in southeastern Idaho yielded a few charred *Juniperus osteosperma* (Utah juniper) seeds. No other identifiable charred macrofloral remains were recovered (Taylor 1986).

Aviator's Cave

Cordage was noted among the perishable remains at Aviator's Cave (Lohse 1989). *Artemisia* (sagebrush) bark has been commonly used as a rough twine in the intermountain west and was used to bind a bundle of hair at Aviator's Cave. Other fibers used as cordage at the site have not yet been identified.

Pence-Duerig Cave

Wooden artifacts from Pence-Duerig Cave in south-central Idaho include parts of arrow shafts constructed of coniferous wood, including juniper, a fragment of a bow constructed of birch, and fragments of reed (*Phragmites communis*) arrow midshafts (Gruhn 1961:9–10).

Corn Creek

Macrofloral remains recovered from Corn Creek at the confluence of the Middle Fork and Main Salmon Rivers in central Idaho included charred *Carex*, Ericaceae, conifer, *Potamogeton*, Ranunculaceae, *Sambucus*, and *Sparganium* seeds (Nowak 1985). All remains were recovered from floor midden deposits, probably representing postoccupational refuse.

Dental Calculus

Dental calculus samples from two prehistoric individuals were compared with that of a historic individual. Phytoliths and starch granules were released from the dental calculus, revealing that the historic individual consumed domesticated cereals such as wheat, whereas the prehistoric individuals ate grass seeds, perhaps as gruel or meal, and cattail roots (Cummings 1998).

Archaeoclimatic Modeling

Archaeoclimatic modeling is a relative newcomer as a tool for interpretation of paleoenvironments (Bryson 1988, 1997). Understanding the local environment through time is essential for interpreting the interaction between people and plants. An example of using archaeoclimatic modeling comes from the eastern edge of the Great Basin, from the KibRidge-Yampa site at the eastern edge of Dinosaur National Monument (Cummings and Bryson 2003). Pollen samples collected at close intervals provide an excellent pollen record for the dated interval 9250 BC to approximately 8050 BC, an interval with human occupation at this site. Modeled temperature, precipitation, and water balance for this interval indicate increasing temperatures (with variations), fluctuating precipitation, and a general increase in spread between precipitation and potential evapotranspiration, indicating increasing aridity. Both the modeled water balance and the stratigraphic pollen record point to two periods of narrowing of this spread, resulting in more water available to plants. The pollen record indicates that the plants that increased in response to these conditions were members of the chicory tribe of the sunflower family (Cummings 2002). Both the modeled conditions and the pollen record are consistent in pointing to increased available moisture that supported springs, which in turn supported birch growing at approximately 9250 BC in an area that today supports a sparse population of sagebrush, xeric grasses, and occasional juniper.

Summary

"Variation between desolate and highly productive areas is the key to understanding the prehistory of the Basin" (Madsen 1982:207). Behavior of Great Basin populations has been modeled primarily using ethnographic analogy, most often centering on a generalized model of Shoshonean subsistence, settlement, and social organization. Models are more rarely built using solely archaeological data and often ignore the wide range of environmental and cultural variability inherent in the Great Basin. Madsen proposes that subsistence adaptation be emphasized and that it be considered along with "variation in available resources as a primary determinant of cultural variation in the Basin" (1982:208).

In the Basin the amount of cultural variation is marked, and extant models are simply not broad enough to explain this range of variation. During most, if not all time periods, groups in the Basin have ranged from almost fully sedentary to fully mobile. This range of variation has occurred despite relatively similar technologies (at any one time) from group to group. This cultural variation can best be explained by reference to the extremely varied environmental conditions to which these groups were adapted. The Great Basin is characterized by rich riverine and lacustrine ecosystems, which form oases between the areas of much more limited resources. These richer resource zones in turn vary in size, and most groups in the Basin incorporated differentially productive areas into their subsistence systems.

In some areas such ecosystems were sufficiently sizable and productive to support large, stable populations throughout the year. In other areas the ecosystems could support only small groups for short periods; they were temporary stops in a year-round patterns of movement. These examples form the ends of a continuum with numerous variations between. [Madsen 1982:207]

The eastern Great Basin, which Madsen (1982:208–209) defines as the area covered by Pleistocene Lake Bonneville and its tributaries, is expanded by other researchers to include more of southern Idaho and southwestern Wyoming, as well as eastern Utah and portions of western Colorado. North–south valleys with relatively flat valley bottoms characterize at least the Utah portion of the eastern Great Basin, making marsh and lacustrine environments important natural resource areas. Odum (1963) notes that marshes are rich ecosystems in terms of both available energy and food productivity. Both diversity and abundance of edible species are far greater in marshes than in other terrestrial ecosystems. Marsh resources, which were more abundant during the early Holocene and Neoglacial, would have been available "either year-round or sequentially, providing a stable year-round subsistence base" (Madsen 1982:208).

Models of prehistoric subsistence based on modern ethnographic data assume consistency in the distribution of resources throughout the Holocene. *Pinus monophylla* has been shown to have reentered the Basin around 7,500 years ago and, thus, was not available as a significant resource for exploitation by the occupants of the northern Great Basin during the early Holocene. Expansion of range of the piñon forest is noted between approximately 5000 and 500 BC, making piñon availability similar to that of the present only for the past 3,000 to 4,000 years (Madsen 1982:208–210). Madsen (1982:210) identifies fluctuations in marsh resources and piñon nuts as the most probable critical elements in understanding prehistoric subsistence. Experimental resource collection and processing, such as that undertaken by Hadden, indicate that *Chenopodium* seeds, when locally abundant, provided a highly nutritious and easily collected food. Based on archaeobotanical evidence, *Opuntia* is emerging as a significant resource at the extreme eastern margin of the Great Basin, primarily in northwestern Colorado and southwestern Wyoming. Distribution might well be greater than this, but evidence is particularly abundant in that area.

Archaeobotanic analysis in the Great Basin has evolved from mere collection of visible, and sometimes spectacular, remains in rockshelters to purposeful sampling. Soil samples are now floated to recover plant remains representing prehistoric activity. Charcoal also is being identified to enhance our description of the local vegetation community and to provide information regarding fuels exploited by prehistoric people. Pollen analysis, both stratigraphic and focused on features, provides a look at both the past environment and plants that people were exploiting. Phytoliths and starches are the two newcomers to archaeobotanic analysis in the Great Basin. Starches have proven to be a valuable tool in interpreting use of ground stone. Recovery of phytoliths from *Zea mays* cobs, for the dual purposes of examining growing conditions and identifying race of maize, shows much promise. The advent of archaeoclimatic modeling, which has been applied only occasionally in the Great Basin, provides a tool for modeling past environmental conditions. The archaeobotanical record provides a description that, taken with the archaeoclimatic model, provides a much more complete view of the past environment. Pollen, phytolith, starch, macrofloral, and charcoal analysis still stand as the best evidence for plant use.

References Cited

Adovasio, James M.
  1970   Textiles. In *Hogup Cave*, by C. Melvin Aikens, pp. 133–153. Anthropological Papers 93. University of Utah Press, Salt Lake City.
Aikens, C. Melvin
  1970   *Hogup Cave*. Anthropological Papers 93. University of Utah Press, Salt Lake City.
Aikens, C. Melvin, David L. Cole, and Robert Stuckenrath
  1977   *Excavations at Dirty Shame Rockshelter Southeastern Oregon*. Tebiwa Miscellaneous Paper 5. Idaho Museum of Natural History, Pocatello.
Ambro, Richard D.
  1967   *Dietary-Technological-Ecological Aspects of Lovelock Cave Coprolites*. Archaeological Survey Reports 70. University of California, Berkeley.
Ambro , Richard D., and Richard A. Cowan
  1966   Coprolite Analysis for Lovelock Cave, Nevada, with Comparisons from the Archaeological and Ethnographic Data for the Area. Paper presented at the 31st Annual Meeting of the Society for American Archaeology and the Great Basin Anthropological Conference, Reno.
Antevs, Ernst
  1948   Climactic Changes and Pre-White Man. In *The Great Basin, with Emphasis on Glacial and Postglacial Times*. Bulletin 39(20), Biological Series 10(7). University of Utah, Salt Lake City.
Barnett, Peggy R., and Nancy J. Coulam
  1980   Plant Macrofossil Analysis. In *Cowboy Cave*, edited by Jesse D. Jennings, pp. 127–134. Anthropological Papers 104. University of Utah Press, Salt Lake City.
Barrett, Stephen W.
  1980   Indians and Fire. *Western Wildlands* 8(3):17–21.

Berry, Michael S.

    1976   Remnant Cave. In *Swallow Shelter and Associated Sites*, by Gardiner F. Dalley, pp. 115–127. Anthropological Papers 96. University of Utah Press, Salt Lake City.

Bryson, Reid A.

    1988   Late Quaternary Volcanic Modulation of Milankovitch Climate Forcing. *Theoretical and Applied Climatology* 39:115–125.

    1997   The Paradigm of Climatology: An Essay. *Bulletin of the American Meteorological Society* 78:449–455.

Burgh, Robert F., and Charles R. Scoggin

    1948   *The Archaeology of Castle Park, Dinosaur National Monument*. Series in Anthropology 2. University of Colorado, Boulder.

Callen, Eric O., and Paul S. Martin

    1969   Plant Remains in Some Coprolites from Utah. *American Antiquity* 34:329–331.

Chamberlin, Ralph V.

    1911   *Ethno-Botany of the Goshiute Indians of Utah*. Memoirs 3, Pt. 5. American Anthropological Association, Menasha, Wisconsin.

Classen, P. W.

    1919   A Possible New Source of Food Supply (Cat-Tail Flour). *Scientific Monthly* 9:179–185.

Cottam, Walter P.

    1961   The Impact of Man on the Fauna of the Bonneville Basin. Lecture presented for Advancement of Learning Series, February 20, University of Utah, Salt Lake City.

Coulam, Nancy J., and Peggy R. Barnett

    1980   Paleoethnobotanical Analysis. In *Sudden Shelter*, edited by Jesse D. Jennings, Alan R. Schroedl, and Richard N. Holmer, pp. 171–195. Anthropological Papers 103. University of Utah Press, Salt Lake City.

Coville, Frederick V.

    1892   The Panamint Indians of California. *American Anthropologist* 5:351–361.

Cowan, Richard A.

    1967   *Lake-Margin Ecological Exploitation in the Great Basin as Demonstrated by an Analysis of Coprolites from Lovelock Cave, Nevada*. Archaeological Survey Reports 70. University of California, Berkeley.

Cully, Anne C.

    1984   *The Analysis of a Pollen Sample from 42UN1103, Dinosaur National Monument, Utah*. University of New Mexico, Albuquerque.

Cummings, Linda Scott

    1990   *Analysis of Fremont Paleobotanic Materials at 42UN1724, Dinosaur National Monument*. Paleo Research Technical Report 90-12. Paleo Research, Golden, Colorado.

    1992   *Analysis of a Prehistoric Fish Hook from 42UN199, Dinosaur National Park*. Paleo Research Technical Report 91-73. Paleo Research, Golden, Colorado.

    1993a   Pollen Analysis for Samples from the Big M Site, Oregon. Manuscript on file, Department of Anthropology, University of Oregon, Eugene.

    1993b   Pollen Analysis of Samples from the Paquet Gulch Bridge Site (35WS125), Oregon. Manuscript on file, Oregon State Museum of Anthropology, University of Oregon, Eugene.

    1993c   Analysis of Fremont Paleobotanical Materials at 42UN1724, Dinosaur National Monument. In *Archeological Investigations at Two Sites in Dinosaur National Monument: 42UN1724 and 5MF2645*, by James A. Truesdale, pp. 45–56. Selections from the Division of Cultural Resources 13. Rocky Mountain Region, National Park Service, US Department of the Interior, Denver.

Linda Scott Cummings

1995   *Pollen Analysis in Drews Valley, Southeast Oregon.* Paleo Research Technical Report 94-16. Paleo Research, Golden, Colorado.

1998   *Microscopic Analysis of Dental Calculus from Two Prehistoric and One Historic Individuals, 10PE20, 10OE5968, and Fort Boise, Idaho.* Paleo Research Technical Report 98-13. Paleo Research, Golden, Colorado.

1999a   *Pollen Analysis of Features at Sites 42DA364, 42DA617, 42DA690, and 42DA693 in the Dutch John Privatization Survey, Uinta Mountains, Utah.* Paleo Research Technical Report 99-50. Paleo Research, Golden, Colorado.

1999b   *Pollen Analysis at the Hanging Hearth Site, 5RB454, Colorado.* Paleo Research Technical Report 99-32. Paleo Research, Golden, Colorado.

2001a   Faunal and Botanical Remains from 26Ch1062: Phytolith Analysis. In *Prehistory of the Carson Desert and Stillwater Mountains: Environment, Mobility, and Subsistence in a Great Basin Wetland*, pp. 251–262. Anthropological Papers 123. University of Utah Press, Salt Lake City.

2001b   *Fiber Identification for Cordage from Willow Creek, East Tavaputs Plateau, Eastern Utah.* Paleo Research Technical Report 00-94. Paleo Research, Golden, Colorado.

2002   Pollen Analysis at the KibRidge-Yampa Site, Northwestern Colorado. In *KibRidge-Yampa Paleoindian Occupation Site (5MF3687), Preliminary Archaeological Excavations (1993–2001)*, by F. Richard Hauck and Michael R. Hauck, Appendix, pp. 1–24. General Studies Series 4. Archaeological Research Institute, Bountiful, Utah.

Cummings, Linda Scott, and Reid A. Bryson

2003   Comparison of Pollen Records and Archaeoclimatic Modeling. Poster presented at the Rocky Mountain Anthropological Conference, Estes Park, Colorado. Available online at www.paleoresearch.com/images/RMAC2003-fnl.jpg.

Cummings, Linda Scott, and Thomas E. Moutoux

1997   *Pollen Analysis at Baker Village (26WP63), Eastern Nevada.* Paleo Research Technical Report 97-06. Paleo Research, Golden, Colorado.

1999a   *Pollen Analysis at Crazy Bird (42SV896), Central Utah.* Paleo Research Technical Report 98-52. Paleo Research, Golden, Colorado.

1999b   *Subsistence and Paleoenvironmental Interpretations of the Pollen and Starch Records along the CIG Pipeline, Northwest Colorado and Southwest Wyoming.* Technical Report 93-61. Paleo Research, Golden, Colorado.

Cummings, Linda Scott, and Curtis Nepstad-Thornberry

2000   *Pollen and Macrofloral Analysis at Site 42CB1407, Central Utah.* Paleo Research Technical Report 00-17. Paleo Research, Golden, Colorado.

Cummings, Linda Scott, and Kathryn Puseman

1992   Fiber and Wood Identification of Remains from a Burial (42UN2012) in Uinta County, Utah. Manuscript on file, Metcalf Archaeological Consultants, Eagle, Colorado, Uinta County Sheriff's Department, Uinta, Utah, and Paleo Research, Golden, Colorado.

1993a   *Examination of Five Pieces of Groundstone from Lander County, Central Nevada, for Pollen, Phytoliths, Starch Granules, and Blood Residue to Interpret Subsistence Activities.* Technical Report 98-36. Paleo Research, Golden, Colorado.

1993b   *Pollen, Starch, and Blood Residue Analysis of Groundstone from Sites in Lander County, Nevada.* Technical Report 92-46. Paleo Research, Golden, Colorado.

2000   *Pollen and Macrofloral Analysis at Site 42GA3817 and Protein Residue Analysis at Site 42GA4735, Bear Creek Canyon, Utah.* Technical Report 00-91. Montgomery Archaeological Consultants, Moab, Utah, and Paleo Research, Golden, Colorado.

2001a   *Pollen and Macrofloral Analysis at the South Temple Site (42SL285), Salt Lake City, Utah.*

Technical Report 98-84. Office of Public Archaeology, Brigham Young University, Salt Lake City, Utah, and Paleo Research, Golden, Colorado.

2001b   *Fiber and Wood Identification at Several Sites on the Ashley National Forest, Utah*. Technical Report 01-45. Paleo Research, Golden, Colorado.

2002   Fiber and Wood Identification at Several Sites on the Ashley National Forest, Utah. In *Prehistoric Uinta Mountain Occupations*, by Clay Johnson and Byron Loosle, pp. A1:22–22. USDA Forest Service, Vernal, Utah.

2003a   *Pollen, Phytolith, and Macrofloral Analysis at Backhoe Village (42SV662), Sevier County, Utah*. Paleo Research Technical Report 02-38. Paleo Research, Golden, Colorado.

2003b   *Pollen, Starch, Macrofloral, and Corn Cob Analyses at the Kuck Site (5RB3157), Rio Blanco County, Colorado*. Paleo Research Technical Reports 01-61, 01-90, 01-89, 02-99. Paleo Research, Golden, Colorado.

Cummings, Linda Scott, Kathryn Puseman, and Thomas E. Moutoux

1998   *Pollen, Phytolith, and Macrofloral Analysis of Samples from the Rimrock Hamlet (5RB2792) and Sky Aerie (5RB104) Sites, Western Colorado*. Technical Report 97-57. Centuries Research, Montrose, Colorado, and Paleo Research, Golden, Colorado.

Cummings, Linda Scott, Kathryn Puseman, Thomas E. Moutoux, and Laura L. Ruggiero

1998a   *Pollen and Macrofloral Analysis at the Hines Site, 35HH2692, Oregon*. Technical Report 98-03. Oregon State Museum of Anthropology, University of Oregon, Eugene, and Paleo Research, Golden, Colorado.

1998b   *Pollen and Macrofloral Analysis at Site 42CB507, Utah*. Technical Report 97-78. Senco-Phenix, Mount Pleasant, Utah, and Paleo Research, Golden, Colorado.

1999   *Pollen and Macrofloral Analysis at 42CB1302, Utah*. Technical Report 99-27A. Montgomery Archaeological Consultants, Moab, Utah, and Paleo Research, Golden, Colorado.

Cutler, Hugh C.

1970   Corn from Hogup Cave, a Fremont Site. In *Hogup Cave*, edited by C. Melvin Aikens, pp. 271–272. Anthropological Papers 93. University of Utah Press, Salt Lake City.

Dalley, Gardiner F.

1970   Artifacts of Wood. In *Hogup Cave*, edited by C. Melvin Aikens, pp. 153–186. Anthropological Papers 93. University of Utah Press, Salt Lake City.

1972   Palynology of the Evans Mound Deposits. In *The Evans Site*, by Michael S. Berry. Special report. Department of Anthropology, University of Utah, Salt Lake City.

1976   *Swallow Shelter and Associated Sites*. Anthropological Papers 96. University of Utah Press, Salt Lake City.

Daubenmire, Rexford F.

1979   *Plants and Environment: A Textbook for Plant Autoecology*. Wiley and Sons, New York.

d'Azevedo, Warren L.

1986   Washoe. In *Great Basin*, edited by Warren L. d'Azevedo, pp. 466–498. Handbook of North American Indians, vol. 11, W. C. Sturtevant, general editor. Smithsonian Institution, Washington, DC.

Elston, Robert G.

1982   Good Times, Hard Times: Prehistoric Culture Change in the Western Great Basin. In *Man and Environment in the Great Basin*, edited by David B. Madson and James F. O'Connell, pp. 186–206. SAA Papers 2. Society for American Archaeology, Washington, DC.

1986   Prehistory of the Western Area. In *Great Basin*, edited by Warren L. d'Azevedo, pp. 135–148. Handbook of North American Indians, vol. 11, William G. Sturtevant, general editor. Smithsonian Institution, Washington, DC.

Linda Scott Cummings

Flannery, Kent V.
    1968   Archaeological Systems Theory and Early Mesoamerica. In *Anthropological Archaeology in the Americas*, edited by Betty J. Meggers, pp. 67–87. Anthropological Society of Washington, Washington, DC.
Follett, W. I.
    1967   *Fish Remains from Coprolites and Midden Deposits at Lovelock Cave, Churchill County, Nevada*. Archaeological Survey Reports 70. University of California, Berkeley.
Fowler, Catherine S.
    1986   Subsistence. In *Great Basin*, edited by Warren L. d'Azevedo, pp. 64–97. Handbook of North American Indians, vol. 11, William G. Sturtevant, general editor. Smithsonian Institution, Washington, DC.
Fowler, Don D., David B. Madsen, and Eugene M. Hattori
    1973   *Prehistory of Southeastern Nevada*. Publications in the Social Sciences 6. Desert Research Institute, Reno.
Fry, Gary R.
    1968   *Prehistoric Diet at Danger Cave, Utah: As Determined by the Analysis of Coprolites*. Unpublished master's thesis, Department of Anthropology, University of Utah, Salt Lake City.
    1970   Preliminary Analysis of the Hogup Cave Coprolites. In *Hogup Cave*, edited by C. Melvin Aikens, pp. 247–250. Anthropological Papers 93. University of Utah Press, Salt Lake City.
    1976   *Analysis of Prehistoric Coprolites from Utah*. Anthropological Papers 97. University of Utah Press, Salt Lake City.
    1977   *Analysis of Prehistoric Coprolites from Utah*. Anthropological Papers 97. University of Utah Press, Salt Lake City.
    1978   *Prehistoric Diet at Danger Cave, Utah, as Determined by the Analysis of Coprolites*. Anthropological Papers 23. University of Utah Press, Salt Lake City.
Gruhn, Ruth
    1961   A Collection of Artifacts from Pence-Duerig Cave in South-Central Idaho. *Tebiwa* 4(1):1–24.
Hadden, Glade V.
    1994   Seed Processing in the Douglas Creek Drainage—New Evidence for the Importance of Cheno/Ams in Fremont Contexts. Paper Presented at the 2nd Rocky Mountain Conference, Steamboat Springs, Colorado.
    1998   Small Seed Resource Processing and Experimental Return Rates for Cheno/Ams. Paper presented at the Great Basin Conference, Bend, Oregon.
    1999   Behold the Lowly Pigweed: Experimental Processing Returns for Cheno/Am Harvests in Northwestern Colorado. Paper Presented at the 5th Biennial Rocky Mountain Anthropological Conference, Glenwood Springs, Colorado.
Hall, Henry J.
    1977   A Paleoscatological Study of Diet and Disease at Dirty Shame Rockshelter, Southeast Oregon. *Tebiwa Miscellaneous Paper* 8:1–14.
Harper, Kimball T.
    1986   Historical Environments. In *Great Basin*, edited by Warren L. d'Azevedo, pp. 51–63. Handbook of North American Indians, vol. 11, William C. Sturtevant, general editor. Smithsonian Institution, Washington, DC.
Harper, Kimball T., and G. M. Alder
    1972   The Macroscopic Plant Remains of the Deposits of Hogup Cave, Utah, and Their Paleoclimatic Implications. In *Hogup Cave*, edited by C. Melvin Aikens, pp. 215–240. Anthropological Papers 93. University of Utah Press, Salt Lake City.

Hauck, F. Richard, Glade V. Hadden, and B. Mueller
  1997   *Archaeological Excavations (1993–1996) in the Douglas Creek–Texas Mountain Locality of Rio Blanco County, Colorado*. AERC Paper 50. Archaeological-Environmental Research Corporation, Bountiful, Utah.
Hauck, F. Richard, Glade V. Hadden, and D. Weder
  1993   *Archaeological Excavations (1988–1992) in the Douglas Creek–Texas Mountain Locality of Rio Blanco County, Colorado*. AERC Paper 50. Archaeological-Environmental Research Corporation, Bountiful, Utah.
Heath, Kathleen M.
  1992   Macrofossil and Micro-Refuse Analysis. In *Archaeological Test Excavations at Kitty's Hot Hole Site (10-OE-42), Owyhee County, Southern Idaho*, edited by Daniel S. Meatte, James C. Woods, and Gene Titmus, pp. 63–70. Herrett Museum, Twin Falls, Idaho.
Heizer, Robert F.
  1960   *Physical Analysis of Habitation Residues*. Publications in Anthropology 28. Viking Fund, New York.
  1966   Analysis of Human Coprolites from a Dry Nevada Cave. Paper presented at the 35th Annual Meeting of the American Association of Physical Anthropologists, Berkeley.
  1967   *Analysis of Human Coprolites from a Dry Nevada Cave*. Archaeological Survey Reports 70. University of California, Berkeley.
  1970   *An Ethnographic Sketch of the Paviotso in 1882*. Archaeological Research 7. University of California, Berkeley.
Heizer, Robert F., and L. K. Napton
  1969   Biological and Cultural Evidence from Prehistoric Human Coprolites. *Science* 165:563–568.
Helzer, Margaret
  2000   Macrobotanical Analysis of a Middle Holocene House Floor in the Fort Rock Basin, Oregon. Paper presented at the 27th Great Basin Anthropological Conference, Ogden, Utah.
Hewitt, Nancy J.
  1980   The Occurrence of Pinyon Pine at Cowboy Cave. In *Cowboy Cave*, edited by Jesse D. Jennings, pp. 135–136. Anthropological Papers 104. University of Utah Press, Salt Lake City.
Hogan, Patrick F.
  1980   The Analysis of Human Coprolites from Cowboy Cave. In *Cowboy Cave*, edited by Jesse D. Jennings, pp. 201–212. Anthropological Papers 104. University of Utah Press, Salt Lake City.
Holmer, Richard N.
  1985   Projectile Points of the Intermontain Region. In *Anthropology of the Desert West: Essays in Honor of Jesse D. Jennings*, edited by Carol J. Condie and Don D. Fowler, pp. 89–115. Anthropological Papers 110. University of Utah Press, Salt Lake City.
Hull, Frank W.
  1976   Comparative Pollen Sampling Techniques at Remnant Cave. In *Swallow Shelter and Associated Sites*, edited by Gardiner F. Dalley, pp. 175–179. Anthropological Papers 96. University of Utah Press, Salt Lake City.
  1980   Animal Skin Bags. In *Cowboy Cave*, edited by Jesse D. Jennings, pp. 137–144. Anthropological Papers 104. University of Utah Press, Salt Lake City.
Janetski, Joel C.
  1980   Wood and Reed Artifacts. In *Cowboy Cave*, edited by Jesse D. Jennings, pp. 75–96. Anthropological Papers 104. University of Utah Press, Salt Lake City.
Jenkins, Dennis L.
  n.d.   Archaeological Investigations at Three Wetlands Sites in the Silver Lake Area of the Fort Rock Basin. Manuscript on file with Dennis L. Jenkins.

Linda Scott Cummings

1994   Settlement-Subsistence Patterns in the Fort Rock Basin: A Cultural-Ecological Perspective on Human Responses to Fluctuating Wetlands Resources of the Last 5000 Years. In *Archaeological Researches in the Northern Great Basin: Fort Rock Archaeology since Cressman*, edited by C. Melvin Aikens and Dennis L. Jenkins, pp. 599–600. Anthropological Papers 50. University of Oregon, Eugene.

Jennings, Jesse D.
1957   *Danger Cave*. Anthropological Papers 27. University of Utah Press, Salt Lake City.
1978   *Prehistory of Utah and the Eastern Great Basin*. Anthropological Papers 98. University of Utah Press, Salt Lake City.
1980   (editor) *Cowboy Cave*. Anthropological Papers 104. University of Utah Press, Salt Lake City.
1986   Prehistory: Introduction. In *Great Basin*, edited by Warren L. d'Azevedo, pp. 113–119. Handbook of North American Indians, vol. 11, William G. Sturtevant, general editor. Smithsonian Institution, Washington, DC.

Judd, Neil M.
1926   *Archaeological Observations North of the Rio Colorado*. Bulletin 82. Bureau of American Ethnology, Smithsonian Institution, Washington, DC.

Kelly, Robert L.
2001   *Prehistory of the Carson Desert and Stillwater Mountains: Environment, Mobility, and Subsistence in a Great Basin Wetland*. Anthropological Papers 123. University of Utah Press, Salt Lake City.

Kelso, Gerald K.
1970   Hogup Cave: Comparative Pollen Analysis of Human Coprolites and Cave Fill. In *Hogup Cave*, by C. Melvin Aikens, pp. 251–262. Anthropological Papers 93. University of Utah Press, Salt Lake City.

Lanner, Ronald M.
1983   The Expansion of Singleleaf Piñon in the Great Basin. In *The Archaeology of Monitor Valley: 2. Gatecliff Shelter*, edited by David Hurst Thomas, pp. 167–171. Anthropological Papers 59, Pt. 1. American Museum of Natural History, New York.

Leach, Larry L.
1970   *Archaeological Investigations at Deluge Shelter in Dinosaur National Monument*. Unpublished PhD dissertation, Department of Anthropology, University of Colorado, Boulder.

Leopold, A. Starker
1950   Deer in Relation to Plant Succession. In *Transactions of the 15th North American Wildlife Conference, March 6–9, 1950, San Francisco*, edited by Ethel M. Quee, pp. 571–578. Wildlife Management Institute, Washington, DC.

Lindsay, La Mar W.
1975   Palynological Analysis and Paleoecology of Innocents Ridge. In *Innocents Ridge and the San Raphael Fremont*, edited by David B. Madsen, pp. 29–66. Anthropological Papers 2. University of Utah Press, Salt Lake City.
1976   Site Paleoecology: Palynology and Macrofossil Analysis. In *Pint-Size Shelter*, edited by La Mar W. Lindsay and Christian K. Lund, pp. 67–74. Antiquities Section Selected Papers 3(9–11). Utah State Historical Society, Salt Lake City.
1980a   Pollen Analysis of Sudden Shelter Site Deposits. In *Sudden Shelter*, edited by Jesse D. Jennings, Alan R. Schroedl, and Richard N. Holmer, pp. 261–272. Anthropological Papers 103. University of Utah Press, Salt Lake City.
1980b   Pollen Analysis of Cowboy Cave Cultural Deposits. In *Cowboy Cave*, edited by Jesse D. Jennings, pp. 213–224. Anthropological Papers 104. University of Utah Press, Salt Lake City.

n.d.   Pollen Analysis of Clyde's Cavern. Manuscript on file, Antiquities Section, Division of State History, Salt Lake City.

Lohse, E. S.

1989   Aviator's Cave. *Idaho Archaeologist* 12(2):23–28.

Loud, Llewellyn L., and Mark R. Harrington

1929   *Lovelock Cave.* Publications in American Archaeology and Ethnology 245(1). University of California, Berkeley.

Lynch, Thomas F., and Lawrence Olsen

1964   The Columbet Creek Rockshelter (Owyhee County, Idaho). *Tebiwa* 7(1):7–16.

Madsen, David B.

1979   The Fremont and the Sevier: Defining Prehistoric Agriculturalists North of the Anasazi. *American Antiquity* 44:711–723.

1982   Holocene Stratigraphy and Palynology at the Saval Ranch, Elko County, Nevada. In *A Class II Cultural Resource Reconnaissance of the Saval Ranch Research and Evaluation Area, Elko County, Nevada.* Bureau of Land Management, Lakewood, Colorado.

Madsen, David B., and La Mar W. Lindsay

1977   *Backhoe Village.* Selected Papers 4(12). Antiquities Section, Utah State Historical Society, Salt Lake City.

Madsen, David B., and David Rhode

1990   Early Holocene Pinyon (*Pinus monophylla*) in the Northeastern Great Basin. *Quaternary Research* 33:94–101.

Madsen, David B., and Steven R. Simms

1998   The Fremont Complex: A Behavioral Perspective. *Journal of World Prehistory* 12: 255–336.

Martin, Paul S.

1963   *The Last 10,000 Years: A Fossil Pollen Record of the American Southwest.* University of Arizona Press, Tucson.

Martin, Paul S., and Floyd W. Sharrock

1964   Pollen Analysis of Prehistoric Human Feces: A New Approach to Ethnobotany. *American Antiquity* 30:168–180.

Marwitt, John

1986   Fremont Cultures. In *Great Basin*, edited by Warren L. d'Azevedo, pp. 161–172. Handbook of North American Indians, vol. 11, William G. Sturtevant, general editor. Smithsonian Institution, Washington, DC.

Meatte, Daniel S., James C. Woods, and Gene Titmus

1992   *Archaeological Test Excavations at Kitty's Hot Hole Site (10-OE-64), Owyhee County, Southern Idaho.* Herrett Museum, Twin Falls, Idaho.

Mehringer, Peter J., Jr.

1985   Late-Quaternary Pollen Records from the Interior Pacific Northwest and Northern Great Basin of the United States. In *Pollen Records of Late Quaternary North American Sediments*, edited by Vaughn M. Bryant Jr. and Richard J. Holloway, pp. 167–189. American Association of Stratigraphic Palynologists Foundation, Dallas.

1986   Prehistoric Environments. In *Great Basin*, edited by Warren L. d'Azevedo, pp. 31–50. Handbook of North American Indians, vol. 11, William G. Sturtevant, general editor. Smithsonian Institution, Washington, DC.

Napton, Lewis K., and Gerald K. Kelso

1969   Part III: Preliminary Palynological Analysis of Lovelock Cave Coprolites. In *Archaeological and Paleobiological Investigations in Lovelock Cave, Nevada: Further Analysis of Human*

Coprolites, by Lewis K. Napton, pp. 19–27. Special Publication 2. Kroeber Anthropological Society, Berkeley.

Nowak, Cheryl
1985 Micro-Refuse. In *Excavations at Corn Creek*, edited by Richard N. Holmer and Jeffrey W. Ross. Reports of Investigations 84-8. Swanson/Crabtree Anthropological Research Laboratory, Idaho State University, Pocatello.

Odum, Eugene P.
1963 *Ecology*. Holt, Rinehart and Winston, New York.

Prouty, Guy L.
1994 Root Crop Exploitation and the Development of Upland Habitation Sites: Paleoethnobotanical and Archaeological Research into the Distribution and Use of Economic Plants in the Fort Rock Basin. In *Archaeological Researches in the Northern Great Basin: Fort Rock Archaeology since Cressman*, edited by C. Melvin Aikens and Dennis L. Jenkins, pp. 573–598. Anthropological Papers 50. University of Oregon, Eugene.

n.d. Macrobotanical Remains from the Indian Grade Spring Site, Appendix A. Manuscript on file, Paleo Research Institute, Golden, Colorado.

Puseman, Kathryn
1994 *Macrofloral Analysis at Nine Sites for the PGT-PG&E Pipeline Expansion Project, Oregon*. Paleo Research Technical Report 93-89. INFOTEC Research, Eugene, Oregon, and Paleo Research, Golden, Colorado.

1995 *Macrofloral Analysis of Samples from Sites in the Ward Charcoal Ovens State Park, Nevada*. Paleo Research Technical Report 96-13. Louis Berger and Associates, Phoenix, and Paleo Research, Golden, Colorado.

1999 *Macrofloral Analysis of Hearth Fill at Site 10-43-1, Utah*. Paleo Research Technical Report 99-46. Office of Public Archaeology, Brigham Young University, Provo, and Paleo Research, Golden, Colorado.

Puseman, Kathryn, and Linda Scott Cummings
1999 *Pollen and Macrofloral Analysis at Site 26CK415, Nevada*. Paleo Research Technical Report 99-53. Harry Reid Center for Environmental Studies, University of Nevada, Las Vegas, and Paleo Research, Golden, Colorado.

2000a *Pollen and Macrofloral Analysis at Sites in the Utah Valley, Utah*. Paleo Research Technical Report 99-86. Brigham Young University, Museum of Peoples and Cultures, Provo, and Paleo Research, Golden, Colorado.

2000b *Pollen and Macrofloral Analysis at Sites in the Texaco Buzzard Bench Well Pads Project, Central Utah*. Paleo Research Technical Report 99-93. Office of Public Archaeology, Brigham Young University, Provo, and Paleo Research, Golden, Colorado.

2001 *Pollen and Macrofloral Analysis and Identification of Botanic Remains from Black Dog Cave, Site 26CK5686/BLM 53-7216, Nevada*. Paleo Research Technical Report 00-60. Harry Reid Center for Environmental Studies, University of Nevada, Las Vegas, and Paleo Research, Golden, Colorado.

Puseman, Kathryn, Linda Scott Cummings, Thomas E. Moutoux, and Laura Ruggiero
1999 *Pollen and Macrofloral Analysis of a Fremont Pit at 42SL285, Salt Lake City, Utah*. Paleo Research Technical Report 99-45. Utah State Historical Society, Salt Lake City, and Paleo Research, Golden, Colorado.

Puseman, Kathryn, Thomas E. Moutoux, and Linda Scott Cummings
1996 *Pollen and Macrofloral Analysis at Sites 42SV2304 and 42SV2229, Fish Lake Area, Central Utah*. Paleo Research Technical Report 96-10. Brigham Young University, Museum of Peoples and Cultures, Provo, and Paleo Research, Golden, Colorado.

Puseman, Kathryn, and Laura Ruggiero

1999a *Macrofloral Analysis of Samples from Sites in the Fort Rock Basin, Oregon.* Paleo Research Technical Report 99-28. University of Oregon, Department of Anthropology, Eugene, and Paleo Research, Golden, Colorado.

1999b *Macrofloral Analysis at 42SL98 (Block 49 Site), Salt Lake City, Utah.* Paleo Research Technical Report 98-87. Office of Public Archaeology, Brigham Young University, Provo, and Paleo Research, Golden, Colorado.

Rhode, David

2001 Faunal and Botanical Remains from 26Ch1062: Macrobotanical Remains. In *Prehistory of the Carson Desert and Stillwater Mountains: Environment, Mobility, and Subsistence in a Great Basin Wetland,* by Robert L. Kelly, pp. 254–262. Anthropological Papers 123. University of Utah Press, Salt Lake City.

Roust, Norman L.

1967 *Preliminary Examination of Prehistoric Human Coprolites from Four Western Nevada Caves.* Archaeological Survey Reports 70. University of California, Berkeley.

Sauer, Jonathan D.

1950 The Grain Amaranths: A Survey of Their History and Classification. *Annals of the Missouri Botanical Garden* 37:561–632.

Scott, Linda J.

1979 Pollen Analysis of Two Sites in the Canyon Pintado Historic District, Rio Blanco, Colorado. Manuscript on file, Laboratory of Public Archaeology, Fort Collins.

1983 Pollen Analysis at Cedar Siding Shelter (42EM1533), Emery County, Utah. Manuscript on file, Grand River Institute, Grand Junction.

1986a Pollen Analysis at 48FR1602: The Paleoenvironmental and Subsistence Records. Manuscript on file, Archaeological Services, Western Wyoming College, Rock Springs.

1986b Pollen Analysis at 48SW5057. Manuscript on file, Archaeological Services, Western Wyoming College, Rock Springs.

Scott, Linda J., and Ronald J. Rood

1986 Subsistence Data from the Pollen, Macrofloral, and Faunal Records at the Texas Creek Overlook Site. Manuscript on file, Bureau of Land Management, Craig, Colorado.

Shellbach, Louis

1967 The Excavation of Cave No. 1, Southwestern Idaho, 1929. *Tebiwa* 10(2):63–72.

Stenholm, Nancy A.

1989a The Botanical Assemblage of Site 35HA1263. Manuscript on file, Paleo Research Institute, Golden, Colorado.

1989b The Botanical Assemblage of Site 35LK2468, Ratz Nest House Ring. Manuscript on file, Paleo Research Institute, Golden, Colorado.

1990 The Botanical Assemblage. In *Archaeology of the Dunn Site (35HA1261), Harney County, Oregon,* edited by Robert R. Musil, pp. 81–86. Report 95. Heritage Research Associates, Eugene.

1992 Fort Rock Basin Botanical Analysis. Paper presented at NWAC, Simon Fraser University. Manuscript on file, Paleo Research Institute, Golden, Colorado.

1994 Paleoethnobotanical Analysis of Archaeological Samples Recovered in the Fort Rock Basin. In *Archaeological Researches in the Northern Great Basin: Fort Rock Archaeology since Cressman,* edited by C. Melvin Aikens and Dennis L. Jenkins, pp. 531–560. University of Oregon Anthropological Papers 50. Department of Anthropology and State Museum of Anthropology, University of Oregon, Eugene.

n.d.   Analysis of Christmas Lake Valley Flotation Samples. Manuscript on file, Paleo Research Institute, Golden, Colorado.

Stewart, Omer C.

1955   Forest and Grass Burning in the Mountain West. *Southwestern Lore* 21(1):5–9.

Taylor, Bill

1986   Plant Macrofossils. In *Shoshone-Bannock Culture History*, edited by Richard N. Holmer, pp. 156–160. Reports of Investigations 85-16. Swanson/Crabtree Anthropological Research Laboratory, Idaho State University, Pocatello.

Thomas, David Hurst

1983   *The Archaeology of Monitor Valley 1, Epistemology*. Anthropological Papers 58, Pt. 1. American Museum of Natural History, New York.

Thompson, Kevin W., and Jana V. Pastor

1995   *People of the Sage: 10,000 Years of Occupation in Southwest Wyoming*. Cultural Resource Management Report 67. Archaeological Services, Western Wyoming Community College, Rock Springs.

Toll, Mollie S.

1985   Flotation and Macro-Botanical Studies at a Small Dry Rock Shelter (42UN1103) in Dinosaur National Monument. In *Site 42UN1103: A Rockshelter in Dinosaur National Monument, Utah*, edited by Terri L. Liestman, pp. 60–80. Occasional Studies in Anthropology 13. Midwest Archaeological Center, National Park Service, US Department of the Interior, Lincoln.

Truesdale, James A.

1992   Analysis and Determination of Archaeological Value for Human Remains and Associated Artifacts Vandalized from 41UN2012, Red Fleet Reservoir State Park, Unitah County, Utah. Manuscript on file, Bureau of Land Management, Vernal, Utah.

1993   *Archeological Investigations at Two Sites in Dinosaur National Monument: 42UN1724 and 5MF2645*. Selections from the Division of Cultural Resources 13. Rocky Mountain Region, National Park Service, US Department of the Interior, Denver.

Tubbs, Deborah Y., and Rainer Berger

1967   *The Viability of Pathogens in Ancient Human Coprolites*. Archaeological Survey Reports 70. University of California, Berkeley.

Wedel, Waldo R., W. M. Husted, and J. H. Moss

1968   Mummy Cave: Prehistoric Record from Rocky Mountains of Wyoming. *Science* 160: 184–185.

Wells, P. V.

1983   Paleobiogeography of Montane Islands in the Great Basin since the Last Glaciopluvial. *Ecological Monographs* 53(4):341–382.

Wells, Philip B., and Clive D. Jorgensen

1964   Pleistocene Wood Rat Middens and Climatic Change in Mohave Desert: A Record of Juniper Woodlands. *Science* 143:1171–1174.

Wheat, Margaret M.

1967   *Survival Arts of the Primitive Paiutes*. University of Nevada Press, Reno.

Wigand, Peter E.

1987   Diamond Pond, Harney County, Oregon: Vegetation History and Water Table in the Eastern Oregon Desert. *Great Basin Naturalist* 47(3):427–468.

2001   Faunal and Botanical Remains from 26Ch1062: Pollen. In *Prehistory of the Carson Desert and Stillwater Mountains: Environment, Mobility, and Subsistence in a Great Basin Wetland*, by Robert L. Kelly, pp. 252–254. Anthropological Papers 123. University of Utah Press, Salt Lake City.

Wigand, Peter E., and Peter J. Mehringer Jr.

    1985   Pollen and Seed Analysis. In *The Archaeology of Hidden Cave, Nevada*, edited by David Hurst Thomas, pp. 108–124. Anthropological Papers 61, Pt. 1. American Museum of Natural History, New York.

Wilke, Philip J.

    1978   *Late Prehistoric Human Ecology at Lake Cahuilla, Coachella Valley, California*. Contributions 38. University of California Archaeological Research Facility, Berkeley.

Winter, Joseph C.

    1973   The Distribution and Development of Fremont Maize Agriculture: Some Preliminary Interpretations. *American Antiquity* 38:439–451.

    1980   Corn Remains from Cowboy Cave. In *Cowboy Cave*, edited by Jesse D. Jennings, pp. 191–192. Anthropological Papers 104. University of Utah Press, Salt Lake City.

Winter, Joseph C., and Henry G. Wylie

    1974   Paleoecology and Diet at Clyde's Cavern. *American Antiquity* 39:303–315.

Woodbury, Richard B.

    1954   *Prehistoric Stone Implements of Northeastern Arizona*. Papers of the Peabody Museum of American Archaeology and Ethnology 34. Harvard University, Cambridge.

Yarnell, Richard A.

    1965   Implications of Distinctive Flora on Pueblo Ruins. *American Anthropologist* 67:662–674.

Paleoethnobotany in California

Julia E. Hammett and Elizabeth J. Lawlor

*N*ative California has more ecological and cultural diversity than any other region in North America (Kuchler 1985; Sturtevant 1967). Ethnohistories document extensive management of plant resources throughout much of Native California (Bean and Blackburn 1976; Lewis 1972). Over the last 20 years paleoethnobotanists have begun to explore the complex ecological relationships between Native California peoples and landscapes and have posited a set of questions, based on ethnohistories, ethnographies, and hard evidence from the archaeobotanical record. This examination of California paleoethnobotany is a candid assessment of past work, our current data base, and directions for further inquiry.

Historical Background

Contacts with Native Californians by Europeans began in 1542 when Cabrillo sailed along the southern coast of California. He was soon followed by Drake, who sailed into the San Francisco Bay in 1569. But the real disruption of Native Californian society began 200 years later in 1769, when Spaniards launched a 50-year effort to establish a mission belt along the southern half of coastal California and also began trading Native American slaves across the desert, over the Old Spanish Trail (Malouf and Findlay 1986). The 1820s brought the Mexican War to California; with it came Mexican rule. In 1848 the Treaty of Guadalupe Hidalgo ceded sovereignty over Alta California to the United States. Shortly thereafter, Euro-American prospectors and settlers reached California from the eastern United States. All of these invasions undermined Native Californian societies, as disease, enslavement, and government-sanctioned genocide caused near annihilation, despite frequents acts of native resistance (Castillo 1978; Heizer 1974; Phillips 1975). Today many surviving groups are trying to regain and preserve material and spiritual aspects of their cultural traditions.

Natural Environments

California has many subregions and microclimates. The state is bisected vertically by the great Central Valley. The mighty Sierra Nevada skirts the valley on the east, and hills hugging the coast of the Pacific Ocean flank it on the west. Northern California comprises the southern tip of the Northwest Coast, the Cascade Range, the Modoc Plateau, and a narrow strip of the western Great Basin. Southern California touches two great American deserts, the Mojave and the Sonoran. The Mojave Desert and the eastern edge of California sometimes are treated as part of the Great Basin (e.g., Grayson 1993); here they are treated as part of California because of the trade relationships that bound those areas to the west in ethnographic times.

Despite this geographic diversity, which is discussed in more detail below, California as a whole is dominated by a Mediterranean climate with a winter precipitation pattern. Extremes in precipitation vary from less than 2 cm/year in parts of Death and Imperial Valleys (Mojave and Sonoran Deserts, respectively) to over 300 cm of rain along the Northwest Coast (Moratto 1984). Northern California receives an average of four times the precipitation of the lower half of the state (McCutchan 1977). In southern California any rain at all in June, July, or August is considered rare. Precipitation in the southern deserts generally is governed by the Gulf of California and thus is primarily the summer phenomenon found in the North American Southwest, which is atypical for California overall.

Southern California is particularly susceptible to a series of seasonal weather conditions that bring about extremely strong, foehn-type winds (warm, dry winds coming off the lee slopes of mountains) known in this subregion as the Santa Anas. These conditions typically involve a surface cold high-pressure center in the Great Basin and a surface trough, or low-pressure area, off the California coast (McCutchan 1977; Serguis 1952). The Santa Ana season, which generally extends from fall until early spring, although most commonly events occur from October through December (Brown 1999), is characterized by very strong winds that originate in the coastal mountain-tops and drive downward toward the coast, lasting for several days at a time. When combined with low moisture availability in the late summer-early fall months, these winds help create conditions that are optimum for fires. It is during this peak fire season that catastrophic fires occur in California (Mc-Cutchan 1977:9). Fires during this season can sweep down canyons, covering hundreds of acres in a matter of hours.

The Central Valley is bordered by the Coast Ranges on the west and the Sierra Nevada on the east. Early historical accounts described the marsh grasslands and prairie grasslands of the Central Valley and the oak woodlands in the bordering foothills as areas that supported large herds of deer, prong-horn antelope, and elk. From historical documentation (Burcham 1957; Wilkes 1845), it is fair to conclude that the numbers of large mammals present in California prior to and at the time of contact with Europeans were sizable. The introduction of European species of plants and animals radically changed the species composition of the grasslands of California more than it did any other vegetation type (Burcham 1957). The most obvious plant food produced in the Central Valley comes from the large oaks and other nut trees that grow throughout the valley floor and accompanying foothills.

The eastern side of California comprises the Sierra Nevada, a significant mountain range rising to a maximum height of 4,753 m (15,594 ft) at Mount Whitney. Notably, this point lies a mere 120 km from the lowest point in the United States, 86 m (282 ft) below sea level in Death Valley. The proximity of these two points demonstrates the immense diversity found within the boundaries of eastern California. The Sierras are characterized by a series of vegetation zones at different elevations. The scrub oak (*Quercus*) in the foothills of the Central Valley gives way to conifer zones at higher elevations, with ponderosa pines (*Pinus ponderosa*) grading to Jeffrey pines (*Pinus Jeffreyi*), then white fir (*Abies concolor*), red fir (*Abies magnifica*), lodgepole pines (*Pinus Murrayana*), and finally foxtail pines (*Pinus balfouriana*). Subalpine and alpine communities occupy high elevations, and Great Basin desert scrub the valley floor at the base of the steep eastern face of the Sierras (Moratto 1984).

Unique to the California region are the redwood belts, one at the south-western end of the Sierra Nevada and the other in the coastal mountain ranges extending from Big Sur and Monterey in central California to northern California. The coastal redwood belt is flanked on most of its eastern side by a mixed evergreen forest of oak (*Quercus* and *Lithocarpus*), madrone (*Arbutus*), and Douglas-fir (*Pseudotsuga*). Northern California is divided by the northern portion of the Central Valley; Great Basin scrub occurs in the far eastern part of this area, and a coniferous zone occupies the far western coast. Northern coastal California is dominated by mixed conifer forests composed of Douglas-fir, cedar (*Thuja*), spruce (*Picea*), and hemlock (*Tsuga*) (Kuchler 1985).

Throughout the California coast, the dominant vegetation is chaparral, which is characterized by woody, stump-sprouting shrubs with broad, leathery (sclerophyllous) evergreen leaves (Barbour et al. 1980; Walter 1973). A vital characteristic of chaparral vegetation is its reliance on fire for rejuvenation. Numerous studies have demonstrated how particular species and vegetation types have developed traits that allow them to resist, tolerate, or even thrive from the impact of fire (i.e., Aschmann 1959; Hanes 1971; Minnich 1983). Southern coastal vegetation is dominated by more drought-resistant species such as chamise (*Adenostoma*), *Ceanothus*, manzanita (*Arctostaphylos*), sumac (*Rhus*), and islay, or holly-leaf cherry (*Prunus ilicifolia*), whereas northern species dominants include coastal redwoods (*Sequoia sempervirens*), madrone (*Arbutus menziesii*), and *Rhododendron*.

The Mojave and Colorado Deserts comprise the southeastern portion of California and receive scant precipitation (usually less than 10 cm/year). The deserts include mountains; wide alluvial fans; both shallow and deep valleys (including Death Valley); dunes; volcanic features, including cinder cones and cooled lava flows; rivers; ephemeral lakes (playas); and a large body of water (the Salton Sea). The Mojave is often considered a transition zone between the Great Basin to the north and the Colorado Desert (i.e., the Sonoran Desert west of the Colorado River) to the south (e.g., Hart et al. 1979). The most characteristic plant communities of the Mojave are creosote-bush–bursage scrub (dominated by *Larrea tridentata* and *Ambrosia dumosa*) and Joshua tree woodland (dominated by grasses and forbs [Rowlands 1978] but with conspicuous *Yucca brevifolia* trees).

California is a geomorphologically dynamic region, and seismic activity has occurred throughout the time of human occupation. At least one volcanic crater is new since humans first arrived in the state (Amboy crater in the Mojave, 4000 BC [Hill 1984:69]). Mount Lassen in north-central California last erupted in 1917, and Mount Shasta, 10 miles away from Lassen, still harbors alpine glaciers (Moratto 1984).

Researchers concur that maritime influences have moderated climatic change in coastal areas (Byrne 1979; Moratto et al. 1978), whereas inland areas, notably the deserts and the Sierra Nevada, have experienced more marked climatic variation. Climatic changes over the long term have taken the deserts from cooler summer temperatures in the early Holocene (about 10,000 to 6000 BC) (Thompson 1990) to a warming trend during the middle Holocene (about 7,500 to 4,500 years ago), when many of the dune systems were formed (Mehringer 1986; Spaulding 1991; Thompson 1992). After that time cooler and moister conditions prevailed (e.g., Mehringer and Wigand 1990), culminating in the Little Ice Age, about AD 1250 to 1850. The Sierra Nevada underwent a similar change, with a cooler climate prior to 9,000 years ago giving way to a warming trend that dominated mountain conditions until about 3,300 years ago. Then a pattern of fluctuating hot-cold and wet-dry conditions prevailed, each episode lasting from 200 to 600 years (Byrne 1979; Moratto et al. 1978). Perhaps most noteworthy is a cool, wet period from AD 150 to 950, with a warmer, drier period after AD 950 (Byrne 1979). The above changes had the greatest impact on resource availability in areas near the Sierra foothills and the desert.

Whereas interior California groups may have been forced to respond periodically to marked climatic change, coastal residents appear to have enjoyed long-term climatic stability. King (1990:79) has posited that for the last 6,000 years, climatic changes in the Santa Barbara Channel have had little effect on the gradual evolution of Chumash society; if true, however, this does not preclude the possibility that wealthier, more secure coastal societies may have asserted their economic influence over more rural and inland populations. Alternatively, groups responding to adverse environmental conditions may have resorted to decreasing population size or migration as solutions to resource shortages.

Overall, California's great natural diversity and richness afforded the state's indigenous inhabitants the ability to survive environmental adversity by juggling their resource base. The best documentation for this pattern is for the Southern Coastal subregion, although throughout the state the importance of trade and craft specialization and of resource control was widely reported by early ethnographers.

Cultural Traditions

Beginning in the early 1900s salvage ethnographers (e.g., Goddard 1903–04; Harrington 1932; Kroeber 1925) and, later, ethnohistorians (e.g., Bean and Lawton 1993; Lewis 1993) and archaeologists (e.g., Cambra et al. 1996; King

1990; King 1982) have pieced together archaeological evidence for what were complex, elaborate sociopolitical and economic systems.[1] Relatively dense populations lived along the central and southern coasts, and inland valley centers near principal water resources (i.e., Clear Lake, Sacramento Delta, Tulare Lake) featured some of the densest human populations anywhere in North America. Archaeological research suggests that some societies occupied the same key locations for thousands of years (Moratto 1984). A stratified social pattern is best documented in the Santa Barbara region, where ranking was manifested in such features as secret societies, an inherited elite, and intermarriage of chiefly families from different territories and villages (Bean 1974; Bean and Lawton 1993). The Chumash of the Santa Barbara area also enjoyed a shell bead money-based economy (King 1971).

More rural parts of California (deserts and mountains) supported much smaller, simpler band-sized populations. These bands practiced a mobile, albeit established, seasonal round, returning annually to key resource patch areas and encampments (Bean and Saubel 1972). Throughout much of California, societies relied on extensive resource management, wild plant manipulation, and integration of a patchwork of resources through an established series of east-west trade partnerships linking different cultural areas (Bean and Blackburn 1976).

Native Californian societies comprised 100 to 500 autonomous units (Bean 1974; Kroeber 1962), each recognizing the territorial boundaries, political rule, and resource claims of neighboring groups but also acknowledging the existence of important interregional leaders. At least six linguistic stocks were present in prehistoric California. Sixty to 80 mutually unintelligible languages were further differentiated into numerous dialects (Shipley 1978). Linguistic and political boundaries were not synonymous. As today, many native people were bilingual or multilingual.

California's size and environmental diversity necessitate geographic subdivision to characterize cultural traditions (Figure 7.1; Table 7.1). Within Northern California, groups living along the Northern Coast were substantially influenced by Northwest Coast cultures; groups in the northeastern part of California interacted with people of the northern Great Basin and the Plateau. Northern and southern coastal areas are separated by the San Francisco Bay, and the great Central Valley is composed of the Sacramento Valley to the north and San Joaquin Valley southward; these geographic divisions correlate to some extent with cultural divisions. Southern subregions of California include the Southern Coast Ranges and the Deserts; both of these sub-

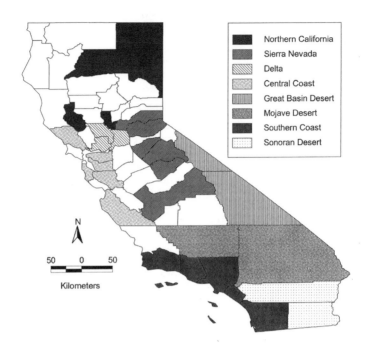

FIGURE 7.1   Regions of California showing counties with sites included in this chapter

regions had interactions through trade with the Southwest region (Baumhoff 1978; Heizer 1978; Kroeber 1925). Although a variety of specific cultural practices existed within these subregions, sociopolitical economies within subregions also shared fundamental patterns.

The population density of California varied from very sparse in the deserts to unusually dense for Native North America north of Mexico (Cook 1976), especially along the coast and in the Central and Owens Valleys. Estimates for different subregions range from 1.25 persons per 25 km² to 250 per 25 km² (.5 to 10 per mi²) (Bean 1978:673). Tribes varied in size from 100 to 1,000 persons and occupied territories ranging from 1,250 to 150,000 km² (50 to 6,000 mi²) (Bean 1978:673–675). The lack of reliable records makes it very difficult to estimate the total native population prior to contact (Jackson 1987).

Table 7.1

California Subregions and Counties

Subregion	County	Abbreviation Used in Site Numbers
Northern California		
	Lake	LAK
	Lassen	LAS
	Modoc	MOD
	Shasta	SHA
	Sutter	SUT
Sierra Nevada		
	Calaveras	CAL
	El Dorado	ELD
	Fresno	FRE
	Mariposa	MRP
	Placer	PLA
	Tuolumne	TUO
Delta		
	Sacramento	SAC
	Solano	SOL
	Yolo	YOL
Central Coast		
	Alameda	ALA
	Contra Costa	CCO
	Monterey	MNT
	San Mateo	SMA
	Santa Clara	SCL
	Sonoma	SON
Southern Coast		
	Los Angeles	LAN
	Orange	ORA
	San Diego	SDI
	Santa Barbara	SBA
	Ventura	VEN
Great Basin Desert		
	Inyo	INY
	Mono	MNO
Mojave Desert		
	Kern	KER
	San Bernardino	SBR
Sonoran Desert		
	Imperial	IMP
	Riverside	RIV

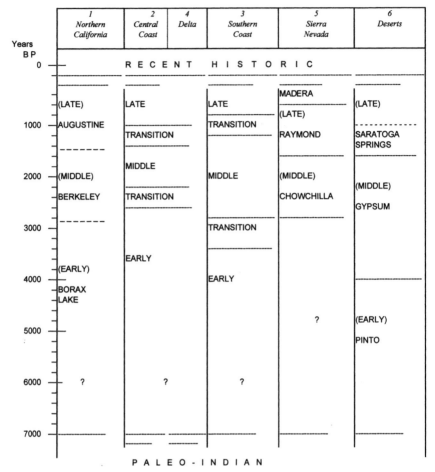

	1 *Northern California*	2 *Central Coast*	4 *Delta*	3 *Southern Coast*	5 *Sierra Nevada*	6 *Deserts*
Years B P 0	—	R E C E N T		H I S T O R I C		
	(LATE)	LATE		LATE	MADERA	(LATE)
1000	AUGUSTINE			TRANSITION	(LATE)	- - - - - - - - - -
		TRANSITION			RAYMOND	SARATOGA SPRINGS
	- - - - - - -					
		MIDDLE				
2000	(MIDDLE)			MIDDLE	(MIDDLE)	(MIDDLE)
	BERKELEY	TRANSITION			CHOWCHILLA	GYPSUM
3000	- - - - - - -			TRANSITION		
		EARLY				
	(EARLY)					
4000	BORAX LAKE			EARLY		- - - - - - - - -
					?	(EARLY)
5000						PINTO
6000	?	?		?		
7000						

P A L E O - I N D I A N

FIGURE 7.2   Culture chronology for California subregions (Chartkoff and Chartkoff 1984 and Moratto 1984)

Culture History

Over 30 localized chronologies have been developed in California, many of which incorporate local names for periods and phases (e.g., Bennyhoff and Hughes 1987; Chartkoff and Chartkoff 1984; King 1990; Moratto 1984; Wallace 1978), but most California archaeologists communicate with each other using an Early/Middle/Late period framework established by King (1990) in the south and Bennyhoff (Bennyhoff and Hughes 1987; Milliken and Bennyhoff 1993) in central California. This chronological framework is roughly comparable to sequences established elsewhere in North America.

(For example, the rise of cultural complexity in Late period California occurred at roughly the same time as the beginning of the classic phases of the Hopewellian culture and the major pueblos at Mesa Verde and Chaco Canyon.) California chronologies are based on radiocarbon dates associated with shell and stone beads and ornaments and, to a lesser extent, changes in projectile points, ceramics, and grinding stone technology (Figure 7.2).

The earliest undisputed evidence for humans in California consists of two fluted points, one found at Borax Lake in the north Coast Range and another at Tulare Lake in the southern Central Valley. No directly datable materials or strata were associated with these finds, and the points are conservatively linked stylistically to Clovis and Folsom projectile point types, which together are characteristic of the Paleoindian period extending from 11,500 to 8,000 years ago (Wallace 1978). The absence of grinding tools associated with the fluted projectile points has been interpreted (Chartkoff and Chartkoff 1984; Wallace 1978) to indicate little or no use of plant foods by California Paleoindians. A more conservative assessment is that the general subsistence patterns of the Paleoindian period are very poorly understood.

Beginning 8,000 to 10,000 years ago, the Early period lasted until about 3,000 years ago (Chartkoff and Chartkoff 1984; Moratto 1984). As is the case for the Paleoindian period, the virtual invisibility of the beginning of the Early period across much of California is problematic. Are the majority of the Paleoindian and Early period sites underwater along the coast? Or have these sites been destroyed by development in prime urban areas throughout California? The archaeological record of the middle part of the Early period is more revealing and has yielded plant data and plant-processing equipment throughout most of the state. For example, Central Valley grinding stones of the Early period, 4,000–5,000 years ago, included milling slabs, basin-shaped bowls, and manolike hand stones (Moratto 1984).

During the Middle period, 2,000–3,000 years ago, the Central Valley tool assemblage shifted from an emphasis on milling stones to increased use of baked-clay balls (probably used as boiling "stones") and mortars (Moratto 1984:200–201). This shift in grinding stone technology has been widely attributed to a hypothesized intensification of the use of acorns and a decreased emphasis on grasses and other small seeds. This marked change in technology, however, is less apparent in other subregions. In the Owens Valley and adjacent northern desert areas, the Middle period saw the beginning of intensive use of piñon (e.g., Bettinger 1976; Garfinkel and Cook 1980; McGuire and Garfinkel 1976). More widespread in the Middle period was an increase in cultural complexity in Native California, which would culminate in the Late period in relatively densely populated, sedentary, autonomous societies with a shell bead currency-based economy.

The Late period, starting around 1,500–1,000 years ago and ending in 1769 with the establishment of the first permanent European settlement, is noted for an increased reliance on trade items and other wealth items. Storable food commodities included acorns, wild cherry pits and other nuts, a host of small seeds, marine resources, and terrestrial mammals. In northwestern California, salmon was an important commodity.

However one reckons California's cultural chronology, whenever paleoethnobotanical data are available, the inescapable conclusion is that local environments supported mixed economies drawing from a variety of riverine, marine, and terrestrial plant and animal resources.

Nature of the Data

Potential sources of archaeobotanical data include macrofossils (including collections of large, dry perishables from caves, floated or sorted seeds and other foodstuff remains, and wood charcoal), microfossils (including pollen, phytoliths, and starch grains), and biochemical residues on ceramics and milling stones. Most sites with subsurface deposits probably contain one or more of these sources of direct information about subsistence, but relatively few studies have taken advantage of them. Curated ethnobotanical, archaeobotanical, and archaeological samples with a high botanical potential (i.e., from intact hearth features) exist at the Phoebe Hearst (Lowie) Museum at the University of California (UC) Berkeley and at other research facilities around the state.

It is difficult to accept the paucity of extant archaeobotanical collections, given the amount of archaeological work that has been done in California, especially considering the frequent attention given to subsistence models (i.e., Basgall 1987; Bergin and Ferraro 1987; Bouey 1987; Glassow 1992; Jones et al. 1998). Most researchers professing concern for subsistence still analyze only faunal assemblages. Plants often are dismissed with a perfunctory ethnobotanical "laundry list" gleaned from available ethnographies. Even archaeologists who consider plant use in subsistence reconstructions rarely collect flotation samples. Ironically, some of the same researchers bemoan the lack of available archaeobotanical data. Although a number of archaeologists working in California consider plant use in their subsistence reconstructions (e.g.,

Elston et al. 1981:77; Glassow 1992:125; Hildebrandt 1983; Lyneis et al. 1989:76–77; Ritter and Coombs 1990; Schroth 1994:377; Taylor et al. 1987; Wade and Hector 1989:16; Warren 1991), rarely do archaeologists collect flotation samples.

The problem is not a lack of appropriate sampling contexts but a mindset. California archaeologists characteristically define terrestrial midden in terms of dark soil with "charcoal flecking" or "organics" and routinely collect radiocarbon samples but not archaeobotanical samples from these contexts. Despite this challenge, California paleoethnobotanists have benefited greatly by borrowing and refining strategies developed in other regions. For example, a 100-percent sampling approach was used during test excavations at Talepop, CA-LAN-229 (King et al. 1982), a prehistoric and protohistoric Chumash village site in southern coastal California. This method, similar to the "blanket-sampling" heralded by Lennström and Hastorf (1992:227), "avoids the problem of predicting where remains will occur" (Pearsall 1989:95).

Research Questions

At present, fundamental research questions are still unanswered for many subregions of California. "What floral resources were important" (Sutton 1988:73) remains to be answered for some areas. Broader questions about scheduling of resource procurement, subsistence changes through time, and responses to environmental stress await systematic sampling of sites across the state. Research questions in California have three themes: subsistence, ecological method and theory, and bioturbation and site taphonomy. Our best archaeobotanical data bases come from the Southern Coast, the San Francisco Bay Area, and the Sacramento Delta.

Anthropologists working in the early 1900s (i.e., Kroeber, Gifford, Merriam) established the environmental framework by which Californian economies were modeled. Merriam (1894, 1898) found that "life zones" in California varied by elevation. Similarly, ethnobotanical work by Stephen Powers (1976) in the 1870s and J. P. Harrington in the early 1900s (Bocek 1984; Harrington 1917, 1981; Lawlor 1995a; Timbrook et al. 1982) recognized the diversity of food resources used by Native Californians. In spite of this early recognition of environmental and economic variation within the region, Gifford (1971), Kroeber (1925), and, to a certain extent, even Merriam (1918) argued that acorns were the single most important staple throughout much of California.

Theoretically, California paleoethnobotany is strongly guided by three key publications, each of which discusses a particular model of California ecological relationships. Lewis (1972) addressed the question of management. He found extensive ethnohistoric evidence for the use of fire as a management tool in Northern California. Within the bounds of north-central California, Baumhoff (1963) formulated a triad of deer, acorns, and salmon as constituting the Northern California economy. Bean and Lawton (1993), responding to Lewis's Northern California data, presented comparative southern California data that indicated several management strategies, including burning, clearing, and pruning, as well as historic evidence for incipient domestication of grasses by riverine desert people.

Archaeobotanical and faunal data attest to the diversity of California's economy. Nevertheless, Baumhoff's students (Gage 1979) perpetuate his tripartite model and have extended its jurisdiction to other parts of California (Basgall 1987; Bouey 1987). Referring to changes in ground stone forms in the Central Valley, they have inferred subsistence practices for California at large and have argued that intensification of acorn use occurred approximately 1,000 years ago (Basgall 1987; Bouey 1987). Until recently no one has used archaeobotanical data to test this acorn-intensification model. Wohlgemuth (1996a) offers the first archaeobotanical data set from the Central Valley appearing to indicate that, if acorn intensification occurred at all, it was 1,000 years earlier than predicted, possibly 2,000 years ago. Prudently, Wohlgemuth stresses the need for much more analysis before solid conclusions can be drawn. Even *if* his model is supported by archaeobotanical data from the Central Valley, it will be important to evaluate its applicability to other Californian subregions. The fact that the research stronghold of Baumhoff's disciples at the University of California, Davis, is located in the heart of the oak woodland belt may contribute significantly to their acorn-centric preoccupation.

Research scientists (Burson 1998; Jones et al. 1998) with Stanford University's Campus Archaeology Program on the San Francisco Bay Area's midpeninsula have recently proposed a new strategy for testing diet breadth models, specifically responding to the acorn-intensification hypothesis and more generally examining the popular use of resource-intensification models along California's coast. Given the assumption that any significant resource intensification would dramatically affect diet breadth, their method is to count all economic taxa (flora and terrestrial and marine fauna) from dated archaeological features and to compare the numbers through time. Initial re-

Julia E. Hammett and Elizabeth J. Lawlor

sults indicate no obvious unidirectional trend or single shift evident over the last 4,000 years of occupation in the San Francisco Bay Area. The high degree of fluctuations in taxa numbers through time may be the result of a combination of factors, including seasonal variation, changes in social access to resources, and possibly the El Niño cycle (Burson 1998), although none of these variables appear to have had a long-term effect on diet breadth. Although noticeable landscape differences exist between the central California delta and the San Francisco Bay peninsula, such divergent findings between data sets from adjacent subregions spark the debate and fuel the need for more systematic sampling in future research.

For the western Mojave Desert (a region where acorns had little importance), M. Sutton has recently proposed a model of changing settlement/subsistence systems in the Middle to Late periods. Based on site locations, Sutton proposes that subsistence focused on riparian habitats in Gypsum times, shifted toward the exploitation of lacustrine resources and lagomorphs, and later (after about AD 950), returned "to a dependence on streams and/or springs, and an apparent (but as yet unknown) shift in resource exploitations" (1996:243). As with previously discussed research questions, systematic sampling for plant remains will be necessary to test this model, and sample sizes likely will need to be in the 10–15-liter range to be productive (Reddy 1999b).

Another important set of research questions is related to the role of aboriginal resource management in altering the landscape and in changing resource yields. To what degree was the native Californian landscape "anthropogenic" in nature? H. T. Lewis's (1993) ethnohistoric work documents the use of fire as an extremely effective management tool in Northern California. Similar work by Bean and Lawton (1993) established evidence for a series of management practices in southern California. Together, these works inspired a generation of young scholars to pursue further research on aboriginal resource management. Notable contributions include additional work with historic records (Lawton et al. 1976; Timbrook et al. 1982), the recording of specific plant management strategies still extant in the Sierra foothills (Anderson 1993), and paleoethnobotanical research on the Southern Coast that led to the development of a testable hypothesis by which to evaluate evidence for prescribed burning as a management tool (Hammett 1991). University of California, Los Angeles (UCLA) paleoethnobotanists L. P. Klug and V. S. Popper (1996a, 1996b, 1996c, 1996d, 1998) have been testing the model with promising but mixed results. In their recent investigation of 20 sites in coastal Orange County, Klug and Popper (1998) focused their exam-

Julia E. Hammett and Elizabeth J. Lawlor

ination on charred seed ubiquities and densities of *Hordeum, Phalaris, Cheno-podium*, and cheno-ams, as well as of several well-known fire followers. Their data indicate traces of small economic seeds in the Early period, a significant rise in small seed utilization beginning in the Middle period, and a slight increase through the Late period, ending just after first contacts with Euro-Americans. In contrast to the abundance of small seeds, these researchers note that acorn nutshells, although present in Middle and Late period contexts, appear never to have been a significant part of the record along the Orange County coast. They speculate that acorn harvesting and processing may have occurred at sites away from the coast.

Finally, in the San Francisco Bay Area charred wood data are being used, in conjunction with other macrobotanical remains, pollen data, and plant survey data to reconstruct prehistoric anthropogenic landscapes (Hammett 1996a, 1997). Initial results indicate the presence of a diverse set of resources obtained from several diverse community associations, with notably higher frequencies of fruiting shrubs (i.e., *Heteromeles arbutifolia* and *Prunus ilicifolia*), nut trees (i.e., *Corylus cornuta*), and bulb/corm plants (i.e., *Calochortus* sp. and *Chlorogalum pomeridianum*) than occur today near these sites.

Another significant question dating back at least to Kroeber (1925:815) is how some of the California groups developed sedentary, relatively complex social organization without the field agriculture that is usually associated with these developments elsewhere. Researchers anticipate that this broad question will be addressed with further extensive data related to the identification of plant resources, their evolution, and related management strategies.

Perhaps the most controversial subsistence question for the southern part of the region involves the development of agriculture in California (Bean and Lawton 1993). Most Californian groups did not practice agriculture in the sense of planted, cultivated fields (Ford 1985; Rindos 1984), but intensive land use and irrigation canals are documented for the Owens Valley Paiute (Lawton et al. 1976). Some desert groups raised domesticated corn, beans, and squash (Winter and Hogan 1986), and a number of groups managed wild plants through burning, tending, and other means. Although it is widely believed that desert agriculture was introduced just prior to European contact (Heizer and Elsasser 1980; Kelly and Fowler 1986:371; Steward 1933), this question has yet to be answered with prehistoric evidence (Fowler 1995).

A final set of research questions pertains to the nature of archaeological deposits in California. In much of the state, site integrity is challenged by various types of bioturbation. This has been the focus of field studies on existing sites (Bocek 1986, 1992; Erlandson 1984) and has also been explored through computer simulations (Pierce 1992). Although such studies are relevant to paleoethnobotany, none have directly addressed the effects of bioturbation on plant remains. One set of potential effects, however, was addressed by Lawlor (1995a) in a series of field experiments investigating horizontal displacement of seeds by rodents and harvester ants at replicated food-processing activity areas in the Mojave Desert. The rodents and harvester ants rejected carbonized seeds when raw seeds were available, though they sometimes damaged or destroyed small quantities of the carbonized specimens. It would be worthwhile to conduct similar experiments in other regions and to investigate whether carbonized seeds are present in burrows (i.e., intentionally cached by rodents and ants at lower stratigraphic levels) at prehistoric sites in all regions of California.

History of Paleoethnobotanical Research

Several ethnobotanies detail important economic plants in California (Barrett and Gifford 1933; Barrows 1900; Bean and Saubel 1972; Bocek 1984; Chestnut 1902; King 1903; Lawlor 1995a). California paleoethnobotanists are fortunate that the first comprehensive ethnobotany was about the Cahuilla of the California deserts (Barrows 1900). Though Barrows conducted his fieldwork as a student at the University of Chicago, he consulted Jepson for plant identifications, and the Barrows-Jepson correspondence implies that Barrows deposited specimens at the Jepson Herbarium at Berkeley. (Whether these collections are extant awaits a massive cataloging project [M. Wetherwax, personal communication to Lawlor, March 1995].)

California paleoethnobotanists also are fortunate to have the legacy of the cultural geography school and biology programs at UC Berkeley. Early ethnobiologists such as C. H. Merriam, E. Gifford, and J. Steward deposited caches of seeds, nuts, medicinal herbs, seed cakes, salt, and sweeteners, to name a few ethnobotanical wonders, in the biology program repositories (Hammett 1991), now curated at the Phoebe Hearst (Lowie) Museum. The cultural geography school, under Carl Sauer, influenced the research questions posed and the observations made by Berkeley's anthropologists and botanists.

J. P. Harrington, working from the 1920s to the 1940s, should be given special attention for having contributed over 10,000 pages of notes on California Indians (Harrington 1981), several important life histories of southern

California Indians, and a treatise on tobacco among the Karuk (Harrington 1932). Recorded in two languages, English and Karuk, the treatise constitutes one of the best original texts in a Native California language. Many of Harrington's plant specimens are curated in the National Anthropological Archives at the Smithsonian Institution in some 160 specimen boxes (J. Kennelly, personal communication to Lawlor, December 1994). Specimens collected during Harrington's Costanoan fieldwork have been analyzed (Bocek 1984), and his Serrano and some other southern California collections have been inventoried by M. Lerch and identified by A. C. Sanders (personal communication to Lawlor, January 2000).

To a certain extent, the historical collections curated at the Phoebe Hearst (Lowie) Museum and elsewhere reflect the degree of botanical training of their collectors. On the whole, however, the historical collections are more complete than some made by more recent researchers. For example, the voucher specimens used to solicit information from Cahuilla elders in the 1960s (Bean 1961; Bean and Saubel 1972) have, unfortunately, been discarded (L. J. Bean, personal communication to Lawlor, November 1994; see Lawlor 1995a:454).

Early investigators did not actively seek plant remains but instead reported serendipitous discoveries of relatively large floral materials in dry caves and rockshelters (e.g., Campbell 1931; Campbell and Campbell 1935, 1937; Harrington 1957), such as baskets, sandals, cordage, netting, and partially processed plant fiber material. Active archaeological sampling for plants in California began in 1974 in two regions simultaneously. K. Johnson and L. Skelstad (1974) collected flotation samples during the salvage excavations of site CA-SHA-177, in the northern part of the state, and M. Gardner and colleagues (1974) collected samples at Lake Perris, at the eastern margin of the Southern Coast subregion near Riverside. This southern California study was followed shortly by those of students from the University of California (UC) Riverside in the middle to late 1970s and included work at Taquitz Canyon (Wilke et al. 1975) and Myoma Dunes (Wilke 1978) in the Sonoran Desert and, a bit later, at Cronise Lake (Drover 1979) and Oro Grande (McCarthy and Wilke 1979) in the Mojave Desert.

Systematic flotation sampling for botanical remains began in 1980 at Talepop, CA-LAN-229 (King et al. 1982), in the Southern Coast subregion in a small valley of the Santa Monica Mountains just north of Malibu. In the early 1980s flotation sampling was also initiated in the Central Coast region by Stanford University researchers, in conjunction with the excavation of a series of prehistoric sites along the San Franscisquito Creek watershed (Bocek 1987; Bocek and Reese 1992).

Although few early endeavors represent systematic sampling strategies and identifications by trained archaeobotanists, the pioneering efforts of specific researchers are laudable. Two California universities in particular have developed strong archaeobotanical research traditions. UC Riverside's P. Wilke, his students, and their students (M. Sutton's students at California State University [CSU] Bakersfield) have contributed the bulk of published reports on flotation, coprolite analysis, and dry cave/rockshelter caches (from UC Riverside: Davis and Smith 1981; Echlin et al. 1981; Farrell 1988; Lawlor 1995b; Pinto 1985; Schneider 1989; Sutton 1984; Sutton and Ritter 1984; Sutton et al. 1987; Swope 1988; from CSU Bakersfield: Osborne 1993; Sutton 1988, 1991; Sutton et al. 1993). Stanford's program has been more systematic and has included flotation conducted by specialists in paleoethnobotany, but publication of the results of research has proceeded slowly (Bocek and Reese 1992; Hammett 1996b, 1997; Jones et al. 1998). In addition to these programs and the very active Paleoethnobotanical Laboratory at UCLA's Institute for Archaeology (e.g., Klug and Popper 1995), some cultural resource management firms have contributed substantial data, notably, Far Western Archaeological Research Group, Inc., in the north (e.g., Wolhgemuth 1996a) and ASM Affiliates, Inc., in the south (e.g., Reddy 1996a).

Beginning in the 1980s several paleoethnobotanists began promoting flotation sampling throughout the state (i.e., Hammett and Wohlgemuth 1982; Wohlgemuth 1988; Wohlgemuth and Basgall 1988). Typically, however, the results of flotation sampling were not widely communicated beyond the areas in which such work was undertaken, nor had paleoethnobotany become a widely accepted part of California archaeology at that time. Then, about ten years ago, a workshop at Stanford University brought several researchers together. The workshop conceived a group of papers on California paleoethnobotany that were presented at the 1994 Society for California Archaeology Meetings at Asilomar at Monterey Bay. Since that workshop, California paleoethnobotanists have used comparable techniques for recovery, identification, data collection, and quantification, they regularly share their data, and several subregional summaries are under way. The systematic reporting of sample volumes and resulting data are generating roughly comparable data sets throughout California (Hammett 1996a, 1997; Klug and Popper 1995, 1996a, 1996b, 1996c, 1996d; Wohlgemuth 1996a). Perhaps the most encouraging sign is that in the last five years, the number of California archaeobotanical reports has more than doubled. Of the several thousand archaeological sites now recorded in the state, paleoethnobotanists can now share archaeobotanical data for well over 100. These data are compiled below.

Most paleoethnobotanists now working in California have achieved concordance in data collection techniques, but this consensus has happened quite recently. For the purposes of this discussion, plant data are presented in terms of presence/absence by subregions, each of which comprises multiple counties (Figure 7.1; Table 7.1). Although counties may belong to more than one physiographic subregion, we made every attempt to assign counties to our subregions on the basis of where the preponderance of plant reporting was conducted. Table 7.2 lists California archaeobotanical remains alphabetically by common name. Table 7.3 provides a full listing of the plant taxa for which macrobotanical remains have been recovered from California sites and specifies the plant parts found. Table 7.4 lists those sites producing archaeobotanical material that have confirmed dates, typically either radiocarbon dates or dates based on diagnostic shell beads or historic markers. Historic sites reported in this chapter are limited to those whose occupants archaeologists are fairly certain were Native Americans. Table 7.5 lists sites with unconfirmed dates. Finally, Table 7.6a–c reports macrobotanical remains according to subregions and temporal periods. Because of its great geographical diversity and the large number of reports, the Desert subregion is subdivided into the three recognized deserts within California, the Great Basin, the Mojave Desert, and the Sonoran Desert (Table 7.6c).

Diet and Subsistence

California archaeological sites have yielded charred seeds and nutshell fragments of over 150 plant taxa; the majority are economic species. In addition, charred wood fragments from nearly 40 taxa have been identified. Overall, California ethnobotanical diversity is astounding. Nevertheless, spatial and temporal patterns emerge from the data. Our most pressing concern here is the identification of staple plant foods.

Northern California boasts a large number of sites with macrobotanical remains but, regrettably, few have confirmed temporal assignments. Most research has centered on campsites and villages along key drainages in Shasta County. Nutshells from several plant taxa, California bay, buckeye, wild cucumber, and several types of pine nuts and acorns have been recovered. The use of fruits and berries in this subregion included manzanita berries and plums. In addition, historic aboriginal sites have yielded seeds or pits of apricots, peaches, and watermelon. Wild grape seeds have been recovered from both historic and prehistoric sites. Small seed taxa from Northern California include buttercups, filaree, mustards, and a number of cheno-ams, legumes, composites, grasses, and other small-seeded plants. The most frequently occurring remains are manzanita seeds, pine nut shells, and, to a lesser extent, acorns. Further research assigning reliable dates to the deposits producing these remains will allow further analysis of temporal patterns.

Along the coastal side of California from the San Francisco Bay Area southward, human settlements comprised a series of shell mounds. Settlements were also located along creeks running perpendicular to the coast. These drainages act as natural corridors through mountains, foothills, and small valleys, connecting the coast and the bay area with the Central Valley. Throughout the coastal subregions people harvested nuts, small seeds, and bulbs and corms. Nut crops included oak and tan oak acorns, California bay, hazelnuts, walnut, wild cucumber, and wild cherry pits. Roots, bulbs, and corms included *Brodiaea*, mariposa lily, soaproot, and wild onions. Significant berries included manzanita and toyon berries. Small seeds included grasses (wild barley, maygrass, and fescue), composites (tarweed and sunflowers), cheno-ams (redmaids, miner's lettuce, spring beauties, goosefoot, and pigweed), and farewell-to-spring. In the Bay Area recovery rates from specific sites indicate that several nuts competed with oak acorns in economic importance. In particular, hazelnut, tanbark oak, wild cucumber, and California bay were all important nut resources throughout the Bay Area. Islay (*Prunus ilicifolia*) was apparently restricted to the peninsula (western) side of the bay area, but it was a more important resource along the Southern Coast, where it occurs with the remains of bulbs and corms, probably wild onion, brodiaea, mariposa lily, and soaproot.

On the Southern Coast, groups used many of the same crops used by their more northern neighbors, except for hazelnut (*Corylus californica*). In addition, south coastal groups used yucca and relied more heavily on islay, walnuts, and sage and redmaids seeds. Sites on the coastal plain reveal an intensive utilization of small seeds, with sage, composite, and grass seeds important resources, along with bulbs and corms (presumably blue dicks, mariposa lilies, and soaproot). On the interior side of the coastal mountain chain, nuts (particularly acorns, islay, and walnuts) and soaproot were important resources, as well as the small seeds, bulbs, and corms listed above. Yucca roasting has been documented as an important subsistence activity. Paleoethnobotanists have recovered good evidence that yucca roasting was the major activity conducted at an interior Chumash site (CA-VEN-1020) (King 1993).

Table 7.2

Plant Names Mentioned in the Text

Common Name	Scientific Name
Agave	*Agave deserti*
Apricot	*Prunus armeniaca* (I)
Apricot, desert	*Prunus* cf. *fremontii*
Aster	*Aster* sp.
Barley (D)	*Hordeum vulgare* (I)
Barley, foxtail	*Hordeum jubatum*
Barley, little	*Hordeum pusillum*
Barley, wild	*Hordeum* sp.
Barnyard grass	*Echinochloa* sp.
Barrel cactus	*Echinocereus/Ferocactus*
Bean, common (D)	*Phaseolus vulgaris* (I)
Beargrass	cf. *Nolina parryi*
Bedstraw	*Galium* sp.
Bentgrass	*Agrostis* sp.
Bird's foot trefoil	*Lotus* sp.
Bitterbrush	*Purshia* sp.
Blackberry/raspberry	*Rubus* sp.
Blazing star	*Mentzelia* sp.
Blow-wives	*Achyrachaena mollis*
Blue dicks	*Dichelostemma* sp.
Boerhaavia	*Boerhaavia* sp.
Borage	*Borage* sp.
Bottle gourd	cf. *Lagenaria siceraria* (I)
Brittlebush	*Encelia farinosa*
Brodiaea	*Brodiaea* sp.
Brome grass	*Bromus* sp.
Buckeye	*Aesculus californica*
Buckthorn	*Rhamnus crocea*
Buckwheat, wild	*Eriogonum* sp.
Bugseed	*Dicoria canescens*
Burdock	*Arctium* sp.
Bursage	*Ambrosia* sp.
Buttercup	*Ranunculus* sp.
Cactus family	Cactaceae
California bay	*Umbellularia californica*
California lilac	*Ceanothus* sp.
Calyptridium	*Calyptridium* cf. *umbellatum*
Carpetweed	*Mollugo* sp.
Carrot, wild	*Daucus carota* (I)
Catchfly	*Silene* sp. (I)
Catclaw	*Acacia greggii*
Cattail	*Typha* sp.
Chamise	*Adenostoma fasciculatum*
Cheno-ams	*Chenopodium-Amaranthus*

Table 7.2 *continued*

Common Name	Scientific Name
Cherry, holly-leaf	*Prunus ilicifolia*
Chia	*Salvia columbariae*
Cholla	*Opuntia* cf. *ramosissima*
Chuparosa	*Beloperone californica*
Cinquefoil	*Potentilla* sp.
Clover	*Trifolium* sp.
Coffee (D)	*Coffea* sp. (I)
Cordgrass	*Spartina* sp.
Cottonwood	*Populus* sp.
Coyote brush	*Baccharis* sp.
Creosotebush	*Larrea tridentata*
Crucillo	*Condalia parryi*
Crypsis	*Crypsis* sp.
Cryptantha	*Cryptantha* sp.
Cucumber, wild	*Marah* sp.
Deer grass	*Muhlenbergia rigens*
Desert tomato	*Lycium* sp.
Desert willow	cf. *Chilopsis linearis*
Ditchgrass	*Ruppia maritima*
Dock	*Rumex* sp.
Dock, willow	*Rumex* cf. *salicifolius*
Dodder	*Cuscuta* sp.
Douglas-fir	*Pseudotsuga menziesii*
Elderberry	*Sambucus* sp.
Epos	*Perideridia* sp.
Eriophyllum	*Eriophyllum* sp.
Farewell-to-spring	*Clarkia* sp.
Fescue	*Festuca* sp.
Fiddleneck	*Amsinckia/Plagiobothrys* sp.
Four o'clock	*Mirabilis* sp.
Galleta grass	*Hilaria rigida*
Globemallow, falsemallow	*Malva* (I)/*Sphaeralcea/Malvastrum*
Goosefoot	*Chenopodium* sp.
Grape, wild	*Vitis californica*
Grass family	Poaceae
Greasewood	*Sarcobatus* sp.
Hairgrass	*Deschampsia* sp.
Hazelnut	*Corylus cornuta*
Hemp, wild	*Apocynum* sp.
Honeysuckle	*Lonicera* sp.
Huckleberry	*Vaccinium* sp.
Incense cedar, California	*Libocedrus decurrens*
Indian hemp	*Apocynum cannibinum*
Ironwood	*Olneya tesota*

Continued on next page

Table 7.2 *continued*

Common Name	Scientific Name
Knotweed	*Polygonum* sp.
Jojoba	*Simmondsia* sp.
Juniper	*Juniperus* sp.
Juniper, California	*Juniperus californica*
Lasthenia	*Lasthenia* sp.
Legume family	Fabaceae
Lemonadeberry	*Rhus integrifolia*
Leptochloa	*Leptochloa* sp.
Locoweed	*Astragalus* sp.
Love grass	*Eragrostis* sp.
Lupine	*Lupinus* sp.
Madrone	*Arbutus menziesii*
Mallow family	Malvaceae
Maize (D)	*Zea mays* (I)
Manzanita	*Arctostaphylos* sp.
Manzanita, bigberry	*Arctostaphylos glauca*
Manzanita, eastwood	*Arctostaphylos glandulosa*
Mariposa lily	*Calochortus* sp.
Maygrass, canary grass	*Phalaris* sp.
Medick, alfalfa	*Medicago* sp. (I)
Melic grass	*Melica* sp.
Mesquite	*Prosopis* sp.
Milkweed	*Asclepias albicans*
Miner's lettuce	*Montia* sp.
Mint	*Mentha* sp.
Mint, wild	*Monardella exilis*
Mistletoe, pine	*Arceuthobium* sp.
Mules ears	*Wyethia* sp.
Muhly grass	*Muhlenbergia porteri*
Mustard family	Brassicaceae
Mustard, field	*Brassica* sp.
Needlegrass	*Stipa* sp.
Nemophila	*Nemophila* sp.
Nightshade	*Solanum* sp.
Nutgrass	*Cyperus* sp.
Oak	*Quercus* sp.
Oak, blue	*Quercus douglasii*
Oak, coastal live	*Quercus agrifolia*
Oak, interior live	*Quercus wislizenii*
Oak, tanbark	*Lithocarpus densiflora*
Oak, valley	*Quercus lobata*
Oat, wild	*Avena sativa* (I)
Ocotillo	*Fouquieria splendens*
Oligomeris	*Oligomeris linifolia*
Onion, wild	*Allium* sp.

Table 7.2 *continued*

Common Name	Scientific Name
Palm, fan	*Washingtonia filifera*
Panic grass	*Panicum* sp.
Paspalum	*Paspalum* sp.
Peach	*Prunus persica* (I)
Peppergrass	*Lepidium* sp.
Phacelia	*Phacelia* sp.
Pigweed	*Amaranthus* sp.
Pine	*Pinus* sp.
Pine, digger	*Pinus sabianana*
Pine, single-leaf	*Pinus monophylla*
Pine, western yellow	*Pinus ponderosa*
Pink family	Caryophyllaceae
Plantain	*Plantago* sp.
Poa	*Poa* sp.
Poison oak	*Rhus diversiloba*
Pondweed	*Potamogeton* sp.
Poppy	*Eschscholzia* sp.
Poppy family	Papaveraceae
Prickly pear/cholla	*Opuntia* sp.
Prickly poppy	*Argemone* sp.
Prunus	*Prunus* sp.
Purslane	*Portulaca* sp. (I)
Rabbitbrush	*Chrysothamnus* sp.
Rabbitbrush, sticky-leaved	*Chrysothamnus* cf. *viscidiflorus*
Redmaids	*Calandrinia ciliata*
Redwood, coastal	*Sequoia sempervirens*
Reed	*Phragmites australis*
Ricegrass	*Oryzopsis* sp.
Rockgrass	*Arabis* sp.
Rose, wild	*Rosa* sp.
Rush	*Juncus* sp.
Sacaton grass	*Sporobolis* sp.
Sage	*Salvia* sp.
Sage, white	*Salvia apiana*
Sagebrush	*Artemisia* sp.
Saltbush	*Atriplex* sp.
Salt grass	*Distichlis* sp.
Sea-blite	*Suaeda* sp.
Sea purslane	*Sesuvium verrucosum*
Sedge	*Carex* sp.
Sedge family	Cyperaceae
Silktassel bush	cf. *Garrya* sp.
Six-week grama	*Bouteloua* sp.
Soaproot	*Chlorogalum pomeridianum*
Spikerush	*Eleocharis* sp.

Continued on next page

Table 7.2 *continued*

Common Name	Scientific Name
Spring beauty	*Claytonia* sp.
Spurge, C.	*Chamaesyce* sp.
Spurge, E.	*Euphorbia* sp.
Squash (D)	*Cucurbita pepo* (I)
Squash/gourd (D)	*Cucurbita* sp. (I)
Squawbush	*Rhus trilobata*
Squirreltail	*Sitanion* sp.
Star thistle	*Centaurea* sp. (I)
St. John's wort	*Hypericum* sp.
Stinging nettle	*Urtica* sp.
Stinkweed	*Cleomella obtusifolia*
Storks bill, filaree	*Erodium* sp.
Sugarbush	*Rhus ovata*
Sumac	*Rhus* sp.
Sumac, laurel	*Rhus laurina*
Sumpweed	*Iva* sp.
Sunflower	*Helianthus* sp.
Sunflower, desert	*Geraea* cf. *canescens*
Sunflower family	Asteraceae
Sweet bush	*Bebbia juncea*
Sycamore	*Platanus racemosa*
Tarweed, H.	*Hemizonia* sp.
Tarweed, M.	*Madia* sp.
Three-awn grass	*Aristada* sp.
Thistle	*Cirsium* sp.
Tobacco	*Nicotiana* sp.
Toyon	*Heteromeles arbutifolia*
Tule	*Scirpus* sp.
Tumble mustard/tansy	*Sisymbrium* (I)/*Descurainia* sp.
Turpentine broom	*Thamnosma montana*
Vervain	*Verbena* sp.
Vetch	*Vicia* sp.
Violet	*Viola* sp.
Walnut	*Juglans* sp.
Water hemlock	*Cicuta douglasii*
Watermelon (D)	*Citrullus lanatus* (I)
Water nymph	*Najas* sp.
Wheat (D)	*Triticum aestivum* (I)
Wheatgrass	*Agropyron* sp.
Wildrye	*Elymus* sp.
Willow	*Salix* sp.
Yucca	*Yucca* sp.

Note: D = domesticated, I = introduced (nonnative taxa).

Table 7.3

Charred Plants Recovered from California Archaeological Sites

Scientific Name	Common Name	Plant Part
GYMNOSPERMAE		
PINACEAE	pine family	
Pinus monophylla	single-leaf pine	N, F, W
Pinus ponderosa	western yellow pine	N, W
Pinus sabianana	digger pine	N, W
Pinus sp.	pine	N, F, W, O
Pseudotsuga menziesii	Douglas-fir	W
TAXODIACEAE	redwood family	
Sequoia sempervirens	coastal redwood	W
CUPRESSACEAE	cypress family	
Juniperus californica	California juniper	S, B
Juniperus sp.	juniper	S, B, W
Libocedrus decurrens	California incense cedar	W
ANGIOSPERMAE: DICOTYLEDONEAE		
LAURACEAE	laurel family	
Umbellularia californica	California bay	N, W
RANUNCULACEAE	buttercup family	
Ranunculus sp.	buttercup	S
MALVACEAE	mallow family	S
Malva (I)/*Sphaeralcea/Malvastrum*	globe-/false-/mallow	S
GERANIACEAE	geranium family	
Erodium sp.	storks bill, filaree	S
EUPHORBIACEAE	spurge family	
Chamaesyce sp.	C. spurge	S
Euphorbia sp.	E. spurge	S
FOUQUIERIACEAE	ocotillo family	
Fouquieria splendens	ocotillo	S, W, O
LOASACEAE	loasa family	
Mentzelia sp.	blazing star	S
HYPERICACEAE	St. John's wort family	
Hypericum sp.	St. John's wort	S
PAPAVERACEAE	poppy family	S
Argemone sp.	prickly poppy	S
Eschscholzia sp.	poppy	S
RESEDACEAE	mignonette family	
Oligomeris linifolia	oligomeris	S
CAPPARIDACEAE	caper family	
Cleomella obtusifolia	stinkweed	S
BRASSICACEAE	mustard family	S
Arabis sp.	rockgrass	S
Brassica sp.	field mustard	S
Lepidium sp.	peppergrass	S
Sisymbrium(I)/*Descurainia* sp.	tumble mustard/tansy	S
CENTROSPERMAE	cheno-ams	S

Continued on next page

Table 7.3 *continued*

Scientific Name	Common Name	Plant Part
CARYOPHYLLACEAE	pink family	S
Silene sp. (I)	catchfly	S
PORTULACACEAE	purslane family	
Calandrinia ciliata	redmaids	S
Calyptridium cf. *umbellatum*	calyptridium	S
Claytonia sp.	spring beauty	S
Montia sp.	miner's lettuce	S
Portulaca sp. (I)	purslane	S
AIZOACEAE	carpetweed family	
Mollugo sp.	carpetweed	S
Sesuvium verrucosum	sea purslane	S
CACTACEAE	cactus family	O
Echinocereus/Ferocactus	barrel cactus	S, F
Opuntia cf. *ramosissima*	cholla	S, F, O
Opuntia sp.	prickly pear/cholla	S, F
POLYGONACEAE	knotweed family	
Eriogonum sp.	wild buckwheat	S
Polygonum sp.	knotweed	S
Rumex cf. *salicifolius*	willow dock	S
Rumex sp.	dock	S
CHENOPODIACEAE	goosefoot family	
Atriplex sp.	saltbush	S, W
Chenopodium sp.	goosefoot	S
Sarcobatus sp.	greasewood	W
Suaeda sp.	sea-blite	S
AMARANTHACEAE	pigweed family	
Amaranthus sp.	pigweed	S
NYCTAGINACEAE	four o'clock family	
Boerhaavia sp.	boerhaavia	S
Mirabilis sp.	four o'clock	S
PLANTAGINACEAE	plantain family	
Plantago sp.	plantain	S
ERICACEAE	heath family	
Arbutus menziesii	madrone	S
Arctostaphylos glandulosa	eastwood manzanita	S
Arctostaphylos glauca	bigberry manzanita	S
Arctostaphylos sp.	manzanita	S, W
Vaccinium sp.	huckleberry	S
APOCYNACEAE	dogbane family	
Apocynum cannibinum	Indian hemp	F
Apocynum sp.	wild hemp	F
ASCLEPIADACEAE	milkweed family	
Asclepias albicans	milkweed	S
CUSCUTACEAE	dodder family	
Cuscuta sp.	dodder	S

Table 7.3 *continued*

Scientific Name	Common Name	Plant Part
HYDROPHYLLACEAE	waterleaf family	
Nemophila sp.	nemophila	S
Phacelia sp.	phacelia	S
BORAGINACEAE	borage family	
Amsinckia/Plagiobothrys sp.	fiddleneck	S
Borage sp.	borage	S
Cryptantha sp.	cryptantha	S
SOLANACEAE	nightshade family	
Lycium sp.	desert tomato	S
Nicotiana sp.	tobacco	S
Solanum sp.	nightshade	S
BIGNONIACEAE	bignonia family	
cf. *Chilopsis linearis*	desert willow	W
ACANTHACEAE	acanthus family	
Beloperone californica	chuparosa	F
VERBENACEAE	verbena family	
Verbena sp.	vervain	S
LAMIACEAE	mint family	
Mentha sp.	mint	S
Monardella exilis	wild mint	S
Salvia apiana	white sage	S
Salvia columbariae	chia	S
Salvia sp.	sage	S
ROSACEAE	rose family	
Adenostoma fasciculatum	chamise	S, W
Heteromeles arbutifolia	toyon	S
Potentilla sp.	cinquefoil	S
Prunus armeniaca (I)	apricot	N
Prunus cf. *fremontii*	desert apricot	N
Prunus ilicifolia	holly-leaf cherry	N, W
Prunus persica (I)	peach	N
Prunus sp.	prunus	S
Purshia sp.	bitterbrush	S, W
Rosa sp.	wild rose	S
Rubus sp.	blackberry/raspberry	S
FABACEAE	legume family	S
Acacia greggii	catclaw	W
Astragalus sp.	locoweed	S
Lotus sp.	bird's foot trefoil	S
Lupinus sp.	lupine	S
Medicago sp. (I)	medick, alfalfa	S
Olneya tesota	ironwood	W
Phaseolus vulgaris (I)	common bean (D)	S
Prosopis sp.	mesquite	S, O
Trifolium sp.	clover	S
Vicia sp.	vetch	S

Continued on next page

Table 7.3 *continued*

Scientific Name	Common Name	Plant Part
PLANTANACEAE	sycamore family	
Plantanus racemosa	sycamore	W
BETULACEAE	birch family	
Corylus cornuta	hazelnut	N, W
FAGACEAE	oak family	
Lithocarpus densiflora	tanbark oak	N, W
Quercus lobata	valley oak	N, W
Quercus agrifolia	coastal live oak	N, W
Quercus douglasii	blue oak	N, W
Quercus wislizenii	interior live oak	N, W
Quercus sp.	oak	N
JUGLANDACEAE	walnut family	
Juglans sp.	walnut	N, W
SALICACEAE	willow family	
Populus sp.	cottonwood	W
Salix sp.	willow	W
ONAGRACEAE	evening primrose family	
Clarkia sp.	farewell-to-spring	S
URTICACEAE	nettle family	
Urtica sp.	stinging nettle	S
VITACEAE	grape family	
Vitis californica	wild grape	S, W
ZYGOPHYLLACEAE	caltrops family	
Larrea tridentata	creosotebush	S
RHAMNACEAE	buckthorn family	
Ceanothus sp.	California lilac	W
Condalia parryi	crucillo	S
Rhamnus crocea	buckthorn	W
BUXACEAE	box family	
Simmondsia sp.	jojoba	S, F
LORANTHACEAE	mistletoe family	
Arceuthobium sp.	pine mistletoe	S
RUTACEAE	rue family	
Thamnosma montana	turpentine broom	W
ANACARDIACEAE	sumac family	
Rhus diversiloba	poison oak	S
Rhus integrifolia	lemonadeberry	S
Rhus laurina	laurel sumac	S
Rhus ovata	sugar bush	S
Rhus trilobata	squaw bush	W
Rhus sp.	sumac	S, W
HIPPOCASTANACEAE	buckeye family	
Aesculus californica	buckeye	N, W
APIACEAE	carrot family	
Cicuta douglasii	water hemlock	S

Table 7.3 *continued*

Scientific Name	Common Name	Plant Part
Daucus carota (I)	wild carrot	S
Perideridia sp.	epos	R
GARRYACEAE	silktassel family	
cf. *Garrya* sp.	silktassel bush	S, O
RUBIACEAE	madder family	
Coffea sp. (I)	coffee (D)	S
Galium sp.	bedstraw	S
CAPRIFOLIACEAE	honeysuckle family	
Lonicera sp.	honeysuckle	S
Sambucus sp.	elderberry	S
CUCURBITACEAE	gourd family	
Citrullus lanatus (I)	watermelon (D)	S
Cucurbita pepo (I)	squash (D)	S
Cucurbita sp. (I)	squash/gourd (D)	S, O
cf. *Lagenaria siceraria* (I)	bottle gourd	O
Marah sp.	wild cucumber	N
ASTERACEAE	composite family	S, W
Achyrachaenamollis	blow-wives	S
Ambrosia sp.	bursage	S
Arctium sp.	burdock	S
Artemisia sp.	sagebrush	S, W
Aster sp.	aster	S
Baccharis sp.	coyote brush	W
Bebbia juncea	sweet bush	S
Centaurea sp. (I)	star thistle	S
Chrysothamnus cf. *viscidiflorus*	sticky-leaved rabbitbrush	W
Chrysothamnus sp.	rabbitbrush	W
Cirsium sp.	thistle	S
Dicoria canescens	bugseed	S
Encelia farinosa	brittlebush	S, F
Eriophyllum sp.	eriophyllum	S
Geraea cf. *canescens*	desert sunflower	S
Helianthus sp.	sunflower	S
Hemizonia sp.	H. tarweed	S
Iva sp.	sumpweed	S
Lasthenia sp.	lasthenia	S
Madia sp.	M. tarweed	S
Wyethia sp.	mules ears	S
VIOLACEAE	violet family	
Viola sp.	violet	S
ANGIOSPERMAE: MONOCOTYLEDONEAE		
POTAMOGETONACEAE	pondweed family	
Potamogeton sp.	pondweed	S
RUPPIACEAE	ditch-grass family	
Ruppia maritima	ditch-grass	S

Continued on next page

Table 7.3 *continued*

Scientific Name	Common Name	Plant Part
NAJADACEAE	water nymph family	
Najas sp.	water nymph	S
LILIACEAE	lily family	
Calochortus sp.	mariposa lily	S
Chlorogalum pomeridianum	soaproot	R, F
ARACEAE	arum family	
Washingtonia filifera	fan palm	O
AGAVACEAE	agave family	
Agave deserti	agave	S, F, O
cf. *Nolina parryi*	beargrass	F
Yucca sp.	yucca	R, F
TYPHACEAE	cattail family	
Typha sp.	cattail	S
AMARYLLIDACEAE	amaryllis family	
Allium sp.	wild onion	S
Brodiaea sp.	brodiaea	R
Dichelostemma sp.	blue dicks	R
JUNCACEAE	rush family	
Juncus sp.	rush	S, F
CYPERACEAE	sedge family	S
Carex sp.	sedge	S
Cyperus sp.	nutgrass	S
Eleocharis sp.	spikerush	S
Scirpus sp.	tule	S, F
POACEAE	grass family	S
Agropyron sp.	wheatgrass	S
Agrostis sp.	bentgrass	S
Aristada sp.	three-awn grass	S
Avena sativa (I)	wild oat	S
Bouteloua sp.	six-week grama	S
Bromus sp.	brome grass	S
Crypsis sp.	crypsis	S
Deschampsia sp.	hairgrass	S
Distichlis sp.	salt grass	S
Echinochloa sp.	barnyard grass	S
Elymus sp.	wildrye	S
Eragrostis sp.	love grass	S
Festuca sp.	fescue	S
Hilaria rigida	galleta grass	F
Hordeum jubatum	foxtail barley	S
Hordeum pusillum	little barley	S
Hordeum vulgare (I)	barley (D)	S
Hordeum sp.	wild barley	S
Leptochloa sp.	leptochloa	S
Melica sp.	melic grass	S

Table 7.3 *continued*

Scientific Name	Common Name	Plant Part
Muhlenbergia porteri	muhly grass	S, F
Muhlenbergia rigens	deer grass	F
Oryzopsis sp.	ricegrass	S
Panicum sp.	panic grass	S
Paspalum sp.	paspalum	S
Phalaris sp.	maygrass/canarygrass	S
Phragmites australis	reed	S, F
Poa sp.	poa	S
Sitanion sp.	squirreltail	S
Spartina sp.	cordgrass	S
Sporobolis sp.	sacaton	S
Stipa sp.	needlegrass	S, F
Triticum aestivum (I)	wheat (D)	S
Zea mays (I)	maize (D)	S

Note: I = introduced (nonnative taxa); D = domesticated; S = seed, N = nutshell/nutmeat pit, B = berry/fruit, R = root/rhyzome/bulb/corm/tuber, W = wood, F = fiber/stem, O = other/scales/spines/anthers/leaves/rind/peduncle/quid.

Table 7.4
California Archaeobotanical Contexts with Confirmed Dates

Site	Site Name/Designation	Time Period	Years B.P.	Date Type	Context	Citation
NORTHERN						
CALIFORNIA						
CA-SHA-350		L	380 ± 100	C14-CH	OS; hearth	Honeysett 1987
CA-SHA-386		M	740 ± 40	C14-CH	OS; hearth	Honeysett 1987
CA-SHA-386		M	860 ± 60	C14-CH	OS; midden	Honeysett 1987
CA-LAS-206		M	2195–2055*C	(2)C14-CH	OS; features	Wohlgemuth 1997a
CA-LAS-206		M	1420–1300*C	C14-CH	OS; feature	Wohlgemuth 1997a
CA-LAS-206		L	1190–930*C	C14-CH	OS; feature	Wohlgemuth 1997a
CA-LAS-377		E	4100–3880*C	C14-CH	OS; feature	Wohlgemuth 1997a
CA-LAS-377		M/L	1380–1260*C	C14-CH	OS; feature	Wohlgemuth 1997a
CA-LAS-377		L	670–450*C	C14-CH	OS; feature	Wohlgemuth 1997a
CA-LAS-1756		L	1070–725*C	(3)C14-CH	OS; features	Milliken and Hildebrandt 1997
CA-LAS-2060		H	100–0*C	hist. art.	OS; feature	McGuire 2000
CA-MOD-3150		H	100–90	hist. art.	OS; feature	McGuire 2000
CA-MOD-3153		L	360–220*C	C14-CH	OS; feature	McGuire 2000
CA-MOD-3153		H	295–5*C	C14-CH; hist. art.	OS; features	McGuire 2000
CA-MOD-3396		L/H	280–180*C	C14-CH	OS; feature	McGuire 2000
CA-MOD-3396		H	80–0*C	(2)C14-CH	OS; features	McGuire 2000
CA-MOD-3448		L	500–380*C	C14-CH	OS; feature	McGuire 2000
CA-MOD-3448		L	330–210*C	C14-CH	OS; feature	McGuire 2000
SIERRA NEVADA						
CA-FRE-632		M/L/H	1150–100	shell beads	OS; midden	Davis and Miksicek 1989
CA-FRE-1671		L/H	1500–100	shell beads	OS; midden	Davis and Miksicek 1988
CA-FRE-2365		M/L	1415–1265*C	C14-CH	OS; feature	Milliken and Meyer 1997

Site	Locality	Period	Date	Material	Context	Reference
CA-FRE-2365		L	525–310*C	C14-CH	OS; feature	Milliken and Meyer 1997
CA-MRP-8	Wawona	L/H	<210	glass beads	OS; midden	Huckell 1981, 1984a
CA-MRP-172	Crossroads	M/L	1690 ± 230	C14-CH	OS; lithic scatter	Huckell 1984a
CA-MRP-173	Crossroads	E	3680 ± 450	C14-CH	OS; lithic scatter	Huckell 1984a
CA-MRP-217	Cemetery	M	1730 ± 70	C14-CH	OS; hearth feature	Huckell 1984a
CA-MRP-645	Windfall	L	820 ± 240	C14-CH	OS; test unit	Huckell 1984a
CA-MRP-645	Windfall	M	1710 ± 80	C14-CH	OS; test unit	Huckell 1984a
CA-TUO-2833		M	ca. 1800	C14	OS; feature	Wohlgemuth in press
CA-TUO-2834		E	ca. 4600	C14	OS; feature	Wohlgemuth in press
CA-TUO-2834		M	ca. 2230	C14	OS; feature	Wohlgemuth in press
DELTA						
CA-SOL-315		M	1850 ± 90	C14-CH	OS; feature	Wohlgemuth 1992a
CA-SOL-315		L	430 ± 105	C14-CH	OS; feature	Wohlgemuth 1992a
CA-SOL-356		L	850–660*C	(2)C14-CH	OS; pit feature, house trash	Wohlgemuth 1996a
CA-SOL-356		L	425–265*C	C14-CH	OS; pit feature, house floor	Wohlgemuth 1996a
CENTRAL COAST						
CA-ALA-555		L	450–210	(2)C14-CH,BO	OS; ash, human cremation	Wohlgemuth 1996b
CA-ALA-555		M	2210–1505	(2)BONECOL	OS; human burial	Wohlgemuth 1996b
CA-ALA-566		L	970–515*C	(2)C14-CH	OS; features	Wohlgemuth 1998
CA-CCO-458		L	565–365*C	C14-CH	OS; feature	Wohlgemuth 1997b
CA-CCO-459		M/L	1390–1260*C	C14-CH	OS; feature	Wohlgemuth 1997b
CA-CCO-459		L	680–560*C	C14-CH	OS; feature	Wohlgemuth 1997b
CA-CCO-637		M	2600–2400*C	C14-CH	OS; feature	Wohlgemuth 1997b
CA-CCO-696	CCO-696 Deep	E	9930–9810*C	C14-CH	OS; feature	Wohlgemuth 1997b
CA-CCO-696	CCO-696 Deep	E	7489–7329*C	C14-CH	OS; feature	Wohlgemuth 1997b
CA-CCO-696	CCO-696 West	M	2440–2340*C	C14-CH	OS; feature	Wohlgemuth 1997b
CA-MNT-1892		L	680–310*C	(3)C14-CH	OS; column samples	Hildebrandt and Jones 1998
CA-SCL-12		E to M	2780–1280	(5)C14-CH	OS; column samples	Klug and Popper 1995
CA-SCL-12		M	1530–1400	(2)C14-CH	OS; column sample	Klug and Popper 1995

Continued on next page

312

Table 7.4 *continued*

Site	Site Name/Designation	Time Period	Years B.P.	Date Type	Context	Citation
CA-SCL-38		M/L	1130 ± 170		OS; human burials	Smith 1996
CA-SCL-30		L	620 ± 60		OS; human burials	Smith 1996
CA-SCL-119		M to L	2005–768	(3)C14-CH	OS; house floor, thermal pits	Hildebrandt and Mikkelsen 1993
CA-SCL-287	Sand Hill Road	E/M,M	2720–2005	(3)C14-CH	OS; thermal rock features	Burson 1998; Jones 1995
CA-SCL-287	Sand Hill Road	M	1495 ± 70	C14-CH	OS; thermal rock feature	Bocek and Reese 1992; Hammett 1996b
CA-SCL-287	Sand Hill Road	L	370 ± 60	C14-CH	OS; thermal rock feature	Bocek and Reese 1992; Hammett 1996b
CA-SCL-308		M	2190–1720*C	C14-CH	OS; house floor	Hildebrandt and Mikkelsen 1993
CA-SCL-464	Stanford West	E	3190 ± 200	C14-CH	OS; human burial	Bocek and Reese 1992
CA-SCL-464	Stanford West	M	1970 ± 50	C14-CH	OS; thermal feature	Bocek and Reese 1992; Burson 1998
CA-SCL-464	Stanford West	M	1600 ± 95	C14-CH	OS; human burial	Bocek and Reese 1992
CA-SCL-464	Stanford West	M/L	1225 ± 90	C14-CH	OS; thermal feature	Bocek and Reese 1992; Burson 1998
CA-SCL-586	Stanford Golf Course	M	1700 ± 65	C14-CH	OS; thermal rock feature	Burson 1998; Jones 1995
CA-SCL-586	Stanford Golf Course	M/L	1340 ± 140	C14-CH	OS; thermal rock feature	Burson 1998; Jones 1995
CA-SCL-698	Stanford Golf Course	M	1510–1313*C	C14-CH	OS; pit feature	Hildebrandt and Mikkelsen 1993
CA-SCL-613	Child. Health Council	E	3640 ± 185	C14-CH	OS; thermal rock feature	Burson 1998; Hammett 1997

Site	Name	Period	Date	Method	Context	Reference
CA-SCL-613	Child. Health Council	E to M	3190–2345	(3)C14-CH	OS; thermal rock features	Burson 1998; Hammett 1997
CA-SCL-613	Child. Health Council	M	1580 ± 60	C14-CH	OS; thermal rock feature	Burson 1998; Hammett 1997
CA-SCL-623	Old Children's Hosp.	M	1710–1520	(2)C14-CH	OS; thermal rock features	Burson 1998
CA-SCL-623	Old Children's Hosp.	L	800–550	(2)C14-CH	OS; thermal rock features	Burson 1998
CA-SCL-639		M/L	1261–1053*C	C14-CH	OS; thermal pits	Hildebrandt and Mikkelsen 1993
CA-SCL-732	Three Wolves	E	6460 ± 150	(4)C14-CH	OS; house post	Hammett 1996a
CA-SCL-732	Three Wolves	E	4720 ± 110	(4)C14-CH	OS; house post	Hammett 1996a
CA-SCL-732	Three Wolves	E	4320 ± 90	(4)C14-CH	OS; rope w/wolf burial	Hammett 1996a
CA-SCL-732	Three Wolves	E	2720 ± 180	(4)C14-CH	OS; human burial	Hammett 1996a
CA-SCL-732	Three Wolves	E to M	2420–1680	(9)C14-CH,BO	OS; human burials	Hammett 1996a
CA-SCL-732	Three Wolves	L/H	490–70	(6)C14-CH,BO	OS; animal burial/house floor	Hammett 1996a
CA-SCR-123		M	3250–2200	(7)C14-CH	OS; midden	Miksicek n.d.a
CA-SMA-204	Jasper Ridge	M/L	1060 ± 60	C14-CH	OS; thermal feature	Bocek and Reese 1992
CA-SMA-204	Jasper Ridge	L	1120–445	(2)C14-CH	OS; human burials	Bocek and Reese 1992
CA-SMA-256	SLAC 2	L	870–590	(3)C14-CH	OS; feature	Bocek and Reese 1992
CA-SMA-263	Oak Knoll	E	3020 ± 160	C14-CH	OS; thermal rock feature	Burson 1998
CA-SMA-263	Oak Knoll	M	2270 ± 80	C14-CH	OS; burial, features	Bocek and Reese 1992; Hammett 1996b
CA-SMA-263	Oak Knoll	M	1820 ± 180	C14-CH	OS; thermal rock feature	Burson 1998
CA-SMA-263	Oak Knoll	M/L	1320 ± 100	C14-CH	OS; thermal rock feature	Burson 1998
CA-SMA-263	Oak Knoll	L	1040–550	(3)C14-CH	OS; thermal rock features	Burson 1998
CA-SON-348	Duncan's Landing	E	7960–6140	(2)C14-CH,SH	RS; midden	Schwaderer 1993; Wohlgemuth 1991a
CA-SON-2098		E	4820 ± 110	C14-CH	OS; features, midden	Wohlgemuth 1993a
CA-SON-2294/H	Rancho Petaluma	H	1834–1850s	hist. art., texts	OS; features, midden	Silliman 2000

Continued on next page

Table 7.4 *continued*

Site	Site Name/Designation	Time Period	Years B.P.	Date Type	Context	Citation
SOUTHERN COAST						
CA-LAN-229	Talepop	L/H	950–126	shell beads	OS; house hearths	Hammett 1991; King et al. 1982
CA-LAN-1032	Buckhorn Flats	M/L	960 ± 60	C14-CH	OS	Klug and Popper 1996a
CA-LAN-1032	Buckhorn Flats	M	2150 ± 60	C14-CH	OS	Klug and Popper 1996a
CA-LAN-1977	Santiago Cyn. #4	L	840–850	C14-CH	OS; earth oven feature	Klug and Popper 1996a
CA-LAN-2327		L	350 ± 60	C14-CH	OS	Klug and Popper 1996a
CA-ORA-225		E	8890 ± 130	C14-SH	OS; test unit	Miksicek 1990
CA-ORA-225		E/M	2900 ± 90	C14-SH	OS; circular feature	Klug and Popper 1996b
CA-ORA-225		M	2120–1480	(2)C14-CH, SH	OS; rock and circle features	Klug and Popper 1996b
CA-ORA-225		M	1550 ± 70	C14-SH	OS; circular feature	Klug and Popper 1996b
CA-ORA-225		L	700 ± 70	C14-SH	OS; feature	Klug and Popper 1996b
CA-ORA-389	Aliso Creek	M/L	1020 ± 70	C14-SH	OS; test unit	Miksicek 1990
CA-ORA-689		L/H	260 ± 40	C14-CH	RS; test unit	Klug and Popper 1996c
CA-ORA-736		L	344 ± 170	C14-CH	RS	Klug and Popper 1996c
CA-ORA-1029		L	524 ± 262	C14-CH	RS	Klug and Popper 1996c
CA-SBA-1816		L/H	450–105	C14-SH, shell beads	OS; sand dunes	Hammett 1989, 1991
CA-SBA-46	Helo, Mescalitan Is.	L/H	250–150	shell beads	OS; house floors	Gamble et. al. 1990; Hammett 1991
CA-SDI-811		M	1330–1510	C14-SH	OS; midden	Reddy1996a
CA-SDI-4538		L	580–940	C14-SH, CH	OS; midden	Reddy1996a
CA-SDI-5137		L	730 ± 50	C14-CH	OS	Reddy 1997a
CA-SDI-5138		L	580–600	C14-CH	OS	Reddy 1997a
CA-SDI-5139		L	590–620	C14-CH	OS	Reddy 1997a
CA-SDI-5145		L	570 ± 50	C14-CH	OS	Reddy 1997a
CA-SDI-5145		H	70–112	C14-CH	OS	Reddy 1997a

Site			Date		Description	Reference
CA-SDI-5146		L	220–450	C14-CH	OS	Reddy 1997a
CA-SDI-6055		L	310–390	(2)C14-CH	OS	Reddy 2000a
CA-SDI-9824		H	100–150	(2)C14-CH	OS	Reddy 2000a
CA-SDI-10,006		L	470–690	(2)C14-SH	OS	Reddy 2000a
CA-SDI-10,700		L	575–730	(2)C14-SH	OS; midden	Reddy 1999a
CA-SDI-10,705		H	150±70	C14-CH	OS	Reddy 1999a
CA-SDI-10,712/13		L/H	170–410	(2)C14-CH	OS	Reddy 2000a
CA-SDI-10,726/A		L	270±70	C14-CH	OS; midden	Reddy1996a
CA-SDI-10,726/A		M/L	1040±50	C14-SH	OS; midden	Reddy1996a
CA-SDI-10,726/B		L	580±50	C14-SH	OS; midden	Reddy1996a
CA-SDI-10,726/B		M/L	1060±50	C14-CH	OS; midden	Reddy1996a
CA-SDI-10,726/B		E	6540–6670	(2)C14-SH	OS; midden	Reddy1996a
CA-SDI-10,728/A		E	7010–7550	(4)C14-SH	OS; midden	Reddy 1997b
CA-SDI-10,728/A		E	6130±80	C14-SH	OS; midden	Reddy 1997b
CA-SDI-10,728/A		L	580–840	(4)C14-SH	OS; midden	Reddy 1997b
CA-SDI-10,728/B		L	590–670	(2)C14-SH	OS; midden	Reddy 1997b
CA-SDI-14,417		L	630±90	C14-SH	OS	Reddy 2000a
CA-SDI-14,665		L	400–420	(2)C14-CH	OS	Reddy 2000a
CA-SCLI-154	LVTA-8	M/L	1080±70	C14-CH	OS	Reddy 2000b
Unspecified (SCLI)	LVTA-9	E	3510±60	C14-SH	OS	Reddy 2000b
Unspecified (SCLI)	LVTA/SE-46	H	160±50	C14-CH	OS	Reddy 2000b
CA-SCLI-1239		L	510±70	C14-CH	OS; midden	Reddy 2000c
CA-SCLI-1249		L	400±90	C14-CH	OS	Reddy 2000c
CA-SCLI-1456		E	3885–4355*C	C14-CH	OS; midden	Klug and Popper 1996d
CA-SLO-165		E	5040–5610*C	(4)C14-SH	OS; midden column	Hammett 1991
CA-VEN-1020		M/L	1090±60	C14-CH	OS; yucca oven	King 1993
CA-VEN-1020		L	280±50	C14-CH	OS; yucca oven	King 1993

DESERTS

CA-IMP-7620		L	200±50	C14-CH	OS; feature in rock enclosure	Klug and Popper 1997
CA-IMP-6467		H	160–222	(10)C14-CH	OS; features, hearth	Reddy 1999b

Continued on next page

Table 7.4 *continued*

Site	Site Name/ Designation	Time Period	Years B.P.	Date Type	Context	Citation
CA-IMP-7750		H	100 ± 60	C14	OS	Reddy 2000d
CA-KER-490		H	170 ± 60	C14-CH	OS	Reddy 1996b
CA-KER-490		L	460–640	C14-CH	OS	Reddy 1996b
CA-KER-490		L	1150 ± 100	C14-CH	OS	Reddy 1996b
CA-KER-2378		L	540 ± 60	C14-CH	OS	Reddy 1996b
CA-KER-2378		L	940 ± 60	C14-CH	OS	Reddy 1996b
CA-INY-30		L	390 ± 90	C14-CH	OS; house floors	Basgall and McGuire 1989
CA-INY-30		M	1600 ± 70	C14-SO	OS; pit feature	Basgall and Wohlgemuth 1989
CA-INY-328	McIrvin Homestead	M	1280 ± 80	C14-CH	OS; hearth	Delacorte et al. 1995
CA-INY-328-H	McIrvin Homestead	L	310 ± 100	C14-CH	OS; hearth	Delacorte et al. 1995
CA-INY-1428		M/L	1305–1050*C	C14-CH	OS; column sample	Gilreath and Holanda 2000
CA-INY-1308		H	<150	sherds, hist. art.	OS; test unit	Wilke 1983
CA-INY-1816		H	160 ± 70	C14-SO	OS; hearth	Gilreath and Hildebrandt 1995
CA-INY-1906		H	110 ± 70	C14-CH	OS; hearth	Gilreath and Hildebrandt 1995
CA-INY-2146	Partridge Ranch	M	1500 ± 100	C14-BO	OS; deer scapula	Delacorte 1984
CA-INY-2750		M	1400–1260*C	C14-CH	OS; feature	Delacorte 1999
CA-INY-3769		L/H	320–40*C	(3)C14-CH	OS; house floor, human burial	Delacorte 1999
CA-INY-3778		L/H	280–10*C	(2)C14-CH	OS; features	Delacorte 1999
CA-INY-3812		M	1340 ± 50	C14-CH	OS; house posts	Delacorte and McGuire 1993
CA-INY-4243		H	130 ± 80	C14-CH	OS; hearth	Gilreath and Hildebrandt 1995
CA-KER-733		L	460 ± 75	C14-CH	OS; hearth	Sutton 1984
CA-KER-2211		M	1300 ± 100	C14-CH	OS; structure	Sutton 1991
CA-MNO-458	Chance Well	H	110 ± 50	C14-CH	OS; house pit	Burton 1985
CA-MNO-584	Sherwin Grade	L	430 ± 150	C14-CH	OS; piñon scales	Garfinkel and Cook 1980

Site	Name	Period	Date	Material	Context	Reference
CA-MNO-584	Sherwin Grade	L	1155 ± 160	C14-CH	OS; piñon scales	Garfinkel and Cook 1980
CA-MNO-2122		H	<150	glass beads	OS; midden, house floor	Arkush 1995; Lawlor 1995
CA-MNO-2206/7		L	450 ± 90	C14-CH	OS; in rock ring	Hemphill 1987
CA-RIV-937	Cottonwood Spring	H	<150	historic pan	RS; cache	King 1976
CA-RIV-1179	La Quinta	L	670 ± 65	C14-CH	OS; hearths, coprolites	Farrell 1988: Swope 1988
CA-RIV-1961		H	200 ± 90	C14-CH	OS; human cremation	Huckell 1985
CA-SBR-72	Oro Grande	L	1050 ± 100	C14-CH	OS; features	Rector 1983
CA-SBR-85	Afton Canyon	L	870 ± 100	C14-CH	OS; hearths	Schneider 1989
CA-SBR-117	Mitchell Caverns	L	480 ± 100	C14-CH	CA; basketry fragments	Pinto 1985
CA-SBR-176	Deep Creek	L/H	800–200	sherds, beads	OS	Altschul et al. 1989
CA-SBR-199	Newberry Cave	M	3765 ± 100	C14-CH	CA; dart shaft	Davis et al. 1981
CA-SBR-199	Newberry Cave	M	2790 ± 250	C14-CH	CA; split-twig figurine	Davis and Smith 1981
CA-SBR-259	Cronise Lake	H	<150	C14-CH	OS; feature	Drover 1979
CA-SBR-2846	Ord Shelter	M	1770 ± 100	C14-CH	RS; wood from snare	Echlin et al. 1981
CA-SBR-334	Southcott Cave	L	230 ± 85	C14-CH	CA; scales, resin	Sutton et al. 1987
CA-SBR-424	Surprise Spring	E	6503 ± 103	C14-CH	OS; midden	Altschul et al. 1990
CA-SBR-6580	Siphon Site	M	3925–3375 *C	(2)C14-CH	OS; hearths	Sutton et al. 1993
CA-SDI-2537	Indian Hill	L	890 ± 50	C14-CH	RS; with ceramics	McDonald 1992
CA-SDI-2537	Indian Hill	E	4070 ± 100	C14-CH	RS; human burial	McDonald 1992
Unspecified	Casa Diablo	L	280 ± 150	C14-CH	OS; charcoal pocket	Cowan and Wallof 1974
Unspecified	Taquitz Canyon	L	245 ± 50	C14-CH	OS; hearth	Wilke et al. 1975
Unspecified	Myoma Dunes	L	365 ± 140	C14-CH	OS; coprolite bed	Wilke 1978
Unspecified	Cave No. 5	H	160 ± 60	C14-CH	CA; basketry fragment	Sutton and Yohe 1988

Note: E = Early, M = Middle, M/L = Middle/Late Transition, L = Late, H = Modern Historic (by region—see Figure 2); *C = corrected date; CH = charcoal, BO = bone, SH = shell, hist. art. = historic artifacts, SO = soil, BONECOL = bone collagen; OS = open site, CA = cave, RS = rockshelter; (#) = number of sample dates.

Dates based on information provided to authors. Date ranges for corrected dates or for multiple specimens where ± values constitute a temporal overlap.

Some dates are from same contexts as at least some archaeobotanical remains; otherwise, date of plant remains has been inferred from dated stratigraphic relationships.

Table 7.5

California Archaeobotanical Contexts without Dates or with Unconfirmed Dates

Site	Site Name	Posited Temporal Period	Archaeobotanical Context	Citation
NORTHERN CALIFORNIA				
CA-LAK-72		M	OS; midden	Wohlgemuth in press
CA-LAK-510		M	OS; midden	Wohlgemuth in press
CA-SHA-47		L, H	OS; features	Wohlgemuth 1991b
CA-SHA-177		M, L	OS; midden	Johnson and Skjelstad 1974
CA-SHA-222		L	OS; midden	Wohlgemuth 1990
CA-SHA-236		L	OS; midden	Wohlgemuth 1991a
CA-SHA-266		L	OS; midden	Wohlgemuth 1985
CA-SHA-279		E, L	OS; midden	Honeysett 1986; Wohlgemuth 1993b
CA-SHA-290		L	OS; features	Wohlgemuth 1985
CA-SHA-294C		E	OS; midden	Honeysett 1986
CA-SHA-294A/B		L	OS; midden	Honeysett 1986
CA-SHA-385		E, L	OS; midden	Honeysett 1987
CA-SHA-396		E, L	OS; midden	Honeysett 1987
CA-SHA-400		E, L	OS; midden	Honeysett 1987
CA-SHA-711/H		?	OS; features	Honeysett 1986
CA-SHA-961		L	OS; midden	Wohlgemuth and Darcangelo 1994
CA-SHA-1109/H		H	OS; midden, features	Honeysett 1986
CA-SHA-1144		H	OS; midden	Honeysett 1986
CA-SHA-1158		?	OS; midden	Honeysett 1986
CA-SHA-1300/H		H	OS; features	Honeysett 1986
CA-SHA-1464		E, L	OS; midden	Honeysett 1987
CA-SHA-1471		M	OS; midden	Honeysett 1987

Site	Site name	Period	Description	Reference
CA-SHA-1474		L	OS; midden	Honeysett 1987
CA-SHA-1544		M, L	OS; midden	Wohlgemuth 1989
CA-SHA-1588		L, H	OS; midden	Wohlgemuth 1989
CA-SUT-17		L/H	OS; house floor, midden	Wohlgemuth 1992b
CENTRAL COAST				
CA-ALA-42		L	OS; features, midden	Wohlgemuth 1997b
CA-CCO-156		?	OS; midden	Wohlgemuth 1992c
CA-CCO-474/H		?	OS; midden	Wohlgemuth 1992d
CA-MNT-234	Moss Landing Hill	E, M, L	OS; shell midden	Wohlgemuth 1999a
CA-MNT-515		L	OS; midden	Miksicek 1993a
CA-MNT-540		?	OS; midden	Miksicek 1993a
CA-MNT-567		L	OS; midden	Miksicek 1993a
CA-MNT-862		?	OS; midden	Miksicek 1993a
CA-MNT-1485/H		L	OS; ash deposits	Miksicek 1992
CA-MNT-1486/H		L	OS; ash deposits	Miksicek 1992
CA-SCL-577		?	OS; midden	Hildebrandt and Mikkelsen 1993
CA-SON-25/H		?	OS; midden	Wohlgemuth and Leary 1993
CA-SON-159		L	OS; midden	Wohlgemuth in press
CA-SON-458		L	OS; midden	Wohlgemuth in press
CA-SON-865		M/L	OS; midden	Wohlgemuth in press
CA-SON-867		?	OS; midden	Wohlgemuth in press
CA-SON-1695		M	OS; midden	Wohlgemuth in press
DELTA				
CA-SAC-133		?	OS; ash, features	Wohlgemuth 1992e
CA-SOL-69		E	OS; midden	Wohlgemuth 1992a

Continued on next page

Table 7.5 *continued*

Site	Site Name	Posited Temporal Period	Archaeobotanical Context	Citation
CA-SOL-355		M	OS; features, midden	Wohlgemuth 1993c
CA-SOL-363		M	OS; features, midden	Wohlgemuth 1994
CA-YOL-132		L	OS; midden	Wohlgemuth in press
SIERRA NEVADA				
CA-CAL-1180/H		E, M, L, L/H	OS; column	Wohlgemuth 1997a
CA-ELD-145		M, L	OS; midden	Wohlgemuth 1999b
CA-FRE-633		?	OS; midden	Davis and Miksicek 1989
CA-FRE-1154		?	OS; midden	Davis and Miksicek 1989
CA-FRE-1155		?	OS; midden	Davis and Miksicek 1989
4-MRP-250C	El Portal	H	OS; house floor, hearth, ashpit	Huckell 1982
4-MRP-250B	El Portal	L/H	OS; artifact scatter	Huckell 1982
FS 05-16-54-19/106		?	OS; midden	Miksicek n.d.b
CA-PLA-695/H	Monte Verde	E, M	OS; midden	Wohlgemuth 2000b
CA-PLA-728/H	Old Joe	L/H	OS; burial, hearth, midden	Wohlgemuth 2000a
SOUTHERN COAST				
CA-ORA-270		?	RS; midden	Miksicek 1990
CA-ORA-736		?	RS; midden	Miksicek 1990
CA-ORA-1029		?	RS; midden	Miksicek 1990
CA-ORA-1082		?	RS; midden	Miksicek 1990
CA-ORA-1083		?	RS; midden	Miksicek 1990
CA-ORA-1089		?	RS; midden	Miksicek 1990
CA-ORA-1090		?	RS; midden	Miksicek 1990
CA-ORA-1091		?	RS; midden	Miksicek 1990

Site	Name	Period	Context	Reference
CA-SBA-3404	Jonjonata	L/H	OS; column	Wohlgemuth in press
CA-SDI-945		L/H	OS; midden	Popper and Martin 2000
CA-SDI-10,697		?	OS	Reddy 2000a
CA-SDI-14,567		?	OS	Reddy 1999a
CA-SDI-14,649		L	OS	Reddy 2000e
DESERTS				
DEVA 83A-7	Timba-Sha	L	RS; fiber sandal	Huckell 1984b
CA-IMP-7750		L/H	OS; house pit	Reddy 2000d
CA-INY-46		L/H	RS; cache	Osborne and Riddell 1978
CA-INY-1308		M	OS; midden	Wilke 1983
CA-INY-2285		L	OS	Wilke 1983
CA-INY-4547		L	OS; bedrock milling feature	Miksicek 1993b
CA-INY-4550		L	OS; midden	Miksicek 1993b
CA-MNO-891		L	OS; midden, above tephra ash	Miksicek 1993c
CA-RIV-4754		L	OS; midden	Martin and Popper 1997
CA-RIV-6059		L	OS	Martin and Popper 1998
CA-SBR-1206		L	CA	Sutton and Ritter 1984
Unspecified	Wadi Beadmaker	L	OS; coprolites	Wilke 1978
Unspecified	near Torres Ranch	L/H	RS; cache	Wilke and Fain 1974

Note: H = recent historic (<250 BP), L = Late period (950–250 BP), M/L = Middle/Late transition (1400–1000 BP), M = Middle period (3000–1400 BP), E = Early period (7000–3000 BP); OS = open site, CA = cave, RS = rockshelter.

Table 7.6a
Plant Taxa Recovered from California Subregions: Northern California and Sierra Nevada

Common Name	Northern California							Sierra Nevada					
Time Period	E	M	M/L	L	L/H	H	All	E	M	M/L	L	L/H	All
Number of Sites	1	1	1	3	1	5	32	1	4	1	4	3	12
GYMNOSPERMS													
Pine family							N		N,F,W	F	N	N,W	N,F,W
Single-leaf pine					N	N	N						
Yellow pine				N			N						W
Digger pine		N				N	N					N	N
Douglas-fir									W				W
Juniper				S	S	S	S	W					W
California incense cedar													W
DICOTS													
California bay							N			N			N
Buttercup							S						S
Mallow family										S	S		S
Globe-/false-/mallow													S
Filaree							S						S
Blazing star		S				S	S						
Mustard family				S			S						
Tansy/tumble mustard							S						
Peppergrass							S			S	S		S
Pink family													S
Catchfly				S									S
Redmaids						S	S						
Miner's lettuce						S	S			S			S
Wild buckwheat						S	S			S			S

Plant								
Knotweed								S
Dock/knotweed	S			S				S
Dock	S	S	S	S			S	S
Saltbush	S		S	S			S	S
Goosefoot		S	S	S			S	S
Sea-blite			S	S		S		S
Pigweed		S		S			S	S
Plantain	S	S		S	N,S		N,S	N,S
Manzanita				N,S	N,S		N,S	N,S,W
Nemophila				S				S
Phacelia		S		S			S	S
Fiddleneck		S		S		S	S	S
Borage family			S	S				S
Cryptantha				S				
Nightshade				S				
Sage				S			S	S
Toyon				S				
Cinquefoil		N		N				
Apricot		N		N				
Peach		N		N				
Sierra plum				S				
Chokecherry				S				S
Bitterbrush	S			S				
Wild rose				S				
Blackberry/raspberry	S		S	S				S
Legume family			S	S			S	S
Lupine				S				S
Common bean (D)								
Clover			S		W		W	S
Sycamore					W		W	W

Continued on next page

Table 7.6a *continued*

Common Name	Northern California							Sierra Nevada					
Time Period	E	M	M/L	L	L/H	H	All	E	M	M/L	L	L/H	All
Number of Sites	1	1	1	3	1	5	32	1	4	1	4	3	12
Oak family				N			N			N	W	N,W	N,W
Valley oak												N,W	N,W
Blue oak												N,W	N,W
Interior live oak												N,W	N,W
Walnut													N
Cottonwood											W	W	W
Willow											W	W	W
Farewell-to-spring							S						S
Wild grape						S	S						
Buckthorn													W
Pine mistletoe							S						S
Buckeye							N						N,W
Carrot family							S						S
Epos						R	R						
Bedstraw		S		S		S	S				S	S	S
Coffee (D)				S			S						
Elderberry							S						S
Watermelon (D)						S	S						
Squash (D)							S						
Wild cucumber							N						N
Composite family							S			S			S
Blow-wives							S						
Burdock							S						
Star thistle							S						
Thistle							S						S

Taxon	E	E/M	M	M/L	L	L/H	H
Eriophyllum							
Sunflower	S				S		
H. tarweed					S		
M. tarweed	S				S		S
Mules ears							F
MONOCOTS							
Soaproot	S	S			S		
Cattail	S	S	S	S			
Brodiaea	R	R		R			
Rush	S	S		S			
Sedge family	S				S		S
Sedge	S	S	S	S		S	S
Tule	S	S	S	S	S	S	S, F
Grass family		S	S		S	F	S
Wheatgrass					S		
Wild oat		S	S				
Brome grass	S	S			S	S	S
Hairgrass	S						S
Wildrye						S	S
Fescue					S	S	S
Barley (D)	S	S					
Wild barley			S		S	S	S
Ricegrass		S					
Panic grass	S	S					S
Maygrass/canarygrass	S	S			S		S
Poa	S	S	S				S
Squirreltail	S	S					
Needlegrass	S	S	S		S		S
Wheat (D)	S	S	S				S

Note: D = domesticated; S = seed, N = nutshell/nutmeat, B = berry/fruit, R = root/rhizome/bulb/corm/tuber, W = wood, F = fiber/stem/leaf; E = Early period, M = Middle period, L = Late period, H = Historic period, E/M, M/L, L/H = transition periods.

Table 7.6b
Plant Taxa Recovered from California Subregions: Delta, Central and Southern Coasts

	Delta			Central Coast							Southern Coast							
Time Period	M	L	All	E	E/M	M	M/L	L	H	All	E	E/M	M	M/L	L	L/H	H	All
Number of Sites	1	1	6	4	2	7	4	5	1	30	7	1	4	7	23	5	4	64
GYMNOSPERMS																		
Pine family	N	N	N			N	N	N		N					W	N		W,N,O,B
Yellow pine							N			N						N		
Digger pine			N	N			N			N								
Coastal redwood										W								
California juniper																S,B		S,B
DICOTS																		
California bay	N	N	N	N		N	N	N	N	N					W	W		N,W
Buttercup		S	S	S		S		S	S	S				S	S		S	S
Mallow family									S	S				S			S	S
Globe-/false-/mallow								S	S	S	S						S	S
Filaree		S	S			S			S	S	S				S		S	S
E. spurge		S	S	S														
C. spurge				S							S							
Blazing star				S	S	S	S	S		S								S
St. John's wort								S		S								
Poppy family						S	S			S								
Poppy														S				
Mustard family								S	S	S						S	S	S
Rockgrass				S		S				S	S							S
Field mustard															S			
Tansy/tumble mustard					S	S					S	S						
Peppergrass		S	S	S	S	S	S	S		S	S	S			S	S	S	S

Plant	1	2	3	4	5	6	7	8	9	10	11	12	13	14	15
Cheno-ams				S	S	S	S	S	S	S		S		S	S
Catchfly								S	S						S
Purslane family						S	S		S						
Redmaids		S	S	S	S	S	S	S	S	S			S	S	S	S
Spring beauty			S	S					S						
Miner's lettuce		S	S	S	S	S	S	S	S				S	S	S
Purslane								S		S			S		S
Carpetweed family													S		S	S
Carpetweed							S		S	S					
Sea purslane										S					
Barrel cactus										S			S		S	
Wild buckwheat			S	S	S		S	S		S	S		S	S		S
Knotweed						S		S	S	S	S		S	S	
Dock/knotweed		S	S					S	S				S		
Dock			S						S		S			S	S	S
Saltbush			S		S		S	S		S	S	S	W, S	S		S,W
Goosefoot		S	S	S	S	S	S	S	S	S	S	S	S	S	S	S
Sea-blite									S						S
Pigweed			S			S	S	S	S	S	S		S	S	S	S
Plantain							S	S		S			S		S
Madrone									S						
Eastwood manzanita													S	S	S
Bigberry manzanita															S
Manzanita	S	S	S	S		S	S	S	S	S			S	S	S	S,W
Huckleberry									S				S		
Phacelia				S	S	S	S	S	S	S			S		S
Fiddleneck		S	S	S		S	S	S	S					S	S	S
Borage family				S	S	S	S	S		S			S		S
Nightshade family												S	S		S

Continued on next page

Table 7.6b continued

Common Name	Delta M	Delta L	Delta All	CC E	CC E/M	CC M	CC M/L	CC L	CC H	CC All	SC E	SC E/M	SC M	SC M/L	SC L	SC L/H	SC H	SC All
Number of Sites	1	1	6	4	2	7	4	5	1	30	7	1	4	7	23	5	4	64
Tobacco				S						S	S							S
Nightshade			S	S		S	S	S	S	S					S	S	S	S
Vervain							S				S				S	S		
Mint family				S				S		S				S	S		S	S
Mint										S								
Wild mint				S						S								
White sage						S				S								
Sage		S	S	S	S	S	S	S	S	S,W	S				S,W	S	S	S,W
Rose family				S				S		S								W
Chamise						S				S,W	S			W	S,W	S		S,W
Toyon		S	S				S			S,W	S		S		S,W		S	S,B,W
Prunus				S							S				S			
Holly-leaf cherry				N	N	N	N	N		N	N					N	N	N
Wild rose					S	N	N	N		S								
Blackberry/raspberry										S								
Legume family		S	S	S	S	S	S	S	S	S	S		S	S	S	S	S	S
Locoweed											S		S	S	S	S	S	S
Bird's foot trefoil			S			S		S		S	S				S	S	S	S
Lupine			S			S				S					S			S
Common bean (D)																S		
Medick, alfalfa									S	S	S			S				S
Clover			S			S			S	S	S				S	S	S	S
Vetch									S	S	S					S	S	S
Sycamore								W		W					W	W		W

Plant													
Hazelnut	N,W	N	N,W	N		N	N	N	N	N	N	N	N	N
Oak family	N,W	N	N,W	N		N	N	N,W	N	N	N	N	N	N
Oak	N,W	N	N	N,W		N	N,W	N	N	W	W		N	W
Valley oak	N	N	N,W		W		N,W	N,W	W	N	N			
Coastal live oak			W				N,W	N,W	N,W					
Blue oak							N,W	W	N,W					
Tanbark oak			N,W	N	N	N	N,W	N	N	N	N		N	
Walnut	N,W	N	N				N,W	N	N,W	N	N		N	
Cottonwood	W	W	W				W	W						
Willow	W	W	W				W	W						
Farewell-to-spring	S		S	S			S	S	S	S	S		S	S
Stinging nettle														S
Wild grape			W				S,W		S					S
Buckthorn family	W													S
California lilac	W		W											
Buckthorn	W							W						
Poison oak									S					
Lemonadeberry	S		S	S			S	S						
Laurel sumac	S		S	S			S							
Sugar bush	W		W				W							
Sumac	S,W		S	N	S									
Buckeye	N	N	S				N	N	N	N	N	N	N	N
Carrot family	S	S	S				S	S	S	S	S		S	S
Carrot	S	S	S				S	S	S	S			S	S
Bedstraw	S	S	S	S	S		S	S	S	S			S	S
Honeysuckle	S	S	S	S	S		S	S	S				S	S
Elderberry	S	S	S	S	S		S,W	S,W	S	S			S	S
Squash/gourd (D)	S	N	N	N	N	N	N	N	N	N	N		N	N
Wild cucumber			S											

Continued on next page

Table 7.6b continued

	Delta			Central Coast							Southern Coast							
Time Period	M	L	All	E	E/M	M	M/L	L	H	All	E	E/M	M	M/L	L	L/H	H	All
Number of Sites	1	1	6	4	2	7	4	5	1	30	7	1	4	7	23	5	4	64
Common Name																		
Composite family		S	S	S	S	S	S	S	S	S	S			S	W	S,W	S	W
Blow-wives		S	S	S				S	S	S								S
Aster															S			
Sunflower			S	S	S	S				S	S			S	S	S	S	S
H. tarweed				S		S		S	S	S	S							S
Sumpweed						S		S										
Lasthenia			S															
M. tarweed		S	S	S		S	S	S	S	S	S				S	S	S	S
Violet								S							S			S
MONOCOTS																		
Pondweed					S				S									S
Water nymph								S										
Lily family		R	R	R	R	R	R	R		R	F				R	R		R
Soaproot				R						R								R
Yucca				S						S	F			F	F	F		F
Cattail										S							S	S
Brodiaea		R	R			R	R	R		R			S					
Rush				S		S		S		S								
Sedge family							S							S				
Sedge				S						S	S			S	S		S	S
Nutgrass															S		S	S
Spikerush			S								S				S			S

Plant												
Tule	S	S					S	S			S	S
Grass family	S	S	S	S	S	S	S	S,F	S	S	S	S,F
Wheatgrass		S					S	S				S
Three-awn grass					S		S					S
Six-week grama							S					S
Brome grass	S	S		S	S	S	S	S	S		S	S
Hairgrass	S	S		S		S	S				S	S
Wildrye	S					S	S		S			S
Love grass	S	S		S	S	S	S	S	S	S	S	S
Fescue	S	S		S	S	S	S	S			S	S
Barley (D)					S	S					S	S
Little barley	S				S?			S	S	S	S	S
Wild barley	S	S				S	S	S	S	S	S	S
Leptochloa		S				S		S				
Melic grass	S			S		S		S	S			
Panic grass					S	S		S	S		S	S
Paspalum							S	S				S
Maygrass/canarygrass	S	S		S	S	S	S	S	S	S	S	S
Poa	S	S	S	S	S		S				S	S
Cordgrass								S			S	S
Sacaton	S						S					
Needlegrass		S			S	S		S		S		S
Wheat (D)				S	S						S	S
Maize (D)				S	S					S	S	S

Note: D = domesticated; S = seed, N = nutshell/nutmeat pit, B = berry/fruit, R = root/rhizome/bulb/corm/tuber, W = wood, F = fiber/stem, O = other/scales/spines/anthers/leaves/rind/peduncle/quid, E = Early period, M = Middle period, L = Late period, H = Historic period, E/M, M/L, L/H = transition periods.

Table 7.6c
Plant Taxa Recovered from California Subregions: Deserts

	Great Basin			Mojave						Sonoran			
Time Period	M	L/H	All	E	M	M/L	L	L/H	All	E	L	H	All
Number of Sites	5	12	23	1	4	1	8	2	18	1	5	5	15
Common Name													
GYMNOSPERMS													
Pine family		N,W,O	N,W,O	N					N		N		N
Single-leaf pine		N,O	N,O			N	N,W,O	N	N,W,O				
California juniper								W	W		W		
Juniper		S,B,W	S,B,W	S			S,B,W		S,B,W		S,W		S,W
DICOTS													
Mallow family						S		S	S				
Globe-/false-/mallow		S	S							S	S		S
Filaree							S		S		S		S
E. spurge							S		S				S
Ocotillo										S,B,W	S,B,W		S,B,W
Blazing star		S	S			S		S	S		S		S
St. John's wort				S									
Prickly poppy				S									
Poppy							S		S				
Oligomeris											S		S
Stinkweed						S							
Mustard family		S	S				S		S				
Tansy/tumble mustard		S	S				S		S				
Peppergrass							S		S		S		S

Plant										
Cheno-ams		S		S	S	S	S	S	S	S
Catchfly	S	S				S	S		S	S
Redmaids									S	S
Calyptridium									S	S
Sea purslane		S		S						S
Cactus family							O			
Barrel cactus								S	S	S
Prickly pear/cholla				S,F	S,F	S,F	S,F	S,F	S,F,O	S,F,O
Cholla				F	F	F	O	S,F,O	S,F,O	S,F,O
Wild buckwheat	S	S		S		S	S			
Willow dock	S									S
Dock/knotweed		S								
Dock	S	S								
Saltbush				S	S	S	S		S,W	S,W
Greasewood	W	W	S							
Goosefoot	S	S		S	S	S	S	S	S	S
Sea-blite									S	
Pigweed	S	S	S	S	S	S	S		S	S
Boerhaavia									S	S
Four o'clock									S	S
Wild hemp	F	F	F	F	F	F	F			
Milkweed									S	S
Dodder									S	S
Phacelia								S		
Fiddleneck									S	S
Cryptantha					S	S	S			S
Desert tomato	S	S		S		S	S			S
Tobacco										
Nightshade							S		S	S

Continued on next page

Table 7.6c *continued*

	Great Basin			Desert									
				Mojave						Sonoran			
Time Period	M	L/H	All	E	M	M/L	L	L/H	All	E	L	H	All
Number of Sites	5	12	23	1	4	1	8	2	18	1	5	5	15
Common Name													
Desert willow							W		W				
Chuparosa											F		F
Vervain							S		S				
Mint family												W	
Wild mint										S			S
Sage	S	S	S			S				S	S	W	S
Chamise					W				W		S		S
Desert apricot								S	S	N	N		N
Bitterbrush		S,W	S,W										
Wild rose		S	S										
Legume family						S			S		S	S	S
Catclaw					W				W		S		S
Locoweed		S	S				S		S				
Bird's foot trefoil		S	S										
Lupine											S		S
Ironwood							W		W				
Mesquite							S	W	S,W		S,F,O,W	W	S,F,O,W
Medick, alfalfa											S	S	S
Clover			S										
Oak family		N	N										N
Cottonwood		W	W	N					N,W	N	N,W		N

Continued on next page

Plant								
Willow	W	W	W	W	W			
Evening primrose family	S	S						
Creosote bush						S,O	S	S
Crucillo								S
Jojoba			W	W	S,O	S,O	S,O	S,O
Turpentine broom				W				
Squaw bush			W	W				
Water hemlock		S		S				
Silktassel bush		S			S,B	S,B		S,B
Bedstraw					S	S		S
Elderberry		W	W	W	S	S		S
Squash (D)					S	S		S
Squash/gourd					S,O	S,O		S,O
Bottle gourd				S	O	O		O
Composite family	W	W		S	S		S	S
Bursage	S		S	S			S	
Sagebrush	S,W	S,W		S	W		S	
Sweet bush	W	W		W	S			
Sticky-leaved rabbitbrush	W	W		S				
Rabbitbrush	W	W						
Bugseed				S	S			
Brittlebush				S	S	F	S	S
Desert sunflower				S	S			F
Sunflower	S	S	S	S				
H. tarweed				S				
Lasthenia	S	S		S			S	S
MONOCOTS								
Ditchgrass	S					O		O
Fan palm						O		O

336

Table 7.6c *continued*

		Desert									Sonoran			
	Great Basin			Mojave						Sonoran				
Common Name	M	L/H	All	E	M	M/L	L	L/H	All	E	L	H	All
Time Period / Number of Sites	5	12	23	1	4	1	8	2	18	1	5	5	15
Agave										S, F, O	S, F, O		S, F, O
Beargrass											O		O
Yucca			F		F		R, F		R, F		F		F
Cattail		S	S			S		S	S				
Wild onion		S	S										
Blue dicks		R	R										
Rush		S	S				S, F	S	S, F		S		S
Sedge family							S						
Sedge		R	R	S					S				
Nutgrass		S	S				S		S				
Tule		S	S			S	S, F	S	S, F		S		S
Grass family	S	S, F	S, F			S	S, F	S	S		S	S	S
Wild oat												S	
Six-week grama					S								
Brome grass											S		S
Crypsis							S		S				
Barnyard grass		S	S								S		S

Taxon							
Wildrye	S	S					S
Love grass	S	S					
Fescue	S	S	S	F		S	S
Galleta grass	S	S	F				
Foxtail barley	S	S					
Little barley	S	S					
Wild barley	S	S				S	S
Muhly grass			F	F			
Deer grass			F	F			
Ricegrass	S		S	S			
Panic grass			S			S	S
Maygrass/canarygrass						F	F
Reed	S	S,F	F			F	F
Poa	S	S	S			S	S
Sacaton	S	S	S	S	S	S	S
Needlegrass	S	S	S,F	S		F	F
Wheat (D)	S	S	S,F	F		S	S
Maize (D)	S	S	S			S	S

Note: D = domesticated; S = seed, N = nutshell/nutmeat pit, B = berry/fruit, R = root/rhizome/bulb/corm/tuber, W = wood, F = fiber/stem, O = other /scales/spines/anthers/leaves/ rind/peduncle/quid, E = Early period, M = Middle period, L = Late period, H = Historic period, E/M, M/L, L/H = transition periods.

Whether or not Wohlgemuth's (1996a) data confirm the economic importance of acorns in the Sacramento Delta, our current data indicate that even within the Central Valley, acorns were part of a quite mixed economy, similar to the economies of coastal subregions. Important resources included nuts (acorns, California bay, buckeye, and wild cucumber), manzanita berries, and small seeds: cheno-ams (especially redmaids), fiddleneck, clover and other legumes, composites (sunflower and tarweed), farewell-to-spring, and grasses (brome, hairgrass, maygrass, and fescue). Bulbs and corms included brodiaea and lilies (probably mariposa lilies).

The western slopes of the Sierra Nevada yielded a less diverse set of resources. Pine nuts and manzanita berries were important resources, as were the seeds of sage, composites, and, apparently to a lesser extent, cheno-ams, mustards, clover, sedge, and various grasses. Relatively few sites from the Sierra Nevada have yielded archaeobotanical remains. Based on what we know of the ethnography, it is unlikely that high-altitude sites were occupied year round. The most likely resources would have been harvested in the lower-altitude foothills; the two key resources were pine nuts and manzanita berries.

Along the eastern edge of California, including the eastern slopes of the Sierra Nevada and portions of the Great Basin and Mojave Deserts, piñon seeds were exploited; discussion of their harvesting and relative dietary importance has occupied much publication space (e.g., Bettinger 1976, 1977; Garfinkel and Cook 1980; McGuire and Garfinkel 1976). As with the acorn issue, much of this discussion concerns camps and tools that probably were associated with piñon harvesting or processing, and few sites have been sampled for paleoethnobotanical data. The earliest recovered direct evidence of piñon use (cone scales from a roasting feature) in eastern California is approximately 1,155 years old. This corresponds closely to Bettinger's earlier estimates based on nonplant archaeological data (Garfinkel and Cook 1980: 285). Interpretations of the relative importance of piñon, and of its changing importance through time, must await more systematic recovery of plant remains from a variety of contexts.

From the data available in the northern and central desert areas, a rough picture of diet is emerging that looks, on the surface, remarkably like that recorded by Julian Steward (1933, 1938). It includes a very wide variety of small-seeded grasses and annual dicots (including goosefoot, pigweed, wild buckwheat, sage, tansy mustard, and ricegrass), supplemented by bulblike foods (including sedges and wild onions) and occasional fruits and seeds from larger shrubs and trees (including juniper, wild rose, bursage, and sagebrush). Toward the southern end of this region, in the Mojave Desert, cactus and mesquite were quite important, also in keeping with the ethnographic record of nearby Nevada (Warren 1994); in contrast, the absence of prehistoric agave and yucca fruits or seeds is surprising, given their importance in Chemehuevi ethnobotany (Lawlor 1995a).

Still further south, the Sonoran Desert pattern is roughly similar, though based on different endemic plants. Most of the recovered seeds represent grasses and annual dicots, but, compared with the deserts to the north, there are more cactus parts, mesquite seeds and pods, and seeds of other shrubs and trees (e.g., ironwood, desert apricot, and fan palm). This region's coprolite record (Farrell 1988; Swope 1988; Wilke 1978), unique in California, provides details not seen elsewhere, such as cattail anthers and chewed seeds of the winter-ripening bugseed, a taxon missing from the ethnobotanical record (Wilke et al. 1979). Also unique to the desert is the presence of gourds, and almost all of the evidence for maize is from the desert (see below).

Summary

Several plant taxa have been recovered from sites throughout California: nutshells of pine nuts and acorns and the small seeds of pigweed, goosefoot, mustards, nightshade, legumes, clover, composites, sedges, and grasses. In all subregions but the deserts, manzanita berries have been found. Elderberries have been found throughout with the exception of the Sierra Nevada subregion. Important small-seed crops in much of California included sage, grasses, composites, phacelia, and fiddlenecks.

Some key economic plants were unique to California. Unique southern California plant foods were sage seeds, yucca, which was widely used, and, in the deserts, palm dates. Along the coast of California islay, sage, and redmaids seeds were harvested. In the central and northern parts of California, especially more inland areas, pine nuts were a key crop, whereas hazelnuts were concentrated in the San Francisco Bay Area. California is unlike other regions where Chenopodiaceae, Amaranthaceae, and Polygonaceae are the most common representatives in the small black seed complex known taxonomically as the Centrospermae (called "cheno-ams" by paleoethnobotanists). In California, the most common members of the cheno-ams are actually members of the purslane family: redmaids, miner's lettuce, and spring beauty. Redmaids are extolled in the California ethnobotanical literature as an im-

Paleoethnobotany in California

portant plant food resource (Chestnut 1974; Timbrook et al. 1982). Based on the recovery of the seeds in human burials, it is safe to conclude they had a significant symbolic value as well.

Plants and Cultural Symbols

California Indian people generally felt a shared existence with and responsibility for plants and animals (Heizer 1978:650); each plant and animal had a soul or spirit (with varying amounts of power) without which nature would not be complete. Plants figured in mythologies and in personal and place names; clearly many plants had symbolic associations.

Plants were less symbolically important, however, than animals, both in ritual and mythology (Bean 1976). There were few taboos associated with gathering, no "first gathering" ceremonies for girls, no prophetic dreams of plant harvests, no totemic plants or any shaman's familiars named for plants, and few personified plants in myths (e.g., Washo [Downs 1966:22]; Chemehuevis [Laird 1976]). Nevertheless, a number of individual plants had particular symbolic significance in California, as shown by their unusual prominence in rituals, prayers, offerings, and myths. Very few of these plants have been recovered from archaeological contexts to date; the only such contexts have been graves along the coast and a dry cave in the Mojave Desert. We discuss these first and then consider other possible symbolic uses of plants that remain to be teased from the prehistoric record.

Plant offerings most commonly recovered from burials include tobacco and redmaids. Tobacco was one of the most important symbolic plants in California. Its psychoactive qualities contributed to its use in mediating communication between people and nonhuman manifestations of power (Bean 1976). Tobacco, smoked or drunk (e.g., Yokuts [Gayton 1976]), was considered so powerful that one spoke to it respectfully during gathering and processing. Recently, tobacco leaves, seeds, and pollen have been recovered from clay and stone pipes in burial contexts at two prehistoric cemeteries in the San Francisco Bay Area, CA-SCL-38 (S. Smith, personal communication 1996) and CA-SCL-732 (Hammett 1997).

Redmaids (*Calandrinia* sp.) have been found with human burials at sites on islands in the Santa Barbara Channel, such as Santa Rosa Island (Timbrook 1986), and inland Chumash sites such as Medea Creek (CA-LAN-243) (King 1982) and CA-LAN- 840 (Wheeler et al. 1989), from at least two burial contexts from Santa Barbara County (Timbrook 1986), and in Northern California from a Wintun burial in Glenn County (Table 7.4). The recovery of hundreds of redmaids seeds from archaeological deposits is a testament to the high lignin content in the seed coats, which preserves the seeds for hundreds of years. It is tempting to infer that their durability may have afforded redmaids seeds a role as an important food for the long journey to the afterworld, but no ethnography specifically documents their use for this purpose. Harrington recorded redmaids seeds as an offering and as a food (Timbrook et al. 1982). The Chumash name for redmaids, *khutash*, was the same as that for Mother Earth (Hudson et al. 1977; Timbrook et al. 1982).

Thus far, the best evidence for plant offerings in burial contexts is derived from two inland Chumash sites, Medea Creek and CA-LAN-840. At Medea Creek, a late prehistoric/protohistoric cemetery, charred and uncharred plant remains were recovered from stone mortars interred with human burials (King 1982). In all, redmaids seeds were associated with eight burials, and acorns were found with 20 burials. Based on the size and shape, the acorns appeared to be from valley oak (*Quercus lobata*). In addition, fragments of seed cakes, containing a variety of seeds, including sage, were recovered from burial contexts (King 1982). Site CA-LAN-840 consisted of the cremations of eight individuals (including two men, two women, and two children), dating to the Middle period. Directly associated with the cremations were concentrations of charred seeds, including redmaids, sage, mustards, plantain, blazing star, tarweed, composites, manzanita, islay, cactus, clover, and grasses. Based on the clumped nature of the recovered seeds, it is likely that they composed seed cakes (Wheeler et al. 1989).

Although some of the plants may merely represent the range of plant foods available for burial offerings, some foods were probably considered more valuable than others. For example, J. P. Harrington observed that when Maria Ignacia (one of his Chumash consultants) lay dying, she wanted to eat clover, perhaps craving the comfort of a food from her childhood (Timbrook et al. 1982). Harrington also noted that *Prunus ilicifolia* was called "islay" by both the Penutian-speaking Costanoan people of central coastal California (Bocek 1984) and by the Hokan-speaking Chumash of the Santa Barbara region on the Southern Coast (Timbrook et al. 1982). Islay has been recovered from burials in both of these cultural areas (Hammett 1996a; Wheeler et al. 1989). According to Harrington's notes on Chumash ethnobotany, two basketry hatfuls of islay were worth three of acorns (Timbrook 1982). The nutmeats may be interpreted as food offerings, perhaps for an afterlife, but the discovery of redmaids seeds, often unburned in burial offerings, is intriguing.

The only other California plant remains with certain symbolic significance are split-twig figurines from Newberry Cave, a Middle period site near Barstow in the Mojave Desert. Eleven nearly whole figurines and over 900 figurine fragments were recovered. All were made of slender willow branches and dated from 840 ± 250 to 1815 ± 100 BC (Davis et al. 1981). The figurines depict quadrupedal animals and were recovered in association with crystals, sinew-wrapped feathers, and sinew-wrapped sheep dung. These items, which indicate magicoreligious hunting activities, attest to the early cultural affinity of the Mojave with the southern Great Basin, where split-twig figurines are more common (Davis and Smith 1981:56–71).

In addition to the plants recovered from graves and from Newberry Cave, it is likely that other symbolically significant plants are awaiting recovery from California archaeological sites. Many probably will be identified in the archaeological record only through creative syntheses of historical, ethnographical, and archaeobotanical evidence. The psychoactive plant jimsonweed (*Datura*), for example, was drunk during coming-of-age ceremonies (e.g., southern subregion [Strong 1972]) and, like tobacco, was addressed respectfully during gathering and processing (e.g., Chemehuevi [Kelly 1934:86; Laird 1976:39–40]). Thus far, no archaeobotanical evidence for jimsonweed has been recovered.

Other plants were symbolically significant because of their role in subsistence, including oaks/acorns throughout much of California (Bean and Saubel 1972; Chestnut 1974; Ortiz 1991) and yucca in the south (Harrington 1981; Laird 1976; Lawlor 1995a). In the Central Valley, colorful blooms of early spring wildflowers were a harbinger of hope for many groups, flowering at the hungriest time of the year and forecasting plentiful seed crops. Men and women picked flowers, sang songs, and made and wore flower crowns in celebration (Gayton 1976). Shared meals (usually the same type of stew or porridge, eaten twice a day) symbolized the social ties of kinship, courtship, and other aspects of community (e.g., Chemehuevi [Lawlor 1995a]). Food also mediated supplication or appeasement of the spirit world (e.g., Chemehuevi [Kelly 1934:154]).

Still other plants that were not inherently symbolic became so because of their uses in religious and other ceremonial contexts. For example, the Luiseño used matting made of a fern (*Woodwardia*) and/or *Juncus* to wrap sacred ceremonial bundles, and they buried or burned a "tule" matting figurine, dressed to represent a deceased person, on the anniversary of that person's death (Strong 1972). Among the Washo, a long, straight elderberry wand, painted red, would be hidden in an upright position to ensure that a girl coming of age would remain straight and strong (Downs 1966). The Mountain Cahuilla used stinging nettles to brush off stinging ants in the adolescent male coming-of-age ceremony (Strong 1972).

To summarize, symbolic uses of plants varied locally across California. So far, such use is better known from the ethnographic record than from prehistoric contexts. The same is true of the current evidence for the manipulation of significant symbolic, food, and other economic plants in Native California.

Evidence for Plant Manipulation

The question of plant manipulation by Native Californians takes two forms. Early research in the state was inspired by work conducted in the neighboring Southwest region, where a corn/beans/squash agricultural complex has been studied extensively. Ethnohistories clearly document a corn/bean/squash agricultural complex in the Death Valley (Fowler 1995; Wallace 1980) and elsewhere in the Mojave (Kelly 1934) and Sonoran Deserts (Lawton and Bean 1972). But was agriculture introduced to California from the Southwest historically or in prehistoric times? Few relevant collections exist; these are either of uncertain age (gourds [Wilke et al. 1977]) or determination (maize [Altschul et al. 1989]). Most members of the crop complex of the North American Southwest have been recovered from the deserts, and maize kernels and common beans have been recovered from a Chumash historic house hearth at Talepop, CA-LAN-299, in the Southern Coast subregion (Hammett 1991). Cultivated wheat and barley were also recovered from the historic Talepop hearth. Maize, wheat, and barley were also found at the historic rancheria of Petaluma (CA-SON-2294/H) on the Central Coast; however, no beans or squash remains were recovered (Silliman 2000). These two coastal sites hint at the possibility that Spaniards imported maize (and beans in the case of Talepop) in their northern coastal expansion. Taken together, these data provide two possible avenues for the introduction of cultigens, at least one during historic times.

Perhaps the more robust question is the degree to which groups of Native Californians practiced various forms of indigenous plant management and manipulation. For example, ethnohistorical data document that Owens Valley Paiutes cultivated blue dicks (*Dichelostemma pulchellum*) and nutgrass (*Cyperus* sp.) in irrigated fields tilled with digging sticks. Their fields were allowed to lie fallow periodically, a system that requires substantial communal labor and that parallels complex farming systems in Southeast Asia and South America (Lawton et al. 1976). Once again, relevant archaeological data are scant, but remains of seven riparian plants reported by Steward (1933) or Lawton et al. (1976) as having been grown in irrigated plots have been recovered from two sites at Fish Springs, an area within the known distribution of Owens Valley Paiute irrigation ditches (Miksicek 1993c). It also has been suggested that the goosefoot seeds from these sites were somewhat larger than goosefoot seeds from sites outside the possibly irrigated area (Miksicek 1993c:A4-18), a suggestion that should be investigated further.

Besides irrigation, prescribed burning has been documented as an important tool for rejuvenating the landscape, from the date palm areas of the deserts to the woodlands of Northern California. Many economically important small-seed plants of California grasslands respond to periodic burning with increased seed production (Hammett 1991; Shipek 1989; Timbrook et al. 1982). In addition, most of the nut- and berry-producing crops of California are stump-sprouters or have other fire-tolerant adaptations (Hammett 1991).

Methods for ascertaining the degree of human intervention within a habitat are evaluations of resource productivity, spatial distributions of plants, and seed morphology. One "resource management" model developed for the Chumash region of southern coastal California (Hammett 1991) uses multidisciplinary data from plant ecology, fire ecology, and ethnobotany. This model predicts possible management regimes and establishes a method for evaluating archaeobotanical data. In outline, frequencies of taxa recovered from archaeological sites are evaluated according to two pairs of criteria: fire-follower/non-fire-follower species and economic/noneconomic taxa. The model assumes that deposits with high frequencies of economic *and* fire-follower species are indicative of an anthropogenic landscape managed by prescribed burning, whereas high frequencies of fire-follower taxa with low economic values will result from nonhumanly set fires, and low frequencies of fire-followers in assemblages with high economic value will lead to rejection of the prescribed burning hypothesis. So far, our best evidence for possible anthropogenic landscapes is from the sand dunes and grasslands of the Southern Coast just north of Santa Barbara (Hammett 1991). Ethnographic data document prescribed burning in that locality (Timbrook et al. 1982). Sites south of Santa Barbara have thus far failed to yield good evidence for prescribed burning (Klug and Popper 1996a, 1996b, 1996c).

One intriguing line of inquiry that several researchers are pursuing focuses on morphological changes and is based on the repeated observation that redmaids seeds from burial contexts appear significantly larger than seeds from modern living stands. Whether the enlarged size is due to a prescribed burning regimen or other cultural selection pressures (i.e., size sorting for burial offerings?), this intriguing ethnobotanical conundrum merits further attention. Redmaids is known to be a fire-follower (Hammett 1991; Timbrook et al. 1982).

Little unequivocal archaeobotanical evidence exists for plant domestication or the use of domesticated plants in Native California. Researchers at the Archaeological Institute at UCLA, however, have collected provocative data indicating the possible use of little barley (*Hordeum pusillum*) and at least one species of maygrass (*Phalaris* sp.) on the Southern Coast (Klug and Popper 1996b, 1998). Previous research at other coastal sites has generated evidence for the use of these two genera (Hammett 1991), but only small quantities of these seeds had been recovered until the more recent UCLA studies. This research is ongoing.

Evidence for arboriculture is more difficult to evaluate because of the longevity of many trees (and some shrubs) relative to that of humans. Nevertheless, two species of important economic plants, the Catalina cherry (*Prunus lyonii*) and a type of native walnut (*Juglans hindsii*), bear fruits (nuts) that are substantially larger than their closest cousins, *Prunus ilicifolia* and *Juglans californica*. *Prunus lyonii* is restricted to several islands (Santa Catalina, San Clemente, Santa Cruz, and Santa Rosa) off the coast of Santa Barbara (Munz and Keck 1968:791), whereas early botanists noted that *Juglans hindsii* tended to grow near old Indian village sites in central California (Jepson 1910:194, 1923:164–165). Neither of these enlarged nut taxa has been identified from archaeobotanical collections, although their fragments would look quite similar to closely related taxa.

Cultivation of bulb, corm, and tuber-producing plants of the lily and amaryllis families is evident from the historic and ethnographic record, although it is all but invisible from the standpoint of the archaeobotanical record. K. Anderson's (1993) doctoral research investigated traditional practices of harvesting, cultivating, and managing Native California crops, particularly in the western Sierra Nevada foothills, through ethnohistory, ethnography, and field experiments. Anderson (1993:153) found that the traditional style of harvesting bulb and corm crops with digging sticks, carefully leaving bulblets, cormlets, or tuber fragments behind, served to ensure future harvests. A similar conservative harvest strategy was employed for the collection of mushrooms and the rhizomes of bracken fern (*Pteridium aquilinum*) and sedge (*Carex* spp.). Similarly, Anderson's informants repeatedly noted that extraction of limbs of various woody shrubs (i.e., willow, ceanothus, and sumac) served to generate future generations of straight shoots.

Julia E. Hammett and Elizabeth J. Lawlor

Only two domesticated nonfood plants were cultivated in California: tobacco and devil's claw (a basketry plant discussed below). Tobacco is the more notable, because it probably was domesticated in California. Two types of tobacco, *Nicotiana quadrivalvis* var. *quadrivalvis* and *N. quadrivalvis* var. *multivalvis*, now apparently extinct, were probably domesticated in northwestern California from a native wild species, *N. quadrivalvis* var. *bigelovii* (Hammett 2000). The species is named for the four-valved capsule associated with *N. quadrivalvis*. var. *quadrivalvis*, which was first collected by Euro-American explorer Meriwether Lewis in 1804 on the Missouri River. The evidence indicates that both cultigens originated from the closely related wild species, which is limited in range to California. Additional specimens of *N. quadrivalvis* var. *quadrivalvis* were collected among the Karok, Yurok, and Hupa tribes of northwestern California in the 1890s. The closely related *N. quadrivalvis* var. *multivalvis*, with a thick seed capsule of five or more chambers, averaging about an inch in diameter, was collected at the turn of the 20th century along river drainages from the southern Oregon border to the Columbia River, and also possibly in the Queen Charlotte Islands off the coast of British Columbia (Hammett 2000). The most detailed description of the management, cultivation, and use of native tobacco among northwestern California groups was published in both English and Karuk (Karok) by J. P. Harrington (1932). Harrington's consultants selected isolated places, typically uphill from the river drainages (where tobacco grew wild) to plant their plots of tobacco. In these "secret" places, old tree stumps were burned, and in their ashes tobacco seeds were planted (Harrington 1932).

The other domesticated nonfood plant found in California was devil's claw (*Proboscidea parviflora* ssp. *parviflora* var. *Hohokamiana*), an important source of black fibers for basketry. Domesticated devil's claw was grown by at least three California Shoshone groups in historic times. Apparently this cultigen, distinguished from wild devil's claw (var. *parviflora*) by its white seeds and disproportionately long, thin "claws," was domesticated in southern Arizona (Bretting and Nabhan 1986). No archaeological evidence of cultivation of either tobacco or devil's claw has yet been identified in California. This is yet another research topic worthy of attention.

Conclusions

The strategies by which Native Californians ensured their economic wellbeing were almost as diversified as their environments. Native Californians relied on a wide range of plant and animal resources from marine, riverine, and terrestrial landscapes. Reliance on important nut crops, including acorns and pine nuts, along with islay, hazelnuts, and California bay in certain subregions, was accompanied by use of a wide range of small-seed crops, including grasses, composites, sage, and cheno-ams, among others. In addition, the berries of manzanita, sumacs, toyon, and elderberry were added to sage and other seeds in the preparation of beverages or were ground and cooked in seed cakes (Hammett 1991; Timbrook et al. 1982). In the southern regions yucca was a dietary component. Throughout California, bulbs, corms, and tubers made an important contribution to the plant portion of the native diet. Together, a mixed set of strategies and resources ensured a livelihood for one of the most diverse and heavily populated regions of Native North America. Significant numbers of economic plant taxa that are distinctive to California subregions have been recovered from chronological contexts spanning the Early period through the first contacts with Euro-Americans. Sites from the northern, central, and southern subregions with multiple dated contexts provide clear evidence that a sedentary way of life was ensured in part by exploiting a wide range of plant resources. These data, combined with the large variety of marine and terrestrial fauna available in the region, point to relatively stable economies throughout much of the California region for thousands of years.

Recommendations for the Future

Several steps should be taken to advance California paleoethnobotany to a status comparable with other regions of North America. First, the California State Research Plan should be updated to rectify its profound inadequacy from the standpoint of paleoethnobotany. Archaeobotanical sampling with ample sample sizes (e.g., 10 to 15 liters in the desert [Reddy 1999b]) should be considered in every data recovery plan recommending excavation. Second, archaeology students in California should be exposed to basic paleoethnobotanical sampling and analytical procedures beginning at the undergraduate level. Third, research concerned with California subsistence should challenge status quo assertions and assumptions that are not based on direct evidence from archaeobotany or historically documented plant use.

Further research is necessary to establish criteria for readily distinguishing among members of certain taxonomic groups, including acorns, grasses, composites, legumes, and bulbs and corms. Finally, refinement of our understanding of temporal variation must await further research and additional data sets with confirmed chronological assignments. This means systematically pairing archaeobotanical samples with radiocarbon-dated samples, and then providing the dates in the plant reports.

Notes

1. We use the past tense because many aspects of these cultures are no longer practiced and our focus is prehistoric, but we emphasize that many California Indian groups have rebounded in population from near genocide. Today many Native Californians retain and are revitalizing identities, attitudes, spiritual beliefs, and many customs characteristic of their traditional cultures throughout the state.

Acknowledgments

We thank the following people for comments and guidance: Karen Adams, Barbara Bocek, Carole Crumley, Scott L. Fedick, Gayle J. Fritz, Matthew C. Hall, Andrea Hunter, Laura Jones, Chester D. King, Lisa Panet Klug, Charles Miksicek, C. Jill Minar, Virginia Popper, Christine Prior, Seetha Reddy, Andrew C. Sanders, Mark Q. Sutton, Philip J. Wilke, Bruce Winterhalder, Joseph C. Winter, Richard Yarnell, and the volume reviewers. Several people graciously provided access to their data, including Lisa Huckell, Lisa P. Klug, Seetha Reddy, Virginia Popper, and Steven Silliman. Eric Wohlgemuth was especially helpful in providing data and background information for the Northern, Delta, Central Coast, and Sierra Nevada subregions. John Varnon helped compile data and format the final draft of this chapter. For funding of this research, we thank the American Association of University Women, Association for Field Archaeology, Muwekma Ohlone Tribe, University of California Natural Reserve System, University of California at Riverside, Stanford Campus Archaeology Program, University of North Carolina, and Wenner-Gren Foundation for Anthropological Research. We are grateful for institutional support from Mount San Antonio College, Santa Monica College, and Truckee Meadows Community College. Finally, we thank Paul Minnis for the opportunity to contribute to this volume.

References Cited

Altschul, Jeffrey H., William C. Johnson, and R. E. Brooks
　　1990　Paleobotanical Analyses. In *Prehistoric Adaptation to a Desert Spring Environment: Archaeological Investigations of Surprise Spring, San Bernardino County, California*, edited by Jeffrey H. Altschul, pp. 97–100. Technical Series 27. Statistical Research, Tucson.

Altschul, Jeffrey H., William C. Johnson, and Matthew A. Sterner
   1989   *The Deep Creek Site (CA-SBR-176): A Late Prehistoric Base Camp in the Mojave River Forks
           Region, San Bernardino County, California.* Technical Series 22. Statistical Research, Tucson.
Anderson, M. Kat
   1993   Native Californians as Ancient and Contemporary Cultivators. In *Before the Wilderness:
           Environmental Management by Native Californians,* edited by Thomas C. Blackburn and
           M. Kat Anderson, pp. 151–174. Ballena Press, Menlo Park, California.
Arkush, Brooke S.
   1995   *The Archaeology of CA-MNO-2122: A Study of Pre-Contact and Post-Contact Lifeways among
           the Mono Basin Paiute.* Anthropological Records 31. University of California, Berkeley.
Aschmann, Homer
   1959   The Evolution of a Wild Landscape and Its Persistence in Southern California. *Annals of
           American Geographers* 49(3)34–56. (Part 2 Supplement: Man, Time, and Space in South-
           ern California.)
Barbour, Michael G., Jack H. Burk, and Wanna D. Pitts
   1980   *Terrestrial Plant Ecology.* Benjamin Cummings, Menlo Park, California.
Barrett, Samuel A., and Edward W. Gifford
   1933   *Miwok Material Culture: Indian Life of the Yosemite Region.* Bulletin of the Public Museum
           of the City of Milwaukee 2(4).
Barrows, David P.
   1900   *The Ethno-Botany of the Coahuilla Indians of Southern California.* University of Chicago
           Press, Chicago.
Basgall, Mark E.
   1987   Resource Intensification among Hunter-Gatherers: Acorn Economies in Prehistoric
           California. In *Research in Economic Anthropology, a Research Annual,* vol. 9, edited by
           Barry L. Isaac, pp. 21–52. JAI Press, Greenwich, Connecticut.
Basgall, Mark E., and Kelly R. McGuire (editors)
   1988   *The Archaeology of CA-INY-30: Prehistoric Culture Change in the Southern Owens Valley, Cali-
           fornia.* Far Western Anthropological Research Group, Davis, California.
Basgall, Mark E., and Eric Wohlgemuth
   1988   Paleobotanical Remains. In *The Archaeology of CA-INY-30: Prehistoric Culture Change in
           the Southern Owens Valley, California,* edited by Mark E. Basgall and Kelly R. McGuire,
           pp. 304–324. Far Western Anthropological Research Group, Davis, California.
Baumhoff, Martin A.
   1963   Ecological Determinants of Aboriginal California Populations. *University of California
           Publications in American Archaeology and Ethnology* 49(2):155–235.
   1978   Environmental Background. In *California,* edited by Robert F. Heizer, pp. 16–24. Hand-
           book of North American Indians, vol. 8, William C. Sturtevant, general editor. Smith-
           sonian Institution, Washington, DC.
Bean, Lowell J.
   1961   The Ethnobotanical Report Sheet: A Field Technique. *University of California Archaeologi-
           cal Survey Annual Report,* pp. 233–236. Department of Anthropology and Sociology, Uni-
           versity of California, Los Angeles.
   1974   Social Organization in Native California. In *Antap: California Indian Political and Economic
           Organization,* edited by Lowell J. Bean and Thomas F. King, pp. 11–34. Ballena Press,
           Ramona, California.
   1976   Power and Its Applications in Native California. In *Native Californians: A Theoretical Ret-*

rospective, edited by Lowell J. Bean and Thomas C. Blackburn, pp. 407–420. Ballena Press, Menlo Park, California.

1978   Social Organization. In *California*, edited by Robert F. Heizer, pp. 673–682. Handbook of North American Indians, vol. 8, William C. Sturtevant, general editor. Smithsonian Institution, Washington, DC.

Bean, Lowell J., and Thomas C. Blackburn (editors)

1976   *Native Californians: A Theoretical Retrospective*. Ballena Press, Menlo Park, California.

Bean, Lowell J., and Harry W. Lawton

1993   Some Explanations for the Rise of Cultural Complexity in Native California with Comments on Proto-Agriculture and Agriculture. In *Before the Wilderness: Environmental Management by Native Californians*, edited by Thomas C. Blackburn and M. Kat Anderson, pp. 27–54. Reprinted. Ballena Press, Menlo Park, California. Originally published 1973, Ballena Press Anthropological Papers 1, Ballena Press, Socorro, New Mexico.

Bean, Lowell J., and Katherine S. Saubel

1972   *Temalpakh: Cahuilla Indian Knowledge and Usage of Plants*. Malki Museum Press, Banning, California.

Bennyhoff, James A., and Richard E. Hughes

1987   Shell Bead and Ornament Exchange Networks between California and the Western Great Basin. *Anthropological Papers of the American Museum of Natural History* 64(2):1–175.

Bergin, Kathleen Ann, and D. D. Ferraro

1987   *Interim Analysis Report: Data Recovery of Bow Willow Wash South*. Research Fort Irwin Archaeological Project Report 20. Coyote Press, Salinas, California.

Bettinger, Robert L.

1976   The Development of Pinyon Exploitation in Central Eastern California. *Journal of California Anthropology* 3(1):81–95.

1977   Reply to McGuire and Garfinkel. *Journal of California Anthropology* 4(1):130–132.

Bocek, Barbara

1984   Ethnobotany of Costanoan Indians, California, Based on Collections by John P. Harrington. *Economic Botany* 38:240–255.

1986   Rodent Ecology and Burrowing Behavior: Predicted Effects on Archaeological Site Formation. *American Antiquity* 51:589–603.

1987   *Hunter-Gatherer Ecology and Settlement Mobility along San Francisquito Creek*. Unpublished PhD dissertation, Department of Anthropology, Stanford University, Stanford.

1992   The Jasper Ridge Reexcavation: Rates of Artifact Mixing by Rodents. *American Antiquity* 57:261–268.

Bocek, Barbara, and E. Reese

1992   *Land Use History of Jasper Ridge Biological Preserve*. Jasper Ridge Biological Preserve Research Report 8. Stanford University, Stanford.

Bouey, Paul D.

1987   The Intensification of Hunter-Gatherer Economies in the Southern North Coast Ranges of California. In *Research in Economic Anthropology, Research Annual*, vol. 9, edited by Barry L. Isaac, pp. 53–104. JAI Press, Greenwich, Connecticut.

Bretting, P. K., and G. P. Nabhan

1986   Ethnobotany of Devil's Claw (*Proboscidea parviflora* spp. *parviflora*: Martyniaceae) in the Greater Southwest. *Journal of California and Great Basin Anthropology* 8:226–237.

Brown, Timothy

1999   Development of a Southern California Weather Severity Index. Final report submitted to the Fire Hazard Reduction Training and Certification Program, Federal Emergency

Management Agency grant 5CA616000. Manuscript on file, University of California Forest Products Laboratory, Berkeley.

Burcham, Levi T.
1957   *California Range Land: An Historico-Ecological Study of the Range Resources of California.* Division of Forestry, State of California Department of Natural Resources, Sacramento.

Burson, E.
1998   *Taxa Diversity and Prehistoric Foraging along the San Francisquito Watershed, California.* Unpublished master's thesis, Department of Anthropology, Stanford University, Stanford.

Burton, J. F.
1985   The Archaeology of the Chance Well Site, Mono County, CA. CA-MNO-458/630. The Mammoth Geothermal Project 4. Copies available from the Eastern Information Center, Department of Anthropology, University of California, Riverside.

Byrne, Roger
1979   Commentary on "Archaeology and California's Climate." *Journal of California and Great Basin Anthropology* 1:196–198.

Cambra, Rosemary, Alan Leventhal, Laura Jones, Julia Hammett, Les Field, Norma Sanchez, and Robert Jurmain
1996   *Archaeological Investigations at Kaphan Umux, CA-SCL-732, a Prehistoric Cemetery on Coyote Creek in South San Jose, California.* Ohlone Families Consulting Services and San Jose State University, San Jose.

Campbell, Elizabeth W. Crozier
1931   *An Archeological Survey of the Twenty Nine Palms Region.* Southwest Museum Papers 7. Los Angeles.

Campbell, Elizabeth W. Crozier, and William H. Campbell
1935   *The Pinto Basin Site: An Ancient Aboriginal Camping Ground in the California Desert.* Southwest Museum Papers 9. Los Angeles.
1937   The Lake Mohave Site. In *The Archeology of Pleistocene Lake Mohave, a Symposium,* edited by Elizabeth W. C. Campbell, and William H. Campbell, pp. 9–44. Southwest Museum Papers 11. Los Angeles.

Castillo, Edward D.
1978   The Impact of Euro-American Exploration and Settlement. In *California,* edited by Robert F. Heizer, pp. 99–127. Handbook of North American Indians, vol. 8, William C. Sturtevant, general editor. Smithsonian Institution, Washington, DC.

Chartkoff, Joseph L., and Kerry Kona Chartkoff
1984   *The Archaeology of California.* Stanford University Press, Stanford.

Chestnut, V. K.
1974   *Plants Used by the Indians of Mendocino County, California.* Reprinted. Mendocino County Historical Society, Ukiah. Originally published 1902, Contributions from the US National Herbarium 7(3):295–408.

Cook, Sherburne F.
1976   *The Population of California Indians 1769–1970.* University of California Press, Berkeley.

Cowan, R. A., and K. Wallof
1974   Final Report: Field Work and Artifact Analysis: Southern California Edison No. 2 Control-Casa Diablo 115 kv Transmission Line. Copies available from the Eastern Information Center, Department of Anthropology, University of California, Riverside.

Davis, C. Alan, and Gerald A. Smith
1981   *Newberry Cave.* San Bernardino County Museum Association, Redlands, California.

Davis, C. Alan, R. E. Taylor, and Gerald A. Smith
  1981   New Radiocarbon Determinations from Newberry Cave. *Journal of California and Great Basin Anthropology* 3:144–147.
Davis, Owen K., and Charles Miksicek
  1988   Macrofossil Analysis of CA-FRE-1671. In *Archaeological Excavations at Site CA-FRE-1671, Fresno County, California: Final Report*, edited by Michael J. Moratto, pp. 593–603. Infotec, Sonora, California.
  1989   Plants. In *Redbank and Fancher Creeks Archeological Data Recovery Program CA-FRE-632, -633, -154, -1155, Fresno County, California*, edited by P. Langenwalter, A. Schroth, P. de Barros, and F. Fenenga, pp. 238–261. MITECH, Santa Ana, California.
Delacorte, Michael G.
  1984   Flotation Analysis. In Archaeological Investigations at the Partridge Ranch Site, Inyo County (CA-INY-2146), edited by Robert L. Bettinger, Michael G. Delacorte, and Kelly R. McGuire, pp. 147–151. Copies available from the Eastern Information Center, Department of Anthropology, University of California, Riverside.
  1999   The Changing Role of Riverine Environments in the Prehistory of the Central-Western Great Basin: Data Recovery Excavations at Six Prehistoric Sites in Owens Valley, California. Copies available from the Eastern Information Center, Department of Anthropology, University of California, Riverside.
Delacorte, Michael G., M. C. Hall, and Mark E. Basgall
  1995   Final Report on the Evaluation of Twelve Archaeological Sites in the Southern Owens Valley, Inyo County, California. Copies available from the Eastern Information Center, Department of Anthropology, University of California, Riverside.
Delacorte, Michael G., and Kelly R. McGuire
  1993   Report of Archaeological Test Evaluations at Twenty-Three Sites in Owens Valley, California. Copies available from the Eastern Information Center, Department of Anthropology, University of California, Riverside.
Downs, James F.
  1966   *The Two Worlds of the Washo.* Holt, Rinehart and Winston, New York.
Drover, C. E.
  1979   *The Late Prehistoric Human Ecology of the Northern Mohave Sink, San Bernardino County, California.* Unpublished PhD dissertation, Department of Anthropology, University of California, Riverside.
Echlin, Donald R., Philip J. Wilke, and Lawrence E. Dawson
  1981   Ord Shelter. *Journal of California and Great Basin Anthropology* 3:49–68.
Elston, R. G., S. M. Seck, and S. James
  1981   An Intensive Archaeological Investigation of Two Proposed Drilling Locations in the Coso Known Geothermal Resource Area, China Lake Naval Weapons Center. Copies available from the Eastern Information Center, Department of Anthropology, University of California, Riverside.
Erlandson, Jon M.
  1984   A Case Study in Faunalturbation: Delineating the Effects of the Burrowing Pocket Gopher on the Distribution of Archaeological Materials. *American Antiquity* 49:785–790.
Farrell, N.
  1988   Analysis of Human Coprolites from CA-RIV-1179 and CA-RIV-2827. In *Archaeological Investigations at CA-RIV-1179, CA-RIV-2823, and CA-RIV-2827, La Quinta, Riverside County, California*, edited by Mark Q. Sutton and Philip J. Wilke, pp. 129–142. Archives of California Prehistory 20. Coyote Press, Salinas, California.

Ford, Richard I.
1985 The Processes of Plant Food Production in Prehistoric North America. In *Prehistoric Food Production in North America*, edited by Richard I. Ford, pp. 1–18. Anthropological Papers 75. Museum of Anthropology, University of Michigan, Ann Arbor.

Fowler, Catherine S.
1995 Some Notes on Ethnographic Subsistence Systems in Mojavean Environments in the Great Basin. *Journal of Ethnobiology* 15:99–117.

Gage, T. B.
1979 The Competitive Interaction of Man and Deer in Prehistoric California. *Human Ecology* 7(3):253–268.

Gamble, Lynn, Natalie Anakaouchine, Douglas B. Bamforth, Carole Denardo, Brian K. Glenn, John R. Johnson, Chester King, Thomas Rockwell, and Phillip L. Walker
1990 *Archaeological Investigations at Helo on Mescalitan Island*. Department of Anthropology, University of California, Santa Barbara.

Gardner, M., L. McCoy, and S. Brown
1974 Floral Remains. In *Perris Reservoir Archeology: Late Prehistoric Demographic Change in Southeastern California*, edited by J. F. O'Connell, Philip J. Wilke, Thomas F. King, and C. L. Mix, pp. 153–158. Archeological Report 14. California Department of Parks and Recreation, Sacramento.

Garfinkel, Alan P., and Roger A. Cook
1980 Radiocarbon Dating of Pinyon Nut Exploitation in Eastern California. *Journal of California and Great Basin Anthropology* 2:283–286.

Gayton, A. H.
1976 Culture-Environment Integration: External References in Yokuts Life. In *Native Californians: A Theoretical Retrospective*, edited by Lowell J. Bean and Thomas C. Blackburn, pp. 79–97. Ballena Press, Menlo Park, California.

Gifford, Edward W.
1971 California Balanophagy. In *The California Indians, a Source Book*, 2nd ed., edited by Robert F. Heizer and Mary Anne A. Whipple, pp. 301–305. Reprinted. University of California Press, Berkeley. Originally published 1936, *Essays in Honor of A. L. Kroeber*, edited by Robert Lowie, pp. 87–98, University of California Press, Berkeley.

Gilreath, Amy J., and William R. Hildebrandt
1995 Prehistoric Use of the Coso Volcanic Field. Copies available from the Eastern Information Center, Department of Anthropology, University of California, Riverside.

Gilreath, Amy J., and Kim L. Holanda
2000 *By the Lake by the Mountains: Archaeological Investigations at CA-INY-4554 and INY-1428*. Far Western Anthropological Research Group, Davis, California.

Glassow, Michael A.
1992 The Relative Dietary Importance of Marine Foods Through Time in Western Santa Barbara County. In *Essays on the Prehistory of Maritime California*, edited by Terry L. Jones, pp. 115–128. Publication 10. Center for Archaeological Research, University of California, Davis.

Goddard, Pliny E.
1903–04 Life and Culture of the Hupa. *University of California Publications in American Archaeology and Ethnology* 1(1):1–88.

Grayson, Donald K.
1993 *The Desert's Past: A Natural Prehistory of the Great Basin*. Smithsonian Institution Press, Washington, DC.

Julia E. Hammett and Elizabeth J. Lawlor

Hammett, Julia E.

    1989   Analysis of Plant Remains from CA-SBA-1816. In Technical Draft Report Transmittal STS and SLC-4 and Security Fence Treatment Programs Draft Report, edited by C. King, pp. 10-1–10-37. Submitted to Martin Marietta Corporation. Copies available from the South Central Coastal Information Center, California State University, Fullerton.

    1991   *The Ecology of Sedentary Societies without Agriculture: Paleoethnobotanical Indicators from Native California.* Unpublished PhD dissertation, Department of Anthropology, University of North Carolina, Chapel Hill.

    1996a   Paleoethnobotany of Site CA-SCL-732. In *Archaeological Investigations at Kaphan Umux, CA-SCL-732, a Prehistoric Cemetery on Coyote Creek in Southern San Jose, Santa Clara County, California*, edited by Rosemary Cambra, Alan Leventhal, Laura Jones, Julia Hammett, Les Field, Norma Sanchez, and Richard Jurmain, pp. 8.1–8.15. Ohlone Families Consulting Services and San Jose State University, San Jose.

    1996b   Paleoethnobotany of the Stanford Golf Course Sites: CA-SCL-623, CA-SCL-287 and CA-SMA-263. Submitted to Campus Archaeology Program, Stanford University Planning Office, Stanford. Copies available from the Northwest Information Center, Sonoma State University, Rohnert Park, California.

    1997   Paleoethnobotany and Cultural Ecology. In *Report of Archaeological Findings at CA-SCL-613, Children's Health Council Santa Clara County, California*, prepared by Laura Jones, pp. 112–133. Stanford University Campus Archaeology Program, Stanford.

    2000   Out of California: Cultural Geography of Western North American Tobacco. In *Tobacco Use by Native North Americans*, edited by Joseph C. Winter, pp. 128–140. University of Oklahoma Press, Norman.

Hammett, Julia E., and Eric Wohlgemuth

    1982   Charred Plant Remains from Talepop. In *Archaeological Investigations at Talepop, (CA-LAN-229)*, edited by C. King, pp. 9.1–9.95. Office of Public Archaeology, University of California, Santa Barbara.

Hanes, Ted L.

    1971   Succession of Fire in the Chaparral of Southern California. *Ecological Monographs* 41(1):27–52.

Harrington, John P.

    1917   Studies among the Indians of California. *Miscellaneous Collections* 68(12):92–95. Smithsonian Institution, Washington, DC.

    1932   Tobacco among the Karuk Indians of California. *Bulletin* 94:1–284. Bureau of American Ethnology, Smithsonian Institution, Washington, DC.

    1981   John P. Harrington Papers: 3. Southern California/Basin. Chemehuevi Field Notes, on file, National Anthropological Archives, Smithsonian Institution, Washington, DC. Microfilm edition, Kraus International Publications, Millwood, New York.

Harrington, Mark R.

    1957   *A Pinto Site at Little Lake, California.* Southwest Museum Papers 17. Los Angeles.

Hart, K. C., Bruce A. Stein, and Sheridan F. Warrick

    1979   Vegetation and Flora. In *Granite Mountains Resource Survey*, edited by Bruce A. Stein and Sheridan F. Warrick, pp. 59–107. Environmental Field Program Publication 1. University of California, Santa Cruz.

Heizer, Robert F.

    1974   *The Destruction of California Indians.* Peregrine-Smith, Santa Barbara.

    1978   Natural Forces and Native World View. In *California*, edited by Robert F. Heizer, pp. 649–653. Handbook of North American Indians, vol. 8. William C. Sturtevant, general editor. Smithsonian Institution, Washington, DC.

Heizer, Robert F., and Albert B. Elsasser

1980   *The Natural World of the California Indians.* University of California Press, Berkeley.

Hemphill, M. L.

1987   Organic Remains. In Recommendations Regarding the National Register Eligibility of Eight Cultural Resources Sites on a Proposed Electrical Interconnection Route, Inyo and Mono Counties, California: US Bureau of Land Management Lands, edited by M. C. Hall, pp. 40, 85, 139, and 163. Copies available from the Eastern Information Center, Department of Anthropology, University of California, Riverside.

Hill, Mary

1984   *California Landscape: Origin and Evolution.* University of California Press, Berkeley.

Hildebrandt, William (editor)

1983   *Final Report, Archaeological Research of the Southern Santa Clara Valley Project.* Far Western Anthropological Research Group, Davis, California.

Hildebrandt, William, and Deborah A. Jones

1998   *Archaeological Investigations at CA-MNT-1892: A Late Period Occupation Site at the Mouth of Limekiln Creek, Monterey County, California,* edited by William Hildebrandt and Deborah A. Jones, pp. 27–31. Far Western Anthropological Research Group, Davis, California.

Hildebrandt, William, and P. Mikkelsen

1993   *Archaeological Test Excavations at Fourteen Sites along Highways 101 and 152, Santa Clara and San Benito Counties, California,* vol. 1 and 2. Far Western Anthropological Research Group, Davis, California.

Honeysett, Elizabeth H.

1986   Seed Remains from Prehistoric and Historic Sites in the Dutch Gulch/Cottonwood Creek Project Area, Shasta County, California. Report on file, Foundation of California State University, Sacramento.

1987   Macrobotanical Remains Recovered from Archaeological Investigations at Lake Britton, Shasta County, California. In *Archaeological Investigations at Lake Britton, California: Pit 3, 4, 5, Project (License No. 233) Archaeological Site Testing,* by Michael S. Kelly, Elena Nilsson, and James H. Cleland, Appendix H. WIRTH Environmental Services, San Diego.

Huckell, Lisa W.

1981   Botanical Remains. In *Archaeology in Yosemite National Park: The Wawona Testing Project,* edited by J. C. Whittaker, pp. 130–153. Publications in Archaeology 18. Western Archaeological and Conservation Center, National Park Service, Tucson.

1982   Plant Remains from the 1981 El Portal Archeological Project. In *Archaeological Investigations in the Central Sierra Nevada: The 1981 El Portal Archaeological Project,* edited by M. R. Baumler and S. L. Carpenter, Appendix H. Western Archaeological and Conservation Center, National Park Service, Tucson.

1984a Botanical Remains from the 1983 and 1984 Wawona Archeological Projects. In *Test Excavations in the Wawona Valley: Report of the 1983 and 1984 Wawona Archaeological Projects, Yosemite National Park, California,* edited by R. G. Ervin, Appendix 3. Publications in Anthropology 26. Western Archaeological and Conservation Center, National Park Service, Tucson.

1984b Botanical Remains. In *The Timba-Sha Survey and Boundary Fencing Project: Archaeological Investigations at Death Valley National Monument,* edited by M. D. Tag, Appendix B. Publications in Anthropology 27. Western Archaeological and Conservation Center, National Park Service, Tucson.

1985   Archaeobotanical Remains from 4-RIV-1961, Joshua Tree National Monument, California. In *Survey and Excavations in Joshua Tree National Monument: Report of the 1985 Joshua Tree Road Improvements Project,* edited by R. G. Ervin, Appendix 3. Publications in An-

Julia E. Hammett and Elizabeth J. Lawlor

thropology 32. Western Archaeology and Conservation Center, National Park Service, Tucson.

Hudson, Travis, Thomas C. Blackburn, R. Curletti, and Janice Timbrook
    1977   *The Eye of the Flute: Chumash Traditional History and Ritual as Told by Fernando Librado Kitsepawit to John P. Harrington*. Santa Barbara Museum of Natural History, Santa Barbara.

Jackson, Robert H.
    1987   Patterns of Demographic Change in the Missions of Central Alta California. *Journal of California and Great Basin Anthropology* 9:251–272.

Jepson, Willis Linn
    1910   *The Silva of California*. Memoirs 2. University of California, Berkeley.
    1923   *The Trees of California*. 2nd ed. Sather Gate, Berkeley.

Johnson, K. L., and L. S. Skjelstad
    1974   The Salvage Archaeology of Site 4-SHA-177, Whiskeytown Recreation Area, Shasta County, California. Manuscript on file, National Park Service, San Francisco, and Northeast Information Center, Department of Anthropology, California State University, Chico.

Jones, Laura
    1995   Summary of Testing at CA-SCL-287, CA-SCL-586, and CA-SMA-263, Proposed Site for Widening of Sand Hill Road at the Bridge Over San Francisquito Creek, Stanford, California. Manuscript on file, Campus Archaeology Program, Planning Office, Stanford University, Stanford.

Jones, Laura, Julia Hammett, and Elizabeth Burson
    1998   Diet, Diversity and Development in Central California: The 3-D Approach to Evaluating Prehistoric Resource Intensification. Paper presented at the 63rd Annual Meeting of the Society for American Archaeology, Seattle.

Kelly, Isabel T.
    1934   Chemehuevi Field Notes: General Ethnological Information. Manuscript on file, Archives Microfilm CU 23.1, No. 138.1. Anthropology Document 17. University of California, Berkeley.

Kelly, Isabel T., and Catherine S. Fowler
    1986   Southern Paiute. In *Great Basin*, edited by Warren L. d'Azevedo, pp. 368–397. Handbook of North American Indians, vol. 11, William C. Sturtevant, general editor. Smithsonian Institution, Washington, DC.

King, Chester D.
    1971   Chumash Inter-Village Economic Exchange. *Indian Historian* 4(1):31–43.
    1990   *Evolution of Chumash Society*. Garland Press, New York.
    1993   Fuel Use and Resource Management: Implications for the Study of Land Management in Prehistoric California and Recommendations for a Research Program. In *Before the Wilderness: Environmental Management by Native Californians*, edited by Thomas C. Blackburn and M. Kat Anderson, pp. 279–298. Ballena Press, Menlo Park, California.

King, Chester D., W. Bloomer, E. Clinger, B. Edberg, L. Gamble, Julia Hammett, J. Johnson, T. Kemperman, Christopher Pierce, and Eric Wohlgemuth
    1982   *Archaeological Investigations at Talepop (LAN-229)*, 3 vols. Office of Public Archaeology, Social Process Research Institute, University of California, Santa Barbara.

King, L. E.
    1903   Some of the Medicinal and Edible Plants of Southern California. *Historical Society of Southern California* 5:237–240.

King, Linda B.
    1982   *Medea Creek Cemetery: Late Inland Chumash Patterns of Social Organization, Exchange and*

Warfare. Unpublished PhD dissertation, Department of Anthropology, University of California, Los Angeles.

King, T. J., Jr.

1976 A Cache of Vessels from Cottonwood Spring (Riv-937). *Journal of California Anthropology* 3(1):136–142.

Klug, Lisa P., and Virginia S. Popper

1995 *Macrobotanical Analysis of Column Samples from CA-SCL-12, Santa Clara County, California*. Paleoethnobotany Laboratory, Cotsen Institute of Archaeology, University of California, Los Angeles.

1996a *Macrobotanical Analysis of Soil and Charcoal Samples from Seven Sites from the San Gabriel Mountains, Los Angeles County, California*. Paleoethnobotany Lab, Cotsen Institute of Archaeology, University of California, Los Angeles.

1996b *Macrobotanical Analysis of Soil Samples from CA-ORA-225, Orange County, California*. Paleoethnobotany Laboratory, Cotsen Institute of Archaeology, University of California, Los Angeles.

1996c *Macrobotanical Analysis of Three Rockshelters: CA-ORA-689, CA-ORA-736, CA-ORA-1029, Orange County, California*. Paleoethnobotany Lab, Cotsen Institute of Archaeology, University of California, Los Angeles.

1996d *Macrobotanical Analysis of Nine Soil Samples from San Clemente Island, California*. Paleoethnobotany Lab, Cotsen Institute of Archaeology, University of California, Los Angeles.

1997 *Macrobotanical Analysis of Four Soil Samples from Site KEA-6, Imperial County, California*. Paleoethnobotany Lab, Cotsen Institute of Archaeology, University of California, Los Angeles.

1998 Prehistoric Subsistence Adaptation in Coastal Orange County, California. Paper presented at the 63rd Annual Meeting of the Society for American Archaeology, Seattle.

Kroeber, Alfred L.

1925 *Handbook of the Indians of California*. Bulletin 78. Bureau of American Ethnology, Smithsonian Institution, Washington, DC.

1962 *The Nature of Land-Holding Groups in Aboriginal California. Two Papers on the Aboriginal Ethnography of California*. Archaeological Survey 56:19–58. Department of Anthropology, University of California, Berkeley.

Kuchler, A. W.

1985 Potential Natural Vegetation. In *National Atlas of the United States of America*. Department of the Interior, US Geological Survey, Reston, Virginia.

Laird, Carobeth

1976 *The Chemehuevis*. Malki Museum Press, Banning, California.

Lawlor, Elizabeth J.

1995a *Archaeological Site-Formation Processes Affecting Plant Remains in the Mojave Desert*. PhD dissertation, Department of Anthropology, University of California, Riverside. University Microfilms, Ann Arbor.

1995b Floral Remains. In *The Archaeology of CA-MNO-2122: A Study of Pre-Contact and Post-Contact Lifeways among the Mono Basin Paiute*, edited by Brooke S. Arkush, pp. 71–73. Anthropological Records 31. University of California, Berkeley.

Lawton, Harry W., and Lowell J. Bean

1972 Preliminary Reconstruction of Aboriginal Agricultural Technology among the Cahuilla. Reprinted in *Temalpakh: Cahuilla Indian Knowledge and Usage of Plants*, edited by Lowell J. Bean and Katherine S. Saubel, pp. 197–210. Malki Museum Press, Banning, California. Originally published 1968, *The Indian Historian* 1(5):18–24.

Paleoethnobotany in California

357

Lawton, Harry W., Philip J. Wilke, Mary DeDecker, and W. M. Mason
    1976   Agriculture among the Paiute of Owens Valley. *Journal of California Anthropology* 3(1):13–50.
Lennström, Heidi A., and Christine A. Hastorf
    1992   Testing Old Wives' Tales in Paleoethnobotany: A Comparison of Bulk and Scatter
            Sampling Schemes from Pancán, Peru. *Journal of Archaeological Science* 19:205–229.
Lewis, Henry T.
    1972   The Role of Fire in the Domestication of Plants and Animals in Southwest Asia: A Hy-
            pothesis. *Man* 7:195–222.
    1993   Patterns of Indian Burning in California: Ecology and Ethnohistory. In *Before the*
            Wilderness: Environmental Management by Native Californians, edited by Thomas C.
            Blackburn and M. Kat Anderson, pp. 55–116. Reprinted. Ballena Press, Menlo Park,
            California. Originally published 1973, Anthropological Papers 1, Ballena Press, Socorro,
            New Mexico.
Lyneis, Margaret M., M. K. Rusco, and K. Myhrer
    1989   *Investigations at Adam 2 (26-CK-2059), a Mesa House Phase Site in Moapa Valley, NV.*
            Anthropological Papers 22. Nevada State Museum, Carson City.
Malouf, Carling I., and John Findlay
    1986   Euro-American Impact before 1870. In *Great Basin*, edited by Warren L. d'Azevedo,
            pp. 499–516. Handbook of North American Indians, vol. 11, William C. Sturtevant, gen-
            eral editor. Smithsonian Institution, Washington, DC.
Martin, S., and Virginia S. Popper
    1997   *Macrobotanical Analysis of Soil Samples and Excavation Specimens from Ca-Riv-4754, Riverside*
            County, California. Paleoethnobotany Lab, Cotsen Institute of Archaeology, University of
            California, Los Angeles.
    1998   *Macrobotanical Analysis of Soil Samples from Ca-Riv-6059, La Quinta, California*. Paleoethno-
            botany Lab, Cotsen Institute of Archaeology, University of California, Los Angeles.
McCarthy, D. F., and Philip J. Wilke
    1979   Plant Remains Recovered by Flotation and Screening. In *Archaeological Studies at Oro*
            Grande, Mojave Desert, California, edited by C. H. Rector, J. D. Swenson, and Philip J.
            Wilke, pp. 98–108. San Bernardino County Museum Association, Redlands, California.
McCutchen, M. H.
    1977   Climatic Features as Determinants of Fire Frequency and Intensity. In *Proceedings of the*
            Symposium on the Environmental Consequences of Fire and Fuel Management in Mediterranean
            Ecosystems, edited by Harold A. Mooney and C. E. Conrad, pp. 1–11. General Technical
            Report WO-3. USDA Forest Service, Washington, DC.
McDonald, Alison Meg
    1992   *Indian Hill Rockshelter and Aboriginal Cultural Adaptation in Anza-Borrego Desert State Park,*
            Southeastern California. PhD dissertation, Department of Anthropology, University of
            California, Riverside. University Microfilms, Ann Arbor.
McGuire, Kelly R.
    2000   *Archaeological Investigations along the California-Great Basin Interface: The Alturas Transmis-*
            sion Line Project: 2. Prehistoric Archaeological Studies: The Pit River Uplands, Madeline Plains,
            Honey Lake and Secret Valley, and Sierran Front Project Segments: Site Reports and Data Ap-
            pendices. Far Western Anthropological Research Group, Davis, California.
McGuire, Kelly R., and Alan P. Garfinkel
    1976   Comment on "The Development of Pinyon Exploitation in Central Eastern California."
            Journal of California Anthropology 3(2):83–85.
Mehringer, Peter J., Jr.
    1986   Prehistoric Environments. In *Great Basin*, edited by Warren L. d'Azevedo, pp. 31–50.

Handbook of North American Indians, vol. 11, William C. Sturtevant, general editor. Smithsonian Institution, Washington, DC.

Mehringer, Peter J., Jr., and Peter E. Wigand

1990 Comparisons of Late Holocene Environments from Woodrat Middens and Pollen: Diamond Craters, Oregon. In *Packrat Middens: The Last 40,000 Years of Biotic Change*, edited by Julio L. Betancourt, Thomas R. Van Devender, and Paul S. Martin, pp. 294–325. University of Arizona Press, Tucson.

Merriam, C. H.

1894 Laws of Temperature Control of the Geographic Distribution of Animals and Plants. *National Geographic* 6:229–238.

1898 Life Zones and Crop Zones of the United States. *US Department of Agriculture Biological Survey Division Bulletin* 10:9–79.

1918 The Acorn, a Possibly Neglected Source of Food. *National Geographic* 34(2):129–137.

Miksicek, Charles

1990 Charred Plant Remains from Sites in the San Joaquin Hills Transportation Corridor. In *Final Test Investigation Report and Request for Determination of Eligibility for 23 Sites along the San Joaquin Hills Transportation Corridors*, edited by P. de Barros and H. C. Koerper, Appendix H. Chambers Group, Santa Ana, California.

1992 *Plant Remains from CA-MNT 1485/H and 1486/H: A Pilot Study*. BioSystems Analysis, Santa Cruz.

1993a Archaeobotanical Results. In *Final Report, Archaeological Resources Evaluation at CA-MNO-891, CA-MNO-2678, and CA-MNO-2679, Mono County, California*, edited by B. Wickstrom and R. Jackson. BioSystems Analysis, Santa Cruz.

1993b Archaeobotanical Remains. In *Archaeological Data Potential Assessment at CA-MNT-515, CA-MNT-540, CA-MNT-567, and CA-MNT-862, Ft. Hunter Liggett Military Installation, California*, edited by B. Wickstrom and T. L. Jackson, pp. 2-14–2-17, 3-13–3-50. BioSystems Analysis, Santa Cruz.

1993c Plant Remains from Sites in the Fish Springs Area. In Archaeological Resources Evaluation at *CA-INY-384, CA-INY-3790, CA-INY-4547, CA-INY-4549/H, and CA-INY-4550, Inyo County, California*, vol. 1, edited by B. Wickstrom, R. Jackson, and T. L. Jackson, Appendix A. Copies available from the Eastern Information Center, Department of Anthropology, University of California, Riverside.

n.d.a Plant Remains from Wilder Ranch (CA-SCR-123). BioSystems Analysis, Santa Cruz. Copies available from the Northwest Information Center, Sonoma State University, Rohnert Park, California.

n.d.b Charred Botanical Remains from FS 05-16-54-19/106, Anderson Valley, Stanislaus National Forest, California. BioSystems Analysis, Santa Cruz. Copies available from the Northwest Information Center, Sonoma State University, Rohnert Park, California.

Milliken, R. T., and James A. Bennyhoff

1993 Temporal Changes in Beads as Prehistoric California Grave Goods. In *There Grows a Green Tree: Papers in Honor of David A. Fredrickson*, edited by G. White, P. Mikkelsen, William Hildebrandt, and Mark E. Basgall, pp. 381–396. Center for Archaeological Research at Davis Publication 11. University of California, Davis.

Milliken, R., and William R. Hildebrandt

1997 *Culture Change along the Eastern Sierra Nevada/Cascade Front: 5. Honey Lake Basin*. Far Western Anthropological Research Group, Davis, California.

Milliken, R., and J. Meyer

1997 *Fire Damage Archaeological Mitigation at CA-FRE-2365, 38-40*. Far Western Anthropological Research Group, Davis, California.

Minnich, Richard D.
  1983   Fire Mosaics in Southern California and Northern Baja California. *Science* 219:1287–1294.
Moratto, Michael J.
  1984   *California Archaeology*. Academic Press, New York.
Moratto, Michael J., Thomas F. King, and Wallace B. Woolfenden
  2002   Archaeology and California's Climate. *Journal of California Anthropology* 5(2):147–162.
Munz, Philip A., and David D. Keck
  1968   *A California Flora, with Supplement*. University of California Press, Berkeley.
Ortiz, Bev
  1991   *It Will Live Forever*. Heyday Books, Berkeley.
Osborne, Carolyn M., and Harry S. Riddell Jr.
  1978   Cache of Deer Snares from Owens Valley, California. *Journal of California Anthropology* 5(1):101–109.
Osborne, Richard H.
  1993   The Archaeological Collection from Ludlow Cave, South-Central Mojave Desert, California. *Journal of California and Great Basin Anthropology* 15:225–234.
Pearsall, Deborah M.
  1989   *Paleoethnobotany: A Handbook of Procedures*. Academic Press, San Diego.
Pierce, Christopher
  1992   Effects of Pocket Gopher Burrowing on Archaeological Deposits: A Simulation Approach. *Geoarchaeology* 7:185–208.
Pinto, Diana G.
  1985   *The Archaeology of Mitchell Caverns*. Unpublished master's thesis, Department of Anthropology, University of California, Riverside.
Phillips, George Harwood
  1975   *Chiefs and Challengers: Indian Resistance and Cooperation in Southern California*. University of California Press, Berkeley.
Popper, Virginia S., and S. Martin
  2000   *Macrobotanical Analysis of Soil Samples from Site CA-SDI-945, San Diego County, California*. Paleoethnobotany Lab, Cotsen Institute of Archaeology, University of California, Los Angeles.
Powers, Stephen
  1976   *Tribes of California*. Reprinted University of California Press, Berkeley. Originally published 1877, *Contributions to North American Ethnology*, vol. 3, US Geographical and Geological Survey of the Rocky Mountain Regions, US Department of the Interior, Washington, DC.
Rector, C. H.
  1983   Field Procedure, Site Structure, and Dating. In *Archaeological Studies at Oro Grande, Mojave Desert, California*, edited by C. H. Rector, J. D. Swenson, and Philip J. Wilke, pp. 20–31. San Bernardino County Museum Association, Redlands, California.
Reddy, Seetha N.
  1996a Paleoethnobotanical Investigations at Las Flores Creek and Horno Canyon, Camp Pendleton. In *Coastal Archaeology of Las Flores Creek and Horno Canyon, Camp Pendleton, California*, edited by Brian F. Byrd, pp. 275–304. ASM Affiliates, Encinitas and Pasadena.
  1996b Paleoethnobotany and Macrobotanical Remains from KER-490 and KER-2378 on Edwards Air Force Base. In *Camping in the Dunes: Archaeological and Geomorphological Investigations of Late Holocene Settlements West of Rogers Dry Lake*, edited by Brian F. Byrd, pp. 233–244. ASM Affiliates, Encinitas and Pasadena.

1997a Macrobotanical Remains and Paleoeconomy at Case Spring. In *Camping and Milling in the Highlands: Archaeological Investigation of Case Spring and Firebreak Sites on Camp Pendleton, San Diego County, California*, edited by Seetha N. Reddy, pp. 215–234. ASM Affiliates, Encinitas and Pasadena.

1997b Macrobotanical Remains and Shell Midden Paleoethnobotany. In *Coastal Archaeology at CA-SDI-10,728, Las Flores Creek, Camp Pendleton, California*, edited by Brian F. Byrd, pp. 117–136. ASM Affiliates, Encinitas and Pasadena.

1999a Macrobotanical Remains from SDI-10,700, SDI-10,705 and SDI-14,567. In *Testing and Evaluation of 14 Archaeological Sites in India LFAM on Camp Pendleton, San Diego County, California*, edited by Brian F. Byrd, pp. 101–112. ASM Affiliates, Encinitas and Pasadena.

1999b Plants, Human Behavior and Archaeological Features: Paleoethnobotany at the Elmore Site. In *Pit and Mortuary Features at a Protohistoric Lake Cahuilla Temporary Camp: Results of Supplementary Phase III Data Recovery at the Elmore Site (CA-IMP-6427)*, edited by Jerry Schaefer, Appendix A. ASM Affiliates, Encinitas and Pasadena.

2000a Paleoethnobotanical Investigations at the Late Holocene Highlands Sites on Camp Pendleton. In *Settling the Highlands: Late Holocene Highland Adaptations on Camp Pendleton, San Diego County, Southern California*, edited by Seetha N. Reddy, pp. 301–319. ASM Affiliates, Encinitas and Pasadena.

2000b Paleoethnobotany on San Clemente Island: Plant Remains from SCLI-154, LVTA-9 and LVTA/SE 46. In *Archaeological Testing of Four Sites near West Cove, Northern San Clemente Island, California*, edited by Brian F. Byrd, pp. 69–79. ASM Affiliates, Encinitas and Pasadena.

2000c Paleoethnobotanical Study of Carbonized Plant Remains from SCLI-1239, SCLI-1249 and PL-100. In *Archaeological Testing of Three Sites along the LVT Road, North-Central San Clemente Island, California*, edited by Brian F. Byrd, pp. 107–120. ASM Affiliates, Encinitas and Pasadena.

2000d Plants Remains and Rock Features: Paleoethnobotany at CA-IMP-7750. In *Archaeological Investigations at a Protohistoric Fish Camp on the Receding Shoreline of Ancient Lake Cahuilla, Imperial County, California*, edited by Jerry Schaefer, pp. 49–61. ASM Affiliates, Encinitas and Pasadena.

2000e Plant Usage and Bedrock Milling: Paleoethnobotanical Investigations at SDI-14,649. In *Data Recovery at SDI-14,649, Case Springs Area, Camp Pendleton*, edited by Dale Cheever and Russ Collett. RECON Technical Report. RECON Environmental, San Diego.

Rindos, David
1984 *The Origins of Agriculture*. Academic Press, New York.

Ritter, Eric W., and Gary B. Coombs
1990 Southern California Desert Archaeology: Settlement-Subsistence Studies. *Pacific Coast Archaeological Society Quarterly* 26(1):24–41.

Rowlands, Peter G.
1978 *The Vegetation Dynamics of the Joshua Tree* (Yucca brevifolia *Engelm) in the Southwestern United States of America*. Unpublished PhD dissertation, Department of Botany and Plant Sciences, University of California, Riverside.

Schneider, J. S.
1989 *The Archaeology of the Afton Canyon Site*. San Bernardino County Museum Association Quarterly 36(1).

Schroth, Adella B.
1994 *The Pinto Point Controversy in the Western United States*. PhD dissertation, Department of Anthropology, University of California, Riverside. University Microfilms, Ann Arbor.

Julia E. Hammett and Elizabeth J. Lawlor

Schwederer, Rae
    1992   Archaeological Test Excavations at the Duncans Point Cave, CA-SON-384/H. In *Essays on the Prehistory of Maritime California*, edited by Terry L. Jones, pp. 55–71. Publication 10. Center for Archaeological Research, Davis, California.

Serguis, L. A.
    1952   Forecasting the Weather: The Santa Ana. *Weatherwise* 5:66–68.

Shipek, Florence C.
    1989   An Example of Intensive Plant Husbandry: The Kumeyaay of Southern California. In *Foraging and Farming: The Evolution of Plant Exploitation*, edited by David R. Harris and Gordon C. Hillman, pp. 159–170. Unwin Hyman, London.

Shipley, William F.
    1978   Native Languages of California. In *California*, edited by Robert F. Heizer, pp. 80–90. Handbook of North American Indians, vol. 8, William C. Sturtevant, general editor. Smithsonian Institution, Washington, DC.

Silliman, Steven W.
    2000   *Colonial Worlds, Indigenous Practices: The Archaeology of Labor on a 19th-Century California Rancho*. Unpublished PhD dissertation, Department of Anthropology, University of California, Berkeley.

Smith, Susan
    1996   Results from Initial Scans of Eleven Pollen Samples from CA-SCL-38. Table on file, Paleoecology Laboratory, Northern Arizona University, Flagstaff.

Spaulding, W. G.
    1991   A Middle Holocene Vegetation Record from the Mojave Desert of North America and Its Paleoclimatic Significance. *Quaternary Research* 35:427–437.

Steward, Julian H.
    1933   Ethnography of the Owens Valley Paiute. *University of California Publications in American Archaeology and Ethnology* 33(3):233–350.
    1938   *Basin-Plateau Aboriginal Sociopolitical Groups*. Bulletin 120. Bureau of American Ethnology, Smithsonian Institution, Washington, DC.

Strong, William D.
    1972   *Aboriginal Society in Southern California*. Reprinted Malki Museum Press, Banning, California. Originally published 1929, Publications in American Archaeology and Ethnology 29. University of California, Berkeley.

Sturtevant, William C.
    1967   Early Indian Tribes, Culture Areas and Linguistic Stocks. In *National Atlas of the United States of America*, Department of the Interior, US Geological Survey, Reston, Virginia.

Sutton, Mark Q.
    1984   Archaeological Investigations at KER-733: A Special Purpose Site in the Antelope Valley. *Pacific Coast Archaeological Society Quarterly* 20(4):33–55.
    1988   *An Introduction to the Archaeology of the Western Mojave Desert, California*. Archives of California Prehistory 14. Coyote Press, Salinas, California.
    1991   *Archaeological Investigations at Cantil, Fremont Valley, Western Mojave Desert, California*. Occasional Papers in Anthropology 1. Museum of Anthropology, California State University, Bakersfield.
    1996   The Current Status of Archaeological Research in the Mojave Desert. *Journal of California and Great Basin Anthropology* 18:221–257.

Sutton, Mark Q., Christopher B. Donnan, and Dennis L. Jenkins
  1987   The Archaeology of Southcott Cave, Providence Mountains, California. *Journal of California and Great Basin Anthropology* 9:232–250.
Sutton, Mark Q., and Eric W. Ritter
  1984   A Basket Fragment from the Lava Mountains, San Bernardino County, California. *Journal of California and Great Basin Anthropology* 6:115–118.
Sutton, Mark Q., J. S. Schneider, and Robert M. Yohe II
  1993   *Archaeological Investigations at the Siphon Site (CA-SBR-6580): A Millingstone Horizon Site in Summit Valley, California.* San Bernardino County Museum Association Quarterly 40(3).
Sutton, Mark Q., and Robert M. Yohe II
  1988   Perishable Artifacts from Cave No. 5, Providence Mountains, California. *Journal of California and Great Basin Anthropology* 10:117–123.
Swope, K. K.
  1988   Plant Remains Recovered by Flotation from CA-RIV-1179. In *Archaeological Investigations at CA-RIV-1179, CA-RIV-2823, and CA-RIV-2827, La Quinta, Riverside County, California,* edited by Mark Q. Sutton and Philip J. Wilke, pp. 119–128. Archives of California Prehistory 20. Coyote Press, Salinas, California.
Taylor, T. T., D. L. Taylor, D. Alcorn, E. B. Weil, and M. Tambunga
  1987   Investigations Regarding Aboriginal Stone Mound Features in the Mojave Desert: Excavations at CA-SBR-221 and CA-SBR-3136, San Bernardino County, California. In *Papers on the Archaeology of the Mojave Desert,* edited by Mark Q. Sutton, pp. 79–114. Archives of California Prehistory 10. Coyote Press, Salinas, California.
Thompson, R. S.
  1990   Late Quaternary Vegetation and Climate in the Great Basin. In *Packrat Middens: The Last 40,000 Years of Biotic Change,* edited by Julio L. Betancourt, Thomas R. Van Devender, and Paul S. Martin, pp. 200–239. University of Arizona Press, Tucson.
  1992   Late Quaternary Environments in Ruby Valley, Nevada. *Quaternary Research* 37:1–15.
Timbrook, Jan
  1982   Use of Cherry Pits as Food by the California Indians. *Journal of Ethnobiology* 2:162–176.
  1986   Chia and the Chumash: A Reconsideration of Sage Seeds in Southern California. *Journal of California and Great Basin Anthropology* 8:50–64.
Timbrook, Jan, John R. Johnson, and David D. Earle
  1982   Vegetation Burning by the Chumash. *Journal of California and Great Basin Anthropology* 4:162–186.
Wade, S. A., and S. M. Hector
  1989   Archaeological Testing and National Register Evaluation of Site LAN-1316, Edwards Air Force Base, California. Manuscript on file, Archaeological Research Unit, Department of Anthropology, University of California, Riverside.
Wallace, William J.
  1978   Post-Pleistocene Aechaeology, 9000 to 2000 B.C. In *California,* edited by Robert F. Heizer, pp. 25–36. Handbook of North American Indians, vol. 8, William C. Sturtevant, general editor. Smithsonian Institution, Washington, DC.
  1980   Death Valley Indian Farming. *Journal of California and Great Basin Anthropology* 2:269–272.
Walter, Heinrich
  1979   *Vegetation of the Earth.* Springer-Verlag, New York.
Warren, Claude N.
  1991   Subsistence Focus and Cultural Change in the Central Mojave Desert. In *Archaeological*

Investigations at Nelson Wash, Fort Irwin, California, edited by Claude N. Warren, pp. 318–364. Fort Irwin Archaeological Project Research Reports 23. Coyote Press, Salinas, California.

1994 The Las Vegas Valley in Prehistory: Misconceptions and Truths. Paper presented at the Kelso Conference on the Prehistory of the Mojave and Colorado Deserts, Little Lake, California.

Wheeler, T. L., P. Walker, E. Honeysett, and W. Wusera

1989 Report and Analysis of Cremated Human Remains from CA-LAN-840. Manuscript on file, California Department of Parks and Recreation, Cultural Heritage Section, Resource Protection Divisions, Sacramento.

Wilke, Philip J.

1978 *Late Prehistoric Human Ecology at Lake Cahuilla, Coachaella Valley, California*. Archaeological Research Facility Contributions 38. University of California, Berkeley.

1983 Final Report: An Archaeological Assessment of Certain Sites on Lower Cottonwood Creek, Inyo County, California. UCRARU #704. Copies available from the Eastern Information Center, Department of Anthropology, University of California, Riverside.

Wilke, Philip J., Mary DeDecker, and Lawrence E. Dawson

1979 *Dicoria canescens* T & G., an Aboriginal Food Plant in the Arid West. *Journal of California and Great Basin Anthropology* 1:188–192.

Wilke, Philip J., and Douglas N. Fain

1974 An Archaeological Cucurbit from Coachella Valley. *California Journal of Anthropology* 1:110–113.

Wilke, Philip J., Thomas F. King, and S. Hammond

1975 Aboriginal Occupation at Tahquitz Canyon: Ethnohistory and Archaeology. In *The Cahuilla Indians of the Colorado Desert: Ethnohistory and Prehistory*, pp. 45–73. Anthropological Papers 3. Ballena Press, Ramona, California.

Wilke, Philip J., T. W. Whitaker, and Eugene Hattori

1977 Prehistoric Squash (*Cucurbita pepo* L.) from the Salton Basin. *Journal of California Anthropology* 4(1):55–59.

Wilkes, Charles

1845 *Narrative of the United States Exploring Expedition during the Years 1838, 1839, 1840, 1841, and 1842*. Lea and Blanchard, Philadelphia.

Winter, Joseph C., and Patrick F. Hogan

1986 Plant Husbandry in the Great Basin and Adjacent Northern Colorado Plateau. In *Anthropology of the Desert West: Essays in Honor of Jesse D. Jennings*, edited by C. J. Condie and Don D. Fowler, pp. 117–144. Anthropological Papers 110. University of Utah Press, Salt Lake City.

Wohlgemuth, Eric

1988 Archaeobotanical Analysis of Column Samples from CA-SHA-290 and CA-TEH-748, Cottonwood Creek Project, Shasta and Tehama Counties, California, Dutch Gulch Lake: Excavation at Six Prehistoric Sites. Copies available from the Northeast Information Center, Department of Anthropology, California State University, Chico.

1989 Floral Remains from CA-SHA-1588 and CA-SHA-1544. In Archaeological Investigations at Flat Creek, CA-SHA-1588, Shasta County, California, edited by M. Kowta and W. R. Dreyer, Appendix. Copies available from the Northeast Information Center, Department of Anthropology, California State University, Chico.

1990 Floral Remains from CA-SHA-222, Redding, California. In Archaeological Investigations at CA-SHA-222, the Ladd Site, Redding, Shasta County, California, edited by

T. Vaughan, Appendix. Copies available from the Northeast Information Center, Department of Anthropology, California State University, Chico.

1991a Charred Plant Remains from Two Ash Samples at SON-348. Submitted to California Department of Parks and Recreation, Sacramento. Copies available from the Northwest Information Center, Sonoma State University, Rohnert Park, California.

1991b Floral Remains from SHA-47 and SHA-236, Redding, California. In Archaeological Investigations at CA-SHA-47 and CA-SHA-236, Redding, Shasta County, California, edited by T. Vaughan, Appendix. Copies available from the Northeast Information Center, Department of Anthropology, California State University, Chico.

1992a Charred Plant Remains from CA-SOL-69 and CA-SOL-315. In Archaeological Investigations at CA-SOL-69 and CA-SOL-315, Green Valley, Solano County, California, edited by R. Wiberg, pp. 179–208. Copies available from the Northwest Information Center, Sonoma State University, Rohnert Park, California.

1992b Seed and Fruit Remains from SUT-17. In Cultural Resources Test Excavations, Sacramento Systems Evaluation, Phase II. Butte and Sutter Counties, California, edited by Paul Bouey, pp. 65–75. Submitted to US Army Corps of Engineers, Sacramento. Copies available from the Northeast Information Center, Department of Anthropology, California State University, Chico.

1992c Plant Remains from CA-CCO-156. In Archaeological Investigations at CA-CCO-156, El Sobrante, California, edited by S. Baker, pp. 40–61. Copies available from the Northwest Information Center, Sonoma State University, Rohnert Park, California.

1992d Report on the 1992 Test Excavations at CA-CCO-474/H near Hercules, Contra Costa County, California. Copies available from the Northwest Information Center, Sonoma State University, Rohnert Park, California.

1992e Floral Remains from CA-SAC-133. In Archaeological Investigations at CA-SAC-133, Sloughhouse, California, edited by Paul E. Bouey and S. A. Waechter, pp. 135–150. Submitted to California Department of Transportation, Marysville, California. Copies available from the North Central Information Center, Department of Anthropology, California State University, Sacramento.

1993a *Floral Remains from CA-SON-2098.* In *The Archaeology of CA-SON-2098: A Buried Archaeological Site in Santa Rosa, Sonoma County, California,* edited by Thomas Origer, pp. 74–97. Origer Consultants, Santa Rosa, California.

1993b Floral Remains from SHA-279. In Archaeology of the Platina Site, CA-SHA-279, Shasta County, California, edited by B. Hamusek, W. Dreyer, R. Bevill, P. Lyden, and Eric Wohlgemuth, pp. 80–93. Copies available from the Northeast Information Center, Department of Anthropology, California State University, Chico.

1993c Floral Remains from CA-SOL-355. In *Archaeological Data Recovery at Prehistoric Site CA-SOL-355/H, Green Valley, Solano County, California,* edited by R. S. Wiberg, pp. 226–250. Holman and Associates, San Francisco.

1994 Floral Remains from CA-363. In Archaeological Investigations at the Pheasant Run Site, CA-SOL-363, edited by J. S. Rosenthal and G. White. Copies available from the Northwest Information Center, Sonoma State University, Rohnert Park, California.

1996a Resource Intensification in Prehistoric Central California: Evidence from Archaeobotanical Data. *Journal of California and Great Basin Anthropology* 18:81–103.

1996b Plant Remains from Flotation Samples. In *Archaeological Investigations and Burial Removal at ALA-483, -483EXT, and -555, Pleasanton, Alameda County, California,* edited by R. S. Wiberg, pp. 189–200. Holman and Associates, San Francisco.

1997a Paleobotanical Remains. In *Culture Change along the Eastern Sierra Nevada/Cascade Front:*

IV. Secret Valley, edited by Kelly R. McGuire, pp. 213–219. Far Western Anthropological Research Group, Davis, California.

1997b Plant Remains. In *Archaeological and Geoarchaeological Investigations at Eight Prehistoric Sites in the Los Vaqueros Reservoir Area, Contra Costa County, California*, edited by Jack Meyers and Jeffrey Rosenthal, Appendix H. Anthropological Studies Center, Sonoma State University Academic Foundation, Inc., Rohnert Park, California.

1998 Charred Plant Remains from CA-ALA-566. In *Results of Archaeological Test Excavations at CA-ALA-566 for the Proposed Route 238 Hayward Bypass Project*, edited by Glenn Gmoser, pp. 100–118. California Department of Transportation District 4. Environmental Planning South, Oakland.

1999a Charred Plant Remains. In *The Moss Landing Hill Site: A Technical Report on Archaeological Studies at CA-MNT-234*, by Randall Milliken, James Nelson, William Hildebrandt, and Patricia Mikkelson, pp. 132–139. Far Western Anthropological Research Group, Davis, California.

1999b Plant Remains from Flotation Samples at CA-ELD-145. In *Once upon a Micron: A Story of Archaeological Site CA-ELD-145 near Camino, El Dorado, California*, edited by Robert Jackson and Hannah S. Ballard, Appendix K. Pacific Legacy, Cameron Park, California.

2000a Analysis of Charred Plant Remains. In *The Archaeology of the Foresthill Divide: The California Forest Highway 124 Project, Placer County, California: 2. The Archaeology of the Old Joe Site, CA-PLA-728/H*, edited by Suzanne Baker, Appendix 9. Archaeological/Historical Consultants, Oakland.

2000b Plant Remains from Flotation Samples at CA-PLA-695/H. In *The Archaeology of the Foresthill Divide: The California Forest Highway 124 Project, Placer County, California: 1. Regional Overviews and the Archaeology of the Monte Verde Site, CA-PLA-695/H*, edited by Suzanne Baker, Appendix 8. Archaeological/Historical Consultants, Oakland.

In press Floral Remains from Project YOSE 92C. In *Dana Meadows Archaeological Testing, Yosemite National Park, Tuolumne County, California*, edited by S. T. Montagne, Appendix F. Publications in Anthropology 19. US Department of the Interior, National Park Service, Washington, DC.

Wohlgemuth, Eric, and Mark E. Basgall
1988 Flotation Analysis. In The Archaeology of Tiefort Basin, Fort Irwin, San Bernardino County, California, edited by Kelly R. McGuire and M. C. Hall, Appendix G. Copies available from the San Bernardino Archeological Information Center, Redlands, California.

Wohlgemuth, Eric, and M. Darcangelo
1994 Floral Remains from SHA-961. In Archaeological Data Recovery, Site CA-SHA-961, Redding, Shasta County, California, edited by Peter M. Jensen, Appendix A. Copies available from the Northeast Information Center, Department of Anthropology, California State University, Chico.

Wohlgemuth, Eric, and Patricia Leary
1993 Floral Remains from SON-25/H. In Archaeological Test Excavations at CA-SON-25/H, -26, -1940, and -1941 in the Los Guilicos Locality, Sonoma County, California, by Katherine M. Dowdall and Susan H. Alvarez, Appendix D. Report on file, CALTRANS District 4, Oakland.

Chapter 8

Paleoethnobotany in the Northwest

Dana Lepofsky

P aleoethnobotany in the Northwest is characterized by extremes. On the one hand, the region has seen some of the most innovative interdisciplinary research in the field of hunter-gatherer paleoethnobotany. On the other hand, many current excavation projects at best may collect a small number of flotation samples as an afterthought and, more typically, conduct no paleoethnobotany at all. Methodologically, there is also great variation. Although new techniques are increasingly being applied to the archaeobotanical record of the Northwest, basic issues of sampling, appropriate flotation procedures, and identification criteria have yet to be resolved. Notwithstanding these unresolved issues, enough data now exist to construct preliminary models of ancient plant use in the Northwest.

The Northwest is a complex area both culturally and environmentally. Past sociopolitical systems ranged from mobile, egalitarian, band-level societies to mostly sedentary, multi-tiered, class-level societies. Subsistence of all groups within the region was based on hunting and gathering. Yet, the ethnographic records recount great variation in the relative reliance on resources that were hunted (and fished) versus gathered. Despite this variation, many models of ancient subsistence practices, and of how those practices were integrated with larger economic and political systems, are focused on animal resources, to the exclusion of plants. The omission of plants from discussions of ancient economies is especially surprising given that the essential role of plants for food, technology, medicines, and ritual in the Northwest is well documented for the historic era (e.g., Compton 1991, 1993; Gunther 1945; Keely 1980; Kuhnlein and Turner 1991; McCutcheon et al. 1992; Palmer 1975; Schlick 1994; Turner 1995, 1996, 1997, 1998; Turner et al. 1980; Turner et al. 1983; Turner et al. 1990). A review of the evidence for ancient plant use in the Northwest is sorely needed to bring some balance to these discussions. This chapter is an attempt at such a review.

Encompassed within the "Northwest" region covered here are the Northwest Coast, including the Willamette Valley and southwestern mountains of Oregon, and the Northern (Canadian) and Southern (Columbian) Plateau (Figure 8.1). Given the cultural and environmental variation within the region, assembling the data needed for a comprehensive review is a monumental task. Much of the direct and indirect evidence of ancient plant use is hidden in the difficult-to-access archaeological gray literature of Alaska, British Columbia, Washington, and Oregon. The indirect evidence of plant use (such as artifacts and features) is often dealt with analytically in a cursory manner, and the analyses of archaeobotanical remains themselves are usually hidden in appendices. As a result, most Northwest archaeologists are unaware that a significant body of data exists that informs about ancient plant use in the region. Though a review of this kind cannot be complete, a sufficient amount of information is compiled here to establish the importance of plant resources in the prehistory of the Northwest.[1]

In this chapter, in addition to a summary of the extant paleoethnobotanical record of the Northwest, I present a review of methodological and theoretical issues of relevance to paleoethnobotany in the region. After defining the study area, I summarize the history of paleoethnobotanical research in the Northwest. The review demonstrates that, although archaeobotanical remains were recovered from some of the earliest excavations in the region and although hundreds of paleoethnobotanical analyses have been conducted since then, very few projects have integrated paleoethnobotany into their research designs. Following this review, I examine some of the current biases Northwest archaeologists have concerning paleoethnobotany, I discuss the nature of the evidence for ancient plant use in the Northwest, and I end with

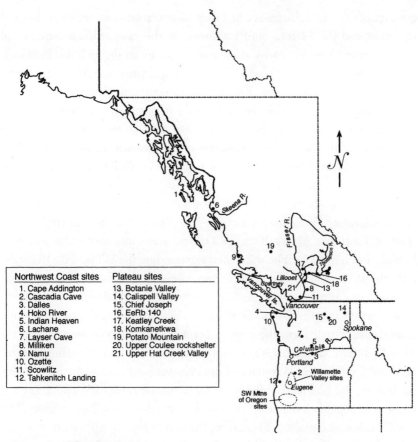

Northwest Coast sites
1. Cape Addington
2. Cascadia Cave
3. Dalles
4. Hoko River
5. Indian Heaven
6. Lachane
7. Layser Cave
8. Milliken
9. Namu
10. Ozette
11. Scowlitz
12. Tahkenitch Landing

Plateau sites
13. Botanie Valley
14. Calispell Valley
15. Chief Joseph
16. EeRb 140
17. Keatley Creek
18. Komkanetkwa
19. Potato Mountain
20. Upper Coulee rockshelter
21. Upper Hat Creek Valley

FIGURE 8.1   The Northwest

a discussion of some of the major issues concerning ancient plant use in the Northwest.

The Study Area Defined

This chapter reviews ancient plant use among the peoples of the Northwest Coast and the Northern and Southern Plateau (Figure 8.1). These regions differ from each other both culturally and ecologically; therefore, I generally treat each area separately. Within the Northwest Coast region, the Willamette Valley of northern Oregon and the southwestern mountains of Oregon are reviewed separately. The placement of these regions within a larger culture area has always been problematic (cf. Walker 1998:Fig. 1) because the

environments and cultures are in many ways transitional between those of the coast and the Plateau (and California in the case of the mountains of southwestern Oregon). Today, these regions are generally included in discussions of the Northwest Coast as a whole (e.g., Ames and Maschner 1999; Suttles 1990). In this review, I discuss them separately from the rest of the coast to highlight the particular importance of plants in those regions.

The boundaries for the Northwest Coast used in this review follow the boundaries of the Northwest Coast culture area as defined in Suttles (1990) and Ames and Maschner (1999). The region is bounded to the west by the Pacific coastline and to the east by the crest of the Chugach and St. Elias Mountains in southern Alaska, the Coast Range in British Columbia, and the Cascade Range in Washington and Oregon. The northern boundary is Cook Inlet in southeast Alaska, and the Oregon state line forms the southern boundary (Figure 8.1). The watershed surrounding the Willamette River defines the Willamette Valley, and the southwestern mountains of Oregon encompass the Umpqua and Rogue River watersheds and their minor tributaries.

The western boundary of the Plateau is defined by the crests of the same coastal ranges that form the eastern boundary of the Northwest Coast region. In British Columbia, the crests of the Cariboo and Monashee Mountains mark the eastern boundary of the Plateau. South of the British Columbia border, the boundary follows the eastern state lines of Washington and Oregon to roughly latitude 44°, where it meets the Great Basin region. The northern boundary of the Plateau region is roughly 52° 30' latitude, which coincides with the traditional boundary marking the northern extent of the Chilcotin peoples of central British Columbia (Lane 1981; Figure 8.1).

The Plateau boundaries used here differ somewhat from those defined in other reviews of Plateau culture, which extend the region to include the Rocky Mountains (Brunton 1998; Ray 1939; Roll and Hackenberger 1998). In this volume, the eastern portion of the Southern Plateau is included with the Great Basin, reflecting the fact that, in many ways, the people and environment of the Rocky Mountains are distinct from other areas of the Plateau. A logistical reason also prompted the inclusion of the eastern periphery of the Southern Plateau with the Great Basin; because the paleoethnobotanists who work in the Great Basin tend to work throughout Idaho, they are in a better position to synthesize the massive amount of unpublished data from the eastern Plateau.

In this review, the northern boundary of the Plateau includes the Chilcotin region. Though the Chilcotin people are often included in the Subarctic culture area (Lane 1981), they are strongly influenced by Plateau cultures (Fladmark 1986; Lane 1981; Pokotylo and Mitchell 1998; Richards and Rousseau 1987). Further, many parts of the Chilcotin region are environmentally more similar to the Plateau than to the northern forests. The similarity in culture and environment between the Plateau and the Chilcotin regions is reflected in ancient plant use.

History of Research

Early "paleoethnobotanical research" in the Northwest was limited to the fortuitous recovery of floral remains found during excavations. It is no coincidence that only those species represented by large specimens were recovered. The first published reference to the recovery of archaeobotanical remains in the Northwest comes from the Upper Coulee rockshelter on the Columbia River in eastern Washington (Mills and Osborne 1951; Figure 8.1). Excavation of this dry rockshelter began in 1947 and produced over 25 plant taxa used for food and technology. No systematic collection was conducted, and the analysis was limited by extensive bioturbation.

In the 1960s, the excavation of three other sites produced large plant specimens. In the Willamette Valley, hazelnuts (*Corylus cornuta*) and acorns (*Quercus* sp.) were recovered from a hearth on the Luckiamute River (Reckendorf and Parsons 1966) and from Cascadia Cave (Newman 1966; Figure 8.1), but in neither study did the discovery of archaeobotanical remains figure prominently. The recovery of large numbers of cherry (*Prunus* sp.) seeds at the Milliken site on the Fraser River of British Columbia (Figure 8.1) led archaeologists to conclude that the site's precarious riverside location was related to the harvest of the fall sockeye salmon run, which corresponds to the time when cherries ripen (Borden 1960:116–117, 1975:63–69). Surprisingly, the obvious conclusion that gathering was also being conducted at the site has only recently been mentioned in the literature (Mitchell and Pokotylo 1996:79).

The late 1970s and early 1980s witnessed the first systematic attempts at paleoethnobotany in the Northwest (Campbell 1985; Chatters 1986; Friedman 1975; Galm and Masten 1985; Ketcheson et al. 1977; Minor and Pickett 1982), probably because of the focus of the "New Archaeology" on the recovery of remains associated with subsistence. Of particular note is the Chief Joseph Dam Cultural Resources Project (1978–1985), which included the excavation of several sites located on the Columbia River below Grand

Coulee Dam (Figure 8.1, Site 15). The analysis of over 400 flotation samples from several sites resulted in the identification of 56 taxa used for food and technology (Stenholm 1985). Unfortunately, nonstandardized sampling and recovery procedures used at these sites limit the possibility for quantitative comparisons of temporal and spatial contexts (Bicchieri 1990:5).

The discovery and excavation of the first water-saturated ("wet") sites along the Northwest Coast in the 1970s had the potential to impact paleo-ethnobotany in the Northwest in a major way. Wet sites are those that contain water-saturated archaeological deposits below the water table. Under such anaerobic conditions, all kinds of vegetal material are extremely well preserved. From the beginning of wet-site archaeology on the coast, however, the primary goal of excavation has been artifact recovery (e.g., Croes 1976; see below).

The first major excavation of a wet site was at the famous Ozette site, at the northern end of the Olympic Peninsula (Figure 8.1). Though there is an earlier dry midden at the site, the focus of the excavation at Ozette from 1970 to 1981 was a Makah village that was buried by a mud slide in approximately AD 1500. The remains include four cedar plank houses and associated areas, which have produced over 50,000 artifacts, the vast majority of which are partially or wholly made of perishable plant materials (Gleeson and Grosso 1976). These artifacts have been analyzed for style (Croes 1977, 1980; Kent 1975; Koch 1975; Mauger 1982) and material type (Friedman 1975). Non-artifactual (i.e., food) plants were examined in only one study (Gill 1983), but the 500,000 seeds on which the analysis was based had been collected inconsistently during wet screening or from in situ contexts (Gill 1983, personal communication 1993).

A second major wet-site excavation was conducted in the 1970s at the Hoko River site, just west of Ozette (Figure 8.1). The site was used primarily as a marine and river fishing camp from 1000 BC to AD 1. Like Ozette, it is composed of wet and dry (rockshelter) deposits. The wet site is characterized by numerous layers of "vegetal debris mats" that are thought to be concentrations of drift materials. Pollen and arboreal cones preserved in these mats were used to reconstruct the environment surrounding the site (Croes 1995; Ecklund 1980; see Munsell 1976 for a similar analysis).

The majority of the perishable artifact assemblage in the Hoko wet deposits is cordage (Croes 1988, 1995; Croes and Blinman 1980), but other culturally deposited remains include seeds, fern roots, and sphagnum moss (Croes 1995). Though the reasons are not clear, it was assumed by the excavators that all or most of the seeds found in the wet-site deposits originated from coprolites (Croes 1995). As at Ozette, the seeds from the Hoko wet deposits were not collected systematically.

Every year since the late 1980s, a small number of archaeological excavations, exclusive of wet sites, have included paleoethnobotanical analyses. The projects are largely confined to those conducted by consulting archaeologists working in Oregon and Washington (see Stenholm references, especially Stenholm 1998a). The number of projects in British Columbia and Alaska that include palaeoethnobotany is slowly increasing. Though nowhere in the Northwest is paleoethnobotany a standard part of archaeological research, well over 100 sites in the region have been examined for archaeobotanical remains. The value of most analyses is limited by the fact that a paleoethnobotanist was not involved in the formation of the project research design, the collection of the material, or the final analysis of the larger project.

In recent years, primarily within university settings, a noticeable shift has occurred in the perceived role of paleoethnobotany in Northwest archaeology. This shift is in large part due to recent hirings of paleoethnobotanists as faculty members, but it is also related to the development of theoretical models that are best evaluated with paleoethnobotanical data (e.g., Ames and Marshall 1980; Chatters 1989; Thoms 1989). As a result, an increasing number of academic archaeologists are regularly incorporating paleoethnobotany into the initial stages of research. In addition, researchers have begun to search for indirect evidence of ancient plant use, such as remains of permanent facilities for cultivation and processing of plant foods (e.g., Deur 1999, 2000, 2002a, 2002b, in press; Peacock 1998, 2002; Thoms 1989). Interdisciplinary approaches, which seek to identify human-plant interactions from several lines of evidence, are also providing new insights into ancient plant use (Lepofsky et al. in press; Lepofsky, Heyerdahl, et al. 2003).

The Status of Palaeoethnobotany in the Northwest

The reluctance of most Northwest archaeologists to incorporate paleoethnobotany into their projects seems to stem from several preconceived notions about traditional plant use in the region as well as about the potential for recovering archaeobotanical remains from the archaeological record (Bicchieri 1990). Perhaps foremost among the biases held by Northwest archaeologists is the notion that plants were not an important part of the palaeoeconomy of the region. This is most dramatically displayed in the Northwest Coast literature, where the importance of salmon dominates discussions of ancient sub-sistence (e.g., Isaac 1988; Matson 1992; Matson and Coupland 1995; but see Ames and Maschner 1999; Monks 1987), but it is also true for the Plateau (e.g., Richards and Rousseau 1982). Particularly frustrating is the misuse of carbon isotopic data—which demonstrate that marine resources were the primary source of *protein* in the diet of coastal and Plateau peoples (Chisholm et al. 1983; Lovell et al. 1986)—to demonstrate that marine resources were the primary component of the *total diet* of peoples in these regions (e.g., Ames 1994:216; Matson and Coupland 1995:30; Mitchell and Donald 1988:335). For many researchers, the importance of salmon on the Northwest Coast and the relatively minor role of all plants in the diet is an unquestioned assumption.

The bias against examining plants in the economy of the Northwest may in part be related to a more general bias against studying women's contribu-tion to the paleoeconomy, given that gathering and processing of plant foods and materials primarily involved women (Bicchieri 1990; Hunn 1981; Norton 1985). This latter bias certainly influenced the work of several early ethno-graphers (Teit [e.g., Steedman 1930] is a notable exception; Wickwire 1993) on whose writings Northwest archaeologists rely heavily.

The reluctance of Northwest archaeologists to incorporate paleoethno-botanical analyses into their research also arises from the preconceived idea that archaeobotanical remains are not preserved in Northwest sites. This idea can be attributed, in part, to the belief that archaeobotanical remains are not preserved in hunter-gatherer sites in general. An additional concern among Northwest archaeologists is that plant remains, which are generally better preserved in acidic environments, will not be preserved in the basic coastal shell middens. This latter concern arises from a lack of understand-ing that *charred* archaeobotanical remains are not affected by pH.

On both the coast and Plateau, most archaeological research concentrates on the recovery of bones and lithics, to the exclusion of plant remains. The systematic collection of archaeobotanical remains from sites is exceedingly rare. Instead, the collection of plants is limited to large specimens retrieved during screening (often through 1/4-inch mesh) or from a few, isolated flota-tion samples.

To some extent, our knowledge of ancient plant use in the Northwest is also limited by the way paleoethnobotany is currently conducted in this re-gion. A major limitation is the lack of reference collections containing a range of plant parts. Collections tend to focus on ethnobotanically important species, and, as a result, it is difficult for archaeobotanists to identify remains of plants that were not used in the historic era. Further, given the importance of "root foods" in the ethnobotanical record of the region (see below), the use of scanning electron microscopy (SEM) to identify geophytes should be standard practice. To my knowledge, however, only one researcher has used this technique in a systematic way (Wollstonecroft 2000).

Our understanding of ancient plant use is also limited by the fact that no standards exist for the kinds of identification criteria that should be included in archaeobotanical reports. The literature is replete with "possible" and "probable" identifications, but no information is provided to assess the strength of such identifications. The problem is made more serious by the fact that, by the time a summary of paleoethnobotanical analyses (based on data provided in an appendix) is included in the main body of a report, tentative identifications have become positive ones. Because paleoethnobotany in the Northwest is a relatively new field and because the comparative collections are somewhat incomplete, it is essential that identification criteria be made explicit. This is especially true for less common taxa. Photographs should be included of taxa whose identifications are tentative, as well as of those that are firmly identified but that are uncommon in the archaeobotanical record.

Quantitative comparisons between contexts and sites are further constrained by the lack of standards for collection procedures. For instance, the volumes of soil collected for flotation range from as much as 8 liters (e.g., Nelson 1992) to less than 1 liter. Developing standard rules of thumb for sufficient volume and number of flotation samples for a given context would ensure that an adequate amount of material is collected by archaeologists not working in conjunction with a paleoethnobotanist. Redundancy plots of numbers of individual taxa (NIT) by numbers of individual specimens (NISP) per context should be a standard part of analysis, to facilitate comparisons and allow evaluation of the strength of interpretations (e.g., Lepofsky et al. 1996; Lyons 2000; Wollstonecroft 2000). Researchers should also be encouraged to standardize all results (i.e., per volume and/or weight of flotation sample) in addition to presenting the raw data.

Finally, standards need to be developed specifically with respect to charcoal identification. Currently, there is no standard guiding how specimens are chosen for identification (e.g., only the biggest pieces? a random selection of all specimens over 2 mm in size?) or how many specimens should be identified. Focusing on one site in coastal British Columbia, Lyons (2000) found that between 25 and 40 charcoal specimens per sample is sufficient to represent the species richness in that sample (based on plots of NISP versus NIT). We do not yet know if this result can be extended to other contexts in the region.

Nature of the Data

Archaeobotanical remains are preserved in a variety of contexts within Northwest sites. At open-air sites in the Northwest, preservation is limited in the same way as at all sites that experience periodic wetting and drying. In general, except for those from deposits that are very recent (100 years old or so), only charred plant remains should be included in paleoethnobotanical analyses. Exceptions to this are western redcedar wood on the coast and birch bark in the Plateau, both of which tend to be more resistant to decay than other wood taxa. Partial charring seems to further increase the likelihood of preservation. I have recovered partially charred redcedar in a coastal shell midden dating to 200–300 years ago and uncharred birch bark from a Plateau site over 1,000 years old. Another notable exception to the rule of collecting only charred remains is red elderberry (*Sambucus racemosa*) seeds, which are preserved uncharred in some deposits for up to 800 years old (Cybulski 1993, personal communication 2002; Losey et al. 2003). This extraordinary preservation may in part be due to poisons contained within the seeds that inhibit insect and microbial decay.

Despite popular belief, if appropriate sampling schemes are employed, a range of charred plant remains can be recovered from coastal shell middens (see below). In my experience, the dark carbon-bearing bands within the middens primarily produce wood charcoal, probably from fuel use. The features within the midden, however, tend to produce a greater range of remains associated with the processing and consumption of plant foods (cf. Lepofsky 1992; Nelson 1992). Keeping these parameters in mind should facilitate the selection of flotation samples that would most benefit the larger project's research goals.

At wet sites on the Northwest Coast, both charred and uncharred plant remains are preserved. Wet sites have been found along much of the Northwest Coast, from southeastern Alaska to the southern Puget Sound, and date from 2000–1000 BC to historic times (e.g., Bernick 1991; Croes 1976, 1988, 1992, 1995; Gleeson 1980; Moss et al. 1990; Nelson 1990:481). It has been estimated that over half of the artifacts (most of them basketry and cordage) included in coastal middens are perishable and can only be found in wet components (Hobler 1990:299). In addition, a range of food plants has also been observed in wet-site deposits (e.g., Croes 1987; Eldridge and Fisher 1997).

As mentioned above, the preservation of uncharred plant material at wet sites presents extraordinary opportunities for investigating ancient plant use.

Borden (1975:257) makes the important point that wet sites provide a fuller range of evidence of women's contribution to the economy than other site types. Some of the most exciting wet-site research on the Northwest Coast has been done by Dale Croes (e.g., 1997, 2001, 2002), who uses stylistic variation represented in basketry and cordage to recognize ethnicity and intergroup relations. With the exception of a few early attempts at retrieving nonartifactual plant remains from wet sites (Gill 1983; Munsell 1976), the potential for such recovery remains largely unexplored. Unfortunately, the time and expense involved in the excavation and subsequent preservation of perishable materials recovered from wet sites constrain the research that is currently being undertaken in these deposits.

One problem often raised by excavators of wet sites is that it is difficult to distinguish naturally versus culturally deposited plant remains (e.g., Eldridge and Fisher 1997). Because the majority of waterlogged deposits were originally situated in locations where water-borne plant parts naturally collected, the deposits are often a mix of human- and water-transported remains (Bernick 1991). It should be possible, however, to distinguish most cultural plant remains by (1) collecting control samples from off-site waterlogged deposits; (2) knowing which plants grow along watercourses; and (3) understanding what plant parts are likely to fall into the water (e.g., seeds and leaves versus bulbs).

At the other extreme of site conditions from the wet sites are "dry" deposits, which are found in a variety of contexts in the Northwest. These deposits are characterized by relatively dry strata and an abundance of uncharred plant remains. Whereas the dry conditions are sufficient to slow microbial decay, the concentration of organic matter produced by the plant remains seems to further encourage preservation by creating hydrophobic deposits that actually repel water. Such deposits have been reported in rockshelters in Oregon (Aikens 1993; Baxter et al. 1983; Ecklund-Johnson 1984; Fowler 1989; Minor 1987; Minor and Connolly 1987; Tuohy 1986), in southeastern Alaska (Lepofsky et al. 2001; Reger and Campbell 1986) and in the Plateau (Chatters 1979; Mills and Osborne 1951), and in rim deposits encircling house pits at open-air sites in the Plateau (Lepofsky 2000a, 2002). Excellent preservation reported from some Plateau pithouses (Stenholm 1985; Stryd 1972, personal communication 1993) may also be due to the same mechanisms. As in wet sites, distinguishing naturally from culturally deposited plant remains in dry deposits requires careful sampling and attention to source and context of the materials (Lepofsky 2000a, 2002).

The collection of off-site control samples to help understand formation processes is particularly important in some Northwest sites. For instance, in many parts of the Plateau, where natural forest fires can occur as frequently as every 10–20 years, the chance of obtaining "naturally" charred floral remains from both noncultural and archaeological deposits is quite high (e.g., Ketcheson et al. 1977). Similarly, in Alaska, where highly acidic soils and cooler temperatures retard microbial decay, uncharred as well as charred remains may have cultural origins (McMahan 1986). In both instances, off-site controls will greatly aid in the interpretation of the archaeological deposits. In my experience, soil samples collected from British Columbia coastal forest soils are devoid of charred seeds (or any seeds), indicating that most charred seeds found within coastal sites are cultural in origin.

Using the ethnographic and ethnobotanical records as the basis for models of ancient plant use can be an important step toward understanding the paleoethnobotanical record (e.g., Lepofsky and Lyons 2003; Lepofsky and Peacock in press; Lyons 2000; Wollstonecroft 2000, 2002). Such models provide insights into which plants are likely to be preserved in the archaeological record and in what contexts. This information can be used both to interpret the record and to design appropriate sampling strategies.

Finally, in addition to actual archaeobotanical remains, ancient plant use in the Northwest can be inferred from a range of artifacts and features (e.g., Peacock 1998, 2002; Thoms 1989). These include tools and features used for the harvesting, processing, consumption, and storage of plants (Tables 8.1 and 8.2). These data are particularly useful for those plants that are less likely to be preserved archaeologically.

The Natural Environment

The following is a general description of the plant communities that characterize the Northwest, including the Northwest Coast, the Willamette Valley and the southwestern mountains of Oregon, and the Plateau. Refer to Chatters (1998), Franklin (1988), Franklin and Dyrness (1988), Habeck (1961), Meidinger and Pojar (1992), Parish et al. (1996), Pojar and MacKinnon (1994), and Schoonmaker et al. (1995) for more complete descriptions of the environments of the Northwest. The following summary is based on the above references as well as personal observations. Table 8.3 lists the common and scientific names of plants mentioned in the text.

Table 8.1

Archaeological Correlates of Plants Used as Food in the Northwest

Activity	Artifacts	Features	Sites Expected
Collection	baskets, berry combs, digging sticks	none	year-round village, summer village, base camp, short-term camp
Food processing	mats, grinders, knives, boiling stones, mortars and pestles, skewers	hearths, earth ovens, drying trenches, drying racks	year-round village, summer village, base camp, short-term camp
Storage	bentwood boxes, baskets, bark lining, cordage	underground pits	year-round village, winter village
Consumption	various implements	hearths for cooking	all

Source: Lyons 2000.

Table 8.2

Archaeological Correlates of Plants Used in Technology in the Northwest

Activity	Artifacts	Features	Sites Expected
Collection of fuel	hammers, bark peelers, bark scrapers, adzes, axes, mauls	none	all
Fuel use	axes	hearths, earth ovens, drying trenches	all
Collection of raw materials	baskets, knives, cordage	none	year-round village, summer village, base camp, short-term village
Working with fibers	bark peelers, bark shredders, bark beaters, spindle whorls, needles, awls, mat creasers, net gauges	none	year-round village, winter village
Woodworking	bark-strippers, adzes, knives, axes, hammers, mauls, drills, chisels, wedges	objects produced (e.g., canoes, posts, poles)	year-round village, winter village

Source: Lyons 2000.

Table 8.3

Plants Mentioned in Text

Common Name	Scientific Name
Alder	*Alnus* sp.
Antelope-bush	*Purshia tridentata*
Balsamroot	*Balsamorhiza sagittata*
Birch, paper	*Betula papyrifera*
Bitterroot	*Lewisia* spp.
Blueberry	*Vaccinium* sp.
Bulrush	*Scirpus* sp.
Camas	*Camassia* sp.
Camas, common	*Camassia quamash*
Camas, great	*Camassia leichtlinii*
Cattail	*Typha* sp.
Chenopod	*Chenopodium* sp.
Cherry	*Prunus* spp.
Cherry, bitter	*Prunus emarginata*
Clover, springbank	*Trifolium wormskjoldii*
Cottonwood	*Populus* sp.
Cow-parsnip	*Heracleum lanatum*
Crabapple, Pacific	*Malus fusca*
Cranberry, highbush	*Viburnum edule*
Currant	*Ribes* spp.
Dogwood, red-osier	*Cornus stolonifera*
Douglas-fir	*Pseudotsuga menziesii*
Elderberry, red	*Sambucus racemosa*
Fern, bracken	*Pteridium* sp.
Fern, spiny wood	*Dryopteris expansa*
Fir, Pacific silver	*Abies amabilis*
Fir, subalpine	*Abies lasiocarpa*
Fir, true	*Abies* sp.
Fireweed	*Epilobium angustifolium*
Glacier lily, yellow	*Erythronium grandiflorum*
Hawthorn	*Crataegus* sp.
Hazelnut	*Corylus cornuta*
Hazelnut, beaked	*Corylus cornuta*
Hemlock, mountain	*Tsuga mertensiiana*
Hemlock, western	*Tsuga heterophylla*
Hemlock-parsley, Pacific	*Conioselium pacificum*
Horsetail	*Equisetum* spp.
Huckleberry	*Vaccinium* spp.
Huckleberry, black	*Vaccinium membranaceum*
Huckleberry, Cascade	*Vaccinium deliciosum*
Incense cedar	*Calocedrus decurrens*
Kinnikinnick	*Arctostaphylos uva-ursa*
Larch	*Larix* sp.
"Lily"	*Fritillaria* spp.

Table 8.3 *continued*

Common Name	Scientific Name
Lily-of-the valley, false	*Maianthemum dilatatum*
Lomatium	*Lomatium* spp.
Lupine, Nootka	*Lupinus nootkatensis*
Lupine, seashore	*Lupinus littoralis*
Manzanita	*Arctostaphylos* spp.
Mock-orange	*Philadelphus lewisii*
Northern rice root	*Fritillaria camschatcensis*
Oak	*Quercus* sp.
Oak, California black	*Quercus kelloggii*
Oak, Garry	*Quercus garryi*
Oak, tan	*Lithocarpus densiflorus*
Onion	*Allium* spp.
Onion, fool's	*Brodiaea hyacinthine*
Onion, nodding	*Allium cernuum*
Oregon-grape	*Mahonia* spp.
Peat moss	*Sphagnum* spp.
Pine	*Pinus* spp.
Pine, lodgepole	*Pinus contorta* var. *latifolia*
Pine, ponderosa	*Pinus ponderosa*
Pine, sugar	*Pinus lambertiana*
Pine, whitebark	*Pinus albicaulis*
Port Orford cedar	*Chamaecyparis lawsoniana*
Prickly pear	*Opuntia* spp.
Raspberry	*Rubus* spp.
Rosehip	*Rosa* spp.
Sagebrush	*Artemisia* spp.
Sagebrush, common	*Artemisia tridentata*
Salal	*Gaultheria shallon*
Salmonberry	*Rubus spectabilis*
Saskatoon	*Amelanchier alnifolia*
Silverweed, Pacific	*Potentilla anserine* spp. *pacifica*
Spring-beauty, western	*Claytonia lanceolata*
Soapberry	*Shepardia canadensis*
Spruce, Engelmann	*Picea engelmannii*
Spruce, Sitka	*Picea sitchensis*
Stoneseed	*Lithospermum ruderale*
Strawberry	*Fragaria* spp.
Strawberry-blite	*Chenopodium capitatum*
Tarweed	*Madia* spp.
Thimbleberry	*Rubus parviflorus*
Tobacco	*Nicotiana attenuata, N. quadrivalvis*
Vetch	*Vicia* spp.
Wapato	*Sagittaria latifolia*
Western redcedar	*Thuja plicata*
Yew, Pacific	*Taxus brevifolia*

The Northwest Coast

Northwest coastal environments are rugged and varied. Along the northern coast from British Columbia into Alaska, the coastlines are characterized by extensive, steep-walled fjords, whose waterways are in the lee of more exposed barrier islands. South of British Columbia, fewer fjords and inland passages occur. Coastal plains and low mountain ranges are broader and dissected by many streams. Much of the Oregon coast is almost unbroken, and few protected bays and estuaries are found along its length. The climate along much of the coast is temperate, with rainy, mild winters and mild summers.

Conifers dominate most Northwest Coast ecosystems. In wetter areas close to tidewater and throughout more northerly parts of the region, Sitka spruce (*Picea sitchensis*), western redcedar (*Thuja plicata*), and western hemlock (*Tsuga heterophylla*) dominate hypermaritime ecosystems. Pacific silver fir (*Abies amabilis*) and yellow-cedar (*Chamaecyparis nootkatensis*) are also important components of these forests. These wet coastal forests can have an exceptionally well developed understory layer dominated by a variety of ericaceous shrubs, including salal (*Gaultheria shallon*) and blueberry and huckleberry species (*Vaccinium* spp.).

From the central British Columbia coast to the southern boundary of the region, low- to moderate-elevation forests away from the wet coastal fringe are dominated by Douglas-fir (*Pseudotsuga menziesii*). Western redcedar and western hemlock are common there as well. Other significant species that also occur in the southern part of the region include noble fir (*Abies procera*) and Port Orford cedar (*Chamaecyparis lawsiniana*). Several other trees characteristic of California coastal forest, such as incense cedar (*Calocedrus decurrens*), tan oak (*Lithocarpus densiflorus*), California black oak (*Quercus kelloggii*), and sugar pine (*Pinus lambertiana*), are found along the southern Oregon coast. The latter two were food sources for the Aboriginal people of that area. Hardwoods tend to be limited to disturbed areas and riparian zones. True firs (*Abies* spp.), mountain hemlock (*Tsuga mertensiana*), and yellow-cedar are common in subalpine and alpine forests throughout most of the region.

All of the major ecosystems along the coast provided an assortment of economically important plants to the Indigenous peoples. A variety of conifers and hardwoods found in each forest association were extensively used by coastal peoples for various technological purposes. The shrub and herb layers of the forests likewise supported numerous economically important plants. Among the most common food plants were salal, various huckleberries or blueberries, raspberries and related berries (*Rubus* spp.), and several ferns. The riparian ecosystems, with their mix of deciduous trees and shrubs, also offered a variety of useful plants. Native peoples living near the coast utilized various seaweeds and important "root" plants that grow on estuarine flats (e.g., springbank clover [*Trifolium wormskjoldii*] and Pacific silverweed [*Potentilla anserina* ssp. *pacifica*] and northern rice root [*Fritillaria camschatcensis*]).

The southeastern area of Vancouver Island, the Gulf and San Juan Islands, and the east side of the Olympic Peninsula stand out as floristically distinct among the coastal ecosystems. These areas fall within the zone of Douglas-fir-dominated forest, but there are large areas within characterized by open oak (*Quercus garryana*) forests and grass prairies. Most of these ecosystems are thought to have been maintained in the past through prescribed burning (see below). The oak savanna supplied the Indigenous people with important food plants such as camas (*Camassia* spp.) and acorns.

The Willamette Valley

The Willamette Valley, along with the Umpqua and Rogue River valleys further south, tends to be drier than the rest of the coast because of the rain-shadow effect of the coastal mountains. Oak savanna forests dominated the low elevation areas of the Willamette Valley prior to European suppression of aboriginally set fires (Boyd 1999a; Thilenius 1968; see below). Today the area is dominated by Garry oak forests, which are characterized by an over-story of oak and an understory of various shrubs. Historically, the habitat was the source of camas, acorns, hazelnuts (*Corylus* sp.), cherry, and various berries and seeds for the local Aboriginal people.

Surrounding the oak savanna, on the edges of the valley and on the mountain slopes, were forests dominated by Douglas-fir. Although a relatively low biomass is characteristic of the forests themselves, openings within the forest and the forest-savanna ecotone provided a variety of edible berries and game habitat (Franklin and Dyrness 1988; Habeck 1961).

The Southwestern Mountains of Oregon

The southwestern portion of Oregon is characterized by a series of river valleys surrounded by steep mountains, which, because of the great vertical ranges, encompass several microenvironments within relatively short distances. The region is floristically transitional between the Northwest Coast and California.

The valley bottoms are characterized by open savannas and grasslands, whose maintenance has relied on human-set fires (see below). These low-elevation areas are bounded by oak woodlands, which cover the foothills of the mountains between elevations of 160 to 1,000 m. The woodlands are dominated by an overstory of oak, which sometimes codominates with Douglas-fir, and an understory of grasses and forbs with some shrubs (Franklin 1992).

The mountains are covered with a mosaic of floristic communities. A western hemlock and Douglas-fir forest generally dominates the Coast Range; however, higher or wetter areas support Sitka spruce or western redcedar, and pines grow in the drier pockets. The higher-elevation areas of the Cascade Range are dominated by true fir forests. The drier interior valley hills, which are characterized by a vegetation mix more similar to California than to Oregon, support forests of Douglas-fir, ponderosa pine (*Pinus ponderosa*), oaks, and manzanita (*Arctostaphylos* spp.) (Franklin and Dyrness 1988).

The Plateau

The Plateau is generally characterized by rolling uplands, river valleys, and surrounding mountains. The largest of the rivers in the region are the Columbia and the Fraser, and many of the smaller rivers ultimately drain into these two. The area is climatically and floristically varied, in large part because of its great topographic variation. The region experiences hot, dry summers and extremely cold, snowy winters.

The alluvial terraces surrounding the major rivers are characterized by shrubby and herbaceous vegetation, the specific composition dependent on local temperature and precipitation. Among the various economically useful plants found in this ecosystem are sagebrush (*Artemisia* spp.), several large perennial grasses, balsamroot (*Balsamorhiza sagittata*), lomatiums (*Lomatium* spp.), onions (*Allium* spp.), mariposa lily (*Calochortus macrocarpus*), prickly pear cactuses (*Opuntia* spp.), and fool's onion (*Brodiaea hyacinthina*).

Open, dry forests, dominated by Douglas-fir and ponderosa pine, are characteristic of slightly higher elevations. Stream gullies support a mixed deciduous habitat, containing many edible shrubs, such as currants (*Ribes* spp.), saskatoons (*Amelanchier alnifolia*), and rosehips (*Rosa* spp.). The subalpine regions are covered in forests dominated by Engelmann spruce (*Picea engelmannii*), subalpine fir (*Abies lasiocarpa*), and pines (*Pinus* spp.). Some of the pines, notably whitebark pine (*Pinus albicaulis*), provided storable nuts that were exploited by many groups. Also in the uplands are large, open meadows. These meadows support a wide array of herbaceous plants. Many of the herbs have edible roots that were extensively collected in the historic and prehistoric periods.

Culture History Summary

The Northwest Coast

The following is a general summary of Northwest Coast culture history. Refer to Aikens (1993), Ames (1994), Ames and Maschner (1999), Carlson and Dalla Bona (1996), Fladmark (1986), and Matson and Coupland (1995) for more detailed summaries.

Though the timing of the initial occupation of the Northwest Coast is debated, scattered finds of fluted points are the earliest archaeological remains. Early Holocene sites, dating from 8000 BC, are dispersed throughout the coast, especially north of Washington State. A distinctive characteristic of early northern assemblages is the prevalence of microblades and the near absence of bifaces, whereas leaf-shaped bifaces and few microblades characterize many southern assemblages. The early coastal occupants were mobile hunters and gatherers who, based on faunal remains, relied on a wide range of marine and terrestrial fauna. The range of plants used is unknown but was likely also diverse.

The post–3000 BC period was characterized by dramatic sociopolitical and economic developments. The number of sites, as well as site size, increased at that time. Large shell middens appeared, indicating an increased reliance on near-shore resources and perhaps semisedentism. A decline in mobility in some areas is also indicated by the appearance of small houses, which were at least semipermanent. Marine resources become increasingly important in many subsistence economies.

After 2000 BC, a storage-based economy developed, technology became more diversified, and there was a trend toward intensifying resource production. The expansion of the woodworking toolkit, in particular, the addition of ground-stone adze blades and mauls, allowed the production of crucial items such as large plank houses, canoes, and bentwood boxes. Semipermanent plank houses and multihouse villages appeared after 2000 BC, and special-use sites and evidence for logistical mobility date to that period. Some evidence for status differentiation appears to date to as early as 2500 BC, and permanent social inequality—with elites and slaves—was well established by 500 BC. Increasing conflict occurred concomitant with shifts to larger, permanent villages and with resource intensification. Though not well understood, at around AD 450–950, many regions experienced changes in settlement, technology, ritual, and art that likely reflect larger social and economic changes.

The Willamette Valley

The archaeological record of the Willamette Valley reflects a hunter-gather economy, with a strong orientation toward gathering plant foods. The majority of archaeological sites in the Willamette Valley dating to ca. 8000 BC are located on floodplains subject to seasonal inundation or on nearby levees that border the active floodplains (Cheatham 1988; Connolly et al. 1999). Even taking into account the destruction of low-lying sites by flooding, fewer sites have been located on the drier, more stable prairies and uplands than in the valley bottom. Local archaeologists believe that the association of sites with inundated areas had to do with the fact that camas and other plant foods are easier to harvest from these low, wet soils than from the upland clayey soils (Connolly et al. 1999). In addition to plants, seasonally available mammals and birds were harvested from floodplain base camps.

After about 3000 BC, a substantial increase occurred in the number of sites in the Willamette Valley, indicating an increase in population. Several middle Holocene sites have a large number of ovens used for the initial processing of camas. Artifacts presumed to be used for plant processing, such as manos, grinding slabs, mortars, and pestles, are common at these sites.[2] Substantial middens indicate the repeated reuse of sites and more extensive use of sites along rivers and streams by 1000 BC. This evidence may in turn indicate increasing territorial circumscription, similar to that documented ethnographically (Connolly et al. 1999:272; Pettigrew 1990).

The Southwestern Mountains of Oregon

As with much of the Northwest, the earliest period of human occupation in the southwestern mountains region is documented by isolated finds of fluted points. The later early Holocene record is characterized by a few small campsites along the major rivers. The scant evidence suggests a generalized diet that included resources from fishing, hunting, and gathering. Specific evidence for gathering comes from stone mortars, pestles, hopper mortar bases, manos, and milling slabs.

The somewhat sporadic archaeological record indicates little change in the culture historical record in the southwestern mountains until about AD 950. At that time, the first permanent pithouses appeared, marking an increase in intensity of settlement. Smaller seasonal campsites with evidence for both hunting and gathering continued to be scattered throughout the hinterlands. The permanent settlements provided easy access to the river fish, as well as constituting home bases from which to make hunting and collecting forays. Why settlement patterns changed at AD 950 is not well understood (Aikens 1993).

The Plateau

The following is a general review of the culture history of the Northern and Southern Plateau regions. Refer to reviews in Ames et al. (1998), Chatters and Pokotylo (1998), Pokotylo and Mitchell (1998), and Richards and Rousseau (1987) for more detailed summaries.

The early Holocene record of human activity on the Plateau is scanty, composed of surface finds of points and low-density lithic scatters. These early people were mobile, generalized hunters and gatherers, but the emphasis placed on different resources varied depending on local resource availability. Evidence for grinding foods in the Southern Plateau (presumably, including plant foods) comes from grinding slabs, small manos, and edge-ground cobbles, and later, from hopper mortar bases and pestles.

The period after 3300 BC was marked by a reduction in mobility in some areas. Small settlements, composed of one to three semisubterranean pithouses, appeared in areas that offered access to resources for most or all of the year. A fairly generalized, opportunistic subsistence strategy is indicated, with a primary focus on valley bottom resources close to the residential base camps. The availability of year-round resources allowed these communities to be sedentary or semisedentary. By 2500 BC, these communities had disappeared, and evidence for pithouses on the Plateau dating to the following 500-year period is rare or absent.

After 2000 BC in many places, important shifts occurred in the regional economy and settlement pattern. Pithouses reappeared in the context of permanent winter settlements that relied on a well-developed storage technology. Concurrent with the winter settlements, specialized seasonal campsites were located in a variety of ecosystems.

After 500 BC, large pithouse settlements appeared on the lower reaches of larger rivers. Evidence exists for increasing specialization in the exploitation of a few resources, particularly salmon, deer, and root crops, but the diet remained broad. The upland zones were extensively used both for harvesting and processing root foods and for hunting. There is increasing evidence for social inequality beginning at this time in areas such as the Dalles on the Columbia and in the mid-Fraser region, around Lillooet. Population increase, circumscription, and private access to and ownership of resources, coupled with increasing socioeconomic competition and environmental changes, are factors thought to have influenced the resource extensification and intensification characteristic of this period (Chatters 1989; Hayden 2000a; Kuijt 1989; Pokotylo and Froese 1983; Richards and Rousseau 1987:57; Thoms 1989). After about AD 950 in many regions, village size and population numbers declined, as does evidence for social inequality.

Ethnographic Seasonal Round and Plant Use

The Ethnographic Record in Context

Paleoethnobotanical researchers in the Northwest are fortunate in that they have access to one of the richest ethnobotanical records in North America. The record provides details about plants used for food (e.g., Turner 1995, 1997), technological materials (e.g., Turner 1998), medicines (e.g., Fortuine 1988), and ritual items (e.g., Compton 1991; Compton et al. 1995). These data allow paleoethnobotanists both to model expectations of plant remains present in the archaeobotanical record and to interpret the remains that are recovered.

Though the information in the ethnographic record and that held by elders today are critical to our understanding of ancient plant use, such information cannot provide the time depth that archaeologists seek.[3] With European contact, many aspects of the traditional lifestyle of Northwest peoples underwent dramatic changes (e.g., Boyd 1990; Carlson 1997; Harris 1994) that ultimately affected patterns of seasonal movement and resource use. The early adoption of the European potato by the Coast Salish (Norton 1985: 136–137; Suttles 1951) is a well-known example of how rapidly such changes occurred.

Changes in land use had profound impacts specifically on traditional plant use. Early habitat destruction from logging, changes in the water table, plowing, and the introduction of grazing animals and exotic plants led to dramatic reductions in traditional plant harvesting areas. Root-gathering locations were especially adversely affected, whereas increased clearing actually may have increased some berry-producing plant populations (Lepofsky 1986; Theodoratus 1989; cf. White 1980). The prohibition of traditional land management practices, such as burning to increase the edible plant harvest, as well as restricted access to traditional collecting grounds, likewise led to a decline in plant use (Lepofsky 1986; Theodoratus 1989). Conversely, the introduction of the horse (and later, roads and wagons) meant a reduction in transportation costs so that upland roots or high-elevation berries could be harvested more frequently and in greater quantities and could be more easily transported back to winter villages (Anastasio 1972; Filloon 1952; Hayden 1992; Theodoratus 1989; Thoms 1989; Turner 1992).

The Northwest Coast Seasonal Round

During the winter months, family groups gathered at the plank house villages, which were located in sheltered locations. Stored food was the primary component of the diet during that time. Fresh plant food was limited in winter to the occasional root vegetable, such as spiny wood fern rootstock (*Dryopteris expansa*). Artifacts such as baskets, mats, tools, and fishing nets were manufactured of plant materials gathered in other seasons.

Springtime undoubtedly brought welcome relief to the monotony of the winter diet. Of the plant foods, fresh green sprouts (e.g., salmonberry [*Rubus spectabilis*], thimbleberry [*R. parviflorus*], fireweed [*Epilobium angustifolium*], cow-parsnip [*Heracleum lanatum*]) were highly valued as much-needed sources of vitamins. These plants were collected near the winter villages and generally were eaten immediately. Small task groups left the village to gather early spring roots (e.g., lupine [*Lupinus littoralis, L. nootkatensis*], springbank clover, Pacific hemlock-parsley [*Conioselinum pacificum*]), and later in the spring, cambium was collected from various trees (e.g., western hemlock). Some of the cambium was processed into cakes for winter consumption.

Summer was the time to gather berries and fruits as they ripened in different habitats and at different elevations. Many of these resources, especially those with low water content (e.g., salal, blueberries, and huckleberries) were dried for winter use. Some were dried in large "fruit leather" rolls, whereas others were dried into "raisins." The end of the summer and fall were primarily spent gathering roots, late-ripening fruits, and, for the more southerly groups, acorns. For the southern Northwest Coast groups particularly, "roots" were an essential source of carbohydrates in the diet. Among these resources, camas bulbs, wild clover rhizomes, and Pacific silverweed roots were especially important. Roots were dug with wooden digging sticks. The majority of the harvested roots were processed and stored for winter consumption. Many of the late-harvest fruits, such as Pacific crabapple (*Malus fusca*) and high-bush cranberry (*Viburnum edule*), were stored in water or grease for later consumption at the winter village. Among some coastal groups, the village heads held inherited rights of ownership of the best berry patches and root grounds.

The Willamette Valley Seasonal Round

The subsistence round of the Kalapuya of the Willamette Valley was one of seasonal movement to exploit the different habitats within their territory (Zenk 1990). Unlike many other coastal groups, for whom salmon was a staple, the people of the Willamette had limited access to salmon. Instead, the economy was broad, with plant resources playing a major role. Small clusters of family groups gathered together in the winter villages located primarily in the shelter of the montane-woodland edge. Houses were semisubterranean, rectangular structures, made of bark, of planks, or both. Winter was a time of minimal subsistence pursuits.

The remainder of the year was spent in transitory camps near seasonal resources. Spring to late summer was the time to harvest camas from the valley bottom. The bulbs were roasted in earth ovens, dried and fragmented, or squashed with a stone mortar and pestle and formed into cakes for winter use. Summer to fall was spent harvesting various seeds, especially tarweed (*Madia* sp.), from burned-over prairies. Once harvested, the seeds were ground into a meal with a stone mortar and pestle. Berries, hazelnuts, and acorns were collected from the oak and montane forests and forest edges in the summer and fall.

The Southwestern Mountains of Oregon Seasonal Round

Culturally, the southwestern mountains of Oregon were transitional between the coast, the Plateau, and northern California (Kendall 1990). The area was occupied by small hunter-gatherer groups whose subsistence rounds were oriented toward river valleys, such as those of the Umpqua and the Rogue. The inhabitants of these areas spent much of the year in rectangular, semisubterranean plank houses clustered along the streams. These house clusters were used as home bases for seasonal forays to harvest resources from the various ecosystems. The grasslands provided camas and tarweed seeds throughout the summer months. Berries and pine nuts were harvested in the summer and fall from the savanna and forested areas. The primary staple, acorns, was harvested from valley bottom and mid-elevation oak forests in the fall; acorns were processed into a meal with mortars and pestles and stored for later use.

The Plateau Seasonal Round

As along the coast, the winter in the interior was a time of minimal subsistence activity. Congregations of families waited out the often very cold winter months in pithouse villages. With the exception of occasional hunting or ice fishing and harvesting of a few plant resources in or under the snow (e.g., rosehips, prickly pear cactus pads, kinnikinnick berries [*Arctostaphylos uva-ursi*]), the village populations relied primarily on stored foods collected during the rest of the year. As on the coast, winter on the Plateau was a time to manufacture various artifacts made of plant materials.

With the coming of spring, the first fresh plant foods were ready for harvest. Early spring roots and fresh green shoots and sprouts were collected close to the winter village, where many of these foods were consumed. Among the greens were cow-parsnip, balsamroot, fireweed, and *Lomatium* spp. The roots included balsamroot, bitteroot (*Lewisia* spp.), *Lomatium* spp., and various lily bulbs (*Fritillaria* spp., *Calochortus macrocarpus*, *Allium cernuum*). As the weather continued to warm, throughout the summer and into the fall, special task groups (primarily women) went to increasingly higher elevations to harvest root crops as they became available. Western spring beauty (*Claytonia lanceolata*), yellow glacier lily (*Erythronium grandiflorum*), and *Lomatium* spp. were the most important of these higher-elevation roots. Many roots were processed (dried, or baked in earth ovens and then dried) at the harvest location and then were brought back to the permanent settlement to be stored for later consumption. The importance of root foods in the Plateau diet as a rich source of carbohydrates has been clearly documented for many areas (Hunn 1990; Hunn and French 1981; Jones and Madsen 1991; Peacock

1998). Not all groups had access to large root-harvesting grounds in their territories; however, for these groups, roots necessarily played a less important role (Anastasio 1972; Turner 1992). Among some groups, as on the coast, root as well as berry grounds were owned or controlled by high-ranking individuals (Peacock and Turner 2000).

The berry and fruit harvest began in early summer, and like the root harvest, moved upland as plants became ready for collecting. The most important summer berry for many Plateau groups was the saskatoon. For many groups, the berry-harvesting season culminated in large late summer gatherings in the uplands to harvest the various blueberry and huckleberry species (especially *Vaccinium membranaceum*). The majority of the berries were dried in the uplands for later use (Filloon 1952; Hunn 1990; Norton et al. 1999). Other berries, nuts (e.g., pine seeds, hazelnuts), and roots were harvested at the mid-to-upper elevations throughout the fall. Again, much of what was harvested was brought back to the winter village for later consumption. The winter village was reoccupied in the late fall.

Ancient Plant Use in the Northwest of North America

The Northwest Coast

Over 100 plant taxa have been identified from sites on the Northwest Coast. They are represented by seeds, wood, needles, leaves, and roots. Remains have been recovered from various contexts dating throughout the Holocene (Table 8.4).

The Early Holocene (pre–3000 BC)

The data that form the basis of our understanding of early Holocene plant use on the Northwest Coast come from three limited paleoethnobotanical analyses, the incidental recovery of remains, and indirect, artifactual evidence. Despite its extremely sparse nature, the record indicates that plants from a range of ecosystems were used and were probably well integrated into the generalized economy of the period.

The Tahkenitch Landing site is the only truly coastal site that has been investigated for paleoethnobotanical remains. The site is located on the southern Oregon coast (Figure 8.1) and dates to sometime before 5,000 years ago

(Moss and Erlandson 1998). The site was identified as a seasonal fishing camp (Minor and Toepel 1986), but the presence of several legume seeds (likely *Vicia* sp.), cherry seeds, and hazelnuts indicate that gathering also took place there (Stenholm 1986a).

A limited paleoethnobotanical analysis conducted at the site of Layser Cave documents the early use of the uplands for plant-gathering activities (Figure 8. 1). The site is located at an elevation of about 600 m in the Cascade Range of southern Washington. It dates to approximately 4500 BC and is interpreted as a spring and summer deer-processing site (Daugherty et al. 1987). Fragments of cherry seeds as well as *Vaccinium* seeds, however, suggest that gathering also took place (Stenholm 1989–90). Stenholm (1989–90) believes the condition of one charred *Vaccinium* fruit suggests the specimen was dried before it was charred, because fresh fruits that are subjected to charring will pop in a characteristic manner. If this interpretation is correct, it indicates that processing plant foods for later consumption began early in prehistory.

Evidence of use of plants at upriver sites comes from the Milliken site on the Fraser River (Mitchell and Pokotylo 1996) and the Dalles Roadcut site on the Columbia (Stenholm n.d.; Figure 8.1). Both sites are situated at major constrictions in the rivers, where salmon can be caught in abundance en route upstream. Both date to the early part of the early Holocene. Archaeobotanical remains from Milliken are limited to cherry seeds found incidentally during excavation. A limited analysis of plant remains from features at the Dalles site, however, produced a range of taxa, including hazelnuts, elderberries, and cherry seeds.

Indirect evidence from artifacts provides additional information on early Holocene plant use on the coast. Edge-ground cobbles (or edged cobbles; Sims 1972) are found at southern coastal sites and may have been used for plant processing as well as the processing of other resources.[4] Early evidence of woodworking, in the form of unifacial pebble choppers, pebble rasps, and core scrapers, comes from the ca. 7000 to 4000 BC levels at Namu on the central coast of British Columbia (Carlson 1996:99; Figure 8.1). An antler wedge and unifacial choppers from the Glenrose site at the mouth of the Fraser River (6500–3000 BC; Matson 1996) also indicate early woodworking technologies. Because redcedar did not recolonize the central and north coast forests (north of the glacial terminus near Seattle) until 5,000 years ago (Hebda and Mathewes 1984), these tools must have been used for working other woods.

Table 8.4

Paleoethnobotanical Remains from the Northwest Coast

Species *Scientific Name* (Common Name)	Part Found	References
BASIDIOMYCOTA		
LYCOPERDACEAE (puffball family)		
Lycoperdon perlatum (puffball)	whole	McPhatter 1985
BRYOPHYTA		
SPHAGNACEAE (sphagnum family)		
Sphagnum sp. (peat mosses)	whole	Croes 1995
PTERIDOPHYTA		
POLYPODIACEAE (fern family)	L, R	Munsell 1976; Stenholm 1992a
GYMNOSPERMAE		
CUPRESSACEAE (cypress family)		
Chamaecyparis sp. (cedars)	W	Connolly and Byram 1997; Inglis 1976; Lepofsky, Heyerdahl, et al. 2003; Lyons 2000; Stenholm 1987c
Juniperus sp. (juniper)	W	Inglis 1976; Stenholm 1987c, 1988c
Thuja plicata (western redcedar)	C, L, W	Barbour 1980; Bernick 1991; Connolly and Byram 1997; Ecklund 1980; Inglis 1976; Lepofsky 1992; Lepofsky, Heyerdahl, et al. 2003; Lyons 2000; McPhatter 1985; Munsell 1976; Nelson 1992; Stenholm 1987c, 1988a, 1988c, 1992a, 1992b, 1995a, 1995b, 1996a, 1996b, 1999
PINACEAE (pine family)		
Abies sp. (true fir)	L, W	Bernick 1991; Burtchard 1990; Inglis 1976; Lepofsky 1992, 1994; Lepofsky, Heyerdahl, et al. 2003; Lyons 2000; Munsell 1976; Stenholm 1987c, 1988a, 1988c, 1995a
Abies sp./*Tsuga* sp.	W	Nelson 1992
Larix sp. (larch)	W	Stenholm 1988a
Picea sp. (spruces)	C, L, S[a], W	Barbour 1980; Bernick 1991; Burtchard 1990; Ecklund 1980; Inglis 1976; Lepofsky 1992, 1994; Lepofsky, Heyerdahl, et al. 2003; Lyons 2000; Moss et al. 1990; Munsell 1976; Nelson 1992; Stenholm 1986a, 1987c, 1992b, 1995a, 1995b, 1999

Taxon	Codes	References
Picea sitchensis (Sitka spruce)	S	Ecklund-Johnson 1984
Pinus sp. (pines)	C, L, S, W	Burtchard 1990; Inglis 1976; Ketcheson et al. 1977; Lepofsky 1994; Lepofsky, Heyerdahl, et al. 2003; Lyons 2000; Mack 1992; Stenholm 1986a, 1987c, 1988a, 1988c, 1992b, 1995a
Pseudotsuga menziesii (Douglas-fir)	C, L, S, W[a]	Baptiste and Wollstonecroft 1997; Bernick 1991; Burtchard 1990; Chatters 1981; Connolly and Byram 1997; Ecklund 1980; Ketcheson et al. 1977; Lepofsky 1992, 1994; Lepofsky, Heyerdahl, et al. 2003; Lyons 2000; Mack 1992; Nelson 1992; Stenholm 1987c, 1988a, 1988c, 1989–90, 1992a, 1992b, 1995a, 1995b, 1996a, 1996b, 1997b, 1999, n.d.
Tsuga sp. (hemlocks)	C, L, W	Bernick 1991; Burtchard 1990; Connolly and Byram 1997; Ecklund 1980; Inglis 1976; Lepofsky 1992; Lepofsky, Heyerdahl, et al. 2003; Lyons 2000; Munsell 1976; Stenholm 1987c, 1988a, 1992a, 1992b, 1995a, 1996a, 1999
TAXACEAE (yew family)		
Taxus sp. (yews)	W	Barbour 1980; Bernick 1991; Inglis 1976; Lepofsky 1992; Lyons 2000; Nelson 1992; Stenholm 1987c
MONOCOTYLEDONAE		
ALISMATACEAE (water plantain family)		
cf. *Sagittaria* sp. (wapato)	R	Croes 1987
CYPERACEAE (sedge family)	St	Stenholm 1992a
Carex sp. (sedges)	S[a]	Ecklund-Johnson 1984; Ketcheson et al. 1977; Lepofsky 1994; Stenholm n.d.
Carex lyngbyei (Lyngby's sedge)	S	Ecklund-Johnson 1984
Eleocharis cf. *palustris* (common spikeweed)	S	Stenholm 1996b
Scirpus sp. (bulrushes)	S	Lepofsky 1992; Mack and McClure 2002; Stenholm 1987c, 1988c
GRAMINEAE (grass family)	S[a], L[a]	Baptiste and Wollstonecroft 1997; Chatters 1981; Ecklund-Johnson 1984; Lepofsky 1992, 1994; Lyons 2000; Stenholm 1996b, n.d.
Elymus sp. (wildrye)	S	Stenholm 1997b
Hordeum sp. (barley)	S	Ketcheson et al. 1977
Panicum sp. (panicum)	S	Ketcheson et al. 1977
Paspalum distichum (knotgrass)	S	Ketcheson et al. 1977
JUNCACEAE (rush family)		
Juncus sp. (rush)	S	Stenholm 1996b

Continued on next page

Table 8.4 *continued*

Species *Scientific Name* (Common Name)	Part Found	References
LILIACEAE (lily family)		
Allium spp. (onion)	S, R	Pettigrew 1980; Stenholm 1987c, 1997b
Camassia spp. (camas)	S, R	Baptiste and Wollstonecroft 1997; Chatters 1981; Pettigrew 1980; Stenholm 1987c, 1996b, 1999
Maianthemum dilatatum (false lily-of-the-valley)	S	Lyons 2000; Patenaude 1985
Xerophyllum tenax (bear-grass)	L	Mack 1992
POTAMOGETONACEAE (pondweed family)		
Potamogeton sp. (pondweed)	S	Stenholm 1996b, 1997b
TYPHACEAE (cattail family)		
Typha latifolia (cattail)	down, L, S, St	Ostapkowicz et al. 2001; Stenholm 1992a
DICOTYLEDONAE		
ACERACEAE (maple family)		
Acer sp. (maples)	W	Bernick 1991; Inglis 1976; Lepofsky 1992, 1994; Lyons 2000; Munsell 1976; Nelson 1992; Stenholm 1987c, 1992a, 1995a, 1996a, 1996b, 1997b, 1999
ANACARDIACEAE (cashew family)		
Rhus sp. (sumac)	W	Stenholm 1987c
AMARANTHACEAE (amaranth family)		
Amaranthus sp. (pigweed)	S	Stenholm 1987c
APIACEAE (carrot family)		
Lomatium spp. (lomatiums)	S, T	Ketcheson et al. 1977; Stenholm 1987c
ASTERACEAE (aster family)		
Aster sp. (asters)	S	Lyons 2000
Madia sp. (tarweed)	S	Ketcheson et al. 1977
BERBERIDACEAE (barberry family)		
Mahonia sp. (Oregon-grape)	S	Nelson 1992; Stenholm 1996b

Taxon		References
BETULACEAE (birch family)		
Alnus sp. (alder)	C, W	Ecklund 1980; Inglis 1976; Lepofsky 1994; Lepofsky, Heyerdahl, et al. 2003; Lyons 2000; Munsell 1976; Nelson 1992; Stenholm 1987c, 1992a, 1992b, 1995a, 1996a, 1997b
Alnus rubra (red alder)	S	Ecklund-Johnson 1984
Betula sp. (birches)	S, W	Inglis 1976; Ketcheson et al. 1977; Lepofsky 1992, 1994; Stenholm 1992a, 1992b, 1995a, 1996b
Corylus sp. (hazelnut)	S[a], W	Croes 1987; Eldridge and Fisher 1997; Munsell 1976; Pettigrew 1980; Pettigrew and Lebow 1987; Stenholm 1986a, 1987c, 1995a, 1996b, 1997a, 1997b, 1999, n.d.
BRASSICACEAE (mustard family)		
Brassica spp. (mustards)	S	Chatters 1988
CAPRIFOLIACEAE (honeysuckle family)		Ketcheson et al. 1977
Lonicera sp. (honeysuckles)	S, W	Lyons 2000 (cf.); Stenholm 1997b
Sambucus sp. (elderberry)	S, W	Chatters 1981, 1988; Croes 1995; Ecklund-Johnson 1984; Hammon 1986; Ketcheson et al. 1977; Lepofsky 1992,1994; Lepofsky, Heyerdahl, et al. 2003; Lyons 2000; Nelson 1992; Stenholm 1987c, 1988c, 1992a, 1992b, 1995a, 1995b, 1996a
Sambucus racemosa (red elderberry)	S	Stenholm 1996b
Sambucus caerulea (blue elderberry)	S[a]	Stenholm 1996b, 1997b, n.d. (cf.)
CARYOPHYLLACEAE (pink family)	S	Stenholm 1987c
CHENOPODIACEAE (goosefoot family)		
Chenopodium sp. (chenopod)	S[a]	Baptiste and Wollstonecroft 1997; Chatters 1981, 1988; Lepofsky 1994; Lyons 2000; Stenholm 1987c, 1995a, 1996a, 1996b, 1997b, n.d.
Suaeda sp. (sea-blite)	S	Chatters 1988
CORNACEAE (dogwood family)		
Cornus sp. (dogwood)	S, W	Lyons 2000 (cf.); Stenholm 1987c, 1995a
Cornus canadensis (bunchberry)	S	Lepofsky 1992; Lyons 2000
Cornus stolonifera (red-osier dogwood)	S	Chatters 1981; Ketcheson et al. 1977
ERICACEAE (heath family)		
Arbutus menziesii (arbutus)	W	Nelson 1992
Arctostaphylos spp. (manzanita)	F, S, T	Lepofsky 1992; Lepofsky, Heyerdahl, et al. 2003; Lyons 2000; Nelson 1992; Stenholm 1986a, 1987c, 1988c, 1996b, 1997b

Continued on next page

397

Table 8.4 *continued*

Species Scientific Name (Common Name)	Part Found	References
Gaultheria sp. (salal)	F, S, T	Lepofsky 1992, 1994; Lyons 2000; Stenholm 1987c, 1992b
Gaultheria sp./*Vaccinium* sp. (salal/blueberry)	S	Ecklund-Johnson 1984; Nelson 1992
Vaccinium sp. (blueberry and huckleberry)	F, L, S, T[a], W	Burtchard 1990; Chatters 1988; Croes 1995; Ketcheson et al. 1977; Lepofsky 1994; Lyons 2000; Mack 1992; Mack and McClure 2002; Martindale 1999; Munsell 1976; Stenholm 1987, 1989–90, 1996b, 1997b
FABACEAE (pea family)		
Lupinus (lupine)	S	Stenholm 1988c
Trifolium sp. (clover)	S	Stenholm 1987c
Vicia sp. (vetch)	S[a]	Chatters 1981; Ketcheson et al. 1977; Stenholm 1986a
FAGACEAE (beech family)		
Quercus sp. (oak)	S, W[a]	Baptiste and Wollstonecroft 1997; Croes 1987; Nelson 1992; Pettigrew 1980; Pettigrew and Lebow 1987; Stenholm 1989–90, 1995b, 1996b, 1999
FUMARIACEAE (fumitory family)		
Dicentra formosa (Pacific bleedinghearts)	S	Lyons 2000
GROSSULARIACEAE (gooseberry family)		
Ribes spp. (currants)	S	Lyons 2000
LABIATAE (mint family)	S	Ecklund-Johnson 1984
Prunella vulgaris (self-heal)	S	Ecklund-Johnson 1984
Satureja cf. *douglasii* (yerba buena)	S	Lyons 2000
OLEACEAE (olive family)		
Fraxinus sp. (ash)	W[a]	Stenholm 1996a, 1996b, n.d.
PLANTAGINACEAE (plantago family)		
Plantago sp. (plantain)	S	Stenholm 1987c
PLUMBAGINACEAE (leadwort family)		
Armeria maritima (thrift)	W	Lepofsky et al. 2001
POLYGONACEAE (buckwheat family)		
Polygonum sp. (knotweed)	S[a]	Ketcheson et al. 1977; Lyons 2000; Stenholm 1988c, 1996a, 1996b, n.d.
Rumex sp. (dock)	S	Stenholm 1996b

PORTULACACEAE (purslane family)		
Montia sp. (miner's lettuce)	S	Stenholm 1992b, 1997b
RANUNCULACEAE (buttercup family)		
Thalictrum sp. (meadowrue)	S	Ketcheson et al. 1977
RHAMNACEAE (buckthorn family)		
Rhamnus sp. (buckthorn)	W	Baptiste and Wollstonecroft 1997; Stenholm 1987c, 1996a, 1996b, 1999
ROSACEAE (rose family)		
Amelanchier sp. (serviceberry)	F, S	Nelson 1992; Stenholm 1987c, 1997b
Crataegus sp. (hawthorn)	F, S	Lyons 2000; Stenholm 1986a (cf.), 1987c
Fragaria spp. (strawberry)	S	Lyons 2000; Stenholm 1987c
Holodiscus discolor (oceanspray)	W[a]	Bernick 1991; Stenholm 1987c, 1989–90, 1995a, 1995b, 1996a, 1996b, 1999
Malus sp. (crabapple)	S, W	Bernick 1991; Ecklund-Johnson 1984; Inglis 1976; Lepofsky, Heyerdahl, et al. 2003; Lyons 2000 (cf.); Stenholm 1987c, 1992b
Oemleria cerasiformis (Indian plum)	S	Lepofsky 1992; Stenholm 1995a, 1997b
Potentilla sp. (silverweed)	S	Ecklund-Johnson 1984; Lyons 2000
Potentilla sp./*Fragaria* sp.	S	Stenholm 1997b
Prunus sp. (cherry)	F, S[a], W	Baptiste and Wollstonecroft 1997; Chatters 1981, 1988; Keddie 1988; Ketcheson et al. 1977; Lepofsky 1992, 1994; Munsell 1976; Pettigrew 1980; Stenholm 1986a, 1992b, 1997a, 1997b
Prunus emarginata (bitter cherry)	S	Croes 1995; Stenholm 1995a, 1997a
Prunus subcordata (Klamath plum)	S	Stenholm 1997a
Prunus cf. *virginiana* (chokecherry)	S[a]	Stenholm n.d.
Rosa sp. (rosehip)	S, W	Chatters 1981, 1988; Croes 1995; Lyons 2000; Nelson 1992; Stenholm 1992a, 1997b
Rosa nutkana (Nootka rose)	F, S	Ecklund-Johnson 1984
Rubus sp. (raspberries and related berries)	F, S, W	Baptiste and Wollstonecroft 1997; Bernick 1991; Chatters 1981; Eldridge and Fisher 1997; Ecklund-Johnson 1984; Ketcheson et al. 1977; Lepofsky 1992, 1994; Lepofsky, Heyerdahl, et al. 2003; Lyons 2000; Munsell 1976; Nelson 1992; Stenholm 1987c, 1988c, 1992a, 1992b, 1995b, 1996b, 1997b, 1999
Sorbus sp. (mountain ash)	S	Stenholm 1987c
Spirea douglasii (hardhack)	W	Bernick 1991

Continued on next page

Table 8.4 *continued*

Species *Scientific Name* (Common Name)	Part Found	References
RUBIACEAE (madder family)		
Galium sp. (bedstraw)	F, S	Chatters 1981; Stenholm 1987c, 1995a, 1995b, 1996a, 1996b, 1997b
SALICACEAE (willow family)		
Populus sp. (cottonwood)	W[a]	Baptiste and Wollstonecroft 1997; Bernick 1991; Lepofsky 1992, 1994; Stenholm 1987c, 1992b, 1995b, 1996a, 1996b, 1999, n.d.
Salix sp. (willow)	W	Lepofsky 1992; Lepofsky, Heyerdahl, et al. 2003; Munsell 1976; Stenholm 1987, 1995a, 1995b, 1996a, 1996b
Salix sp./*Populus* sp.	W	Lyons 2000; Stenholm 1988c, 1999
SAXIFRAGACEAE (saxifrage family)		
Philadelphus sp. (mock-orange)	W	Stenholm 1988c, 1995a
Tellima grandiflora (fringecup)	S	Ecklund-Johnson 1984
Tiarella trifoliate (foamflower)	S	Ecklund-Johnson 1984
SCROPHULARIACEAE (figwort family)		
Collinsia sp. (blue-eyed Mary)	S	Stenholm 1988c
SOLANACEAE (nightshade family)		
Solanum sp. (nightshade)	S	Chatters 1981; Stenholm 1996b
URTICACEAE (nettle family)		
Urtica sp. (nettles)	S	Lyons 2000
ZOSTERACEAE		
Zostera marina (seawrack)	S	Ketcheson et al. 1977

Note: C = cone, F = fruit, L = leaf/needle, R = bulbs, corms, rhizomes, etc., S = "seed" (exocarp, endocarp, etc.,), St = stem, T = other nonwoody tissue, W = wood, bark, branch, etc.

[a] Found in deposits older than 3000 BC as well as those postdating 3000 BC

Though the post–3000 BC archaeobotanical record on the coast is more extensive than that of the early Holocene, in some cases it is no easier to interpret. A large number of isolated sediment samples have been examined for plant remains, but only a handful of systematic paleoethnobotanical studies have been conducted. The record is particularly scarce for sites in southeastern Alaska.

Although numerous village sites have been excavated on the coast, few have been examined for paleoethnobotanical remains (Chatters 1981, 1988; Gill 1983; Lepofsky 1994; Lepofsky and Lyons 2003; Lyons 2000; Stenholm 1986a, 1987c, 1992a, 1992b, 1995b, 1996b, 1997a, 1997b). With the exception of three sites, the villages producing plant remains that have been studied are located in Washington State. Most of the sites were occupied during the last 1,000 years of prehistory, but village deposits at the Tahkenitch Landing site date from 3200 to 1000 BC and those at Scowlitz (Figure 8.1) date to 400 BC to AD 200.

Despite the relatively small sample size, an impressive list of plants from a range of ecosystems has been recovered from village sites (Table 8.4). The taxa indicate a wide range of plant-related activities, including the consumption of fresh and processed plant foods, the processing of plants for future consumption, and the use of plants for various technologies. Nonlocal species recovered at the Ozette site on the Olympic Penninsula (Friedman 1975; Gill 1983) and at the Lone Pine site on the Columbia River (Stenholm 1997a) suggest that some plant taxa may have been traded over long distances. Unfortunately, the sample of investigated village sites is not yet large enough to detect trends in plant use through time.

Seeds from berries and fruits are the most common plant food remains recovered from coastal village sites. Salal, *Vaccinium* sp., red elderberry (*Sambucus racemosa*), and *Rubus* often dominate village archaeobotanical assemblages.[5] The density and context of these remains suggest that they were eaten fresh and were also processed en masse and eaten during the winter months. Evidence of salal processing comes from flattened, mature berries (Stenholm 1992a) and an abundance of seeds in hearths within houses (Lyons 2000) and middens outside houses (Gill 1983). Seeds of nonlocal *Vaccinium* sp. found at a Chinookan village in the Lower Columbia River valley, were likely transported from upland berrying sites (Stenholm 1997b; see below). Compelling evidence for *Vaccinium* processing and storage comes from the protohistoric

Tsimshian village of Psacelay on the Skeena River in northern British Columbia, where hundreds of thousands of *Vaccinium* seeds (and staining from the berry juice) were recovered from hearths and storage areas associated with high-status families (Martindale 1999).

At the Ozette site, almost 30,000 elderberry seeds were recovered in association with *Rubus* seeds, suggesting the two fruits were mixed to increase the palatability of the otherwise insipid elderberries (Gill 1983). The seeds were found together both inside and outside the houses (in the middens). Because the mud slide at Ozette is thought to have occurred in the spring, before berries ripen, the co-occurrence of the two fruits inside the house indicates storage (Norton 1981:435). Ethnographically, various *Rubus* species (but not salmonberry) were boiled and dried for future consumption, but elderberries were boiled and made into a sauce. Their co-occurrence at Ozette suggests these species were processed and stored in a manner not documented in the ethnographic literature.

Several additional species of berries and fruits are found in small amounts in coastal village sites. They include bitter cherry (*Prunus emarginata*, which was not eaten in the historic period), *Vaccinium* spp., *Rosa* spp., red-osier dogwood (*Cornus stolonifera*), kinnikinnick, Pacific crabapple, Oregon-grape (*Mahonia* sp.), and strawberry (*Fragaria* spp.). Many of these species could have been processed for winter use, but some (e.g., strawberries) could only have been eaten fresh, in season.

Direct evidence for the processing and consumption of "roots" at villages comes from the site of Cathlapotl, a year-round Chinookan village, located north of Portland. A series of rock ovens located in the front of a house produced an abundance of camas, possible wapato (*Sagittaria latifolia*), and a range of other plant foods (Stenholm 1996b). Stenholm (1996b) notes that the camas bulbs were small to average in size, suggesting that the large bulbs were removed from the ovens with greater care and only the smaller specimens remained.

Additional evidence for the use of roots at village sites is sparse. A single camas bulb recovered in the screen is the only direct evidence for camas use in any British Columbia site (Baptiste and Wolstonecroft 1997). At the Duwamish village site, near Seattle (Stenholm 1987c), the midden produced the remains of camas, onion, and another, unidentified "root." At the nearby White Lake site, identified as a processing area associated with another Duwamish village, wapato and a range of other plant foods were recovered from features (Stenholm 1996a). The archaeobotanical records from Cathlapotl and the Duwamish sites suggest that at villages plant food processing in general, and root food processing in particular, often may have occurred at some distance from the houses themselves.

Given that the ethnographic model of plant use indicates the importance of various wild root foods among many coastal peoples, root remains should be relatively common components of the archaeobotanical record. Their absence can be explained in part by the care with which the root foods were initially cooked in earth ovens. In addition, most paleoethnobotanists in the Northwest are unable to identify parenchymous tissues in the archaeobotanical record. Flotation samples from coastal middens contain an abundance of small, disassociated pieces of plant tissue (Stenholm's "possible edible tissue" [PET]), which, if examined with scanning electron microscopy, would undoubtedly reveal a range of plant remains (cf. Stenholm 1987c).

Nuts have also been recovered from several village sites along the south coast. Direct evidence consists of the remains of hazelnuts found at both Duwamish (Stenholm 1987c) and Ozette (Gill 1983), and charred acorns and hazelnuts from the Meier site (Ames et al. 1992), Cathlapotl (Stenholm 1996b), and Sunken Village (Croes 1987; Pettigrew and Lebow 1987), all on the Lower Columbia River. No direct evidence for the use of seed plants has been found at any coastal site.

On the whole, more paleoethnobotanical research has been conducted at short-term camps than at village sites, though both site types are poorly represented in this regard. A range of plant remains has been recovered from most sites, regardless of the sites' primary functions. This indicates that at least some plant gathering and use always occurred in tandem with other resource extraction activities. This is true for low-elevation camps as well as for those in the uplands (e.g., Burtchard 1990; Stenholm 1989).

As at village sites, elderberry, *Rubus*, and salal or *Vaccinium* sp. often dominate the archaeobotancial assemblages of short-term lowland camps (e.g., Ecklund-Johnson 1984; Hammon 1986; Lepofsky 1992; Lepofsky et al. 2001; Lepofsky and Lyons 2003; Lyons 2000; Mierendorf 1986; Stenholm 1995a, 1996a), but a range of other species are recovered in minor amounts. At the Barnett site, on the Fraser River in Vancouver, British Columbia (Lepofsky 1992), and at the Scowlitz site 100 km inland on the Fraser (Figure 8.1), huge quantities of these three berry taxa were found together in a series of shallow cooking features. These features, together with the fact that the berries are often found associated at village sites, support the notion that the plants were processed together en masse (with the seeds) for winter consumption. These and other summer berries were recovered from the deposits at the Hoko River campsites (Ecklund-Johnson 1984), which are thought to have been occupied in spring/summer and late summer/fall (Croes 1995:69; Figure 8.1). This suggests either that processed fruits were eaten throughout the year, not just at winter villages, or that the sites were occupied for additional seasons than previously suggested.

A unique example of plant food processing comes from the Pitt River site, located east of Vancouver, on the Fraser River. Though generally thought of as a fishing camp, a late deposit contained over 80 hearths that produced hundreds of thousands of charred lily-of-the-valley (*Maianthemum dilatatum*) seeds, as well as abundant hemlock needles. The needles likely originate from the boughs used as pit lining. Detailed descriptions of the features are not provided in the site report, but from drawings, they appear to be circular to linear, up to 4–6 m long, and 2–3 m wide. The absence of lily-of-the-valley seeds at village sites suggests that processing involved making a seedless sauce that was stored for future consumption. Several of the features at the Pitt River site show evidence of having been repeatedly used for plant processing. This, in turn, may indicate an owned or preferred harvesting location.

A recent discovery of a series of late prehistoric and historic sites near the crest of the southern Washington Cascades provides new insights into the importance of upland berry gathering and processing. At "Indian Heaven" sites in southern Washington (Figure 8.1) large quantities of *Vaccinium* berries (in particular, *V. membranaceum* and *V. deliciosum*, based on elders' interviews) were dried for future consumption using reflected heat from a log fire (Mack 1992; Mack and McClure 2002). The sites are located in upland meadows, from 900 m to over 1,500 m in elevation, with the majority occurring above 1,280 m. Today many of the features are located within forested areas that do not support blueberries, which may indicate changes in fire regime in these areas (see prescribed burning, below).

To date, well over 200 berry-drying features have been identified (Cheryl Mack, personal communication 2000). Archaeologically, these appear as subtle linear depressions or trenches (average 1 m wide, 6 m long, and 20 cm deep) with a mound of earth on one side. There is often a line of rocks inside the trench that is sometimes visible on the surface or that can be located with a soil probe or by excavating. A thin, dense lens of charcoal is often found at the base of the trench, and a decaying or charred log occasionally parallels the trench (Mack and McClure 2002). Many of the sites are associated with bark-stripped trees and the remains of temporary structures. Archaeobotanical analyses of these features have yielded *Vaccinium* seeds and fruits as well as *Scirpus* seeds, likely from the mat used to dry the berries (Mack and McClure 2002).

Recently, additional berry-drying sites have been identified in the Coast Range of northern Washington (elevation 1,365 m; Miss and Nelson 1995), in the North Cascades of British Columbia just north of the international border (elevation 1,600 m; Franck 2000), and near Mt. Garibaldi, about 90 km north of Vancouver (elevation 1,660 m; Reimer 2000). The trench features in northern Washington (the ones in British Columbia were not excavated) differ from those at Indian Heaven in that they contain large quantities of charcoal but no rocks. They have yielded radiocarbon dates ranging from 700 BC to AD 400. This evidence indicates that some variation existed in the method of drying and that some of these features are quite old. A concerted effort to systematically survey high-elevation meadows should locate many more berry-processing sites (Lookabill 1998).

Direct evidence for "root" processing and consumption at short-term camps is sparse. Low-elevation earth ovens (undated) have been recorded on eastern Vancouver Island and in northwestern Washington State (Capes 1964; Reagan 1917; Thoms 1989:296–299). These have been identified as camas-processing features, which, based on their location and form, is likely. Although there has not been systematic collection of plant remains from these features, in addition to bulbs (presumed to be camas), several unidentified seeds have been observed.

The only other possible evidence for the use of root foods comes from the Hoko River wet site, dating to 100 BC–AD 200 (Croes 1995; Figure 8.1). Croes (1995:68) notes that it is common to find fern rhizomes (unidentified) in the wet-site layers. He believes that these were discarded after being ground—likely with the stone bowls and grinding stones found in the associated dry deposits of the site—as described in the ethnographic literature on the use of bracken (*Pteridium aquilinum*) rhizomes (Norton 1979b). If Croes is right, the Hoko River evidence not only documents the antiquity of fern rhizome processing but also points to the value of conducting systematic paleoethnobotanical analyses in wet-site deposits.

The only possible identification of root harvesting at higher elevations comes from the Naches site, located at 1,500 m above sea level, on the crest of the Washington coast mountains. The site, dated to ca. AD 1, has been identified as a special lithic processing site, but starchy tissues were recovered from a hearth (Stenholm 1988a). The unidentified tissues are the only potential evidence of high-altitude root gathering on the coast.

Only limited evidence exists for the use of nuts in short-term camps on the coast. Small numbers of acorns and hazelnuts were recovered from a late prehistoric campsite south of Seattle (Stenholm 1996a). In addition, a site near Victoria, BC, dating from 450 BC to AD 450, is thought to be an acorn-processing site (Baptiste and Wollstonecroft 1997). Indirect evidence for nut processing and consumption (see below) suggests that the apparent absence of acorns and hazelnuts in sites located in suitable ecosystems is the result of sampling bias.

Finally, there is extensive indirect evidence for plant food harvesting and use over the last 5,000 years of coastal prehistory. Indirect evidence for seeds, nuts, and "roots" comes from manos, grinding slabs, mortars, and pestles recovered from several sites along the southern Oregon coast and the Columbia River that date to at least 2000 BC (Aikens 1993; Ames et al. 1992; Burtchard 1990; Pettigrew 1981). Grinding slabs and manos (but not mortars and pestles) have also been recovered from sites in Washington and southwestern British Columbia that date to the same time (Larson and Lewarch 1995; Mitchell 1971). These tools may indicate acorn processing. Large grinding or pounding slabs ("tabular palettes") and edge- and end-battered pebbles were recovered from the Maurer site, a 4,500-year-old house in the Fraser Valley. These items may have been used to process plants (Schaepe 1998), but it is not clear which species were involved. Root crops are also indirectly represented by antler digging stick handles and digging sticks recovered from village sites on the Oregon coast (Aikens 1993; Connolly 1992), the Columbia River (Ames et al. 1992; Pettigrew 1981), and the Lachane site in northern British Columbia (Inglis 1976; Figure 8.1), all dating to ca. 500 BC.

The Late Holocene (post-3000 BC): Nonfood Plants

The combined records from villages and campsites on the coast provide data on technological uses of plants in the past. Charcoal identifications from most sites demonstrate a strong preference for conifer woods, in particular Douglas-fir, over hardwoods (e.g., Lepofsky 1992, 1994; Stenholm 1987c, 1992a, 1995a, 1995b, 1997b). In most cases, the dominance of Douglas-fir cannot be explained simply by its abundance in the surrounding forest. Assuming that the bulk of the charred wood was used as fuel, selection of Douglas-fir makes sense. It burns well and is easily collected because it is a good self-pruner (i.e., the branches regularly fall off by themselves). Of the hardwoods, cottonwood (*Populus* sp.) is fairly well represented, but alder (*Alnus* sp.) is exceedingly rare, especially in comparison with its current dominance in many coastal habitats. In general, the diversity of taxa represented by charcoal may be greater at village sites than at shorter-term occupations, both because of the greater need for warmth at winter villages and because wood tends to be used for a greater range of tasks at villages (e.g., tool production and repair) than at camps (Lepofsky and Lyons 2003; Lyons 2000).

The sheer abundance of charcoal from most sites reflects the importance of fuelwoods on the coast. Not only was fuel needed for warmth and basic cooking, but it was also critical for drying foods for winter consumption. The ethnographic records are replete with passages that document the value of fuel on the Northwest Coast (Lepofsky, Lyons, et al. 2003). A paleoethnobotanical analysis from a campsite on Cape Addington in southeast Alaska indicates that driftwood, particularly Douglas-fir, was an important source of fuelwood (Lepofsky et al. 2001; Figure 8.1).

Wet sites are a tremendous source of data on the use of plants for technology. The oldest waterlogged materials are stakes that were part of fish weirs (Moss et al. 1990). These are found throughout the coast, dating to as early as ca. 1550 BC (Moss et al. 1990), and have been identified as a variety of coniferous woods (Bernick 1991; Moss et al. 1990). Basketry and cordage from wet sites have been extensively studied. In addition to contributing to discussions of style and ethnicity (see above), these analyses provide detailed information on the technical use of fibers in the past (e.g., Bernick 1991; Connolly and Byram 1997).

Examination of wood artifacts from Ozette and, to a lesser extent, Hoko River and the Lachane site in northern British Columbia (Barbour 1980; Friedman 1975; Inglis 1976; Figure 8.1) provides valuable information on the selection of woods for manufacturing artifacts. At Ozette, Friedman (1975) clearly demonstrates the preference for western redcedar for most artifact types, followed by yew (*Taxus brevifolia*) and Sitka spruce. Sitka spruce is generally considered a second choice to yew as a tough wood needed for such tools as wedges. Yews, however, are rare and slow growing and would have been easily overexploited. The people at Ozette compensated for this by only choosing compression wood from the spruces when they needed a tougher wood. The findings at Hoko, although not quantified to the same extent, seem to parallel those from Ozette. At the Lachane site, there was a strong preference for true fir, followed by hemlock and then by western redcedar, for the many digging sticks recovered at the site.

Indirect evidence for large-scale woodworking increases dramatically in the post–3000 BC archaeological record, with the appearance of artifacts such as mauls, adzes, and wedges. The prevalence of the woodworking tool-kit in the late Holocene is tied to the establishment of western redcedar on the coast at approximately the same time (Hebda and Mathewes 1984). Other evidence for plant processing over the last 2,000 years comes from artifacts such as bark shredders (e.g., Dewhirst 1980; MacDonald 1983; McMillan and St. Claire 1994), bark beaters (e.g., Dewhirst 1980; McMillan and St. Claire 1992), spindle whorls, possibly for spinning plant fibers (Carlson 1972), matting needles (Chatters 1988), probable net shuttles (Chatters 1988), and possible net gauges (Dewhirst 1980). The earliest possible mat creaser comes from the Hoko River wet site and dates to approximately 850 BC (Croes 1995). Two bark peelers were discovered at an early historic village on the central coast (Philip Hobler, personal communication 2002).

"Culturally Modified Trees" (CMTs) are an important source of information on the use of trees on the Northwest Coast. In British Columbia, a CMT has been formally defined as "a tree which has been intentionally altered by Native people as part of their traditional use of the forest" (Stryd 1997; Stryd and Eldridge 1993). Tree alteration results from a range of activities, including the removal of bark for weaving and shelter (e.g., Bergland 1992; Davis 1991, 1993), cambium, pitch, or sap extraction (Eldridge 1982; Hadley 1999), harvesting of medicines, and the removal of logs or planks (Mobley and Eldridge 1992). Each activity results in unique morphological variation in the altered tree (Davis 1992; Mobley and Eldridge 1992; Stryd 1997). The most common CMTs on the coast are bark-stripped yellow-cedars and red-cedars that have had the outer bark removed to access the softer inner bark so highly valued for weaving items such as clothing and baskets. These trees have characteristic healing lobes over the scars, some of which have been dated, using dendrochronological techniques, from the mid-15th century AD to the historic period (Mobley and Eldridge 1992). Cultural alterations have also been identified on coastal western hemlock, spruce, and pine, but these are less common, reflecting both Aboriginal use patterns and the fact that these species are less likely to survive after the bark has been damaged. CMTs have been documented from the Oregon Cascades to the Kodiak Archipelago in Alaska and from sea level to high-elevation zones.

Few examples exist from the coast of late-period ritual and medicinal uses of plants. At a historic burial site near Victoria, BC, concentrations of cherry seeds were thought to be evidence of ritual "feeding the dead" (Keddie 1988);

however, lack of proper excavation controls in burial and nonburial contexts weaken the argument. At a historic burial in Toquart Bay on the west coast of Vancouver Island, an individual was recovered with two clusters of puffballs (*Lycoperdon* sp.) around the neck, likely placed there for medicinal or ritual purposes or both (McPhatter 1985).

The only precontact coastal example of plants in ritual contexts comes from the Greenville Burial site on the Nass River in northern British Columbia. Several burials at this site dating to ca. AD 250–1250 were found associated with layers of elderberry seeds. This is consistent with Tsimshian and Nishga origin myths, which associate elderberries with death (Cybulski 1993).

The Willamette Valley

The importance of plant resources in the subsistence round of the earliest prehistoric people of the Willamette Valley is well documented (Table 8.5), despite the fact that only a few sites from the valley have been systematically investigated for plant remains (Cheatham 1988; Connolly et al. 1999; Minor and Pickett 1982). The earliest definitive evidence for plant use comes from the Hannavan Creek site, located on a small tributary of the Long Tom River, just west of Eugene. Hearths and earth ovens are common at the site, as are fragments of ground stone that may have been used for grinding and pounding. One earth oven produced several hundred charred camas bulbs, which were radiocarbon dated to about 6000 BC (Cheatham 1988). Remains of camas, acorns, and hazelnuts are also reported from other pre–4000 BC sites along the Long Tom River (O'Neill 1987).

Extensive evidence exists for plant harvesting, processing, consumption, and storage in lowland sites dating after 4000 BC in the Willamette Valley. The emphasis on plant use varies with site type, but most sites have evidence of plant exploitation. Evidence for plant use comes from a range of site types, including seasonal camps (Connolly et al. 1999; Miller 1975; Minor and Pickett 1985; O'Neill 1987; Pettigrew 1980; Prouty et al. 1999; Sanford 1975; Wilson 1993), multiseason base camps (Cheatham 1988; Connolly et al. 1999; Pettigrew 1980), and winter residential sites (Aikens 1993:195, 206–209; Cheatham 1988; White 1975). Direct evidence comes from camas bulbs, acorns, and hazelnuts found during excavation. Minor amounts of other plants have also been recovered when flotation has been employed, but the camas-acorn-hazelnut triad dominates the record. Indirect evidence comes from manos and grinding slabs, mortars and pestles, and earth ovens. A stone

Table 8.5

Paleoethnobotanical Remains from the Willamette Valley

Species *Scientific Name* (Common Name)	Part Found	References
PTERIDOPHYTA		
POLYPODIACEAE (fern family)		
Pteridium aquilinum (bracken fern)	L	Tuohy 1986
MONOCOTYLEDONAE		
CYPERACEAE (sedge family)		
Carex sp. (sedges)	S	Minor and Pickett 1985
GRAMINEAE (grass family)	S	Minor and Pickett 1982
Hordeum sp. (barley)	S	Minor and Pickett 1985
LILIACEAE (lily family)		
Allium spp. (onion)	S	Minor and Pickett 1985
Camassia spp. (camas)	R	Cheatham 1988; Miller 1975; O'Neill 1987; Prouty et al. 1999; Sanford 1975; White 1975
DICOTYLEDONAE		
BETULACEAE (birch family)		
Corylus sp. (hazelnut)	S	Minor and Pickett 1982; Newman 1966; O'Neill 1987; Prouty et al. 1999
ERICACEAE (heath family)		
Vaccinium sp. (blueberry and huckleberry)	S	Minor and Pickett 1982

Taxon	Part	References
FABACEAE (pea family)		
Cercis occidentalis (redbud)	L	Touhy 1986
FAGACEAE (beech family)		
Quercus sp. (oak)	S	Minor and Pickett 1982, 1985; O'Neill 1987; Prouty et al. 1999
JUGLANDACEAE (hickory family)		
Juglans sp. (walnut)	S	Minor and Pickett 1985
POLYGONACEAE (buckwheat family)		
Rumex sp. (dock)	S	Minor and Pickett 1982; Prouty et al. 1999
PORTULACACEAE (purslane family)		
Claytonia perfoliata (miner's lettuce)	S	Prouty et al. 1999
RHAMNACEAE (buckthorn family)		
Rhamnus sp. (buckthorn)	S	Minor and Pickett 1982
ROSACEAE (rose family)		
Amelanchier alnifolia (Saskatoon)	S	Minor and Pickett 1982
Oemleria cerasiformis	S	Prouty et al. 1999
Prunus sp. (cherry)	S	Cheatham 1988; Minor and Pickett 1982, 1985; Prouty et al. 1999
Prunus emarginata (bitter cherry)	S	Minor and Pickett 1985
Prunus subcordata (Klamath plum)	S	Minor and Pickett 1985
Rosa sp. (rosehip)	O, S	Minor and Pickett 1982, 1985
Rubus sp. (raspberries and related berries)	S	Minor and Pickett 1982, 1985; Prouty et al. 1999
RUBIACEAE (madder family)		
Galium sp. (bedstraw)	S	Prouty et al. 1999

Note: L = leaf/needle, S = seed, R = bulbs, corms, rhizomes, etc., O = other (thorns).

bowl recovered from a burial contained an abundance of Compositae pollen, likely from the grinding of tarweed (Jim Chatters, personal communication 2000). Several antler digging stick handle fragments were also recovered from the residential sites at Fuller and Fanning Mounds, likely dating within the last 2,000 years (Aikens 1993:206–209).

Camas-processing sites in particular, are a major component of the late Holocene archaeological record after about 2500 BC (Thoms 1989:301–325). The Long Tom site, west of Eugene, is a well-documented example of such a camas-processing site. The site was most intensively occupied between 3000 and 2000 BC; however, the earliest occupation dates to 9,000 years ago. The use of magnetometry at the site allowed the excavators to identify more than 100 earth ovens, ranging in diameter from 1 to 3 m. Each contained abundant fire-altered rock, charcoal, and charred camas bulbs, as well as lesser amounts of acorns and hazelnuts (Connolly et al. 1999; Prouty et al. 1999).

In addition to the earth ovens, the Long Tom site produced a feature that may have been used to dry plants. Unlike the earth ovens, this feature was linear (3.5 m by 1 m), contained little rock, and was found within the residential part of the site. Camas, acorn, and hazelnuts were recovered from it. Based on its morphology, the excavators suggest it was used to dry rather than bake plants, similar to the berry trenches found in the uplands along the coast (see above; Connolly et al. 1999).

Camas processing sites in the Willamette Valley were used repeatedly, especially by 1000 BC to AD 1. Reuse is indicated by formalized discard and activity areas, reuse of features, and lids to cover the camas ovens. Reuse, in turn, may indicate local ownership of camas grounds and a focusing in on the camas resource, as is documented ethnographically (Cheatham 1988; Connolly et al. 1999; Wilson 1993).

The Halverson site, a later prehistoric campsite located several miles east of Eugene, produced a different plant record than most sites in the Willamette Valley (Minor and Pickett 1982). The systematic collection of plant remains at this site produced saskatoons, *Vaccinium* sp., *Rubus*, rose, and cherry, among other species. Hazelnuts and oak together comprise only a small percentage of the total plant remains, and earth ovens and milling stones are absent from the assemblage. The site seems to be a task-specific site for the collection of fruits and seeds, rather than of camas and nuts, as is typical of other Willamette Valley sites.

Evidence for plant use in upland sites in the Willamette Valley comes from rockshelters that are thought to have been used primarily as spring or fall hunting camps. The earliest evidence of upland plant use comes from Cascadia Cave, located in the montane forests to the west of the Willamette Valley and dating from 6000 BC to sometime between 4000 and 1000 BC. Evidence of plant use consists of hazelnuts, edge-ground cobbles, and manos and grinding slabs found during excavation (Newman 1966). The presence of ovens and ground stone tools at upland sites dating to the later Holocene (Aikens 1993) suggests that plant harvesting and processing may have been more important at upland sites than previously assumed (cf. Aikens 1993). This possibility should be evaluated with systematic investigations of paleoethnobotanical remains in upland sites.

The Southwestern Mountains of Oregon

The paleoethnobotanical record of the southwestern mountains of Oregon is even sparser than that of the Willamette Valley (Table 8.6). Few systematic studies have been conducted, and some of the strongest data for ancient plant use comes from indirect evidence, that is, from artifacts and features. Based on the ethnographic record of plant use, plants undoubtedly played a significant role in the palaeoeconomy of the region. The role of plants in prehistory, however, has not yet been thoroughly documented.

Evidence for early Holocene plant use in the region is limited to indirect evidence from sites such as JA53b on the Applegate River, just north of the California-Oregon border (Aikens 1993). The site, which dates from 6000 to 2000 BC, is thought to be a hunting and gathering camp. Plant use is indicated by stone bowl mortars, pestles, hopper mortar bases, manos, and milling slabs.

Saltsgaver site, located on a tributary of the Rogue River, just northeast of the Applegate River, provides evidence for mid-Holocene plant use (Prouty 1989). The site, which dates from 3350 BC to the historic period, produced over 100 earth ovens. No paleoethnobotany was conducted, but based on the similarity of the ovens to archaeological features in the Willamette Valley and to ethnographic descriptions from the region, all of the ovens are thought to have been used primarily for the roasting of camas. One pit (dating to AD 50) yielded the remains of a possible camas bulb (Prouty 1989). The pits range is diameter from 60 cm to 1 m—smaller than those reported from the Willamette Valley. This difference in size may be due to the fact that the Rogue River soils are clayey and, thus, more difficult to dig than the loose floodplain soils of the Willamette Valley. The use of this site over such

414

Table 8.6

Paleoethnobotanical Remains from the Southwestern Mountains of Oregon

Species Scientific Name (Common Name)	Part Found	References
GYMNOSPERMAE		
CUPRESSACEAE (cypress family)		
Calocedrus decurrens (incense cedar)	S, W	Davis and Miksicek 1987; Pickett 1987
PINACEAE (pine family)		
Abies sp. (true fir)	L, S, W	Davis and Miksicek 1987
Pinus sp. (pines)	L, S, W	Davis and Miksicek 1987; O'Neill et al. 1996; Pickett 1987; Stenholm 1994
Pseudotsuga menziesii (Douglas-fir)	S, W	Davis and Miksicek 1987; O'Neill et al. 1996; Pickett 1987; Stenholm 1994
MONOCOTYLEDONAE		
GRAMINEAE (grass)		
Elymus sp. (wildrye)	S	Davis and Miksicek 1987
Festuca sp. (fescue)	S	Davis and Miksicek 1987
Panicum sp. (panicum)	S	Davis and Miksicek 1987
Poa sp. (bluegrass)	S	Davis and Miksicek 1987
LILIACEAE (lily family)	S	Pickett 1987
Camassia spp. (camas)	R	Prouty 1989 (cf.), 1991
DICOTYLEDONAE		
ASTERACEAE (aster family)		
Cirsium sp. (thistle)	S	Davis and Miksicek 1987
Madia sp. (tarweed)	S	Davis and Miksicek 1987
BETULACEAE (birch family)		
Alnus sp. (alder)	W	Davis and Miksicek 1987
Corylus sp. (hazelnut)	S	Davis and Miksicek 1987; Pickett 1987; Prouty 1991
BORAGINACEAE (borage family)	S	Davis and Miksicek 1987
CAPRIFOLIACEAE (honeysuckle family)		
Sambucus sp. (elderberry)	S	Davis and Miksicek 1987
CHENOPODIACEAE (goosefoot family)		

Chenopodium sp. (chenopod)	S	Davis and Miksicek 1987; Prouty 1991
CRUCIFERAE (mustard family)		
Brassica spp. (mustard)	S	O'Neill et al. 1996
ERICACEAE (heath family)		
Arbutus menziesii (arbutus)	S	Davis and Miksicek 1987
Arctostaphylos spp. (manzanita)	S	Davis and Miksicek 1987
Vaccinium sp. (blueberry and huckleberry)	S	Davis and Miksicek 1987; Pickett 1987
FABACEAE (pea family)	S	Davis and Miksicek 1987
Lotus sp. (lotus)	S	Davis and Miksicek 1987
cf. *Lupinus* (lupine)	S	Davis and Miksicek 1987
cf. *Medicago* sp.	S	Davis and Miksicek 1987
FAGACEAE (beech family)		
Quercus sp. (oak)	S, W	Davis and Miksicek 1987; O'Neill et al. 1996; Stenholm 1994
OLEACEAE (olive family)		
Fraxinus sp. (ash)	W	Davis and Miksicek 1987
PLANTAGINACEAE (plantago family)		
Plantago sp. (plantain)	S	Davis and Miksicek 1987
POLYGONACEAE (buckwheat family)		
Eriogonum sp. (buckwheat)	S	Davis and Miksicek 1987
Rumex sp. (dock)	S	Davis and Miksicek 1987
RHAMNACEAE (buckthorn family)		
Rhamnus sp. (buckthorn)	W	Davis and Miksicek 1987
ROSACEAE (rose family)	S	Pickett 1987
Prunus sp. (cherry)	S	Pickett 1987; Prouty 1991
Rubus sp. (raspberries and related berries)	S	Davis and Miksicek 1987
RUBIACEAE (madder family)		
Galium sp. (bedstraw)	S	Davis and Miksicek 1987
SALICACEAE (willow family)		
Salix sp. (willow)	W	Davis and Miksicek 1987

Note: L = leaf/needle, R = roots, bulbs, corms, rhizomes, etc., S = "seed" (exocarp, endocarp, etc.), W = wood, bark, branch, etc.

a long time may indicate repeated occupation by one group or by related social groups who had rights to harvest camas from this location.

Winter residential sites dating to the last 3,000 years have also produced both indirect and direct evidence of plant use. Indirect evidence comes from a variety of sites in the form of earth ovens, mortars and pestles, hopper mortar bases, and manos and grinding slabs (Aikens 1993). Direct evidence comes from paleoethnobotanical investigations at a series of late (post–AD 1) pithouse sites along Elk Creek, a tributary of the Upper Rogue River. Paleoethnobotanical analyses from various contexts identified a wide array of edible seeds, nuts, and berries, as well as wood charcoal (Davis and Miksicek 1987). The density of plant remains is higher in middens associated with pithouses than on the pithouse floors, but nowhere is the density particularly high. A notable exception is the high number of chenopod (*Chenopodium* sp.) seeds, which may indicate that chenopods were processed and eaten at this site.

Also notable at the Elk Creek sites is the identification of a pit, associated with two pithouses dating to the last 1,000 years. The feature was 1 m in diameter, 60 cm deep, and filled with fire-altered rock. Associated with the pit were several charred acorns, presumably harvested in the oak groves found at intermediate elevations and then brought back to the site for processing. The usual array of artifacts associated with plant processing was found at the Elk Creek sites (Aikens 1993:243–250). Camas is notably absent from these sites, possibly because of sampling bias or the season of occupation.

Direct evidence for plant use at seasonal base camps is less compelling than that found at pithouse sites. Archaeobotanical remains have been recovered from a series of rockshelters at South Umpqua Falls, dating from ca. 1000 BC to historic times (Minor 1987), from the Standley site on the Coquille River, dating from ca. 350 BC to the late prehistoric period (Connolly 1991), and from site 35JA189 on the Upper Rogue River, dating from AD 450 to 950–1500. (Connolly et al. 1994). The South Umpqua Falls sites produced charred and uncharred pine seeds, hazelnuts, and rose seeds; however, problems with bioturbation common to dry rockshelters limit interpretations about the role of plants (Minor 1987; Pickett 1987). The Standley site produced an abundance of plant remains, but many could not be identified. Hazelnuts and an unidentified bulb, likely camas, dominated the assemblage (Prouty 1991). Finally, samples from fire-cracked rock features at site 35JA189 produced an abundance of conifer charcoal, but little else (Stenholm 1994).

The full range of artifacts thought to be associated with camas and nut and seed processing were recovered at the Standley site and at 35JA189. At the

Standley site, the evidence includes earth ovens, mortars and pestles, manos, and edge-ground cobbles. Indirect evidence of plant processing at 35JA189 includes edge-ground cobbles, manos, hopper mortar bases, grinding slabs, and anvils. Their presence indicates that these tool types—including edge-ground cobbles, usually associated with the early Holocene—persisted throughout the sequence in southwestern Oregon.

The Plateau

The Early Holocene (pre–2000 BC)

As is the case with the other regions discussed, direct evidence for early Holocene plant use on the Plateau is extremely sparse and comes from the end of the time period (Lepofsky and Peacock in press; Table 8.7). Charred camas bulbs were recovered from 5,500-year-old earth ovens at the Calispell site, in northwestern Washington (Andrefsky 2000; Thoms 1989; Figure 8.1), and a pithouse site in the Chief Joseph project area (Figure 8.1) produced saskatoon and hawthorn (*Crataegus* sp.) seeds and possible *Lomatium* tissue (Stenholm 1984a). All of the hawthorn seeds had been crushed, possibly as a result of pulverizing the fruit to remove the large seeds from the flesh.

Indirect evidence for early plant use on the Southern Plateau is relatively common, but to my knowledge, such evidence is lacking from the Northern Plateau. Grinding slabs, manos, and edge-ground cobbles are found in many southern assemblages dating to ca. 11,000–8,000 years ago. After 8,000 years ago, hopper mortar bases and pestles began to replace the manos and edge-ground cobbles, and at some sites they are common (Ames and Marshall 1980; Chatters and Pokotylo 1998; Thoms 1989). This shift in artifacts may reflect the increased importance of root foods that require pounding (e.g., camas).

The multiseason availability of root foods may have been an important factor in attempts at sedentism on the Plateau between 5,300 and 4,500 years ago (cf. Ames and Marshall 1980). Compelling evidence for the importance of plant foods comes from the many hopper mortar bases and anvil stones or grinding slabs recovered from Chief Joseph and other pithouse sites in the Columbia Plateau (Ames et al. 1998:109). The artifacts are part of the "furniture" of these early houses, similar to the grinding slabs recovered from the early Maurer house on the coast (see above). Their presence suggests that grinding and pounding of roots and other plants was both a common and an important part of the economy of these early households.

Table 8.7

Paleoethnobotanical Remains from the Plateau

Species *Scientific Name* (Common Name)	Part Found	References
BASIDIOMYCOTA		
LYCOPERDACEAE (puffball family)		
Bovista sp.	carpophores	Matthewes 1980
Bovista dakotensis	carpophores	Compton et al. 1995
Bovista tomentosa	carpophores	Compton et al. 1995
Abstoma reticulatum	carpophores	Compton et al. 1995
PTERIDOPHYTA		
POLYPODIACEAE (fern family)		
Pteridium aquilinum (bracken fern)	R	Ketcheson 1979
SALVINIACEAE (salvinia family)	St	Stenholm 2000a
Azolla sp.	sporocarp	Stenholm 2000a
ARTHROPHYTA		
EQUISETACEAE (horsetail family)		
Equisetum sp. (horsetail)	R, St	Stenholm 2000a
GYMNOSPERMAE		
CUPRESSACEAE (cypress family)		
Chamaecyparis sp. (cedars)	W	Stenholm 1984e, 1985
Juniperus sp. (juniper)	L, W[a]	Ketcheson 1979; Leney 1984; Lepofsky 2000a; Stenholm 1984a, 1985, 1986b, 2000a
Thuja plicata (western redcedar)	W	Galm et al. 1985; Rhode 1986; Stenholm 1984b, 1984d, 1984e, 1985, 1987b, 2000a
PINACEAE (pine family)		
Abies sp. (true fir)	C, L, W	Ketcheson 1979; Leney 1984; Rhode 1986; Stenholm 1986b, 2000a
Larix spp. (larches)	W[a]	Leney 1984; Stenholm 1984a, 1984b, 1984c, 1985, 1986b, 1988b, 2000a
Picea sp. (spruces)	W	Ketcheson 1979; Lepofsky et al. 1987; Rhode 1986; Stenholm 1984e, 1985, 1986b, 2000a
Pinus sp. (pines)	C, L, W[a] S, St	Leney 1984; Lepofsky 1990, 2000a; Nicholas et al. 1997; Peacock 2002; Rhode 1986; Stenholm 1986b, 1987b
Pinus albicaulis (whitebark pine)	C, S, W	Eldridge 1996; Matthewes 1980; Stenholm 1984d, 1985, 1986b, 1987b, 2000a

Pinus contorta (lodgepole pine)	C, L, S, W[a]	Chance and Chance 1982; Ketcheson 1979; Stenholm 1984a, 1984b, 1986b, 1987b, 1997c, 2000a
Pinus ponderosa (ponderosa pine)	C, L, S, W[a]	Chance and Chance 1982; Ketcheson 1979; Lepofsky 1988; Lepofsky et al. 1987; Lepofsky et al. 1996; Matthewes 1980; Mossop-Cousins 2000; Nicholas et al. 1997; Peacock 2002; Stenholm 1984a, 1985, 1986b, 1991, 1997c, 2000a; Wollstonecroft 2000
P. ponderosa/P. contorta	W[a]	Stenholm 1984b, 1984c, 1984d, 1984e, 1985, 1986b, 1987a, 1988b, 1997c
Pseudotsuga menziesii (Douglas-fir)	B, C, L, S, W[a]	Galm et al. 1985; Ketcheson 1979; Leney 1984; Lepofsky 1988, 1990, 2000a; Lepofsky et al. 1987; Lepofsky et al. 1996; Matthewes 1980; Mossop-Cousins 2000; Nicholas et al. 1997; Peacock 2002; Rhode 1986; Stenholm 1984a, 1984b, 1984c, 1984d, 1984e, 1985, 1987b, 1997c, 2000a; Wollstonecroft 2000
Tsuga sp. (hemlocks)	W[a]	Galm et al. 1985; Ketcheson 1979; Rhode 1986; Stenholm 1984a, 1984b, 1984e, 1985, 1987b, 2000a
TAXACEAE (yew family)		
Taxus sp. (yews)	W	Stenholm 1985
MONOCOTYLEDONAE		
CYPERACEAE (sedge family)		
Carex sp. (sedges)	S	Lepofsky 1988, 2000a; Lepofsky et al. 1996
Eleocharis palustris (common spikeweed)	S[a]	Stenholm 2000a
Scirpus sp. (bulrushes)	S[a]	Stenholm 2000a
GRAMINEAE (grass family)	L, R, S[a], St	Lepofsky 2000a; Lepofsky et al. 1996; Stenholm 1984d, 1986b, 2000a; Ketcheson 1979; Lepofsky 2000a; Lepofsky et al. 1996; Mossop-Cousins 2000; Nicholas et al. 1997; Stenholm 1984a, 1984c, 1984d, 1984e, 1985, 1987a, 1991, 2000a; Wollstonecroft 2000
Calamagrostis sp. (reedgrass)	S	Ketcheson 1979
Elymus sp. (wildrye)	S	Chance and Chance 1982; Stenholm 1985 (cf.)
Elymus cinereus (giant wildrye)	S, St	Stenholm 1985, 1998b
Muhlenbergia sp. (muhly)	S	Ketcheson 1979
Panicum sp. (panicum)	S	Stenholm 1986b
Phalaris sp. (canarygrass)	S	Stenholm 1986b
Poa sp. (bluegrass)	T	Ketcheson 1979
Sporobolus cryptandrus (sand dropseed)	St	Stenholm 1985
LILIACEAE (lily family)	R	Ketcheson 1979; Stenholm 1998b
Allium spp. (onion)	S, R	Chance and Chance 1982; Ketcheson 1979; Wollstonecroft 2000

Continued on next page

Table 8.7 *continued*

Species *Scientific Name* (Common Name)	Part Found	References
Brodiaea sp. (cluster lily)	R	Stenholm 1991
Camassia spp. (camas)	R	Stenholm 1984b, 1985, 1986b, 1991, 1997c
Camassia quamash (common camas)	R, S[a]	Stenholm 2000a
Erythronium grandiflorum (yellow glacier lily)	R	Stenholm 2000a
Smilacina racemosa (false Solomon's seal)	S	Lepofsky 2000a
Smilacina stellata (star-flowered false Solomon's seal)	S	Lepofsky et al. 1996
TYPHACEAE (cattail family)		
Typha spp. (cattail)	T	Stenholm 2000a
DICOTYLEDONAE		
ACERACEAE (maple family)		
Acer sp. (maples)	W	Lepofsky 2000a; Lepofsky et al. 1987; Stenholm 1984d, 1984e, 1985
AMARANTHACEAE (amaranth family)		
Amaranthus sp. (amaranth)	S	Stenholm 1986b, 2000a
ANACARDIACEAE (cashew family)		
Rhus sp. (sumac)	S	Stenholm 1985
APOCYNACEAE (dogbane family)		
Apocynum sp. (dogbane)	St	Stenholm 1984e, 1985
APIACEAE (celery family)		
Lomatium spp. (lomatiums)	R	Stenholm 1984a, 1984b, 1985
ARACEAE (arum family)		
Lysichiton americanus (American skunkcabbage)	R	Stenholm 2000a
ASTERACEAE (aster family)	S,R	Ketcheson 1979; Wollstonecroft 2000
Artemisia spp. (sagebrush)	L[a], S, W[a]	Leney 1984; Lepofsky 2000a; Rhode 1986, 1987; Stenholm 1984a, 1984c, 1984d, 1985, 1987a, 1987b, 1998b; Wollstonecroft 2000

Species	Code	References
Balsamorhiza sp. (balsamroot)	S	Rhode 1986
Chrysothamnus sp. (rabbitbrush)	B, W[a]	Rhode 1986; Stenholm 1984c, 1984d, 1985
Helianthus annuus (sunflower)	S	Stenholm 1984b, 1984d, 1985
Wyethia sp. (wyethia)	S	Stenholm 1986b, 2000a
BETULACEAE (birch family)		
Alnus sp. (alder)	W	Ketcheson 1979; Lepofsky 2000a; Lepofsky et al. 1996; Stenholm 2000a
Betula sp. (birches)	W[a]	Chance and Chance 1982; Ketcheson 1979; Lepofsky 1988, 1990, 2000a; Lepofsky et al. 1987; Matthewes 1980; Nicholas et al. 1997; Stenholm 1984a, 1984b, 1984e, 1985, 1986b, 2000a
Betula papyrifera (paper birch)	W	Lepofsky et al. 1996; Wollstonecroft 2000
Corylus sp. (hazelnut)	S	Chance and Chance 1982; Stenholm 2000a;Wollstonecroft 2000
BORAGINACEAE (borax family)	S	Lepofsky et al. 1996
Amsinckia menziesii (small-flowered fiddleneck)	S	Lepofsky 2000a
Lithospermum sp. (gromwell)	S	Chance and Chance 1982; Nicholas et al. 1997; Wollstonecroft 2000
BRASSICACEAE (mustard family)	S	Wollstonecroft 2000
CACTACEAE (cactus family)		
Opuntia spp. (prickly pear cactuses)	S	Lepofsky 2000a; Lepofsky et al. 1996
CAPRIFOLIACEAE (honeysuckle family)		
Sambucus sp. (elderberry)	S, W	Ketcheson 1979; Lepofsky 1988, 1990, 2000a; Mossop-Cousins 2000; Stenholm 1991
Sambucus cerulea (blue elderberry)	S	Stenholm 1998b
Symphoricarpos sp. (snowberry)	W[a]	Rhode 1986
CARYOPHYLLACEAE (pink family)		
Arenaria sp. (sandwort)	S	Stenholm 2000a
Silene sp. (silene)	S	Lepofsky 1988, 2000a; Lepofsky et al. 1996; Stenholm 2000a
CHENOPODIACEAE (goosefoot family)		

Continued on next page

Table 8.7 *continued*

Species *Scientific Name* (Common Name)	Part Found	References
Chenopodium sp. (chenopod)	S[a]	Lepofsky 1988, 2000a; Lepofsky et al. 1996; Matthewes 1980; Mossop-Cousins 2000; Nicholas et al. 1997, 2002; Stenholm 1984a, 1984b, 1985, 1986b, 1987b, 1998b, 2000a; Wollstonecroft 2000
CORNACEAE (dogwood family)		
Cornus sp. (dogwood)	S	Chatters 1984
Cornus nuttallii (Pacific dogwood)	W	Stenholm 1986b
Cornus stolonifera (red-osier dogwood)	S	Lepofsky 1988, 2000a; Lepofsky et al. 1996; Nicholas et al. 1997; Rhode 1986; Stenholm 2000a; Wollstonecroft 2000
ERICACEAE (heath family)	S	Lepofsky et al. 1996; Wollstonecroft 2000
Arctostaphylos spp. (manzanita)	F, L, S[a]	Ketcheson 1979; Lepofsky 1988, 2000a; Lepofsky et al. 1996; Mossop-Cousins 2000; Stenholm 1986b, 1997c, 2000a
Vaccinium sp. (blueberry and huckleberry)	L, S	Ketcheson 1979; Mossop-Cousins 2000; Wollstonecroft 2000
EUPHORBIACEAE (spurge family)		
Euphorbia sp. (spurge)	S	Stenholm 1991
FABACEAE (pea family)		
Astragalus sp. (milkvetches)	L, S	Ketcheson 1979
Oxytropis sp. (crazyweed)	S	Stenholm 1998b
GROSSULARIACEAE (gooseberry family)		
Ribes spp. (currants)	F, S, W	Leney 1984; Lepofsky 1988, 2000a; Wollstonecroft 2000
HYDROPHYLLACEAE (waterleaf family)		
Phacelia sp. (phacelia)	S	Lepofsky 1988, 1990, 2000a; Lepofsky et al. 1996; Mossop-Cousins 2000; Stenholm 1985, 2000a
LABIATAE (mint family)		
Hedeoma sp. (pennyroyal)	S	Stenholm 1985
PLANTAGINACEAE (plantago family)		
Plantago sp. (plantain)	S	Stenholm 1985

POLYGONACEAE (buckwheat family)		
Polygonum sp. (knotweed)	S	Stenholm 1984d, 1984e, 1985, 1986b, 2000a
Rumex sp. (dock)	S	Stenholm 1986b, 1998b, 2000a; Wollstonecroft 2000
POLEMONIACEAE (phlox family)		
Collomia linearis (narrowleaf mountain trumpet)	S	Stenholm 2000a
RANUNCULACEAE (buttercup family)		
Clematis sp. (clematis)	W	Stenholm 1984a, 1985
RHAMNACEAE (buckthorn family)		
Rhamnus sp. (buckthorn)	W	Stenholm 1997c
ROSACEAE (rose family)	W[a]	Stenholm 1985
Amelanchier sp. (serviceberry)	F, S[a], W[a]	Lepofsky 1988, 1990, 2000a; Lepofsky et al. 1987; Lepofsky et al. 1996; Matthewes 1980; Mossop-Cousins 2000; Nicholas et al. 1997; Rhode 1986; Stenholm 1984a, 1984b, 1984c, 1984d, 1984e, 1985, 1986b, 1991, 1998b, 2000a; Wollstonecroft 2000
Crataegus sp. (hawthorn)	S, W	Chance and Chance 1982; Chatters 1984; Lepofsky 1988, 1990; Rhode 1986; Stenholm 1984b, 1984c, 1984d, 1984e, 1985, 1986b, 1991, 1998b, 2000a
Fragaria spp. (strawberry)	S[a]	Stenholm 1984a (cf.), 1985
Holodiscus discolor (oceanspray)	L, W	Leney 1984; Rhode 1986; Stenholm 1984b, 1984e, 1985, 1986b, 2000a
Prunus sp. (cherry)	F, S, W	Chance and Chance 1982; Chatters 1984; Ketcheson 1979; Lepofsky 1988, 2000a; Lepofsky et al. 1987; Lepofsky et al. 1996; Matthewes 1980; Nicholas et al. 1997; Rhode 1986; Stenholm 1984c, 1984e, 1991, 1998b, 2000a
Prunus cf. *virginiana* (chokecherry)	S	Stenholm 1985; Wollstonecroft 2000
Purshia sp. (bitterbrush)	W[a], S[a]	Chatters 1984; Rhode 1986, 1987; Stenholm 1984a, 1984b, 1984c, 1984d, 1984e, 1985, 1987a
Rosa sp. (rosehip)	S	Lepofsky 1988; Stenholm 1985
Rosa cf. *woodsii* (Woods' rose)	S, T	Lepofsky 2000a; Lepofsky et al. 1996; Stenholm 1998b
Rubus sp. (raspberries and related berries)	S, W[a]	Lepofsky 1988, 1990; Lepofsky et al. 1987; Matthewes 1980; Nicholas et al. 1997; Rhode 1986; Stenholm 1986b, 2000a; Wollstonecroft 2000
Sanguisorba sp. (burnet)	S	Stenholm 1986b, 2000a
Sorbus sp. (mountain ash)	S	Stenholm 2000a

Continued on next page

423

Table 8.7 *continued*

Species *Scientific Name* (Common Name)	Part Found	References
RUBIACEAE (madder family)		
Galium sp. (bedstraw)	S	Lepofsky 1988; Stenholm 1998b, 2000a
SALICACEAE (willow family)		
Populus sp. (cottonwood)	S, W[a]	Ketcheson 1979; Lepofsky 2000a; Lepofsky et al. 1987; Lepofsky et al. 1996; Nicholas et al. 1997, 2002; Rhode 1986; Stenholm 1984b, 1985, 1986b, 1987b, 1997c, 1998b, 2000a
Salix sp. (willow)	W	Ketcheson 1979; Leney 1984; Lepofsky 2000a; Rhode 1986; Stenholm 1984b, 1984d, 1985, 1986b, 1998b, 2000a
Salix sp./*Populus* sp.	W	Lepofsky 1988; Stenholm 1987a; Wollstonecroft 2000
SANTALACEAE (sandalwood family)		
Comandra umbellata (bastard toadflax)	S	Stenholm 1984d, 1985
SAXIFRAGACEAE (saxifrage family)		
Philadelphus lewisii (Lewis' mock-orange)	W[a]	Stenholm 1984a, 1984b, 1984d, 1984e, 1985
SCROPHULARIACEAE (figwort family)		
Collinsia sp. (blue-eyed Mary)	S	Stenholm 2000a
Collinsia parviflora (small flower blue-eyed Mary)	S	Lepofsky 1988, 2000a
ULMACEAE (elm family)		
Celtis douglasii (hackberry)	L, W	Stenholm 1984b, 1984c, 1985, 1987a

Note: B = bud, C = cone, F = fruit, L = leaf/needle, R = roots, bulbs, corms, rhizomes, etc., S = "seed" (exocarp, endocarp, etc.), St = stem, T = other nonwoody tissues, W = wood, bark, branch, etc.

[a] Found in deposits older than 3000 BC as well as those postdating 3000 BC.

A full complement of plant remains is found at a range of site types post-dating 2000 BC and the beginning of the winter pithouse settlement pattern (Table 8.7). Detailed paleoethnobotanical studies were conducted at several pithouses associated with the Chief Joseph project on the Columbia Plateau (Stenholm 1984a, 1984b, 1984c, 1984d, 1984e, 1985; Figure 8.1) and at the late prehistoric pithouse village of Keatley Creek on the Fraser River in the Canadian Plateau (Lepofsky 2000a, 2000b; Mossop-Cousins 2000; Figure 8.1). These studies, combined with more limited paleoethnobotanical analyses and the incidental recovery of plant remains during excavation (Chance and Chance 1982; Lepofsky 1988, 1990; Mathewes 1980; Stenholm 1988b; Stryd 1972), have resulted in an extensive list of plant taxa that were used at pithouse villages on the Plateau. In general, though the diversity of remains within pithouses is often high, relatively low densities suggest that the houses were regularly swept clean (Lepofsky 2000a, 2002). Despite such low densities, plant processing and consumption areas can be identified on pithouse floors (Lepofsky 2000b; Lepofsky et al. 1996).

Of the plant foods recovered from pithouse sites, berries are the best represented. Of the berries, saskatoons are by far the most ubiquitous of the taxa, in both Northern and Southern Plateau pithouse sites. (Chenopods, which are also ubiquitous at pithouse sites, are discussed below.) Saskatoons are highly prized by Plateau groups today because they are abundant, flavorful, and easily dried. These qualities make the berries an ideal winter staple food, as is reflected in the archaeobotanical record of pithouses. Dried Saskatoon berries were embedded in matting recovered from the Mitchell pithouse site, located just north of the Keatley Creek village (Mathewes 1980).

Nuts and seeds are also found in pithouse deposits in small amounts. Hazelnuts have been recovered from the Columbia River (Chance and Chance 1982), and conifer seeds have been recovered from various sites. Whitebark pine seeds and cones were found at the Fountain site, just downstream from and contemporaneous with the Keatley village (Stryd 1972). Whitebark pine is a high-elevation conifer, the green cones of which were gathered in the fall and then roasted over a fire to extract the seeds. According to Turner (personal communication 1993), in historic times, people brought down sacks of cones from higher elevations to process at home. The cones from the Fountain site suggest that this is an ancient practice.

"Root foods" are represented at pithouse sites by both direct and indirect evidence. On the Southern Plateau, lomatium, camas, and unidentified parenchymous tissues were recovered from several pithouses in the Chief Joseph project (Stenholm 1984a, 1984b, 1984c, 1984e, 1985) but never in great abundance. A single specimen of possible balsamroot is reported from a pithouse on the Columbia River in northeast Washington (Chance and Chance 1982), and Apiaceae pollen recovered from 3–4,000-year-old house floors may represent the processing of *Lomatium* sp. or some other member of this family (Cummings 1993).

Earth ovens are reported from the larger pithouse villages on the Canadian Plateau (Keatley Creek and the Bell site; Hayden and Mossop-Cousins in press; Stryd 1973), but they are notably uncommon given the sizes of the villages. A preliminary archaeobotanical analysis of the ovens at Keatley Creek, dating to late prehistoric times, produced an abundance of (unidentified) charcoal, unidentified tissues of different kinds, and possible *Allium* bulbs (Hayden and Mossop-Cousins in press).

Though root foods were clearly processed and consumed at pithouse villages, the record from these villages alone does not indicate extensive use of root foods. One explanation for the relative paucity of remains is simply that the consumption of roots at pithouse villages was sometimes low, depending on whether a group had rights to root collecting grounds and on the distance to the collecting grounds from the village site (Lepofsky 2000a; Turner 1992). Alternatively, the paucity of roots may be due to the fact that few roots were processed at village sites. Off-site processing, combined with the fact that most Northwest paleoethnobotanists cannot identify root tissue fragments, could account for the amounts recovered. This latter explanation is more consistent with the evidence for extensive and intensive root processing at nonpithouse sites throughout the Plateau (see below).

Indirect evidence of plant foods at pithouses comes from various artifacts. Antler digging stick handles have been recovered from pithouse sites in British Columbia (Hayden and Schulting 1997; Stryd 1972, 1983). Most have been found by local collectors and are undated; the handle from the earliest dated context comes from a 450 BC pithouse site in Kamloops, British Columbia (Eldridge and Stryd 1983). Root and nut foods are indicated by pestles and hopper mortar bases and by manos and grinding slabs from several pithouses in Oregon and Washington (Aikens 1993; Ames et al. 1998; Galm and Masten 1985; Thoms 1989) and British Columbia (Smith 1899).[6] Artifacts used to remove bark for cambium extraction from coniferous trees ("bark peelers"; Hayden 2000b) and to remove the cambium from the bark ("sap-scrapers"; Stryd 1973) were recovered from late prehistoric pithouses on the Canadian Plateau. The scrapers are the oldest evidence for cambium harvesting in the Northwest.

Though most short-term camps in Plateau archaeology are identified as fishing (salmon) or hunting camps, paleoethnobotanical analyses rarely fail to produce at least some evidence of plant food consumption or processing. In general, plant remains seem to be concentrated in features (hearths and earth ovens; e.g., Chance and Chance 1982; Gough 1998, Lepofsky et al. 1987; Stenholm 1988b, 1991), but inadequate and uneven sampling usually prevents an unbiased assessment of overall plant use at these sites. Collectively, the plant remains recovered at short-term camps represent a wide range of plants used in food and technology on the Plateau.

One recent study challenges the conclusion that most short-term camps on the Plateau were primarily focused on nonplant pursuits. Wollstonecroft (2000, 2002) conducted the first extensive, systematic paleoethnobotanical analysis of a mid-elevation campsite in the northern Plateau. The site (EeRb 140; Figure 8.1) is one of many open-air sites located on old river terraces above the Fraser-Thompson River system. In the past, the immediately obvious abundance of lithics (especially because many sites are deflated) led people to conclude that such sites were likely used for hunting (and some have been termed "men's sites"). Wollstonecroft's thorough analysis, however, demonstrated that in late prehistory, site EeRb140 functioned at least in part as a base camp for plant processing and consumption. A large sample size, the use of SEM to identify tissues, careful attention to context, and explicit identification criteria resulted in a list of 30 plant taxa that were used for food, technology, and medicine.

Despite the inability of most Northwest archaeologists to identify parenchymous tissue fragments, evidence is mounting to suggest that root foods were harvested at many lowland campsites. Identified species include onion (Stenholm 1991; Wollstonecroft 2000), camas (Stenholm 1991), lomatium (Schalk 1987; Stenholm 1987a), and fool's onion (corm nets) (Chance et al. 1977, cited in Chance and Chance 1982). Most sites date to the late prehistoric period, but the fool's onion corm nets were recovered from a site dating to 2300–2000 BC (Chance and Chance 1982). Indirect evidence of root processing at lowland sites comes from earth ovens in the Southern Plateau, dating from 1000 BC (Chance and Chance 1982; Gough 1998), and from pestles, grinding slabs (Schalk 1987), and hopper mortar bases (Gough 1998), also from the Southern Plateau.

The strongest evidence for the importance of root foods in the post–2000

BC period comes from a series of processing sites in the uplands of the Canadian and Columbian Plateau (Aikens 1993; Alexander et al. 1985; Andrefsky et al. 2000; Baker 1974; Gough 1997; Magne 1984, 1985; Matson and Alexander 1980; Peacock 1998, 2002; Rousseau et al. 1991; Thoms 1989; Thoms and Burtchard 1986). Though these localities differ in specifics, they share two fundamental characteristics: (1) they are located in upland meadows where one or more root foods flourish, and (2) earth ovens are a main component of the archaeological record. Some of the localities were popular root harvesting grounds in the historic era (e.g., Botanie Valley in the Canadian Plateau; Figure 8.1).

Detailed archaeobotanical investigations of these upland root processing sites has been conducted in the Calipsell Valley in eastern Washington (Stenholm 1986b, 1997c, 2000a, 2000b; Thoms 1989; Figure 8.1), at Komkanetkwa (Peacock 1998, 2002; Figure 8.1), and, to a lesser extent, in the Upper Hat Creek valley (Ketcheson 1979; Pokotylo and Froese 1983; Figure 8.1). At Calipsell, paleoethnobotanical analyses produced an abundance of charcoal and the remains of camas in the form of bulbs, seeds, and processed cake fragments (Stenholm 1986b, 2000a, 2000b). The analysis of the Komkanetkwa material produced only fuelwoods (though based on site location, balsamroot was likely processed there; Peacock 1998, 2002), and the limited analysis of the Hat Creek material yielded abundant charcoal, small amounts of onion, and an unidentified bulb and rhizome (Ketcheson 1979). In all cases, the remains of roots themselves are rare, especially relative to charcoal abundance. Determinations of which roots were processed at other sites are largely based on which plants are found in abundance in the meadows today (e.g., spring beauty at Potato Mountain; Matson and Alexander 1980; Figure 8.1). Given the sheer abundance of charcoal in earth ovens and the fact that earth ovens were traditionally lined with plant materials to facilitate the removal of cooked roots, large samples of oven remains need to be examined to recover remains other than charcoal.

As a result of identification of a relatively large number of dated earth ovens from the Plateau, it is possible to discern regional trends in earth oven frequency and size. In the Calispell Valley, the earliest camas ovens date to 3500 BC, but earth ovens were not used extensively until after 1500 BC (Thoms 1989). Between 1500 BC and 500 BC, and again after AD 450, there were peaks in oven use (Gough 1997; Thoms 1989). In Calispell, there may also have been a trend through time of declining oven size (Thoms 1989; but see Gough 1997). In the Yakina Valley, to the south and west, the number of ovens suggests oven use peaked after AD 950 (Gough 1998). In the Canadian

Plateau, the earliest recorded upland ovens date to 1150 BC (Rousseau et al. 1991), but they were not common on the upland landscape until after 450 BC. Between AD 450 and AD 1150, there were fewer earth ovens in the uplands, but this appears to have been contemporaneous with the appearance of large ovens in lowland pithouse villages. Finally, after AD 1150, the size of upland ovens decreased dramatically, but this may have been coupled with a concurrent increase in the overall number of these features (Lepofsky and Peacock in press). Researchers across the Plateau region have provided various explanations for these complex shifts in the intensity of earth oven use, including changing access to other, more preferred resources (Thoms 1989), fluctuations in groups size, different species being cooked (Peacock 1998), and shifts in social structure at nearby pithouse communities (Hayden 2000a; see "Intensification of Plant Resources" below).

At higher elevations, whitebark pine nutlets were likely a valued resource. In historic times, as mentioned above, forays were made into the subalpine zone to collect the oil-rich pine nutlets. Evidence of ancient collecting and processing comes from the nutlets found at the lower-elevation pithouse site mentioned earlier (the Fountain site) and from the Paradise Creek site, west of Keatley Creek in the Canadian Plateau (elevation 2,000 m; Eldridge 1996). At Paradise Creek, several storage pits and earth ovens were found containing an abundance of whitebark pine nutlets. Though this is the only recorded whitebark pine processing site on the Plateau, the recent increase in the number of archaeological surveys conducted in high-elevation forests (initiated by increased logging activity) should result in the recording of more such processing sites.

Finally, CMTs have been an important source of information about ancient use of tree cambium on the Plateau (e.g., Marshall 2002; Prince 2001). As on the coast, CMTs are the result of a range of activities, but those modified to extract food seem to have been relatively more common on the Plateau. In particular, bark-stripped lodgepole pine (*Pinus contorta* var. *latifolia*) is a relatively common CMT in Plateau forests. Lodegpole pine cambium, an important food for Plateau peoples, was harvested by removing the outer bark in a strip and then scraping the cambium inside. The healed scar from the bark stripping can be dated using dendrochronological techniques.

The Late Holocene (post–2000 BC): Nonfood Plants

The most comprehensive study of technological uses of plants on the Plateau comes from the Chief Joseph Project (Stenholm 1985). The study resulted in the identification of coniferous and deciduous wood (for fuel), branches, grasses, and bark (for flooring, bedding, and pit lining), wood, bark, and Indian hemp (*Apocynum cannabinum*; for weaving), conifer pitch for adhesives, and several plants that may have been used as dyes. Indirect evidence of use of plants in technology comes from striae on bones and on steatite artifacts that indicate the use of horsetail (*Equisetum* sp.) as a fine abrasive.

The long chronological sequence at the Chief Joseph sites indicates shifts in fuel use through time. Tracking fuel use through the 7,000 years of occupation represented at these sites, Stenholm (1984c, 1985) notes that there was a decline in forest species, such as pines and larches (*Larix* spp.), and a slight increase in Douglas-fir through time. Conversely, use of xeric steppe shrubs, in particular, common sagebrush (*Artemisia tridentata*), antelope-brush (*Purshia tridentata*), and possibly mock-orange (*Philadelphus lewisii*), increased through time, especially during the last 1,000 years of prehistory. As fuelwoods, sage and antelope-brush differ from the conifers, in that the shrubs produce hot fires but are quick to burn to ash, whereas the conifers tend to sustain a hot fire longer. Stenholm (1985) offers no explanation for the observed shift in fuel use, but depletion of preferred fuelwoods near the villages is one possibility. A similar shift in fuel use has been demonstrated at sites located at Wells Reservoir, just downstream from the Chief Joseph sites (Rhode 1986), and possibly at sites in the Calispell Valley (Stenholm 2000b).

On the Canadian Plateau, the few studies that have identified charred wood taxa have demonstrated an overwhelming preference for *Populus* sp., pine, and Douglas-fir as fuelwoods (Lepofsky 2000a; Peacock 2002; Wollstonecroft 2000, 2002). No study of changes in fuel use over time has been completed.

The preservation of uncharred woods in the Chief Joseph sites allowed Stenholm to distinguish woods that were used for fuel and those that were likely intended for technological purposes. Stenholm found both local and nonlocal woods in her assemblage, but nonlocal woods were rarely charred. Nonlocal taxa (hemlock, redcedar, yellow-cedar, spruce, true fir, and possibly yew) were collected on long-distance harvesting trips and as driftwood from the Columbia River. Instead of being used for fuel, they were largely reserved for technological purposes, such as structural members for pithouses. The importance of driftwood for fuel and other purposes has also been demonstrated at the Wells River sites (Rhode 1986) and possibly at Avey's Orchard site, approximately 60 km further downstream on the Columbia River (Galm and Masten 1985).

More limited information is available on the use of nonwoody taxa for technological purposes on the Plateau. To my knowledge, few woven materials have been recovered from Plateau sites. These include a basket dating to AD 1700 recovered from a pithouse at the Keatley Creek site (Hayden 2000b) and an uncharred tule (*Scirpus* sp.) mat from a 500-year-old burial in the Chief Joseph region (Stenholm 1985). Various grasses, rushes, and conifer boughs have been identified as liners for earth ovens and storage pits (e.g., Stenholm 1998b, 2000b; Wollstonecroft 2000) and as bedding (Lepofsky 2000a). The occupants of site EeRb140 (Figure 8.1) traveled up to a half-day from the site to gather conifer boughs for pit lining. The bark of paper birch (*Betula papyrifera*) has been recovered at several sites on the Plateau. It was used to line storage pits (Nicholas et al. 1997; Wollstonecroft 2000, 2002), for basketry (Hayden 2000b; Matthewes 1980), possibly for torches (Hayden 2000c), and for other, unidentified functions (Stenholm 2000b). Finally, a few examples are known of western redcedar, birch, hemlock, and spruce CMTs that have had the bark removed, presumably for various technological purposes (Stryd 1997).

Though important food plants elsewhere in North America, chenopods were likely used only for technological purposes on the Plateau. Northwest paleoethnobotanists have debated the role of chenopods in the Plateau paleo-economy,[7] but the extant data suggest they were mostly likely used for lining pits and as bedding. Scattered chenopods (*Chenopodium capitatum*) have been recovered from most Plateau sites, as expected of a taxon that colonizes disturbed soils. In addition, the seeds have been recovered in high concentrations in hearths on the Canadian and Columbian Plateau (Stenholm 1985; Wollstonecroft 2000, 2002) and mixed with conifer needles presumed to have been used for bedding in the Keatley Creek pithouses (Lepofsky 2000a). In these latter contexts, the sheer number of chenopod seeds argues for their deliberate introduction, likely attached to the plant. This suggests chenopods were used to line pits and as bedding, but it is not known why they were selected for those purposes.

Evidence for ritual and medicinal use of plants on the Plateau is scant. Medicinal use of some plants has been suggested on the basis of ethnobotanically documented use (e.g., Compton et al. 1995; Lepofsky 2000a; Wollstonecroft 2000, 2002), but the context of recovery does not strongly support these interpretations. More definitive ritual use of plants comes from burials in the Plateau, which have produced seed fluff (likely cattail [*Typha latifolia*]; Ostapkowicz et al. 2001). Cattail fluff has a strong association with death among coast and interior Salish peoples (Ostapkowicz et al. 2001). Uncharred stoneseeds (*Lithospermum ruderale*) were recovered in abundance on skeletons during an early excavation of graves on the Fraser River (Smith 1899:135), but because the seeds are often cached by rodents, we cannot be confident of their archaeological context. Birch bark was also used to line and cover the graves (Smith 1899:135).

Issues in Northwest Paleoethnobotany

During the historic era, Northwest peoples used ecological, technological, and social mechanisms to increase the availability of desired plants (Lepofsky and Peacock in press). Ecological mechanisms included a variety of plant management practices, such as cultivation and the setting of prescribed fires (Deur 2000; Peacock and Turner 2000; Turner and Peacock in press). Technological innovations, such as berry rakes, digging sticks, pit cooking, and various methods of preservation, allowed Northwest people to efficiently harvest and process large quantities of plants. Finally, social mechanisms included ownership of harvesting plots, increasing access to plants through kin-based trade networks, and elite control over the harvest and use of certain plants.

Undoubtedly, each of these mechanisms was also central to plant use in the precontact era. In fact, as populations increased and became more socially complex through time, there was likely a concomitant intensification in the ecological, technological, and social mechanisms that increased access to plant resources. The challenge for paleoethnobotanists is to document these components of past plant production, because in many cases these aspects of plant use are not visible in the archaeobotanical record (Lepofsky and Peacock in press). As a result, researchers are increasingly turning to innovative methods, which go beyond the confines of palaeoethnobotany per se, to document all aspects of ancient plant use.

Plant Cultivation

In the historic era, Northwest peoples used a variety of cultivation techniques to enhance plant productivity (Peacock and Turner 2000; Turner and Peacock in press). Both ritual and food substances were actively tended and included tobacco (*Nicotiana quadrivalvis* and *N. attenuata*; Boyd 1999a; Dixon 1933; Hunn 1990; Meilleur 1979; Palmer 1975; Setchell 1921; Turner and

Taylor 1972), "root foods" (e.g., camas, wapato, springbank clover rhizomes; Deur 1999, 2000; Suttles 1951), and berries (Lepofsky et al. in press). Family- and village-owned plots were often fertilized, mulched, tilled, and weeded. Starchy roots were selectively harvested, and small bulbs and tubers were often replaced in the ground for future harvests. Berry bushes were pruned and coppiced, and fire was often used to clear plots or individual bushes. Of the taxa that were traditionally managed, only tobacco could be considered a domesticate in the traditional sense, because it was grown from seed and may have been genetically altered through selection (Turner and Peacock in press).

Though the strength of the ethnographic evidence suggests that cultivation practices are long-standing in the Northwest, little concrete evidence exists for ancient cultivation. Evidence for the cultivation of tobacco should be the most archaeologically visible, because tobacco is clearly a nonnative plant and was processed and used in particular ways. The seeds, however, have yet to be recovered from the archaeobotanical record, and evidence of tobacco use is limited to somewhat tenuous indirect evidence. For instance, it has been suggested that stone mortar bowls recovered from several archaeological contexts on the north coast dating to "at least the first millennium A.D." were used to grind tobacco leaves (MacDonald 1983:116; also Duff 1975). Based on ethnographic analogy, this is a reasonable assumption; however, until residue analyses are conducted, the function of the bowls will remain uncertain. Similar stone bowls have been recovered from elsewhere on the coast (e.g., Borden 1983; Carlson 1983a), but their function is also not known with certainty.

Stone pipes found archaeologically may have been used to smoke tobacco, yet only Plateau groups are reported to have smoked the leaves (northern coastal groups chewed the leaves; Turner and Taylor 1972). Pipes have been recovered from several southern coastal sites, dating to the last 1,500 years or so of prehistory (Borden 1983; Carlson 1983b; Mitchell 1990; Ross 1990: Figs. 2, 3). Several pipes have also been recovered from undated contexts on the Plateau (Stryd 1983). A pipe recovered from a Keatley Creek pithouse (Figure 8.1) dating to AD 750–950 is the only prehistoric pipe that has been subjected to residue analyses. Though the laboratory that undertook the analyses demonstrated that the pipe contained abundant organic compounds, nicotine and its breakdown product, cotinine, were definitely not among them (Hayden 2000b:197).

Solid evidence for the ancient cultivation of two rhizomatic species on the coast has emerged recently as a result of innovative research conducted by

Douglas Deur (1999, 2000, 2002a, 2002b, in press). By compiling ethnographic and ethnohistoric information, Deur has demonstrated that in the historic era, groups on the central mainland coast and the west coast of Vancouver Island intensively cultivated springbank clover and silverweed in estuarine gardens. Remnant garden plots are visible throughout the archaeological record of these regions, marked by stone walls in estuarine areas. Deur notes that several of the previously recorded rock features were identified as fish traps or as structures of unknown function. To determine the age of these features, Deur dated carbon samples trapped between the original estuarine surface and the deposits laid down after the plots were constructed. In this way, he has been able to demonstrate that the features definitively date to the precontact era.

A recent study of Garry oak genetics by Y. A. El-Kassaby, University of British Columbia, provides another example of the kind of innovative approaches that are required to document ancient cultivation in the Northwest. Today, oaks are distributed more or less continuously from southern Oregon northward to southeast Vancouver Island. In addition, two isolated populations are located in the Fraser Valley: one on a dry, south-facing rocky slope on Sumas Mountain (south of Scowlitz; Figure 8.1) and the other near Yale on the coast-interior transition (near Milliken; Figure 8.1). The rich archaeological record of the area surrounding the Yale oak stands indicates intensive occupation in the past, whereas the Sumas population is located on terrain too steep to be inhabitable. Two alternative hypotheses explain the origin of the disjunct Fraser Valley populations. The oaks could be Pleistocene relicts, or they could have been established more recently as a result of human transport.

The study of Garry oak DNA indicates distinct histories for the Yale and Sumas Mountain populations (Yousry El-Kassaby, personal communication 2000). Whereas the Sumas oaks are most closely related to southern populations, those located near Yale are most closely related to oaks in the northern Gulf Islands (east of Courtney; Figure 8.1). This genetic evidence suggests that humans were responsible for the origin of the Yale stand and that the Sumas population is a Pleistocene relict. Whether acorns or shoots were consciously transplanted to the Yale area is unknown. Given that the concept of planting was well integrated into the ecological knowledge of many Northwest groups, however, and that acorns were a highly valued food among Northwest people, establishment of oaks near Yale likely was deliberate. Future archaeological and paleoethnobotanical investigations in the sites around

Yale should provide information on the antiquity of acorn use by the inhabitants of that region.

Landscape Burning

Historical and ethnographic accounts from Oregon, Washington, and British Columbia demonstrate that prescribed burning was a common management practice among the Northwest Indigenous people in the historic era (Boyd 1999a, 1999b; Gottesfeld-Johnson 1994; Norton 1979a; Turner 1999). Controlled fires were set to enhance the growth of successional plant species for consumption, medicines, and technology, to provide forage for animals to be hunted, and to create trails and other openings. Anthropogenic fires were carefully timed and placed and reflect an in-depth knowledge of local ecology and plant requirements.

Though the historic use of prescribed fires is well documented, demonstrating use of fire in precontact times has been problematic. Most ethnobotanists agree that though the documentation for prescribed burning in the historic era of the Northwest is sparse overall, the accounts are so widespread that they likely represent a management practice with a long time depth. Physical evidence for prescribed burning in the past, however, is limited.

Several lines of evidence may suggest the antiquity of prescribed burning practices in the Northwest. The recent encroachment of fire-tolerant plant communities into fire-maintained ecosystems, such as the Garry oak-camas woodlands of southeastern Vancouver Island, may indicate a recent cessation of ancient burning practices. Because European settlers restricted both natural and cultural fires, however, the role of Aboriginally set fires is difficult to tease out. Similarly, the encroachment of coniferous trees into high-elevation *Vaccinium* harvesting areas—such as has been observed in the Indian Heaven region (Cheryl Mack, personal communication 2000)—may indicate the cessation of prescribed burning. Alternatively, however, 20th-century warming, which is coincident with the time when many Native peoples ceased to set prescribed fires, is also known to be responsible for the recent encroachment of conifer forests (Brink 1959; Franklin et al. 1971).

The presence of camas in spruce-hemlock forests on the Oregon coast is another possible indicator of ancient prescribed burning practices (Deur 1999, 2000, in press). Two species of camas (*Camassia quamash* and *C. leichtlinii*) were traded from their native, open ecosystems to the dense coastal forests, where they grew in abundance at contact. To allow camas to survive in these forests, openings were created through regular, prescribed burning. Today, with the cessation of prescribed fires, the camas meadows have been taken over by encroaching vegetation, and camas are almost entirely absent from this portion of the coast.

Shifts in fire frequency after European contact could also indicate ancient prescribed burning practices. Based on tree-ring analyses of fire scars in a Willamette Valley meadow, Hadley (1999) demonstrated that fires increased in frequency immediately after contact but then decreased dramatically once fire suppression regulations were introduced. In general, fires were more common prior to European arrival and more common in the meadow than in the surrounding forest.

Finally, changes in the pollen record have been cited as possible evidence for anthropogenic fires. In a pollen record from the northern coast of British Columbia, an increase in lodgepole pine after 250 BC may be evidence of prescribed burning of the landscape (Gottesfeld et al. 1991). The increase, however, may also be due to the onset of a warm, dry period that has been recently documented elsewhere on the coast (Hallett et al. 2003). In many instances, documenting the onset of anthropogenic fires in the pollen record is difficult because shifts from conifer-dominated ecosystems to herb- and shrub-dominated ecosystems may not be reflected in overall pollen counts. This is because many plants that flourish with increased fire frequency (e.g., *Vaccinium* and camas) produce little pollen and rely on insects for dispersal, whereas conifer pollen is produced in abundance and is widely dispersed via wind.

Surprisingly, few studies in the Northwest have been designed explicitly to document the history of prescribed burning in particular regions. This is in large part because researchers have been unable to distinguish natural versus cultural fires in the archaeological and paleoecological records, because cultural fires often mimic natural ones, and because the record of small, controlled fires is obliterated by the occasional large, natural fire (Lepofsky et al. in press). In my research, I am attempting to tackle the problem by working with multidisciplinary teams who bring together expertise in areas such as oral traditions, ecology, paleoecology, archaeology, and palynology (Lepofsky et al. in press; Lepofsky, Heyerdahl, et al. 2003). Our approach has been to formulate explicit testable hypotheses that allow us to understand the interaction between humans and other forces causing changes in ecosystems. Our research demonstrates that modern ecosystems reflect a long, complex interaction between humans, climate, and the landscape (Hallett et al. 2003; Lepofsky, Heyerdahl, et al. 2003)

Plants and Society

Historically, plants were well integrated into the social systems of all Northwest groups. Many plant-harvesting areas were owned and managed by families, and in some regions the harvest was subject to the control and supervision of a chief (Turner 1995, 1997). Further, certain plants were associated with high status and were served at feasts (e.g., the long, thick rhizomes of silverweed and springbank clover, soapberry [*Shepherdia canadensis*], and possibly yellow-cedar inner bark [Turner 1995, 1998]), and many plants were obtained through kin-based trade networks (e.g., camas, wapato, blueberries, and soapberries [Turner 1995]).

Evidence for ancient management and control of plants comes from isolated examples from the coast and the Plateau. Repeated use of berry-harvesting sites on the coast (e.g., Pitt River site; Patenaude 1985) and root-processing sites in the Willamette Valley and on the Plateau may indeed represent family-owned harvesting grounds that were exploited yearly by kin holding rights to those lands. Stands of yellow-cedar and redcedar CMTs that exhibit multiple bark-strip scars of different ages may reflect not only a conservation ethic (i.e., a prohibition against ring-barking trees) but also the management of those stands by certain families (e.g., Lepofsky and Pegg 1996). More concrete evidence for elite control over plant resources comes from the protohistoric Tsimshian village of Psacelay, where a box of *Vaccinium* sp. was found associated with the living area of high-status families (see above; Martindale 1999).

The connection between plants and the elite is also illustrated by the differential use of digging sticks handles. Though digging stick technology is undoubtedly very old, the practice of using digging stick handles, specifically, seems to correlate with more recent changes in social structure. Digging stick handles first appear in the archaeological record in contexts postdating 450 BC, when many Northwest groups appear to have undergone increasing sociopolitical complexity. If, as has been suggested, digging stick handles are status markers (Hayden and Schulting 1997), digging roots with one of these tools would have been a highly visual way of affirming a (woman's?) status.

Trade is one aspect of the social connection to plants that has been difficult to document archaeologically. The presence of nonlocal plants at the Ozette site (Friedman 1975; Gill 1983) and at the Lone Pine site (Stenholm 1997a) on the coast and at EeRb 140 (Wollstonecroft 2000, 2002) may indicate that those plants were traded in to those sites. Given that the extent of ancient plant harvesting territories is unknown, however, these plants also may have been collected by the sites' inhabitants. To my knowledge, no plant recovered at any archaeological site could not have been gathered within a few days' walk from that site.

Intensification of Plant Resources

Models of culture change in both Northwest Coast and Plateau prehistory share similar themes of increasing population, circumscription, and competition, concomitant with an intensification of resources. Until recently, these models have focused on the role of animal foods, in particular, salmon, to the exclusion of plants (but see Ames and Marshall 1980; Thoms 1989). The argument presented to support this focus is that salmon offers a reliable, predictable, and localized food source that can be harvested en masse, stored, and then owned (e.g., Matson 1983, 1992; Matson and Coupland 1995).

In fact, many plant resources are well suited to the process of intensification for the same reasons salmon is. Whereas salmon harvests were increased primarily through specialized extractive and processing techniques (e.g., Moss et al. 1990), however, plant production could be increased both through technological innovations and by managing the resource itself. Though the record for ancient plant management is too sparse to track shifts in plant intensification through time, various kinds of technological innovations can be used as proxies for changes in plant production (Lepofsky and Peacock in press).

Of the technological innovations, processing tools and features have been used as measures of plant intensification. In a seminal article, Ames and Marshall (1980) argued that the abundance of grinding and pounding implements at early pithouse sites on the Southern Plateau indicated the importance of root foods at those sites. These tools, as well as those recovered from the Maurer site on the coast (Schaepe 1998), may indicate an initial intensification of plant harvesting associated with early attempts at sedentism. Unfortunately, the mid-Holocene archaeobotanical record is too scant to provide concrete support for this proposition.

Perhaps a more significant measure of plant intensification is the changing frequency of earth ovens through time. Pit cooking in earth ovens was an important part of plant production because it converted foods—primarily root foods—into more storable and nutritious forms (Peacock 1998). Though the technology of pit cooking is likely quite old, at distinct periods in the past earth ovens are more common than at other times. On the Southern Plateau, ovens were numerous between 1550 and 350 BC and then again after AD 450 (Gough 1997; Thoms 1989). On the Canadian Plateau large and medium-sized ovens appeared in the uplands in abundance beginning at 450 BC. After 450 BC, in both the uplands and in pithouse villages, the number and size of ovens shifted through time (Lepofsky and Peacock in press). In the Willamette Valley, an increase in the number of earth oven sites occurred from 1000 BC onward. Though climate, increased population, and changes in mobility have been posited to explain periods of intensive root processing (Peacock 1998; Thoms 1989), temporal changes in these factors do not correspond well to changes in the number of earth oven sites. Shifts in the intensity with which plants were harvested and processed were likely associated with a range of factors, including changes in social structure (Lepofsky and Peacock in press). Our current understanding of many of these processes, however, is not sufficiently detailed to understand the role of plant production in the larger socioeconomic system.

The Potential of Paleoethnobotany in Northwest Archaeology

The foregoing review clearly demonstrates that paleoethnobotanical remains are preserved in Northwest sites and that they are a significant component of the archaeological record. What is now needed is for paleoethnobotany to be regularly included in all archaeological research designs in the Northwest. Concerted efforts need to be made to focus investigations on site types or components that are likely to yield paleoethnobotanical remains. Sufficient sample sizes must be analyzed, and special techniques, such as SEM to iden-tify problematic specimens and residue analyses of supposed plant processing artifacts, must be used. Paleoethnobotanists also have the responsibility of collecting extensive reference materials, providing explicit information on sampling and identifications (e.g., Friedman 1978), and publishing the re-sults of their analyses to make them accessible to a wide audience.

Comparatively speaking, the field of paleoethnobotany in the Northwest is young. Yet we have already learned a considerable amount about prehistoric plant use in the region. With sufficient methodological rigor, we can move be-yond simply gathering data and begin to form testable models of prehistoric plant use, such as models of intensification of plant production through time.

Dana Lepofsky

There is little doubt that the potential contribution of paleoethnobotany to Northwest archaeology is great. All that is needed is a concerted effort on the part of Northwest archaeologists working together with paleoethnobotanists to bring the potential to fruition.

Notes

1. Whenever possible, I have used names rather than number designations for the sites discussed in this chapter. The different numbering systems used in Oregon, Washington, British Columbia, and Alaska can be confusing and are certainly difficult to remember. To standardize among reports, I have also converted all dates to approximate BC (uncalibrated) dates.

2. Terminology for grinding and pounding implements in the Northwest is often inconsistent and is rarely explicitly defined. Flat cobble- and boulder-sized rocks that have evidence of grinding across much of their surfaces are variously referred to in the literature as grinding slabs, abrasive slabs, metates, and milling stones. In this review, I use the term "grinding slab" to refer to this general class of artifacts. Hand-held grinding stones, often used with grinding slabs, are referred to as manos, abrading stones, and milling stones. I use the term "mano" in this review. Both types of artifacts are found throughout the Southern Plateau and southern Northwest Coast.

   Grinding slabs are distinct from hopper mortar bases, which typically are flat cobble- or boulder-sized rocks with evidence of grinding, percussion (pounding), or both, on one or both surfaces. The wear usually takes the form of a central circular depression on which a hopper was placed. The hopper, often a basket, was filled with plant and possibly animal foods, which were then ground and pounded into a flour or meal. Hopper mortar bases are found in southwestern Oregon and throughout the Southern Plateau.

   The use of the term "anvil" in the literature is particularly problematic, because it is often not defined. Ames et al. define anvils as "large flat stones that lack the evidence of pounding but are in contexts that suggest their use" (1998:109). This definition contrasts with that of Connolly et al., who describe boulder anvils as large cobbles and boulders that "exhibit non-localized percussion damage across the surface" (1994: 101). Anvils have roughly the same geographical distribution as hopper mortar bases.

   It is generally assumed that manos and grinding slabs were used for seed and nut processing and that mortars, pestles, hopper mortar bases, and anvils were used to pound roots, in particular, camas bulbs (Ames and Marshall 1980). Mortars and pestles were also used historically in the Canadian Plateau to grind tobacco, berries, and other foods such as salmon (Alexander n.d.), and in the Colombia Plateau they were used to pound both roots and seeds. That these artifacts are largely confined to the Southern Plateau and southern coast—where various seed plants, camas, and acorns grow—argues strongly that they were most commonly used to process these particular plant foods.

3. The seeming completeness of the historic record of plant use may in part explain why many Northwest archaeologists recount detailed ethnobotanical information in site

reports yet conduct no paleoethnobotanical analyses to evaluate the ethnographic information.

4. Edge-ground cobbles are river cobbles with one or more edges that have been ground. The cobbles are found throughout the Northwest and northern Great Basin. In the Northwest, they are most commonly associated with Plateau sites, but they have also been reported from early Holocene sites on the southern half of the coast (e.g., Namu on the central coast; Carlson 1996:99; Figure 8.1). They are sometimes associated with what are thought to be grinding slabs or anvils (Butler 1962:46). In the original definition of the Old Cordilleran culture, Butler (1965:1127) proposed that edge-ground cobbles were used for the processing of root crops, in particular camas, but others have suggested they were used for hide scraping (Sims 1972). Since Butler originally described these artifacts, edge-ground cobbles found in early period contexts are often assumed to have been used for "plant processing"—but the type of processing is unspecified. The association of cobbles with areas where camas never grew (e.g., Namu) suggests that they were multipurpose tools that were used for processing a variety of plant and nonplant resources. Residue analyses of these tools are sorely needed.

5. Though *Rubus* has been identified to species in many paleoethnobotanical reports from the coast and the Plateau, I have lumped all determinations into the single genus. Considerable morphological variation occurs within a species of *Rubus*, so that distinguishing between species is problematic. Some *Rubus* species generally do not overlap in characteristics, and with a large enough sample, reliable determinations at the species level should be possible in those cases. Because paleoethnobotanists do not provide identification criteria in their reports, however, there is no way to evaluate the basis for species determinations. On the coast, *Rubus* seeds are usually assumed to be from salmonberries because they are the most abundant *species* in coastal environments. Because salmonberries fruit one or two months earlier than most other berries, definitive identification can be important for determining site seasonality.

6. The abundance of artifacts associated with root processing found at pithouses stands in contrast to the paucity of direct evidence for root processing in those contexts (i.e., earth ovens, remains of tissues). This pattern is consistent with Thoms's (1989) observation that tools associated with root collecting and processing are often recovered from winter villages but not from harvesting locales. Because of the labor involved in making them, and because they may have been status markers (Hayden and Schulting 1997), these artifacts were obviously curated.

7. Ethnographically, the berries of strawberry-blite (*Chenopodium capitatum*) were commonly used as a dye, but they were considered inedible by most groups (Turner 1998). Only the Klamath of southern Oregon are reported to have collected chenopods (species unspecified) in late summer and ground them into a meal (Spier 1930).

Acknowledgments

Numerous people greatly facilitated the research for this chapter. I especially thank Nancy Stenholm (Botana Labs, Seattle) for her generous help and advice and, especially, for her enthusiasm for Northwest paleoethnobotany.

Many archaeologists and anthropologists sent published and unpublished material, for which I am greatly appreciative. They are Mel Aikens (Department of Anthropology, University of Oregon), Diana Alexander (Archaeological Consultant, Vancouver, BC), Sarah Campbell (Department of Anthropology, Western Washington University), Brian Compton (Department of Botany, University of British Columbia), Tom Connolly (Museum of Anthropology, University of Oregon), Dale Croes (Southern Puget Sound Community College), Jeff Davis (Vancouver, WA), Morley Eldridge (Millennia Research, Sidney, BC), Jerry Galm (Eastern Washington University), Richard Haines (BLM State Archaeology Office of Oregon), Lynn Larson (LAAS, Seattle), Dave McMaham (Department of Natural Resources, Office of History and Archaeology, Anchorage), Cheryl Mack (National Park Service, Mt. Adams), Rick Minor and Chip Oetting (Heritage Research Associates, Eugene), Helen Norton (Silverdale, WA), Brian O'Neill (Oregon State Museum of Anthropology), Guy Prouty (Confederated Tribes of Warm Springs, OR), Arnoud Stryd (Arcas Associates, Coquitlam, BC), Jeanne Schaaf (National Park Service, Anchorage), Roderick Sprague (Laboratory of Anthropology, University of Idaho), Bob Mierendorf (National Park Service, Marblemount), Douglas Wilson (Archaeological Investigations, Northwest, Portland), and Michele Wollstonecroft (University College of London). Roy Carlson and Alan McMillan (Department of Archaeology, Simon Fraser University) provided information on the indirect evidence of plant remains on the Northwest Coast. I appreciate the time Nancy Turner, Brian Hayden, Ken Lertzman, and Nancy Stenholm took the to read over and comment on an earlier version of this chapter. I am also indebted to the interlibrary loan department at the University of British Columbia for putting up with my endless obscure requests. Kim Ng was very helpful with the final compilation of this chapter.

References Cited

Aikens, C. Melvin
    1993   *Archaeology of Oregon*. Bureau of Land Management, US Department of the Interior, Portland, Oregon.
Alexander, Diana
    n.d.   Material Culture on the Interior Plateau. Manuscript in possession of Diana Alexander.
Alexander, Diana, R. Tyhurst, L. Burnard-Hogarth, and R. G. Matson
    1985   A Preliminary Ethnoarchaeological Investigation of the Potato Mountain Range and the Eagle Lake Area. Report on file, BC Provincial Archaeology Branch, Victoria, British Columbia.

Ames, Kenneth M.

    1994   The Northwest Coast: Complex Hunter-Gatherers, Ecology, and Social Evolution. *Annual Review of Anthropology* 23:209–229.

Ames, Kenneth M., Don E. Dumond, Jerry R. Galm, and Rick Minor

    1998   Prehistory of the Southern Plateau. In *Plateau*, edited by Deward E. Walker Jr., pp. 103–119. Handbook of North American Indians, vol. 12, William G. Sturtevant, general editor. Smithsonian Institution, Washington, DC.

Ames, Kenneth M., and Alan G. Marshall

    1980   Villages, Demography, and Subsistence Intensification on the Southern Columbia Plateau. *North American Archaeologist* 2:25–52.

Ames, Kenneth M., and Herbert D. G. Maschner

    1999   *Peoples of the Northwest Coast: Their Archaeology and Prehistory.* Thames and Hudson, London.

Ames, Kenneth M., Doria F. Raetz, Stephen Hamilton, and Christine McAfee

    1992   Household Archaeology of a Southern Northwest Coast Plank-House. *Journal of Field Archaeology* 19:275–290.

Anastasio, Angelo

    1972   The Southern Plateau: An Ecological Analysis of Inter-Group Relations. *Northwest Anthropological Research Notes* 6:109–229.

Andrefsky, William, Jr.

    2000   Summary. In *The Calispell Valley Archaeological Project Final Report: 4. Artifact Analysis*, edited by William Andrefsky Jr., Gregg C. Burtchard, Kira M. Presler, Steven R. Samuels, Paul H. Sanders, and Alston Thoms, pp. 19.1–19.11. Center for Northwest Anthropology, Washington State University, Pullman.

Andrefsky, William, Jr., Gregg C. Burtchard, Kira M. Presler, Steven R. Samuels, Paul H. Sanders, and Alston Thoms (editors)

    2000   *The Calispell Valley Archaeological Project Final Report: 4. Artifact Analysis.* Center for Northwest Anthropology, Washington State University, Pullman.

Baker, J.

    1974   Report on the Archaeological Research Done in the Lytton Region, May to August 1974. Permit 1974-27. Report on file, BC Provincial Archaeology Branch, Victoria, British Columbia.

Baptiste, G., and Michele Wollstonecroft

    1997   Plant Remains. In *Vancouver Island Highway Project, Victoria Approaches Archaeological Data Recovery DcRu-92*, vol. 1, pp. 129–139. Millennia Research, Victoria and Vancouver, British Columbia.

Barbour, R. J.

    1980   Microscopic Identification of Artifactual Plant Materials. In *Hoko River: A 2500 Year-Old Fishing Camp on the Northwest Coast of North America*, edited by Dale R. Croes and Eric Blinman, pp. 151–159. Report 58. Laboratory of Anthropology, Washington State University, Pullman.

Baxter, Paul W., Richard D. Cheatham, Thomas J. Connolly, and Judith A. Willig

    1983   *Rigdon's Horse Pasture Cave: An Upland Hunting Camp in the Western Cascades.* Anthropological Papers 28. University of Oregon, Eugene.

Bergland, Eric O.

    1992   Historic Period Plateau Culture Tree Peeling in the Western Cascades of Oregon. *Northwest Anthropological Research Notes* 25:31–53.

Bernick, Kathryn

    1991   Wet-Site Archaeology in the Lower Mainland Region of British Columbia. Manuscript on file, BC Provincial Archaeology Branch, Victoria, British Columbia.

Dana Lepofsky

Bicchieri, Barbara
    1990   Paleoethnobotany and Plateau Research. *Archaeology in Washington* 2:3–10.
Borden, Charles Edward
    1960   DjRi3, an Early Site in the Fraser Canyon, British Columbia. In *Contributions to Anthro-*
            pology 1957, pp. 101–118. Bulletin 162. Anthropological Series 45. National Museum of
            Canada, Ottawa.
    1975   *Origins and Development of Early Northwest Coast Culture to about 3000 BC* Archaeological
            Survey of Canada Paper 45. Mercury Series, National Museum of Man, Ottawa.
    1983   Prehistoric Art of the Lower Fraser Region. In *Indian Art Traditions of the Northwest Coast*,
            edited by Roy L. Carlson, pp. 148–165. Archaeology Press, Simon Fraser University,
            Burnaby, British Columbia.
Boyd, Robert
    1990   Demographic History, 1774–1874. In *Northwest Coast*, edited by Wayne Suttles, pp. 135–
            146. Handbook of North American Indians, vol. 7, William G. Sturtevant, general editor.
            Smithsonian Institution, Washington, DC.
    1999a Strategies of Indian Burning in the Willamette Valley. In *Indians, Fire and the Land in the*
            Pacific Northwest, edited by Robert Boyd, pp. 94–138. Oregon State University Press,
            Corvallis.
    1999b (editor) *Indians, Fire and the Land in the Pacific Northwest*. Oregon State University Press,
            Corvallis.
Brink, V. C.
    1959   A Directional Change in the Subalpine Forest-Heath Eco-Tone in Garibaldi Park,
            British Columbia. *Ecology* 40:10–16.
Brunton, Bill B.
    1998   Kootenai. In *Plateau*, edited by Deward E. Walker Jr., pp. 233–227. Handbook of North
            American Indians, vol. 12, William G. Sturtevant, general editor. Smithsonian Institu-
            tion, Washington, DC.
Burtchard, Gregg C.
    1990   *The Posy Archaeological Project. Upland Use of the Central Cascades, Mt. Hood National Forest,*
            Oregon. Laboratory of Anthropology, Portland State University, Portland, Oregon.
Butler, B. Robert
    1962   *Contributions to the Prehistory of the Columbia Plateau. A Report on Excavations in the Palouse*
            and Craig Mountain Section. Occasional Papers 9. Idaho State University Museum,
            Pocatello.
    1965   The Structure and Function of the Old Cordilleran Concept. *American Anthropologist*
            67:1120–1131.
Campbell, Sarah K.
    1985   *Summary of Results of the Chief Joe Dam Cultural Resource Project, Washington.* Office of
            Public Archaeology, University of Washington, Seattle.
Capes, Katherine H.
    1964   *Contributions to the Prehistory of Vancouver Island.* Occasional Papers 15. Idaho State Uni-
            versity Museum, Pocatello.
Carlson, Keith Thor
    1997   *You are Asked to Witness: The Stó:lo in Canada's Pacific Coast History.* Stó:lo Heritage Trust,
            Chilliwack, British Columbia.
Carlson, Roy L.
    1972   *Salvage '71: Reports on Salvage Archaeology Undertaken in British Columbia in 1971.* Publica-
            tion 1. Department of Archaeology, Simon Fraser University, Burnaby, British Columbia.

1983a   Prehistoric Art of the Central Coast. In *Indian Art Traditions of the Northwest Coast*, edited by Roy L. Carlson, pp. 121–129. Archaeology Press, Simon Fraser University, Burnaby, British Columbia.

1983b   Change and Continuity in Northwest Coast Art. In *Indian Art Traditions of the Northwest Coast*, edited by Roy L. Carlson, pp. 197–205. Archaeology Press, Simon Fraser University, Burnaby, British Columbia.

1998   Early Namu. In *Early Human Occupation in British Columbia*, edited by Roy L. Carlson and Luke Dalla Bona, pp. 83–102. University of British Columbia Press, Vancouver.

Carlson, Roy L., and Luke Dalla Bona (editors)

1996   *Early Human Occupation in British Columbia*. University of British Columbia Press, Vancouver.

Chance, David H., and Jennifer V. Chance

1982   *Kettle Falls: 1971/1974*. Anthropological Research Manuscripts Series 69. University of Idaho, Moscow.

Chance, David H., Jennifer V. Chance, and John L. Fagan

1977   *Kettle Falls 1972: Salvage Excavations in Lake Roosevelt*. Anthropological Research Manuscripts Series 31. University of Idaho, Moscow.

Chatters, James C.

1979   *Exploratory Excavations at the Wa-pai-ixie Archaeological Site Complexes (45-KT-241)*. Reconnaissance Report 23. Office of Public Archaeology, Institute for Environmental Sciences, University of Washington, Seattle.

1981   *Archaeology of the Shabadid Site 45K151, King County Washington*. Office of Public Archaeology, Institute for Environmental Studies, University of Washington, Seattle.

1984   *Dimensions of Site Structure: The Archaeological Record from Two Sites in Okanogan County, Washington*. Central Washington Archaeological Survey, Central Washington University, Ellensburg.

1986   *The Wells Reservoir Archaeological Project: 1. Summary of Findings*. Central Research Report 86-6. Washington Archaeological Survey, Central Washington University, Ellensburg.

1988   *Tualdad Altu (45K159) a Fourth Century Village on the Black River, King County, Washington*. First City Equities, Seattle.

1989   Resource Intensification and Sedentism on the Southern Plateau. *Archaeology in Washington* 1:3–19.

1998   Environment. In *Plateau*, edited by Deward E. Walker Jr., pp. 29–48. Handbook of North American Indians, vol. 12, William G. Sturtevant, general editor. Smithsonian Institution, Washington, DC.

Chatters, James C., and David L. Pokotylo

1998   Plateau Prehistory: Introduction. In *Plateau*, edited by Deward E. Walker Jr., pp. 73–80. Handbook of North American Indians, vol. 12, William G. Sturtevant, general editor. Smithsonian Institution, Washington, DC.

Cheatham, Richard D.

1988   *Late Archaic Settlement Pattern in the Long Tom Sub-Basin, Upper Willamette Valley, Oregon*. Anthropological Papers 39. University of Oregon, Eugene.

Chisholm, Brian S., D. Erle Nelson, and Henry P. Schwarcz

1983   Marine and Terrestrial Protein in Prehistoric Diets on the British Columbia Coast. *Current Anthropology* 24:396–398.

Compton, Brian D.

1991   "It Pulls Everything to You": North Wakashan Herbal Talismans. In *Collected Papers of the*

Dana Lepofsky

26th International Conference on Salish and Neighbouring Languages, Held 15–17 August, 1991, pp. 33–79. University of British Columbia, Vancouver.

1993   *Upper North Wakashan and Southern Tsimshian Ethnobotany: The Knowledge and Usage of Plants and Fungi among the Oweekeno, Hanaksiala (Kitlope and Kemano), Haisla (Kitamaat) and Kitasoo Peoples of the Central and Northwest Coasts of British Columbia.* Unpublished PhD dissertation, Department of Botany, University of British Columbia, Vancouver.

Compton, Brian D., Rolf Mathewes, and Gastón Guzmán

1995   Puffballs from the Past: Identification of Gasteromycetes from a Lillooet Archaeological Sites and Speculation Regarding their Aboriginal Use. *Canadian Journal of Archaeology* 19:154–159.

Connolly, Thomas J.

1991   *The Standley Site (35DO182): Investigation into the Prehistory of Camas Valley, Southwest Oregon.* Anthropological Paper 43. University of Oregon, Eugene.

1992   *Human Responses to Change in Coastal Geomorphology and Fauna on the Southern Northwest Coast. Archaeological Investigations at Seaside, Oregon.* Anthropological Paper No. 45. University of Oregon, Eugene.

Connolly, Thomas J., J. E. Benjamin, B. L. O'Neill, and Dennis L. Jenkins

1994   *Archaeological Investigations at Two Sites on the Upper Rogue River (35JA189 and 35JA190) Southwest Oregon.* Anthropological Paper 48. University of Oregon, Eugene.

Connolly, Thomas J., and R. S. Byram

1997   Oregon Wet-Site Basketry: A Review of Structural Types. In *Contributions to the Archaeology of Oregon 1995–1997*, edited by Albert C. Oetting, pp. 185–204. Occasional Paper 6. Association of Oregon Archaeologists, Eugene.

Connolly, Thomas J., B. L. O'Neill, and D. E. Friedel

1999   Cultural and Landscape History of the Upper Willamette Valley: Summary and Discussion. In *The Long Tom and Chalker Sites: A Holocene Geoarchaeological Record for the Upper Willamette Valley*, edited by B. L. O'Neill, Thomas J. Connolly, and D. E. Friedel, pp. 261–272. Report 99-6. Oregon State Museum of Anthropology, University of Oregon, Eugene.

Croes, Dale R.

1976   (editor) *The Excavation of Water Saturated Archaeological Sites (Wet-Sites) on the Northwest Coast of North America.* Archaeological Survey of Canada Paper 50. Mercury Series, National Museum of Man, Ottawa.

1977   *Basketry from the Ozette Village Archaeological Site: A Technological, Functional, and Comparative Study.* Unpublished PhD dissertation, Department of Anthropology, Washington State University, Pullman.

1980   *Cordage from the Ozette Village Archaeological Site: A Technological, Functional, and Comparative Study.* Project Report 9. Washington Archaeological Research Center, Washington State University, Pullman.

1987   Sunken Village Site (35MU4). Archaeological Potential as a Northwest Coast Site. Report in possession of Dale R. Croes.

1988   The Significance of the 3000 B.P. Hoko River Waterlogged Fishing Camp in Our Overall Understanding of the Southern Northwest Coast Culture Evolution. In *Wet-Site Archaeology*, edited by Barbara A. Purdy, pp. 131–152. Tilford Press, Caldwell, New Jersey.

1992   An Evolving Revolution in Wet Site Research on the Northwest Coast of North America. In *The Wetland Revolution in Prehistory*, edited by Byrony Coles, pp. 99–112. Occasional Paper 6. Wetland Archaeology Research Project (WARP), Exeter, England.

1995   *The Hoko River Archaeological Site Complex, the Wet/Dry Site (45CA213), 3,000-2,600 B.P.*
Washington State University Press, Pullman.

1997   The North-Central Cultural Dichotomy on the Northwest Coast of North America: Its
Evolution as Suggested by Wet-Site Basketry and Wooden Fish-Hooks. *Antiquity*
71:594–615.

2001   North Coast Prehistory—Reflections from Northwest Coast Wet Site Research. In *Perspectives on Northern Northwest Coast Prehistory*, edited by Jerome S. Cybulski, pp. 45–173.
Mercury Series Paper 160. Canadian Museum of Civilization, Hull, Quebec.

2002   Birth to Death: Northwest Coast Wet Site Basketry and Cordage Artifacts Reflecting a
Person's Life-Cycle. In *Enduring Records: The Environmental and Cultural Heritage of Wetlands*, edited by Barbara A. Purdy, pp. 92–109. Occasional Paper 15. Wetland Archaeology Research Project (WARP), Oxford.

Croes, Dale R., and Eric Blinman (editors)

1980   *Hoko River: A 2500 Year-Old Fishing Camp on the Northwest Coast of North America.* Report
58. Laboratory of Anthropology, Washington State University, Pullman.

Cummings, Linda Scott

1993   Pollen and Starch Analysis of Living Surfaces and Features at Heathcliff's Site, 35Je319,
Oregon. Manuscript in possession of Linda Scott Cummings.

Cybulski, Jerome S.

1993   *A Greenville Burial Ground.* Archaeological Survey of Canada Paper 146. Mercury Series,
National Museum of Man, Ottawa.

Daugherty, Richard D., J. J. Flenniken, and J. M. Welch

1987   *A Data Recovery Study of Layser Cave (45-LE-223) in Lewis County, Washington.* Studies in
Cultural Resource Management 7. USDA Forest Service, Portland, Oregon.

Davis, Jeffrey D.

1991   Data Recovery on the Peeled Cedar Component of the Paradise Creek Headwalls Site
(45SA233). Paper presented at the 44th Northwest Anthropological Conference, Missoula.

1992   Culturally Modified Trees Working Group. Information handout at 45th Northwest
Anthropological Conference, Burnaby, British Columbia.

1993   Five, Six, Pick Up Sticks . . . Further Data Recovery on the Fall Creek Peeled Cedar
Sites. Paper presented at 46th Northwest Anthropological Conference, Bellingham,
Washington.

Davis, O. K., and Charles H. Miksicek

1987   Plant Remains From Archaeological Sites in the Elk Creek Drainage, Southern Oregon,
In *Data Recovery at Sites 35JA27, 35JA59, and 35JA100, Elk Creek Lake Project, Jackson
County*, vol. 2, edited by Richard M. Pettigrew and Clayton Lebow, pp. B.1–B.12. Infotec
Research, Eugene.

Deur, Douglas

1999   Salmon, Sedentism, and Cultivation: Towards an Environmental Prehistory of the
Northwest Coast. In *Northwest Lands, Northwest Peoples: An Environmental History Anthology*, edited by Dale D. Goble and Paul W. Hirt, pp. 119–144. University of Washington
Press, Seattle.

2000   *A Domesticated Landscape: Native American Plant Cultivation on the Northwest Coast.* Unpublished PhD dissertation. Department of Geography and Anthropology, Louisiana State
University, Baton Rouge.

2002a   Plant Cultivation on the Northwest Coast: A Reassessment. *Journal of Cultural Geography*
19(2):9–35.

Dana Lepofsky

2002b Rethinking Precolonial Plant Cultivation on the Northwest Coast of North America. *Professional Geographer* 54(2):140–157.

In press Tending the Garden, Making the Soil: Northwest Coast Estuarine Gardens as Engineered Environments. In *Keeping It Living: Traditions of Plant Use and Cultivation on the Northwest Coast*, edited by Douglas E. Deur and Nancy J. Turner. University of Washington Press, Seattle.

Dewhirst, J.

1980 *The Yuquot Project: 1. The Indigenous Archaeology of Yuquot, a Nootkan Outside Village*. History and Archaeology 39. Parks Canada, Ottawa.

Dixon, R. N.

1933 Tobacco Chewing on the Northwest Coast. *American Anthropologist* 35:146–150.

Duff, Wilson

1975 *Images: Stone: B.C.* Oxford University Press, Toronto.

Ecklund, Debra J.

1980 Macroflora Analysis. In *Hoko River: A 2500 Year-Old Fishing Camp on the Northwest Coast of North America*, edited by Dale R. Croes and Eric Blinman, pp. 91–100. Report 58. Laboratory of Anthropology Washington State University, Pullman.

Ecklund-Johnson, Debra J.

1984 *Analysis of Macroflora from the Hoko River Rockshelter, Olympic Penninsula, Washington*. Unpublished master's thesis, Department of Anthropology, Washington State University, Pullman.

Eldridge, Ann

1982 Cambium Resources of the Pacific Northwest: An Ethnographic and Archaeological Study. Manuscript on file, BC Provincial Archaeology Branch, Victoria, British Columbia.

Eldridge, Morley

1996 Archaeological Impact Assessment of Paradise Creek Area Cutblocks in the Lillooet Forest District. Report on file, BC Provincial Archaeology Branch, Victoria, British Columbia.

Eldridge, Morley, and T. Fisher

1997 St. Mungo Cannery Wet-Site, DgRr 2: An Evaluation. Report on file, BC Provincial Archaeology Branch, Victoria. British Columbia.

Eldridge, Morley, and Arnoud H. Stryd

1983 CN Rail Rail-Yard Expansion Project Heritage Mitigation Study, Kamloops Junction, B.C. Report on file, BC Provincial Archaeology Branch, Victoria, British Columbia.

Filloon, R.

1952 Huckleberry Pilgrimage. *Pacific Discovery* 5:4–13.

Fladmark, Knut R.

1986 *British Columbia Prehistory*. National Museums of Canada, Ottawa.

Fortuine, R.

1988 The Use of Medicinal Plants by the Alaska Natives. *Alaska Medicine* 30:186–226.

Fowler, Catherine S.

1989 Appendix E: Perishable Artifacts. In Times Square Rockshelter (35DO212): A Stratified Dry Rockshelter in the Western Cascades, Douglas Country, Oregon, by Lee Spencer and others, pp. 396–443. Lee Spencer Archaeology Paper 1989-4, on file at the Umpqua National Forest, Roseburg, Oregon.

Franck, Ian Christian

2000 *An Archaeological Survey of the Galene Lakes Area in the Skagit Range of the North Cascade Mountains, Skagit Valley Park, B.C.* Unpublished master's thesis, Department of Archaeology, Simon Fraser University, Burnaby, British Columbia.

Franklin, Jerry F.

1988   Pacific Northwest Forests. In *North American Terrestrial Vegetation*, edited by Michael G. Barbour and William Dwight Billings, pp. 104–130. Cambridge University Press, Cambridge.

1992   Foothill Oak Woodlands of the Interior Valleys of Southwestern Oregon. *Northwest Science* 66:66–76.

Franklin, Jerry F., and C. T. Dyrness

1988   *Natural Vegetation of Oregon and Washington*. Oregon State University Press, Corvallis.

Franklin, Jerry F., W. H. Moir, G. W. Douglas, and C. Wiberg

1971   Invasion of Subalpine Meadows by Trees in the Cascade Range, Washington and Oregon. *Arctic and Alpine Research* 3:215–224.

Friedman, Janet Patterson

1975   *The Prehistoric Uses of Wood at the Ozette Archaeological Site*. Unpublished PhD dissertation, Department of Anthropology, Washington State University, Pullman.

1978   *Wood Identification by Microscopic Examination*. Heritage Record 5. British Columbia Provincial Museum, Victoria.

Galm Jerry R., and R. A. Masten (editors)

1985   *Avey's Orchard: Archaeological Investigations of a Late Prehistoric Columbia River Community*. Reports in Archaeology and History 100-42. Archaeological and Historical Services, Eastern Washington University, Cheney.

Galm, Jerry R., R. A. Masten, and D. G. Landis

1985   The Houses and Their Contents. In *Avey's Orchard: Archaeological Investigations of a Late Prehistoric Columbia River Community*, edited by Jerry R. Galm and R. A. Masten, pp. 159–242. Reports in Archaeology and History 100-42. Archaeological and Historical Services, Eastern Washington University, Cheney.

Gill, Steven J.

1983   *Ethnobotany of the Makah and Ozette People, Olympic Peninsula, Washington*. Unpublished PhD dissertation, Department of Botany, Washington State University, Pullman.

Gleeson, Paul F.

1980   *Ozette Woodworking Technology*. Unpublished PhD dissertation, Department of Anthropology, Washington State University, Pullman.

Gleeson, Paul F., and Gerald Grosso

1976   Ozette Site. In *The Excavation of Water-Saturated Archaeological Sites (Wet Sites) on the Northwest Coast of North America*, edited by Dale R. Croes, pp. 13–44. Archaeological Survey of Canada Paper 50. Mercury Series, National Museum of Man, Ottawa.

Gottesfeld, A. S., Rolf W. Mathewes, and L. M. J. Gottesfeld

1991   Holocene Debris Flows and Environmental History, Hazelton Area. *Canadian Journal of Earth Science* 28:1583–1593.

Gottesfeld-Johnson, L. M.

1994   Aboriginal Burning for Vegetation Management in Northwest British Columbia. *Human Ecology* 22:171–188.

Gough, Stan

1997   *Data Recovery Excavations at Site 45PO422: A Camas Processing Site in Calispell Valley, Pend Oreille County, Washington*. Reports in Archaeology and History 100-99. Archaeological and Historical Services, Eastern Washington University, Cheney.

1998   (editor) *Yakima Training Center Expansion Area Archaeology: Investigations in the Johnson Creek Drainage Basin Kittitas County, Washington*. Reports in Archaeology and History 100-93. Archaeological and Historical Services, Eastern Washington University, Cheney.

Dana Lepofsky

Gunther Erna
1945   *Ethnobotany of Western Washington: The Knowledge and Use of Indigenous Plants by Native Americans.* University of Washington Press, Seattle.

Habeck, J. R.
1961   The Original Vegetation of the Mid-Willamette Valley, Oregon. *Northwest Science* 35: 65–77.

Hadley, K. S.
1999   Forest History and Meadow Invasion at the Rigdon Meadows Archaeological Site, Western Cascades, Oregon. *Physical Geography* 20:116–133.

Hallett, D. J., Dana Lepofsky, Rolf W. Mathewes, and Kenneth P. Lertzman
2003   11,000 Years of Fire History and Climate in the Mountain Hemlock Rainforests of Southwestern British Columbia Based on Sedimentary Charcoal. *Canadian Journal of Forest Research* 33:292–312.

Hammon, D.
1986   Excavations at the Whalen Farm Site (Canadian) Dg Rs 14, Boundary Bay, B.C. Report on file, Heritage Conservation Branch, Victoria, British Columbia.

Harris, Cole
1994   Voices of Disaster: Smallpox around the Strait of Georgia in 1782. *Ethnohistory* 41: 591–626.

Hayden, Brian
1992   Conclusions: Ecology and Complex Hunter/Gatherers. In *A Complex Culture of the British Columbia Plateau: Traditional Stl'átl'imx Resource Use*, edited by Brian Hayden, pp. 527–563. University of British Columbia Press, Vancouver.
2000a   An Overview of the Classic Lillooet Occupation at Keatley Creek. In *The Ancient Past of Keatley Creek: II. Socioeconomic Interpretation*, edited by Brian Hayden, pp. 255–286. Archaeology Press, Simon Fraser University, Burnaby, British Columbia.
2000b   Prestige Artifacts at Keatley Creek. In *The Ancient Past of Keatley Creek: II. Socioeconomic Interpretation*, edited by Brian Hayden, pp. 189–202. Archaeology Press, Simon Fraser University, Burnaby, British Columbia.
2000c   Site Formation Processes at Keatley Creek. In *The Ancient Past of Keatley Creek: I. Taphonomy*, edited by Brian Hayden, pp. 229–355. Archaeology Press, Simon Fraser University, Burnaby, British Columbia.

Hayden, Brian, and Sara Mossop-Cousins
In press   The Social Dimensions of Roasting Pits in a Winter Village Site. In *Complex Hunter-Gatherers: Evolution and Organization of Prehistoric Communities on the Plateau of Northwestern North America*, edited by Bill Prentiss and Ian Kuijt. University of Utah Press, Salt Lake City.

Hayden, Brian, and Rick J. Schulting
1997   The Plateau Interaction Sphere and Late Prehistoric Cultural Complexity. *American Antiquity* 62:51–85.

Hebda, Richard J., and Rolf W. Mathewes
1984   Holocene History of Cedar and Native Indian Cultures of the North American Pacific Coast. *Science* 225:711–713.

Hobler, Philip M.
1990   Prehistory of the Central Coast of British Columbia. In *Northwest Coast*, edited by Wayne Suttles, pp. 289–305. Handbook of North American Indians, vol. 7, William G. Sturtevant, general editor. Smithsonian Institution, Washington, DC.

Hunn, Eugene S.
1981   On the Relative Contribution of Men and Women to Subsistence among Hunter-

Gatherers of the Columbia Plateau: A Comparison with Ethnographic Atlas Summaries. *Journal of Ethnobiology* 1:124–134.

1990   *Nch'i-Wána, The Big River.* University of Washington Press, Seattle.

Hunn, Eugene S., and D. H. French

1981   Lomatium: A Key Resource for Columbia Plateau Native Subsistence. *Northwest Science* 55:87–94.

Inglis, Richard I.

1976   'Wet' Site Distribution—The Northern Case GbTo33—The Lachane Site. In *The Excavation of Water-Saturated Archaeological Sites (Wet Sites) on the Northwest Coast of North America*, edited by Dale R. Croes, pp. 158–185. Archaeological Survey of Canada Paper 50. Mercury Series, National Museum of Man, Ottawa.

Isaac, Barry L. (editor)

1988   *Research on Economic Anthropology, Prehistoric Economies of the Pacific Northwest Coast.* JAI Press, Greenwich, Connecticut.

Jones, Kevin T., and David B. Madsen

1991   Further Experiments in Native Food Procurement. *Utah Archaeologist* 4:68–76.

Keddie, Grant

1988   The 6-Mile Rockshelter. Report on file, BC Provincial Archaeology Branch, Victoria, British Columbia.

Keely, Patrick Byron

1980   *Nutrient Composition of Selected Important Plant Foods of the Pre-Contact Diet of the Northwest Native American Peoples.* Unpublished master's thesis, School of Nutritional Science and Textiles, Washington State University, Pullman.

Kendall, Daythal L.

1990   Takelma. In *Northwest Coast*, edited by Wayne Suttles, pp. 589–592. Handbook of North American Indians, vol. 7, William G. Sturtevant, general editor. Smithsonian Institution Press, Washington, DC.

Kent, S.

1975   *An Analysis of Northwest Coast Combs with Special Emphasis on Those from Ozette.* Unpublished master's thesis, Department of Anthropology, Washington State University, Pullman.

Ketcheson, Maureen V.

1979   Floral Analysis of Archaeological Sites in the Hat Creek Valley. Manuscript on file, Department of Anthropology and Sociology, University of British Columbia, Vancouver.

Ketcheson, Maureen V., M. Norris, and D. A. Clark

1977   Floral Analysis of the 1976 Hope Archaeological Project. Manuscript on file, BC Provincial Archaeology Branch, Victoria, British Columbia.

Koch, J.

1975   *Miniatures from the Archaeological Inventory at the Ozette Village Site.* Unpublished master's thesis, Department of Anthropology, Washington State University, Pullman.

Kuhnlein, Harriet K., and Nancy J. Turner

1991   *Traditional Food Plants of Canadian Indigenous Peoples: Nutrition, Botany, and Use.* Gordon and Breach, Philadelphia.

Kuijt, Ian

1989   Subsistence Resource Variability and Culture Change during the Middle-Late Prehistoric Cultural Transition on the Canadian Plateau. *Canadian Journal of Archaeology* 13:97–118.

Lane, Robert B.

1981   Chilcotin. In *Subarctic*, edited by June Helm, pp. 402–412. Handbook of North American Indians, vol. 6, William G. Sturtevant, general editor. Smithsonian Institution, Washington, DC.

Dana Lepofsky

Larson, Lynn L., and Dennis E. Lewarch
  1995   *The Archaeology of West Point, Seattle, Washington: 4,000 Years of Hunter-Fisher-Gatherer Land Use in Southern Puget Sound.* Vol. I and II. Larson Anthropological/Archaeological Services, Seattle.
Leney, L.
  1984   Plant Macrofossil Identifications: Analysis and Results. In *Human Adaptation along the Columbia River 4700–1600 B.P. A Report of Test Excavation at River Mile 590, North Central Washington,* edited by James C. Chatters, Appendix F. Research Reports 84-1. Central Washington University, Ellensburg.
Lepofsky, Dana
  1986   The Effects of Development in the Georgia Strait on Traditional Plant Use. In *Island Waters, Perspectives on the Sound,* edited by E. Richard Hart, pp. 7–9. Institute of the North American West, Seattle.
  1988   Floral Remains from EeQw 30. In *Archaeological Excavations at the Sahhaltkum Bridge Site (EeQw 30), Chase, B.C.,* edited by Mike K. Rousseau and Arnoud H. Stryd, pp. 279–288. Arcas Associates, Vancouver and Kamloops, British Columbia.
  1990   Floral Remains. In *Impact Mitigation and Archaeological Sites EfQv121, EfQv123 and EfQv133 near Squilax, B.C.,* pp. 345–356. Arcas Associates. Vancouver and Kamloops, British Columbia.
  1992   Paleoethnobotanical Report for Barnett Highway Mitigation Project. In The 1991 Archaeological Excavation at the Barnett Highway Site, Port Moody, BC (DhRr 69), by L. C. Hamm and A. Yip. Report on file, BC Provincial Archaeology Branch, Victoria, British Columbia.
  1994   Botanical Remains. In *Archaeological Investigations at Tsawwassen, B.C.,* vol. II, pp. 36–37, 54, 91–93, 136, 149, 180–181, 218–219. Arcas Consulting Archaeologists, Vancouver and Kamloops, British Columbia.
  2000a Site Formation Processes at Keatley Creek: The Palaeoethnobotanical Evidence. In *The Ancient Past of Keatley Creek: I. Taphonomy,* edited by Brian Hayden, pp. 105–135. Archaeology Press, Simon Fraser University, Burnaby, British Columbia.
  2000b Socioeconomy at Keatley Creek: The Botanical Evidence. In *The Ancient Past of Keatley Creek: II. Socioeconomic Interpretations,* edited by Brian Hayden, pp. 75–86. Archaeology Press, Simon Fraser University, Burnaby, British Columbia.
  2003   Plants and Pithouses: The Archaeobotany of Complex Hunter-Gatherers on the British Columbia Plateau. In *The Archaeobotany of Temperate-Zone Hunter-Gatherers,* edited by Sarah L. R. Mason and Jon G. Hather, pp. 62–73. Institute of Archaeology, London.
Lepofsky, Dana, D. Hallett, Kenneth Lertzman, K. Washbrook, Albert (Sonny) McHalsie, and Rolf Mathewes
  In press Documenting Precontact Plant Management on the Northwest Coast: An Example of Prescribed Burning in the Central and Upper Fraser Valley, British Columbia. In *Keeping It Living: Traditions of Plant Use and Cultivation on the Northwest Coast,* edited by Douglas E. Deur and Nancy J. Turner. University of Washington Press, Seattle.
Lepofsky, Dana, E. Heyerdahl, Kenneth Lertzman, D. Schaepe, and Robert Mierendorf
  2003   Climate, Humans, and Fire in the History of Chittenden Meadow. *Conservation Ecology* 7:5. Electronic document, http://www.consecol.org/vol7/iss3/art5.
Lepofsky, Dana, Karla D. Kusmer, Brian Hayden, and Kenneth P. Lertzman
  1996   Reconstructing Prehistoric Socioeconomies from Palaeoethnobotanical and Zooarchaeological Data: An Example from the British Columbia Plateau. *Journal of Ethnobiology* 16:31–62.

Lepofsky, Dana, S. Lawhead, Arnoud H. Stryd, and Karla Kusmer
1987 Archaeological Investigations of Site EeRl 12, Lillooet, B.C. Report on file, BC Provincial Archaeology Branch, Victoria, British Columbia.
Lepofsky, Dana, and Natasha Lyons
2003 Modeling Ancient Plant Use on the Northwest Coast: Towards an Understanding of Mobility and Sedentism. *Journal of Archaeological Science* 30:1357–1371.
Lepofsky, Dana, Natasha Lyons, and Madonna L. Moss
2003 The Use of Driftwood on the North Pacific Coast: An Example from Southeast Alaska. *Journal of Ethnobiology* 23:125–141.
Lepofsky, Dana, Madonna L. Moss, and Natasha Lyons
2001 The Unrealized Potential of Paleoethnobotany in the Archaeology of Northwestern North America: Perspectives from Cape Addington, Alaska. *Arctic Anthropology* 38:48–59.
Lepofsky, Dana, and Sandra Peacock
In press A Question of Intensity: Exploring the Role of Plant Foods in Northern Plateau Prehistory. In *Complex Hunter-Gatherers: Evolution and Organization of Prehistoric Communities on the Plateau of Northwestern North America*, edited by Bill Prentiss and Ian Kuijt. University of Utah Press, Salt Lake City.
Lepofsky, Dana, and Brian Pegg
1996 Archaeological and Ethnographic Assessment. In *The Kowesa Watershed Assessment: Summary Report*, prepared by Interrain Pacific with the Nanakila Institute, the Hausla Nation, Ecotrust Canada, and Ecotrust, pp. 38–44. Interrain Pacific, Portland, Oregon.
Lookabill, Anna B.
1998 A Predictive Model for Locating *Vaccinium*-Huckleberry Processing Sites in the Northern Cascades of Washington. *Northwest Anthropological Research News* 32(2):173–180.
Losey, R. J., Nancy Stenholm, P. Whereat-Phillips, and H. Vallianatos
2003 Exploring the Use of Red Elderberry (*Sambucus racemosa* spp. *pubens*) Fruit on the Southern Northwest Coast of North America. *Journal of Archaeological Science* 30:695–707.
Lovell, Nancy C., Brian S. Chisholm, D. Erle Nelson, and Henry P. Schwarcz
1986 Prehistoric Salmon Consumption in Interior British Columbia. *Canadian Journal of Archaeology* 10:99–106.
Lyons, Natasha
2000 *Investigating Ancient Socioeconomy in Stó:lo Territory: A Palaeoethnobotanical Analysis of the Scowlitz Site, Southwestern BC*. Unpublished master's thesis, Department of Archaeology, Simon Fraser University, Burnaby, British Columbia.
MacDonald, George
1983 Prehistoric Art of the Northern Northwest Coast. In *Indian Art Traditions of the Northwest Coast*, edited by Roy L. Carlson, pp. 99–121. Archaeology Press, Simon Fraser University, Burnaby, British Columbia.
Mack, Cheryl A.
1992 In Pursuit of the Wild *Vaccinium*—Huckleberry Processing Sites in the Southern Washington Cascades. *Archaeology in Washington* 4:3–16.
Mack, Cheryl A., and R. McClure
2002 Vaccinium Processing in the Washington Cascades. *Journal of Ethnobiology* 22:35–60.
Magne, M.
1984 Taseko Lakes Prehistory Project: Report on a Preliminary Survey. Manuscript on file, BC Provincial Archaeology Branch, Victoria, British Columbia.
1985 Taseko Lakes Prehistory Project. Phase II. Preliminary Excavations. Manuscript on file, BC Provincial Archaeology Branch, Victoria, British Columbia.

Marshall, A. L.
  2002 *Culturally Modified Trees of the Nechako Plateau: Cambium Ultilization amongst Traditional Carrier (Dakhel) Peoples*. Unpublished master's thesis, Department of Archaeology, Simon Fraser University, Burnaby, British Columbia.
Martindale, Andrew
  1999 *River of Mist: Cultural Changes in the Tsimshian Past*. Unpublished PhD dissertation, Department of Anthropology, University of Toronto, Toronto.
Mathewes, Rolf W.
  1980 Plant Remains from the Lillooet Archaeological Project, B.C. *Abstract Botanical Society of America*, p. 71. Miscellaneous Series 158. Botanical Society of America, St. Louis.
Matson, R. G.
  1983 Intensification and the Development of Cultural Complexity: The Northwest versus the Northeast. In *The Evolution of Maritime Cultures on the Northeast and the Northwest of America*, edited by Ronald J. Nash, pp. 125–148. Publication 11. Department of Archaeology, Simon Fraser University, Burnaby, British Columbia.
  1992 The Evolution of Northwest Coast Subsistence. In *Long-Term Subsistence Change in Prehistoric North America*, edited by Dale Croes, Rebecca A. Hawkins, and Barry L. Issac, pp. 367–428. Research in Economic Anthropology Supplement 6. JAI Press, Greenwich, Connecticut.
  1996 The Old Cordilleran Component at the Glenrose Cannery Site. In *Early Human Occupation in British Columbia*, edited by Roy L. Carlson and Luke Dalla Bona, pp. 111–122. University of British Columbia Press, Vancouver.
Matson, R. G., and Diana Alexander
  1980 Potato Mountain: The Archaeology of Alpine Root Procurement. Paper presented at the Canadian Archaeological Association, Whitehorse, Yukon.
Matson, R. G., and Gary Coupland
  1995 *The Prehistory of the Northwest Coast*. Academic Press, San Diego.
Mauger, Jeffrey E.
  1982 Ozette Kerf-Corner Boxes. *American Indian Art Magazine* 8(1):72–79.
McMahan, J. D.
  1986 Analysis of Archaeological Deposits from SEW-214 and SEW-216: 1985–1986 Supplement. In *Supplement Report: Sterling Highway Archaeology, 1985–1986*. Alaska Archaeological Surveys, State of Alaska Department of Natural Resources, Anchorage.
McMillan, Alan D., and Denis E. St. Claire
  1992 The Toquaht Archaeological Project: Report on the 1992 Field Season. Manuscript on file, British Columbia Heritage Trust, Victoria; BC Provincial Archaeological Branch, Victoria; and Toquaht Band, Ucluelet.
  1994 The Toquaht Archaeological Project: Report on the 1994 Field Season. Manuscript on file, BC Provincial Archaeological Branch, Victoria, and Toquaht Band, Ucluelet.
McCutcheon, A. R., S. M. Ellis, R. E. W. Hancock, and G. H. N. Towers
  1992 Antibiotic Screening of Medicinal Plants of the British Columbian Native Peoples. *Journal of Ethnopharmacology* 37:213–223.
McPhatter, B.
  1985 Analysis of Found Human Remains at Toquart Bay, Historical Period Box Burial. Permits. Report #1985-4 on file, BC Provincial Archaeology Branch, Victoria, British Columbia.
Meidinger, Dell, and Jim Pojar
  1992 *Ecosystems of British Columbia*. BC Special Report 6. British Columbia Ministry of Forests, Victoria.

Meilleur, Brien A.

1979 Speculations on the Diffusion of *Nicotiana quadrivalvis* Pursh to the Queen Charlotte Islands and Adjacent Alaskan Mainland. *Syesis* 12:101–104.

Mierendorf, Robert R.

1986 People of the North Cascades. Report on file, Pacific Northwest Region, National Park Service, US Department of the Interior, Seattle.

Miller, F. E.

1975 The Benjamin Sites (35 LA 41, 42). In *Archaeological Studies in the Willamette Valley, Oregon*, edited by C. Melvin Aikens, pp. 311–347. Anthropological Papers 8. University of Oregon, Eugene.

Mills, John E., and Carolyn Osborne

1951 Material Culture of an Upper Coulee Rockshelter. *American Antiquity* 17:352–359.

Minor, Rick (editor)

1987 *Archaeology of the So: Umpqua Falls Rockshelters, Douglas County, Oregon.* Report 64. Heritage Research Associates, Eugene.

Minor, Rick, and Thomas J. Connolly

1987 *Archaeological Testing at Times Square Rockshelter, Douglas Country, Oregon.* Report 55. Heritage Research Associates, Eugene.

Minor, Rick, and Christine Pickett

1982 Botanical Remains from the Halverson Site, Upper Willamette Valley, Oregon. *Tebiwa* 19:15–26.

1985 Botanical Remains from the Flanagan Site. In *The Flanagan Site: 6,000 Years of Occupation in the Upper Willamette Valley, Oregon*, by Kathryn Anne Toepel, pp. 187–195. Unpublished PhD dissertation, Department of Anthropology, University of Oregon, Eugene.

Minor, Rick, and Kathryn Anne Toepel

1986 *The Archaeology of the Tahkenitch Landing Site: Early Prehistoric Occupations on the Oregon Coast.* Report 46. Heritage Research Associates, Eugene.

Miss, Christian J., and Margaret A. Nelson

1995 *Data Recovery at the Mule Spring Site, 45KL435, King County, Washington.* Manuscript on file, Mt. Baker-Snoqualmie National Forest, Mountlake Terrace, Washington.

Mitchell, Donald H.

1971 *Archaeology of the Gulf of Georgia Area: A Natural Region and Its Culture Types.* Syesis 4 (Supp. 1).

1990 Prehistory of the Coasts of Southern British Columbia and Northern Washington. In *Northwest Coast*, edited by Wayne Suttles, pp. 340–358. Handbook of North American Indians, vol. 7, William G. Sturtevant, general editor. Smithsonian Institution, Washington, DC.

Mitchell, Donald H., and Leland Donald

1988 Archaeology and the Study of Northwest Coast Economies. In *Prehistoric Economies of the Northwest Coast*, edited by Barry L. Isaac, pp. 293–351. Research in Economic Anthropology Supplement No. 3. JAI Press, Greenwich, Connecticut.

Mitchell, Donald H., and David Pokotylo

1996 Early Period Components at the Milliken Site. In *Early Human Occupation in British Columbia*, edited by Roy L. Carlson and Luke Dalla Bona, pp. 65–82. University of British Columbia Press, Vancouver.

Mobley, Charles M., and Morley Eldridge

1992 Culturally Modified Trees in the Pacific Northwest. *Arctic Anthropology* 29:91–110.

Dana Lepofsky

Monks, Gregory G.
  1987   Prey as Bait: The Deep Bay Example. *Canadian Journal of Archaeology* 11:119–142.
Moss, Madonna L., and Jon M. Erlandson
  1998   Early Holocene Adaptations of the Southern Northwest Coast. *Journal of California and Great Basin Anthropology* 20(1):13–25.
Moss, Madonna L., Jon M. Erlandson, and R. Stuckenrath
  1990   Wood Stake Weirs and Salmon Fishing on the Northwest Coast: Evidence from Southeast Alaska. *Canadian Journal of Archaeology* 14:143–158.
Mossop-Cousins, Sara
  2000   A Palaeoethnobotanical Comparison of Four Small House-Pits. In *The Ancient Past of Keatley Creek: II. Socioeconomic Interpretations*, edited by Brian Hayden, pp. 87–102. Archaeology Press, Simon Fraser University, Burnaby, British Columbia.
Munsell, David A.
  1976   Excavation of the Conway Wet Site, 45SK95b, Conway, Washington. In *The Excavation of Water-Saturated Archaeological Sites (Wet Sites) on the Northwest Coast of North America*, edited by Dale R. Croes, pp. 86–121. Archaeological Survey of Canada Paper 50. Mercury Series, National Museum of Man, Ottawa.
Nelson, Charles M.
  1990   Prehistory of the Puget Sound Region. In *Northwest Coast*, edited by Wayne Suttles, pp. 481–484. Handbook of North American Indians, vol. 7, William G. Sturtevant, general editor. Smithsonian Institution, Washington, DC.
Nelson, Margaret A.
  1992   Shell Midden Deposits and the Archaeobotanical Record: A Case from the Northwest Coast. In *Deciphering a Shell Midden*, edited by Julie K. Stein, pp. 239–259. Academic Press, Seattle.
Newman, Thomas M.
  1966   *Cascadia Cave*. Occasional Papers 18. Idaho State Museum, Pocatello.
Nicholas, G. P., Michele Wollstonecroft, and G. Baptiste
  1997   *Long-Term Secweoemc Plant-Use: Initial Results of Archaeobotanical Investigations in the Interior Plateau*. Archaeological Research Reports 2. Archaeology Department, Secwepemc Cultural Education Society-Simon Fraser University Program, Burnaby, British Columbia.
Norton, Helen H.
  1979a   The Association between Anthropogenic Prairies and Important Food Plants in Western Washington. *Northwest Anthropological Research Notes* 13:175–200.
  1979b   Evidence for Bracken Fern as a Food for Aboriginal Peoples of Western Washington. *Economic Botany* 33:384–396.
  1981   Plant-Use in Kaigani Haida Culture: Correction of an Ethnohistorical Oversight. *Economic Botany* 35:434–449.
  1985   *Women and Resources of the Northwest Coast: Documents from the 18th and Early 19th Centuries*. Unpublished PhD dissertation, Department of Anthropology, University of Washington, Seattle.
Norton, Helen H., Robert Boyd, and Eugene S. Hunn
  1999   The Klickitat Trail of South-Central Washington: A Reconstruction of Seasonally Used Resource Sites. In *Indians, Fire and the Land*, edited by Robert Boyd, pp. 65–93. Oregon State University Press, Corvallis.
O'Neill, Brian L.
  1987   *Archaeological Reconnaissance and Testing in the Noti-Veneta Section of the Florence-Eugene Highway, Lake City, Oregon*. Report 87-6. Oregon State Museum, Eugene.

O'Neill, Brian L., Thomas J. Connolly, and D. E. Friedel

1996   *Streamside Occupations in the North Umpqua River Drainage Before and After the Eruption of Mount Mazama*. Report 96-2. Oregon State Museum of Anthropology, Eugene.

Ostapkowicz, Joanna, Dana Lepofsky, Rick Schulting, and Albert (Sonny) McHalsie

2001   The Use of Cattail (*Typha latifolia* L.) Down as a Sacred Substance by the Interior and Coast Salish. *Journal of Ethnobiology* 21:77–90.

Palmer, Gary B.

1975   Shuswap Indian Ethnobotany. *Syesis* 8:29–81.

Parish, Roberta, Ray Coupé, and Dennis Lloyd

1996   *Plants of Southern Interior of British Columbia*. BC Ministry of Forests and Lone Pine Press, Vancouver.

Patenaude, Val

1985   The Pitt River Archaeological Site (DhRg 21): A Coast Salish Seasonal Camp on the Lower Fraser River. Manuscript on file, BC Provincial Archaeology Branch, Victoria, British Columbia.

Peacock, Sandra L.

1998   *Putting Down Roots: The Emergence of Wild Plant Food Production on the Canadian Plateau*. Unpublished PhD dissertation, Interdisciplinary Degree Program, University of Victoria.

2002   Perusing the Pits: The Evidence for Prehistoric Geophyte Processing on the Canadian Plateau. In *Archaeobotany of Temperate Hunter-Gatherers*, edited by Sarah L. R. Mason and Jon G. Hather, pp. 44–61. Institute of Archaeology, London.

Peacock, Sandra L., and Nancy J. Turner

2000   "Just Like a Garden": Traditional Resource Management and Biodiversity Conservation on the Interior Plateau of British Columbia. In *Biodiversity and Native America*, edited by Paul E. Minnis and Wayne J. Elisens, pp. 133–179. University of Oklahoma Press, Norman.

Pettigrew, Richard M.

1980   *Archaeological Investigations at Hager's Grove, Salem, Oregon*. Anthropological Papers 19. University of Oregon, Eugene.

1981   *A Prehistoric Culture Sequence in Portland Basin of the Lower Columbia Valley*. Anthropological Papers 22. University of Oregon, Eugene.

1990   Prehistory of the Lower Columbia and Willamette Valley. In *Northwest Coast*, edited by Wayne Suttles, pp. 518–529. Handbook of North American Indians, vol. 7, William G. Sturtevant, general editor. Smithsonian Institution, Washington, DC.

Pettigrew, Richard M., and Clayton G. Lebow

1987   *Archaeological Investigations at the Sunken Village Site (35MU4) Multonmah County, Oregon*. Report PNW87-10. Infotec Research, Eugene.

Pickett, Christine

1987   Botanical Remains. In *Archaeology of the South Umpqua Falls Rockshelter, Douglas County, Oregon*, edited by Rick Minor, pp. 97–103. Report 64. Heritage Research Associates, Eugene.

Pojar, Jim, and Andy MacKinnon

1994   *Plants of Coastal British Columbia including Washington, Oregon, and Alaska*. British Columbia Ministry of Forests and Lone Pine Publishing, Vancouver.

Pokotylo, Donald L., and Patricia D. Froese

1983   Archaeological Evidence for Prehistoric Root Gathering on the Southern Interior Plateau of British Columbia: A Case Study from the Upper Hat Creek Valley. *Canadian Journal of Archaeology* 7:127–157.

Pokotylo, David L., and Donald Mitchell
    1998   Prehistory of the Northern (Canadian) Plateau. In *Plateau*, edited by Deward E. Walker Jr., pp. 81–102. Handbook of North American Indians, vol. 12, William G. Sturtevant, general editor. Smithsonian Institution, Washington, DC.

Prince, Paul
    2001   Dating and Interpreting Pine Cambium Collection Scars from Two Parts of the Nechako River Drainage, British Columbia. *Journal of Archaeological Science* 28:253–263.

Prouty, Guy L.
    1989   Ancient Earth Ovens at the Saltsgaver Site, Southwestern Oregon. In *Contributions to the Archaeology of Oregon 1987–1988*, edited by Rick Minor, pp. 1–36. Occasional Papers 4. Association of Oregon Archaeologists, Eugene.
    1991   Macrobotanical Analysis of Specimens from the Standley Site. In *The Standley Site (35DO182): Investigations into the Prehistory of Camas Valley, Southwestern Oregon*, edited by Thomas J. Connolly, pp. 189–191. Anthropological Papers 43. University of Oregon, Eugene.

Prouty, Guy L., Brian L. O'Neill, and Thomas J. Connolly
    1999   Aboriginal Plant Use at the Chalker and Long Tom Sites. In *The Long Tom and Chalker Sites: A Holocene Geoarchaeological Record for the Upper Willamette Valley*, by Brian L. O'Neill, Thomas J. Connolly, and D. E. Friedel, pp. 249–260. Report 99-6. Oregon State Museum of Anthropology, University of Oregon, Eugene.

Ray, Verne F.
    1939   *Cultural Relations on the Plateau of Northwest America*. Publication 3. Frederick Webb Hodge Anniversary Publication Fund, Los Angeles.

Reagan, Albert B.
    1917   Archaeological Notes on Western Washington and Adjacent British Columbia. *Proceedings of the California Academy of Sciences* 7:1–131.

Reckendorf, Frank F., and Roger B. Parsons
    1966   Soil Development Over a Hearth in Willamette Valley, Oregon. *Northwest Science* 40: 46–55.

Reger, Douglas R., and C. R. Campbell
    1986   *Early Historic Use of Sakie Bay Cave, CRG-230*. Alaska Archaeological Surveys, Alaska Department of Natural Resources, Anchorage.

Reimer, Rudy
    2000   *Extreme Archaeology: The Results of Investigations at High Elevation Regions in the Northwest*. Unpublished master's thesis, Department of Archaeology, Simon Fraser University, Burnaby, British Columbia.

Rhode, David E.
    1986   Archaeobotanical Investigations in the Wells Resevoir Archaeological Project, Eastern Washington. In *The Wells Reservoir Archaeological Project: 1. Summary of Findings*, edited by James C. Chatters, Appendix A-3. Report 86-6. Central Washington Archaeological Survey, Central Washington University, Ellensburg.
    1987   Analysis of Charred Plant Remains from 45KT250 and 45KT285. In *Archaeology of Eight Sites in the Multipurpose Range Complex, Yakima Firing Center, Washington*, edited by James C. Chatters and M. K. Zweifel, Appendix B. Report 87-2. Central Washington Archaeological Survey, Central Washington University, Ellensburg.

Richards, Thomas H., and Michael K. Rousseau
    1982   Archaeological Investigations on Kamloops Indian Reserve No. 1, Kamloops, British Columbia. Manuscript on file, Heritage Conservation Branch, Victoria, British Columbia.

1987 *Late Prehistoric Cultural Horizons on the Canadian Plateau.* Archaeology Press, Simon Fraser University, Burnaby, British Columbia.

Roll, Tom E., and Steven Hackenberger
 1998 Prehistory of the Eastern Plateau. In *Plateau*, edited by Deward E. Walker Jr., pp. 120– 137. Handbook of North American Indians, vol. 12, William G. Sturtevant, general editor. Smithsonian Institution, Washington, DC.

Ross, Richard E.
 1990 Prehistory of the Oregon Coast. In *Northwest Coast*, edited by Wayne Suttles, pp. 554– 559. Handbook of North American Indians, vol. 7, William G. Sturtevant, general editor. Smithsonian Institution, Washington, DC.

Rousseau, Michael, R. Muir, D. Alexander, J. Breffit, S. Woods, K. Berry, and T. van Gaalen
 1991 Results of the 1989 Archaeological Investigations Conducted in the Oregon Jack Creek Locality, Thompson River Region, South-Central British Columbia. Permit no. 1989-76. Report on file, BC Provincial Archaeology Branch, Victoria, British Columbia.

Sanford, Patricia R.
 1975 The Lynch Site (35 LIN 36). In *Archaeological Studies in the Willamette Valley, Oregon*, edited by C. Melvin Aikens, pp. 229–271. Anthropological Papers 8. University of Oregon, Eugene.

Schaepe, David M.
 1998 *Recycling Archaeology: Analysis of Material from the 1973 Excavation of an Ancient House at the Maurer Site.* Unpublished master's thesis, Department of Archaeology, Simon Fraser University, Burnaby, British Columbia.

Schalk, Randall F. (editor)
 1987 *Archaeology of the Morris Site (35GM91) on the John Day River, Gillman City, Oregon.* Office of Public Archaeology, University of Washington, Seattle.

Schlick, Mary Dodds
 1994 *Columbia River Basketry: Gift of the Ancestors, Gift of the Earth.* University of Washington Press, Seattle.

Schoonmaker, Peter K., Bettina von Hagen, and Edward C. Wolf (editors)
 1995 *The Rain Forests of Home: Profile of a North American Bioregion.* Island Press, Washington, DC.

Setchell, William Albert
 1921 Aboriginal Tobaccos. *American Anthropologist* 23:397–413.

Sims, Cort
 1972 Edged Cobbles of the Pacific Northwest. *Tebiwa* 14(2):21–38.

Smith, Harlan I.
 1899 *Archaeology of Lytton, British Columbia.* Memoirs Vol. 1, Pt. 3. American Museum of Natural History, New York.

Spier, Leslie
 1930 *Klamath Ethnography.* Publications in American Archaeology and Ethnology 30. University of California, Berkeley.

Steedman, Elsie Viault (editor)
 1930 *The Ethnobotany of the Thompson Indians of British Columbia. Based on Field Notes of James A. Teit.* 30th Annual Report, 1908–1909:22–102. Bureau of American Ethnology, Smithsonian Institution, Washington, DC.

Stenholm, Nancy A.
 1984a Botanical Analysis of 45-OK-11. In *Archaeological Investigations at Site 45-OK-11, Chief Joseph Dam Project*, edited by E. S. Lohse, pp. 193–211. University of Washington, Seattle.

1984b Botanical Analysis of 45-OK-250. In *Archaeological Investigations at Sites 45-OK-250 and 45-OK-4, Chief Joseph Dam Project*, edited by Sarah K. Campbell, pp. 161–177. University of Washington, Seattle.

1984c Botanical Analysis of 45-OK-18. In *Archaeological Investigations at Site 45-OK-18, Chief Joseph Dam Project*, edited by Manfred E. W. Jaehnig, pp. 101–110. University of Washington, Seattle.

1984d Botanical Analysis of 45-OK-287/288. In *Archaeological Investigations at Sites 45-OK-287 and 45-OK-288, Chief Joseph Dam Project*, edited by Christian J. Miss, pp. 128–151. University of Washington, Seattle.

1984e Botanical Analysis of 45-DO-214. In *Archaeological Investigations at Site 45-DO-14, Chief Joseph Dam Project*, edited by Christian J. Miss, pp. 97–119. University of Washington, Seattle.

1985 Botanical Assemblage. In *Summary of Results, Chief Joseph Dam Cultural Resources Project, Washington*, edited by Sarah K. Campbell, pp. 421–453. Office of Public Archaeology, University of Washington, Seattle.

1986a Botanical Remains from Tahkenitch Landing. In *The Archaeology of the Tahkenitch Landing Site: Early Prehistoric Occupations on the Oregon Coast*, by Rick Minor and Kathryn Anne Toepel, pp. 73–77. Report 46. Heritage Research Associates, Eugene.

1986b Botanical Analysis for the Calispell Valley Project. In *Calispell Valley Archaeological Project: Interim Report for 1984 and 1985 Field Seasons*, edited by Alston Thoms and Gregg C. Burtchard, pp. 479–512. Center for Northwest Anthropology, Washington State University, Pullman.

1987a Analysis of Botanical Samples. In *Archaeology of the Morris Site (35GM91) on the John Day River, Gillman City, Oregon*, edited by R. F. Schalk, pp. 8.1–8.10. Office of Public Archaeology, University of Washington, Seattle.

1987b Flotation Analysis of 45BN329. In *Archaeological Investigations at 45BN329, Benton County, Washington*, edited by Stan Gough, pp. 61–68. Reports in Archaeology and History 100-58. Archaeological and Historical Services, Eastern Washington University, Cheney.

1987c Botanical Analysis. In *The Duwamish No. 1 Site. 1986 Data Recovery*, pp. 13.1–13.31. URS and BOAS, Seattle.

1988a The Botanical Array at CR05-07-31. In *Naches Lithic Scatter. CR05-07-31, Data Recovery Report*, edited by Astrida R. Blukis Onat, pp. 96–99. BOAS, Seattle.

1988b Macrobotanical Analysis. In *Archaeological Investigations at River Mile 590: The Excavations at 45DO189I*, by Jerry R. Galm and R. Lee Lyman, Appendix 6. Reports in Archaeology and History 100-61. Archaeological and Historical Services, Eastern Washington University, Cheney.

1988c Botanical Analysis. In *Data Recovery for Headwaters-Extension Site 45-CH-208*, by Hal Kennedy and Astrida R. Blukis Onat, pp. 143–152. BOAS, Seattle.

1989 Botanical Analysis. In *Evaluation of the Burton Creek Rockshelter Site 45-LE-266*, edited by Christian J. Miss, pp. 15–18. Northwest Archaeological Associates, Lewis County, Washington.

1989–90 The Botanical Assemblage of Layser Cave, Site 45LE223. Report prepared for Randle Ranger District, Gifford Pinchot National Forest, USDA Forest Service, Randle, Washington. Manuscript in possession of Nancy A. Stenholm.

1991 Centennial Trail Botanical Analysis. In *Archaeology of the Middle Spokane River Valley: Investigations along the Spokane Centennial Trail*, edited by J. A. Draper and William Andrefsky Jr., Appendix O, pp. O.1–O.12. Report 17. Center for Northwest Anthropology, Department of Anthropology, Washington State University, Pullman.

1992a Botanical Analysis. In *Daishowa America Port Angeles Mill Shell Midden, 45CA415, Clallam County, Washington*, by D. E. Lewarch, L. L. Larson, and L. S. Phillips, pp. 73–81. Technical Report, 92-7. Larson Anthropological/Archaeological Services, Seattle.

1992b Flotation Results from the North Nemah River Bridge Site (45PC101). Report prepared for Archaeological and Historical Services, Cheney. Manuscript in possession of Nancy A. Stenholm.

1994 Results of Botanical Analysis, Site 35JA189. In *Archaeological Investigations at Two Sites on the Upper Rogue River (35JA189 and 35JA190) Southwest Oregon*, edited by Thomas J. Connolly, J. E. Benjamen, Brian L. O'Neill, and Dennis L. Jenkins, pp. 185–188. Anthropological Papers 48. University of Oregon, Eugene.

1995a Botanical Analysis. In *The Archaeology of West Point, Seattle, Washington. 4,000 Years of Hunter-Fisher-Gatherer Land Use in Southern Puget Sound*, vol. I and II, edited by L. L. Larson, and D. E. Lewarch, Apendix 7. Larson Anthropological/Archaeological Services, Seattle.

1995b Botanical Remains. In *Archaeology of the Cape Creek Shell Midden, Cape Perpetua Scenic Area, Central Oregon Coast*, by Rick Minor and R. L. Greenspan, pp. 79–86. Coastal Prehistory Program, Oregon State Museum of Anthropology, University of Oregon, Eugene.

1996a Botanical Analysis. In *King County Department of Natural Resources Water Pollution Control Division Alki Transfer/CSO Project. Allentown Site (45KI431) and White Lake Site (45KI438 and 45KI1438A) Data Recovery*, edited by L. L. Larson, Appendix 3. Larson Anthropological/Archaeological Services.

1996b Botanical Analysis of Floral Samples. In *Archaeological Investigations (1991–1995) at 45CL1 (Cathlapotle): Clark County Washington: A Preliminary Report* by Kenneth M. Ames, W. L. Cornett, and S. C. Hamilton, Appendix B. Wapato Archaeology Project Report 6. Department of Anthropology, Portland State University, Portland, Oregon.

1997a Botanical Remains. In *The Lone Pine Site (35WS247) and the Late Prehistory of the Dalles Area, Oregon and Washington*, by Rick Minor, p. 67. Report 209. Heritage Research Associates, Eugene.

1997b Botanical Remains. In *The Archaeology of Skamanyak (45SA16): Late Prehistoric–Early Historic Indian Settlement at the Middle Cascades, Lower Columbia River Valley*, by Rick Minor, pp. 77–87. Report 201. Heritage Research Associates, Eugene.

1997c Botanical Analysis of Flotation Samples from Camas Ovens at Site 45PO422. In *Data Recovery Excavations at Site 45PO422: A Camas Processing Site in Calispell Valley, Pend Oreille County, Washington*, edited by Stan Gough, pp. A4.1–A4.10. Reports in Archaeology and History 100-99. Archaeological and Historical Services, Eastern Washington University, Cheney.

1998a Two Decades of Archaeobotanical Work in Washington. *AWA News* 3(2):3.

1998b Archaeobotany of Yakima Training Center Expansion Sites 45KT979, 45KT980, 45KT1003, 45KT1011, and 45KT1012. In *Yakima Training Center Expansion Area Archaeology: Investigations in the Johnson Creek Drainage Basin Kittitas County, Washington*, edited by Stan Gough, Appendix 4. Reports in Archaeology and History 100-93. Archaeological and Historical Services, Eastern Washington University, Cheney.

1999 Botanical Analysis. In *The SR-101 Sequim Bypass Archaeological Project: Mid- to Late-Holocene Occupations on the Northern Olympic Peninsula, Clallam County, Washington*, vol. 2, edited by Vera E. Morgan, pp. K.1–K.24. Reports in Archaeology and History 100-108. Archaeological and Historical Services, Eastern Washington University, Cheney.

2000a Botanical Analysis Taxonomic Classifications. In *The Calispell Valley Archaeological Project Final Report: 5. References and Appendices*, edited by William Andrefsky, Gregg C. Burt-

Dana Lepofsky

chard, Kira M. Presler, Steven R. Samuels, Paul H. Sanders, and Alston Thoms, pp. C.1–C.23. Center for Northwest Anthropology, Washington State University, Pullman.

2000b   Botanical Analysis for the Calispell Valley Archaeological Project. In *The Calispell Valley Archaeological Project Final Report: 4. Artifact Analysis*, edited by William Andrefsky, Gregg C. Burtchard, Kira M. Presler, Steven R. Samuels, Paul H. Sanders, and Alston Thoms, pp. 14.1–14.66. Center for Northwest Anthropology, Washington State University, Pullman.

n.d.   Botanical Analysis of Floral Samples from 35WS8. In Report on the 1993 Excavation at the Dalles Road-Cut Site: An Early-Mid Holocene Site on the Columbia River, Oregon, by Virginia Butler. Report on file, Department of Anthropology, University of Oregon, Eugene.

Stryd, Arnoud

1972   Housepit Archaeology at Lillooet, British Columbia: The 1970 Field Season. *B.C. Studies* 14:17–46.

1973   *The Later Prehistory of the Lillooet Area, British Columbia*. Unpublished PhD dissertation, Department of Archaeology, University of Calgary.

1983   Prehistoric Mobile Art from the Mid-Fraser and Thompson River Areas. In *Indian Art Traditions of the Northwest Coast*, edited by Roy L. Carlson, pp. 165–181. Archaeology Press, Simon Fraser University, Burnaby, British Columbia.

1997   *Culturally Modified Trees of British Columbia*. British Columbia Ministry of Forests, Nanaimo.

Stryd, Arnoud, and Morley Eldridge

1993   CMT Archaeology in British Columbia: The Meares Island Studies. *B.C. Studies* 99:184–234.

Suttles, Wayne

1951   The Early Diffusion of the Potato among the Coast Salish. *Southwestern Journal of Anthropology* 7:272–288.

1990   (editor) *Northwest Coast*. Handbook of North American Indians, vol. 7, William G. Sturtevant, general editor. Smithsonian Institution, Washington, DC.

Theodoratus, R. J.

1989   Loss, Transfer, and Reintroduction in the Use of Wild Plant Foods in the Upper Skagit Valley. *Northwest Anthropological Research Notes* 23:35–52.

Thilenius, J. F.

1968   The *Quercus garryanna* Forests of the Willamette Valley, Oregon. *Ecology* 49:1124–1133.

Thoms, Alston

1989   *The Northern Roots of Hunter-Gatherer Intensification: Camas and the Pacific Northwest*. Unpublished PhD dissertation, Department of Anthropology, Washington State University, Pullman.

Thoms, Alston, and Gregg C. Burtchard

1986   *Calispell Valley Archaeological Project. Interim Report for 1984 and 1985 Field Seasons*. Contributions in Cultural Resource Management. Center for Northwest Archaeology, Washington State University, Pullman.

Tuohy, Donald R.

1986   A Maidu Coiled Basket from the North Fork of the Willamette River, Oregon. *Journal of California and Great Basin Anthropology* 8(2):260–263.

Turner, Nancy J.

1992   Plant Resources of the Stl'átl'imx (Fraser River Lillooet People): A Window into the Past. In *A Complex Culture of the British Columbia Plateau. Traditional Stl'átl'imx Resource Use*, edited by Brian Hayden, pp. 405–469. University of British Columbia Press, Vancouver.

1995   *Food Plants of Coastal First Peoples*. University of British Columbia Press, Vancouver.

1996   "Dans une Hotte": L'Importance de la Vannerie dans l'Économie des Peuples Chasseurs-Pêcheurs-Cuilleurs du Nord-Ouest de l'Amérique du Nord ("Into a Basket Carried on the Back": Importance of Basketry in Foraging/Hunting/Fishing Economies in Northwestern North America). *Anthropologie et Sociétiés* 20:3:55–84. (Special issue of *Contemporary Ecological Anthropology: Theories, Methods and Research Fields*.)

1997   *Food Plants of Interior First Peoples*. University of British Columbia Press, Vancouver.

1998   *Plant Technology of First Peoples in British Columbia*. University of British Columbia Press, Vancouver.

1999   "Time to Burn". Traditional Use of Fire to Enhance Resource Production by Aboriginal Peoples in British Columbia. In *Indians, Fire and the Land*, edited by Robert Boyd, pp. 185–218. Oregon State University Press, Corvallis.

Turner, Nancy J., Randy Bouchard, and Dorothy I. Kennedy

1980   *Ethnobotany of the Okanagan-Colville Indians of British Columbia and Washington*. Occasional Paper 21. British Columbia Provincial Museum, Victoria.

Turner, Nancy J., and Sandra L. Peacock

In press   Solving the Perennial Paradox: Evidence for Plant Resource Management on the Northwest Coast. In *Keeping It Living: Traditions of Plant Use and Cultivation on the Northwest Coast*. Douglas E. Deur and Nancy J. Turner, editors. University of Washington Press, Seattle.

Turner, Nancy J., and R. L. Taylor

1972   A Review of the Northwest Coast Tobacco Mystery. *Syesis* 5:249–257.

Turner, Nancy J., John Thomas, Barry F. Carlson, and Robert T. Ogilvie

1983   *Ethnobotany of the Nitinaht Indians of Vancouver Island*. Occasional Paper Series 24. British Columbia Provincial Museum, Victoria.

Turner, Nancy J., Laurence C. Thompson, M. Terry Thompson, Annie Z. York

1990   *Thompson Ethnobotany: Knowledge and Use of Plants by the Thompson Indians of British Columbia*. Memoir 3. Royal British Columbia Museum, Victoria.

Walker, Deward E., Jr.

1998   Introduction. In *Plateau*, edited by Deward E. Walker Jr., pp. 1–7. Handbook of North American Indians, vol. 12, William G. Sturtevant, general editor. Smithsonian Institution, Washington, DC.

White, John R.

1975   The Hurd Site. In *Archaeological Studies in the Willamette Valley, Oregon*, edited by C. Melvin Aikens, pp. 141–225. Anthropological Papers 8. University of Oregon, Eugene.

White, Richard

1980   *Land Use, Environment, and Social Change. The Shaping of Island County, Washington*. University of Washington Press, Seattle.

Wickwire, Wendy

1993   Women in Ethnography: The Research of James A. Teit. *Ethnohistory* 40:539–562.

Wilson, Douglas C.

1993   Exploring Late Archaic Refuse Disposal and Site Structure at a Camas Processing Site in the Willamette Valley, Oregon. Paper presented at the 46th Annual Northwest Anthropological Conference, Bellingham.

Wollstonecroft, Michele M.

2000   *The Fruit of Their Labour: A Paleoethnobotanical Study of Site EeRb 140, a Multi-Component Open-Air Archaeological Site on the British Columbia Plateau*. Unpublished master's thesis, Department of Archaeology, Simon Fraser University, Burnaby, British Columbia.

Dana Lepofsky

2002 The Fruit of Their Labour: Plants and Plant Processing at EeRb 140 (860 ± 60 uncal to 150 ± 50 uncal B.P.), a Late Prehistoric Hunter-Gatherer Site on the Southern Interior Plateau, British Columbia, Canada. *Vegetation History and Archaeobotany* 11:61–70.

Zenk, Henry B.

1990 *Kalapuyans*. In *Northwest Coast*, edited by Wayne Suttles, pp. 547–553. Handbook of North American Indians, vol. 7, William G. Sturtevant, general editor. Smithsonian Institution, Washington, DC.

Authors

Karen R. Adams
2837 Beverly Dr.
Tucson, AZ 85716
agave@dakotanet.com

Linda Scott Cummings
Paleo Research Institute
2675 Youngfield
Golden, CO 80401
linda@paleoresearch.com

Suzanne K. Fish
Arizona State Museum
University of Arizona
Tucson, AZ 85721
sfish@u.arizona.edu

Richard I. Ford
Museum of Anthropology
University of Michigan
Ann Arbor, MI 48109
riford@umich.edu

Authors

Julia E. Hammett
Department of Social Sciences/
    Sierra 200K
Truckee Meadows Community
    College
700 Dandini Blvd.
Reno, NV 89512
jhammett@tmcc.edu

Lisa W. Huckell
Maxwell Museum of Anthropology
University of New Mexico
Albuquerque, NM 87131
lhuckell@unm.edu

Elizabeth J. Lawlor
Mt. San Antonio College
1100 N. Grand Ave.
Walnut, CA 91789
elawlor@mtsac.edu

Dana Lepofsky
Department of Archaeology
Simon Fraser University
Burnaby, BC V5A 1S6
dlepofsk@sfu.ca

Paul E. Minnis
Department of Anthropology
University of Oklahoma
Norman, OK 73019
minnis@ou.edu

Mollie S. Toll
Office of Archaeological Studies
Museum of New Mexico
Santa Fe, NM 87501
mtoll@oas.state.nm.us

Botanical Index

467

Subject Index

The complete listing of plants by genus and family is in the Botanical Index. Only those plant taxa cited on 30 or more pages in the Botanical Index are included by common name in the Subject Index.

472